Guide
to
Teaching Woodwinds

Guide to Teaching Woodwinds

Second Edition

FREDERICK W. WESTPHAL
California State University, Sacramento

wcb
WM. C. BROWN COMPANY PUBLISHERS
Dubuque, Iowa

Consulting Editor

Frederick W. Westphal
California State University, Sacramento

Library of Congress Catalog Card Number: 73—89023

ISBN 0—697—03507—7

Printed in the United States of America

Contents

Preface vii

Introduction 1
Musical Learning 1
Organization of Instruction 3
Instructional Materials 3
Beginning Methods 5
Practice 6
Breathing and Breath Control 7
Organization of Chapters 7

Clarinet 9
The Clarinet Family 9
Playing Ranges 10
Parts of the Instrument 11
Assembling the Instrument 12
Checklist for Assembly 20
Holding Positions for the Clarinet 21
Hand Positions 27
Checklist for Holding and Hand Positions 34
Embouchure Formation 35
Checklist for Embouchure Formation 39
Tuning 40
Intonation 41
Tone 44
Tonguing 46
Technique Problems 52
Play Alto, Bass, and Contrabass Clarinet 62
Transpositions for the Clarinetist 63
Selection of Instruments 65
Student Qualifications and Aptitudes 66
Care of the Clarinet 66
Bibliography of Study Materials 71
Study and Achievement Questions 76

Flute 79
Playing Ranges 79
Assembling the Instrument 80
Parts of the Instrument 80
Checklist for Assembly 84
Holding Positions for the Flute 85
Holding Position for Other Instruments 87
Hand Positions 88
Checklist for Holding and Hand Positions 92
Embouchure Formation 93
Tuning 93
Checklist for Embouchure Formation 97
Intonation 98
Tone 100
Tonguing 101
Technique Problems 105
Harmonics 109
Transposition for the Flutist 111
Selection of Instruments 111
Student Qualifications and Aptitudes 112
Care of the Flute 113
Bibliography of Study Materials 115
Study and Achievement Questions 117

Oboe and English Horn 119
Playing Ranges 119
Assembling the Instrument 119
Parts of the Instrument 120
Checklist for Assembly 124
Holding Positions for Oboe 125
Holding Positions for English Horn 127
Hand Positions 129
Checklist for Holding and Hand Positions 133
Embouchure Formation 134
Checklist for Oboe Embouchure Formation 140
Tuning 141
Intonation 141
Tone 144
Tonguing 146
Technique Problems 149
Harmonics 152
Transposition for the Oboist 153
Selection of Instruments 153

Student Qualifications and Aptitudes 154
Care of the Oboe 155
Bibliography of Study Materials 158

Bassoon 163
Parts of the Bassoon 163
Assembling the Instrument 163
Checklist for Assembly 168
Holding Positions for Bassoon 168
Hand Positions 172
Checklist for Holding and Hand Positions 175
Embouchure Formation 176
Tuning 178
Checklist for Embouchure Formation 179
Intonation 180
Tone 183
Tonguing 185
Technique Problems 188
Selection of Instruments 192
Student Qualifications and Aptitudes 192
Care of the Bassoon 193
Accessories 197
Bibliography of Study Materials 198

Saxophone 201
The Saxophone Family 201
Playing Ranges 202
Parts of the Saxophone 202
Assembling the Instrument 203
Checklist for Assembly 207
Holding Positions for the Saxophone 208
Hand Positions 214
Checklist for Holding and Hand Positions 222
Embouchure Formation 223
Checklist for Embouchure Formation 226
Tuning 227
Intonation 227
Tone 230
Tonguing 231
Technique Problems 235
Transpositions for the Saxophone 240
Selection of Instruments 242
Student Qualifications and Aptitudes 243
Care of the Saxophone 243
Bibliography of Study Materials 246

Mouthpieces and Reeds 251
Parts of the Mouthpiece 252
Criteria for a Good Mouthpiece 253
Recommendation for a Mouthpiece 253
Mouthpiece Deficiencies 254
Reeds 255
Criteria for a Good Reed 256
Clarinet and Saxophone Reeds 256
Adjusting the Single Reed 259
Care of the Reed 261
Oboe and English Horn Reeds 262
How an Oboe Reed Is Made 263
Types of Oboe Reeds Available 267
Types of Cut 268
Selecting the Reed 269
Tools and Materials for Adjusting Oboe Reeds 269
Areas of Reed to Be Scraped for Adjustment 270
Testing and Correcting Reed Response 273
English Horn Reeds 276
Care of the Oboe and English Horn Reed 276
Bassoon Reeds 277
Parts of the Bassoon Reed 278
How a Bassoon Reed Is Made 278
Types of Bassoon Reeds Available 279
Types of Cut 279
Selecting the Reed 279
Tools and Materials for Adjusting Bassoon Reeds 280
Areas of Reed to Be Scraped for Adjustment 280
Adjusting Bassoon Reed with Wires 282
Testing and Correcting Reed Response 282
Care of the Bassoon Reed 285
Study and Achievement Questions 286

Vibrato 289
Definition 289
Confusion about Vibrato 289
What Is Good Vibrato? 289
Methods of Producing a Vibrato 290
Developing a Vibrato 292

Appendix 1—Acoustics and Woodwind Instruments 293

Appendix 2—Phonograph Recordings 297

Appendix 3—Sources of Music for Woodwinds 301

Fingering Charts 307
Flute 309
Oboe 315
Clarinet 320
Bassoon 326
Saxophone 332

Preface

This book is written primarily for the college student who is preparing for instrumental teaching in the schools and secondly, as a general reference book for those interested in the teaching and study of woodwinds. The material contained within represents a consensus of the best contemporary practices and procedures. It is a comprehensive treatment of all aspects of teaching woodwinds from the very beginning of study to the most advanced.

The preparation of a new edition of the book provided an opportunity to expand certain sections significantly. The sections on technique problems have been expanded to include numerous additional items of a more sophisticated and advanced nature. In all sections new material devoted to the specific performance problems of contemporary music has been added as an aid to those students and teachers who are becoming more and more involved in music of this style.

The sections on study materials have been expanded and brought up to date to provide a broader base for selection. Here too, materials in contemporary styles have been added. Basic fingering charts have been expanded and the pitch range extended to the limits of today's musical requirements. Trill fingering charts have also been expanded as have the special harmonic fingering charts. Supplementary resource material has been increased through the expansion of bibliography. A more detailed chapter on vibrato with discussions of specific instruments has been provided.

A primary problem in presenting information such as that contained in this book is found in the selection and use of words to describe a particular element of performance. Words have different meanings, and are subject to different interpretations by different readers. Each teacher has his or her own vocabulary and few agree on the exact terms to be used in explaining the same thing. Much of the difference of opinion on how a particular thing should be achieved on an instrument comes from the descriptive words and imagery used rather than in the intended end product.

There is a wide variety of points of view on all aspects of woodwind instruction and performance. Authorities differ on a great many specifics of woodwind playing. The very fact that there is such a variety of successful approaches to the problems is a clear indication that there are several ways in which each of these problems can be solved.

Where there are several prevailing points of view on a particular procedure an attempt has been made to present them. It is obviously impossible to present all views, or the many possible variations of one of the views presented. The reader is left free to choose that which he prefers on his own concepts and experiences and those of the instructor. In each instance the point of view presented first is the personal choice of the author, but the reader may use any of them with confidence in success and with the weight of authority behind the choice.

In organizing the material for maximum use and understanding, the step-by-step method of presentation with liberal utilization of photographs is employed for many sections. Other features of the book include identification of commonly found faults in each aspect of performance together with causes and suggestions for correction; identification of technique problems unique to each instrument with the correct procedures suggested; discussions of alternate fingerings and when and how to use them; a bibliography of study material for each instrument; a consideration of mouthpieces for clarinets and saxophones; the selection and adjustment of single and double reeds; check lists for various aspects of study; study and achievement questions for each chapter and finally, complete fingering charts for each instrument making use of a standardized nomenclature in an easy to read format.

The material in this book is based on many years of research which included all available printed material, a detailed study of the widest variety of methods books, the expressed needs of teachers on all educational levels, the performance abilities of students on various levels, and a variety of teaching experiences. In this way the standard practices and procedures of a wide variety of skilled teachers and professional players on each instrument were discovered and the information correlated and organized into a single body of information consistent with the needs of teachers.

Each chapter is complete within itself. Readers interested in a particular subject or in a particular instrument may refer to that chapter for complete information without cross references. For this reason it is felt that the book will be a useful permanent reference when the student enters the teaching profession, and also for those teachers who may feel the need for additional information of this type.

The author is especially indebted to Donald L. Gerhauser for the photographs which were taken from the previous edition and to Lynn Cramer for his work in providing the many new photographs for this edition. To my friends and colleagues who successfully combine the jobs of professional musicians and teachers for the tedious job of posing for photography the author is most grateful. These include Edna Comerchero and Robert Klump, flute; Norman Gillette, oboe; Ben Glovinsky, oboe and English horn; Daniel Kingman and Daniel McAullife, bassoon; Herbert Harrison and William Wood, saxophone; Gerry Greer and Dennie Green; and to Robert Humiston for the sequence on making and adjusting oboe reeds.

Chapter 1

Introduction

Teaching the woodwind instruments with good results becomes a fairly simple process when the instruments themselves are fully understood and when appropriate techniques, procedures and materials are used in an abundant variety. The instruments in the woodwind family have a great many things in common and when these are understood and advantage taken of them understanding the instructional process becomes more efficient. Rather than five distinct and separate instruments they become a unified whole.

Careful selection of the students who will study a woodwind instrument as well as helping the prospective student select the specific instrument he wishes to study is basic to success. This must be a cooperative decision between the teacher and student. The student's responsibility is to have a real interest in the instrument and to consider it worth learning so that he will conscientiously apply himself to the study. The teacher's responsibility is to see that the student has the intellectual capacity to comprehend and utilize instruction and musical information, that he has sufficient innate musical talent to succeed, and preferably that he has a natural aptitude for the instrument selected.

The natural progress of success or failure during the first year or so of study of the instrument eliminates those with insufficient interest, little musical talent and lacking the intellectual capacity for the instruction. Those who continue with an instrument will succeed or fail, will make rapid, slow or no progress depending partly upon themselves but to a great extent upon the skill of the teacher in motivating them through instruction which is carefully planned to proceed in small increments of learning and which build to a goal that the student can recognize and accomplish.

MUSICAL LEARNING

The things which must be taught are surprisingly few in number but of unlimited depth so that they must be developed over a period of years. These may be classified generally as notation, tone production, ear training, technical facility, and sight reading. Each is independent of the others yet a deficiency in one area will handicap development in others. They are separate but at the same time closely interrelated.

Notation

Notation, the written language of music, is not difficult to learn provided the information is well organized and presented. It is best learned independently and then applied to the instrument although this may be impossible in many situations. By learning notation independently, the student can focus his attention upon it without distraction.

In either independent study or in conjunction with the study of an instrument, the teacher can make use of drills, memory devices, workbook sheets, regular reviews, and tests until the subject is thoroughly learned. In this way both pitch and rhythmic notation can be quickly assimilated to provide a sound basis for instrumental study.

Tone Production

Tone production, the development of a beautiful sound on the instrument, is the goal of every musician. Without a beautiful sound musical expression is limited. Tone production is dependent upon several things, each of which can be isolated, described, and understood by the student. These include the instrument; the mouthpiece and/or reed or embouchure hole; embouchure formation, development and control; and inhalation, exhalation and support of breath. Each of these factors is considered in detail in the chapters on each instrument. Tone is the object of all performance, its quality the result of all performance and practice.

Ear Training

Ear training is an aspect of woodwind instruction which is frequently considered only incidentally or indirectly if at all, yet is one of the important determining factors in the musical development of the student. The ear is concerned with hearing, identifying, comparing and controlling the four basic aspects of a musical tone: pitch, loudness, rhythm and tone quality. If the student clearly recognizes that he is responsible for hearing only four different kinds of things the process of learning to hear and control them becomes much easier for him.

The ability to hear and discriminate these four aspects of a musical sound is an innate capacity which every student has to a greater or lesser degree. Some students are born with a high capacity for this type of discrimination and it is easy for them to develop, others are born with less capacity and have more difficulty in developing a proficiency. These differences in innate capacities must be recognized and students handled accordingly.

Pitch

In hearing pitch the student is involved hearing the exact pitch of the note and any intonation faults it might have. He is involved in hearing a series of melodic intervals. He hears the note he is playing as one of the notes in a harmonic structure. He is involved in hearing and correctly performing melodic ornaments such as grace notes, trills, turns, etc. All of these can be isolated or combined but can and must be developed to the student's level of musical understanding and technical proficiency on the instrument.

Loudness

In hearing loudness the student is involved in hearing the exact degree of loudness of any particular note. He is hearing changes in dynamics as in crescendo, diminuendo, attacks, and releases. He is hearing volume of sound of both himself and the other players and the interrelation between the two. He can detect imbalance in loudness or erratic and incorrect changes.

Rhythm

Rhythm is the most basic of all musical elements. Everyone can feel the beat of heavily accented music such as marches. The student in hearing rhythm or time is involved in much more than simply hearing the beat. He is concerned with the actual duration of each individual tone he produces and of each individual rest. He is concerned with tempo and tempo changes. He is concerned with the precision of attack and release both in relation to what he is playing and in relation to any other performers. He is concerned with the length of notes in various articulations: staccato, marcato, half-staccato, legato, etc. He is concerned with changes in tempo—accelerando, ritards, fermatas, etc. He hears and is sensitive to small degrees of erratic and incorrect tempo and in the duration of notes and rests.

Tone Quality

The ability to discriminate good, bad, or indifferent tone quality either in himself or in others is one of the most difficult aspects of ear training to develop. This ability is dependent to a great extent upon having a mental image of what the ideal tone quality should be so that a comparison between what he hears and the mental image can be made. It is for this reason that it is so important for every student on any level of achievement to hear live and record performances of music, especially that featuring their own instrument, as often and as consistently as possible. Innumerable other benefits occur from this experience in addition to acquiring a concept of tone quality. Appendix II is concerned with recordings which may be used for this purpose. Teachers should encourage, or even require, attendance at public concerts.

In hearing tone quality the student will develop an exact and objective concept of tone quality. He will become sensitive to variations in tone quality from one instrument to another, from one player to another on the same instrument, and in variations in tone quality on an instrument which are the result of the register in which it is played, in loudness or softness of the tone, and in how the breath supports the tone.

The goals of ear training as a portion of woodwind instruction are not achieved quickly. They are a portion of the student's work as long as he continues to play the instrument. As he gains experience on the instrument and in listening to music his powers of discrimination increase. The degree of acuity of discrimination which the teacher expects of him and he demands of himself must increase simultaneously. As he gains facility in hearing, the accumulated knowledge is transferred to his own playing which improves accordingly.

Technical Facility

Technical facility is the product of neuro-muscular patterns which are established through repetition. It is not an isolated factor in performance, but must be based on ear training so that technique is developed and controlled to achieve the highest musical results.

Technical facility is the result of intelligent conscientious practice of appropriate musical materials. Suitable materials for this are listed in the chapter on each instrument. These materials must be at the level of the student—neither too easy nor too difficult. They must be varied and interesting.

In practicing the student should recognize what he is learning. He should repeat each new pattern or sequence until its use becomes habitual. He should review regularly and in cycles so that he loses nothing that he has acquired. Most teachers will assign specific music to review rather than depending on the student to do it for himself. If these suggestions are followed, a sound technical facility will be acquired.

The ability to read at sight is one of the most valuable assets any performer can have. It is the culmination of musical learning as it combines the student's knowledge of notation, tone production, ear training and technical facility. Musicians gain facility in sight reading only by reading at sight as much as possible. A portion of every lesson, every band or orchestra rehearsal should be spent in sight reading in order to develop this facility. Students should be provided with material and encouraged to sight read regularly outside of lessons and rehearsals. Once this ability is developed other aspects of musical performance become easier to control.

The process of learning to play a woodwind instrument is one in which the various segments of learning are clearly defined, in which the objectives in each segment are clear, and in which the teacher can offer guidance and assistance. The teacher must not lose sight of the objectives of each facet of learning: notation, tone production, ear training, technical facility and sight reading. Concentrate attention on the portion of each which is appropriate to the student or class, rather than simply on "playing" the instrument.

ORGANIZATION OF INSTRUCTION

The typical beginner on a woodwind instrument is started in one of three types of instruction: (1) A heterogeneous grouping of instruments such as a beginning band, (2) a homogeneous grouping of instruments such as a beginning clarinet class, or (3) individual instuction. Each of these types of instruction is dictated by the particular circumstances of the school or personal situation and each has its advantages.

Heterogeneous Groups

A heterogeneous grouping of instruments is advantageous in that the situation provides maximum motivation for the young student, but has certain disadvantages as well. Beginning band or orchestra books which provide instructional material for all woodwind, brass, string, and percussion instruments must of necessity compromise the amount and sequence of material to accommodate the various instruments

Material which is naturally adapted to the woodwinds is difficult for brasses. Material which is naturally adapted to the beginning brass student has little or no functional value for the woodwind student. For this reason progress is at a snail's pace for every instrument and the actual accomplishment of the individual student is not at all commensurate with the amount of time consumed in the effort.

If the heterogeneous grouping is used the method selected for class use must be supplemented with additional material designed specifically for each instrument. Instruction from the supplementary material can be distributed through the lesson period alternating the use of specific instruments and the entire group. Additional material from other sources must be given to those students who are high achievers so that even within the basic class organization each student is constantly working at his own maximum level.

This is admittedly a difficult problem in class management. It requires that the teacher have a great knowledge of available materials and the ability to organize their use. This information is part of the tools of the trade and is most certainly not too much to expect, nor is it difficult to acquire if direct attention is paid to it. A wealth of suitable materials for all the woodwind instruments which can be used as a starting point for this information is listed in the chapter on that instrument.

Homogenous Grouping

The homogeneous grouping for instruction—like instrument classes—may be used on beginning, intermediate or advanced levels of instruction. It provides incentive for the student while at the same time permitting the selection of music suitable for that instrument which is uncompromised by being adjusted to problems of other instruments.

Even on the beginning level like instrument classes are preferable. Once past the elementary stage student ability and accomplishments become so diverse that like instrument classes or individual instruction are the only way in which real progress can be accomplished.

Individual Instruction

Individual instruction, or private lessons, is by far the most successful way of teaching and learning a woodwind instrument. Some will make the point that class instruction gives better motivation for the very beginner than individual instruction. There is no doubt that competition with other players is a great incentive to many students, and many instructors wisely take full advantage of this.

On the other hand the larger the class the less individual attention each student receives. This may lead to the establishment of incorrect habits in embouchure, hand position, fingering, breath support, articulation and other facets of performance. Habits established at the beginning level are extremely difficult to change and require considerable effort on the part of the student and considerable skill and patience on the part of the instructor to correct. It would be a more efficient use of student and instructor time to use the individual attention necessary to correct bad habits earlier in the instructional process to keep them from developing.

Private lessons in addition to the beginning class instruction are ideal to combine the advantages of each and should be encouraged. Any student who is seriously interested in learning to play his instrument should be strongly encouraged to take private lessons no matter what his level of advancement. It is safe to say, and all authorities will agree, that no real advanced level of technical or musical accomplishment is possible without individual instruction.

INSTRUCTIONAL MATERIALS

The best organization of instructional materials on any technical level involves a five classification program. Material in each of these classifications is used simultaneously to provide a well-rounded musical experience, provide stimulation to the study of the instrument, to maintain interest through a variety of materials and to assure a continual advancement in technical and musical proficiency.

One assignment in each of the five classifications might well be given for each lesson. The amount of material available for each instrument is sufficient to introduce this type of instruction early in the beginning stage and carry it through to a high artistic level. Except for information about solo and ensemble literature which is readily available elsewhere, a broad cross section of materials available in the other classifications is given in the chapter on each instrument.

The five classifications of materials and musical experiences may be listed as follows:

1. *A methods book.* These are basic to the study of the instrument and provide continuity. Methods books for every instrument are available which are suitable for students from the very beginning stages to the most advanced. American publishers have been very active in providing methods books for the elementary levels of study, and they exist in large numbers for virtually every instrument. Theoretically they are organized to progress in easy stages and to provide sufficient material for the establishment of the factors being learned. In practice the various beginning methods vary tremendously in the success with which they do this.

Three American publishers in particular—Belwin, Rubank, and Carl Fischer—have made special efforts to provide materials for the public school age student on the beginning and intermediate levels. These materials have been written or selected by authors who are both music educators and specialists in woodwinds. Beginning, intermediate, and advanced methods and supplementary materials by these publishers in particular should be examined. Other American publishers have materials of the same type and quality available, but not to the extent of these three publishers. The study material lists for each chapter includes a selected list of all of these.

Many teachers have found it desirable to use two or three beginning methods simultaneously and to coordinate assignments in them in order to provide sufficient material on the same problem for the beginner to firmly establish the technical facility being learned. Teachers of students on the elementary level have a general tendency to expect too little of their students and to give them too little to do. Instructors of woodwind instruments would be wise to model their instructional procedures on the successful private piano teacher of young beginners who normally has each student working out of three or four books of similar material at the same time. For example, in the beginning study of clarinet Paul van Bodegraven's *Adventures in Clarinet Playing* and James Collis' *Modern Course for the Clarinet* make an excellent pair. Other combinations are possible for the clarinet and effective combinations for the other instruments can be easily selected. Material in the other four classifications should be introduced as soon as the student progresses to the point where suitable material is available.

Methods books for other levels of advancement are available for each instrument. These are listed in the chapter for each instrument in sections called "Beginning Methods" which includes series made up of two or three volumes sometimes under the same title and sometimes called beginning, intermediate, and advanced even though they are in reality different levels of beginning books.

The second group of methods books is described as "Standard Methods." These are the traditional methods such as Klose for clarinet, Altes for flute, Barret for oboe, Weissenborn for bassoon, and Mayeur for saxophone. For the most part these are more than fifty years old, are not arranged progressively, and do not take advantage of contemporary teaching techniques and are not suitable for beginning study of the instrument.

These must be used, however, in some point of the study of the instrument since the material they contain is basic to the study of the instrument. It is incumbent upon the teacher to assign the material in the correct order for a particular student. None of these is suitable for a beginning student, but most contain material from the intermediate to the most advanced level. Most students will use one or more of these over a period of a year or two or more in combination with other materials. The total number of standard methods books for all the woodwind instruments is not large and a skilled teacher will become familiar with all of them.

2. *Technical studies.* Technical studies are the mechanical note patterns which are common to all musical styles and in which the student develops a basic technical facility which can be applied to all his playing. These involve major and minor scales; major, minor, diminished and augmented triads; dominant, diminished, and other forms of seventh chords all in various patterns, various ranges, and in every key. To these is added mechanical exercises to establish finger patterns which are difficult on that particular instrument and which will enable the student to gain facility in using all possible alternate fingerings.

Such studies are available which are suitable for students on any level of advancement past the beginning stage. Many of these are incorporated in the standard methods, others are published separately. The Pares studies which are available for all woodwind instruments are almost exclusively scale studies suitable for the lower intermediate level. For clarinet the Albert *Twenty-four Varied Scales and Exercises;* Books I, II, and III of the Kroepsch *416 Progressive Daily Studies;* and Part III of the Baermann *Method for Clarinet* are typical of this material. The three volume *Scales and Daily Exercises* for bassoon by Oubradous; the *Scales and Arpeggios—480 Exercises* of Moyse for flute; sections of the Andraud *Vade Mecum* for oboe; and Arnold's *Fingered Scales* or Rascher's *Scales for the Saxophone* for saxophone are representative of this kind of material on a more advanced level. Other material of this nature on every level of advancement is listed in the "Additional Study Materials" section of each chapter.

The skilled teacher will take full advantage of this common core of technique which has universal application and keep his students working with it at their maximum level. Consistent use of this type of study is a shortcut to technical proficiency on any instrument.

3. *Études or studies.* These are books of studies of varying lengths each of which is concerned with developing a facility in a particular segment of study. Such studies concern themselves with tone control, phrasing, staccato, articulation patterns, a particular key, etc., and differ from technical studies in that they are musical rather than mechanical. The student practices them primarily for musical results with technical facility a subordinate objective. Material of this kind is available for every level of technical advancement past the early beginning stage. It is the core of the study of any instrument.

Much of the study material available for each instrument is of this nature, since it is possible to include all musical styles from baroque through contemporary so that the student becomes familiar with various styles as they apply to his instrument. So much of the available material of this nature is in the nineteenth century style that it is necessary to make a real effort to find suitable materials in other styles. Even so, much of the study of style must be relegated to the solo and ensemble classifications.

Typical of the books of études available are the Lo Presti *20 Melodic Studies for Clarinet* which are of lower intermediate level of difficulty. The *40 Studies* and *32 Studies* for clarinet by Rose; the Ferling *48 Studies* for oboe or saxophone; the studies by Berbiguier and Anderson for flute; the Weissenborn *Studies, Op. 8* and the Jancourt studies for bassoon. Much material in this classification is listed in the "Additional Study Materials" section in the chapter for each instrument. The teacher must become familiar with as many of these as possible.

4. *Duets or other ensemble music.* The opportunity to play with another instrument or instruments is an integral part of the study of any instrument on any level. Ensemble experience is an important aspect of ear training in that the student must relate his pitch, loudness, rhythm and tone quality to other players.

Duets for like instruments are especially valuable since the clear texture gives an opportunity for hearing and comparing. If the student is taking private lessons playing duets with the teacher gives him an auditory model to follow in the matters of tone quality, phrasing, intonation and style. Much musical learning is accomplished by the process of imitation and this experience is invaluable.

Playing duets, trios, quartets, etc. with other student players provides a different kind of valuable experience for all. Learning to play together, to become sensitive to the playing of others, and to become an integral part of a musical group is a part of becoming a good player. Such experiences can be encouraged and provided on a regular organized basis, on a volunteer basis or as a recreational activity which the student does on his own. The more of this type of activity the better for the student.

Duets are frequently included in the standard methods books. Volumes of duets by a single composer are available as well as compilation of selected duets of various composers. These are available on virtually every level of technical advancement.

5. *Solos.* Every woodwind instrument is a solo instrument. Opportunities for performing a solo with piano accompaniment must be provided for every student. Such performances provide an incentive for practice and develop self confidence to a degree no other activity can provide. Solos on every level from the most elementary to the most advanced are available for every instrument. So many are available in fact that the problem is not finding a solo but in finding the best solo for a particular student at a particular time.

Solo experience can be provided for students in any type of class instructions as well as those taking individual instruction. Every student should have several solos of various kinds ready to play at any time and should be preparing others at the same time. They should be encouraged to play all of them from memory and over a period of time develop complete confidence in their ability to do so.

The *Selective Music Lists* published by the Music Educators National Conference has graded lists of solos and ensembles for the public school age player. These lists are highly selective and do not include a very high percentage of available material for any instrument. This list is a useful starting point but must be considerably expanded in most categories to acquire sufficient teaching materials. Various authors whose books make literature recommendations are indicated at the beginning of the Study Materials section in each chapter.

BEGINNING METHODS

There are numerous beginning methods for each instrument, some of them very excellent both from the standpoint of pedagogy and musical content, others strong on pedagogy and weak on musical content, and still others weak on both points.

Since the excitement in starting the study of a new and strange instrument wears off rapidly once the student realizes that a real effort is necessary, his initiative and interest must be sustained by the material he is studying. Dreary mechanical exercises, endless repetition of the same thing, difficult technical problems introduced without sufficient preparation or material to accomplish them, and the lack of musically satisfying melodies soon turn what could be pleasant into a dissatisfying experience. Students lose interest and either fail to make satisfactory progress or drop the study of the instrument entirely.

Probably the most important decision a teacher will ever make for a student is what book or books to use for his very beginning experience.

Examine and evaluate all beginning methods for each instrument. Do they progress in small increments of learning, are the problems presented in logical order, is sufficient material included to establish habits for each problem, is the musical content varied and interesting or is it trite and mechanical? What books can be combined to give the student sufficient material on the same level of difficulty? At what point in the book, if at all, can solos with piano accompaniment be introduced? Does the book contain duets or trios, and if not at what point can this experience be introduced? Beginners need a variety of approaches to the same problem. The young beginners, especially, do not realize the value of many repetitions of the same music but will practice different music containing the same problems and achieve the same result. Take full advantage of this fact.

New beginning methods for each instrument appear regularly. Examine these carefully and compare them with those previously selected. There is a tendency among music teachers to consider a new publication superior to all others simply because it is new. This is not necessarily true. The new publication may well be inferior to older publications. Excellent new material is being published and should be used, but not simply because it is new, but because a careful evaluation points out its usefulness.

PRACTICE

All teachers assign music for the students to practice, but few tell them how to practice. Practice is a habit with students and the sooner this habit is established the more successful he will be. He must understand that a certain amount of daily practice is required, and that daily means seven days a week. He should have a specific time to practice each day, rather than changing times from day to day according to his other activities. Schedule a specific hour of the day, with the cooperation of the parents of younger children, which is set aside for practice. If this is done, other activities do not interfere and a habit of regular practice is established. It is effective to have the student keep a record of the time practiced each day and report regularly to his teacher.

Materials

Daily practice on all five classifications of materials is required. In addition regular reviews of previously learned material must be scheduled so that the player does not lose command of that particular facility. The review makes excellent material with which to begin the practice session, or the practice session can begin with typical warm-up material such as long tones, slow scales, etc.

The student should learn to devote his full mental powers to his practicing, rather than letting his mind wander. Suggestions by the teacher of specific items in each portion of the assignment to which he must pay attention will help the student. The student should alternate periods of complete concentration with periods of rest and relaxation. Many students, especially the younger ones, will profit more from two shorter practice periods during the day rather than one long one.

Speed

Many students both experienced and inexperienced practice too fast. One of the most difficult problems of the teacher is to make the student realize the value of slow practice, and to teach him restraint in the matter of tempo. Use of a metronome is helpful provided the student is instructed on when and how to use it, and does not let it become a crutch. Practicing too fast makes rough technique, poor musicianship in the matter of musical values and phrasing, establishes uncontrolled articulation, and eliminates much of the value of the practice period in the important areas of ear training. Showing the student frequently in class or lesson how to practice will help impress upon him the old axiom that haste makes waste.

Planning

A carefully planned assignment plus the efficient use of practice time can help the student overcome any weaknesses he might have in tone, technique, intonation and phrasing. During the practice session he can listen to his tone quality carefully, correct or develop his embouchure with the use of a mirror, select and experiment with reeds if he is playing a reed instrument, spending as much time as necessary to accomplish his assignment.

New Material

New material is best practiced first slowly and completely through. This first impression is the most important so the student must go slowly enough that every note is correct and that correct fingering choices are made. Fingerings can be marked on the music if desirable.

This is followed by several slow repetitions to establish notes and fingerings. By this time the difficult sections of a few notes or a measure or so can be identified. Practice is continued by isolating and practicing only these difficult sections until the sequence is established. If the sequence is particularly difficult practice two or three notes, add another note and continue to repeat, then add other notes one by one until the entire sequence can be played easily.

Finally practice the phrase in which this sequence occurs. When this is done with each section the entire study can be practiced slowly at first and then with gradually increasing speed until the proper tempo is reached. Practicing the entire study, especially if it is a page or two in length, without working out the difficult sections is a poor use of time and will not achieve the desired results.

Intonation

Individual practice sessions where the player can hear himself are invaluable in developing intonation on the instrument. Students must be taught to hear correct intonation by using an electronic device or by playing with an experienced player. They become accustomed to the temperament of their own instrument and accept it as being correct even though it might not be. Hearing correct intonation does not come naturally, it must be acquired. A study of intonation and how to correct deficiencies must be a continual part of instruction if the students is to become able to help himself acquire perfection.

Phrasing

Phrasing is worked out in practice, and is the final objective of all the other aspects of performance. Instruction in phrasing is frequently neglected in favor of instruction in technique. Technique without good phrasing is valueless.

Students must be taught to recognize phrases, periods and sections of a composition, together with repetitions and contrasting sections which make up good musical form. An understanding of the simple structures of music is easy to acquire and gives the student a concrete basis upon which to build his phrasing.

Developing good phrasing is a slow process in which the student needs considerable help. Ends of phrases, places to breathe, slight nuances in dynamics should be marked in the music by the teacher so the student can practice intelligently. As the student gains musical experience and technical facility various musical styles must be introduced together with details of how each style is phrased and how they differ from each other.

BREATHING AND BREATH CONTROL

Correct inhalation, exhalation and breath support form the foundation for woodwind performance without which only limited success is possible. The only correct breathing is that described as diaphragmatic. This is exactly the same breathing process that is taught in playing brass instruments, singing and public speaking.

Details of diaphragmatic breathing are so widely known and taught that they need not be repeated here. Those who are interested in the physiology of the breathing process should consult the article on inhalation in one of the large standard encyclopedias where it is thoroughly and simply explained. Once this is understood teaching it becomes simpler.

Every teacher has his or her own set of words to describe correct breathing as well as procedures used in teaching it. The reader is encouraged to observe as many skilled teachers as possible in their teaching procedures and techniques which they feel will be successful. A variety of ways of explaining and doing the same thing is valuable.

In teaching the woodwinds correct breathing and breath support must be taught from the very beginning of study, reviewed regularly, checked regularly and corrected if necessary until it becomes habitual with the student. Many many problems which woodwind players have can be traced to incorrect breathing and breath support. The importance of doing it properly cannot be emphasized enough.

ORGANIZATION OF CHAPTERS

The chapters dealing with each instrument follow the same plan of organization for easy reference. A brief summary of this organization follows. Where necessary, basic similar material is repeated in more than one chapter so that the reader will not have to make cross references. If the reader is interested in the saxophone, for example, all pertinent material for that instrument is in that chapter.

The Family of Instruments

All of the commonly used instruments of the family with their transpositions and playing ranges are listed. The ranges are given for beginning, intermediate, and advanced players. These are normal, commonly accepted ranges, but may vary considerably from player to player.

Assembling the Instrument

A standard procedure is given for assembly of each instrument and illustrated with detailed photography. This is a matter of some importance for every beginning student and more so for some instruments than others. Learning this procedure and following it carefully will avoid many future problems. The section includes a list of the commonly found faults and a checklist.

Holding Positions

Holding positions—seated, standing, and resting—are presented and illustrated. This general position is followed by a detailed, illustrated section on hand positions. Where there is more than one commonly accepted position, it is also noted. This section also includes a list of commonly found faults and a checklist.

Embouchure Formation

One or more standard embouchure formations are described in detail, and directions for setting the embouchure given. A checklist is provided for judging embouchure formation.

Tuning and Intonation

Details of tuning the instrument are given, followed by a section on intonation in which the natural intonation tendencies of the instrument are discussed. This is followed by a discussion of various items which effect the intonation of a particular player on a specific instrument. The effect of such things as embouchure, dynamics, playing position, mechanical factors, and alternate fingerings on intonation are presented with directions for correcting any problem areas.

Tone

Tone is discussed, and the various registers of the instrument identified. In this connection the recommendation is made for the student to study a variety of recorded performances to get an aural concept of the best tone quality for this instrument. The section includes a listing and discussion with remedial measures to be taken for the commonly found problems in tone.

Tonguing

Tonguing is discussed in detail, including tongue placement for fundamental articulation, followed by legato and staccato articulation procedures. For more advanced players double, triple, and flutter tonguing are included. The section concludes with the common problems in articulation with suggestions on how to correct them.

Technique Problems

All common technique problems, which vary greatly from instrument to instrument, are presented in this section, with suggestions for the solution of each. Standard alternate fingerings, special fingerings, trill fingerings, etc., are presented along with directions for when to use each. The production and use of harmonics on the instrument are in this section where applicable.

Transpositions for the Player

This section is for the more advanced players who are called upon to transpose parts from another instrument. The commonly needed transpositions for each instrument are included.

Selection of Instruments

Various models of the instrument under discussion are described, along with alternatives in key mechanism which are available.

Student Qualifications and Aptitudes

A brief discussion of student qualifications and aptitudes for a particular instrument is found here. Authorities vary greatly in their attitudes toward specific qualifications and aptitudes for undertaking the study of any particular instrument. Some teachers have great success in applying specific standards, others use none at all other than physical size of the student. This section presents items of a general nature, with no attempt to resolve differences of opinion.

Care of the Instrument

Proper care of an instrument is basic to success. This section discusses these problems in detail and concludes with suggestions for the regular maintenance of the instrument.

Bibliography of Study Materials

This section includes a selective list of study materials for the instrument. It is divided into Beginning Methods, Standard Methods, and Additional Study Materials. Solo and ensemble material is not included as it is beyond the scope of this book, but sources for specific information for the instrument under discussion are given.

A listing of composers, titles, and publishers is only the starting point for acquiring teaching materials. Only a knowledge of the music itself can give the answer to the quality of the music and how and when it could be used. The reader is urged to examine as many of the titles listed as possible, and to evaluate them whenever possible through actual use. Many books do not give the results in practice that a visual examination would indicate. The greatest problem a teacher has is to select the right music for a particular student at a specific stage in his development.

Study and Achievement Questions

A number of questions on the content of the chapter are provided. These are only suggestive and both instructors and students will be able to provide others for their own use.

The details of each item in each chapter represent the best concensus of opinion on that particular problem. Where more than one commonly used procedure is widely used, alternates are presented. It is not expected that every specialist on every instrument will agree completely with every detail. Music is an art, not a science, and various ways of doing things give equally good results. But unless the instructor has different recommendations, the contents of these chapters may be followed with the confidence that they represent a standard of the profession.

Chapter 2

Clarinet

The clarinet is considered the basic instrument of the woodwind family and it is the appropriate instrument with which to begin the study of teaching the woodwinds. In the schools there are probably more clarinet students than all the other woodwinds combined. It is by far the most common beginning woodwind instrument and countless thousands of youngsters begin the study of the clarinet each year. Some to continue on the clarinet, others to transfer to another woodwind instrument, and unfortunately many to discover that they have too little interest, motivation or talent to continue.

For these reasons as well as to insure continued development of more advanced players the basics of teaching clarinet must be thoroughly understood. While it is desirable for all teachers to have as much experience on all the woodwinds as possible, the greatest experience should be on the clarinet. The basics learned on it can be successfully applied to all the other woodwinds.

THE CLARINET FAMILY

From the high E-flat to the B-flat Contra-Bass the clarinet family forms a choir whose pitch range and tone color more nearly approximates that of the string family than any other family of woodwind instruments. A full compliment of instruments in the clarinet family forms the basis of the modern concert band. Late nineteenth and twentieth century orchestral composers have taken advantage of the variety of clarinet sounds and have used all the instruments.

Fingerings for all the instruments are identical except for minor adjustments on the lower pitch instruments made to help tonal control. The basic embouchure is the same for all instruments with adjustments made according to the size of the mouthpiece of the instrument.

The discussions in this chapter will center around the B-flat clarinet with special problems and differences between it and the other instruments in the family noted in the course of the discussion.

All the instruments in the family have the same theoretical *written* playing range:

but all are transposing instruments and *sound* in different ranges.

The transpositions and ranges in which each instrument sounds is as follows:

1. *E-flat Clarinet*: Sounds a minor third higher than written.[1]

Written Sounds Range of actual sounds[2]

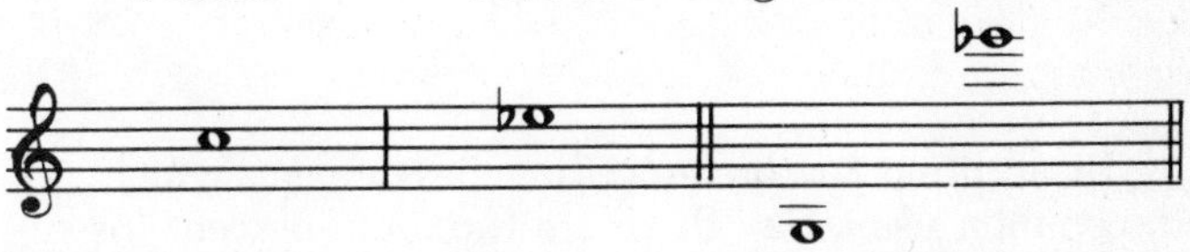

2. *B-flat Clarinet*: Sounds a major second lower than written.

Written Sounds Range of actual sounds

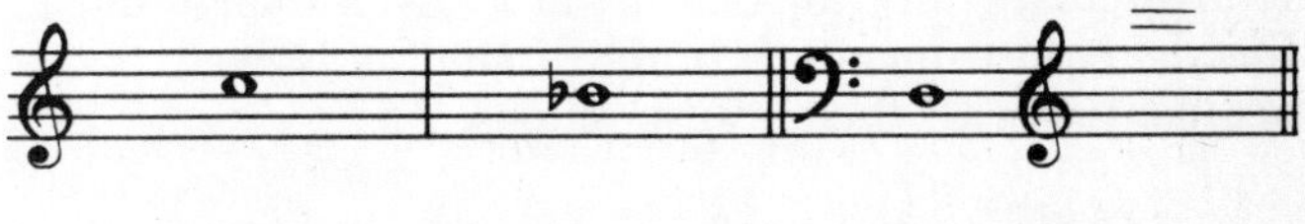

3. *E-flat Alto Clarinet*: Sounds a major sixth lower than written.

Written Sounds Range of actual sounds

1. As an aid in remembering transpositions of instruments a written "C" sounds the designated pitch of the instrument. A written "C" for any E-flat instrument sounds E-flat; a written "C" for any B-flat instrument sounds B-flat. The octave in which the sounding note is heard is determined by whether it is a soprano, alto, tenor, bass or contra-bass member of the family.

2. In the range of actual sounds for each of the instruments the highest note is the limit of the intermediate playing range given in this chapter, rather than the theoretical upper limit.

4. *B-flat Bass Clarinet*: Sounds an octave plus a major second lower than written.

Written Sounds Range of actual sounds

5. *E-flat Contra-Bass Clarinet*: Sounds an octave plus a major sixth lower than written.

Written Sounds Range of actual sounds

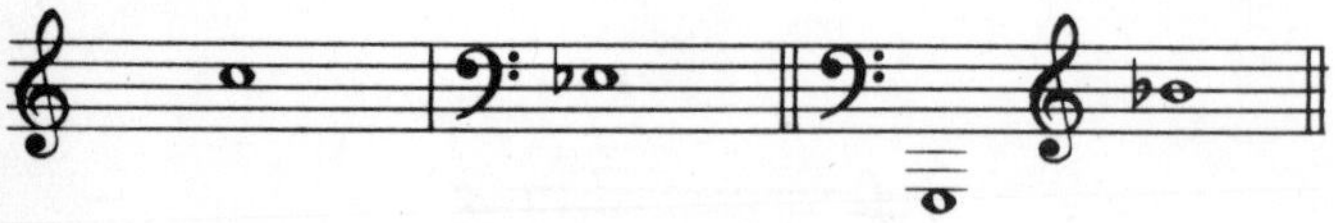

6. *B-flat Contra-Bass Clarinet*: Sounds two octaves plus a major second lower than written.

Written Sounds Range of actual sounds

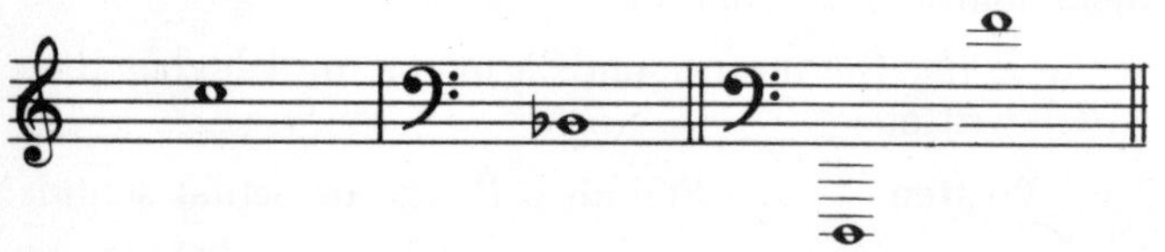

In addition to the preceding instruments which are in common use today there are three obsolescent instruments in the clarinet family for which parts are found in orchestral scores. They are the D clarinet, another version of the E-flat soprano; the C clarinet which has been replaced by the modern B-flat instrument; and the Basset Horn, actually an Alto Clarinet in F. Even though music for these instruments is rarely found it is well to be acquainted with their transpositions.

7. *D Clarinet*: Sounds a major second higher than written.

Written Sounds

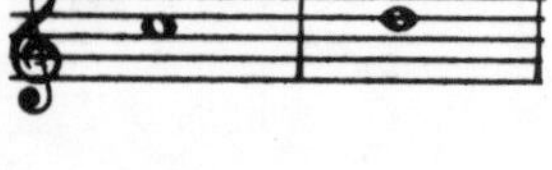

8. *C Clarinet*: Sounds as written.

Written Sounds

9. *Basset Horn*: Sounds a perfect fifth lower than written.

Written Sounds

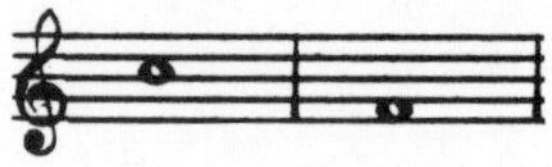

PLAYING RANGES

Although all the instruments in the clarinet family have the same theoretical written playing range, but in practice this complete range is rarely if ever called for. Certain portions of the playing ranges of the various instruments are technically easier than others for students in various stages of development, and on the lower pitched instruments notes in the extreme high register are rarely used because the tone quality produced is not really satisfactory and contributes little to the sonority of an orchestra or band.

There are generally accepted playing ranges for each of the instruments which are useful in teaching situations so that one may know what to expect from students. For convenience these have been designated as *Beginning*, the range a typical elementary school player should have by the end of his first year of study; *Intermediate*, the range which can be expected from the average good high school player; and *Advanced*, the range in which the professional player is called upon to perform. The differences in these ranges for clarinets are primarily in the upper limits, since the lowest notes do not present major difficulties either in tone production or fingering. As in any technical skill great variation in accomplishment from individual to individual can be expected, and these playing ranges are given simply as general indications.

The E-flat and A clarinets are not generally considered beginning instruments, but are usually assigned to players with previous experience on the B-flat clarinet. Students transferring to these instruments from the B-flat clarinet would not be considered beginners on these instruments and can be expected to have a much greater range than that indicated for beginners. The beginning range is, however, that which students transferring will be able to play easily and with good tone quality without too much experience on the new instrument.

1. *B-flat Clarinet* (*E-flat and A*)

Beginning Intermediate Advanced

Parts of the Instrument

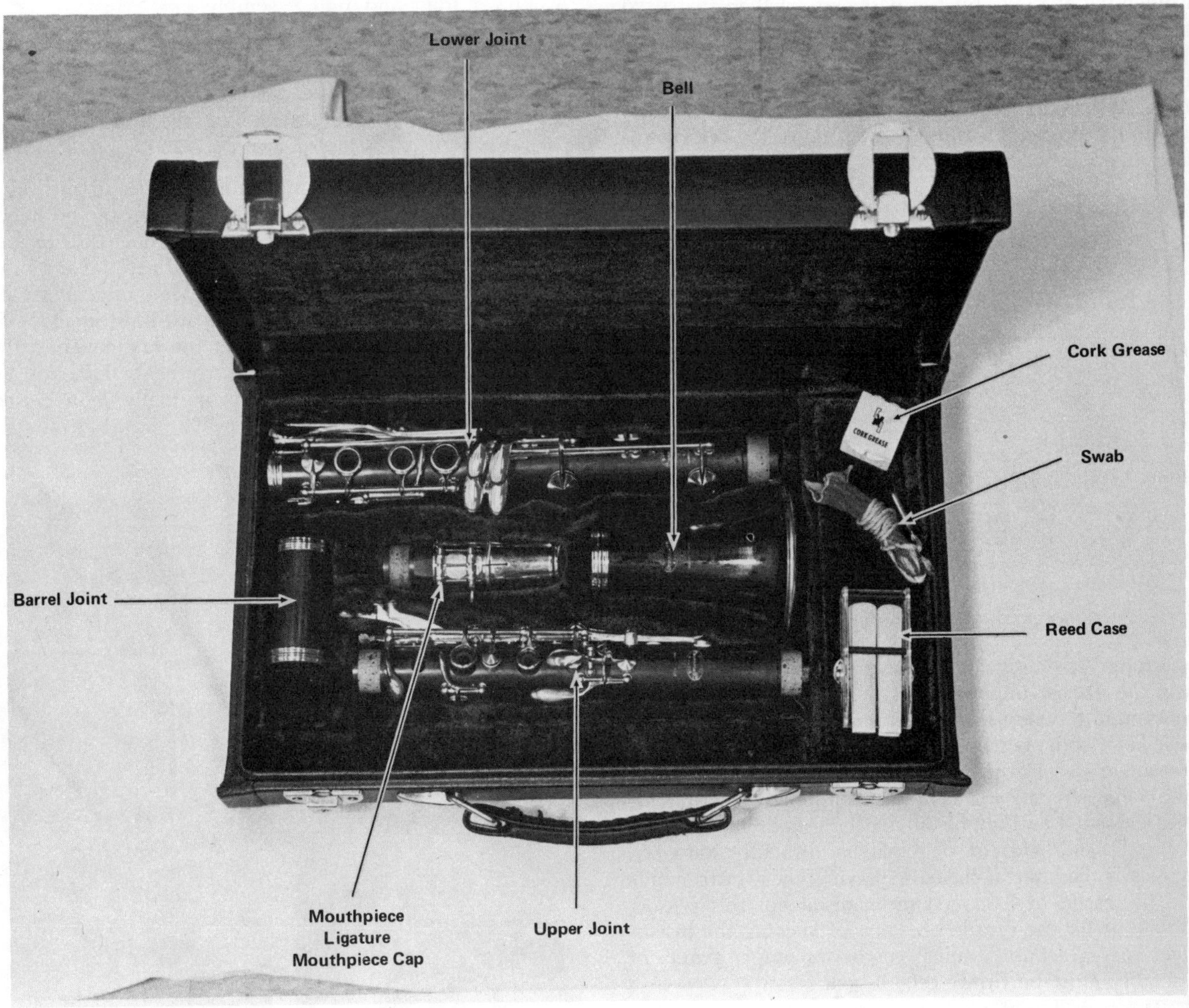

Figure C-1

The Alto, Bass and Contra-Bass instruments, like the E-flat and A, are usually given to players who have developed a basic facility on the B-flat clarinet. As the fundamental pitch of the instrument gets lower the higher notes are increasingly unsatisfactory in quality, and for this reason most arrangers write for the Bass and Contra-Bass instruments primarily in the range indicated below as *Intermediate.*

Orchestral composers and orchestrators normally use a much wider range for the Bass clarinet than that used in band, approximately that range indicated below as *Advanced,* since the tone quality of the instrument in the upper portion of the range blends well with the string tone. All three of these instruments demand special attention to the fingering for those notes above the Intermediate range.

2. *Alto, Bass, Contra-Bass Clarinets.*

Intermediate

Advanced

ASSEMBLING THE INSTRUMENT

Proper assembly and disassembly of the instrument is of the utmost importance, and must be taught to students from the very first lesson. Probably more damage—bent keys, rods, bent connecting levers, etc.— is done to instruments in putting them together and taking them apart than by all other means combined. Instruments with damaged and out-of-line mechanism do not respond properly, and a great deal of the difficulty students, especially beginners, have in playing their instruments can be traced to damaged mechanism. For this reason, as well as for the simple necessity of keeping the instrument in perfect mechanical condition, proper habits of assembly must be firmly established.

The assembly of an instrument must be accomplished without putting pressure on any key or rod which will bend it in any way. It is obviously impossible to put the clarinet together without touching the keys, so in selecting the way in which the parts are held the hands and fingers must be against posts or keys and rings which are not affected by the pressure put upon them. There are, of course, various possibilities.

The following step-by-step procedure is given in detail, and every student should practice it carefully until each procedure is correct and automatic. Before starting the process make sure that all cork joints are well greased with prepared cork grease so that undue pressure will not have to be applied. Study the photograph and directions for each step carefully and repeat the operation several times before proceeding to the next.

Assembling the B-flat Clarinet (E-flat and A)

A. Lower Joint and Bell Assembly

1. Figure C-2. Grasp the lower joint with the left hand, palm of the hand against the wood of the instrument beneath the keys, and with the flesh between the thumb and the forefinger against the thumb rest.

2. Figure C-3. With the palm in position, the first and second fingers cover and press the second and third rings holding the joint firmly in the palm of the hand. The other two fingers are free, and do not press on the keys. The base of the thumb is held firmly against the wood at the side of the instrument, but there must be no pressure against the rod underneath it. Students with small hands may need to press on the key covering the tone hole on the side of the instrument. There is no danger of bending it since it is normally in a closed position.

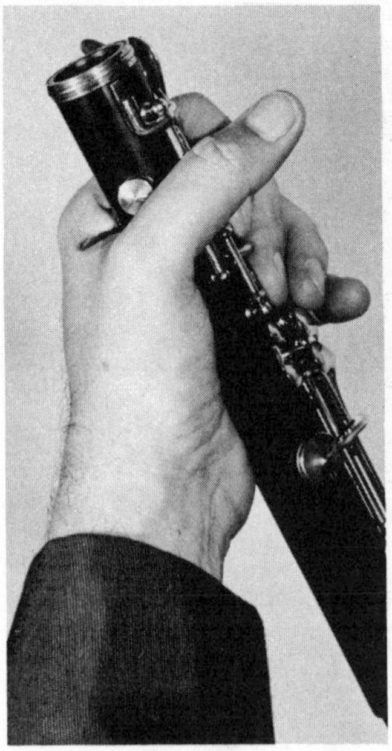

Figure C-2

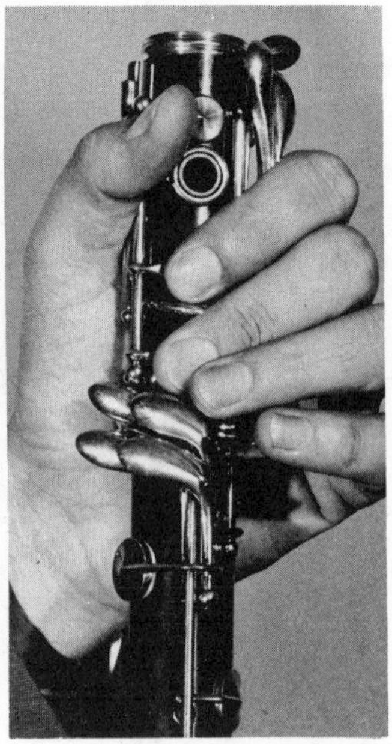

Figure C-3

3. Figure C-4. The right hand graps the bell with the large end of the palm of the hand with the fingers holding it securely.

Figure C-4

4. Figure C-5. The bell is then pushed on the lower joint with a twisting motion until it rests solidly against the joint.

Figure C-5

B. Lower Joint to Upper Joint Assembly

1. Figure C-6. The upper joint is held in the left hand with the palm of the hand against the wood on the under side of the instrument.

2. Figure C-7. The first finger of the hand presses on the first tone hole, and the remaining three fingers fall naturally over the remaining tone holes and the one key on the top of this joint. Pressure down on this key will not bend it as it fits solidly against the the body of the instrument when pressed down.

The ring of the second hole must be held completely down throughout the assembly of these two sections as it raises the connecting lever between the upper and lower joints so that they may be fitted together without bending. Bending this connecting lever out of line is the most common fault of improper assembly.

3. Figure C-8. The thumb rests against the lever keys on the side of the instrument. It may exert some pressure against these keys since they are not subject to bending if the pressure is downward in their normal plane of movement against the body of the instrument.

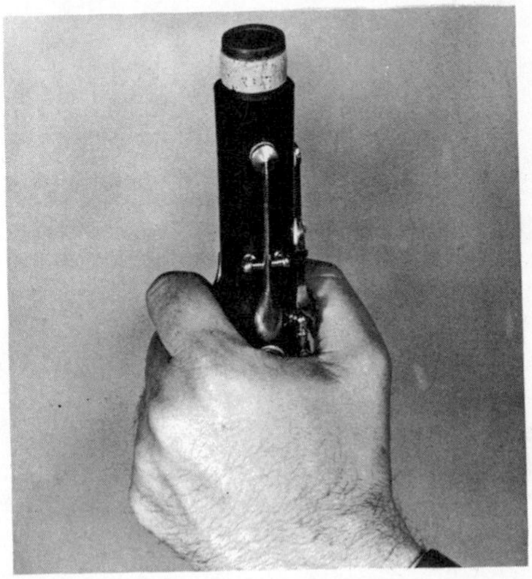

Figure C-6

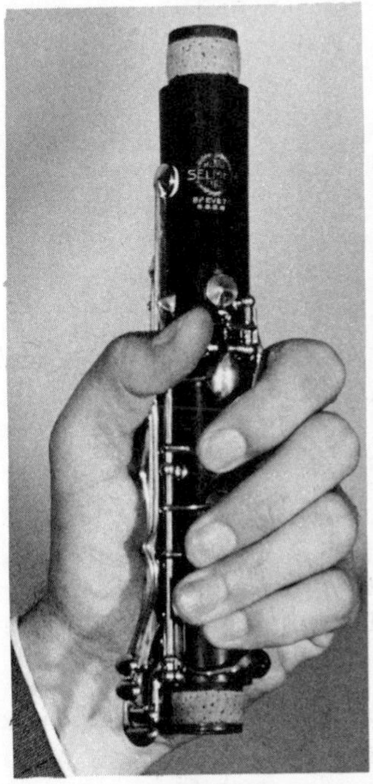

Figure C-7

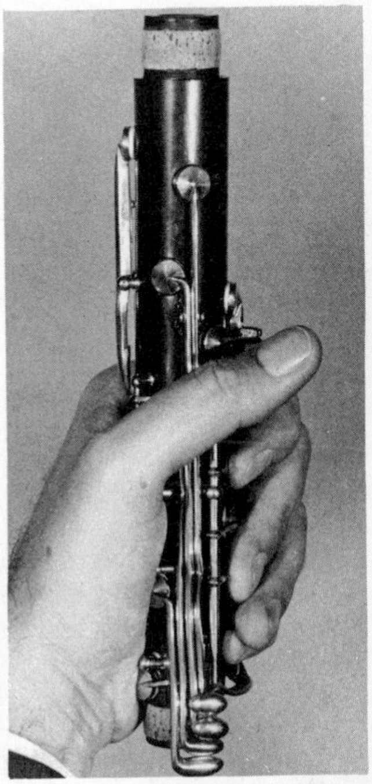

Figure C-8

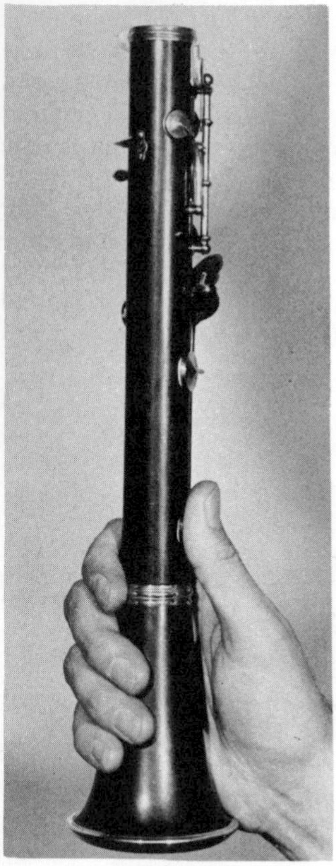

Figure C-9

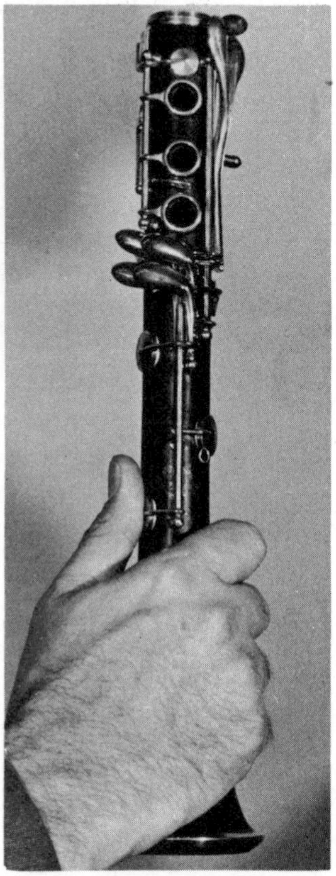

Figure C-10

Figure C-11

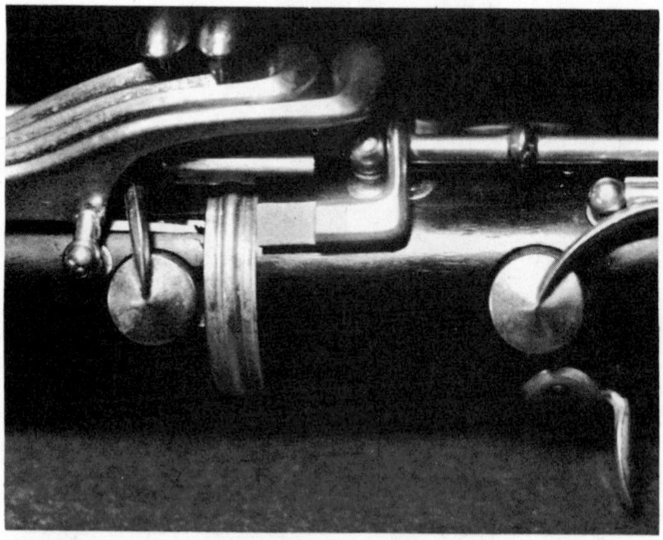

Figure C-12

4. Figure C-9. The previously assembled lower joint and bell are held in the right hand. First finger on the wood of the lower joint, the remaining three fingers on the bell pressing the instrument against the palm of the hand.

5. Figure C-10. The ball of the thumb presses down on the key covering the bottom tone hole on the side of the instrument to add stability and control to the procedure.

6. Figure C-11. With the left hand and right hand holding the two sections properly, they are pushed together with a slight rotary motion back and forth. They must not be twisted too far from their normal alignment or the overlapping keys on either side will be bent.

7. Figure C-12. If the ring covering the second hole of the upper joint is closed, the connecting lever is raised to allow connection on the lower joint to move freely under it.

8. Figure C-13. When the two sections are firmly together line up the two sections of the connecting lever.

Figure C-13

C. Adding the Barrel Joint

1. Figure C-14. Hold the barrel joint in the palm of the right hand with the thumb over the upper end and the fingers curled around it.

2. Figure C-15. Rest the end of the bell on the leg

Figure C-14

Figure C-15

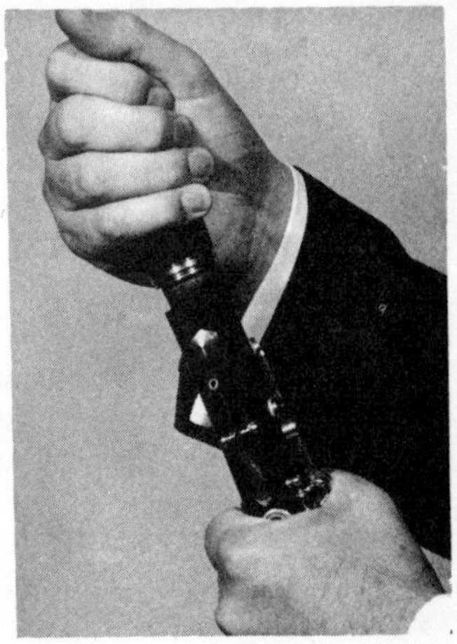

Figure C-16

with the left hand holding the upper joint the same way the upper joint was held when it was connected with the lower joint. Slide the barrel joint on with a twisting motion.

D. Adding the Mouthpiece

1. Figure C-16. Hold the mouthpiece in the palm of the right hand with the tips of the fingers over the flat portion. With the clarinet resting on the leg, and the left hand holding the upper joint as before, insert the mouthpiece with a twisting motion until it is firmly seated.

2. Figure C-17. Line up the flat part of the mouthpiece so that it is centered exactly on the register key on the bottom of the clarinet. The final step in the process is to add the reed. This is discussed at the end of this section of the chapter.

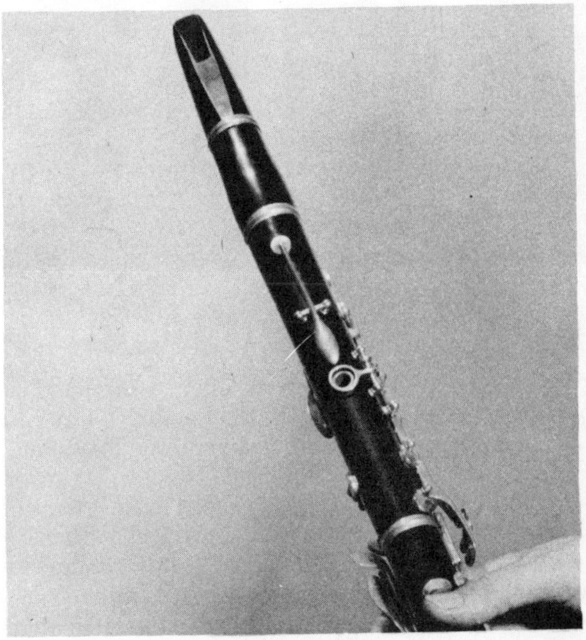

Figure C-17

Assembling the Alto and Bass Clarinet

The way in which the Alto and Bass Clarinet are assembled differs from the procedure for the soprano instruments in only one major way. Because the bell extends up and over some of the key mechanism on the lower joint when it is in place, the upper and lower joints are put together first, then the bell is added. The metal neck on which the mouthpiece fits, replaces the tuning barrel of the soprano instruments and poses no difficulty in assembly. Because the keys and rods on these instruments are longer they are even more susceptible to the danger of being bent than the smaller instruments and must be handled with great care. Be sure all cork joints are well greased before starting the assembly. In the photographs a Bass Clarinet is used, but the procedures for the Alto and Contra-Bass instruments are identical.

A. Lower and Upper Joint Assembly

1. Figure C-18. The upper joint is held in the left hand with the palm of the hand against the wood on the underside of the instrument.

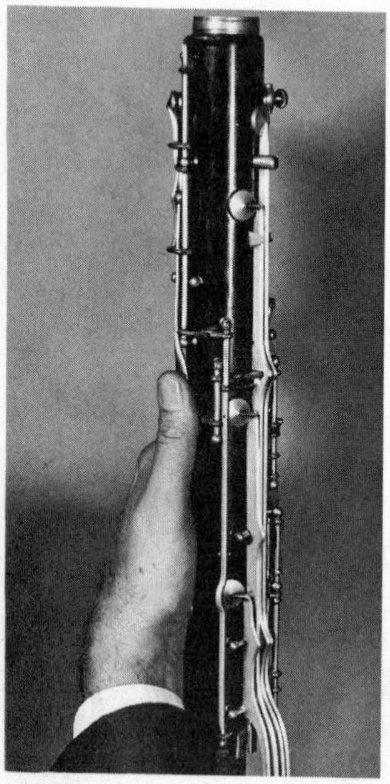

Figure C-18

Figure C-19

2. Figure C-19. The first finger of the hand presses on the first tone hole, and the remaining three fingers fall naturally over the remaining tone holes and the one key on the top of this joint. Pressure down on this key will not bend it as it fits solidly against the body of the instrument when pressed down. The cover of the second hole must be held down firmly throughout the assembly of these two sections as it raises the connecting lever between the upper and lower joints so that they may be fitted together without danger of bending.

3. Figure C-20. The lower joint is held in the right hand, with the long rods of the keys operated by the right little finger protected against pressure by the palm of the hand cupped over them.

4. Figure C-21. The ball of the thumb presses the upper pad of the two tone holes on the right side, and the base of the thumb presses the lower. Avoid any pressure against the rods of these keys.

The second finger of the right hand covers and presses the pad on the left side of the instrument, and the remaining three fingers grasp the wood of the joint. Make slight adjustment in hand position if necessary to avoid any pressure on the long rods of these keys.

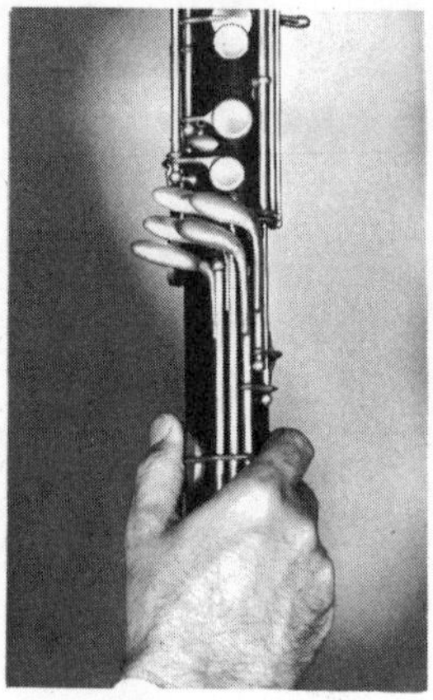

Figure C-20

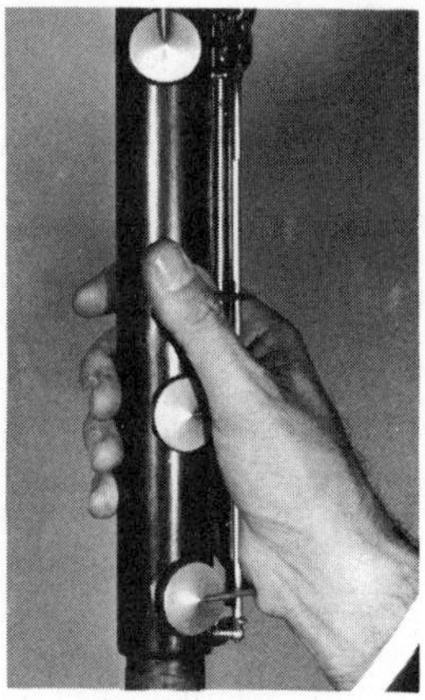

Figure C-21

5. Figure C-22. With the left and right hands holding the two sections properly, they are pushed together with a slight rotary motion back and forth. They must not be twisted too far from their normal alignment or the overlapping keys on either side will be bent. When the two sections are firmly together line up the connecting lever or levers.

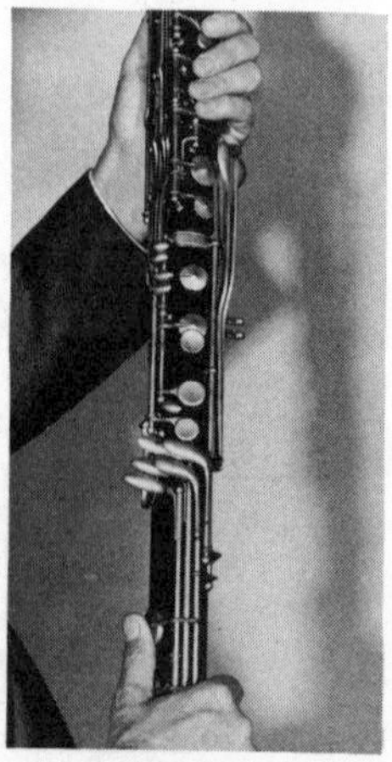

Figure C-22

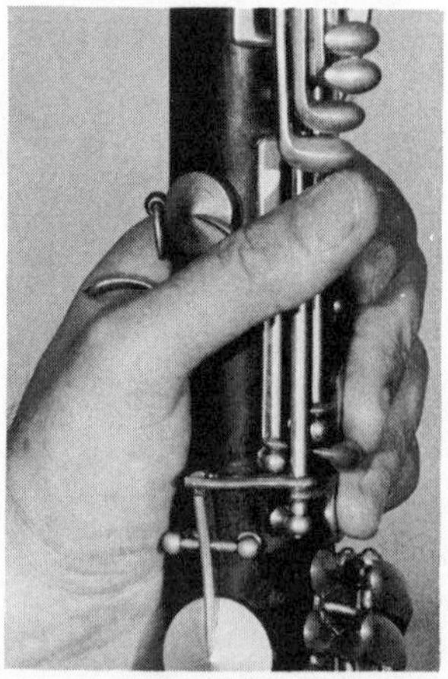

Figure C-23

B. Adding the Bell

1. Figure C-23. The lower joint of the two sections already assembled is held in the left hand, with the palm of the hand against the wood of the instrument beneath the keys, and with the flesh between the thumb and forefinger near or against the thumb rest.

2. Figure C-24. With the palm in position, the first and second fingers cover and press the second and third rings, holding the body of the instrument firmly in the palm of the hand. The other two fingers are free and do not press on the keys beneath them.

3. Figure C-25. The base of the thumb is held firmly against the wood at the side of the instrument, but there must be no pressure against the rod under the finger.

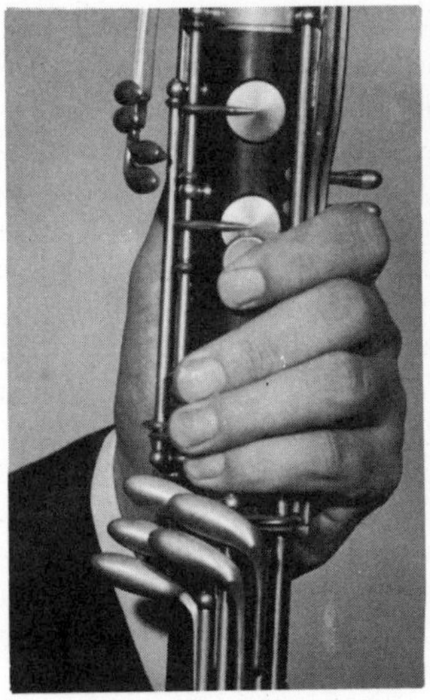

Figure C-24

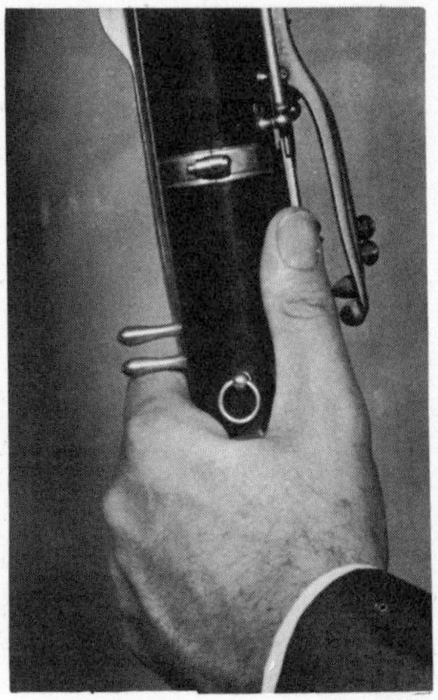

Figure C-25

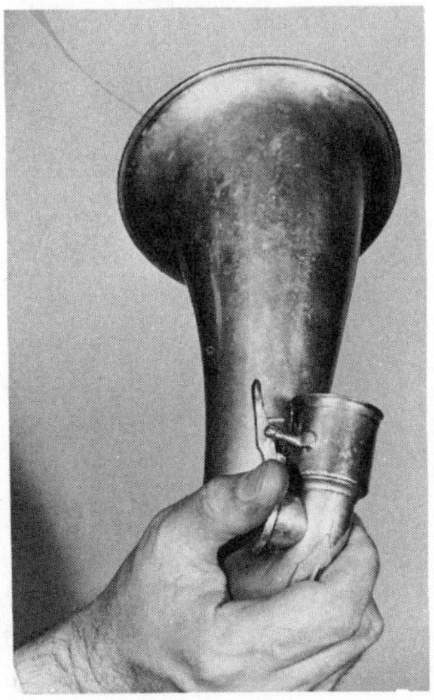

Figure C-26

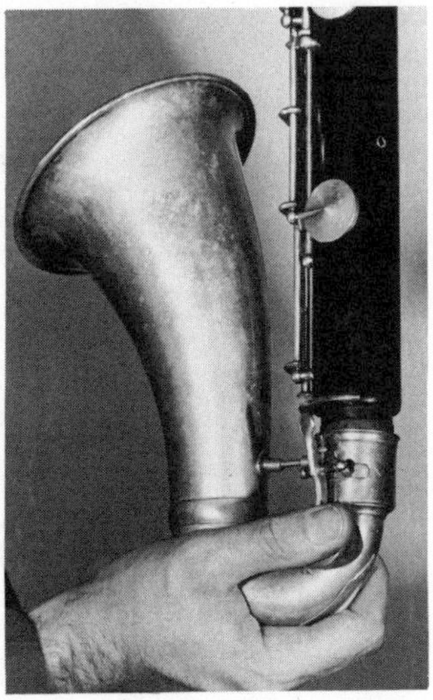

Figure C-27

4. Figure C-26. The right hand grasps the bell with the lower part of the front firmly placed in the crotch of the thumb. The thumb and forefinger hold the bell firmly on either side. The thumb presses the key on the bell so that it will clear the operating lever on the lower joint.

5. Figure C-27. The bell is pushed on the lower joint with a slight rotary motion from right to left to properly connect the key on the bell. Center the bell on the tone holes of the lower joint, and test keys to see that pad or pads on bell close firmly.

D. Adding the Neck

1. Figure C-28. Grasp the neck with the right hand fingers, the little finger just above the cork joint. Holding the upper joint with the left hand as described in section A (p. 16) and the instrument across the legs, push on the neck section and center it on the register key beneath the instrument.

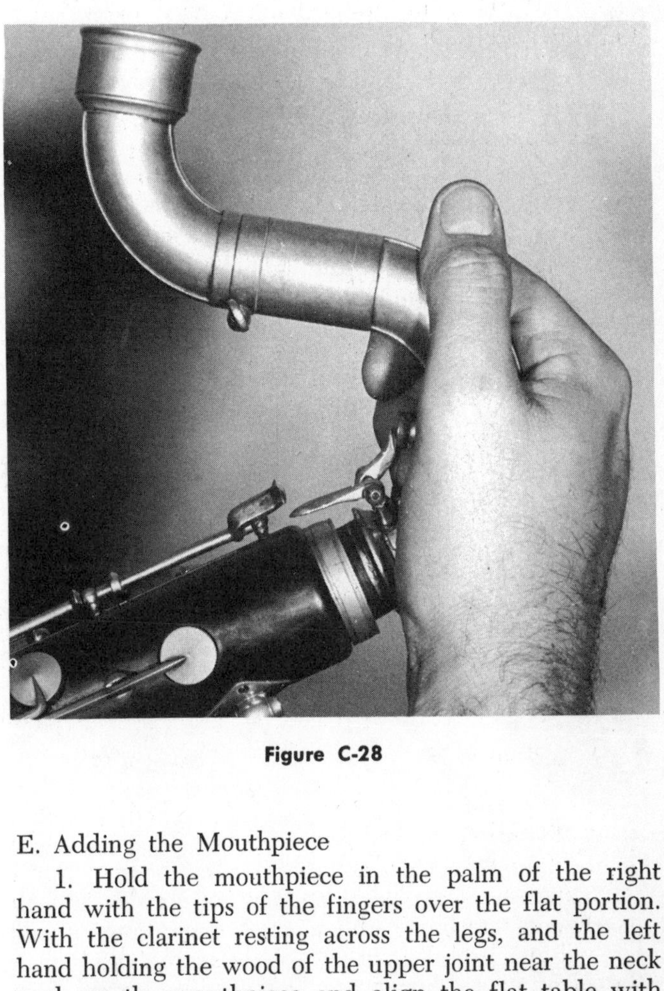

Figure C-28

E. Adding the Mouthpiece

1. Hold the mouthpiece in the palm of the right hand with the tips of the fingers over the flat portion. With the clarinet resting across the legs, and the left hand holding the wood of the upper joint near the neck push on the mouthpiece and align the flat table with the body of the instrument. Avoid any pressure against a rod with the left hand while performing this operation. Placement of the reed on the mouthpiece is discussed later in this section of the chapter.

Placing the Reed on the Mouthpiece

Placement of the reed on the mouthpiece is highly critical since the way in which it is fitted to the mouthpiece determines its response and tone quality to a considerable degree. Placement and procedure is the same for all instruments in the clarinet family. If the reed is put on the mouthpiece and the ligature slipped over it, there is danger that the ligature will chip or split the reed if it touches it. Many reeds are damaged this way by students, and even professionals have been known to ruin a good reed by hitting it with the ligature.

To avoid the slightest chance of damage, and as a matter of efficient procedure, it is recommended that the ligature be put on first and the reed slipped under it. The following step-by-step outline should be followed assiduously by all clarinetists from the beginning to the most advanced stage of development.

1. Figure C-29. Place the ligature over the end of the mouthpiece about half way down, holding it away from the flat portion of the mouthpiece with the left forefinger. (Screws on the double-screw model ligature are on the flat side of the mouthpiece, while the screw of the single-screw model is on the side away from the flat portion.) Tension type ligatures without screws are not recommended.

2. Figure C-30. Holding the reed with the thumb and forefinger of the right hand slip it under the ligature.

3. Figure C-31. Slide the ligature down so that the edges are over the guidelines etched in the mouthpiece. Figure C-32. Center the reed exactly at the butt so an equal amount of reed extends over each side of the flat table and at the tip so that it exactly matches the curvature of the mouthpiece.

Figure C-29

Figure C-30

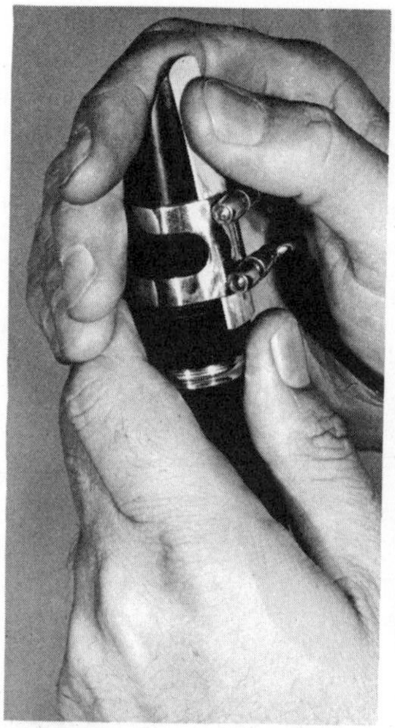

Figure C-31

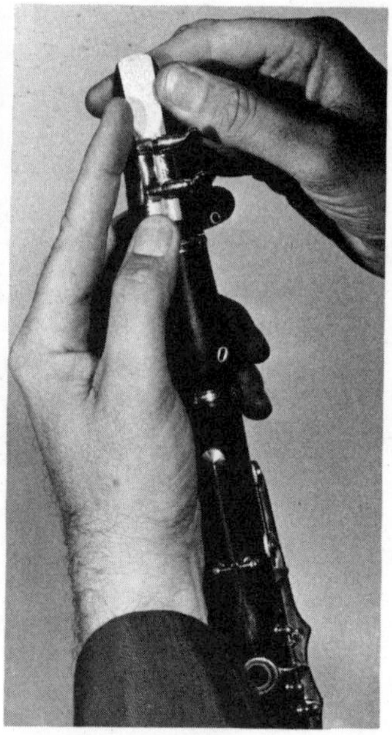

Figure C-32

4. Figure C-33. The reed is the proper distance from the tip when a hairline of black can be seen when the tip is pressed against the lay.

5. Figure C-34. Holding the reed in place with the thumb and forefinger of the left hand tighten the two screws just to the point at which they are holding the reed firmly. Avoid getting the screws too tight, which restricts the vibration of the reed.

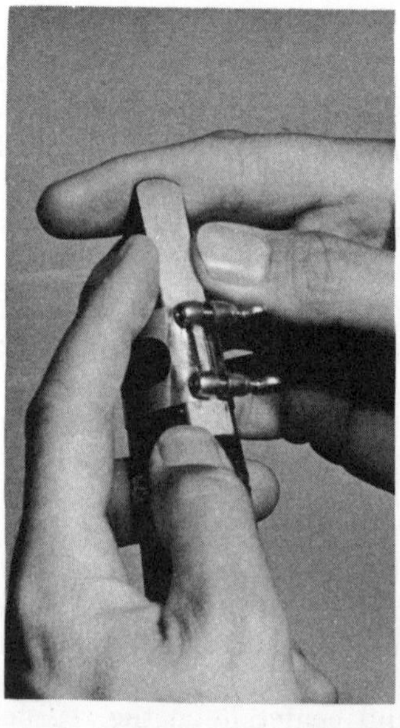

Figure C-33

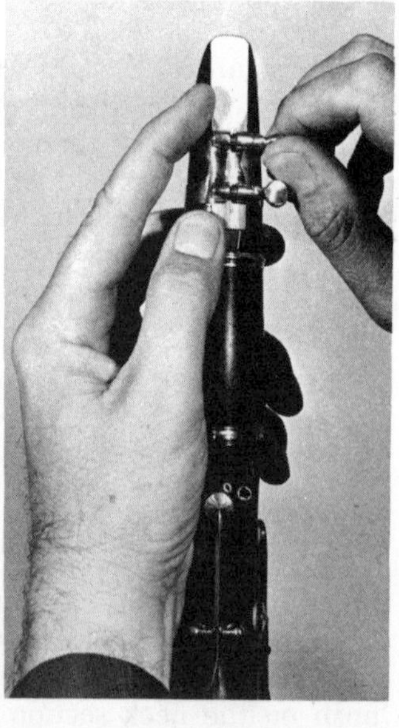

Figure C-34

6. Figure C-35. When the instrument is not in use, the mouthpiece cap should be in place. In order to avoid chipping the end of the reed with the cap, the upper portion of the cap should be placed lightly against the curved portion of the mouthpiece and slid into position keeping contact with the mouthpiece.

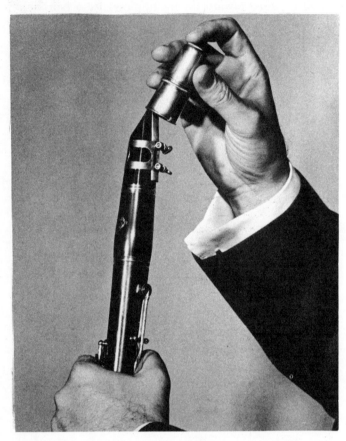

Figure C-35

Common Faults in Assembly

There are incorrect procedures in assembling a clarinet which are commonly seen among students. The younger the student and the less experienced he is the more often he violates the best procedures. Advanced players have learned through experience the value of careful assembly, and rarely, if ever, deviate from an accepted method of preparing his instrument for playing. If the opportunity arises, observe carefully how a professional clarinetist takes his instrument from the case and puts it together, the care and detail with which the reed is put on the mouthpiece, and the way in which the instrument is tested to assure that everything is operating properly.

The following items are the most frequent faults.

1. *Holding the joints improperly.* This puts undue pressure on keys and rods which eventually forces them out of adjustment. Bent keys rub against each other and move sluggishly or stick; bent rods cause the key to stick against its pivot screw. Some keys, especially those operated by the little finger of the left hand, are bent so that it is difficult for the fingers to reach them. Key 4x on the upper joint, operated by the first finger of the right hand, is especially vulnerable.

2. *Failure to grease cork joints.* A small container of prepared cork grease is a must for every clarinet case, and every case has a place for it. Teachers should make sure that every student has it in his case. Assuming that the cork fits properly a small amount of grease applied once a week or oftener if necessary and spread evenly over the cork will make the joints slide together easily. Excess grease must be wiped off with a soft cloth.

Corks which are too large, or which are not greased make it difficult to assemble the instrument causing excess pressure against the mechanism of the instrument and possible damage.

3. *Connecting lever out of line.* The small connecting lever or levers between the upper and lower joints are the most vulnerable pieces of the clarinet mechanism. An examination of the typical elementary school beginning clarinet class would reveal that at least fifty percent of the instruments have this lever bent out of line to a lesser or greater degree. This is caused by failure to hold down the ring of the second hole of the upper joint which raises the lever so that the connecting portion on the lower joint can slide under it easily. This point must be repeatedly emphasized with young or beginning students.

An out of line or bent connecting lever does one of two things to the mechanism of the instrument. (1) The rings for the keys of the lower joint are kept from going down far enough for the pad connected with them on the same rod to close completely. If this happens, notes which call for the fourth or fifth finger to be down either play with difficulty, squeak, or do not respond at all. If students are having difficulty in producing notes involving the fourth or fifth fingers the connecting lever is the first place to check. (2) If the portion of the lever on the upper joint is bent upward, there is no difficulty in playing notes with the right hand, but alternate fingerings for the B-flat above the staff (100 400 and 100 050) do not respond. If, when these important alternate fingerings are introduced, they are difficult to play, check first the condition of this lever.

4. *Bent keys or rods.* Bent keys or rods are most frequently the result of improper assembly of the instrument. The clusters of keys played by the left and right little fingers, and the first finger of the right hand are very carefully arranged to fit under these fingers for the most efficient operation. It is possible to play with one of them bent even though the pad does not leak, but this builds in the technique of the player an im-

proper relationship between the keys which frequently makes technique rough and uneven.

Bent keys or rods should be realigned by a repairman as soon as they are discovered. They must be removed from the instrument for straightening—never attempt to straighten a key while it is on the instrument. This puts tremendous pressure on the small posts and can easily break them or the key, making a major repair job out of a minor one.

5. *Reed improperly placed on the mouthpiece.* The way in which the reed is placed on the mouthpiece determines to a large degree how the instrument responds. Inexperienced players do not understand the importance of perfect reed placement, and teachers must check constantly to see that it is done properly.

Check first to see that it is properly centered both at the tip and at the butt. A reed which is crooked is hard to blow, squeaks, or does not respond properly. If the reed is centered properly, check the distance of the tip from the tip of the mouthpiece. When looking directly across the tip of the reed toward the mouthpiece just a hairline of black of the mouthpiece should be seen. Reeds which are too far down from the tip or which extend past the tip of the mouthpiece require greater wind pressure to produce a tone than when they are properly placed. There are minor deviations from this rule of placement which can be used in emergencies.

Checklist for Assembly

Observe the student in the operation of assembling and disassembling the instrument and check the following items. Incorrect items for older students should not be called to their attention until the entire process is completed; younger students should be corrected immediately. If any mistake is made, the entire process should be repeated until perfect.

	Yes	No	Comments
1. Were corks examined to see if they were well greased?			
2. Upper joint held properly?			
3. Lower joint held properly?			
4. Bell joint held properly?			
5. Barrel joint or neck held properly?			
6. Mouthpiece held properly?			
7. Connecting lever(s) perfectly aligned?			
8. Flat part of mouthpiece aligned?			
9. Ligature placed over mouthpiece before reed?			
10. Reed correctly placed on mouthpiece?			
11. Ligature tightened to proper degree?			
12. Parts assembled in the right order?			
13. Parts disassembled in the right order?			
14. Parts properly placed in case?			

HOLDING POSITIONS FOR THE CLARINETS

The manner and position in which the clarinet is held affects both directly and indirectly such important musical items as tone quality, intonation and technical facility. The proper position is one in which the body is in a comfortable erect position, in which the hands and arms fall naturally into position, and which permits the formation and development of the best embouchure. Authorities are in virtually unanimous agreement on what the proper playing positions are for all the instruments in the clarinet family, and the ones given here follow this standard. Basic seated, standing and rest positions are given here, with details of hand and finger positions following in the next section.

B-flat, E-flat and A Clarinets

Seated Position. The B-flat, E-flat or A Clarinet is held directly in the center of the front of the body. The instrument is at about a 40 degree angle with the body, and is balanced between the right thumb and the mouth, assisted by the left thumb. Head erect, chin up, eyes straight ahead, with shoulders up but relaxed. Elbows hang free from the body. Both feet flat on the floor. Shoulders and back must not touch the back of the chair when playing. Adjust the height of the music stand so that music can be easily read in this position. When two students are playing from the same music, angle the chair slightly toward the center of the stand so that the position of the body and instrument can remain correct.

Figure C-36. Seated Position (Front View).

Figure C-37. Seated Position (Side View).

Standing Position. The position of the instrument when the player is standing should be identical with the seated position. Only the position of the body itself is changed. Stand erect with feet slightly apart, one foot ahead of the other to help maintain balance. Head remains erect, with chin up and eyes straight ahead. Shoulders up but relaxed, and elbows free from body. Raise the music stand, if one is being used, so that head does not tilt downward. Every player should regularly spend a portion of his practice time standing to become at ease playing in a standing position.

Rest Position. In the standard rest position, the clarinet is placed diagonally across the legs with the tone holes down. Some players prefer to turn the instrument so the

Figure C-38. Standing Position (Front View).

Figure C-39. Standing Position (Side View).

tone holes are up. From either position it can be quickly picked up and returned to playing position. If the instrument is to be left in this position any length of time the cap should be put over the reed to protect it from possible damage.

The alternate rest position for these instruments is

Figure C-40. Standard Rest Position.

Figure C-41. Semi-Rest Position.

one which is used effectively by many band directors because it looks well from the audience. It is actually a semi-rest position since the right hand remains in contact with the instrument. The bell is rested on the right leg with the clarinet in a vertical position with the right hand remaining in playing position. The clarinet can be returned to playing position quickly. This position is most effectively used during rests when the entire clarinet section of the band arrives at this position and returns to the playing position simultaneously.

Alto and Bass Clarinets

Seated Position. The Alto or Bass Clarinet (shown in photograph) is held between the legs of the player directly in front of the body. In a vertical position the bell is slightly closer to the player's body than the top of the instrument in order to put the mouthpiece at the best angle for correct embouchure formation. The weight of the instrument is held by the neck strap, with the right thumb carrying practically none of the weight, but simply controlling the position of the instrument, and balancing it in the mouth with the aid of the left thumb. Head erect, chin up, eyes straight ahead, with shoulders up but relaxed. Elbows hang free from the body. Both feet flat on the floor. Sit forward so the instrument does not touch the chair, and shoulders and back do not contact the back of the chair.

Adjust the height of the music stand for easy reading. When two players are using the same music, angle the chairs slightly toward the center of the stand so that the position of the body and instrument can remain correct.

The preceding position is the standard one for these instruments and it is mandatory that boys use it. However, girls who play these instruments frequently find it necessary, because of clothing styles, to hold the instrument to their right resting the instrument against their right leg rather than between the legs. This position is widely used, and is accepted in most sections of the country as a necessary alternative.

There are some disadvantages to this position, however, since the long keys which are against the leg do not have guards to protect them from the pressure which results. For this reason they are subject to being bent either by the pressure or by catching on the clothing, and frequently operate sluggishly. Use this alternate holding position for the instruments only in case of necessity, and impress on the player the importance of protecting the keys. If this position is used then the neck and mouthpiece must be adjusted so that the proper embouchure can be formed.

Figure C-42. Seated Position (Front View).

Figure C-43. Seated Position (Side View).

Standing Position. The Alto Clarinet is shown in these photographs. When the player is standing the position of the instrument itself and its relationship to the body should be identical with the seated position. Only the position of the body itself is changed. Stand erect with feet slightly apart, one foot ahead of the other to maintain balance. Head remains erect, with chin up and eyes straight ahead. Shoulders up but relaxed, and elbows free from the body. A certain amount of regular practice time should be spent standing in order to develop ease playing in this position.

Figure C-44. Standing Position (Front View).

Figure C-45. Standing Position (Side View).

Rest Position. In the rest position for the Alto and Bass Clarinets, the neck strap is lengthened or unhooked and the instrument laid diagonally across the legs with the tone holes down. From this position it can be quickly picked up and returned to playing position, although players must allow sufficient time for adjusting or hooking the neck strap. If the instrument is to be left in this position for any length of time, the cap should be put over the reed to protect it from possible damage.

Figure C-46. Rest Position.

If the rest position is to be held for a very brief time, many players prefer to leave the neck strap hooked and rest the bell against the leg as in the photograph or simply lay the instrument across the legs with the bell joint resting on the right leg.

Figure C-47. Alternate Rest Position.

Contra-Bass Clarinet

Figure C-48. Seated Position (Front View).

Figure C-49. Seated Position (Side View).

Seated Position. The seated position for the B-flat Contra-Bass instrument is similar to that of the Alto or Bass Clarinet. The Contra-Bass is held between the legs of the player directly in front of the body. The instrument is slightly out of perpendicular with the bell closer to the player's body in order to put the mouthpiece at the best angle for the correct embouchure formation, and to allow for a comfortable position of the right hand. The weight of the instrument may be held by a neck strap as in the photographs or by an end-pin which may be added to the instrument. In either case none of the weight of the instrument is supported by the right thumb. Head erect, chin up, eyes straight ahead, with shoulders up but relexed. Elbows hang free from the body. Both feet on the floor. Sit forward on the chair so that the instrument does not touch the chair.

Common Faults in Holding Positions

The proper holding position for an instrument can further rapid musical development, or it can make progress difficult. Teachers must continually check students positions for it is important that any deviations be corrected immediately before they develop into habits. Once an incorrect position is established, it is extremely difficult to correct. Students themselves must learn to *feel* the right position, and should be encouraged to check their positions daily in front of a mirror both at school and at home. A full-length mirror is an integral part of the well-equipped instrumental room of every school.

The following are the most commonly found faults in holding positions, and most apply to all the instruments in the clarinet family.

1. *Instrument not centered on body.* Some students allow the instrument to point toward one knee or the other rather than straight ahead. This is sometimes found when two students are reading from the same music and direct the instruments toward the center of the stand rather than turning their chair and their entire body, but most of the time there is no discernible reason at all.

This position affects the embouchure, and thereby tone quality and control, since more of the reed is in the mouth on one side than the other thus making the line of support by the lip slightly diagonal across the reed rather than straight across. This adds a roughness or edge to the tone quality since the reed is vibrating unevenly. The slightest unevenness is magnified many times in the tone which is produced.

2. *Bell resting on leg.* This is a common fault with the B-flat Clarinet, and is done by the student to take the weight of the instrument off of his right thumb, or perhaps simply because he is tired or lazy or both. Some students compensate by turning their head in the direction of the leg on which the bell is resting, but even this does not correct the adverse effect on the embouchure. Sometimes the head is tilted slightly back, putting the mouthpiece into the mouth at a too small angle, which in turn puts too much pressure against the reed

restricting its vibration as well as changing the direction of the breath entering the instrument.

All of these have an influence on the tone quality being produced. With some students it is possible to hear the tone quality improve if they will sustain a tone while moving the instrument from their leg into the proper position. Resting the instrument on a leg is an easy habit to fall into and should be corrected promptly every time it is seen.

3. *Fingers assisting thumbs in holding the instrument.* At the beginning stage of experience on a clarinet many students do not feel secure in holding and balancing the instrument between the right thumb and mouth, and add other fingers to secure and stabilize the instrument. This feeling is by no means restricted to very young students. Various fingers are found out of position to help hold the instrument—little fingers under the instrument or under keys, first finger of the right hand pressing on the rod on which the rings of the lower joint operate, etc.

Any deviation from the standard holding position will affect smoothness of technique, or make some notes difficult to play, and in general impede progress on the instrument. Beginners will need continual checking and correction, but even more advanced students will sometimes fall rather quickly into a bad habit.

4. *Head inclined downward.* This problem is encountered in students at all stages of development. When the head is inclined downward, the effect on the embouchure is the same as if the clarinet were being held straight out. The angle at which the reed enters the mouth is so great that the lips cannot control the reed, and the tone which results is reedy and open in quality, and the intonation is inevitably poor. Some advanced players drift into this position when the music stands which they use are too low. This is especially true in a standing position.

One remedial measure which can be taken is to put the music stand higher than it would normally be, forcing the student to raise his head, but at the same time keep the instrument at its normal 40 degree angle with the body. More often than not a decided change for the better in tone quality can be heard if the student will sustain a tone (open G, for example) while moving the head and instrument into the proper relationship. An advanced player can clearly demonstrate why this position is poor by sustaining a tone while moving the clarinet from its proper position to the straight position and back again. Even when demonstrated by a good player the change in tone quality is easily noticeable.

5. *Slouched body.* Varying degrees of poor posture occur almost universally—shoulders slumped or curved forward, leaning against the back of the chair with spine curved, feet crossed or hung over a rung on the chair or various combinations of these. Poor posture affects breathing and breath control to the point the students may find it impossible to support the tone adequately. It pulls the arms, and consequently the fingers out of position making technique rough.

Poor posture is contagious in an instrumental group and a good teacher will see that it never starts. Emphasize to the students in as many ways as possible that good posture minimizes fatigue while poor posture increases it, and at the end of a long rehearsal players with good posture might not be physically tired at all while those with poor posture might well be physically exhausted even though their contributions to the rehearsal were not their best because of the poor posture.

6. *Moving the body while playing.* Nothing is more distracting to other members of the group or to the director than a player who beats time with his instrument, or who makes grandiose movements of body and instrument to emphasize a phrase or a difficult technical spot. An audience is also distracted and frequently amused by these movements. Moving the instrument up and down or back and forth changes the position of the reed in the mouth, moving the body itself alters the coordination of the muscles involved in breath support. Both the body and the instrument must be held in the proper position without any undue motions if the best musical results are to be achieved.

7. *Alto and bass clarinet angle.* The most prevalent violation of a good position on the Alto and Bass clarinets involves having the bell of the instrument pushed too far forward or pulled too far back. With the bell out of position in either direction the angle of the mouthpiece and reed in the mouth and consequent control by the embouchure is changed. The proper relationship between mouthpiece and embouchure is built into the instruments through the shape of the neck if the instruments are almost perpendicular. Slight deviations from the exact perpendicular come naturally to players as they gain experience on the instruments and is to be expected.

8. *Adjustment of neck strap.* The adjustment of the neck strap on the Alto, Bass, and Contra-Bass instruments allows little deviation from the ideal if it is to be used to the best advantage. The standard adjustment of the neck strap is one in which the mouthpiece falls naturally into the embouchure without tilting the head up or down and with the weight of the instrument supported by the neck strap rather than the right thumb. An adjustment which is too high or too low forces the student to raise or lower his head which is not only a muscular strain if continued over a period of time, but also forces the embouchure formation into an unnatural shape.

Because of the weight of these instruments it is virtually impossible for the right thumb to support it without cramping the right hand and forcing the fingers out of position. When a student transfers to the Alto or Bass clarinet it is well worth the time spent to help him find the proper adjustment of the neck strap since the correct and natural playing position for the instrument is so dependent on it.

HAND POSITIONS

The same basic hand position is used on all instruments in the clarinet family, the only difference being the slightly increased space between the fingers on the larger instruments. This position may be defined as one in which the fingers fall naturally into place and are completely relaxed without any muscular tension in the fingers, wrists, arms or shoulders. It is only in this perfectly relaxed condition that it is possible to develop rapid, accurate and dependable facility.

Proper position and shape of the hands on the instrument must be stressed from the very beginning of clarinet study, and checked in detail regularly until it is habitual. Even the youngest students can achieve this correct position, and indeed, progress much faster with the correct placement than with one which deviates even slightly. Almost all the difficulties beginners have in playing across the break, in playing the throat tones with facility, and in playing the lowest tones on the instrument can be traced to faulty hand and finger positions and placement.

Figure C-50

It is very easy for beginners who have not acquired a feel for the instrument to deviate to a position which temporarily feels better or gives them a greater sense of security. But the fact remains that the proper placement of the hands develops both a faster sense of security and feeling right than an incorrect one. Perhaps the greatest service a teacher can be to a student is to insist that he establish and maintain this correct position.

The following step-by-step procedure for establishing the hand position should be studied thoroughly, preferably with an instrument with which to experiment. Study both the text and the photographs carefully until they are perfectly clear. The "Guide Position" which is given is the fundamental position for hands and fingers and should be maintained at all times except when the fingering for a note involves moving a finger to another location. This position on the instrument may be compared to the guide position on the typewriter which makes it possible to develop speed and accuracy so quickly on that machine. It is used on the clarinet for the very same reason.

A. Right Hand Position

1. Figure C-50. The right thumb contacts the thumb rest on the flesh to the side of and at the base of the nail. The ball of the thumb is against the body of the instrument.

2. Figure C-51. The right little finger touches lightly Key F, and the remaining fingers are no more than an inch above the three tone holes. When closing the holes, the tips of the fingers overlap the rings slightly so that the ball of the finger directly beneath the fingernail is in the center of the tone hole. The fingers fall into a natural curve without tension which allows maximum control and accuracy of movement.

Figure C-51

B. Left Hand Position

1. Figure C-52. The left thumb has the double duty of closing the tone hole and operating the register key beneath the instrument either independently or together. It is placed at a diagonal angle across the instrument so that the fleshy part of the ball is closing the hole, and the side of the tip just touching, but not pressing the register key. The register key is controlled by vertical movements of the first joint of the thumb.

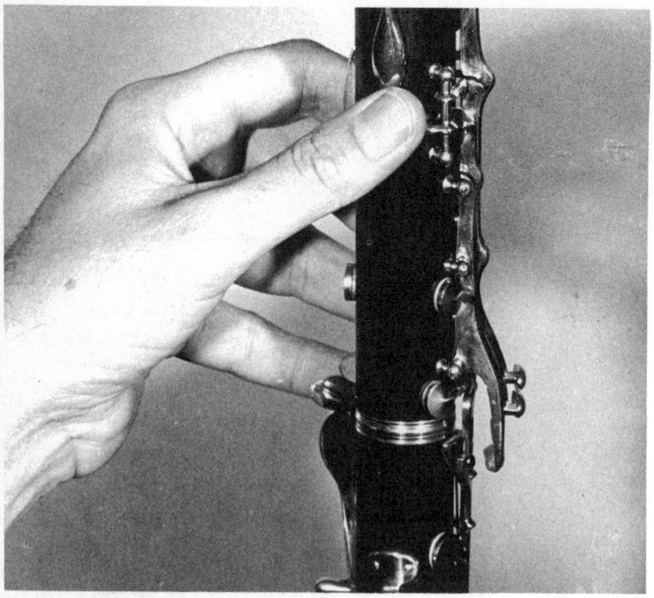

Figure C-52

2. Figure C-53. The left little finger touches lightly Key E, and the remaining fingers cover the tone holes.

Figure C-53

3. Figure C-54. The tips of the fingers overlap the rings slightly so that the ball of the finger directly beneath the fingernail is in the center of the tone hole. The fingers are in a natural curve.

Figure C-54

C. Guide Position

1. Figure C-55. With the thumbs and little fingers in place as described above and the remaining fingers over the tone holes a guide position is established which should be maintained constantly. Note that the fingers are at approximately a ninety degree angle to the instrument, and the wrists flat. The entire finger moves from the knuckle and closes the tone holes with a snap or click, pressing just hard enough to close the holes. Avoid too much pressure against the holes with the fingers. Fingers are kept no more than an inch directly above their hole.

Figure C-55

Alternate Hand Position

A second commonly used hand position calls for the fingers of the left hand to approach the instrument at a slight downward angle. The hand is tilted upward so that the edge of the first finger touches the "A" key. The little finger remains in contact with the "B" key for the guide position. The right hand fingers angle slightly downward so that the side of the first finger is directly above the first side key (see Figure C-56).

Figure C-56. Alternate Hand Position.

The advantage of this position is that it shortens the amount of roll the first finger must do in order to play "A," and the "G-sharp" key is directly under the first finger. It also puts the fourth finger into close position for playing the side keys.

The position does have the disadvantage with some students of pulling the little fingers away from the keys they operate, making the little fingers stretch into flat positions to reach them. This is not a problem for the player who has long fingers, but it is a problem for the player with short fingers. However, many fine teachers feel that the advantages outweigh the disadvantages and recommend this as the standard position. With the exception of the angle of the fingers, the guide position remains the same as that previously described.

Movement of Fingers from Guide Position

Fingerings for certain notes on the instrument tend to pull the hands out of position unless fingers are moved efficiently and with minimum motion. These movements do not seem to come naturally to all students, but can be readily developed if they are understood and the teacher provides music which isolates the problem. A constant check on finger positions for these notes is necessary until the movements become habitual.

1. Figure C-57.
The left thumb fingering B-flat: 

The hole is opened and the register key is opened by a vertical motion of the first joint of the thumb. The thumb contacts the register key at the side of the tip. The register key is opened with the same motion while the hole is kept closed for notes in the upper register.

2. Figure C-58.
Left hand fingering A: 

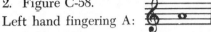

The first finger is rolled toward the A key pressing it with the side of the first joint. The little finger must remain touching the E key and the other two fingers directly over their tone holes.

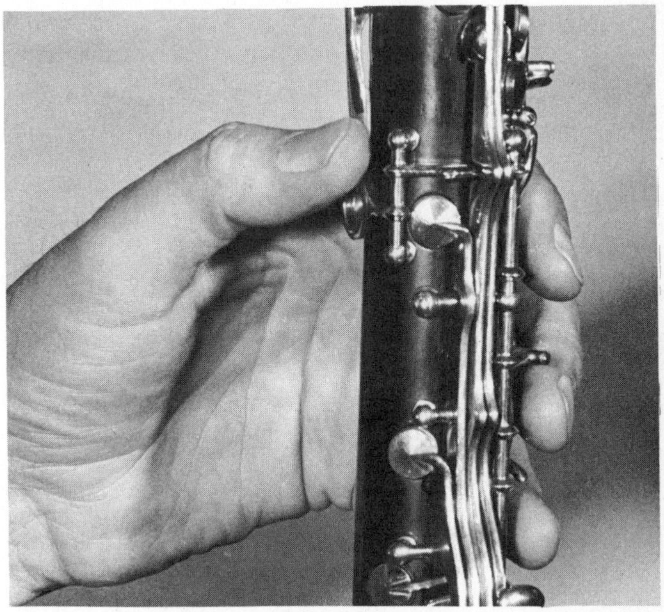

Figure C-57

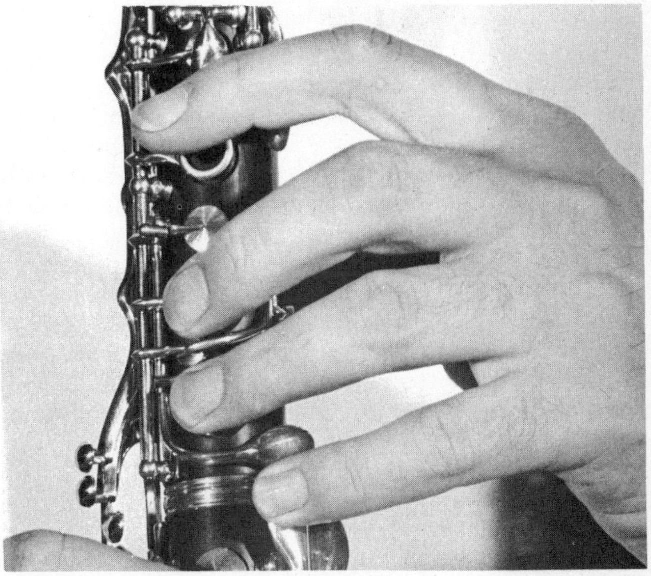

Figure C-58

3. Figure C-59.
Left hand fingering G-sharp: 

The first finger is straightened and brought directly down to contact the G-sharp key on the bottom of the finger between the first and second joints. The remaining fingers must remain in the guide position.

4. Figure C-60.
First finger right hand fingering E-flat-B-flat: 
The first finger of the right hand is straightened and extended to open key 4x with a downward motion. The remaining fingers must remain in the guide position.

The same motion is used for the chromatic fingering of F-sharp: 
which involves the use of two of the side keys rather than one.

Common Faults in Hand and Finger Position

A clarinetist with perfect hand position both at rest and in playing is a rare individual, but at the same time a player whose hand and finger positions are poor develops facility slowly and seldom if ever becomes what would be considered a good performer. A beginning student who persists in quickly establishing the proper positions makes rapid progress in acquiring technical facility.

There is a direct relationship between how the instrument is held, hand and finger positions, and success on the instrument. The closer to the standard position the faster the rate of progress, and conversely the poorer the position the slower the rate of progress. Extremely poor positions make any progress on the instrument virtually impossible and quickly discourages the student.

It is of the utmost importance that proper positions be established from the very beginning of clarinet study, through careful continuous checking by the teacher who must insist on the proper position. Some teachers take the attitude that positions are not important for elementary school beginners, and that poor positions can be corrected when they become more advanced. Nothing could be more unfortunate than this attitude since many students are discouraged from continuing, and even those who do continue with the instruments have great difficulty in correcting non-standard positions once the muscular pattern is established incorrectly. It is so easy and simple to do it correctly in the beginning and so difficult to correct that every teacher who is truly interested in his pupil's progress will do everything possible to establish the proper habits from the very beginning.

The common faults which are listed here occur over and over again in students. All of these faults have an adverse affect on facility and technique–making some progressions rough, some difficult, and others impossible.

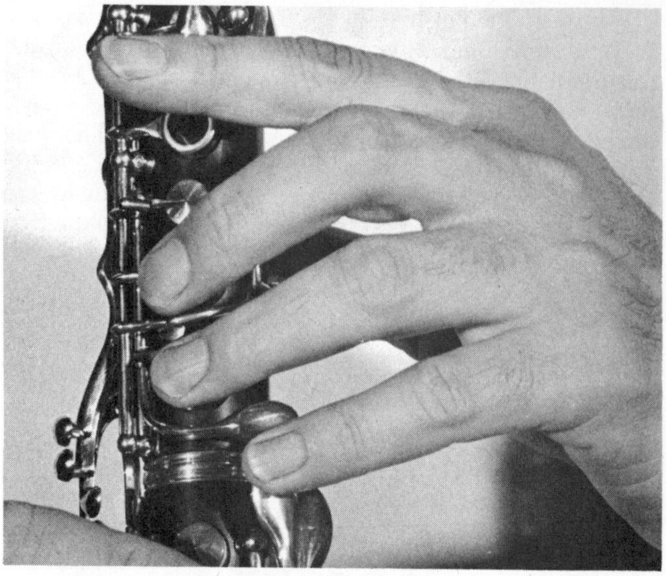

Figure C-59

Figure C-60

1. *Right thumb.* There are two common faults with the position of the right thumb:

(a) Pushing the thumb too far under the instrument so that it contacts the thumb rest away from the nail, some students contacting at the first joint of the thumb and some even higher. This condition can frequently be detected by merely looking at the student's thumb since an incorrect position will cause a callous on any player who spends enough time playing the instrument to be considered an average performer. No callous will develop if the thumb is in the proper position.

When the thumb is too far under the instrument the fingers are forced into an unnaturally acute angle so that the fingers must cover the tone holes toward the tip or even with the tip rather than with the natural pad on the finger beneath the nail. Younger students especially have difficulty in covering the tone holes at or toward the tip since their fingers are small, and the result is squeaks or difficulty in producing a tone at all. Further, when the fingers are at an acute angle which approaches the tone hole directly, there is considerable muscular tension which makes rapid movement difficult. When this condition is corrected with intermediate or advanced students there is a noticeable improvement in facility and smoothness of technique in the space of a few days.

The right thumb must contact the thumb rest in the natural hollow on the side near the base of the nail as indicated in Figure C-61.

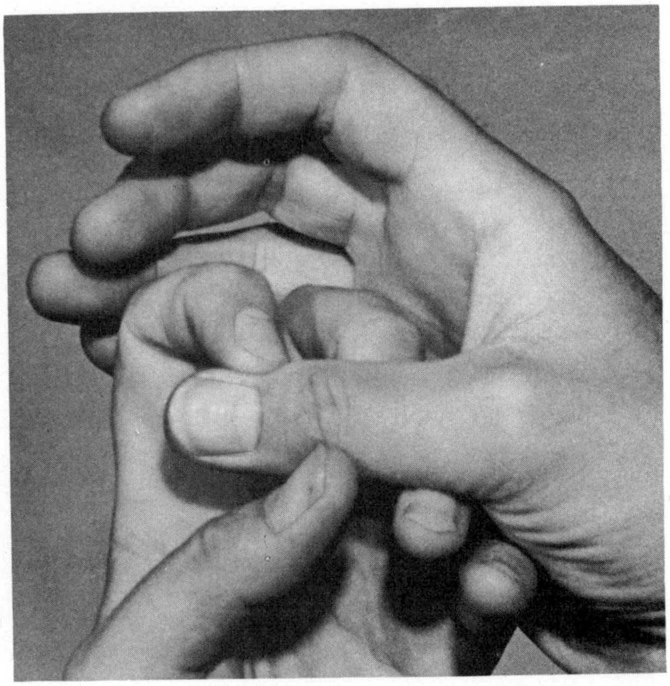

Figure C-61

(b) The second fault is that of contacting the thumb rest with the nail itself so that the side of the finger rather than the ball is against the body of the instrument. This condition is more prevalent in beginners than it is with intermediate and advanced students, since if the condition persists advancement on the instrument is virtually impossible and the student does not continue playing. This puts the weight of the instrument on the thumb in such a way that a tremendous amount of muscular tension is needed to support the instrument and the student tires quickly. It also turns the hand slightly downward making it difficult for the fingers to contact the holes and keys in the correct way. Fortunately this faulty position is easy to correct if discovered before it becomes habitual. Students are grateful for the correction since they are immediately more comfortable playing the instrument.

2. *Little fingers.* The guide position calls for each little finger to be in contact with a key so that they will be in a position to move rapidly and easily to other keys which they operate. If they are not on the guide keys, then there is a slight delay in putting the finger in place making for rough technique. Beginners whose little finger position has not been established frequently go so far as to take their instrument out of the mouth to look at the keys to see exactly where the little finger should go. If the fingers are on the proper key then they soon move naturally to the desired location.

The most frequently found fault in the placement of the little fingers is to find them sticking straight up in the air—a tense position sometimes referred to as the "teacup" position. From this position they must feel for the proper key. The right little finger is frequently found hooked under the keys, apparently to help support the instrument. The left little finger frequently is placed entirely underneath the instrument for the same reason. The best, and perhaps the only, remedial measure is to insist that the fingers remain in the guide position actually touching their respective keys.

3. *Fingers over tone holes.* There are several commonly found faults in the position of the fingers over the tone holes, each of which affects technical facility.

(a) Lifting the fingers too high, i.e., more than an inch above the tone holes. This is extremely common, even among advanced players, and causes unevenness in rapidly moving passages. Since the fingers usually are unequal distances above the holes it takes a slightly longer space of time for the finger highest above the holes to close the hole than it does for the finger which is closest. This space of time is frequently microscopic, but it is enough that unevenness can be heard. It is significant to note that this fault is never found among the finest players or among the professionals.

(b) Closing the holes with the tips of the fingers. This problem is most frequently encountered with beginners or inexperienced players, but also occurs with more advanced students. It happens when the fingers do not fall in the natural curve, and may occur even though the remainder of the hand position is correct. It is frequently the result of a faulty position of the right thumb (see above), and if this is the case is easily corrected by correcting the placement of the thumb. Using the tips of the fingers to close the holes causes the fingers to fall into an unnatural position which creates muscular tension and stiff movements. Younger students with small fingers have difficulty in closing the holes entirely and get squeaks or no tone at all.

The remedial action for this problem is to insist that the pad of the finger close the tone hole with the tips of the fingers lapping over and touching the ring. Figure C-62 shows a pencil pointing at the center of the natural pad on the finger. Most fingers have a natural bump which can be easily seen by looking at the fingers in profile. This natural bump must fit exactly in the center of the tone hole. This determines the amount of the overlap at the tip of the finger which varies according to the size and shape of the fingers. Check also to be sure that the wrists are flat.

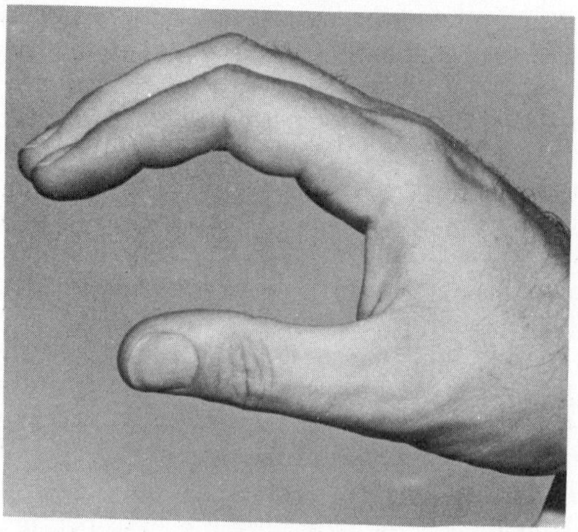

Figure C-63

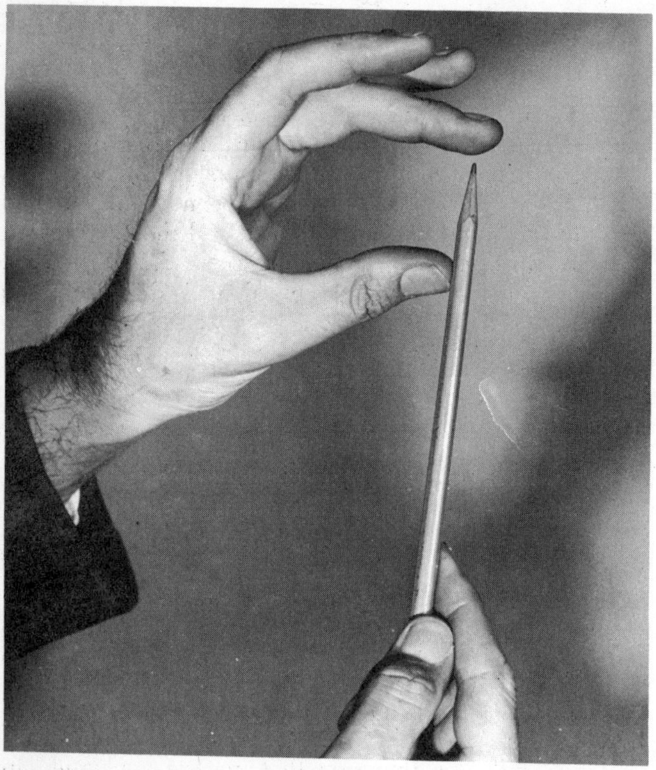

Figure C-62

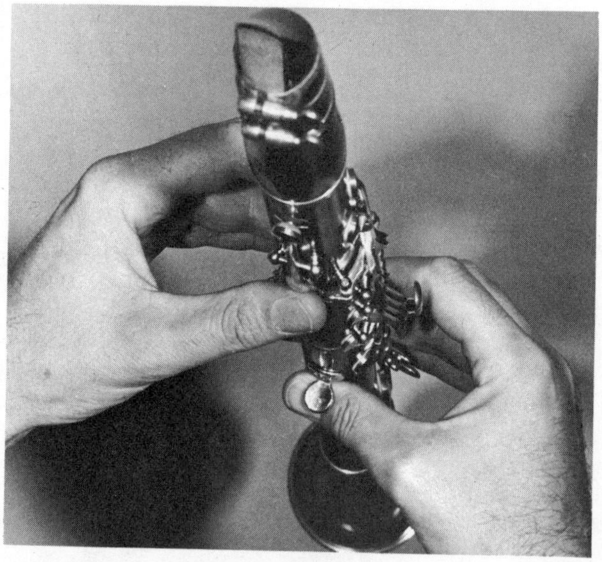

Figure C-64

4. *Fingers not curved.* This problem is directly related to the preceding discussion, since a proper curve will normally result in the tone holes being closed by the pad of the finger. However, it is almost always the result of a greater or lesser degree of misplacement of the thumb. If the thumbs and first fingers of both hands are properly placed they will form a "U." Figure C-63 shows the position of the right thumb and forefinger. That of the left is similar. The other fingers follow exactly the same curve as the forefinger. Figure C-64 shows the curve of the fingers in position on the instrument.

5. *Left thumb.* The left thumb must be positioned so that it can open and close both the tone hole and the register key singly or together. The diagonal angle described in the holding position, with the tone hole covered by the pad of the thumb, and the corner of the finger operating the register key is the position which produces the best results, and which is almost universally accepted as correct. There are several common deviations from this standard position:

(a) The thumb is held almost parallel with the body of the instrument rather than diagonal. While it is possible to operate the register key properly from this position, the fingers are pulled out of position on the top of the instrument sometimes to the point that the student cannot reach the keys with the left little finger, and there is general difficulty in technique involving the left hand.

Remedial measures include changing the direction of the thumb to the diagonal so that the thumb and forefinger form the "U" as pictured above, and insisting that the left little finger remain in contact with its guide key.

(b) The thumb slides back and forth over the tone hole to open and close the register key rather than operating it with a vertical movement of the joint. This will not normally happen if the thumb is in the proper relation to the body of the instrument, but it does occur and must be checked.

The best remedial measure is to position the thumb properly and then have the student play intervals of the twelfth from the chalumeau to the clarion register which involve only opening the register key. It should be noted that intervals of the twelfth can not be slurred down over the break. The following example is typical of the material which can be used for this purpose.

(c) The thumb is removed from the tone hole and put on the body of the instrument when playing the throat tones G, G-sharp, and A which do not involve the use of the left thumb. The thumb should be no more than an inch directly below the tone hole just as the fingers on the tone holes above the instrument are kept within an inch. Beginning students are especially susceptible to this difficulty, and frequently have trouble replacing the thumb for the following note.

Practicing a pattern such as the following will impress on the student the correct use of the thumb in this connection, although persistent effort is necessary to make the correction if it has become habitual.

6. *First finger left hand.* The first finger of the left hand is involved in covering a tone hole and operating two keys, and as a result is constantly changing position. There are two common faults in the way in which this finger is used:

(a) The finger hops from the tone hole to the "A" key rather than rolling, and the result is an unwanted "G" grace note preceding the "A" unless the tone is completely stopped. The rolling motion of the finger is controlled from the knuckle and involves a rather wide movement of the second joint. The movement can be seen and understood by the student making use of a pencil. Put four fingers on the pencil and hold it against them with the thumb, lining up the four fingers as if on the instrument. Hold the end of the pencil with the other hand and move the second joint of the first finger from side to side, so that none of the other fingers move. The rolling motion of the tip of the finger is exactly that used on the instrument.

A musical example such as the following one applies this movement to the instrument. In practicing it the left little finger should press down firmly on its guide key closing it completely so that the hand will be held in the correct position.

(b) The finger presses the G-sharp key with the side of the finger by rolling the entire hand over rather than by straightening the finger and pressing the key with the bottom of the finger at the second joint, or the curve of the finger will be increased and the key pressed with the tip of the finger. Both of these draw the hand out of position and cause technical difficulties with the note or notes which follow. The following exercise makes use of notes which will illustrate the correct usage of the finger.

7. *First finger right hand.* In addition to covering a tone hole the first finger of the right hand operates four keys on the side of the instrument, but is primarily concerned with the first one of the group which produces E-flat and B-flat in the two registers of the instrument, and it is with this fingering that we are concerned in the first of the two problems presented:

(a) The first finger presses the key with the side of the finger by turning the entire hand rather than stretching the finger and playing it with the bottom of the finger. Turning the hand pulls the rest of the fingers out of position which in turn creates technical problems. In correcting this make sure that the little finger is kept firmly in place on the guide key.

Practice the following exercise with the little finger pressing and closing the guide key so that the hand will be kept in place, and making sure that the key is pressed with the bottom of the finger near the second joint.

Checklist for Holding and Hand Positions

The following list of items provides a thorough check of holding positions and hand positions, and is limited to the seated positions for the instruments. The check should be performed while the student is playing and perferably when he is not aware that the check is being made. Any items which are checked "No" should be corrected with the deviation explained to the student, what effect it has on his playing, and why the correct position is important. Students make a more serious effort to correct mistakes if they thoroughly understand the reasons for them.

A. Holding Position	Yes	No	Comments
1. Instrument in center of body?			
2. Angle with body correct?			
3. Head up?			
4. Shoulders up and relaxed?			
5. Elbows free from body?			
6. Height of music stand correct?			
7. Body posture good?			
8. Feet in place?			
9. Neck Strap (if any) adjusted properly?			

B. Hand Positions

1. Right thumb contacting thumb rest properly?			
2. Left thumb at diagonal across instrument?			
3. Tip of left thumb touching register key?			
4. Fingers curved?			
5. Fingers across instrument at proper angle?			
6. Right little finger touching guide key?			
7. Left little finger touching guide key?			
8. Thumbs and forefingers form a "U"?			
9. Wrists flat?			
10. First finger roll to "A" key?			
11. Register key operated by vertical movements of the first joint?			
12. Side G-sharp played with bottom of straight finger?			
13. Right hand kept in position when forefinger plays a side key?			
14. Guide position consistently maintained?			
15. Balls of fingers closing holes?			

(b) A second, and fortunately less common, fault in the use of the first finger of the right hand is found when the bottom of the finger underneath the second joint is pressed against the rod to which the rings of the tone holes are connected, or when this finger is hooked underneath the first side key. Beginners do this to help steady the instrument. If not corrected immediately, it becomes habitual and extremely difficult to correct.

If this finger is pressing the rod or hooked underneath the key, the tone hole is opened and closed by movements of the second joint of the finger rather than a movement of the entire finger. Some students will move the entire hand to close the hole. Remedial action is to insist on the "U" shape formation between the thumb and forefinger, and the proper curve on all the fingers.

EMBOUCHURE FORMATION

> The embouchure is the interpreter of our sensations and of our musical ideas. A good embouchure is therefore indispensable, and all our labours must tend to this result.—H. Klose

An embouchure may be defined as the formation of the performer's lips with supporting muscles, teeth and jaws in relation to the mouthpiece and reed which have to do with tone production. The criteria for a good embouchure may be stated as follows:

A good embouchure is one which over the entire range of the instrument:

1. Produces (or has the potential of producing) a rich, full bodied, clear tone.
2. Plays perfectly in tune.
3. Allows the player to use the full scope of articulations from a hard short staccato to the smoothest legato at all dynamic levels and without adverse effect on tone quality.
4. Allows the player to use the full range of dynamics from the very softest to the very loudest under complete control and without affecting either pitch or tone quality.
5. Plays and is controlled with a minimum amount of physical exertion.
6. Once developed can be maintained with a reasonable amount of practice.

Conversely a poorly formed embouchure is one in which:

1. The tone quality is reedy, thin, nasal, or which changes quality from register to register on the instrument.
2. Plays upper register, lower register or throat tones out of tune consistently, or with which it is difficult or impossible to adjust the pitch of individual tones.
3. Produces staccato notes which are hard, with mechanical noises, or which have poor tone quality.
4. Has a restricted dynamic range in which tonal body is lost at soft levels, and very loud levels impossible to produce.
5. Requires an undue amount of physical exertion.
6. Deteriorates rapidly without an undue amount of daily practice.

Among fine clarinet teachers, there is considerable difference of opinion on exactly how the best embouchure should be formed, but at the same time there are many points on which there is unanimous agreement. Much of the difference of opinion can be traced to the semantics with which the formation is explained, since it is difficult to write and talk about something which is physical and musical.

However, it becomes clearly apparent that there are basically only two clarinet embouchures in general use today. Each is subject to minor differences from teacher to teacher but the fundamental and basic formation is the same. The major difference between the two is found in the shape of the lower lip, one embouchure bunches the lower lip to a greater or lesser degree, the other stretches it to a lesser or greater degree. Both descend from a long line of illustrious performers and teachers and both meet the criteria for a good embouchure when properly developed.

Historically, the first is an Americanized version of the old French school of playing, while the second is an Americanized version of the old German school of playing. Both can be traced back through generations of students and teachers to fine emigrant clarinetists who came to this country around the turn of the century as principal clarinetists in major symphony orchestras and whose teachings have been modified and refined to fit the demands of the contemporary American musical scene.

For convenience and clarity the bunched lower lip formation is called a "Soft Cushion" and the stretched lower lip a "Hard Cushion." The words "hard" and "soft" are relative and must not be taken literally. Those familiar with embouchure formation on other instruments will recognize immediately that the same dichotomy exists not only in the other woodwind instruments but on instruments in the brass family as well.

The Soft Cushion Embouchure

The basic formation of the soft cushion embouchure can be achieved through the following step-by-step procedure: Check each step with a small mirror on the music stand.

1. Keeping the lips lightly together drop the lower jaw so that the teeth are about three-eighths of an inch apart.
2. Shape the lips as if saying the letter "O." The corners of the mouth are slightly compressed and there are wrinkles in the lips, especially the lower one.
3. With the teeth dropped and the lips in the "O" position the rim of the lip which divides it from the chin should be directly in front of the top edge of the front teeth. Feel this with a finger and raise or lower the jaw until this relationship is correct.
4. Maintaining this position insert the mouthpiece of the clarinet into the mouth allowing the reed to push the lower lip over the teeth. If the wrinkles in the lower lip are maintained, the line dividing the lip from the chin is directly over the front edge of the lower teeth. Students with thicker than average lips will probably adjust so that less lip is over the teeth. Contract the lips and especially the corners of the mouth inward and around the mouthpiece so that no air can escape.
5. The end of the reed must be clear of any contact with the lip for three-eighths to a half-inch in order to vibrate freely. Feel this with the tongue.
6. The upper teeth rest, but do not press, on the top of the mouthpiece about a half inch from the end.
7. The lower teeth remain in the open position established in step three above, and must not bite or exert pressure against the lower lip.
8. The chin is held in a firm flat position with a slight downward pull of the muscles.
9. The first efforts at tone production should be with the mouthpiece alone. Check the embouchure formation in the mirror, and using standard breath support produce a tone by blowing without using the tongue. Continue practicing with the mouthpiece alone until a steady natural tone of the higest pitch (approximately C, second line above the treble clef) can be sustained for at least ten seconds. Check constantly in the mirror to be certain that the effort of blowing and producing a tone does not change the shape of the embouchure. When this is accomplished the student is ready to proceed with tone production on the entire instrument.

The following illustrations show a typical soft cushion embouchure formation. As in all photographs in this book where the embouchure is visible the photographs of the mouthpiece in the embouchure were taken during performance on the instrument. Figure C-65 shows the shape of the lips as described in steps two and three of the step-by-step procedure. Notice the wrinkles in the lips which are produced when the corners of the mouth are pushed toward the center. Support of the reed and mouthpiece by this inward pressure from the corners is basic to this type of formation.

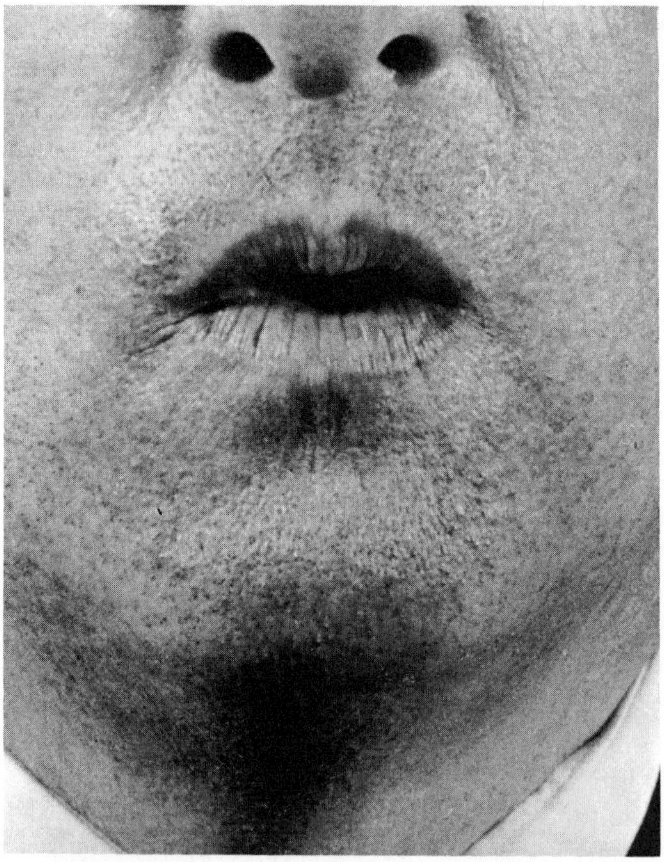

Figure C-65

Figure C-66 and Figure C-67 show the front and side views of this embouchure in action. Observe how much of the mouthpiece is in the mouth and the angle of the mouthpiece in relation to the chin. Notice the shape of the chin in the side view where the chin muscles are firm and pulling down.

Any experienced teacher will verify the fact that while it is fairly simple to explain and form the embouchure in the manner given above, maintaining it in

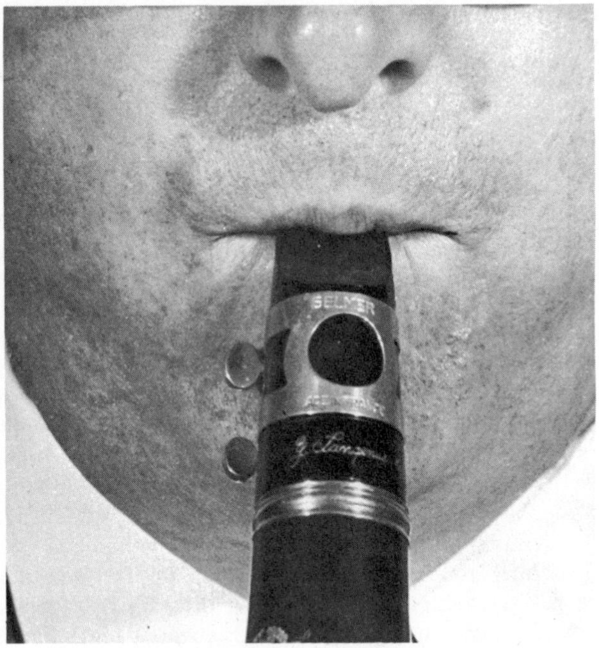

Figure C-66. Front View.

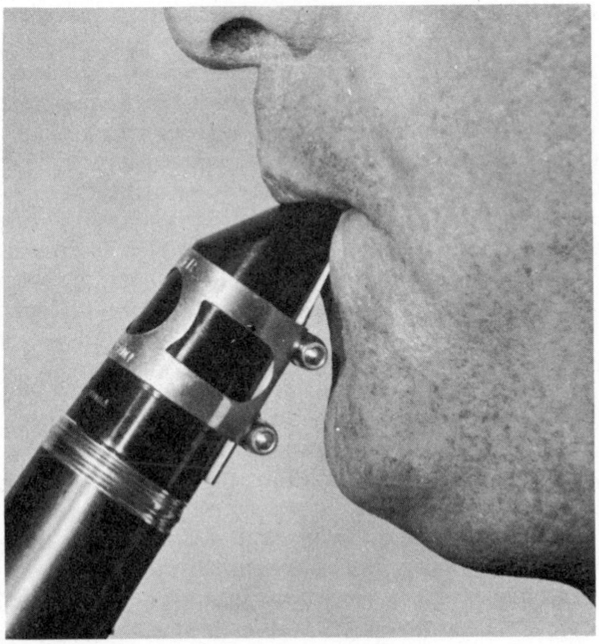

Figure C-67. Side View.

perfect condition over a period of weeks and months while the student is struggling with tone production and fingering problems is an entirely different matter. For this reason it is suggested that every student who is working on embouchure formation, whether he is at the beginning, intermediate, or advanced level, have a small mirror on the music stand for constant reference.

The teacher will have to check frequently to catch any deviations from the standard. Students, especially beginners of any age, are not always capable of discovering their own mistakes, or of actually knowing when they are right and when they are wrong. The embouchure must be established by how it feels in the mouth and how the tone sounds, as well as how it looks in the mirror. The teacher must tell the student when he is right so he can discover the right feel, hear the right sound, and see the right shape.

Common Faults in Soft Embouchure Formation.

1. *Dimples in cheek.* Perhaps the most frequent mistake in the formation of the soft cushion embouchure is indicated by the presence of a dimple in one or both cheeks. These are caused when one muscle is pulling back the corner of the mouth, while at the same time another muscle is attempting to contract the lower lip. This situation is much easier to discover than it is to correct, and the only solution is long sustained tones while the student watches himself in a mirror to see that the dimple doesn't return. This is a serious problem since the pulling back of the corners lessens the support of the lip against the reed with a consequent loss of tone quality. Students with this condition tire easily since two sets of muscles are pulling against each other.

2. *Amount of lip.* A second problem which must be checked is the amount of lower lip over the teeth. Too much lip over the teeth produces an open tone with many squawks but too much mouthpiece in the mouth produces the same symptoms so a visual check and experimentation with the amount of mouthpiece in the mouth is necessary. Too little lip over the teeth produces a cushion which is too small to control the vibrations of the reed and produces a very nasal reedy tone quality which is usually quite flat in pitch, especially in the upper register. But again, too little mouthpiece in the mouth produces much the same sound so a visual check for this is also necessary. It is virtually impossible to produce a smooth pleasing tone which is in tune if there is too little mouthpiece in the mouth, or too little lip over the lower teeth. The ensemble quality of many school bands which is objectionable because of the clarinet section sound could often be remedied by simply adjusting distance of the mouthpiece in the mouth and/or amount of lower lip. These adjustments are relatively easy to make, requiring a minimum amount of attention to establish by intermediate and advanced students.

3. *Biting.* Biting the reed with the lower teeth to a greater or lesser degree is a frequently found condition. This presure against the reed restricts the amount of vibration possible, and produces a thin stuffy tone with little body, and requires considerably more breath pressure to produce a tone than the correct pressure. Reducing

this pressure by dropping the jaw back into the open position immediately frees the tone and improves both body and quality. Students with this excess pressure find it difficult to produce tones above high "C" and this difficulty is usually a sure sign of excess pressure. The position of the lower jaw in relation to the lip remains the same throughout the entire range of the instrument. As an aid in getting this open position the student may play low "E" as loudly as he can which forces the lower jaw down and demands quite a relaxed condition if the note is to be played very loudly. He can then be directed to play over his entire range with this same embouchure adjustment. While this position is much too open for high notes, it does put across the point.

4. *Amount of mouthpiece.* The amount of mouthpiece to put in the mouth is dependent on several variables—facial characteristics, mouthpiece, and reed—and the final determination is made by ear, moving the mouthpiece back and forth slightly, to secure the best tone quality. The physical characteristics of the student's dental-facial formation are an important factor. Students with thicker lips will use less of the lower lip over the teeth than the average given in the step-by-step procedures, while students with thin lips will need the entire red of the lip over the teeth. Students with mouth formation wider than average will use fewer wrinkles in the lower lip. The adjustments are made to secure a firm but not hard cushion for the reed to rest on, which has sufficient area to control vibrations of the reed with a minimum of effort.

5. *Type of mouthpiece.* The type of mouthpiece being used is a second factor to be considered in shaping the embouchure. The length and amount of curvature of the lay, and the size of the opening at the tip help determine the exact location of the mouthpiece. The lower teeth must be slightly forward, i.e., toward the tip of the mouthpiece, of the point at which the lay starts breaking away from the reed in order that the cushion may control its vibration. A mouthpiece with a slight curvature and small opening at the tip requires that the lower teeth be fairly close to the break-away point, while a mouthpiece with a larger curvature and wide opening at the tip requires that the lower teeth support the cushion closer to the tip of the mouthpiece farther away from the break-away point. The exact placement can be determined only by hearing the student play and adjusting the distance of the mouthpiece into the mouth to achieve a tone with the best body which is well in tune and which is easily controlled.

6. *Reed.* The third variable—the reed—is directly related to, and must be chosen for a particular mouthpiece and an individual student. However a general observation concerning the strength of the reed used on a mouthpiece and embouchure formation is possible. Stiffer reeds require more pressure of the cushion against them for control than do softer ones, and a reed which is too stiff tends to encourage biting. If less mouthpiece is used for stiff reeds than for soft ones the tendency to bite with the lower teeth is reduced.

7. *Puffing cheeks.* Puffing cheeks is a problem with many beginners as well as with some more advanced students. They indicate a lack of support by the cheek muscles which may or may not affect the support corners of the mouth are giving the mouthpiece. It always indicates that breath support necessary to produce the tone is not properly focused and directed into the mouthpiece. This problem must be corrected if the student is to achieve his goal of becoming a fine player. Frequently the student does not realize that the cheeks are puffed, and the use of the mirror to check embouchure formation is valuable. When the student can see that the cheeks are not puffed he can feel the muscular support which is necessary to keep them in place and make the correction. It is sometimes useful to have him feel the cheeks with one hand while playing open "G."

8. *Relaxed lip.* Some students will achieve a good embouchure except for the fact that the upper lip is somewhat relaxed which either allows a little air to escape or which puts too much pressure by the upper teeth against the mouthpiece. If this occurs the student may be told to push down with the upper lip to push the mouthpiece entirely away from the upper teeth while playing so that he can feel the muscular movement. The amount of downward pressure can then be relaxed to the proper amount.

9. *Escaping air.* Escaping air from one corner of the mouth while playing is another clear indication that something is wrong with the embouchure formation. Normally it means that the lips are not being kept in a circle with pressure against the mouthpiece from all directions, but are being relaxed at that corner. The imagery of suggesting that the lips act as a draw-string closing around the mouthpiece is frequently helpful. This is described as the "laundry-bag" concept by one teacher, and seems to have real and effective meaning to many students.

10. *Chin muscles.* A very commonly found problem with beginners is their failure to keep the chin muscles firm. Instead of pulling downward the chin is pushed upward and the muscles bunched under the reed. This carries with it an excess of pressure against the reed both with the lip and in association with the lower jaw. Only a minimum amount of success is possible for the student who has this condition, and unless it is corrected the student will soon drop the instrument. This condition is extremely difficult to correct once it has become fixed, and for this reason must be observed and corrected and measures taken to keep it from occurring from the very first day of study. A mirror will help the student check himself while practicing.

The Hard Cushion Embouchure

The hard cushion embouchure is formed in virtually diametric opposition to the soft cushion, and like the soft cushion is subject to many slight variations.

The basic formation of this embouchure can be achieved through the following step-by-step procedure. Use a mirror on the music stand to check each step.

1. Drop the lower jaw so that the teeth are about three-eighths of an inch apart, allowing the lips to open also.
2. Draw the lower lip over the teeth so that approximately one-half of the red of the lip is covering the teeth. Test by putting a finger against the lip to see that the front edge of the upper teeth is in the center of the lip.
3. Using the "smile" muscles pull the corners of the mouth back in a smiling position.
4. The chin is held firm in a flat and pointed position pulling the lower lip against the teeth, forming a smooth hard cushion upon which the reed rests.
5. Put the mouthpiece in the mouth so that the upper teeth are resting approximately a half-inch from the lip. This distance is adjusted in or out for students with a greater than normal underbite or with an over-bite.
6. The corners of the mouth are pushed together to prevent air from escaping while maintaining the smiling position.
7. A slight downward pressure of the upper lip and a slight upward pressure of the lower lip provide the support for the mouthpiece and reed.
8. First efforts at tone production should be made with the mouthpiece alone as described in step 8 of the soft cushion formation. Continue to check constantly with the mirror to maintain the proper shape.

Common Faults in Hard Cushion Embouchure Formation. Problems encountered forming the proper hard cushion embouchure may be summarized as follows:

1. *Amount of lip.* The amount of lip over the lower teeth is dependent on the size and thickness of the lips of the individual student. Students with very thin lips may need to put the entire lip over the lower teeth, while students with thick lips may need to use as little as one-third of the lower lip. The correct distance can be determined by a visual check and by the tone quality produced.

2. *Amount of mouthpiece.* The amount of mouthpiece in the mouth is determined by the nature of the teeth of the individual student. The position described above is satisfactory for the average or normal formation, and is suggested as a means of putting the lower teeth at the proper supporting point under the lower lip against the reed. This distance is determined in the same manner as described for the soft cushion formation. Students with protruding upper teeth will need to place them farther than a half inch on the mouthpiece. If the lower teeth or jaw protrude he will need less than a half inch distance from the tip of the mouthpiece.

3. *Chin.* The chin must be kept pointed at all times as it is this muscular tension in a downward direction which maintains the hard cushion over the lower teeth. If the chin is relaxed or pushed up the cushion is lost and there is too much pressure against the reed which restricts its vibration resulting in a poor tone quality. A stretched flabby hard cushion formation produces the poorest imaginable tone quality on the instrument.

4. *Corners of mouth.* The corners of the mouth should maintain the smile position and the most frequently encountered problem in this connection is that they are pulled back too far into a position similar to the make-up on a happy circus clown. This exaggerated position makes control difficult and often causes air leakage around the mouthpiece. This condition can be corrected by pushing the corners of the mouth slightly toward the mouthpiece, while relaxing the tension on the smile muscles.

5. *Biting.* Biting or excess pressure of the lower teeth against the reed is as frequent with this embouchure formation as with the soft cushion formation. Excess pressure restricts the reed vibration, demands excess breath pressure to produce a tone, makes high tones difficult to play in tune, and inhibits the development of a good tone quality. Insist that the teeth remain apart as described. If there is too much pressure the student can feel well-defined indentations on the inside of his lower lip with his tongue and will complain of a "sore" lip.

The problems involving the mouthpiece, the reed, and puffing cheeks are similar with those encountered with soft cushion formation and need not be repeated here.

Comparison of the Soft and Hard Cushion Embouchure

Both the soft cushion and the hard cushion type of embouchure are subject to infinite variation, all of which are slight, depending on the training of the person using them. None of these variations affect the basic formation, but primarily involve the semantics used in describing them. No two teachers will agree exactly on how to describe the correct formation. The production of pleasing musical sounds as the end product of developing an embouchure is the goal of every teacher and performer, and is the same no matter what road is taken to get there. The final judgment of whether an embouchure is good or bad cannot be made on how it is described or how it is formed but how it actually sounds.

The decision on whether to use the soft cushion or the hard cushion approach is dependent on the ultimate type of tone quality desired. Both styles produce musically pleasing sounds. A comparison between fine players using both styles will reveal that generally speaking the soft cushion embouchure produces a dark full-bodied

Checklist for Embouchure Formation

The following check on embouchure formation must be made while the student is playing and preferably when he is not aware that a check is being made. Any errors should be carefully explained to the student, the correction worked out with him while he is observing the embouchure in a mirror. Remedial exercises can be assigned on the basis of this list.

A. Soft Cushion Embouchure	Yes	No	Comments
1. Lips rounded with wrinkles?			
2. Mouthpiece proper distance in mouth?			
3. Corners of lips pushed inward?			
4. Sufficient lip over lower teeth?			
5. Are lower teeth biting?			
6. Cheeks puffed?			
7. Dimples in cheek?			
8. Air escaping?			
9. Chin firm and down?			

B. Hard Cushion Embouchure			
1. Mouthpiece proper distance in mouth?			
2. Proper amount of lip over lower teeth?			
3. Chin firm and pointed?			
4. Cheeks in proper smiling position?			
5. Lower lip smooth and firm?			
6. Corners pushed in slightly?			
7. Are lower teeth biting?			
8. Cheeks puffed?			
9. Air escaping?			

tone quality capable of great shading, while the hard cushion produces a clear flute-like quality somewhat less full-bodied but capable of a variety of shading. Few teachers or students have the opportunity of making direct comparisons between the two approaches, but should take advantage of the opportunity if it arises. People like the sound with which they are most familiar which is as it should be.

Other Embouchure Formations

Double Embouchure. This formation calls for the upper lip as well as the lower lip to be over the teeth, hence the designation "double embouchure." Except for the upper lip over the teeth, this embouchure is formed using either the soft cushion or the hard cushion shape, or a formation between the two.

The double embouchure is favored by a rather small minority of players. In a survey of college and university clarinet teachers and professional players, Gold found that only twelve percent made use of the double embouchure.[3] This figure may be misleadingly high, for a number of respondents indicated that they used the double embouchure only occasionally.

Some of the relatively few teachers who play with the double embouchure do not always insist that their students use it. It is a very difficult embouchure to develop since only those players with a longer than normal upper lip can pull it over the teeth easily. Those with normal upper lips have some difficulty, and a short upper lip makes it impossible. Strength and control is achieved very slowly with this embouchure, but its most serious drawback is that constant daily practice is necessary to maintain it, since strength and control is lost rapidly if the instrument is not played. Unless there is a strong personal preference for the double embouchure, a formation using only the lower lip over the teeth should be used.

The German Embouchure. This embouchure differs from all the previous embouchures in that neither the upper lip nor the lower lip is over the teeth. With this embouchure the clarinet is pushed firmly against the upper teeth by the right thumb, and the lower lip is placed against the reed from a position in front and beyond the front edge of the lower teeth. The upper teeth contact the top of the mouthpiece almost an inch from the tip—twice as far as other embouchures. This embouchure is infrequently used and taught in this country, since it demands a mouthpiece with a long lay and preferably reed with the German cut which are not commonly available.

This is the most difficult of all embouchure formations to develop. Considerable lip pressure is required for control, and this is acquired slowly since so few muscles, compared to other embouchures, can be involved. One authority mentions the fact that it is difficult to make the delicate shadings required by contemporary standards of interpretation with this embouchure.

In order to reduce the amount of lip pressure and to gain a greater control of the tone, the embouchure is modified considerably when used in this country. These modifications include the use of a shorter lay on the mouthpiece which allows the use of a less stiff reed and requires a little less mouthpiece in the mouth. But the fact remains that even with these modifications this embouchure formation is much more difficult to develop, lacks flexibility, and is much more difficult to develop a fine tone than either of the standard formations.[4]

Old Italian Embouchure. This embouchure formation is mentioned as a curiosity rather than as having any practical value, since it has not been used for many, many years. The formation of this embouchure calls for both lips to be over the teeth as in the French formation, but with the mouthpiece turned over with the reed against the *upper* teeth. This formation is said to have required a very soft reed which made intonation a real problem, and variety in articulation was obviously impossible. It is interesting to speculate on how players using this embouchure actually sounded!

TUNING

All clarinets must be carefully and regularly tuned to the standard international pitch of A-440. Tuning for them as for all wind instruments is best done with an electronic aid which provides a visual check on pitch. Tuning bars and tuning forks are useful for checking single notes through the use of "beats" or direct comparisons, but are not as useful as an instrument which could check the pitch of all the notes on the instrument. The piano is perhaps the poorest source of tuning notes that it is possible to imagine, unless it has been tuned by an expert tuner within the previous few days. Piano pitch is affected by temperature changes which cause the string to stretch or contract, raising and lowering the pitches, and over a period of time the over-all pitch of the instrument sinks lower than the standard A-440. Temperature affects the piano and wind instruments in reverse directions. A low temperature raises the pitch of the piano and lowers the pitch of wind instruments, while a high temperature lowers the pitch of the piano and raises the pitch of wind instruments. Obviously, a player who is playing a solo with piano accompaniment, or in an ensemble which includes a piano must tune and play in tune with it. But other than this the piano should not be used for tuning purposes. Use tuning bars, tuning forks, or preferably an electronic instrument.

On woodwind instruments the pitch of a given note

3. Cecil V. Gold. *Clarinet Performing Practices and Teaching in the United States and Canada* (Moscow, Idaho: University of Idaho, School of Music, 1972).

4. Those interested in greater details about the German Embouchure should consult W. M. Eby. *The Clarinet Embouchure* (New York: Walter Jacobs, Inc.), pp. 11-16. Copyright 1927 by W. M. Eby.

is determined by the distance from the tip of the mouthpiece or double-reed to the first open hole. Thus, the pitches of two successive notes on a clarinet—say C and B-flat which are one tone hole apart in fingering—is not determined by the distance between the two tone holes involved, but by the ratio of the distance from each of the tone holes to the tip of the mouthpiece. For this reason the ratios between the tip of the mouthpiece and the various first open holes must be maintained as close to the original as possible when tuning adjustments are made.

A B-flat clarinet when tuning to an A-440 tuning bar plays B-natural on the third line. If the tuning barrel is pulled a quarter of an inch or more to bring the clarinet pitch down to A-440, it will be found that the throat tones are quite flat. In changing the ratio of the distance for the B-natural, the ratios for the throat tones was made out of proportion and they respond by being flat. The further out the tuning barrel is pulled for the B-natural to be in tune, the flatter the throat tones will be. A similar situation prevails on the other instruments in the clarinet family.

For this reason, if the intonation of the clarinet is to remain good over its entire range, tuning adjustments must be made in *three* places on the instrument: at the barrel joint, at the middle joint and at the bell joint. The three tuning notes for each instrument of the clarinet family and the corresponding concert pitch is given below. They must be used in the order given tuning the barrel joint, middle joint, and bell joint in that sequence. If all three notes cannot be tuned perfectly, distribute the difference between them. Once the instrument itself is accurately tuned, the remainder of the intonation on the instrument is dependent on the player.

1. *E-flat Clarinet*

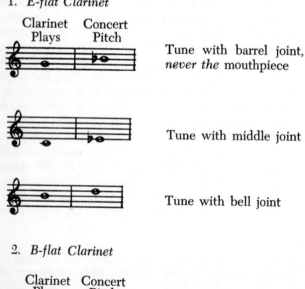

Clarinet Plays — Concert Pitch

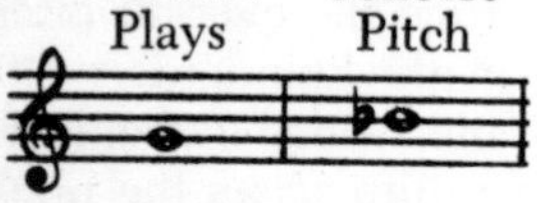

Tune with barrel joint, *never the* mouthpiece

Tune with middle joint

Tune with bell joint

2. *B-flat Clarinet*

Clarinet Plays — Concert Pitch

Tune with barrel joint, *never the* mouthpiece

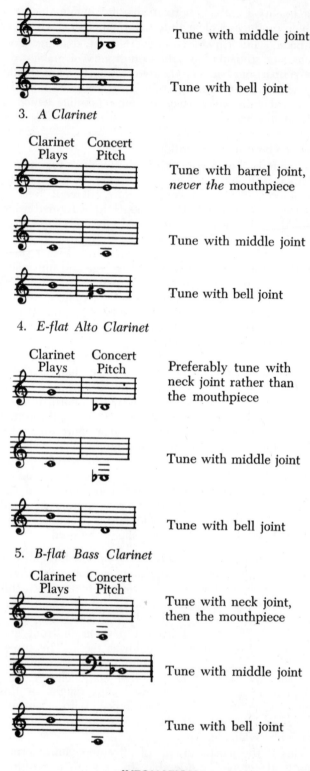

Tune with middle joint

Tune with bell joint

3. *A Clarinet*

Clarinet Plays — Concert Pitch

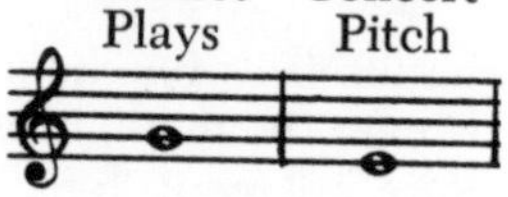

Tune with barrel joint, *never the* mouthpiece

Tune with middle joint

Tune with bell joint

4. *E-flat Alto Clarinet*

Clarinet Plays — Concert Pitch

Preferably tune with neck joint rather than the mouthpiece

Tune with middle joint

Tune with bell joint

5. *B-flat Bass Clarinet*

Clarinet Plays — Concert Pitch

Tune with neck joint, then the mouthpiece

Tune with middle joint

Tune with bell joint

INTONATION

Natural Tendencies of the Instrument

The process of tuning the instrument just described produces the best possible foundation upon which to build good intonation, since the instrument is as nearly in tune with itself as it is possible to get. It is not possible for a manufacturer to build an instrument which is absolutely perfectly in tune throughout its entire range. On clarinets all notes above third line B-flat are products of partial vibrations of the air column or overtones of the pitches below. The pitches of overtones are determined by the natural acoustical laws of vibration. The first harmonic is an octave, and the second harmonic an octave plus a fifth, or the interval of a twelfth. Because of the acoustical properties of the clarinet, the octave and other even numbered notes in the harmonic series cannot be produced. Hence the clarinet overblows a twelfth, or to put it simply when the register key is added to a fingering of a tone in the chalumeau register the resulting tone is a twelfth. Other woodwind instruments overblow an octave, which is why the key operated by the left thumb is called a register key on the clarinet, and an octave key on the oboe and saxophone.

Notes produced as overtones in the natural harmonic series have different rates of vibration than the same interval in the tempered scale.[5] The higher in the harmonic series the greater the discrepency between the natural overtones and the corresponding note in the tempered scale. The first harmonic, or octave above the fundamental, is perfectly in tune, while the next—the twelfth—is slightly out of tune in comparison with the tempered scale.

The following example shows a comparison of the pitches of three notes when produced with the same fingering on the clarinet showing the natural frequency of the tones with the frequencies of the same notes demanded by equal temperament in which the clarinetist plays.[6]

Natural Frequency	220	660	1100
Equal Temperament	220	659.2	1108.5

The "A" is the fundamental vibration and is the same. The "E" a twelfth above is the third note in the harmonic series and is eight-tenths of a vibration sharper than it should be for the equal tempered scale. The C-sharp, two octaves and a major third above the fundamental is the fifth note in the overtone series, and is eight and one-half vibrations flat. This extreme flatness of the C-sharp is compensated for by raising the first finger of the left hand. If a stroboscope is available a clarinetist in the class can demonstrate this relationship on these notes as well as other similar series of notes using different fundamentals.

The clarinet, using the twelfth for notes in the clarion register, has greater intonation problems than the oboes or saxophones which use the octave for their second register. However, instrument manufacturers have made the most effective compromises possible to bring the entire range into tune with the tempered scale and as players devolop the continual process of adjusting the embouchure to accommodate the slightly out-of-tuneness becomes a natural response, and playing in tune becomes automatic. As a result of this situation, the clarinet has natural tendencies in intonation with which every teacher and player should be familiar.

Tendency to be sharp:

Tendency to be flat:

Sharp or flat depending on embouchure:

Reed and Intonation

A reed which is too hard tends to make the instrument sharp while a reed which is too soft tends to make the instrument flat. A soft reed emphasizes the natural tendencies of the notes and does not respond to embouchure adjustments. so in addition to a general flatness the instrument is out of tune with itself. A student who consistently plays flat, but whose embouchure formation is correct, is playing on a reed which is too soft. If he is given a harder reed the overall flatness disappears rather quickly, although he will probably protest that it is too hard to blow, which simply means that he is not accustomed to supporting the tone as much. Most students make the adjustment to slightly stiffer reeds quite readily. If the student has been playing on an extremely soft reed, he should be gradually brought to playing on the proper strength through a succession of increasingly stiff reeds.

The student who has been using a reed which is too hard compensates for the overall sharpness by pulling out the barrel joint and other joints of the instrument. Unfortunately the instruments do not permit pushing in an equal amount to compensate for the habitually flat player. Providing the embouchure formation is correct, a student who has to pull the instrument out an excessive amount to play at the standard pitch is playing

5. Refer to the appendix on acoustics of woodwind instruments for details of this harmonic structure.

6. Donald W. Stauffer. *Intonation Deficiencies of Wind Instruments in Ensemble* (Washington, D. C.: Catholic University of America Press, 1954), p. 77. This is the most complete study of intonation of wind instruments available.

on a reed which is too stiff. This tuning habit is frequently the best clue to an overly stiff reed. If he is given a softer reed, the pitch will be lowered, although he will complain about the tone quality he is producing, no change in quality will be apparent to the listener.

Embouchure and Intonation

The embouchure is the primary controlling factor in intonation as well as tone quality, two aspects of performance which must be well done if the musical effect is to be pleasing. It is for this reason that so much emphasis is given to proper embouchure formation, and justly so.

Too little mouthpiece in the mouth emphasizes the flatness of the clarion and high registers. It is virtually impossible to play the high register in tune without sufficient mouthpiece in the mouth no matter how hard the student bites—and he will. Too much mouthpiece in the mouth tends to make the general pitch a little flat, but even more important makes pitch control of individual notes difficult.

The angle at which the clarinet is held determines the way in which the embouchure can control it. If the bell is too far out from the body—i.e., farther than a forty degree angle—the embouchure cannot support the reed and there is an overall flatness in pitch. If the bell is held closer to the body than normal the overall pitch is sharpened. This can be verified by having a student sustain an open G while moving the bell of the instrument back and forth. There will be a marked change in both pitch and tone quality.

Mouthpiece and Intonation

Mouthpieces with a close lay tend to be sharper than mouthpieces with an open lay, although through proper reed selection and embouchure formation the player can compensate for these natural tendencies of the mouthpiece.

All mouthpieces do not have the same internal dimensions—i.e., throat and bore size and shape—and the same type of mouthpiece does not fit all instruments. If the size of the bore does not match the bore of the clarinet itself the instrument is difficult to play in tune with itself. If a student is having serious intonation problems and other possible causes have been checked, have him try other mouthpieces of different brands. If the mouthpiece construction is the problem some quite serious intonation difficulties can be solved by changing mouthpieces, although the student will not suddenly cease playing out of tune and start playing in tune because of the automatic adjustments his embouchure has been making to accommodate the out-of-tune mouthpiece. However, the mouthpiece has its greatest influence on tone *quality,* and is not to be blamed for poor intonation until all other causes have been checked and corrected.

Dynamics and Intonation.

There is an unfortunate tendency for the clarinetist to play flatter as he gets louder and sharper as he gets softer, the degree of flatness or sharpness increasing as the degree of dynamics approaches the extremes. This must be compensated for by embouchure adjustments. The student has the tendency to increase the pressure of the lower lip when playing softly and to decrease the pressure as he gets louder. This tendency is especially apparent in students who do not use the proper abdominal breath support.

To overcome sharpness when playing softly relax the embouchure slightly, decrease the velocity of the air through the instrument but maintain the same firm support of the breath with the diaphragm and abdominal muscles that is used when playing loudly.

To prevent becoming progressively flatter and flatter as the loudness of a tone increases, drop the lower teeth slightly but increase the pressure of the lips around the mouthpiece, especially the pressure of the lower lip against the reed.

Relaxing the embouchure when playing softly allows a greater length of the reed to vibrate which lowers the natural pitch of the reed itself and hence the pitch of the tone being played. Dropping the lower jaw and increasing the pressure around the mouthpiece when playing loudly allows the maximum length of the reed to vibrate in order to produce a loud tone with the increased pressure of the lower lip against it raises its natural rate of vibration to maintain the proper pitch. The dynamic levels between a normal mezzo piano and mezzo forte usually require little or no adjustment for intonation. Dynamic levels of piano, pianissimo and softer, and forte, fortissimo and louder demand increasing compensation.

The following tone exercises are excellent practice in control of pitch through wide dynamic levels. Practice them slowly enough to use an entire breath. Maintain constant firm breath support while controlling the dynamics by changing the velocity of the breath through the instrument.

Practice exercise "a" in major or minor scale patterns to include the range of the instrument in which the student is proficient. Exercise "b" is best practiced chromatically from low E to F in the staff as indicated.

a. adagio

b. adagio 

This is also a good exercise for developing register crossing, and it is well to check to see that the student is operating the register key by vertical movements of the joint of the thumb and not sliding the thumb.

Intonation in Ensemble

The ability to tune the clarinet to the standard pitch and to play the instrument in tune with itself is essential. However, very few woodwinds other than practicing do much playing alone, but rather with other instruments in ensembles of two or three up to a full orchestra or band. Hence playing the instrument in tune with itself is only the starting point for good intonation. The student must listen to other instruments and make slight adjustments so that he is exactly in tune with the other players. The worst possible situations intonation-wise are the result of not listening to the others, or when a player insists that his pitch is right and everyone else is wrong.

Other woodwind instruments have natural tendencies toward out of tuneness which are different than those on the clarinet, brass instruments have different problems, and strings still others. The musically intelligent player will recognize these different problems, and will compromise his intonation for the sake of perfect ensemble intonation. Training in listening and hearing intonation is a valuable contribution which an instrumental teacher can make to his students. But it must be emphasized that the basis for good intonation must be the ability to play an instrument in tune with itself at the standard pitch.

Deviations from the Standard A-440 Pitch

There is an unfortunate tendency for some groups to use as a standard tuning note a pitch which is higher than A-440. One large university even went so far as to have its tuned percussion retuned to the standard of A-445. Even if groups don't deliberately tune to note higher than A-440 they have a tendency to drift to a higher pitch while playing. The result of a higher pitch is a multiplicity of intonation problems.

Clarinets and other woodwind instruments, as well as the brasses are manufactured so that they play in tune at A-440. They are simply not in tune with themselves at higher pitches and the players must force the pitch higher, biting on the reed, and make constant adjustments. Some of the poor intonation in school bands and orchestras can be attributed to this situation. If a group which has been playing high is brought down to the A-440 standard and held at this pitch, there is an amazingly rapid improvement in intonation.

Adjusting Intonation of Individual Notes

Because the various standard fingerings for many notes, especially those in the high register, may produce slight differences in pitch from what the player may want for the best intonation, it is frequently necessary to adjust the tuning of a standard fingering. This is accomplished by opening or closing one or more tone holes in addition to those called for in the standard fingering. Some experimentation by the player will be necessary to discover exactly what is needed.

These are basic principles to be used in making intonation adjustments in standard fingerings.

1. In general, opening tone holes will raise the pitch and closing tone holes will lower the pitch.
2. At least one tone hole below the last closed hole involved in the fingering must remain open.
3. The closer to this tone hole that additional holes are open or closed, the greater the effect on the pitch will be; conversely, the farther from this tone hole the less effect on the pitch.
4. More than one finger may be added to the basic fingering to correct the pitch.
5. The degree of correction which may be needed varies from player to player and with the given musical situation.
6. Whether or not a correction is called for varies with the dynamic level being used.

The following examples illustrate these principles.

1. The range  is frequently sharp at softer dynamic levels. To flatten the pitch slightly, add key "F"; to flatten the pitch more add key "E."
2. The range 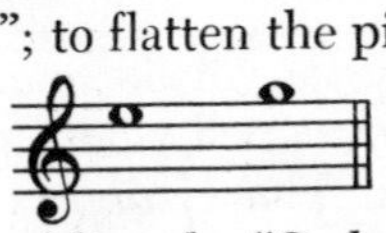 may be raised slightly in pitch by adding the "G-sharp" key with the right little finger, and lowered slightly in pitch by add ing the "F" or "F-sharp" key.
3. The range  may be raised slightly in pitch by adding key "6x", and lowered in pitch by omitting the "G-sharp" key.

The use of a stroboscopic device is extremely valuable in checking and developing correct intonation. It should be a part of every well-equipped instrumental program and used regularly. It should be available for students to use individually for personal checks—indeed, this should be insisted upon. Serious use of such a device will develop intonation rapidly and efficiently. And, since it is built to the A-440 standard will help maintain the proper pitch level.

TONE

Basically the tone quality on a clarinet must be the same over the entire range of the instrument. It must not vary greatly from note to note, nor from register to register. In developing a good tone a great deal of attention must be given to this problem of matching quality. The better the balance of quality over the instrument the better the musical results and the better the response of the listeners.

In the preface of his method for clarinet Gustave Langenus makes the following statement regarding tone on the clarinet.

> Everything should be sacrificed for a beautiful tone. No amount of technic, when the tone is coarse, will give such pleasure as a simple phrase played with a clear and pleasing tone quality. A beautiful voice is expected from a singer; if he does not possess this, his high notes and vocalisms do not charm, but leave us cold. The same is true of the clarinetist. No instrument can emit such a rough, disagreeable sound as the clarinet, and, on the other hand, no wind instrument can equal it in golden tones. The tone of the lower register resembles the contralto in richness and mellowness, while the clarion register possesses the sweet and tender qualities of the soprano.[7]

The range of the clarinet is divided into four registers, which should be memorized since so much of the literature about the instrument makes reference to them.

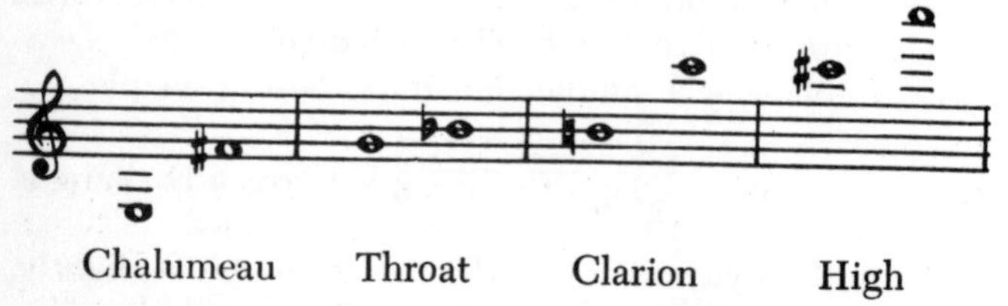

The chalumeau register gots its name from the instrument from which it developed whose playing range was limited to these notes. The clarion register was added during the course of the development of the instrument for when these notes were added to the clarinet it was used to replace a primitive valveless brass instrument called the clarion. The throat tones are so labeled because in the early development their pitch was primarily controlled by the player's throat. The reason for the designation *high register* is obvious.

Referring back to the use of harmonics on the clarinet we find that notes in the chalumeau register and the throat tones are produced as fundamentals of the vibrating column of air; those in the clarion register by the third notes in the overtone series; and those in the high register by either the fifth or seventh tone in the overtone series.

There is no single standard for a good tone on instruments of the clarinet family. The two basic embouchures described for the instruments produce different qualities, both fulfilling all the criteria for a good tone, and both equally pleasing when fully developed. Deviations from these two basic embouchures produces slightly different qualities. But no matter what the differences a clarinet still sounds like a clarinet and if the tone is pleasing, it is a good tone.

Every teacher and clarinetist should avail themselves of every opportunity to hear live performances of fine instrumentalists. Or if this is not possible study the recorded performances of repertoire for the clarinet listed in an appendix on a high quality phonograph where realistic reproduction can be heard. Compare the tone qualities of the various artists in so far as it is possible to separate quality from phrasing, technique, and general musicianship. A comparison of the recorded performances of French artists, German artists, English artists, and American artists will be quite revealing. All will be quite different, all will be pleasing, and in spite of the intermingling of cultures national differences will be readily discernible.

Common Problems in Tone

A good tone is the product of all the elements involved in playing: instrument, mouthpiece, reed, embouchure and breath support. If any of these is defective then tone quality suffers accordingly.

Problems of tone production and quality are many and varied, but may usually be traced to their source, and should be corrected immediately. Refer also to the sections on mouthpiece, reed, and embouchure.

Following are some of the most prevalent problems or faults in tone.

1. *Small, pinched, or muffled tone.* Assuming a proper mouthpiece and reed, a small, pinched, or muffled tone may be caused by too much pressure on the reed with the lower jaw, or by having too little mouthpiece in the mouth. Adjust the distance in the mouth by experimentation to the point of optimum quality and fullness, yet avoiding the tendency of the tone to break into the next upper partial which is caused by too much mouthpiece in the mouth. Too much pressure against the reed can be remedied by asking the student to play flatter. This will cause him to relax the pressure of the lower jaw and free the reed. Unless he also relaxes the support of the lip against the reed, he will not actually play flatter in pitch, the effect will simply be a freer tone quality.

2. *Squawky tone.* The squawky tone which can be described as lacking in body and focus, generally uncontrolled, and commonly flat in pitch is caused by one of three things. Not enough support for the reed with the lower lip; poor embouchure formation evidenced by not enough pressure around the mouthpiece with the

7. Gustav Langenus, *Complete Method for Boehm Clarinet,* part I. (New York: Carl Fischer, Inc., 1923), p. x.

upper lip, the corners of the mouth, as well as the lower lip; or by a poor reed. Corrections for these have been discussed in previous sections.

3. *Hard, cold tone.* A tone which is inflexible and which lacks the intangible quality of vitality is described as hard and cold. This is caused by a mouthpiece which has a lay which is too open and too long, or by a reed which is too hard.

4. *Squeaking.* Squeaking on a clarinet is usually caused by a hole not being completely covered by one of the fingers, a condition most common with beginners; by a leaky pad which must be identified and replaced; by the reed; or by an incorrect embouchure which is putting pressure unequally on the reed.

5. *Weak, colorless tone.* A tone which is otherwise smooth in quality, but is lacking in body, quality, and carrying power is most often due to lack of proper breathing and breath support.

6. *Loud, racous tone.* This quality is always the result of too much breath support which overblows the instrument and presses it beyond its true dynamic range. Insisting on a full dynamic range, and limiting the volume the student is allowed to produce will correct this problem. This condition is also associated with a mouthpiece which has a longer lay with an open tip, and with the use of reeds which are too stiff. In school bands, it is never one clarinet which has this problem but the entire section which indicates clearly that the director is responsible for letting it develop.

7. *Control of soft tone.* Difficulty in producing and controlling a soft tone is principally due to the inability of the player to project a steady concentrated small stream of air into the instrument. Check breathing and breath support, and have the student practice focusing a steady stream of air into the palm of his hand. Other possible causes may be a reed which is too stiff, a mouthpiece which is too open, or a poorly shaped embouchure. Check all three if breath support is not the solution.

8. *Throat tone resonance.* Even advanced players are frequently concerned with a lack of resonance in the throat tones especially at softer dynamic levels. These tones are quite sensitive to breath support and embouchure. If both of these are satisfactory, it is possible to increase the resonance in this register by adding the fourth, fifth, and sixth fingers to the basic fingering. This will usually result in a noticable increase in resonance. The player should also experiment with adding the third finger, then the second finger, and finally the first, although with some players adding these fingers may flatten the pitch slightly.

9. *Dynamics and tone quality.* Some students will loose their tone quality when playing at extremes of loudness and softness. This is normally due to an undeveloped embouchure. Keep the volume of tone within the ability of the embouchure to retain control, and concentrate on embouchure development through the use of the proper exercises.

TONGUING

Tonguing refers to the manner in which the tongue operates in relation to the reed and breath support in order to articulate the tones. This placement and action must be rapid and under complete control at all speeds. It must, in coordination with breath support, be able to produce on the clarinet all varieties of articulation from the hardest staccato to the softest legato. In short, the clarinetist must be able to match sound for sound the entire gamut of bow strokes used on the violin.

The manner in which the tongue touches the reed, the place it touches, and how it moves is dependent somewhat upon the embouchure formation. There are several points of view on how this is done and each is effective.

In essence the tongue acts as a valve to control the flow of breath through the mouthpiece, stopping the breath and vibration when it touches the reed, and allowing the vibration to begin again when it is removed and the air flow begins again. Effective articulation is entirely dependent upon the flow of air, and hence upon proper breath support and control. The interrelationship between breath pressure and tongue pressure against the reed allows the production of every conceivable kind of attack from the hardest marcato-staccato to the very smoothest legato within the widest dynamic range. The amount of pressure of the tongue against the reed determines the hardness of the attack, the amount of wind pressure against the tongue determines the loudness of the attack.

There are three basic methods of tongue placement used on the clarinet, each subject to variations according to the personal desires of the teachers using them. They have several things in common however: (1) the tongue is relaxed. A tongue under tension cannot move rapidly enough, nor can it be controlled; (2) Tongue movement is confined to the forward part of the tongue; and (3) The tongue acts as a valve for the air and is dependent on good breath support. The three methods may be outlined as follows:

First Method. This method is used with the soft cushion embouchure previously described and is the method taught by many fine clarinetists. It produces maximum flexibility and facility, and is adaptable to solo, chamber music, band, and orchestra performance. This method in combination with the soft cushion embouchure is recommended by the author.

With the mouthpiece in playing position, and the embouchure correctly formed, feel with the tip of the tongue the junction of the reed and the lower lip. The reed and lip form a small "V" shaped pocket. The tongue should be in this pocket with the top of the tip of the tongue curved up and touching the reed lightly about three-eighths of an inch from the tip.

To start the tone put the tongue in place on the reed and build up wind pressure against it. Release the air into the instrument with tongue action similar to that in pronouncing the syllable "too." The center of the tongue is depressed slightly so that the tongue will not lie flat on the reed. Figures C-68 and C-69 show this tongue position.

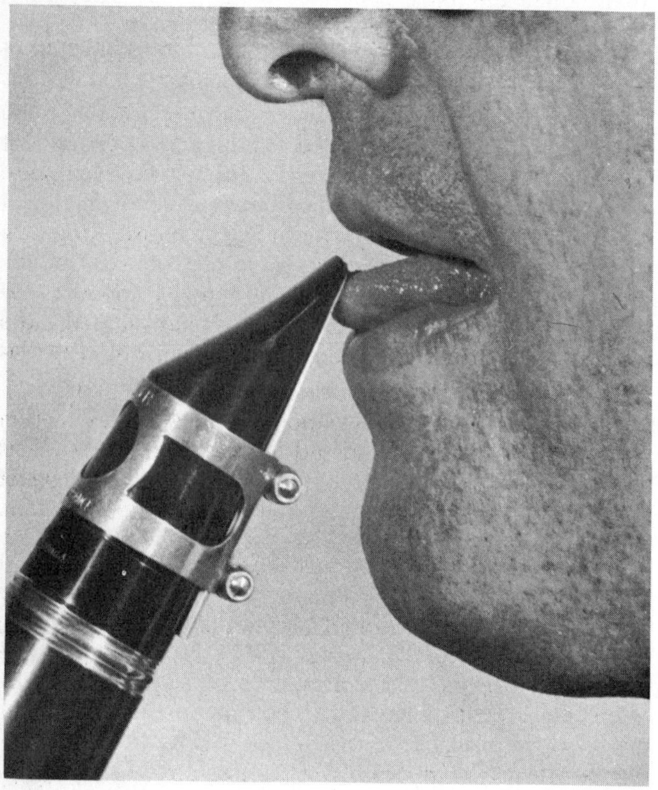

Figure C-68

Second Method. This method is used with the hard cushion embouchure previously described, and is recommended by many fine clarinet teachers. It produces great flexibility and is adapted to all types of performance.

With the mouthpiece in place and the embouchure properly formed, the tongue is drawn up and back with the tip pointed. The center of the tongue is arched and the throat kept open. Action of the tongue is foward contacting the reed an eighth or sixteenth of an inch from its tip with the top of the tongue about an eighth of an inch from its tip. Pressure of the tongue against the reed may be light or heavy depending on the type of articulation desired. To start the tone place the tongue against the reed, build up air pressure against it, and release the air with a tongue action similar to that in pronouncing "du" to start the tone. Figure C-70 shows the tongue in position on the reed for this type of articulation.

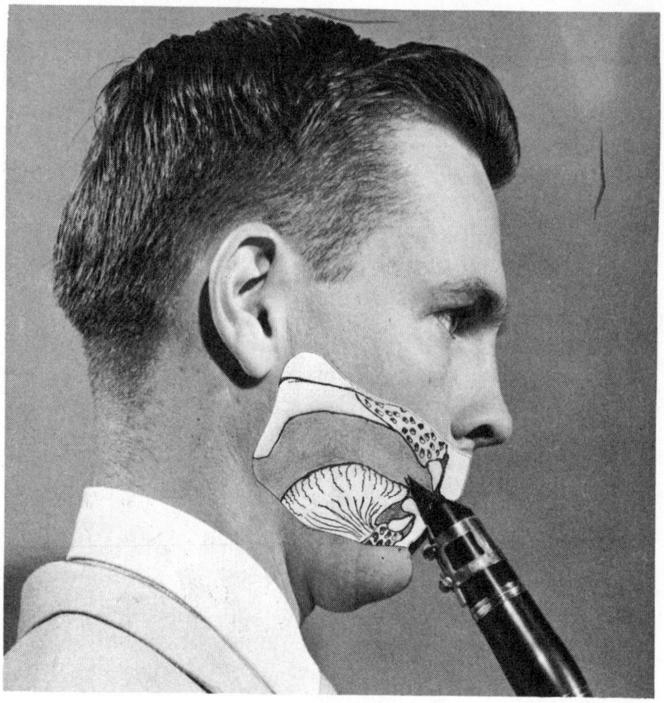

Figure C-69

Third Method. This method is used with either the soft cushion or the hard cushion embouchure. With the mouthpiece in place and the embouchure properly formed, the tip of the tongue is anchored against the

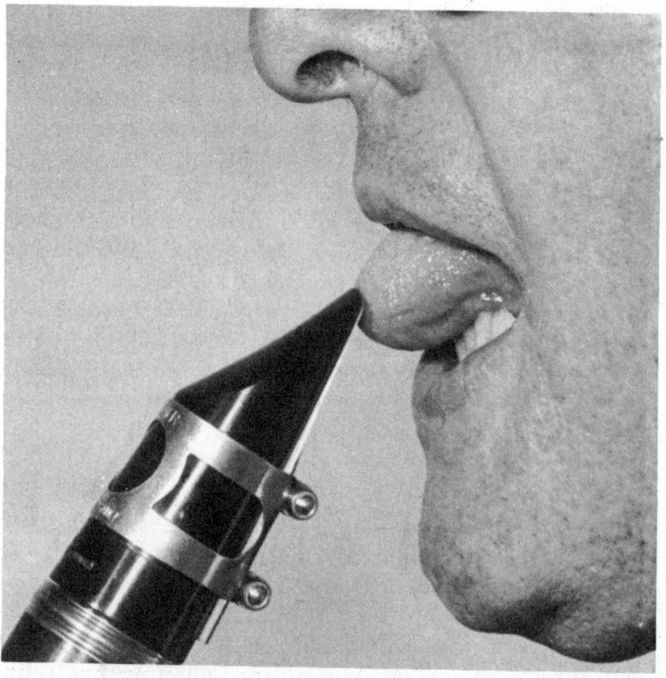

Figure C-70

base of the lower teeth. Keeping the tongue anchored against the teeth the tongue moves up and forward to contact the reed an eighth to half inch from its tip. The point on the tongue which contacts the reed is found naturally and is determined by its natural placement. Experience with advanced students who use this method has indicated that this technique of using the tongue does not have the potential of as great a variety of articulations as either of the previous methods, nor is speed and control developed as rapidly or to as great an extent. Unless there is a strong personal preference for this method, it should be used with caution.

The reader may compare the placement and action of the tongue for the three methods by forming an embouchure using the thumbnail or a pencil to replace the reed. Compare the ease, natural feeling, and rapidity of motion possible on each of the three. The method which feels most comfortable and which provides the most rapid movement will probably be the one which you as a clarinetist would develop fastest. Experience on other woodwinds, or on a brass instrument will help determine the result.

Alto, Bass, and Contra-Bass Clarinets

Any of the three methods of tongue placement and action described can be successfully used on the Alto, Bass, or Contra-Bass clarinet. Normally these instruments are played after some experience on the B-flat clarinet and the same system should be used as on that instrument. The difference between these instruments and the soprano instruments will be found in the point at which the tongue contacts the reed. Since there is more reed in the mouth because of the larger mouthpiece, the point of contact is further away from the tip of the reed. But the placement of the tongue in relation to the lower lip and teeth remains essentially the same.

It may be found that additional pressure of the tongue will be needed to close the reed if the mouthpiece has an open lay. Because of the larger reed its response is slower and it becomes increasingly difficult to produce a short staccato or to articulate as rapidly as we go from Alto to Bass to Contra-Bass. A short staccato on the Contra-Bass instrument is not only difficult to produce but is not musical in sound. Staccato on this instrument should more nearly reproduce the pizzicato sound of the string bass.

Developing Tongue Action

For the purposes of developing articulation on the clarinet the position of the tongue *against* the reed is considered the normal (home, or rest) position. For it is from this position that it starts the tone. There is no forward movement preceding the beginning of the tone since the breath support is against the tongue.

One writer has compared this concept with a pipe organ. There is wind pressure against the opening into the pipe before a key is pressed. When a key is pressed electrical contacts open the pipe, the air is released through it and a tone produced. When the key is lifted the pipe is closed, the tone stops but wind pressure against the pipe remains. So it is on the clarinet—tongue against the reed, and breath pressure against the tongue before the tone is started.

The commonly used word "attack" to describe the articulation of a tone is most unfortunate since it implies, if only subconsciously, both violence and forward movement. It has come into use in the English language as a mistranslation of the Italian word "attacca" which means *begin* and not attack. The words articulate and articulation are more meaningful in English, and the word attack should not be used when discussing articulation with students.

The first step in developing correct tongue action is to develop the starting and stopping of a tone. This is accomplished by a continual pressure of air against the mouthpiece with standard abdominal support. The tongue acts as a valve, releasing and stopping the flow of air through the instrument with the pressure remaining constant, much as the flow of water through a faucet is turned on and off. The water pressure doesn't fall to zero when the faucet is closed, and neither must the breath pressure when the tongue closes the reed against the mouthpiece.

Breath support and articulation are inseparable, so proper breath support must be developed before articulation is started. Almost all teachers insist that beginning clarinetists establish the beginnings of a good embouchure and breath control through developing a satisfactory tone in the chalumeau register before using the tongue against the reed. This is done by simply blowing to start the tone and stopping the air flow to end the note. If this is done then favorable conditions are set up for beginning the learning of articulation.

The following exercises are widely used to establish tongue action. They are mechanical exercises for tongue action and not music. If the students play them musically they are not deriving the full benefits. They must be played fortissimo and very slowly. No movement of the breathing mechanism is involved, diaphragm and abdominal muscles remain in tight support from beginning to end and *must not* move either at the beginning or end of the notes. Breath pressure against the tongue and mouthpiece remains the same during the rests as it is during the time the notes are sounding.

1. 

2. 

3. 

4. 

After breath pressure is built up against the mouthpiece the tongue moves away quickly with a motion similar to pronouncing the syllable "Too," or "Du" depending on placment of the tongue, and the note will start fortissimo and with an accent. Without diminishing the loudness of the one the tongue returns to its position on the reed with a motion like saying the letter "t." Thus the action of the tongue during the exercise is "T-o-o-o-o-o-t" or "D-u-u-u-t." If the notes were short, the tongue action would be a simple "toot" or "duut." Mechanical noise of the tongue leaving and returning to the reed must be heard. If it is not, then the pressure of the tongue is too light. These exercises should be practiced at least five minutes a day until the tongue action is secure.

When these have been established on the open G, practice them also on the following notes:

Having established the loudest and hardest articulation, it is necessary to establish the pianissimo with a soft articulation. Tongue action is the same. Support from the diaphragm and abdominal muscles remains the same, but the velocity of the air is reduced so that the loudness level of the tone is pianissimo. Sustain the open G as softly as possible. When it is established return the tongue to the reed quickly and with only enough pressure to stop the vibration of the reed but so that the tip of the reed does not close the mouthpiece, and air continues to go through the instrument. The same amount of air moves through the instrument during the rests as during the time the note is sounding! Hence breath pressure and velocity remains constant throughout. Play the exercise very softly and very slowly. Both beginnings and ends of the note are slow to respond. Include it in the daily practice routine until facility is established.

adagio

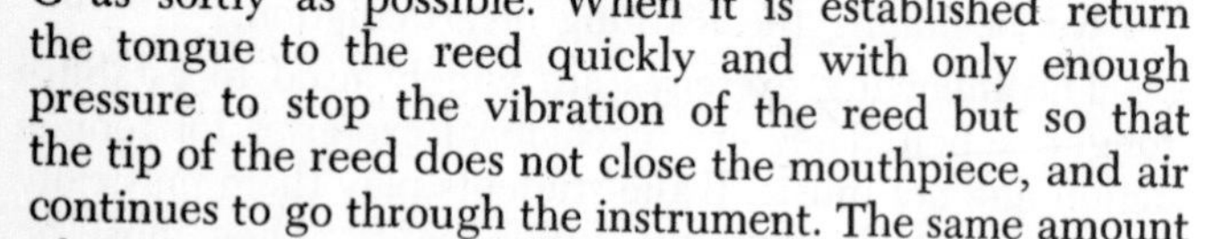

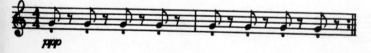

When this exercise is performed successfully on the open G practice also the following notes:

When both the fortissimo and pianissimo tongue actions are established, further development can be applied to melodic figures through the use of the "45 exercises upon different combinations of articulation, etc." in Part I of the *Klose Method for Clarinet*. Carl Fischer Edition. So that the articulation patterns will move slowly enough to develop security and accuracy in tongue action and breath support the speed must be greatly decreased. Sixteenth notes are played as half-notes at a slow speed.

The examples on page 51 indicate the manner in which they are played. Follow the dynamic markings exactly. All notes are started with the tongue. All notes at ends of slurs and all staccato notes are stopped with the tongue. Breath support remains constant throughout, with dynamics controlled by changes in velocity. Breath pressure against the reed continues during the rests. Careful practice of these will establish complete control of tongue action in a few weeks.

The basic principles illustrated by these four examples can be applied to all the 45 exercises: First notes under slurs are forte and a diminuendo is made for the duration of the slur mark so that the last note under the slur is piano. The final note is stopped by the tongue. All staccato notes are piano and started and stopped by the tongue. Eliminate all movements of any portion of the abdominal muscles or the diaphragm, support remains constant. These principles may also be applied to the Joseph Küffner *Fifty Progressive Duets* in the Klose Method Part I, but also published separately in several editions. These are technically easy and can be used by the students in the lower intermediate stage of development to begin musical application of articulation. More advanced students find ready adaptation of these principles of articulation in the C. Rose *Forty Studies for Clarinet* Books I and II, and the C. Rose *32 Studies for Clarinet*, all published by Carl Fischer.

No. 2. Written:

Played:

No. 5. Written:

Played:

No. 7. Written:

Played:

No. 10. Written:

Played:

Variety in Articulation

Once correct tongue action is established according to the method selected, variety in articulation can be developed. The exact sounds desired are determined by musical taste and style. A tremendous variety of articulations is possible on the clarinet through the use of varying degrees of pressure of the tongue against the reed combined with varying amounts of breath support and velocity of wind through the instrument. This can be illustrated by a member of the class playing in the following ways:

1. Sustain an open G at a good solid forte level. While maintaining this dynamic level and keeping the lengths of the notes the same start with maximum tongue pressure against the reed and play a series of notes with gradually diminishing pressure of the tongue.

2. Do the same maintaining a piano level for the open G, but starting with minimum pressure against the reed and play a series of notes with gradually increasing pressure of the tongue. It will be found that tongue pressure beyond a certain point will introduce an objectionable amount of mechanical noise.

3. Starting with an open G softly play a series of staccato notes simultaneously increasing both loudness of the tone and pressure of the tongue against the reed. Be sure to eliminate any movement of the breathing mechanism. Experimentation will show that the louder the staccato note the greater the tongue pressure needed to control it and if the result is to be musically pleasing, the louder the staccato the longer duration it must have. Staccato at loud dynamic levels automatically become marcato notes.

The success of these experiments depends on the degree of advancement of the player performing them. An advanced player will be able to carry the illustrations much farther and show a greater variety of articulated sounds.

Accents, Sforzando, Forte-piano

Accents, sforzando, and forte-piano notes must be played in relation to the dynamic level of the musical phrase. A sforzando is not a note played as loudly as it is possible to play, but simply an isolated note one or two degrees louder than the notes which precede or follow it in the phrase. It demands assistance from the breath so that the breathing mechanism supplies additional support and velocity simultaneously with the release of the reed by the tongue.

The forte-piano requires immediate relaxation of support and velocity by the breathing mechanism, coupled with whatever degree of simultaneous support at the instant the tone starts demanded by the music itself. Accents indicated above or below the notes must be only one dynamic level above the notes which precede or follow them. Many accents may be accomplished by only increased tongue pressure against the reed, others demand slight movements of the breathing muscles. It must be clearly understood that there are no rapid movements of any breathing muscles in support of tongue action except for accents, sfzorando, and forte-piano note.

Common Articulation Problems

There are a multitude of problems connected with articulation on members of the clarinet family, and the following are the most common:

1. *Movement of the jaw in tonguing.* This is the result of too large or too violent movements of the tongue. Rather than confining the movement to the front portion of the tongue the student is moving the entire tongue. The solution is to ask the student, no matter what his technical advancement, to practice the basic exercises for developing articulation constantly checking in a mirror on the music stand to eliminate all movement. Jaw movements can occur with all methods of correct tongue placement, as well as with incorrect tongue placement.

2. *Sluggish tongue.* Assuming that placement of the tongue is correct this can be corrected only by diligent practice. The use of major and minor scales, scales in the third pattern, major and minor arpeggios using various patterns of slurred and tongued notes will provide the most rapid cure for a sluggish tongue. The playing of staccato chromatic octaves up and down is excellent. The student should use a metronome while doing this practice in order that the best can be kept constant, or he will slow down and speed up according to the technical difficulty of the note patterns. More advanced students who have this problem can profit by using the *Kell 17 Staccato Studies.*

3. *Hard attack.* This is the result of too much tongue pressure against the reed in relation to the amount of breath support, or because too much tongue is in contact with the reed. Review the fundamental pianissimo exercises suggested for developing tongue action and continue practice until it can be done successfully. The hard attack is frequently associated with movements of the lower jaw which must also be eliminated. Use a mirror constantly for checking.

4. *Poor staccato.* A poor staccato or no staccato at all, if tongue placement is otherwise correct, is caused by lack of sustained, continuous breath support. The support is being relaxed between staccato notes and then tightened simultaneously with the beginning of the note by the tongue. Check breathing carefully, since if this is the case, the air is most frequently being inhaled with a chest movement rather than by the diaphragm and abdominal muscles. A good staccato is rarely possible with incorrect breath placement.

If a check reveals that all is well with placement of breath and the support is continuous, then a poor staccato is the result of incorrect tongue placement or movement. Frequently the cause is simply that the student is not returning the tongue quickly enough to its place on the reed to stop the vibration. This can be developed by practicing slow repeated notes at a very soft dynamic level, increasing the dynamic level as proficiency is attained. Many students are simply afraid to stop a note with their tongue and need encouragement.

5. *Lack of coordination between tongue and fingers.* This is the result of practicing and playing too fast without the essential slow working out process. Slow down the tempo until the tongue and fingers are perfectly coordinated, and increase speed gradually. Do not allow the student to exceed the maximum tempo at which there is perfect coordination between tongue and fingers. Use of a metronome to maintain a constant tempo is mandatory. Often there are gaps in the speeds at which the tongue and fingers can be coordinated, i.e., coordination is perfect at slower speeds and at faster speeds, but impossible at that particular speed. These gaps can be located with the use of the metronome, and the same exercises suggested for the correction of a sluggish tongue used for correction.

In developing tonguing action, facility and variety a constant check must be kept on placement and use of the tongue, and especially on maintaining the proper breath support. Students at all levels of advancement can lapse into incorrect procedures which will become habitual if not caught and corrected promptly. Good articulation is simple and easy to develop correctly if the proper attention is given to it.

Flutter Tonguing

Flutter tonguing is being called for more and more by twentieth century composers. Technically it is not an articulation but a special tonal effect, the nature of which depends on the register in which it is being used and the dynamic level. There is no standard notation for flutter tonguing. When it is required, written directions are given in the printed music. Some of the words used in other languages to indicate this effect include *flatterzung, coupe de langue roule, enroulant la langue, tremolo dental,* and *frullante.* Flutter tonguing seems to come naturally to some players, while others have difficulty in developing the technique. In any event, it should be a part of the basic technique of every advanced clarinetist.

In developing a flutter tongue which is always dependable and under control certain things should be observed. (1) The tongue should always be as relaxed as possible; (2) the embouchure must not move out of its normal position although it may be relaxed to open the reed; and (3) the stream of air must be very firmly supported and move rapidly through the mouthpiece.

There are three methods of flutter tonguing on the clarinet. The player should experiment with each to see which method works best for him. Some players may want to use more than one method to meet the various musical requirements they will find. The methods may be outlined as follows:

Tongue on Reed. In this method the flutter is produced by rolling the tongue rapidly against the reed as in rolling the letter "r" in "b-r-r-r." This method changes the basic tone quality less than the other two methods.

Dental Flutter. Place the tip of the tongue against the upper edge of the upper teeth. A fast stream of air will flutter the tongue against the teeth.

Hard Palate Flutter. Flatten the tongue and place the front portion against the front of the hard palate. A fast, well-supported stream of air will vibrate the tongue rapidly against the palate. This method produces a greater change in normal tone quality than the other two methods.

Double and Triple Tonguing

The technique of double or triple tonguing used for very rapid articulations can be used effectively by advanced clarinetists. It is most useful in the throat and chalumeau registers for rapid repeated notes of the same pitch. It is used less frequently in the clarion register and almost never in the high register. The development of a good double and triple tonguing on the clarinet requires considerable persistence and should be studied only by advanced players who have mastered the standard staccato articulation.

Double tonguing is executed by rapid movements of the tongue as in pronouncing the syllables "tu-ku." The "tu" is articulated in the usual fashion on the reed, while the "ku" is produced by the tongue against the palate to stop the flow of air. The problem in developing a useful double tonguing technique is in matching the attack and tone qualities of the two syllables. Practice slowly at first on throat tones and notes in the upper chalumeau register. Breath support must be firm. Avoid any movement of the jaw and any changes in the embouchure. Increase the speed of the repeated notes gradually, making sure that the attacks of all notes match.

Triple tonguing is done with the same syllables as those used in double tonguing, either "tu-ku-tu" or "tu-tu-ku." Unfortunately, the standard literature for clarinet does not include any specific material for the development of double or triple tonguing. Clarinetists who are developing this technique can adapt material from that written for flute.

TECHNIQUE PROBLEMS

In the course of acquiring a technical proficiency on the instrument which is accurate, under control, and facile, certain out of the ordinary problems are encountered which will slow the progress of the student unless they are approached in logical ways. The importance of solving the technical problems in the correct way must be impressed on the student, as well as the reasons for a particular solution. Many technical problems on the clarinet demand that the player make a choice between two or more alternatives. Each alternative must be practiced until it becomes an involuntary part of his technique and how each alternative is used must be made so much a part of his technique that the correct choice becomes involuntary and instantaneous. The following problems are those which are most frequently found.

1. *Use of left and right little fingers.* The mechanism of the standard Boehm system clarinet has some notes which can be played with either the right or left little fingers, others only with the right or left little finger. These are as follows:

Left or right:

Right only:

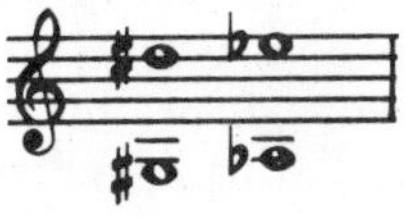

Left only:

Using the basic rule of good fingering choice which says that the same finger is not used in two different places for successive notes, the little fingers are used alternately when two or more consecutive notes involving their use occur. Following are examples of how this selection is made: "L" indicating left and "R" indicating right little finger. Students should be encouraged to put either an L or an R under the first note in a pattern involving the little fingers. Even professionals do this occasionally to assure smoothness and accuracy. It is necessary to read ahead to see if a G-sharp-D-sharp or a note in the high register involving the use of this key is in the pattern and plan ahead so that the correct little finger is free to contact this key without sliding.

2. *Sliding the little fingers.* There are instances where even the best finger choice will not eliminate the necesity for sliding a little finger from one key to another for consecutive notes. If a student is sliding a finger, first make sure that no alternative pattern is possible. If sliding is called for then be sure he follows the correct procedure.

Sliding is done from one key to another which is lower so that the finger slides down toward the body of the instrument. With the right little finger slide from the F or G-sharp key to the E or F-sharp key but not in the reverse. With the left little finger slide from the E key to the F, C-sharp, or F-sharp keys but not the reverse. Most students find it better to do the necessary sliding with the right little finger since the keys are better arranged for this purpose than those on the left, and it is almost always possible to arrange the fingering pattern so this is possible.

The proper sliding is done by increasing the curvature of the finger and pressing down so that it slides off of the top key onto the lower one. If the finger does not slide easily an old professional trick is to rub the finger beside the nose where the skin is oily and the finger picks up enough of this oil to slide easily. Rubbing the finger in the hair works equally well.

Following are some examples showing correct sliding. L and R indicate left and right little fingers while the notes marked ∧ indicate that the finger slides from the first to the second.

3. *Organ fingering.* As an alternative in some situations where sliding a finger is called for, the organ fingering technique is a solution which will produce a sure legato. The term "organ fingering" is taken from the organ technique of changing from one finger to another on a single key while it is depressed, the tone continuing to sound without interruption. The technique applied to the clarinet utilizes the notes which can be played by both the left and right little fingers. The procedure is to exchange the right and left little fingers while a note is being sustained.

The greatest usefulness of organ fingering is in slowly moving legato pasages where sliding a finger might break the legato. The change from left to right or right to left little fingers is made in rhythm, making sure the continuity of the tone is not broken. The following examples illustrate a typical situation where organ fingering can be used. Where the organ fingering is used, the fingers are changed in an eighth note rhythm, but the note itself sounds as a quarter.

4. *Crossing the break.* The "break" on the clarinet occurs between the third-line B-flat throat tone and B-natural in the clarion register where the production of the tone changes from the fundamental vibration to the third harmonic. The fingering pattern starts duplicating that for notes a twelfth lower. Developing facility in crossing the break is one of the major problems for beginning students, although the problem is considerably simplified if the proper procedure is used. Above all never tell the student that it is going to be difficult since this automatically sets up a psychological block and makes it difficult even though that particular student would otherwise have little difficulty.

Crossing from the chalumeau to the clarion register must not be introduced until the student is secure in the chalumeau register, playing with a reasonable good tone and with accurate fingerings. The process of crossing should then be introduced by slurring an interval of a twelfth from the chalumeau register which demands only the opening of the register key with the left thumb. Check to see that the left thumb is opening the register key by vertical movements of the first joint and not by sliding it onto the register key.

Exercises similar to the following are used in several methods books to introduce the clarion register.

Once the student is playing the clarion register notes, he should establish some security in this register before attempting to cross back and forth between the chalumeau range or throat tones to the clarion register. Finger positions must be perfect so that they cover the tone holes accurately or the student will squeak. If finger placement is accurate, crossing from chalumeau notes to clarion notes can be developed without too much difficulty.

Crossing back and forth through the break between throat tones and the clarion register develops more slowly since so much finger movement is involved. Here is a most useful device for both developing this facility and making these changes perfectly smooth once the facility is developed.

Organ fingering

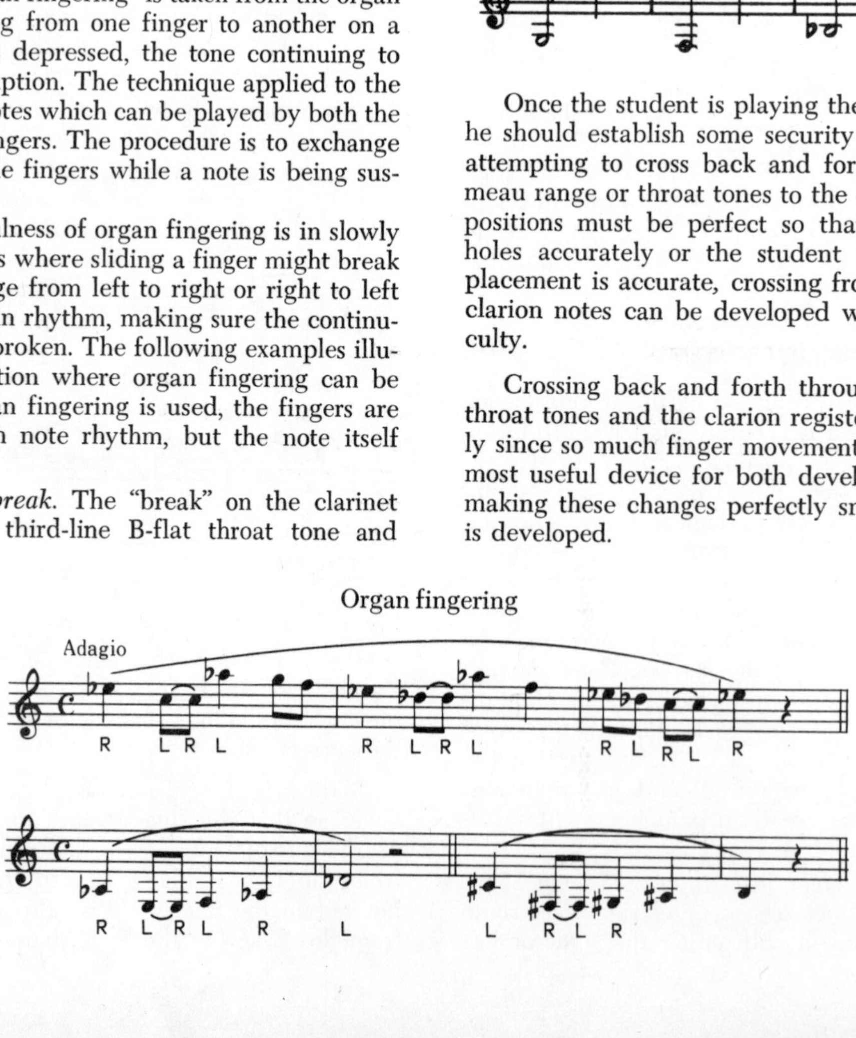

The right hand portion of the fingering for any one of these notes:

can be kept down while playing any of these notes:

This technique is utilized in two kinds of passages: (1) when the note in the clarion register precedes the throat tone, the right hand fingers are kept in place for the throat tone, and (2) when the note in the throat tone register precedes those in the clarion register, the clarion note is prepared in advance by putting the right hand portion of the fingering in place while playing one of the throat tones. Keeping the fingers of the right hand down when playing the throat tones does not effect the pitch of the throat tones. In fact, many clarinetists feel that the right hand fingers down improves the sonority of the throat tones.

The following example illustrates how this technique is used when the clarion notes precede throat tones. Fingers of the right hand are kept in place for the duration of the brackets.

These examples illustrate the technique when throat tones precede the clarion notes. On the first note under the bracket the right hand portion of the first clarion note is added to the fingering of the throat tone.

5. *Slurs into the high register.* Even though the notes in the high register can be played well many, if not all, clarinetists have difficulty in slurring from the clarion register to a note in the high register. The notes in the higher register seem to pop when they start. This is due to acoustical properties of the instrument since a different series of overtones produce the high tones than produce the clarion tones.

Some of the roughness in slurring to the high tones can be corrected through adjusting breath support. High notes require less breath support for the same dynamic level than do notes in the clarion register. This difference can be demonstrated by playing octaves into the clarion register using the same amount of breath support for each note. The upper note will be considerably louder than the lower. The necessary adjustments in breath support can be readily made once the player is conscious of their need.

A second technique, and one which is mandatory if perfect slurs from clarion to high registers are to be achieved, is the use of the half-hole with the first finger. This use of the first finger half-hole is part of the standard fingering for oboe and bassoon, and can be effectively put to a similar use on the clarinet.

Most fingerings for notes in the upper register call for the first finger to be up to open the hole. If instead of being lifted off the hole, the first finger is rolled down toward the second finger so that half of the hole is opened we have the half-hole position for the tone hole. It is important that the finger roll and not slide if facility is to be achieved. In order to make a perfect slur from a note in the clarion register to one in the high register roll the first finger into the half-hole position instead of lifting it off and reduce the amount of breath support. Figure C-71 shows the half-hole position on the B-flat clarinet and Figure C-72 the position on Bass clarinet.

Figure C-71

In the following example the half-hole is used to slur to each of the upper notes:

The half-hole technique is used only for slurring to the notes. Do not use a half-hole if the note is tongued. Do not keep the finger to the half-hole position for notes

Figure C-72

in the clarion register other than the one slurred to. The Bass clarinet uses the half-hole position as part of the standard fingering for all notes in the clarion register.

6. *Slurring downward from register to register.* In slurring from notes in the high register to notes in the clarion register many players, even advanced ones, get a small glissando. Some players are unable to make this kind of slur at all. The problem is an acoustical one of changing the vibration of the air column from the fifth harmonic to the third. In order to help force the change to the clarion note the first finger of the left hand should close the hole with a fast, firm movement. This technique is useful in intervals such as the following:

In slurs to the chalumeau register from the clarion (or high registers) the chalumeau note will frequently not respond or will sound a twelfth too high. The problem is an acoustical one of changing the vibration of the air column from the third (or fifth) harmonic to the fundamental. Less advanced players, especially, have problems with this kind of slur. The only solution, and it is a perfectly acceptable one is to tongue the chalumeau note very lightly. Do not change the embouchure or head position to make the slur. In intervals such as the following, the lower note may have to be lightly articulated.

7. *Articulated G-sharp key.* Some model clarinets have an articulated G-sharp key (G-sharp first space above the staff which also plays C-sharp first line below the staff). Advantages and disadvantages of this mechanism are discussed in the section of selection of instruments. This key facilitates certain passages. It makes easy trills and shakes on these notes:

since the little finger can be kept down on the G-sharp–C-sharp key and the trill or shakes made with the right hand alone. Passages such as the following are easier since the little finger can be kept in position and there are no movements in the left hand.

If the instrument has an articulated G-sharp key take full advantage of it. The articulated key is standard on all saxophones and oboes.

8. *Use of seventh ring.* Some models of B-flat, E-flat, and A clarinets have seven instead of six rings. It is the ring for the tone hole of the third finger, so it is simple to see whether a particular instrument has it or not. It is not found on Alto, Bass, or Contra-Bass Clarinets because of the covered tone holes on these instruments.

The seventh ring adds an important and most useful alternate fingering for:

which are fingered with only the first and third fingers down. The seven ring model instrument is highly recommended since it facilitates such passages as the following:

9. *Selection and use of basic alternate fingerings.* There are basic alternate fingerings for many notes on the clarinet which must be a part of the technique of any good player. Some of these, such as the chromatic fingerings for B-natural and the two F-sharps must be introduced when first needed at the beginning level. Others are best introduced when needed at any advanced level. Neither special trill fingerings nor other alternate fingerings described as special purpose auxiliary fingerings are included here. Both are discussed later. This section includes only basic standard alternate fingerings which should be considered the basic minimum in clarinet technique. It is necessary that the clarinetist learn them, and learn when to use each fingering. The best choice is the one which gives the smoothest progression and the best facility and intonation.

Choice of fingerings which involve using either the left or right little fingers has already been discussed. Review this if necessary. Following are some of the more common usages for certain fingerings. Study them carefully and try them, or have some clarinetist illustrate the correct choice and other possible choices to determine the reason for using this particular fingering.

(a) B-natural: 

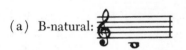

Two Fingerings: (1) T 123 050 (Diatonic)
(2) T 123 406x (Chromatic)

Typical uses for each fingering are illustrated below:

Use fingering 1:

Use fingering 2:

(b) D-sharp:
E-flat: 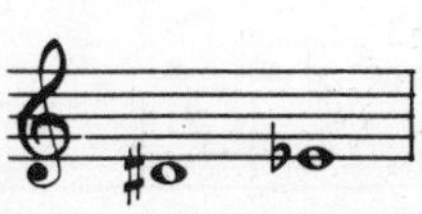

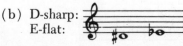

Four Fingerings: (1) T 120 4x00
(2) T 123x 000
(3) T 100 400
(4) T 103 000 (7-ring)

The first is the normal fingering which must be used unless there is a particular reason for using one of the others. The second keeps the fingering for the note entirely in the left hand and is recommended for chromatic passages and for trilling. The third fingering is quite sharp and is used only for rapid arpeggiated passages where the duration is so short that the out-of-tuneness is not heard. Fingering four can be used only on a 7-ring model instrument. Following are typical uses for each fingering.

Use fingering 1:

Use fingering 2:

Use fingering 3:

Use fingering 4:

(c) F-sharp:
G-flat: 

Two Fingerings: (1) 0 100 000 (Diatonic)
(2) T 000 4xy00 (Chromatic)

The first is the normal diatonic fingering. The second is mandatory in chromatic passages, and is frequently the best choice when the F-sharp is approached or left chromatically. Following are typical uses of each:

Use fingering 1:

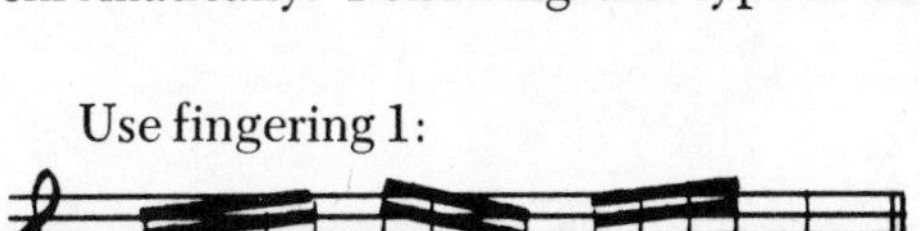

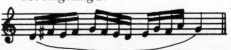

Use fingering 2:

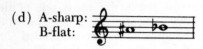

(d) A-sharp:
B-flat:

Two Fingerings: (1) R A00 000
(2) A00 4z00

The first is the normal fingering which is used both in diatonic and chromatic passages. The second is useful only in slow moving passages where maximum sonority is desired, since its sound is much bigger than the normal fingering and it is perfectly in tune. It cannot be used where the note which follows uses fingers of the right hand, since the hand must be out of place in order to reach key 4z. Following are typical uses of each:

Use fingering 1:

Use fingering 2:

(e) F-sharp:
G-flat:

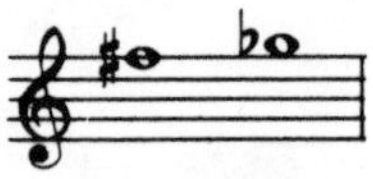

Two Fingerings: (1) TR 123 050 (Diatonic)
(2) TR 123 45x0 (Chromatic)

The first is the normal diatonic fingering, the second mandatory in chromatic passages. The second is also frequently the choice when the F-sharp is approached or left chromatically, or to lead smoothly to or from a fingering for a note in the high register.

Following are typical uses of each:

Use fingering 1:

Use fingering 2:

(f) G-sharp:
A-flat:

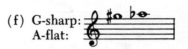

Two Fingerings: (1) TR 123C-sharp 000
(2) TR 120 450

The first is the normal fingering for both diatonic and chromatic passages. Since it involves the use of the left little finger, its use must be properly prepared for in any pattern involving the little fingers. The second is used only in rapid arpeggiated passages since its quality does not normally match perfectly the other notes of the clarion register, and on some instruments it is slightly out of tune. The following illustrate typical uses of each:

Use fingering 1:

Use fingering 2:

(g) A-sharp:
B-flat:

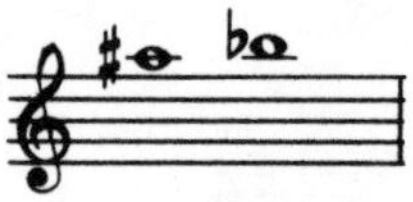

Five Fingerings: (1) TR 120 4x00
(2) TR 123x 000
(3) TR 100 400
(4) TR 100 050
(5) TR 103 000 (7-ring only)

The first is the normal fingering and is a safe choice for any passage. The second is suggested, but not mandatory for chromatic passages, and trills, but has limited usefulness because the third finger must not slide to or from its tone hole; misuse of this fingering is very common. The third fingering produces a tone of excellent quality well in tune and is used in either slow or fast arpeggiated passages. The fourth produces a good quality of tone, but is slightly sharp and its use is restricted to rapid arpeggiated passages. The fifth can be used only on a 7-ring model instrument. The following illustrate typical uses of each:

Use fingering 1:

Use fingering 2:

Use fingering 3:

Use fingering 4:

Use fingering 5:

(h) D-sharp:
E-flat:

Three Fingerings: (1) TR 023 45x0 G-sharp
(2) TR 023 006 G-sharp
(3) TR 023 050 G-sharp

The first is the normal fingering used for either diatonic or chromatic passages, and should be the choice unless there is a particular reason for not using it. The second is an excellent alternate fingering of good quality and well in tune and is particularly useful when slurring from the lower portion of the clarion register to the high E-flat. The third choice is quite flat in pitch, although the tone quality is good. It is used in rapid passages in the high register where facility is more important than tone quality. Over use of this third fingering, frequently as first choice, is a common fault among inexperienced clarinetists. The following illustrate typical uses of these fingerings.

Use fingering 1:

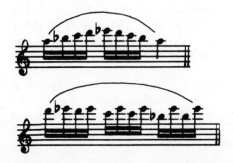

Use fingering 2:

Use fingering 3:

(i) F natural:

Two Fingerings: (1) TR 023C-sharp 000 G-sharp
(2) TR 123C-sharp 456 (no G-sharp)

The first is the normal fingering used for both diatonic and chromatic passages. The second is a special fingering which is useful for slurring from the clarion or lower registers to this note, or when playing softly in the high register and there is the slightest chance that the other fingering will not speak, or when it is played in a long diminuendo. The second finger is of good tone quality and well in tune (provided the G-sharp key is not used) and will produce only this F. When it is used, there is no chance of getting another note by mistake—it either plays F or nothing, and will not squeak. The following illustrates typical uses of these fingerings.

Use fingering 1:

Use fingering 2:

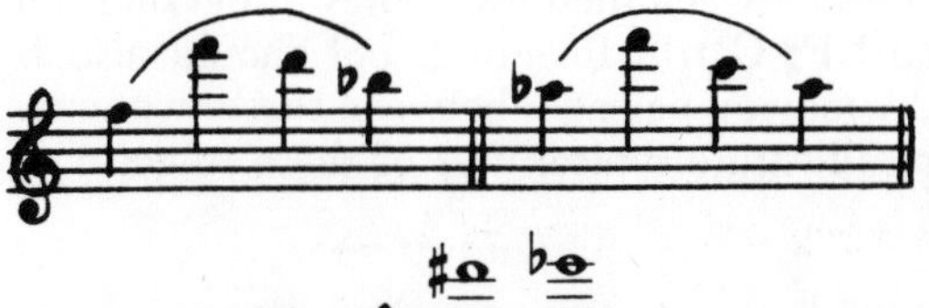

(j) F-sharp:
G-flat:

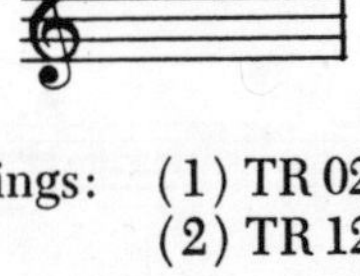

Two Fingerings: (1) TR 020 000 G-sharp
(2) TR 120 456 G-sharp

Fingering one is the basic fingering used in both diatonic and chromatic passages. Some players find this fingering unstable and sometimes difficult to articulate precisely. Nor does it sustain easily and softer dynamic levels. Fingering two is more stable than the first and is preferred for slurs from the clarion register, for precise attacks when the passage in which it occurs does not involve an overcomplicated sequence of fingerings, and for the best control at both extremes of dynamic range. The following examples illustrate typical uses of these fingerings.

Use fingering 1:

Use fingering 2:

(k) G: 

Four Fingerings:
(1) TR 020 450 G-sharp
(2) TR 100 450 G-sharp
(3) TR 003 C-sharp 000 G-sharp
(4) TR 020 5x00 G-sharp

From the multitude of fingerings for this note, these are the most useful alternates. Although fingering one is considered the basic fingering, many clarinetists find that fingering two responds better for them and use it rather than one as their basic fingering. Fingering two is especially useful in upward slurs where the first finger is down on the preceding note. Fingering three is the standard F-G trill fingering, but should also be used in rapidly moving passages between these two notes. Fingering four is the standard F♯-G trill fingering, but should also be used in rapidly moving passages between these two notes. The following illustrate typical uses of these fingerings.

Use fingering 1:

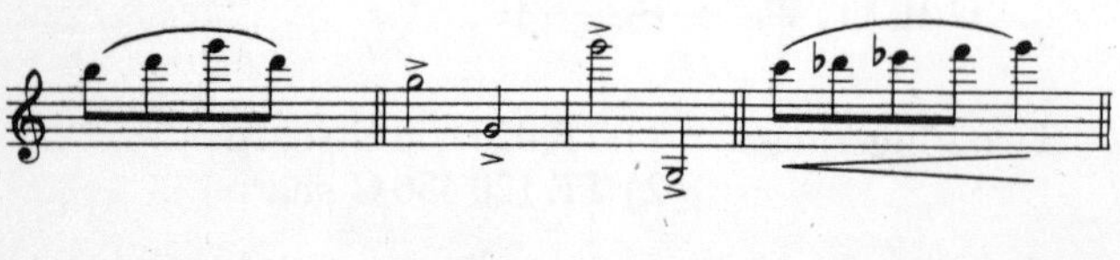

Use fingering 2:

Use fingering 3:

Use fingering 4:

10. *Selection and use of auxiliary fingerings.* As the clarinetist becomes more and more advanced, the increased technical demands will require frequent use of auxiliary fingerings (i.e., alternate fingerings other than the standard basic ones) if his performance is to be accurate and smooth. This is especially true when the music involves notes in the high register where numerous auxiliary fingerings are available.

When problems of technical facility or accuracy in tone placement occur, the player should consult the fingering chart for possible auxiliary fingerings. Try each in the musical pattern involved and select the one which best fits the need. Frequently, more than one of the auxiliary fingerings will be satisfactory, and the choice becomes a matter of personal preference. Sometimes none of the auxiliary fingerings will be any better than the basic or alternate fingering. And, unfortunately, there are not auxiliary fingerings for every note to solve every problem.

Not all auxiliary fingerings respond equally well for all players. There will be slight differences between the response of the same auxiliary fingering for the same player on the B-flat and A clarinets. There will be even greater differences and a greater number of the auxiliary fingerings which will not respond well on the Alto and Bass clarinets.

The response and intonation of a given auxiliary fingering may vary with the volume. The ease of response will vary with the notes which precede and follow it, and will vary with the individual player's embouchure, mouthpiece, and reed.

Auxiliary fingerings are usually selected for technical facility, but they are also selected to achieve a particular tone quality to meet musical demands, for intonation, and for ease of control in specific situations. Following are some typical examples.

(a) Auxiliary fingering for facility:

A-sharp:
B-flat: 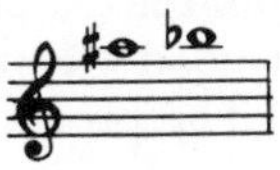 TR 023C-sharp 000

This auxiliary fingering is useful for passages such as the following:

(b) Auxiliary fingering for control:

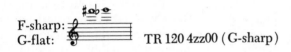

F-sharp:
G-flat:  TR 120 4zz00 (G-sharp)

This fingering is more stable than the basic fingering, but its use is somewhat limited by the fact that key 4zz moves the first finger of the right hand out of position for quick use on the hole of the next note. It is most useful for slowly moving passages and for slurs up from the lower registers in the soft dynamic range.

(c) Auxiliary fingering for tone quality and facility:

D:  TR G-sharp 00 (4x) 00 G-sharp

Although this fingering is the basic C-D trill fingering, it is also useful in rapidly moving passages where the "D" is the only note in the high register. In this situation this fingering will match the tone quality of the clarion register notes better than the basic fingering, and may at the same time solve a difficult technical problem. If the fingering is too flat, the use of the 4x key will raise the pitch. The following examples are typical uses.

11. *Trill fingering.* These are a special type of alternate fingering intended for trilling but which may also be used in certain other circumstances. Many trills may be executed with standard or basic alternate fingerings for the notes involved, but others require special fingerings. A chart of these special trill fingerings is given following the standard clarinet fingering chart. These special fingerings may tend to sacrifice intonation and/or tone quality on the upper note for the sake of facility. Some are noticeably out of tune when played slowly, but this out-of-tuneness is tolerable at the rapid speed of the trill.

The use of trill fingerings in situations other than trills is most useful, even mandatory, if technique is to be smooth. The accomplished clarinetist will use them as substitutes for basic fingerings on grace notes, mordents, turns, and for upper neighbor tones in diatonic passages. But as with any alternate fingering, trill fingerings must not be used when the ear can hear faulty intonation.

12. *Tremolo.* A tremolo involving the interval of a third or larger occurs occasionally, and is being used more and more in contemporary music. The problems involved in accomplishing the rapid alternation of notes are similar to those found in the half and whole-step trills. Good tremolos are not possible on all note combinations on the clarinet, but careful choice of fingerings will keep these to a minimum.

The basic principle in the selection of the best fingering is to select a basic, alternate, or auxiliary fingering for the lower note of the tremolo in order to move as few fingers as possible for the upper note. Preferably the fingering for the upper note can also be selected from one of the standard fingerings. But as in the standard procedure for trill fingerings, there are places where the intonation and/or tone quality of the upper note must be compromised for the sake of facility.

The procedure for selecting fingerings is:

1. Check all possible fingerings for both notes.
2. Select the combination which involves the least finger movement.
3. If too much finger movement is involved to accomplish the necessary speed of alternation, experiment with leaving additional fingers in place in the upper note fingering which will have the least effect on its intonation and tone quality.

Clarinetists who have not made this kind of experiment will be surprised to discover how many fingers can be kept down and keys open or closed without a serious adverse effect on intonation or quality. Take advantage of the fact that in a tremolo neither note is sustained long enough for the ear to accurately appraise intonation or quality. Needless to say, the ear must determine the degree of deviation from normal which can be tolerated, but make this judgment with the notes moving at normal tremolo speed rather than slowly. It is useful to know, for example, that the keys operated by the little fingers may be kept down in tremolos for they have only a minor effect on notes in which the sixth, fifth, or fourth finger is up.

Following are some typical examples of tremolo fingerings. Fingers which move to produce the tremolo are circled.

(a) Tremolos using standard fingering:

(b) Tremolos leaving extra fingers in place:

(c) Special effect tremolo.

Some contemporary composers make use of the tremolo for special musical effects. Directions for the technical execution may be given in the printed music for they frequently alter the intonation and/or tone quality of the upper note more than normal. Following is a typical example. The lower notes use standard fingerings and the tremolo is produced by moving only the third finger of the left hand.

13. *Glissando and portamento.* A glissando may be defined as the execution of a rapid scale passage as when the pianist draws a finger rapidly up or down the white keys, or the harpist a finger over the strings. Wind players frequently confuse the glissando with the portamento which is a gliding from one pitch to another through all the intermediate pitches as when a violinist slides a finger up or down the strings, or with the trombonist the slide up or down through all the pitches between the half steps.

When a glissando is called for in clarinet music, the procedure is to play a rapid chromatic scale from the beginning to the final note. This is what is intended in a cadenza, for example, when the music has a low "F" connected by a line and the word "glissando" to the "F" three octaves higher.

Ocassionally in contemporary music a clarinetist is expected to play portamento, as in Gershwin's *Rhapsody in Blue* even though the printed music may say glissando. The musical style will dictate whether a glissando or portamento is used. A true portamento can be produced in the clarion and high registers of the clarinet with a lot of hard practice. Because of the acoustics of the instrument it is virtually impossible in the chalumeau register, although some players are able to produce an illusion of the effect.

Only advanced players should attempt to develop the portamento, for it requires a good flexible embouchure and dependable finger action. The procedure for producing the portamento is to start with a very loose relaxed embouchure. The fingers slide very slowly one at a time off the holes to produce a gradual rise in pitch. At the same time the embouchure is gradually tightened until it is in its normal state on the final note.

For practice purposes, the interval from fourth line "D" to "C" above the staff is excellent. Once this is established, various smaller intervals within this range may be used. The downward portamento is rarely called for, but can be developed once the upward direction is mastered.

14. *Special problems above high G.* The intermediate clarinetist can successfully extend his range to the "G" in the high register. The advanced clarinetists have developed good facility and control in this range and have the foundation for extending this facility and control to the top of the clarinet range. In practice most clarinetists will have encountered only a few of these notes in their musical experiences. If the clarinetist has studied Book III of the Kroepsch *Daily Studies* or the Third Division of the Baerman *Method*, he will have an opportunity to develop some facility in this range. He will have encountered a few such notes if he has played the concertos by von Weber or Spohr.

Contemporary composers are using this range quite freely and it has become necessary for clarinetists to develop facility with notes above the high G equal to that in the lower ranges if they are to perform this music successfully. Advanced clarinetists who are interested in developing this portion of their playing range to its maximum usefulness should study *The Twentieth Century Clarinetist* by Allen Sigel.

Before venturing into this range, the clarinetist should have developed a strong flexible embouchure to avoid distastrous results of increased upward jaw pressure, have mastered breath control and support, and be playing on a mouthpiece and using reeds which in combination will respond in this register.

The increased difficulty in playing the notes above "G" is found in the acoustics of the instrument. The notes in the high register up to and including the "G" are produced by the fifth harmonic in the overtone series, while the notes above that are produced by the seventh or ninth harmonics. The natural seventh harmonic in the series is out of tune with the tempered scale so the fingering of the fundamental of the series must be adjusted to bring the seventh harmonic in tune. This explains the multitude of possible fingerings for these notes.

As an introduction to understanding these notes, play the following series of harmonics. Tongue each note. The top note in each series will be out of tune for these fingerings are not useful ones as they stand. Use the normal fingering for the first note, add the register key for the second, lift first finger of the left hand for the third, increase velocity of breath and increase embouchure support for the final note. Not all players will be able to play this example readily, and should not be concerned if they can not.

In developing this register players will find that (1) intonation is extremely sensitive; (2) fingerings are more complex than fingerings in the lower ranges; (3) these complex finger patterns of many of the fingerings cause technical problems both in facility and accuracy; and (4) considerable persistence is necessary to achieve facility.

When a player encounters a note in this range, he should check the fingering chart and try each fingering for each note in the pattern, not just the fingerings for the high note. Frequently, the best results are achieved by using an alternate or auxiliary fingering for the note which precedes or follows the high note. The fingering selected should be the one which speaks easily and in tune in that particular passage. Response, intonation, and tone quality of the fingerings varies greatly with the player. Only with experimentation and practice can a player discover the best fingering for him in a given situation. Eventually the player should have several fingerings for each note at his command.

The chromatic scale is a good introduction to this range for it requires a series of fingerings which are accurate, in tune, and capable of being played rapidly and smoothly. The fingerings indicated are considered the standard ones if any fingering can be considered standard in this register.

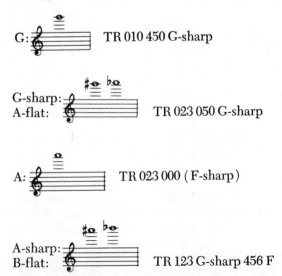

G:  TR 010 450 G-sharp

G-sharp:
A-flat:  TR 023 050 G-sharp

A:  TR 023 000 (F-sharp)

A-sharp:
B-flat:  TR 123 G-sharp 456 F

B:  TR 120 450 (F-sharp)

C:  TR 100 400 G-sharp

Following are some of the most prevalent problems encountered in playing in this register.

1. *Note does not sound.* Presuming the correct fingering is used, possible causes are insufficient breath support with not enough air moving through the instrument, the reed is too soft, insufficient support by the embouchure, player is biting and closing tip of reed so it won't vibrate. Frequently more than one of these causes are present.

2. *Intonation.* Pitch is quite sensitive in this register and small deviations in intonation can be adjusted by loosening or tightening embouchure support. Flatness throughout the range may be caused by insufficient breath support and velocity, insufficient support by the embouchure, or a reed which is too soft. Sharpness throughout the range is caused by too much embouchure support (biting) or a reed which is too hard.

If breath support, embouchure, and reed are correct and individual notes are out of tune beyond embouchure control, another fingering must be selected. Or if none of the fingerings on the chart will bring the note in tune, the player must experiment and devise his own fingering by adding or subtracting fingers from one of these fingerings. If a good fingering results, the player should use it even though it doesn't appear on a fingering chart.

PLAYING ALTO, BASS AND CONTRA-BASS CLARINET

The Alto, Bass, and Contra-bass clarinets are not beginning instruments. Interested students should be transferred to them only after they have reached at least the early intermediate level of proficiency on the B-flat clarinet. A smooth transition from the soprano instrument to one of lower pitch can be made if the following things are observed.

1. *Embouchure.* The basic embouchure formation remains the same but is progressively more relaxed as the player moves from soprano to alto, to bass, and to contrabass. As the pitch ranges move down, reeds move slower and need a wider amplitude of vibration.

2. *Amount of mouthpiece.* The amount of mouthpiece in the mouth is critical. The standard procedure for determining the correct amount for all clarinets should be used. This procedure calls for playing a series of open G's, each with a little more mouthpiece in the mouth, until the note produced is not a "G" but a harmonic. The correct placement of lip support is just forward of this point. Taking too little mouthpiece in the mouth is the

most common fault of students transferring to larger instruments. A mouthpiece with medium length lay and medium tip opening is recommended.

3. *Reed strength.* There is a tendency for students to select reeds which are too stiff for the proper response on the instrument in an effort to match the resistance they felt on the soprano instrument. Resistance should decrease with the increasing size of the instrument if the normal medium length-medium tip mouthpiece is selected to allow for the increased flow of air needed to produce the most desirable tone. Medium-soft or medium reeds are recommended.

4. *Mouthpiece angle.* The angle at which the mouthpiece enters the mouth for the bass and contra-bass instruments is not the same as for the B-flat clarinet. They enter the mouth at an almost straight line similar to the saxophone when the instrument is held in the proper playing position. Attempting to duplicate the soprano instrument's upward angle pinches off the tone. The alto clarinet is designed so that the mouthpiece enters the mouth at a slight angle, but not as great as that for the soprano instrument.

5. *Breath support.* Good firm breath support, as well as a good capacity, is necessary. As the instruments increase in size a greater amount of well-supported air is needed, with a corresponding decrease in velocity. A full resonant tone quality in the chalumeau register will indicate that the proper relationship between support and velocity has been achieved. An open throat is mandatory to achieve the best flow of air.

6. *Tongue placement.* Tongue placement on the reed for articulation is in the same relationship as for the B-flat clarinet. Some adjustment in the amount of force against the reed to close the tip will be necessary, depending on the mouthpiece and strength of reed. As the instruments get larger there are greater differences between the amount of force used in the chalumeau and clarion registers; the player must be very conscious of the kind of attack he is achieving. Too much tongue on the reed will produce a hard attack with a small pop, or even a slap tongue effect.

7. *Neck straps and end-pins.* Neck straps or end-pins for the bass and contra-bass instruments must be adjusted so that the mouthpiece is held firmly against the upper teeth when the instrument is in playing position. If it is not, the pressure on the low lip restricts tone production and forces the head out of position so that breathing is restricted.

8. *Fingerings.* With one important exception fingerings on these instruments are identical with those used on the B-flat instrument. The exception is critical and is very frequently overlooked. Notes in the high register which are played on the B-flat clarinet with the first finger open are played on these instruments with the finger in the half-hole position so that the small hole in the first finger plate is open. Slide the first finger down to the small plate attached to the one covering the tone hole. If the half-hole position is not used on these instruments, the high register is difficult to control and tone quality is not the best.

TRANSPOSITIONS FOR THE CLARINETIST

The clarinetist is frequently expected to transpose and play on this instrument from parts written for an instrument in a different key. The professional must be able to do this, and advanced school players should develop some facility, at least on the more common transpositions. This ability is acquired only by doing it, slowly at first, and then with increasing speed. These transpositions, many of which are encountered even on the high school level include:

1. *Playing piano, violin, or "C" clarinet on the B-flat clarinet.* The need for this transposition is so frequent that every clarinetist past the lower intermediate stage of development should begin to acquire facility. This is the transposition from the concert key to the B-flat clarinet. Playing from piano music is frequently recreational in nature which helps encourage development. Parts for "C" clarinets are frequently found in the original editions of symphonic music from the classic period, although modern school editions transpose them to the B-flat instrument. The process of making the transposition from the concert pitch to B-flat clarinet involves adding two sharps or subtracting two flats from the key signature and reading the notes a tone higher than written. The following examples illustrates the interval and key signature transpositions.

Piano Key: C — B-flat Clarinet Key: D

Piano Key: A-flat — B-flat Clarinet Key: B-flat

Piano Key: G — B-flat Clarinet Key: A

2. *Playing "A" clarinet parts on the B-flat clarinet.* Much of the orchestral literature includes parts written for the "A" clarinet as well as for the B-flat. While the "A" instruments are common enough, frequently being owned by the school and loaned to the student, this transposition is so frequent that facility should be acquired. To play "A" clarinet parts on the B-flat clarinet

transpose each note down one-half step either through changing the key signature or simple reading down. The "A" instrument is chosen by the composer in order to avoid asking the clarinets to play in a large number of sharps or flats, so when an A part is being played on the B-flat the technical demands on the player are greater than if it were being played on the A instrument. The following examples illustrate the interval and key signature transpositions.

A Clarinet Key: C — B-flat Clarinet Key: B

A Clarinet Key: B-flat — B-flat Clarinet Key: A

A Clarinet Key: A-flat — B-flat Clarinet Key: G

3. *Playing alto saxophone parts on the B-flat clarinet.* It is mandatory that a player who doubles on Alto saxophone and clarinet be able to transpose and play the saxophone parts on the clarinet. There are other occasions where this facility is needed as well. To play the E-flat Alto saxophone parts on the B-flat clarinet transpose a perfect fifth lower, or add one flat or subtract one sharp from the saxophone key signature and play a fifth lower making the proper adjustments for accidentals. The following illustrate the interval and key relationships.

Alto Saxophone Key: C — B-flat Clarinet Key: F

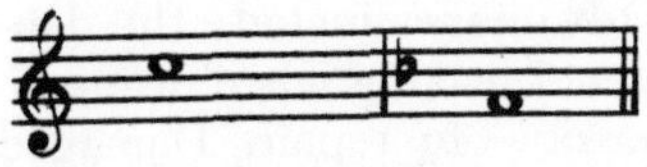

Alto Saxophone Key: D — B-flat Clarinet Key: G

Alto Saxophone Key: B-flat — B-flat Clarinet Key: E-flat

4. *Playing "D" clarinet parts on the E-flat clarinet.* The high D clarinet is used in some orchestral music of the nineteenth and early twentieth centuries in place of the E-flat clarinet. In this country these parts are almost invariably played on the E-flat instrument. The transposition involved is exactly the same as that for playing music for A clarinet on the B-flat intsrument. Each tone is played a half-step lower.

5. *Playing string bass or tuba parts on the E-flat contra-bass clarinet.* The E-flat contra-bass clarinet is coming more and more into general use as a permanent member of the concert band. Since a great many band arrangements do not publish a printed part for this instrument, a string bass or tuba part is substituted, and the player is expected to make a direct transposition. This is a purely mechanical transposition. Substitute a treble clef for the bass clef, add three sharps to the key signature and play as written, making the necessary adjustments for accidentals. School musicians rapidly gain facility in this transposition until it becomes automatic.

Tuba Key: C — Clarinet Key: A

Tuba Key: A-flat — Clarinet Key: F

Tuba Key: G — Clarinet Key: E

Summary of Transpositions

1. *Playing "C" parts on B-flat clarinet:* Up a whole tone, add two sharps.
2. *Playing "A" parts on B-flat clarinet:* Play each note a half-step lower or read a tone lower and add five sharps.
3. *Playing alto saxophone parts on B-flat clarinet:* Perfect fifth down, add one flat.

4. *Playing "D" clarinet parts of E-flat clarinet:* Play each note a half-step lower or read a tone lower and add five sharps.
5. *String bass or tuba parts on E-flat contra-bass clarinet:* Change bass clef to treble clef; add three sharps. Accidentals inflected same degree as original.

SELECTION OF INSTRUMENTS

The system of fingering used on present day instruments was adapted from the principles first applied to the flute by Carl Boehm. This mechanical system, called the Boehm System clarinet, was developed in Paris between 1835 and 1845 by Klose who was professor of clarinet at the Paris Conservatory and whose method is still widely used, and by Auguste Buffet, founder of the Buffet company. The Boehm system is now the standard for all clarinets, although it took over fifty years after its introduction for it to be accepted.

The fingering mechanism which preceded it is known as the Albert System, an instrument with thirteen keys and two rings. It had many deficiencies, among them poor intonation, and it was virtually impossible to play in all keys. This mechanical difficulty in playing in all keys with the Albert System and the models which preceded it, made it necessary for composers to use the B-flat, A, and C instruments according to the key of the music, and all professional clarinetists used all three. Albert System clarinets were widely distributed in this country up until about 1925, and some of the instruments are still for sale in loan shops. Needless to say, no student should be handicapped by starting to play an Albert System even though the instrument would be inexpensive.

Models of the Boehm System Clarinet

Various models of clarinets are available and are usually designated by two numbers indicating the number of keys and the number of rings.

1. 17-6, seventeen keys and six rings. This is the standard model of the instrument, and a fair estimate would indicate that probably over 85% of all instruments in use are this model. Few if any student grade instruments are available in anything other than this model.

2. 17-7, seventeen keys and seven rings. This model differs from the preceding model in that a ring is added to the one hole covered by the third finger. This ring operates an additional small tone hole covered by a pad and makes possible an extremely useful alternate fingering for E-flat and B-flat: 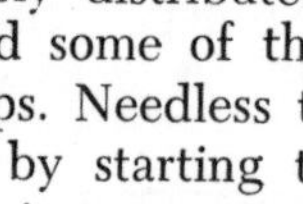 commonly called the "Fork B-flat" fingering, since the B-flat is produced by closing the first and third tone holes. This additional ring adds no complication to the mechanism of the instrument, but improves intonation of certain notes, and makes certain technical passages smoother and easier. It adds very little to the cost of the instrument, and it is this model which should be purchased for a student past the intermediate level of instruction, or who aspires to becoming a fine clarinetist.

3. Articulated G-sharp. This key is found both on the 17-6 and 17-7 models and although it is designated as the articulated G-sharp key it also produces C-sharp:  An articulated G-sharp key is one which is connected to the rings operated by the fingers of the right hand so that if the G-sharp key is being held open by the left little finger, it is automatically closed when the rings on the lower joint are down. This facilitates trills involving G-sharp or C-sharp, as well as certain other passages. The addition of this key has two disadvantages: it adds complicated mechanism to the instrument involving two springs working against each other which seem to get out of order frequently, and it eliminates the use of the alternate fingering for F in the high register. For these reasons an instrument with the articulated G-sharp is not recommended.

4. Full Boehm. A full Boehm clarinet has twenty keys, seven rings, and an articulated G-sharp. It is rarely seen, and never recommended for use, being more of a curiosity than anything else. The three additional keys are added to those already operated by the little fingers and create a very heavy and complicated mechanism on the lower joint. The disadvantages of this model far outweigh its advantages.

Plastic Instruments

Most student model instruments are made of plastic. Plastic has the advantage of being molded into shape rapidly and economically, and some plastics are even harder than wood. Not only are B-flat clarinets made of plastic, but also alto and bass instruments. The chief advantage of plastic instruments lies in their cost; therefore, they are recommended for use on the beginning level. In order to keep the price down, the manufacturing process is highly automated and there is relatively little handwork on the instrument. For this reason, and not because they are made of plastic, the musical potential of these instruments is limited and most teachers would agree that their use on any level higher than beginning is undesirable.

The plastic clarinet in the hands of beginners has the tremendous advantage of not being subject to cracks as are wooden instruments. Disadvantages include the danger of the body of the instrument breaking when dropped, and plastic is virtually impossible to repair. Damaged joints on plastic instruments are replaced with a new one, with the key mechanism of the broken joint transferred to the replacement. This is a simpler process than repairing a crack in a wooden instrument. Posts knocked loose on a plastic instrument pose a more difficult repair job than on a wooden instrument. But for beginners the advantages of a plastic instrument outweigh the disadvantages.

Bass Clarinet

As an alternate to the standard Boehm System Bass clarinet, most manufacturers offer a model with an additional key for low E-flat. This model is recommended for advanced players. The low E-flat is only occasionally called for in contemporary band music, but this extra note is essential for the orchestral player. Some of the standard symphonic repertoire using the bass clarinet is written for bass clarinet in "A"—an instrument that is not used in the United States. In order to transpose the "A" part for performance on the B-flat instrument, the low E-flat is necessary to get the full range called for in the "A" part.

STUDENT QUALIFICATIONS AND APTITUDES

A certain amount of innate musical talent is necessary to play any instrument successfully, and the fact that the student does not possess this necessary minimum of talent may be determined either by testing or by permitting experiment on the instrument.

Standards of physical aptitudes for the clarinet are not always reliable. It goes without saying that the student must be physically large enough so that he may hold the instrument with the proper hand position and cover the holes properly. Students who are too small to play the instrument develop poor hand positions which are extremely difficult to correct, make slow progress, and tend to become discouraged because of the physical handicap. Any student with normal teeth, lip and chin formation can play the clarinet successfully. Thick lips and thin lips, overbite and underbite, crooked teeth and straight teeth can all be compensated for the embouchure formation without any adverse results on future development.

A natural aptitude for the clarinet may be determined by the success of the student in producing a steady natural tone of the highest pitch (approximately concert "C" above the staff) with the mouthpiece and reed alone after some instruction on embouchure formation. The student should be able to produce strong clear tones in this manner and sustain them five to ten seconds before preceding with the complete instrument. Some students will accomplish this quickly, others may fail for some time but with instruction and guidance may develop an equal facility.

The clarinet is the best and most common beginning instrument of the woodwind family, and large numbers of students should be started on the instrument in the elementary school. Once facility is developed on the clarinet, the student can easily transfer to flute, oboe, bassoon, or saxophone with little loss in facility, and will pick up his musical progress on the new instrument without difficulty.

In selecting students for any instrument it must be remembered that interest and persistence are the greatest of all aptitudes.

CARE OF THE CLARINET

Assemble and disassemble with care. Keep the instrument in its case when not in use. It is most important that the instrument be thoroughly dried after each playing. The process of drying it and putting it into the case does not take much time, and is well worth the time spent. The habit of thorough drying should be established from the very beginning of clarinet study. The suggested step-by-step process is efficient and should be checked regularly by the instructor until it is easily accomplished by the student.

1. *Drying the clarinet.* Take the instrument apart in the reverse order of assembly. Shake moisture out of each end of each joint and place the parts carefully in the case. Then swab each piece using a chamois swab made of a single piece of chamois with a strong cord long enough to reach through the length of the upper and lower joints and with a weight on the end of the string. The weight should be absolutely smooth so as not to scratch the bore of the instrument. Swabs of this type in sizes to fit the B-flat, alto, and bass clarinets are available commercially and are inexpensive.

A B-flat clarinet swab can be made of a well-tanned piece of chamois four inches by six inches. Tie a heavy nylon cord eighteen inches long to one corner, and tie a smooth weight like a small lead fishing weight to the end of the cord. Swabs for alto, bass or contrabass instruments may be similarly made in increasingly larger sizes. An old linen handkerchief which is lint free may be substituted for the chamois if desired as it is equally efficient.

2. The mouthpiece must be cleaned from both ends. Place the forefinger in the center of the chamois and wipe out tone chamber (Figure C-73). Twist chamois and clean bore (Figure C-74). Wipe outside of mouthpiece. The chamois must not be pulled through the

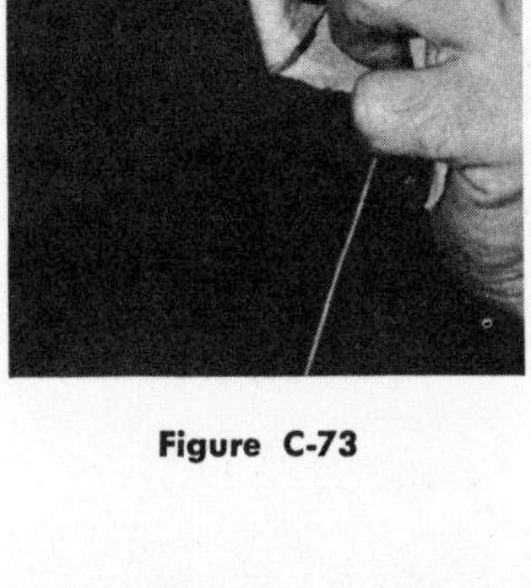

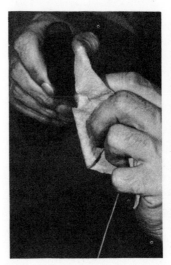

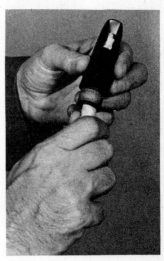

Figure C-73

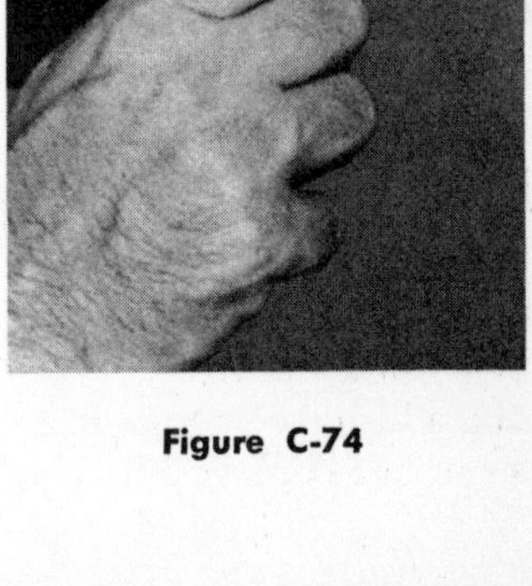

Figure C-74

mouthpiece as the metal weight may scratch the lay or chip the tip.

3. The barrel joint is cleaned by drawing the swab through once or twice (Figure C-75). Then fold the chamois over the forefinger and carefully wipe all moisture out of both the connecting sleeves (Figure C-76).

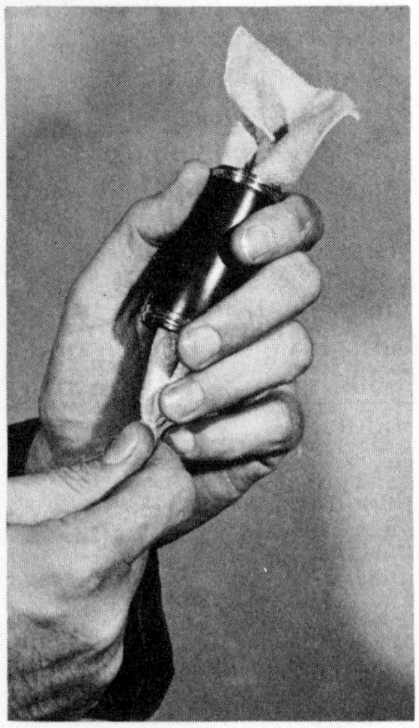

Figure C-75

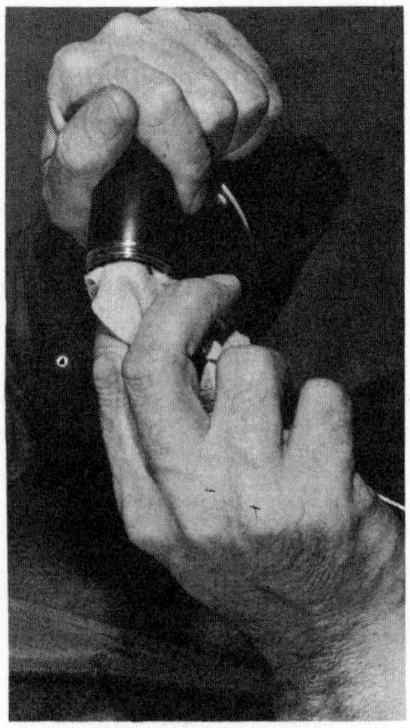

Figure C-76

4. The upper joint is cleaned by dropping the weight from the top (Figure C-77) and drawing it through several times (Figure C-78). Then wipe moisture off the cork end. The swab must be dropped from the top down as the bore of the instrument increases gradually toward the bottom of the joint. A swab put in from the larger end frequently sticks and is difficult to remove. Teachers of beginning classes will save them many hours of time spent in removing stuck swabs from the upper joint if they will insist on always starting the process from the top of each joint.

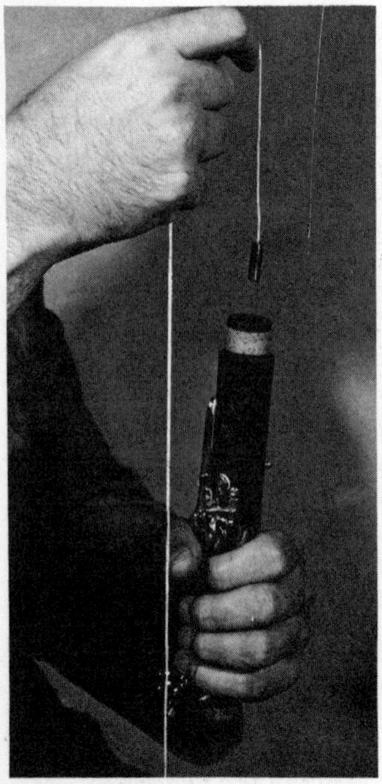

Figure C-77

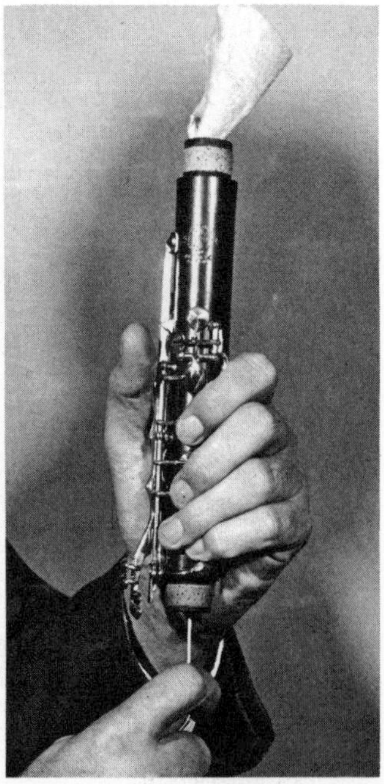

Figure C-78

5. The lower joint is cleaned by dropping the weight on the swab from the top (Figure C-79) and drawing it through several times (Figure C-80). Put the fore-

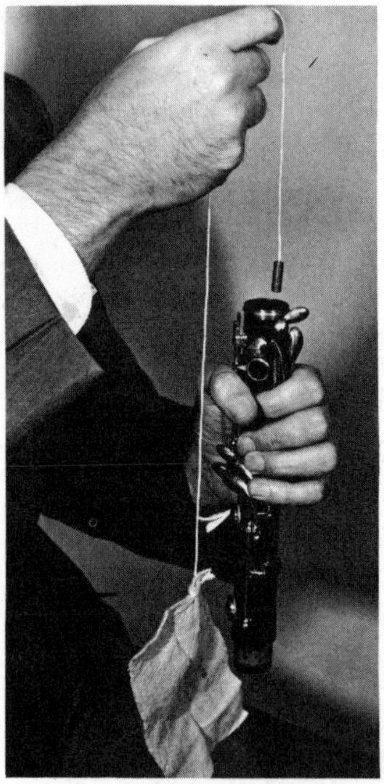

Figure C-79

Figure C-80

finger in the center of the chamois and wipe out the upper end (Figure C-81). Then wipe off cork end as before.

6. The bell should be wiped out from the large end with the chamois as shown in Figure C-82. Clean the upper end in the same fashion as on the lower joint.

Parts are replaced in the case as they are dried. Beginners cases must be checked to be sure that the parts are properly in place. Tone holes up, side keys on both joints fitted exactly into the space provided in the case, ligature and mouthpiece cap in place on the mouthpiece. Cases must never be forced closed. If they do not close easily, check the placement of the parts. The photograph earlier in the chapter identifying parts of the clarinet shows a typical arrangement of parts in the case.

The reed must be removed from the mouthpiece, carefully dried, and placed in the reed case so that it will dry flat without warping.

Figure C-81

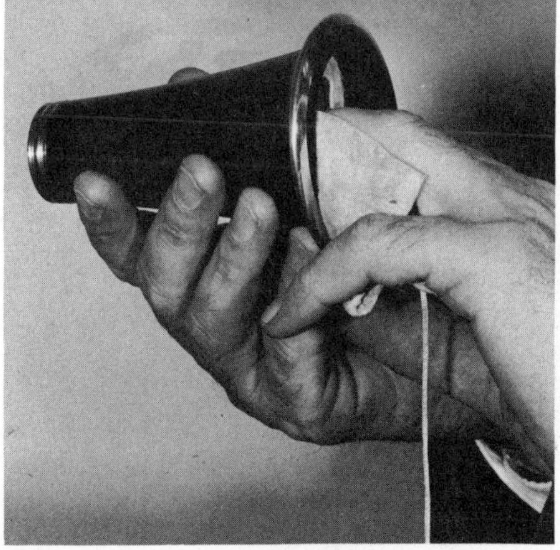

Figure C-82

Regular Maintenance of the Instrument

1. *Oiling the bore.* Even though they are made of the hardest wood available—Grenadilla—the wooden clarinets are subject to cracking. Careful swabbing after each playing will help avoid this, but authorities recommend that the wood be protected by oiling the bore with specially prepared bore oil. Owners of new instruments should follow manufacturers directions for oiling. In the absence of directions, oil at least once a month for the first year. Older instruments should be oiled several times a year.

This must be done with care so that no oil gets on the pads, since it dries out and hardens the pads and they no longer cover the holes without leaking. The oiling can be done with a commercial oiler, or with a swab kept for this purpose. The swab should be lightly oiled, not saturated, and drawn through the parts of the instrument once or twice so as to coat the inside very lightly. The outside of the instrument is not oiled as a rule, although it may be given a very light coat of oil occasionally where temperature and humidity extremes are common.

2. *Dusting the instrument.* After an instrument has been in use over a period of time, dust collects under the key mechanism. This can and should be removed with a soft watercolor brush (Figure C-83).

3. *Oiling the mechanism.* The mechanism, if it is to remain in the best playing condition, must be oiled regularly four or five times a year. Special oil for this purpose is commercially available. A drop of oil on the end of a toothpick should be put at each pivot point

Figure C-83

of each key (Figure C-84). Do this carefully so that no oil can get onto the pads.

Figure C-84

4. *Shining the keys.* Silver polish should never be used on the keys. If keys become excessively dull, they must be polished by a repairman who will remove them from the instrument. They are never polished while they are on the instrument. Keys may be kept in good condition if they are wiped regularly with a soft cloth or a chamois to remove perspiration and dirt. Using silver polish on the keys while they are on the instrument will foul pivot points on the mechanism, and damage pads so that they will leak. It is well to caution students against polishing the keys.

5. *Bent keys.* In spite of the best of care keys become bent out of line. No attempt should be made to straighten them while they are on the instrument. This puts excessive pressure on both the keys and their posts and the instrument may be damaged even more. Keys must be removed from the instrument by a repairman who has the tools to straighten and align them. Bent keys will cause unevenness in technique, since some of them stick, or become out of line so that the fingers do not fall on them naturally.

6. *Sticking pads.* If the instrument is not thoroughly dried before it is put into its case, or if the humidity is excessive even temporarily, some pads on the instrument will stick tightly, or will stick momentarily before opening. Moisture can be removed from them by placing a cigarette paper between the pad and the tone hole, pressing down on the key firmly. Then release the key and repeat the process until the key no longer sticks. If this does not relieve the sticking, put the cigarette paper in place, press on the key, and pull it slowly from under the pad. Repeat the process several times. If the condition reoccurs regularly have the pad replaced. Never use powder on pads to stop sticking.

7. *Water in tone holes.* Some instruments tend to collect water in certain tone holes under pads that are normally closed, producing a bubbling tone when these keys are opened. This may be removed by opening the key and blowing firmly into the hole. If time permits, take the instrument apart and swab the joint on which this occurs thoroughly. If a particular hole collects water regularly, it may frequently be corrected by removing the key and coating the inside of the tone hole lightly with vaseline. Avoid a heavy coat of vaseline as it will soak into the pad.

8. *Leaky pads.* Pads on an instrument wear out with use. Some wear out more rapidly than others and begin to leak causing the instrument to respond with difficulty on certain notes or if the leak is a large one to squeak on certain notes. To test for leaks take the instrument apart. Plug the lower end of the joint with a cork or with the palm of the hand. Cover the tone holes and close all keys as if playing, avoiding using more pressure against the holes or keys than is used when playing. Blow through the other end with as much pressure as possible. Leaky pads can be identified by leaking air. If a tone hole normally covered by a key and pad held closed by a spring leaks when maximum wind pressure is applied, the spring on that key must be strengthened or replaced. A joint in perfect condition will not leak air no matter how much breath pressure is applied.

If the leak cannot be located by the above method, an alternative method which assures positive seating of all pads is to use cigarette papers (or feeler papers if purchased commercially). The cigarette paper should be cut or torn into strips about a quarter inch wide. Slide one end of the paper under the pad, put the normal amount of pressure against the pad if the key is not held closed with a spring, and slowly draw the paper out. As long as the pressure against the paper remains constant there is no leak. If the pressure suddenly lessens, the pad is not properly seated. Repeat the process completely around the pad so that all edges are tested.

The process of blowing cigarette smoke through the instrument to identify a leak through seeing the cigarette smoke coming out of the leak is not recommended. The nicotine in the smoke coats the pads and if this is done frequently will damage them so that they harden and leak.

Pads may leak because they are not seated properly, or because they are worn. A loose membrane on the bottom of the pad indicates that it should be replaced immediately, even though it is not leaking at that time. It soon will be, and if the condition persists it will produce a buzz when that particular key is used to play a note.

9. *Loose tenon rings.* Tenon rings are fitted at the ends of joints to reinforce the wood at those points where it is thinnest. There are two rings on the barrel joint, one on the lower joint, one at the top of the bell and a ring at the bottom of the bell. If the wood shrinks so that any of these are loose, they are no longer reinforcing the wood

and the instrument is subject to splitting at that point. Have the rings tightened immediately by a repairman.

10. *Corks and felts.* A number of keys on the clarinet have corks or felts cemented on them. These serve to control the amount of opening of a key (as on the G-sharp and "A" keys in the throat tones), to close a pad in conjunction with the operation of another key (as on the bridge key between the upper and lower joints), or to eliminate noise in the action (as on the keys operated by the right little finger). It is essential that all of these corks or felts be kept at the right thickness.

Corks which control the amount of opening of a key have a major function in the pitch of that tone. If the cork is worn and the key opens too far, the note will be a little sharp; and conversely, if the cork is too thick and the key doesn't open far enough the note will be a little flat and probably have a stuffy sound.

Corks which articulate the closing of pads with another ring or key are the source of many problems. If the cork on the bridge key between the upper and lower joints is too thin the 100 400 fingering for the clarion B-flat will not respond properly. Probably the most critical of these corks are those under the E and F-sharp keys played by the right little finger. When either of these keys are depressed, the pad on the low F key must close completely or neither tone will respond. This response is particularly noticeable on middle line B-natural or third space C-sharp. The difficulties that many beginners have in getting these two notes to respond can be traced directly to corks that are not thick enough.

A deficiency in a cork or felt used to eliminate noise in the action is obvious to both the player and a listener and detracts from the performance if they are not replaced.

11. *Cork on tenons.* Corks on the tenons which are excessively tight after being greased may be rubbed down to the proper size with very fine sandpaper. Avoid sanding the wood in the process. After an instrument has been used over a period of time the corks may be permanently compressed so that the instrument fits together loosely. Some may be compressed so much that the joint leaks or the instrument falls apart.

As a temporary measure if the cork is only slightly loose, it may be heated over an alcohol burner, candle, or even a lighted match to increase its size. Avoid getting the flame too close so that the cork will be burned. If the cork cannot be returned to the correct size by this method, it must be replaced by a repairman. Replacing all tenon corks are a normal part of the regular overhaul.

12. *Regular overhaul.* The condition of every instrument must be checked at least once a year by the instructor or by a repairman. Regular maintenance keeps an instrument in playing condition over a period of years, rather than allowing it to gradually deteriorate becoming increasingly difficult to play. Every instrument must have a complete overhaul every three to five years depending on amount of usage. If fine instruments receive a yearly checkup and regular overhauls, they will last in virtually perfect condition for many years. The services of a competent repairman is invaluable and an asset to any program of instrumental instruction.

BIBLIOGRAPHY OF STUDY MATERIALS

The wealth of musical material for study and performance on clarinet is so extensive that it is impossible to include more than a selective listing of study materials. Additional information on music for clarinet may be found in the books by Coleman, Gold, Heller, Opperman (the most complete), Rasmussen-Mattran, Stein, and Thurston as listed in the bibliography at the end of this book and in the MENC Selective Music Lists.

Except for the very beginners, a student should be studying in several books at the same time in order to get a well-rounded experience. Chapter one discusses five types of materials which can be used simultaneously. As examples of how this material can be grouped for clarinet study the following are typical. The groups are not progressive but simply illustrative of what can be used at various stages of development.

Group I. Suitable for a beginning student:
- a. Bodegraven, Paul Van. *Adventures in Clarinet Playing,* Book I.
- b. Collis, James. *Modern Course for the Clarinet,* Book I.
- c. Endresen, P. *Supplementary Studies for Clarinet.*
- d. Kueffner, J. *Fifty Progressive Duets, op. 80.*
- e. Appropriate solo material.

Group II. Suitable for an intermediate student:
- a. Langenus, Gustave. *Method for Clarinet,* Part I.
- b. Klose, H. *Method for Clarinet,* p. 123-135. Technical Studies.
- c. LoPresti, Ronald. *20 Melodic Studies for Clarinet*
- d. Voxman, H. *Selected Duets for Clarinet,* Vol. I.
- e. Appropriate solo material.

Group III. Suitable for an upper-intermediate student:
- a. Baermann, Carl. *Complete Method for Clarinet,* Part II.
- b. Albert, J. B. *Twenty-four Varied Scales and Exercises.*
- c. Rose, C. *40 Studies for Clarinet.*
- d. Bach-Langenus. *J. S. Bach Clarinet Duos.*
- e. Appropriate solos.

Group IV. Suitable for an advanced student.
- a. Langenus, Gustave. *Method for Clarinet,* Part III.
- b. Baermann, Carl. *Complete Method for Clarinet,* Part III.
- c. Perier, A. *Études De Gener Et D'Interpretation,* Vol. I.
- d. Mozart, W. A. *Three Duos.*
- e. Appropriate solos.

The sections which follow list typical materials in various classifications. The use of the words beginning, intermediate, and advanced to indicate levels of difficulty are simply general indications since the words have different meanings to different people. Experience with the materials will soon classify and identify exact grade of difficulty.

Beginning Methods

In the beginning study of the clarinet authorities are almost unanimous in agreement on at least two points: that a reasonable good tone and facility should be developed in the chalumeau register before the clarion register is introduced, and that articulation, or tonguing, must not be started until the chalumeau tone is established and in the process of developing.

Many beginning methods books violate the second of these by introducing articulation with the first or second lesson through the attempt to teach rhythmic reading, simultaneously with tone production. This sets up almost insurmountable problems for the student who must learn to hold the instrument, form an embouchure, establish breath support, learn to articulate, and learn fingerings for the notes. With all these problems presented at the same time it is a wonder that any student succeeds, and accounts for the very slow progress of many classes.

Taking the student into the clarion register before the chalumeau register is well established causes serious problems in embouchure development, since an unsettled embouchure will make incorrect adjustments in order to play the clarion register. If the problem of crossing the break is introduced at the same time, the difficulties are multiplied many fold. Some beginning methods do this.

In selecting a method book for the beginning clarinet all these things must be taken into account. Several standard beginning method books are listed below. As many of these as possible should be examined before making a selection for actual use.

Group I. These books present the technical problems in good order, establish the chalumeau register first, delay articulation, and have material of musical interest. Two or more of them may be used simultaneously with good results. Paul Van Bodegraven's *Adventures in Clarinet Playing* and the method by James Collis are an excellent pair.

Bodegraven, Paul Van. *Adventures in Clarinet Playing.* Book I, Book II. Staff Music Publishing Co.

Bodegraven, Paul Van. *A Clarinet Method for Grade Schools.* Carl Fischer.

Collis, James. *Modern Course for the Clarinet.* Book I, Book II. Henri Elkan Music Publishers.

Phillips, Harry I. *The Clarinet Class.* Summy-Birchard Publishing Co.

Stubbins, William H. *The Study of the Clarinet.* George Wahr Publishing Co.

Waln, George. *Elementary Clarinet Method.* Belwin.

Group II. Many of these books use the rhythm approach and introduce articulation from the very beginning. Others present problems without sufficient foundation for solving them, or lack musical interest. All have many assets, and may be preferred as the beginning text. Any of them can be used with one of the Group I books after the student is established. Some of them progress faster and farther than others, approaching the technical level of those in Group III.

Anzalone, Valentine. *Breeze-Easy Method for Clarinet,* 2 vols. M. Withark & Sons.

Dalby, Cleon E. *All Melody Method for Clarinet.* 2 vols. Pro-Art Publications.

Gekeler-Hovey. *Belwin Clarinet Method.* 3 vols. Belwin-Mills.

Hovey, Nilo. *Rubank Elementary Method for Clarinet.* Rubank, Inc.

Liegel, Leopold. *Basic Method for the Clarinet.* Carl Fischer.

Manring, Ernest. *Elementary Method for Clarinet.* Mills Music, Inc.

Lindeman, Ben. *Melodious Fundamentals for Clarinet.* Charles Colin, Inc.

Weber-Lowry. *Student Instrumental Course for Clarinet,* 3 vols. Belwin, Inc. The three volumes are correlated with supplementary volumes of solos, duets, and studies.

Group III. These books progress farther or faster or both than either of the previous groups. The second volume of these in both the first and second group would fall into this classification as well. These books can be used to follow those previously considered, or picked up before they are completed.

Hendrickson, Clarence V. *Hendrickson Method for Clarinet,* 2 vols. Belwin, Inc.

Hovey, Nilo W. *Daily Exercises for Clarinet.* (Compiled from the works of Albert and Pares.) Belwin, Inc.

Kell, Reginald. *The Kell Method for Clarinet,* vol. I. Boosey & Hawkes.

Langenus, Gustave. *Complete Method for the Boehm Clarinet,* part I. Carl Fischer. By far the best choice to follow any beginning method, or to be introduced after the student is past the easy beginning stage.

Mitchell, Albert. *Mitchell's Class Method for the Clarinet.* Oliver Ditson.

Snavely, Jack. *Clarinet Method for Beginning Students,* 2 vols. Leblanc Publications, Inc.

The Standard Methods

There are four standard methods for the clarinet which are widely used, and all except one, that by Langenus, are about a hundred years old. None of them are suitable for the beginning student according to present day pedagogy since methods of instruction have undergone many changes in the years since they were written. A thoroughly schooled clarinetist will have studied portions, or all of each of them at one stage or another in his development. All are quite different in their content, unlike the present day beginning methods which seem to have been cast from the same mold, and all have valuable contributions to make. The four are discussed below in some detail, and should be examined carefully.

I. Langenus, Gustave. *Complete Method for the Boehm Clarinet.* Part I, Part II, Part III. Carl Fischer, Inc.

This is the only one of the standard methods which was written in the twentieth century, and which makes use of contemporary teaching techniques. Gustave Langenus was a distinguished New York clarinetist who has had tremendous influence on the clarinet through his teaching and his many publications of original works and arrangements for the instrument. Parts I and II are progressive, and Part I can be started after completion of a beginning method, or toward the end of the beginning method, depending on which one is selected. Part II is a continuation of Part I. Part III is Virtuoso Studies and Duos and represents a wide jump in technical requirements over the end of Part II and is for advanced students.

Part I of this method is without doubt the best organized and presented method for any of the woodwind instruments. It presents and develops the various technical problems for the instrument logically and musically. Any student who thoroughly studies Parts I and II will have both an excellent technical as well as musical foundation upon which to build his performance. Any teacher who is responsible for the development of clarinetists on any level should study these books thoroughly, and should be able to play Part I in order to thoroughly understand the instrument.

All three volumes make extensive use of duets which add interest to the study of the instrument. All are carefully edited in the most musical fashion, and contain written comments and instructions which clarify the purpose of the study.

II. Baermann, Carl. *Complete Method for Clarinet, Op. 63.* Two editions. Revised and edited by Gustave Langenus. Carl Fischer, Inc. Parts I, II, III complete or Parts I and II in a single volume and Part III in a single volume. No piano accompaniments. Cundy-Bettoney Co., Inc. Revised by Harry Bettoney and published as follows: Parts I & II in a single volume; Piano accompaniment to Part II; Part III; Part IV; Piano accompaniment to Part IV; Part V.

Carl Baermann (1820-1865) was the most noted German clarinetist of his day, and a prolific composer for the instrument. His father was also a noted clarinetist and it is probable that father and son collaborated on this method. Both Baermanns worked toward the technical improvement of the mechanism of the clarinet at the same time Theobald Boehm was working on the improvement of the flute. They developed a Baermann System clarinet which was similar to the Albert System clarinet, but which was never widely used outside of Germany, having been superceded by the Boehm System clarinet which was developed in France at about the same time. The Cundy-Bettoney edition indicates fingering choices for the Albert-Baermann System as well as for the Boehm System.

Part I, or the 1st Division, is purely theoretical introductory material which is interesting but of little practical value. In the Carl Fischer edition it is eleven pages long, and in the Cundy-Bettoney edition the complete general instructions by Baermann are reprinted along with additional technical information by the editor to the extent of 52 pages.

Part II is useful for the upper intermediate level of study. It develops gradually and thoroughly the facility for different fingerings through occasional pages of one measure mechanical studies, but primarily through a series of very musical studies, some of them given names to indicate that they are solos, progressively through major and minor keys up to and including three flats. All facets of nineteenth century musical style are developed, with emphasis on the development of a sense of phrasing as well as technical development. A piano accompaniment is available for all the fifty studies in Part II except for the mechanism and scale studies. The use of the piano accompaniment is recommended, and is quite valuable in giving the student continual experience playing with accompaniment and all the values inherent in this experience. The accompaniments are not pianistically difficult and can be played easily by a pianist with average technique. This piano accompaniment is published only by Cundy-Bettoney, but the rehearsal letters are identical with those in the Carl Fischer edition so that it can be used with either edition.

Part III is designated as daily studies and are for advanced players. All studies are in all keys, and encompass the entire professional range of the instrument. These include scales, chromatic scales, major and minor arpeggios, diminished seventh chords, interrupted scales, broken major and minor chords, returning scales, dominant seventh chords, scales in thirds, scales in sixths, and four general studies on octaves and staccato. Mastery of this volume is a must for the advanced clarinetist, for it provides a technical facility in all keys which forms the basis for much of the music he will be playing.

Part IV is a continuation of Part II of this method, and is Opus 64 of Baermann's works. It is published in this country only by Cundy-Bettoney and a piano accompaniment is available. It does not continue progressively through the keys from where Part II left off, but is devoted to certain technical problems. Many of the studies in this part as well as in Part II would make interesting and satisfactory solos for public performance.

Part V is published by Cundy-Bettoney and is a collection of excerpts from the works of Baermann other than Opus 63 and 64. It is for the advanced student, and if the previous four parts have been covered, there is little need for studying this volume as it will add little to the advancement of the student. The music is repetitious and boring.

III. Klose, H. *Celebrated Method for the Clarinet.* Revised and Enlarged by Simeon Bellison. Carl Fischer, Inc. Published complete or Parts I and II separately.

This is perhaps the most widely used of the standard methods for clarinet, for it contains much valuable material. Klose was professor of clarinet at the Paris Conservatory around 1850, and with August Buffet is credited with the development of the Boehm System Clarinet. His method was the first written for this system, and the mechanism studies were intended to introduce the various uses of this new system.

The Klose method is not a beginning method, nor is it progressive in difficulty. In order to use it effectively the teacher must skip around through the volume. Excerpts designed for the advanced beginner and intermediate level students are published by the Carl Fischer company under the title *Klose-Prescott* method. It is less expensive, and although it is not progressive it contains essential material from both Parts I and II of the complete edition.

Use of the Klose method can start with the advanced beginner. The 68 and 141 mechanical exercises present in capsule form fingering problems which can be mastered and put to use by the beginner who has a basic facility in the chalumeau and clarion registers of the instrument, and who has learned to cross the break without too much difficulty. The *Fifty Progressive Duets* by Joseph Kuffner, Op. 80 are useful on this stage of development and are reprinted in this edition of the Klose mehod. These duets are also published separately by Carl Fischer, for those who don't wish to purchase the method, and are very useful in the young clarinet class since both parts of the duet are written for the student, rather than the student-teacher pattern used in some methods.

The Klose *Scales and Exercises* are in duet form and take the student through major keys only, and are more difficult than those by Kuffner. The scale and arpeggio exercises at the beginning of Part II are basic to the study of the clarinet, and should be studied by the intermediate student as the first of a series of progressively more difficult studies of this type.

The *Fifteen Grand Duets* pages 136-201 of Part II are for the advanced student, and are widely used, although they require considerable editing by the teacher in order to bring them into line with contemporary performance styles. The *Twenty Studies* on pages 216-255 are quite advanced technically and present various technical problems. These too require considerable editing since these, as well as the entire book, are basically a reprint of the 1898 edition with very minor additions to the original plate by the editor in order that a new copyright could be secured.

The present edition concludes with a reprint of Book II of the Kroepsch *416 Progressive Daily Studies for the Clarinet,* which starts with exercises in three flats and progresses through the keys to six flats. The Kroepsch studies are considered in detail later.

IV. Lazarus, Henry. *Method for Clarinet in Three Parts,* available complete, or each part singly. Cundy-Bettoney, Revised by Gustave Langenus. Carl Fischer, Revised by Simeon Bellison.

Henry Lazarus (1815-1895) was the most famous English clarinetist of his time. From 1858 he was professor at Kneller Hall, the great English school of music. His method was written for use with his students at Kneller Hall, and the duets it contains are among the most interesting and challenging in clarinet literature.

In addition to the original method by Lazarus each edition includes certain works by other composers. The Cundy-Bettoney edition includes: Berr—Fifteen Progressive Duets, Kuffner—Fifty Progressive Duets, Albert—Twenty-Four Varied Scales, Schmidt—Twenty-Four Technical Exercises, Klose—Scale Studies, Blancou—Forty Studies from the works of Mazas, Cavallini—Thirty Caprices. The Carl Fischer Edition adds: Kuffner—Fifty Progressive Duets, Klose—Scale Studies, Albert—Twenty-Four Varied Scales, and Kroepsch—416 Exercises for the Clarinet, Book I.

The range of difficulty in this method is from lower intermediate to quite advanced. The Cundy-Bettoney edition has a greater variety of material in both the intermediate and advanced range of difficulty and would be the better choice.

Summary

The methods by Baermann, Klose and Lazarus were all written at about the same time—the middle of the nineteenth century. The danger in using these methods to the exclusion of all other material lies in the fact that the musical style is exclusively that of the mid nineteenth century. Limiting the experience of the student to this style is not the best procedure, and although these either singly or in combination must be used, care should be taken to include material of other styles from baroque to contemporary.

The Langenus method, unlike the other three, does include a wide variety of musical styles in the three volumes from baroque to the early twentieth century. It should be the basic method for the student, and can be supplemented by Baerman, Klose and sections of Lazarus in order to get a wide variety of material on approximately the same level of technical difficulty. None of these methods should be considered a beginning method, and must be preceded by one of the standard beginning methods books.

Additional Study Materials

The supply of study materials for the clarinet is practically inexhaustible, and it is impossible to make an exhaustive analysis of the entire scope. Particular attention should be paid to the materials printed in France. The major development of the study of clarinet and other woodwind instruments has been in France through the influence of the Paris Conservatory which has been in continuous existence for over one hundred and fifty years. There have been a series of outstanding artist-teachers at this institution from Berr and Klose to the present day. Each has made significant contributions to the study literature for the instrument, in particular Perier and Jean-Jean whose works have become classics for the instrument.

The following list of material represents a typical cross section of that which is most useful in varying situations, but is by no means all inclusive. These and others should be examined and put into use to determine what results will be obtained. Different teachers will obtain different results from the same material, so it is necessary to adapt material not only to the individual student, but to the pedagogy and concepts of the teacher.

Albert, J. B. *Twenty-Four Varied Scales and Exercises.* Carl Fischer. Basic to the development of good technical facility.

Bach, J. S. *21 Pieces for Clarinet.* Ricordi. From suites for solo violin and solo cello.

Baermann, C. *Daily Studies.* Boosey & Hawkes.

Baermann, H. *Twelve Amusing Exercises, Op. 30.* Cundy-Bettoney.

Balassa-Kerkes. *Clarinet Tutor,* 4 vols. Boosey & Hawkes.

Bellison, S. *Scales and Chords.* Carl Fischer.

Bitsch, Marcel. *12 Rhythmical Studies for Clarinet.* Leduc. Difficult twentieth century rhythmic patterns.

Blancou, V. *40 Studies from the Works of Mazas,* 2 vols. Cundy-Bettoney. Nineteenth century style, intermediate difficulty.

Bonade, Daniel. *Sixteen Phrasing Studies.* Leblanc Publications Inc. These are slow studies from the Rose *32 Études,* with meticulous detailed phrasing in the best contemporary performance style.

Bordogni-Clark. *20 Solo Studies.* Southern Music Company. With piano accompaniment. Transcribed from the famous Bordogni vocalises, they are excellent phrasing studies on the lower intermediate level.

Cailliet, L. *Clarinet Studies.* Belwin Mills.

Cavallini, E. *30 Caprices.* Ricordi, International, Carl Fischer.

Coward, G. *Secret to Rapid Tonguing and Finger Technique.* Carl Fischer.

Delecluse, U. *15 Études from the Works of J. S. Bach.* Leduc.

Demnitz, F. *Fundamental Scale and Chord Studies.* G. Schirmer.

Dies, W. *Anleitung zur Improvisation für Klarinette (Jazz Studio).* Schott (Belwin-Mills).

Dolezal. *24 Easy Studies.* Boosey & Hawkes.

Druart, Henri. *Eleven Modern Études.* Leblanc Publications, Inc. In a conservative twentieth century style, these are designed to supplement the Rose studies.

Endresen, P. *Supplementary Studies for Clarinet.* Rubank, Inc. Useful on upper beginning levels.

Faulx, J. *20 Virtuoso Studies after Bach.* Henri Elkan.

Folland-Zwick. *Adventures in the Lower Register.* Belwin-Mills. Piano accompaniment available.

Gambaro, J. *10 Caprices, Op. 9.* International.
12 Caprices, Op. 18. International.

Gates, Everett. *Odd Meter Études.* Sam Fox. Excellent studies in twentieth century meters.
Odd Meter Duets. Sam Fox. Designed to supplement the Études.

Hite, David L. *Melodious and Progressive Studies,* 3 vols. Southern Music Co.
Style Études and Technical Exercises. Southern Music Co.
Intermediate Style Études and Technical Studies. Southern Music Co.
Volume one of Melodious studies is on the intermediate level, volume two more advanced material selected from standard clarinet literature. Volume 3 has both the Rose 32 and 40 studies. The Style études are the works of various authors and both volumes are on the intermediate level. Much useful material in this series.

Hovey, N. *Practical Clarinet Studies,* 2 vols. Belwin-Mills.
Section Studies for Clarinets. Belwin-Mills.

Jean-Jean, Paul. *Progressive and Melodic Studies for Clarinet,* 3 vols. Leduc. Excellent musically, these provide basic concepts in phrasing and the French style of playing. The three volumes have études through the circle of keys and are on the advanced level.
Twenty-Five Technical and Melodic Studies. Leduc. Style is carried into early twentieth century. A second volume has second and third clarinet parts and a few studies arranged for four clarinets.
18 Études de Perfectionment. Andrieu Freres. Intended to follow the preceding volume, these are less interesting musically.
16 Études Modernes pour Clarinette. Buffet-Crampon & Cie. Extremely difficult studies in twentieth century idioms. Essential for any serious clarinet student.
Vade-Mecum du Clarinettiste. Leduc. Designed to help the advanced clarinetist keep in shape when there is no time for regular practice.

Jettl, Rudolf. *Preliminary Studies to the Accomplished Clarinetist,* 3 vols. Joseph Weinberger.
The Accomplished Clarinetist, 3 vols. Joseph Weinberger.
Modern Clarinet Practice. (3 clarinets). Joseph Weinberger. This is excellent twentieth century material for the most advanced clarinetist. *Modern Clarinet Practice* is a series of 17 studies for three clarinets "for perfection in ensemble playing" and is less difficult than the other material.

Jones, Marquis. *Virtuoso Studies for the Clarinet.* Leblanc Publications, Inc. Traditional style. Level of difficulty similar to Rose 32 Studies.

Kell, Reginald. *17 Staccato Studies.* International.
30 Interpretative Studies. International.
The staccato studies are excellent material for improv-

ing the staccato of advanced students. The interpretative studies are in traditional style.

——— *The Kell Method for Clarinet.* 3 vols. Boosey & Hawkes. An important recent addition to clarinet study materials. Volume 1 is a beginning method using legato approach, but moves faster than most beginning methods. Musically rewarding. Has a number of duets. Volume Two is a continuation of the first on the upper intermediate level. Volume three has the subtitle "Clarinet Staccato from the Beginning." An excellent presentation of staccato. Technical demands on upper intermediate level.

Klose, H. *20 Characteristic Studies.* International.

20 Technical Studies. International.

Kroepsch, F. *416 Progressive Daily Studies,* 4 vols. Carl Fischer. International. Volumes one and two go through the circle of keys with two or three line exercises. Book three goes through circle of keys in the form or scale and arpeggio studies. All three are lower advanced level. Volume four is a collection of études in every key, which are difficult and not very interesting.

Langenus, Gustav. *Fingered Scale Studies for the Boehm Clarinet.* Carl Fischer.

Practical Transposition. Carl Fischer.

Twenty-Seven Original Studies. Carl Fischer.

Clarinet Cadenzas: How to Phrase Them. Carl Fischer.

LaPorta, John. *A Guide to Improvisation.* Berklee Press. Has a director's manual, three l.p.'s and a book for B-flat instruments, treble.

Langey, O. *Practical Tutor for Clarinet.* Boosey & Hawkes.

Lester, L. *Melodious Studies.* Henri Elkan. Good lower intermediate material.

LoPresti, R. *20 Melodic Studies for Clarinet,* 2 vols. Luverne Publications. Outstanding collection of studies for lower intermediate level.

Manevich, A. *Ten Studies.* International.

McCarty, Keith. *Methods for New Music,* 2 vols. Lariken Press. For the clarinetist who wants to develop facility in performance of avant-garde music.

McGinnis-Siennicki. *Études for the Advanced Clarinetist.* Shawnee Press. Contemporary idiom. Has a recording for illustration.

Mohr. *8 Grand Études.* Editions Salabert.

Mueller, Ivan. *22 Easy Studies,* 2 vols. International. Intermediate grade, interesting and useful.

Opperman, Kalmen. *Modern Daily Studies for the Clarinet,* 2 vols. M. Baron.

Pares, G. *Daily Technical Exercises for Clarinet.* Carl Fischer.

Foundation Studies for Clarinet. Rubank, Inc. Two editions of the same material, intermediate level.

Perier, A. *20 Études Faciles et Progressives.* Leduc. Excellent studies on the level of the Rose 40 studies.

Études De Genre Et D'Interpretation. 2 vols. Leduc. Diverse styles for advanced student.

30 Études. Leduc. From the works of Bach, Handel, Paganini, Dont, etc. these studies have a wide range of difficulty.

Polatschek, Victor. *Advanced Studies for the Clarinet.* G. Schirmer. Twenty-eight studies on the advanced level, each in the style of a standard composer in styles ranging from Bach to Barber.

Purseglove, A. *Crossing the Register.* Belwin. To supplement a beginning method when this problem is involved.

Rose, C. *26 Études for Clarinet.* Leduc.

40 Studies for Clarinet, 2 vols. Carl Fischer or 1 vol. Charles Hansen Music Corp.

32 Studies for Clarinet. Carl Fischer.

20 Studies from the Works of Rode. Cundy-Bettoney. The Rose studies, especially the 32 and 40, are a part of virtually every clarinetists course of study. These are on the lower advanced level of difficulty.

Russo, John P. *Twenty Modern Studies,* 2 vols. Henri Elkan. Good studies in contemporary styles. A piano accompaniment has been announced for each volume.

Schaeffer. *Reading Rhythms* Pro-Art Publications.

Sigel, Alan. *The Twentieth Century Clarinetist.* Franco Columbo. The best set of studies available for contemporary music. Should be a part of every advanced player's study.

Stark, R. *24 Studies in all Tonalities.* International.

Arpeggio Studies, Op. 39. International.

24 Grand Virtuoso Studies, 2 vols. International.

Uhl, Alfred. *48 Études for Clarinet,* 2 vols. Schott Edition. Designed to familiarize the clarinetist with technical problems of twentieth century music, these studies have become as standard in clarinet study on the advanced level as the Rose studies.

Voxman, H. *Selected Studies for Clarinet.* Rubank, Inc. Advanced études, scales, and arpeggios in all major and minor keys.

——— *Classical Studies for Clarinet.* Rubank. From the works for solo violin, solo cello and other works of Bach and Handel.

Viola, Joseph. *Developing Sight Reading Skills in the Jazz Idiom.* Berklee Press.

Wiedemann, L. *32 Clarinet Studies.* G. Schirmer.

Alto and Bass Clarinet

Weber-Lowry. *Student Instrumental Course,* 3 vols. Belwin, Inc. For Alto clarinet, for Bass clarinet. Each of the three volumes is correlated with solos and studies for each instrument.

Baermann-Rhoads. *Baerman for Alto and Bass Clarinet.* Southern Music Co.

Mimart, P. *Method for Alto and Bass Clarinets.* Cundy-Bettoney.

Rhoads. *Eighteen Selected Studies.* Southern Music Co.
Études for Technical Facility. Southern Music Co.
35 Technical Studies. Southern Music Co.
21 Foundation Studies. Southern Music Co.

Study and Achievement Questions

1. What is the theoretical playing range of the clarinet?
2. Select a band arrangement scored for a full compliment of clarinets. Transpose the clarinet parts to the pitches they actually sound and make a two-line piano score of these parts.
3. Indicate on a staff the beginning, intermediate, and advanced playing ranges of the Soprano clarinets; the Alto and Bass clarinets.
4. Identify the various parts of a clarinet making use of an instrument for illustration.
5. Perform the correct assembly process for the B-flat clarinet showing the correct holding position for each step. Do the same with an Alto or Bass clarinet.
6. Demonstrate the correct procedure for placing a reed on the clarinet mouthpiece. Add the protective cap.
7. Observe one or more beginning clarinet students assemble their instrument and fill out the checklist for assembly. Do the same for intermediate and advanced level students. Correct any improper procedures if there is an opportunity to do so. This observation may be done in the college class, but is especially valuable if it can be done in an actual public school situation.
8. Demonstrate the correct holding position for the B-flat, Alto or Bass, and Contrabass instruments.
9. Consider the advantages and disadvantages of holding the Alto or Bass clarinet to the right of the right leg rather than between the legs.
10. Describe and demonstrate the basic guide position of the hands on one or more instruments in the clarinet family.
11. Using a student who is unfamiliar with the clarinet give him complete instructions on the holding position and detailed instructions on establishing the correct hand position.
12. Describe and demonstrate the position and movements of the left thumb in playing from the lower to the upper register. In playing the third-line B-flat.
13. Describe and demonstrate the positions and movements of the first finger in playing second-line G-sharp. In playing second space A. Do the same for first finger right hand in fingering first-line E-flat or first-space F-sharp.
14. Observe one or more beginning players and fill out the checklist for holding and hand positions. Do the same for intermediate and advanced players. If there is an opportunity to do so correct any improper procedures suggesting remedial measures. Make this observation in the public school situation if possible.
15. Describe and discuss the various types of clarinet embouchure formations. Indicate your choice and reasons for it. Then describe and demonstrate the step by step procedure for its formation. Do the same with a student who is unfamiliar with the instrument.
16. Observe one or more beginning, intermediate and advanced players and fill out the checklist for embouchure formation for each. Suggest corrections and remedial measures.
17. Describe and perform the tuning process for one or more instruments in the clarinet family using intermediate or advanced players and an electronic tuning device if available.
18. What are the factors which will make a clarinet flat? sharp? Instruct an advanced player on how to demonstrate some of them.
19. Identify the four registers of the clarinet's range.
20. Listen to beginning, intermediate, and advanced clarinet players. Diagnose any problems in tone quality and suggest corrections.
21. Discuss various ways of placement and use of the tongue in articulation. Select the one you prefer and describe it in detail. Discuss various ways of developing articulation.
22. Select a musical example which has successive notes making use of the little fingers. Mark the sequence of left and right.
23. Indicate a procedure for making "crossing the break" easier. For slurring into the high register.
24. List the notes which have alternate fingerings, demonstrate each, and illustrate how each is used.
25. Identify the various transpositions which may be required of a clarinetist and describe how each is done.
26. Discuss the selection of an instrument for various purposes, and the basis for each. Discuss the brands available and make recommendations for various levels of performance.
27. Discuss student qualifications and aptitudes. If there is an opportunity, observe the process of selection, and discuss it with a public school teacher.
28. Perform the process of disassembly and swabbing. Discuss regular maintenance of the instrument. Test an instrument for leaks. Examine one or more instruments for needed repairs or adjustments.
29. Make a comparative analysis of as many beginning methods as you have available. Select and rank them in order of preference.
30. Examine available standard methods and additional study materials for clarinet and list them with comments.
31. Prepare a suggested list of material to include all five types of materials suggested for simultaneous study for an upper beginner, an intermediate, and an advanced student.
32. Listen to several phonograph records of clarinet literature, comment on and compare tone quality, phrasing, articulation, and general facility.

33. Attend a woodwind event in a solo and ensemble festival. Observe the players and make a detailed critique of as many as possible on details of holding positions, hand positions, embouchure formation, tuning, intonation, tone quality, articulation, and technique. Describe any faults found in any of these, the symptoms, possible causes, and corrections for each.

Flute

Flutes are the most ancient of the woodwind instruments since their tone is the product of an edge tone rather than a vibrating reed. Flutes have appeared historically in many forms from the earliest civilizations. The present day family of instruments include the C flute, the piccolo in C (the D-flat piccolo is considered obsolescent), the E-flat flute, the Alto flute in G and the Bass flute in C.[1]

All the instruments in the flute family currently in use are built in the Boehm system and have identical fingerings for the same written notes. All but the C flutes are transposing instruments. The transpositions and ranges in which each instrument sounds is as follows:

1. *C Flute*

Written Sounds Range of actual sounds

2. *C Piccolo*

Written Sounds Range of actual sounds

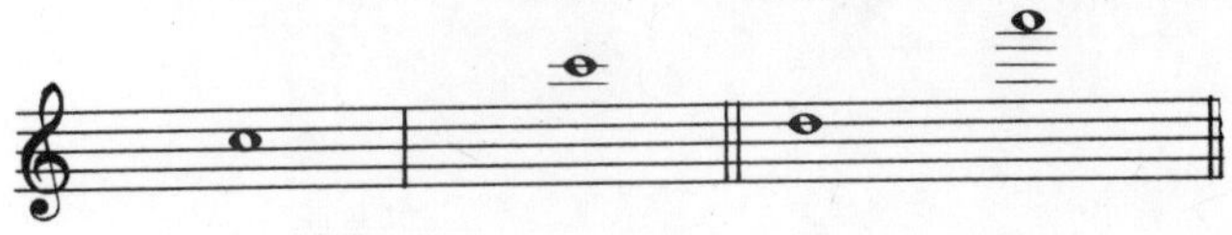

3. *D-flat Piccolo*

Written Sounds Range of actual sounds

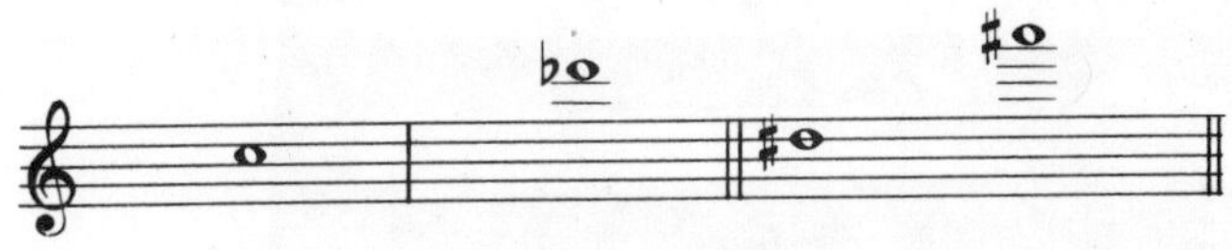

4. *E-flat Flute*

Written Sounds Range of actual sounds

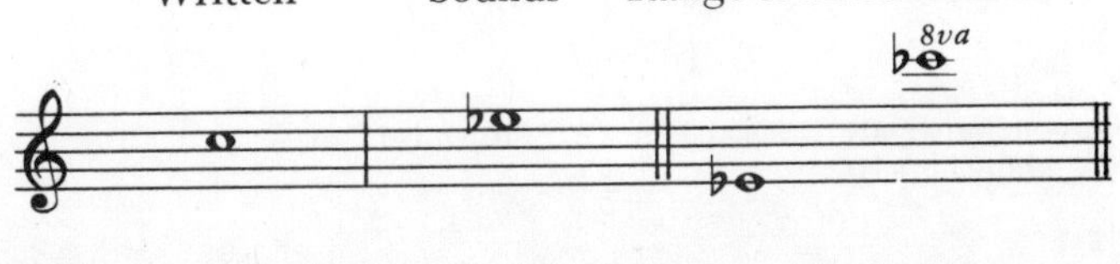

5. *Alto Flute in G*

Written Sounds Range of actual sounds

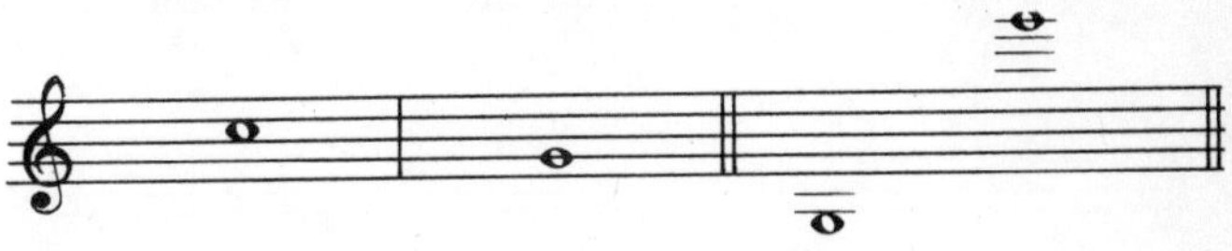

6. *Bass Flute in C*

Written Sounds Range of actual sounds

PLAYING RANGES

With the exception of the two lowest notes which are not on the piccolo all the instruments in the flute family have the same theoretical written playing range.

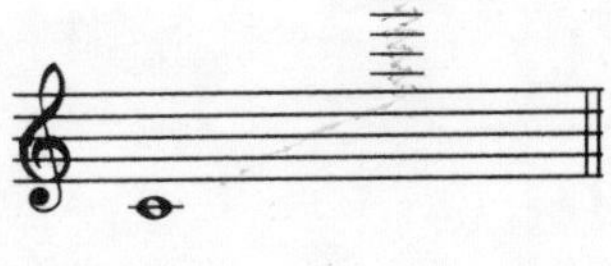

There are commonly accepted playing ranges for the flute which for convenience may be designated as *beginning,* the range a typical young beginner can be expected to play by the end of the first year of experience; *intermediate,* the range commonly required for the average good high school player; and *advanced,* the range in which the professional is expected to perform.

1. A recording, *The Flute Family Album,* containing unaccompanied solos for C flute, piccolo, E-flat, Alto and Bass flutes is available from the W. T. Armstrong Co., Elkhart, Indiana.

These ranges are very flexible with some beginning students achieving tone production in the intermediate range rather quickly. Only the C flute is considered a beginning instrument. The other instruments of the family, including the piccolo, are not beginning instruments and should be played by a student who has had experience on the C flute.

1. *Flute*

Beginning Intermediate Advanced

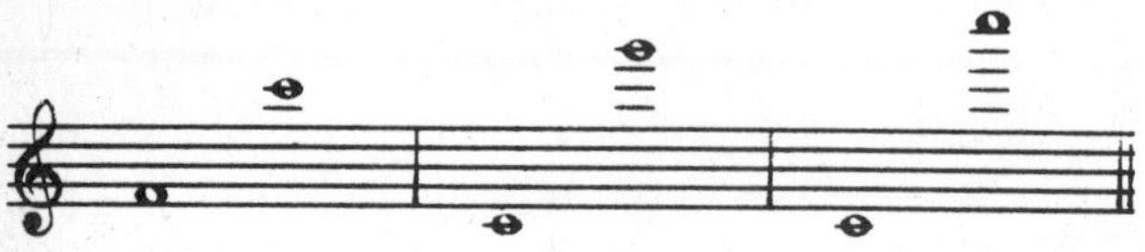

2. *Piccolo*

Beginning Intermediate Advanced

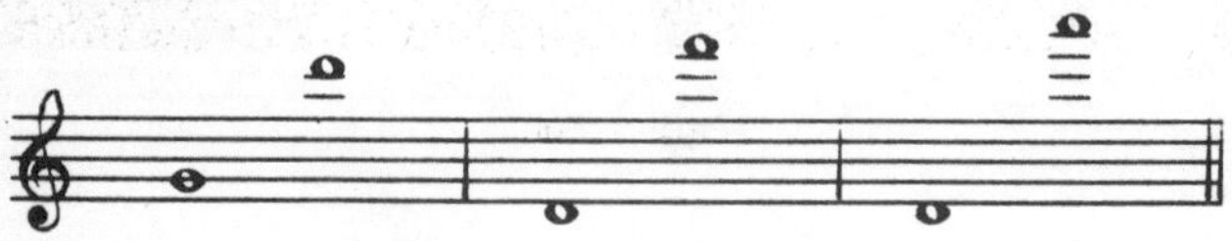

ASSEMBLING THE INSTRUMENT

Although in comparison with the oboe and clarinet, the mechanism of the flute is sturdy; it must nevertheless be assembled and disassembled with care. The assembly of the instrument must be accomplished without putting pressure on any key or rod which will bend it in any way.

Before starting the process of assembly, check to see that the connecting tenon and tuning sleeve on the head joint and the tenon on the middle section are clean. The instructor should check to see that the sections fit together without difficulty before asking the student to assemble the instrument. These connections require no lubrication if the instrument is in good condition. If they fit together with difficulty, a very small amount of prepared cork grease may be applied to reduce the amount of friction.

The way in which the flute is assembled is subject to some variation according to the desire and experience of the teacher. No matter what procedure is used students must be taught from the very first lesson to perform the process correctly. The following step-by-step process of assembly is a standard one which can be understood and performed easily by beginners. Study the photograph and directions for each step carefully and repeat the operation several times before proceeding to the next.

1. Figure F-2. Hold the open flute case in the lap. Take the head joint out of the case with the right little finger in the end. Parts of the instrument fit tightly in the average case and removing them in this way avoids picking them up by the keys and puts the hand into a good position for grasping the joint.

Parts of the Instrument

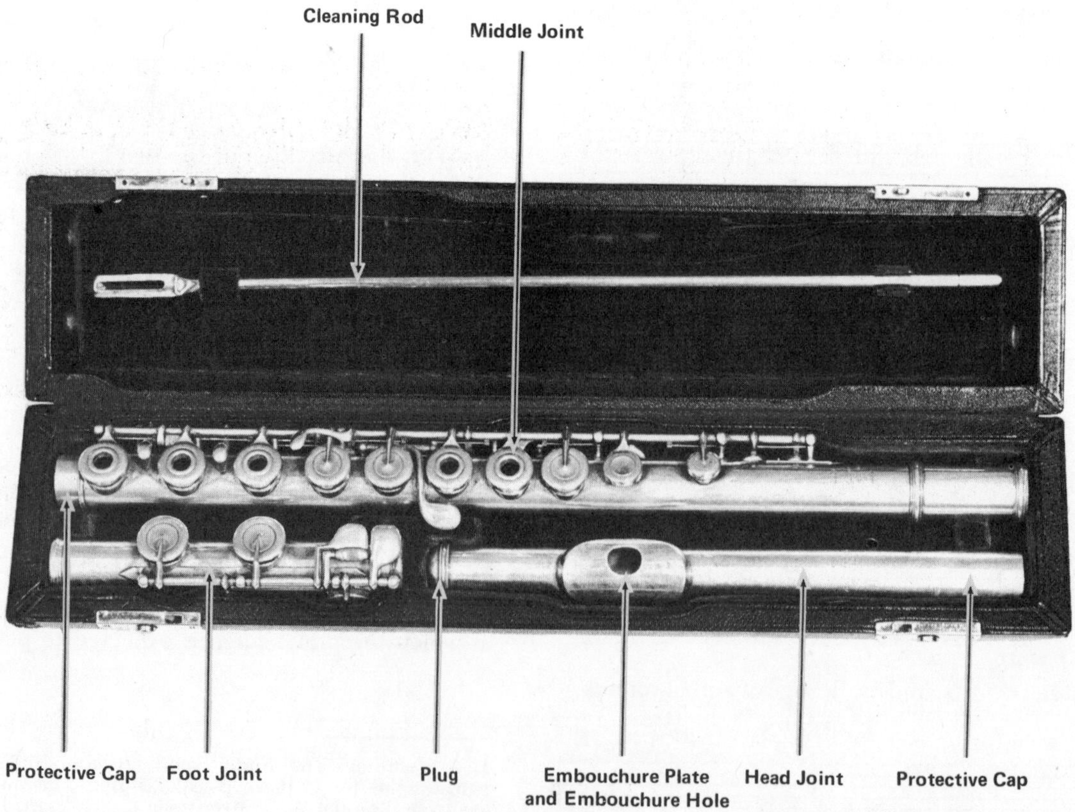

Figure F-1

Figure F-2

2. Figure F-3. With the joint partially out of the case, roll the hand over as shown and pick up the joint, transferring it to the left hand.

Figure F-3

3. Figure F-4. Holding the joint in the left hand remove the protective cap and return it to the case. Teachers must insist that the protective caps be kept on the instrument when it is in the case to avoid bending or damaging the connecting sleeves. Students have an unfortunate tendency to lose these caps.

Figure F-4

4. Figure F-5. Take out the middle joint with the little finger of the right hand in the same way the head joint was removed, holding the middle joint at the end away from the keys. Remove the protective cap and return it to the case.

Figure F-5

5. Figure F-6. To assemble the head and middle joints, hold the middle joint in the right hand at the end away from the key mechanism. The palm of the hand is on the top of the instrument, fingers are curled around the body, and the joint is held firmly by the

thumb and forefinger. With this holding position there is no pressure against key mechanism.

6. Figure F-7. Hold the head joint in the palm of the left hand, with the thumb over the embouchure plate and the fingers firmly around the pipe.

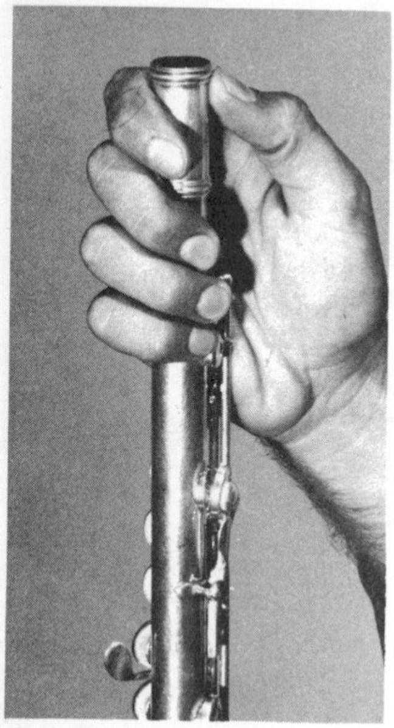

Figure F-6

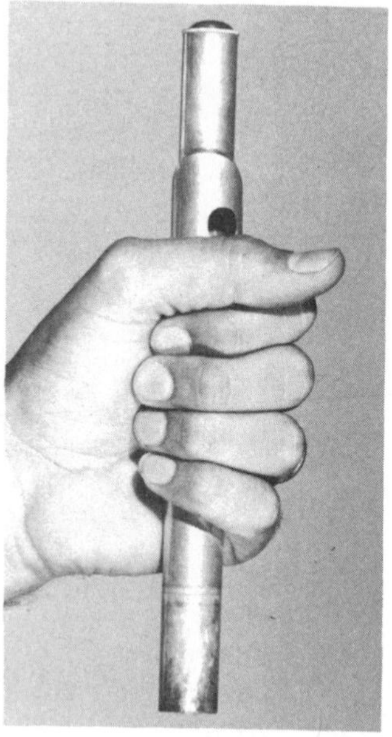

Figure F-7

7. Figure F-8. Holding the head and middle joints as described push the parts together with a twisting motion. Line up the hole in the embouchure plate so that it is centered on the tone holes on the top of the instrument in their *closed* position.

Figure F-8

8. Figure F-9. Take the foot joint from the case again using the end of the little finger. Place the thumb against the rim at the end which fits on the middle joint below the keys operated by the right little finger. The joint fits loosely in the palm of the hand, held firmly by the thumb and forefinger with the remaining fingers around the pipe.

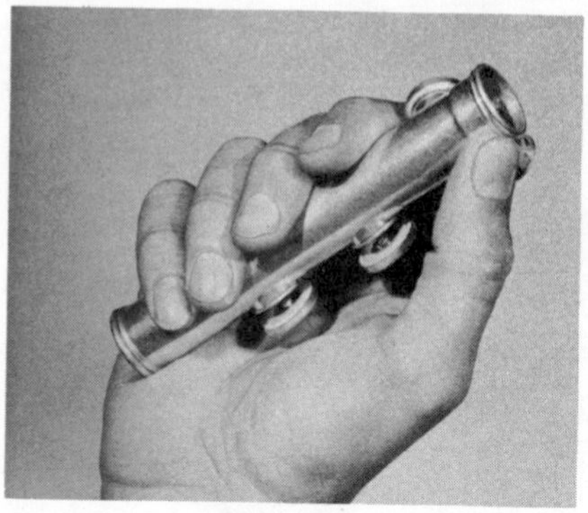

Figure F-9

9. Figure F-10. Hold the assembled head and middle joints in the palm of the left hand near the lower end for their connection with the foot joint. Fingers are over the tone holes and thumb over the connecting rods on the left side of the instrument. The joint is held by pressure of the base of the thumb pushing the flute against the palm. Avoid pressure against the rods. This particular holding position is the most critical of all because of the possibility of bending the rods. Check this position carefully.

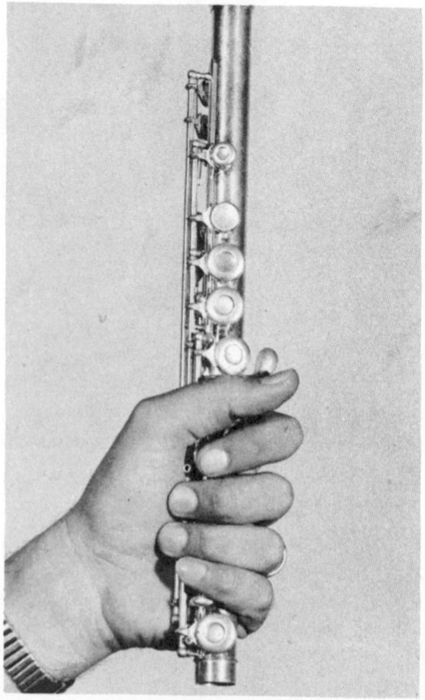

Figure F-10

10. Figure F-11 and F-12. Holding the foot joint and the middle joint as described put on the foot joint with a twisting motion to the right. Figure F-11 shows the beginning of this process and Figure F-12 the conclusion. The foot joint is in the correct position when the rod on which the keys pivot is centered on the closest tone hole. This puts the keys on the foot joint in the best position for efficient operation by the little finger.

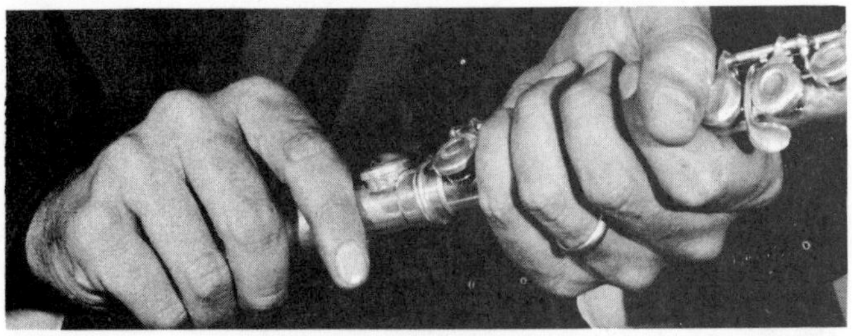

Figure F-11

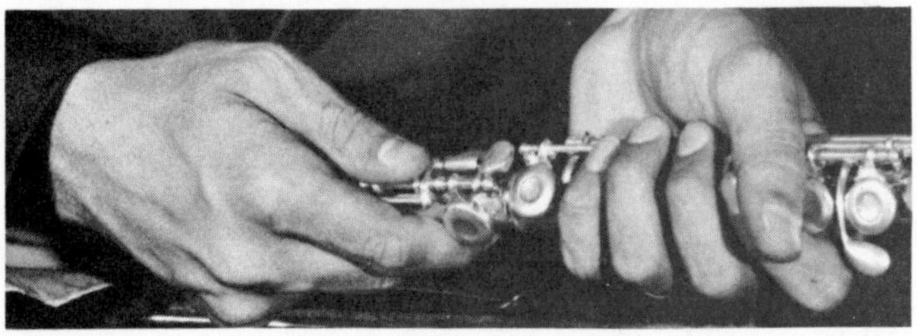

Figure F-12

Figure F-13. This photograph shows the assembled flute with the head and foot joints properly positioned. Check the head joint to see that the tone hole is centered on the tone holes on the top of the instrument, and that the pivot rod on the foot joint is centered on the bottom tone hole. This is the basic position of the parts. Experienced students will vary this position slightly to accommodate shape and size of hands, and embouchure formation. Avoid wide deviations from this standard.

Figure F-13

Common Faults in Assembly

There are, of course, several ways in which the flute may be assembled, and various teachers will have different procedures and methods. The only criteria for a good procedure is that no pressure is put on rods, plates or keys during the process. The procedure outlined above is a common standard one and may be safely used for beginners. As familiarity with the instrument increases, students may change the procedure to suit themselves. The following items are the most common faults or inaccuracies in the assembly of the flute.

1. *Failure to clean connecting sleeves.* All connecting sleeves both inside and out must be kept absolutely clean and smooth if the instrument is to be assembled easily. With a soft lint-free cloth wipe the outside and inside of the connecting portions thoroughly and regularly. No lubrication of these connecting parts is necessary on an instrument in good condition. However, if they fit together with difficulty even though they are clean a very light coating of petroleum jelly or prepared

cork grease will make them slide together easily. Avoid a heavy coating, and wipe off excess. When the connecting sleeves do not slide together easily the alignment of the parts is difficult and excess pressure is put on keys and rods.

2. *Failure to Align Head Joint.* The center of the embouchure hole must be lined up exactly with the tone holes on the top of the instrument. As a convenient and accurate way to insure proper alignment some authorities recommend scratching lines on the side of these two parts of the instrument once the exact correct alignment is established. When this is done it is simple to match the lines.

If the head joint is not properly aligned the holding position of the instrument becomes somewhat unnatural resulting in unsteady hand positions which in turn make holding and fingering the instrument more difficult than necessary. Improper alignment of the head joint does not normally affect the embouchure placement of the flutist, except early beginners, as the student will almost invariably turn the instrument to put the embouchure plate in the proper position sacrificing the most comfortable holding position of the instrument.

3. *Failure to align foot joint.* The foot joint must be aligned so that the rod on which the keys pivot is centered on the nearest tone hole. The most common mistake which inexperienced flute students make is to align the rod on the foot joint with the rod on the middle joint. The purpose of the correct alignment is to put the three keys on the foot joint in the best position for the little finger of the right hand to operate them. Improper alignment will pull the right hand out of position so that holding the instrument is unsteady and will make development of finger technique in the right hand difficult, as well as affecting embouchure development.

If the foot joint is turned too far up the student will of necessity put the fingers of the right hand too far over the tone holes so that the little finger can reach the keys. If the foot joint is too far down, the little finger must push forward or punch the keys rather than depressing them in the proper fashion.

4. *Holding the joints improperly.* In the preceding section on assembly, the exact holding position of each section for each operation was described in detail. If this is not done properly, there is undue strain on rods and keys which will bend them out of alignment. This will cause leaks in the pads covering holes which in turn make some notes impossible or difficult to produce, and these leaks are difficult to locate and correct. Mechanism which is seriously bent will cause sluggish movement of keys to the point where technical development is adversely affected.

Checklist for Assembly

Observe the student in the operation of assembling the flute and check the following items. Incorrect items for older students should not be called to their attention until the entire process is completed; younger students should be corrected immediately. If any mistake is made the entire process should be repeated until perfect.

	Yes	No	Comments
1. Were parts removed from case carefully and in approved manner?			
2. Were protective caps in place on instrument in the case?			
3. Middle joint held properly in assembly with head joint?			
4. Head joint held properly in assembly with middle joint?			
5. Embouchure hole properly aligned with middle joint?			
6. Foot joint held properly in assembly with middle joint?			
7. Middle and head joints held properly with assembly of foot joint?			
8. Rod of foot joint properly aligned with middle joint?			
9. Were final checks and adjustments of alignment of head and foot joints made after completion of assembly?			

HOLDING POSITION FOR THE FLUTE

The way in which the flute is held influences both directly and indirectly the type of tone quality produced, the embouchure formation, intonation, and the development of technical facility. The proper position is one in which the head and body is in a comfortable relaxed position, in which the hands and arms fall naturally into position, and which permits the formation and development of the best embouchure as well as the efficient development of accurate and useful technical facility.

There is almost unanimous agreement among authorities on what the best playing position for flute is. The description and illustrations given here follow this standard. Seated, standing, and rest positions are given with details of hand and finger positions following in the next section.

Seated Position

The flute is held to the right of the body with the left hand closest to the head. The head is turned slightly (20° to 30°) to the left so that the right arm can be held in a comfortable position. The instrument angles slightly downward with the head tilted so that the line of the lips is parallel with the line of the flute. A downward angle of fifteen to twenty degrees is standard, although the exact angle is not as important as keeping the line of the lips parallel with the embouchure plate.

The instrument is held firmly in position through three points of contact with the body: (1) the base of the left forefinger, (2) the right thumb, and (3) the right little finger depressing the E-flat key. Head erect except for a slight tilt to the right, chin up, eyes straight ahead, with shoulders up but relaxed. Elbows are free from the body in a relaxed position. Both feet flat on the floor. Shoulders and back must not touch the back of the chair when playing. Turn the chair slightly to the right so that the back corner will not interfere with the right arm or shoulder.

Adjust the music stand so that music can be easily read in this position. When two students are playing from the same music, angle the chairs slightly toward the center of the stand so that the position of the body and instrument can remain correct.

Figure F-14. Seated Position (Front View).

Figure F-15. Seated Position (Side View).

Standing Position

The position of the instrument itself when the player is standing should be identical with that in the seated position. Only the position of the body itself is changed. Stand erect with feet slightly apart, one foot ahead of the other to help maintain balance. Head remains erect, with chin up and eyes straight ahead. Shoulders up but relaxed, and elbows free from the body. Raise the music stand, if one is being used, so that the head does not tilt downward. Every player should regularly spend a portion of his practice time standing to become at ease playing in a standing position.

Figure F-16. Standing Position (Front View).

Figure F-17. Standing Position (Side View).

Rest Position

In the standard rest position the flute is placed squarely across the legs with the tone holes up to keep moisture off of the pads. From this position the instrument can be quickly picked up and returned to playing position.

Figure F-18. Standard Rest Position.

HOLDING POSITIONS FOR OTHER INSTRUMENTS

The holding positions for other instruments in the flute family are identical with the C flute except for the adjustments in hand position which are necessary to accomodate the differing sizes of instrument. Most students will automatically assume the same positions that they use for the C instrument, but it is well for the instructor to check. The same basic principles apply.

1. The instrument angles slightly downward with the head tilted so that the line of the lips is parallel with the line of the instrument.
2. Elbows must be kept free of the body in a relaxed position.
3. Head is erect, except for a tilt to the right, chin is up, eyes straight ahead, and shoulders up but relaxed.

Rest positions across the legs with tone holes up are used for all instruments except the piccolo. Because of its small size, there is no rest position across the legs of the player in which the instrument can be placed with any safety at all. In the rest position it must be held loosely in the player's hand as shown in the photograph. If the player is wearing a coat it may be safely tucked into the outside breast pocket. Some players who double piccolo keep the instrument in an inside coat pocket both for safety and to keep the instrument warm. Do not put the instrument on a music stand where it can easily fall or be knocked off!

Common Faults in Holding Position

The way in which the flute is held influences the rate and potential degree of musical progress. Progress can be facilitated by a perfect holding position or it can be drastically slowed or even made impossible by a poor position. The instructor must check continually, especially during the first few months of study on the instrument, to correct any deviations before they become habitual. The player must learn to feel the correct position, and a continual check will help him achieve this. Every player should be encouraged to check his position daily in front of a mirror.

Figure F-19. Picolo Rest Position.

The following are the most commonly found faults in holding positions for the flute, and to some extent the piccolo. Since the piccolo is normally played by a flutist, any deviations from the standard will be transferred to that instrument. The effect of certain deviations is greatly magnified when the player transfers to the piccolo resulting in poor intonation, restricted range, and poor tone quality.

1. *Angle of flute.* Two angles are involved in the relationship between the flute and the embouchure.
   a. The horizontal or up and down, illustrated in the front view of the holding position. How far down from parallel is the end of the flute?
   b. The front to back relationship, illustrated in the side view of the holding position. Is the end of the flute forward or backward from a right angle with the body?

A check of photographs of the holding position given in various methods and texts reveals that the recommended horizontal angle of the instrument is between fifteen and twenty degrees from parallel with the floor. An angle of less than fifteen degrees puts undue strain on the right arm since it must be held up higher if the correct hand position is to be achieved.

An angle of more than twenty degrees demands an unnatural tilt of the head to the right if the proper relationship of the embouchure plate and the lips is maintained with consequent difficulty in breath control and support. This angle is all-important in the success which the student will have in forming and developing an embouchure, tone control, and in achieving the optimum hand positions. Remember, *the line of the lips must be parallel with the flute.* Have the student check frequently with a mirror.

The front to back angle of the instrument is also highly critical because of its effect on the formation and function of the embouchure. The flute should be held at a ninety-degree angle with the head, or to put it another way the end of the flute in playing position must be parallel with the lips. If the flute is pushed or pulled back from this parallel relationship, the angle of the embouchure hole with the lips is changed causing inefficient use of the breath which would then be directed toward a corner of the blow hole rather than directly across it. This situation results in a thin breathy tone, in difficulty in playing the lowest notes with full volume, in playing at all in the highest register, as well as multiplying intonation problems.

2. *Head inclined downward.* This problem is encountered in students at all stages of development, and is frequently encouraged by the habit of playing with a music stand which is too low, or by practicing at home with the music on a chair or table. When the head of a flute student is inclined downward one of two undesirable things happens: (1) the lower jaw is thrust out and held in a rather rigid position in order to produce an acceptable tone, or (2) the flute is rolled forward to help shape the embouchure putting hands in a cramped position. Frequently these happen together. A rigid lower jaw prohibits accurate control of intonation and makes intervals difficult and inaccurate, as well as reducing the potential tone quality. The cramped hand position tires the young student quickly and encourages poor posture, frequently to the extent of encouraging him to drape the right arm over the back of the chair. A cramped hand, usually caused by a bent wrist, makes technical advancement slow and inaccurate. The inclined head is easy to detect and should be corrected immediately. Have the student check frequently in a mirror to establish the proper position.

3. *Slouched body.* Varying degrees of poor posture occur in almost every student, especially the younger ones. Good posture must be stressed from the very first lesson, in every lesson, and in every rehearsal until good posture becomes a habit. Degrees of poor posture include shoulders slumped or curved forward, leaning against the back of the chair with the spine curved, feet crossed or hung over a rung on the chair, or unique with the flute, hanging the right arm over the back of the chair to help support the instrument. More often than not these occur in combination.

Poor posture affects breathing and breath control to the point that the students may find it impossible to support the tone adequately. This is especially important with the inexperienced flutist where problems of breath control are more acute than on other woodwinds. Poor posture pulls the arms, and consequently the fingers out of position making technical advancement slow, and technique rough and inaccurate. Emphasize to the students in as many ways as possible that good posture minimizes fatigue while poor posture increases it. Frequent checks by the student in a large mirror are invaluable in establishing the best posture.

4. *Arms and elbows.* The position of the arms and elbows in playing the flute tend to tire the beginning student more than on any other woodwind instrument, just as beginners tire quickly when studying the violin or viola. Good body posture and absolutely correct holding position of the instrument will help minimize this fatigue. Because of the physical discomfort of playing the instrument for long periods of time in the early stages of study, beginners should be instructed to practice no more than twenty minutes at a time without a break of a half hour or more. As the students become physically tired poor posture and holding position is greatly encouraged. It is at this point that the right arm begins to be hung over the back of the chair and the body to slouch.

5. *Moving the body while playing.* Excessive body movements while playing is more frequently found in advanced players than in beginners because the instrument itself does not restrict these movements in any way. Beating time with the end of the instrument, swaying back and forth in time with the music, grandiose flourishes of the instrument at the end of difficult passages, etc., are extremely distracting to the conductor of a group and to the other players, and frequently humorous to an audience.

All movements have a tendency to change the position of the embouchure plate on the lips, interfere with the coordination of the muscles controlling breath support and in general make for a poorer performance. The habit of body movement during performance is very difficult to correct once it becomes ingrained, since the player frequently doesn't realize he is doing it. Any such movements must be corrected immediately and firmly.

6. *Use of crutch.* A crutch on the flute is a device, similar to the right hand-rest used on the bassoon, which fitted into a socket on the body of the flute and rested in the crotch of the left thumb and index finger. Use of the flute crutch has virtually disappeared, and instruments being manufactured today are not equipped with the device, although some older instruments will still have the socket on them. The crutch was intended to assist in holding the flute, and to keep the right hand fingers in the best playing position. That it ever succeeded is doubtful, and its disappearance causes no regrets. No authority of today recommends its use, and if an older instrument which was provided with a place for the crutch is used, the socket into which it fitted should be removed from the body of the instrument. The socket, if allowed to remain will interfere with the establishment of the proper contemporary hand position.

HAND POSITIONS

The flute is supported at the base of the left forefinger, the right thumb and right little finger, and steadied with a slight pressure of the embouchure plate against the lower lip. If all of these are in the right place, the instrument is held firm and steady and there is no feeling of insecurity on the part of the student. It is easier to achieve a good hand position on the flute than on any other woodwind because of the way in which the key mechanism is arranged. There is no need for any muscular tension in the fingers, wrists, arms or shoulders. A comfortable relaxed position allows facility to develop rapidly.

The exact placement of the hands and shape of the fingers on the instrument will vary slightly from student to student according to the length of the fingers, especially the thumbs, but the basic procedure must be the same. The following step-by-step procedure for establishing the hand position on the flute should be studied thoroughly, perferably with an instrument so that a feel for the right position can be developed. Study both the text and the photographs carefully until they are perfectly clear.

The "Guide Position" which is given is the fundamental position for hands and fingers and should be maintained at all times except when the fingering for a note involves moving a finger temporarily to another location—a situation which is less frequent on the flute than on other woodwinds. This guide position puts all fingers into the best position for developing speed and accuracy.

A. Left Hand Position

1. Figure F-20. The body of the flute rests at the base of the index finger between the knuckle and first joint. The structure of the finger provides a small shelf for the instrument.

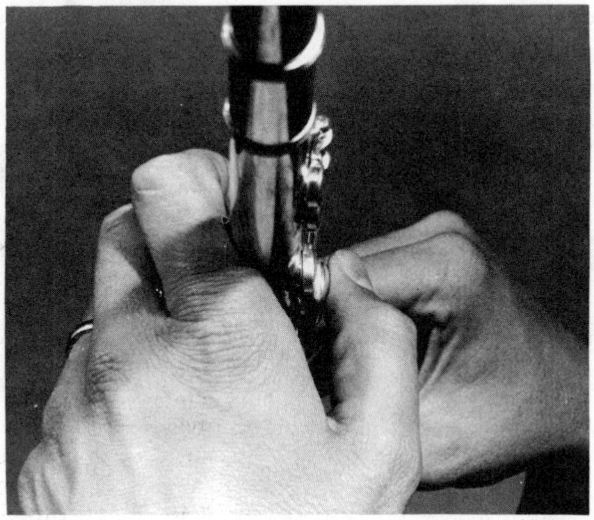

Figure F-20

2. Figure F-21. The thumb of the left hand is curved slightly to contact the B-natural lever with the ball of the finger.

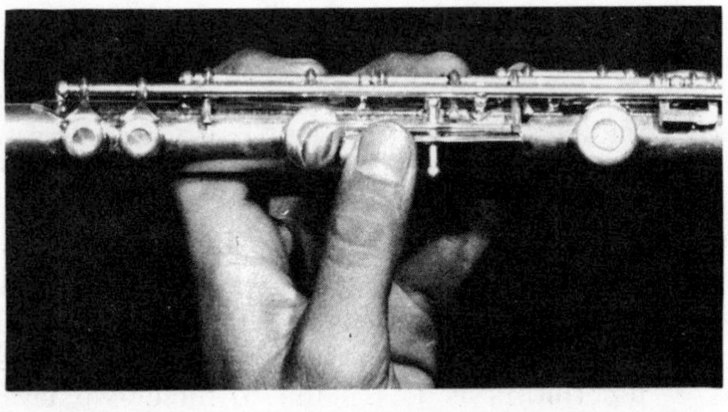

Figure F-21

3. Figure F-22. The remaining fingers are curved to contact the proper plates with the flesh beneath the nail. The index finger has considerable curve, the other fingers less and less curve, with the little finger only slightly curved and touching lightly the G-sharp key.

Figure F-22

B. Right Hand Position

1. Figure F-23. The body of the flute is supported on the cushion of the right thumb contacting the tube opposite the space between the first and second fingers.

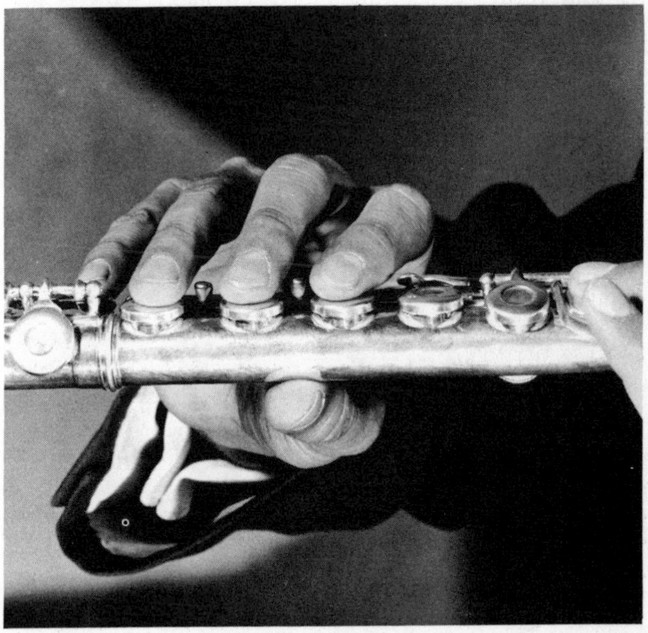

Figure F-23

2. Figure F-24. The little finger helps balance the instrument by depressing the D-sharp key (on all except four notes in the normal playing range). Cushions of the remaining fingers contact the center of the indentations of their keys. Fingers are at a right angle with the flute.

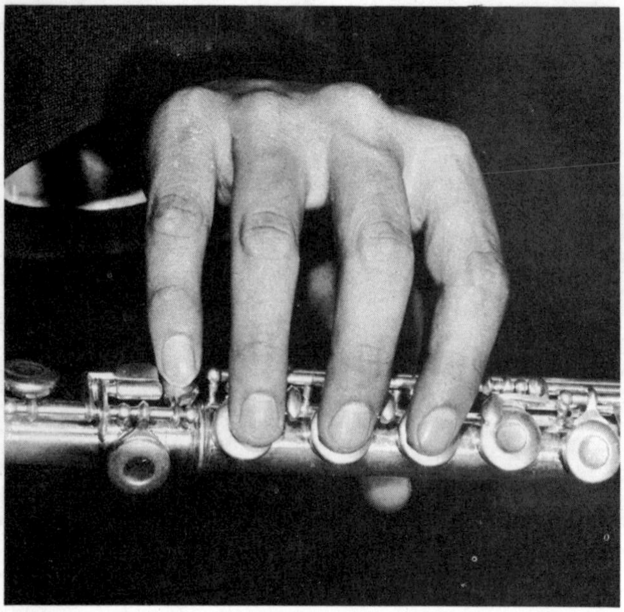

Figure F-24

C. Guide Position

1. Figure F-25. With the thumbs and little fingers in position there will be a definite "U" shape between the thumb and index finger of each hand. This is important if the fingers are to lie in a natural curve and not cramped. Keeping the little fingers in place adjust the position of instrument on the left index finger and the point of contact of the right thumb to achieve this shape.

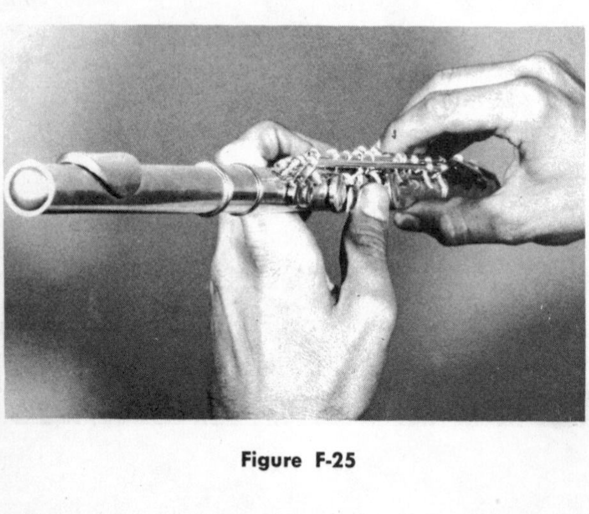

Figure F-25

2. Figure F-26. The photograph shows the guide position as observed by the teacher. Note the curve on the fingers of the left hand, and that the fingers of the right hand are at a right angle with the instrument. Little fingers are touching their keys. This position should be kept at all times while playing except when a finger of the right hand is moved to a trill key, or the little finger to a low C or C-sharp. Maintaining this guide position will help facilitate rapid progress. Check the guide position often until it becomes established and is automatic.

Figure F-26

Because of the physical construction of the flute in the Boehm System, the hand position is more comfortable and the fingerings less complicated than on any other woodwind instrument. There are no complex fingerings to pull the hand out of position to reach a side key, and the guide position can be established and maintained somewhat more easily and efficiently than on the other woodwinds. There is no excuse at all for a poor hand position on the flute.

The only alternate placement of fingers involves the use of the B-flat lever with the left thumb, three trill keys in the right hand, and the keys for low C and C-sharp with the right little finger. These are discussed in the following.

1. *Use of B-flat lever.* The left thumb may be as conveniently placed on the B-flat lever as on the B-natural lever. Figure F-27 shows the thumb in position on the B-flat lever. The normal position is on the B-natural lever. There is considerable confusion on the part of non-flutists as to the use of these two levers. Contemporary professional teaching treats this B-flat

as a trill or special fingering, to be used only on special occasions with the 100 400 fingering used as the standard fingering in both diatonic and chromatic passages. Keep the thumb on the B-natural lever except when the music clearly calls for the use of the B-flat lever. Never slide the thumb from th natural to the flat lever for two consecutive notes.

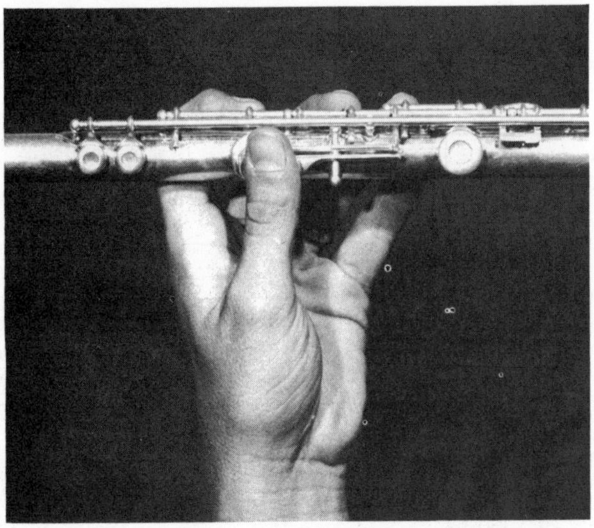

Figure F-27

The thumb does not slide easily and technique will be rough and uneven if this is done. The student will eventually learn to use both fingerings with equal facility and apply them according to the demands of the music. Refer to section on technique problems for a fuller discussion.

2. *Right hand trill keys.* The three trill keys operated by the three fingers of the right hand are: (1) the side B-flat key operated by the fourth finger; (2) the D-natural trill key operated by the fifth finger; and (3) the D-sharp trill key operated by the sixth finger. In operating these keys the hand must stay in the guide position with only the finger or fingers being used on these keys moved out of position. Figure F-28 shows the first finger moved out of guide position to operate the side B-flat lever. Keeping the little finger in place depressing the E-flat key helps maintain the correct position. Trills on which these keys are used are given in the trill fingering chart.

3. *Right little finger.* The previous discussion of finger position indicated that the right little finger should depress the E-flat key on all except a very few tones. It is important that the habit of using the E-flat key correctly be developed from the very beginning of flute study to help steady the instrument as well as to assist intonation and tone quality.

The right little finger is involved in the fingering for the low C and C-sharp. In playing these notes the little finger must be kept in a curved position and the key depressed with the ball of the finger. If necessary, adjust the foot joint so that those students with short fingers can reach these keys easily with the correct finger position. The low C key is provided with a roller on most flutes so that the finger can be rolled from the C to the C-sharp key and vice versa in a slurred chromatic passage. This rolling must be practiced at the time these low notes appear in the course of study in a chomatic relationship—normally after the student has been playing several months.

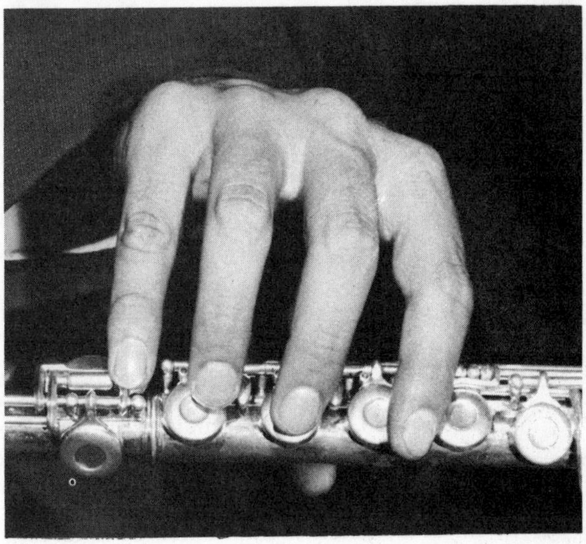

Figure F-28

Common Faults in Hand and Finger Positions

A good hand position is a great asset to the study of the flute, and is relatively easy to achieve. It will help develop facility and control, while a poor hand position retards this development. The first experiences with the instrument must emphasize hand position, and it must be continually checked until the best position for that particular player is established. Physical differences among students must be taken into account, but allow as little deviation from the standard as possible. The small hands of the grade school student frequently forces compromises, but with physical growth this should gradually change into the most desirable position. Some students do this naturally, while others must have constant reminders from the instructor.

A beginning player who persists in quickly establishing the proper positions makes rapid progress. The use of a mirror of sufficient size so that the student can see the entire length of the instrument is an asset in establishing position.

The items which are listed here are those with which problems occur most frequently, and are those to which the instructor should be alerted. Deviations in any of these will have an adverse affect on facility and technique and a combination of several will be a severe handicap to progress.

Checklist for Holding and Hand Positions

The following list of items provides a means of quickly checking holding positions and hand positions. The check should be performed while the student is playing and preferably when he is not aware that the check is being made. Any items which are checked "no" should be corrected with the deviation explained to the student, what effect it has on his playing, and why the correct position is important. Students make a more serious effort to correct mistakes if they thoroughly understand the reason.

A. *Holding Position*	Yes	No	Comments
1. Correct horizontal angle with body?			
2. Correct vertical angle with body?			
3. Head tilted to follow line of flute?			
4. Shoulders up but relaxed?			
5. Elbows free from body?			
6. Body posture good?			
7. Feet well placed?			
8. Height of music stand correct?			
9. Uses correct rest position?			
10. Excessive body movements?			

B. *Hand Positions*

1. Left index finger contacting flute at proper place for best support?			
2. Right thumb correctly placed?			
3. Left little finger touching G-sharp key?			
4. Right little finger depressing D-sharp key?			
5. Left thumb contacting key properly?			
6. Balls of fingers contacting keys			
7. "U" shape between thumbs and index fingers?			
8. Basic guide position maintained?			
9. Wrist flat?			
10. No muscular tension?			
11. Left thumb kept on B-natural lever?			
12. Fingers no more than one inch above tone plates?			
13. Fingers curved?			

1. *Left thumb.* The point at which the left thumb contacts the B-natural lever is highly critical in achieving the best position of the left hand. The most common error is to put the thumb too far up on the plate. This pulls the wrist down and forces the other fingers into a cramped position—especially the first finger which must have considerable curve under normal circumstances. This upward extension of the thumb is sometimes caused by having the flute too far down on the index finger. Check this first of all.

The normal position calls for a "U" shaped opening between the thumb and index finger, and achieving this, with the little finger in position on its key, will usually put the thumb in the proper place. In the correct position the wrist is virtually flat. An upward hump in the wrist will pull the thumb too far down on the plate, pulling the first finger over the instrument so that it is no longer curved, but in a right angle at the first joint.

2. *Left little finger.* The normal position for the left little finger is a natural curve, touching but not pressing the G-sharp key. Common errors in this position include the habit of putting the finger beneath the key to help support the instrument, or extending it upward in a stiff position. Both errors cause muscular tension in the entire hand, and must be avoided. Check frequently in the early stages of development for once this habit is established it is difficult to correct. The student should be encouraged to check himself in a mirror frequently until the proper position is achieved.

3. *Right thumb.* The exact position for the right thumb for an individual player is determined by the length of his thumb in relation to the other fingers. The body of the flute must rest on the ball of the thumb normally orientated between the first and second fingers above the flute. This position usually gives the most security to the holding of the instrument. However, it can be moved up or down the instrument to put it slightly closer to the first or to the second finger if necessary to put the other fingers at a right angle with the instrument.

The thumb can be moved forward or backward on the instrument to the place where the fingers fall in a natural curve over the top. There is considerable fluctuation in the exact place on the ball of the finger contacting the instrument. Some authorities, and these are in the minority, recommend that the thumb contact the side of the flute with the tip of the thumb. While an experienced player can hold the flute in this way, an inexperienced student will have a strong feeling that the instrument is not being held securely with the result that the embouchure plate moves on the lower lip. If the thumb is too far under the instrument contacting it near or on the joint, the fingers are forced into a sharp curve and contact the keys with the tips rather than the ball of the fingers. This tense and cramped position is a decided handicap to technical development.

4. *Right little finger.* The most common fault with the right little finger is the failure to keep the D-sharp key depressed. This is especially prevalent in those students who have transferred from the clarinet or another woodwind as a continually depressed key is unique with the flute. This depressed key is quite important as it is one of the points of support and control of the instrument, and if not used, gives the student a feeling of insecurity in holding the instrument. In addition the open key adds resonance to the tone, and must be open if all tones on the instrument are to be perfectly in tune. Check carefully and continually from the very beginning of study on the instrument on the use of this finger.

5. *Sliding left thumb.* Use of the left thumb on the B-natural and B-flat levers has been discussed. Some students develop the unfortunate habit of using only the thumb B-flat which forces them to slide the thumb from one lever to the other. The instrument is not constructed to facilitate this procedure, and as a result technique is uneven, and in fact, many incorrectly inflected B's result from this habit. Most authorities agree that the 100 400 fingering for B-flat should be the only fingering used in the beginning stages of flute study, with the thumb B-flat introduced after some facility is attained. If a student has developed the habit of sliding the thumb, introduce the other fingering for B-flat and insist that he use it exclusively until facility is developed.

6. *Right hand trill keys.* While these keys are not used to a great extent in the beginning stages of study, it is nevertheless necessary that they be used properly. Insist that the hand be kept in the full guide position except for the finger concerned. Most students will be well into the intermediate stage of development before encountering the need to use these keys, and hand position will be well established. For this reason it is not difficult to maintain the correct position of all fingers.

EMBOUCHURE FORMATION

An embouchure may be defined as the formation of the performer's lips with supporting muscles, teeth and jaws in relation to the embouchure hole which have to do with tone production. A good embouchure may be defined as one which, over the entire range of the instrument, produces (or is capable of producing) a rich, full-bodied, clear tone; plays perfectly in tune; allows the full scope of articulations with minimum effort; allows the full range of dynamics to be played with complete control; plays and is controlled with a minimum of physical exertion. A poor embourchure is one in which any one of these criteria is lacking or is deficient in any way.

The flute is unique among the woodwinds in that there is no vibrating reed for the performer to contend with. Embouchure formation and development, lies entirely within the physical control of the player who does not have to be involved with the complexities of mouthpieces and/or reeds. Unlike those instruments which produce a tone with a reed which is constantly changing and having to be replaced, the embouchure plate and hole on the flute remain constant and unchanging. This is an advantage, but the flute has the disadvantage, since the entire control does lie with the player, of requiring a highly flexible and accurate embouchure development.

The flute tone is technically described as an "edgetone" in the study of acoustics. Briefly this means that the stream of air is concentrated and directed toward a sharp edge where it is set into turbulence. In the instance of the flute, part of the turbulent air is going into the flute and part escaping into the open air. This concept of splitting the air stream into two parts is basic to understanding how the flute embouchure works. The function of the embouchure is to direct the air stream toward the far edge of the embouchure hole in such a way as to produce the desired quality and pitch of tone.

There is probably more unanimity of opinion on the desirable embouchure for the flute than on any other woodwind instrument. The wide divergence of opinion on the proper formation found with the other woodwinds simply doesn't exist for the flute, although there are slight differences which occur because of physical differences in the players themselves. The following is the standard procedure for shaping the embouchure. Use the head joint alone until the student's embouchure is set.

1. Hold the head joint with the embouchure hole against the lips. Feel with the tongue so that the hole is centered on the lips.
2. Roll the joint forward until the embouchure hole is parallel with the floor, and so that the lower lip covers one-fourth to one-third of the hole.
3. Keeping the lower lip relaxed, pull the corners of the mouth back slightly to firm the upper lip.
4. Allow the center of the upper lip to relax to produce an opening no more than one-sixteenth of an inch high and one-half inch long. This opening desirably should be more of a diamond shape than an oval. It is never circular. Figures F-29, F-30, and F-31 show three views of the properly formed embouchure.

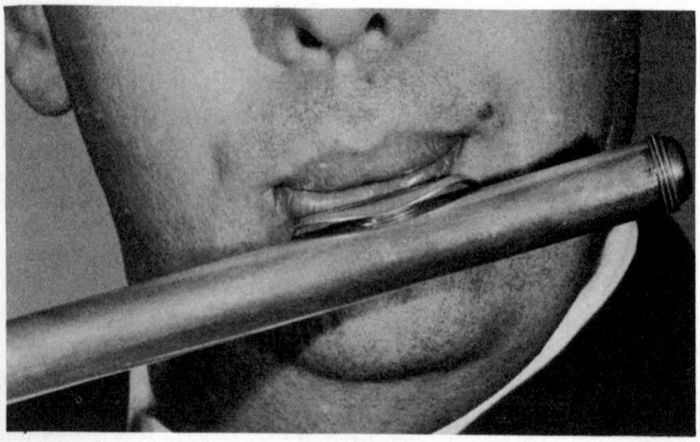

Figure F-29

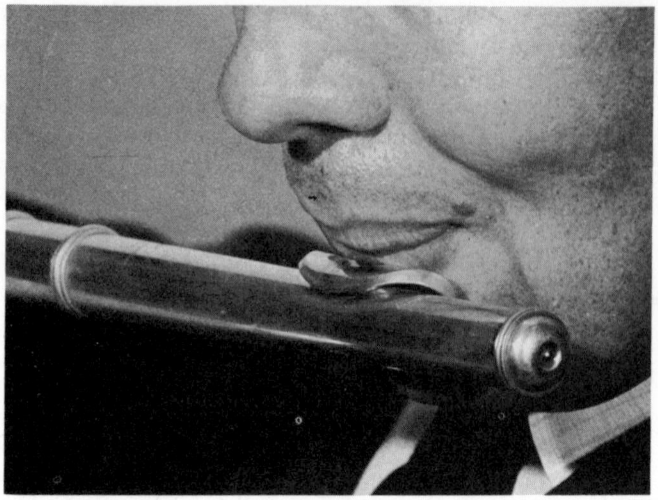

Figure F-30

Figure F-31

Setting the Embouchure

The following should be done in front of a mirror. Using the head joint alone, form the basic embouchure as described. Hold the joint with the left hand and stop the open end with the right. Using standard abdominal breath support, blow a gentle concentrated stream of air through the hole in the lips directed toward the opposite edge of the embouchure hole rather than down into it. Move the lower jaw and lips slowly back and forth until a tone which approximates the pitch of second space "A" is produced. Continue to experiment with the speed of air through the lips and the adjustment of the lower jaw and the lips until a rather full steady tone can be sustained for at least ten seconds.

Open the end of the head joint and repeat the process, this time producing a pitch which approximates the "A" first time above the treble clef. It will be found that to produce this pitch requires a slightly greater pressure of the breath, and a change in its direction achieved by pushing the jaws and lips slightly more forward to direct it more across the hole rather than down. Continue to experiment with wind velocity and direction until a full steady tone on this pitch can be sustained for at least ten seconds. When these tones produced by the closed and open head joint can be produced easily, the student is ready to assemble the complete instrument and proceed with the regular course of instruction.

However older students and students with a strong natural aptitude for the flute can experiment further with the head joint alone to produce harmonics in addition to the two fundamentals. With the end of the head joint closed a pitch of approximately "E" third line above the staff can be produced, and with the end of the head joint opened a pitch approximating "A" fifth space above the clef can be produced. These are produced by using a greater velocity of air and by adjustments of the lower jaw and lips. They are not easily produced by many students, and it is not wise to insist that all students be able to produce them before continuing with the complete instrument. Those students who are able to produce these harmonics easily will be able to make more rapid progress in tone production in the early stages of instruction than those who cannot. These approximate pitches are produced with the head joint closed and open.

Closed end Open end

Success in producing a clear full tone on the flute is determined by: (1) the amount of embouchure plate covered by the lower lip, (2) the direction of the stream of air, (3) the focusing of a concentrated stream of air determined by the size and shape of the aperture formed by the lips; and (4) the use of standard abdominal breathing and breath support. Each of these factors is closely related with all others and cannot be altered without changing another factor. The problem in achieving a fine flute embouchure is to bring all these factors into the proper relationship with each other. These factors are not static in performance but constantly changing to control pitch, intonation, dynamics, and tone quality. The influence of each is considered separately in the following:

1. *Standard abdominal breathing and breath support.* This procedure is standard for all wind instruments, and without it no great progress on an instrument is possible. The flute is especially critical in respect to breathing as the production of an edge tone is inherently wasteful of breath. Beginning flutists are notoriously short of breath because they have not learned to use the embouchure and instrument efficiency.

Dizziness is a common complaint of the beginning flutist. It is the result of hyperventilation (more than normal breathing both in amount and frequency of breaths taken which puts too much oxygen into the blood stream). The body soon adjusts to this and the dizziness will pass. However, when a student becomes dizzy he should stop playing until the dizziness is gone. Breathing exercises, combined with regular and brief practice sessions on the flute will soon eliminate the dizzy spells. Some students become alarmed at the dizziness and it is well to explain its cause and how it can be eliminated.

2. *Aperture shape and size.* The size and shape of the aperture formed by the lips is of prime importance to control the amount, direction and shape of air being directed across the embouchure plate. The exact size and shape can be seen only when the student is producing a sound. It should be roughly diamond shaped as shown in Figure F-32. The exact size of the aperture varies directly with the octave being played: larger for the first octave, smaller for the second octave, and still smaller for the third octave: larger for softer dynamic levels and smaller for louder ones within the basic size for the octave being played.

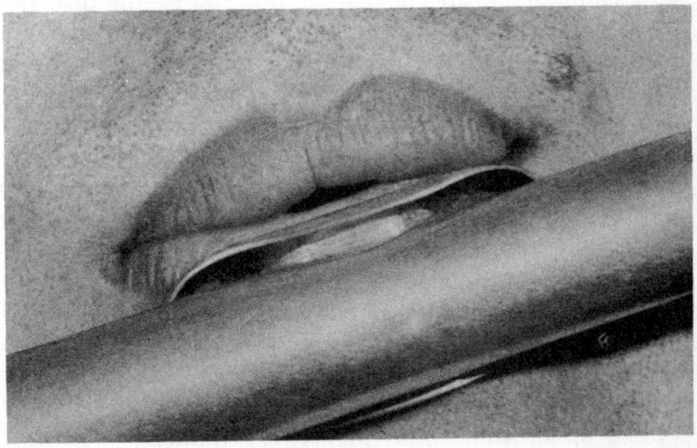

Figure F-32

The function of this aperture is to first, shape the stream of air into a concentrated and well-focused flow, and secondly to control the amount and intensity of the flow. The shape of the air stream must be wide enough from side to side to strike the entire width of the embouchure hole and narrow from top to bottom to avoid wasting air. This shape can best be achieved when the corners of the lips are pulled back slightly with the upper lip firm and the lower lip relaxed. Avoid a pucker in the lips which shapes a round aperture. The round shape of the air stream produced strikes only a portion of the opposite edge of the embouchure hole and produces a breathy noisy tone quality.

The air stream coming from the lips must be centered in the side to side relationship with the embouchure hole. Move the flute from side to side on the lower lip until this hole is centered. Many normal lips do not naturally form the aperture exactly in the center of the lips, and the flute must be adjusted to the student's lip formation. This adjustment is basic, and must be done at the very beginning of flute study.

3. *Amount of embouchure plate covered by lower lip.* In the first octave of the flute range in which the beginning student first plays approximately one-fourth to one-third of the embouchure hole is covered by the lower lip. The exact amount to be covered varies from individual to individual depending on the other factors involved, and must be the subject of considerable experimentation.

A good starting position for this experimentation is to put the inner edge of the embouchure hole at the lower edge of the lip on the line where the lip and the chin meet. The exact adjustment is then done by ear. More of the hole may be covered by: (1) moving the flute down on the lip, or (2) rolling the flute in slightly. Less of the hole will be covered by: (1) moving the flute up on the lip, or (2) by rolling the flute out slightly.

The exact adjustment is strongly affected by the size and shape of the aperture in the lips and by the direction of the stream of air. The first experiments in determining the amount of hole to be covered are best done by rolling the flute back and forth, then if a major adjustment is necessary moving the flute up or down on the lip.

If too little of the hole is covered by the lower lip: (1) the air stream is used inefficiently and too much is required to produce a tone, (2) very little dynamic range is possible and the general amount of tone produced is small, (3) a tone of poor quality—uncontrolled and breathy—is produced, (4) the range is limited, and (5) notes in the third octave will be difficult to produce and control.

If too much of the hole is covered by the lower lip: (1) a small thin tone quality is produced, (2) very little dynamic range is possible—the tone will disappear entirely when the student attempts to play softly, (3) articulation is limited and slow in response, (4) a true legato is difficult in certain passages. Covering too much of the embouchure hole is a great temptation for beginners as it requires less than the normal amount of air to produce a tone. Watch this closely.

Once the basic amount of hole to be covered is discovered and established the small adjustments in this amount which are required for playing in the various octaves of the instrument, for controlling dynamics, and for controlling intonation, are made by a slight back and forth movement of the lower jaw and lips. The lower jaw and lips are pulled back for the low tones and forward for the high ones.

This movement of the lower jaw and lips also controls the direction of the air stream, and it must be emphasized again that the amount of hole covered and the direction of the air stream are very closely interrelated. In a performance by an advanced flutist these movements of the jaw and lips are quite noticeable and almost constant as he adjusts for tone placement, intonation, and dynamics.

Avoid at all costs making these adjustments in amount of hole covered and direction of the air stream by rolling the flute in and out or by moving the head up and down. Such movements hinder rather than help progress on the instrument; it is not possible to make the rapid and delicate adjustments necessary for fine performance in this way.

4. *Direction of the stream of air.* The tone of the flute is produced by a stream of air which is blown toward the opposite edge of the embouchure hole, part of it going into the flute and part into the open air. Contrary to the unfortunate popular opinion blowing a flute is *not* the same as making a sound on a jug or pop bottle. The size, shape, and location of the flute embouchure plate and hole are the result of the most careful acoustical calculations and it resembles only slightly the acoustical conditions of a jug. A student who begins his study of the flute with the concept that blowing a flute is like blowing a pop bottle begins with a severe handicap which is difficult to overcome.

The direction of the air stream determines how much air will go into the instrument and how much into space, producing corresponding changes in the turbulence of the air which in turn control both pitch and volume. The actual direction is controlled by forward and backward movements of the corners of the lips working with corresponding movements of the lower jaw. While for the purposes of this discussion we are isolating the direction of the air stream, in actual practice it is closely interrelated to and is inseparable from breath support, intensity of the air stream, and amount of embouchure hole covered by the lower lip.

The actual direction of the air must be determined by considerable experimentation, and control established by experience and practice. As a guide to the effect of the direction of the air stream some general statements may be made. The more downward the air stream: (1) the lower in pitch the flute will respond, and (2) the louder the volume of sound produced. Conversely the more outward the air stream is directed: (1) the higher in pitch the flute will respond, and (2) the softer the volume.

In performance, then, the direction of the air stream is used with extremely small adjustments to control the intonation on individual notes, and with somewhat greater adjustments to control the octave in which a note will sound. As a general guide to students on the beginning and intermediate levels the concept of the direction of the air stream changes with the octave. Once a good embouchure is established, the student may visualize the direction of the air more downward in the octave:

More across the hole in the octave:

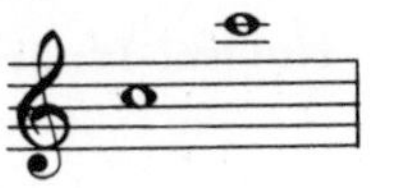

and more in an upward direction in the octave:

These slight changes, which are more conceptual than literal, are accomplished by slight forward and backward movements of the lower jaw. Octave skips, for example, will result in quite noticeable movements of the lips and lower jaw changing the direction of the air stream as well as the amount of embouchure hole covered by the lower lip. The movement of the lips has many similarities to the movement of a brass instrument player as he changes pitch on his instrument.

TUNING

As a non-transposing instrument, the flute sounds the pitch written for it. The instrument is designed so that it will sound A-440 when the head joint is pulled about an eighth of an inch from the middle joint. This allows some margin of safety so that the instrument can be played slightly sharper than standard pitch if necessary. For the proper development of temperament and intonation on the instrument it is important that all students tune regularly to A-440, making use of a tuning bar or an electronic tuner, and practice with the instrument adjusted to this pitch. If the instrument is in tune with the head joint pulled out an eighth of an inch, all practice which the student does should be done with it in this adjustment.

The pitch adjustment of the instrument in basic tuning is made only at the head joint-middle joint juncture. If the instrument is being played so flat that it is still low in pitch with the head joint all the way in, or conversely if it is being played so sharp that the head joint must be pulled out more than a quarter of an inch, the problem lies in the embouchure formation and not in the instrument. If the head joint is pulled out more than three-eighths of an inch in order to bring the instrument down to pitch, intonation on the instrument suffers and it is virtually impossible to play the instrument in tune with itself.

Cork in Head Joint

The tuning cork (or plug) in the end of the head joint is there simply to close the end of the pipe. The exact location of this cork is highly critical for tuning and intonation, and once it is properly located must not be moved. The end of the cork must be exactly seventeen millimeters from the center of the embouchure hole. So that this distance can be checked, the cleaning rod which is provided with the instrument has a line etched in the metal at this distance from one end. To check the distance, insert the

Checklist for Flute Embouchure Formation

The following check on flute embouchure formation must be made while the student is playing and preferably when he is not aware that a check is being made. Any errors should be carefully explained to the student, and the correction worked out with him while he is observing the embouchure in a mirror. Remedial measures can be assigned on the basis of this list.

	Yes	No	Comments
1. Flute parallel with line of lips?			
2. Aperture in lips centered in side-to-side relationship with embouchure hole?			
3. Proper amount of embouchure hole covered by lower lip?			
4. Size and shape of aperture in lips correct?			
5. Air stream properly directed?			
6. Corners of mouth pulled back slightly?			
7. Direction of air stream controlled by lips and lower jaw?			
8. Produces clear, full-bodied tone?			

cleaning rod carefully into the end of the head joint until it is touching the stopper. The etched line, as shown in Figure F-33, should be exactly in the center of the embouchure hole. If the tuning plug is too far toward the closed end, unscrew the cap on the end, and push the plug into place. If it is too far toward the open end, tighten

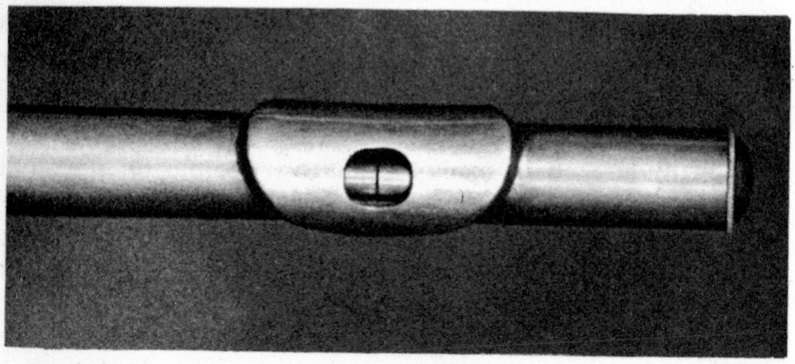

Figure F-33

the cap slowly until it is pulled into place. If it is necessary to unscrew the cap, tighten it so that it moves gently into place. Screwing the cap firmly will pull the cork out of place. In the absence of an etched cleaning rod, the plug can be adjusted by tuning the three octave "D's" to as close to perfect octaves as possible.

Beginning students should be warned rather early in their study about keeping the plug in place. Frequently it is pulled out of place by the student who will loosen or tighten the cap without thinking or who will push it out of place inadvertently when the instrument is being cleaned after use.

Should it ever be necessary to remove the plug from the instrument, remove the screw cap and push the plug out the end of the head joint which fits into the middle joint of the instrument. The head joint of the instrument is slightly conical with the closed end appreciably smaller than the open end. Forcing the plug out the small end could damage the cork so that it will leak. This plug should be removed only under the most urgent circumstances, and preferably by an expert repairman. Students who are curious about the construction of their new instruments must be warned not to remove or tamper with the plug.

INTONATION

The basic mechanical design of the flute as developed by Boehm produced an instrument which is inherently as well in tune as it is possible to produce an instrument which plays in the tempered scale. While there are small differences from manufacturer to manufacturer the temperament of the instrument is such that, with the proper embouchure formation and control, it can be played perfectly in tune. With modern manufacturing techniques and research in the production of instruments, any serious intonation problems can be traced to their source and corrected.

Natural Tendencies of the Instrument

The first octave of the flute is produced by the fundamental vibrations of the pipe, the second octave by the first (or octave) overtone, the third octave by the second or third overtone (the twelfth and double octave above the fundamental). Since the frequencies of the natural overtones do not correspond exactly with the corresponding frequencies demanded by the tempered scale, the intonation of the flute is comprised somewhat by the design in order that all notes in all octaves can be played in tune with the average good embouchure.

The natural tendencies of the instrument are as follows:

Tendency to be sharp:

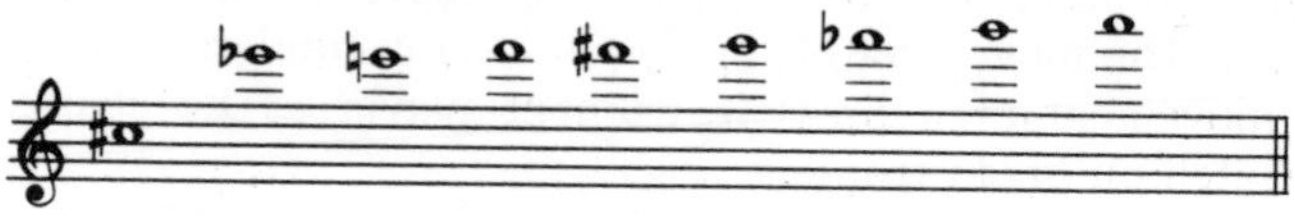

Tendency to be flat:

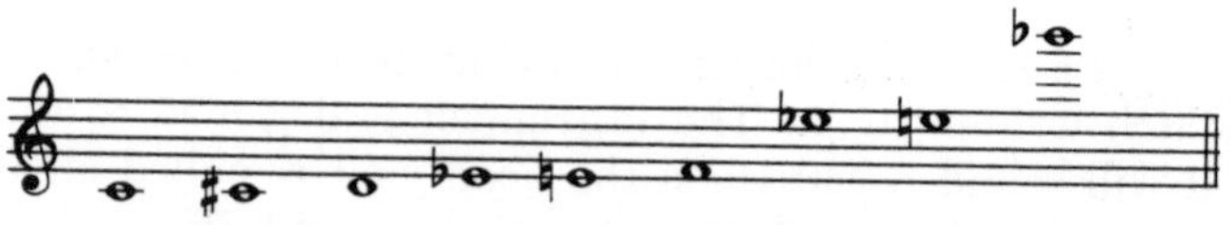

The notes in the first and second octaves may, with some experience and a well-controlled embouchure, be easily adjusted to play in tune. The third octave requires more adjustment, although fingerings have been selected which overcome to some degree the natural tendencies of the instrument. Because of the embouchure adjustments needed to produce and play tones in the third octave in tune, it is well to delay extending the range of the student into this area until he is playing and controlling notes in the first and second octaves with ease and precision.

Effect of Embouchure on Intonation

The all-important role of the embouchure on intonation has been alluded to several times. In reality all intonation problems, other than mechanical ones with the instrument, can be traced to and corrected by the embouchure working in conjunction with breath support. It is for this reason that so much stress must be placed from the very beginning of study on accurately forming and developing the embouchure.

Two factors of embouchure which effect the pitch are:

1. The direction of the stream of air can be changed slightly to alter the pitch of individual notes.

The more downward the air is directed into the embouchure hole, the flatter the pitch; and conversely, the more across the hole the higher the pitch. Changes in direction of the air stream are accomplished by moving the jaw forward and backward for major adjustments. As the jaw is pulled back, air is directed more into the hole; and as it is moved forward, the air is directed more across the hole. Minor adjustments in the pitch of individual notes are accomplished more efficiently by small movements of the corners of the mouth, with jaw movements reserved for large adjustments and changes in the octave in which the notes appear.

2. The placement of the embouchure plate on the lower lip effects overall pitch as well as intonation.

If the plate is too low, the overall pitch will be flat; if the plate position is too high on the lip, the overall pitch will be sharp. This is one of the first things to look for when a student is playing consistently flat or sharp beyond the normal range of tuning with the head joint. This high or low placement of the plate has an adverse effect on tone quality as well.

These adjustments are the product of critical listening on the part of the player whose attention must be called to the necessity of making them very early in beginning study. The use of an electronic aid is highly recommended for establishing normal intonation in the student's ear. With experience, these embouchure adjustments become automatic.

Dynamics and Intonation

Dynamics—loudness or softness—on the flute are controlled by the velocity of the air stream striking the embouchure hole. The greater the velocity the louder the tone. The pitch of the flute and other instruments, such as the tonette and song flute, on which the sound is produced by an edge-tone is directly affected by the velocity of the air stream. The greater the velocity the sharper the pitch. Thus, in making a diminuendo the pitch will get flatter and flatter and in a crescendo the pitch will get sharper and sharper unless the embouchure compensates. This compensation is done by simultaneously changing the direction of the air stream striking the embouchure hole. As the velocity of the air diminishes and the tone becomes softer the direction of the air stream is gradually raised by a forward movement of the lips and lower jaw so that it is directed more across the hole. In a crescendo as the velocity of the air increases to make the tone louder the direction of the air stream is gradually changed so that it is directed more and more into the embouchure hole. This delicate and demanding relationship between velocity and direction of the air stream must be consciously developed, and progresses simultaneously the development of the embouchure only if attention is devoted to it. The regular practice of long tones with crescendo and diminuendo should be a part of every flutist's daily schedule.

Playing Position and Intonation

A playing position which is incorrect in any aspect can have an adverse effect on intonation.

1. A slouched position which makes breath support inadequate makes control of wind velocity difficult or impossible with the consequences usually being flatting in pitch.

2. The angle at which the instrument is held is important and becomes a problem in intonation if the angle of the flute doesn't follow the line of the lips. This deficiency results in the air stream striking the embouchure hole at an angle rather than directly and accentuates the natural tendencies of the instrument toward being out of tune.

3. Tilting the head up or down changes the direction of the stream of air, and will produce an overall flatness or sharpness in pitch. Tilting the head to change the pitch is not recommended.

Mechanical Factors and Intonation

If a player is to achieve the very best intonation, the instrument upon which he is playing must be in perfect mechanical condition. On the flute two mechanical factors influence intonation, leaky pads and the height of the pads above the tone holes.

1. Leaky pads may be caused by bent rods or keys, by incorrectly set adjusting screws, or by simple deterioration of the covering of the pads. Pads deteriorate so slowly that frequently the student is not aware of any change at all, so a regular inspection of their condition is called for. A leaky pad will cause a note or notes to respond with difficulty and somewhat sharp in pitch.

Leaky pads caused by bent rods or keys seem to occur most frequently on the lower end of the instrument, especially the foot joint. Many students cannot produce low C or C-sharp because of leaks, and if they can the pitch is impossible to control. These notes are naturally quite flat in pitch and do not readily respond to embouchure adjustments when there is a leak.

2. The height of pads above the tone holes is quite critical for perfect intonation. Frequently, the pad cups are bent up or down by various kinds of accidents or through careless assembly. Look for this condition when one or two notes are consistently out of tune.

A pad which is too close to the tone hole tends to flatten the pitch, while a pad which is too far above the tone hole will sharpen the pitch. An unadjusted pad will have the greatest effect on the note which is the first hole down the pipe from the head joint, as well as other notes to a lesser degree. It does not, of course, affect a note when it is in the closed position.

Inspect the instrument regularly for height of the pad cups. All of them should be the same distance above their tone holes. If any of them are out of line, the correction should be made by an expert repairman, unless the correction can be made by an adjusting screw. Do not attempt to bend keys on the instrument yourself unless you have the proper tools.

Alternate Fingerings and Intonation

The flute has fewer alternate fingerings than any other woodwind instrument except the saxophone. The most useful alternate fingerings in the first two octaves are those for B-flat which does not effect pitch, and an alternate fingering for F-sharp which may effect pitch to a slight degree.

There are many useful alternate fingerings for notes

in the third octave. The alternate fingerings in this register provide one means of controlling intonation both with the instrument and in ensemble playing. Different instruments and different players will produce slightly different pitches with alternate fingerings in this register. The first fingering provided in the fingering chart is the one that the greatest percentage of players will find to be closest in tune. If, for some reason it is not, then try another fingering.

The player should be aware of the alternate fingerings for the various notes and should be able to use them with facility. He should check the pitch relationships between the fingerings for the same note and be aware of them. The pitch differences between alternate fingerings will vary from player to player and it is impossible to make a positive statement on what these differences will be. It is frequently necessary to select a fingering for the sake of perfect intonation rather than the fingering that offers the best facility. The player must never hesitate to put intonation before facility.

TONE

The most valuable asset of any flutist is a beautiful tone, and it is to this purpose that the student must direct his constant attention. The quality of the tone must be the same over the entire range of the instrument and at all dynamic levels. The better the balance of quality over the instrument the better the musical results and the more favorable the playing is to the listener.

The range of the flute is divided into three registers commonly called the first octave, the second octave, and the third octave:

First Octave   Second Octave   Third Octave

Notes above high C in the third octave can be played by professional level players, and are called for in the music of some contemporary composers. This is called the *fourth octave,* or the *extended range.* Notes in this range are included in the fingering chart at the end of the book. Notes in the first octave are produced by the fundamental vibration of the air column, those in the second octave by the column of air vibrating in two segments (the first partial), and the notes in the third and fourth octaves produced by the column of air vibrating in three, four or possibly five segments (the third, fourth, and fifth partials of the overtone series).

Beginners on the instrument tend to have a discernibly different tone quality in each of the three octaves as they extend their playing range. In addition to the details of tone production much of the student's attention needs to be directed to the problem of matching quality over the entire instrument.

There is no single standard for determining what is a good tone on the flute, although there tends to be less difference in tone qualities of the best professionals than on any of the other woodwind instruments. Every teacher and flute student should take advantage of every opportunity to hear live performances of fine instrumentalists. If this is not possible, study the recorded performances of the flute repertoire on a high quality phonograph. Compare the tone qualities of the various artists.

With the universality of the phonograph record, it is quite possible to study the sounds of fine musicians from France, Germany and other nations as well as our own artists. A careful comparison of tone qualities produced by artists from other nations will reveal some differences, although these differences are not as easily detected via the phonograph recording as they are in personal performance. In spite of the differences all the tone qualities will be pleasing as they will have in common the essential elements of a good tone: clarity, body, and perfect intonation.

Common Problems in Tone

A good tone is the product of all the elements involved in performance: instrument, embouchure and breath support. If any of these is defective, then the tone quality suffers accordingly. Problems of tone production and quality are many and varied, but may usually be traced to their source and must be corrected immediately. Following are some of the most prevalent problems or faults in tone:

1. *Small or weak tone.* This is a common fault with beginning flutists, but is found among more technically advanced students as well. In most instances it can be traced directly to poor breathing habits and lack of support. Check the inhalation process of the student to see that the breathing is diaphragmatic rather than in the chest, and that the student has the proper concept of support with the diaphragm and abdominal muscles. Remedial measures should be assigned. If breathing appears to be correct, it is possible that the throat is tight restricting the flow of air at this point. Work for an open relaxed throat so that the air can get out.

The second condition which could produce a small, weak tone is the placement of the embouchure plate on the lower lip. If thé plate is too far down on the lower lip, too much of the embouchure hole is covered and not enough air is entering the instrument to produce the desired tonal body. Move the plate on the lower lip so that no more than one-fourth of the embouchure hole is covered.

2. *Hollow tone.* The hollow unfocused sound is a typical problem in tone for a great many students. It, like other tonal problems, is caused by the lack of a

etc. to comfortable limit of range

mental standard of sound on the part of a student who doesn't know that this particular quality is undesirable in the instrument. This sound is achieved when too little of the embouchure hole is covered, and is usually accompanied by a chronic shortage of breath. This sound is also achieved by those students who have the concept of, and form the embouchure for a pop bottle or jug. And if the student is allowed to progress in this fashion without correction the flute begins to sound like a chromatic jug band. Students with the hollow tone sound will always have difficulty in playing in the third octave of the instrument.

The correction for this sound is simply to move the embouchure plate to the correct position on the lower lip and to correct the direction and control of the air stream. Since major changes in embouchure formation and control are increasingly difficult to achieve as the student's technical facility and experience increases, this type of tone quality must be detected early in the beginning stage and remedial measures taken immediately.

3. *Shrill high register.* The tones of many players who have acceptable quality in the first two octaves tend to thin out and become shrill in the third octave. Theoretically, if the student is achieving an acceptable quality in the lower octaves, this should not happen. If it does, it usually means that he simply isn't listening to his tone and attempting to match the quality over the entire range of the instrument. This condition sometimes exists when the extension of the student's range into the third octave is delayed too long, or when the tone studies—long tones, crescendo, diminuendo—are not applied to this octave with regular practice. This tone quality is frequently found when too little of the embouchure hole is covered by the lower lip which, in the third register, emphasizes the upper partials in the tone produced.

When this shrill quality exists in a student, check first the amount of embouchure hole covered and the forward movement of the lips and lower jaw necessary to close more of the embouchure hole and to redirect the air stream in a more upward direction for this register. If this situation is correct, assign tone studies of various kinds in the third register. Octave studies from the second to third register in crescendo and diminuendo as shown at the top of this page are excellent if the student is listening critically to both the tone quality and intonation.

4. *Control of soft tone.* Difficulty in producing and controlling a soft tone is principally due to the inability of the player to project a steady concentrated stream of air in the proper direction across the embouchure hole. Check breathing and breath support, and have the student practice focusing a steady stream of air into the palm of his hand or to bend steadily the flame of a candle.

A second possibility might be an aperture in the lips which is too large and which permits an air stream which is too large. This is causing the student to reduce support to make the tone soft, which in turn makes him lose control of the tone.

A third possible cause is that the air stream is directed too far down into the embouchure hole. As softer and softer dynamic levels are reached, the size of the opening in the lips must be slightly and gradually decreased, and the direction of the air stream gradually raised by a forward movement of the lips and lower jaw. There is a very close interrelation between the amount of air being used and the direction of the air stream which must be discovered and used by the player.

5. *Dynamics and tone quality.* Students with otherwise good tone quality will lose it when playing at extremes of loudness or softness. This is caused by an undeveloped, poorly formed or inadequately controlled embouchure, or by lack of proper breath control or a combination of both.

If tone quality and intonation are to be maintained in a cresendo, the amount of opening in the lips must gradually be increased, and the direction of the air stream gradually lowered through pulling back the lips and lower jaw while increasing the intensity of the air stream. To maintain tone quality in a decrescendo gradually decrease the size of the opening in the lips, change the direction of the air stream by a forward movement of the lips and lower jaw.

Briefly, the louder the tone the greater the intensity of the air stream, the larger the aperture in the lips, and the less of the embouchure hole covered. Conversely, the softer the tone the less the intensity of the air stream, the smaller the aperture in the lips, and the more embouchure hole covered. Good control is a combination of these three factors, and if they are in the proper balance both tone quality and intonation will remain good.

Recommended Material for Tonal Development

A book by Marcel Moyse *De La Sonorite: Art et Technique*, published by Alphonse Leduc has almost become the standard material for tone development. It lays out an organized plan for developing and matching tones, explained by a frequently awkward English text. Much of the material can be used by students on the intermediate level. Regular daily practice, properly done, on material from this book would be invaluable for any student.

TONGUING

Tonguing refers to the manner in which the tongue operates in relation to the aperture in the lips and breath support in order to articulate the tones. The placement and action of the tongue must be rapid and under complete control at all speeds, and at all dynamic levels. It must, in coordination with breath support, be able to produce on the flute all varieties of articulation from the hardest staccato to the softest legato. By skillful use of the tongue and breath the flutist is able to reproduce the sound and effect of the multitude of bow strokes used by a fine string player, plus the effects of double tonguing, triple tonguing, and flutter tonguing.

The absence of a mouthpiece and reed or a double reed to contend with makes articulation on the flute considerably simpler than on other woodwinds, for the tongue can physically act as a valve in controlling the flow of breath into the instrument. There is considerable unanimity of opinion among authorities on the placement of the tongue in flute articulation, although there are small differences in the imagery used to achieve this placement.

Fundamental Articulation

Fundamental articulation is the basic movement of the tongue used to start a note in the absence of any other marking on the music such as a staccato and for the first note under a slur. This articulation and the legato style must be thoroughly mastered by the beginning student before proceeding to any other type of articulation.

Fundamental articulation should be introduced and first practiced on notes in the mid-range of the instrument (within the staff). Use a mirror to check that the embouchure formation does not change and that there is no movement of the lips and jaw during articulation. The following step-by-step process will introduce this articulation.

1. Place the tip of the tongue on the front teeth at the base of the gum.
2. With the tongue in place so that no air can pass through the lips, build up air pressure against the tongue using standard abdominal support.
3. Release the air to produce the tone with a movement of the tongue as in pronouncing the syllable "tu," "ta," "du," or "da." The tone should start without a sudden increase in loudness.
4. Stop the tone (assuming a rest follows) by stopping the flow of air. Do not put the tongue back on the gum to stop the flow of air.
5. During the silence of the rest, repeat steps one and two and start the next tone.

When a series of articulated notes which are not separated by rests are played, the tongue moves in pronouncing the syllable selected to start each tone. Sustain each note for its full value. The process of starting the next tone automatically stops the preceding one. The tone is never stopped by the tongue except in such a series, and in practicing such a series the student must concentrate his attention solely on the beginnings of the notes. If the beginnings are correct, the endings of the preceding notes will also be correct.

An open throat for a free flowing stream of air is absolutely necessary for any type of articulation. Check the student visually for any sign of tenseness in the throat muscles. The syllables "tu," "ta," "du," and "da" have become standard to provide the imagery for the tongue action because when the tongue movement is correct they force an open throat and a low tongue.

With some experience the student will notice a difference in the type of articulation produced by "tu" or "ta" and "du" or "da"—the "du" movement producing a softer attack than the other syllables. More advanced flutists will take advantage of this difference to produce the exact sound demanded by the musical style. Beginners may find it helpful to try all four syllables to discover which works best for them at this stage.

The exact placement of the tip of the tongue is subject to some variation from teacher to teacher, but depends primarily on the length of the players tongue and the exact concept of the sound to be produced. Some authorities suggest that the tongue, in this type of articulation, be placed on the gum above the teeth, others suggest that it be placed somewhat down on the teeth so that the tip does not touch the gum at all. The placement of the tip against the teeth at the gum line is without a doubt the most common and the safest for the beginning student, who will automatically make adjustments of the placement up or down to suit his own physical characteristics as his facility is developed.

In the hands of experienced flutists the placement of the tongue varies directly with the loudness of the attack and with the octave, or pitch range, in which the note appears. As a general rule the tongue moves downward on the teeth as the notes get louder or as the pitch range gets lower, and moves higher on the teeth and onto the gum itself as the notes get softer or as the pitch range gets higher. These changes in location of the tongue for the attack are very slight, but are necessary if the sound of the attack is to remain the same over the entire dynamic range and pitch range of the instrument. Most students will make these adjustments automatically, although if they are having problems, it is well to discuss the procedure with them.

In developing fundamental articulation keep the following points in mind:

1. The tongue touches the front teeth at the gum line to stop the flow of breath.
2. The breath is released, after being built up in pressure, by tongue action using "tu," "ta," or "du," or "da."
3. Support of the breath by the diaphragm and abdominal muscles remains constant throughout a series of articulated notes. Supporting muscles do not and must not move in conjunction with the tongue.
4. Position of tongue is higher for lower pitch range and lower for high pitch range.

5. Position of tongue is lower for loud dynamic levels and higher for soft dynamic levels.
6. Avoid starting notes with an accent, or increasing or decreasing the volume of the tone after the attack.

Legato Articulation

Once the fundamental articulation is established the student may easily progress to other types of articulation of which those described as legato or staccato are basic. Various types of articulations demand varying lengths of silence between successive notes, and in combination with dynamic variations will produce a variety of effects required for various musical styles. Basically the legato articulation is one in which the action of the tongue makes a minimum interruption in the flow of sound.

In developing this type of articulation there must be a continuing emphasis on the steady flow of air, unchanged by movements of the breathing muscles, with rapid and gentle strokes of the tongue. Using the syllable "du" rather than "ta" or "tu" will produce the soft articulation usually associated with the music in which this type of articulation is demanded. The following is a typical example of legato articulation.

Staccato Articulation

Staccato articlulation should not be introduced until both the fundamental and legato styles of articulation have been mastered. The same tongue movement and placement and the same steady stream of air is used in staccato articulation. The only difference is that in staccato articulation the tongue returns to its place on the teeth or gums to stop the flow of air, but the air pressure against the tongue remains the same during the period of silence as during the production of tone. Staccato articulation is the only type in which the tongue is used to stop the tone.

Because of the longer period of silence between notes in this type of articulation students are frequently tempted to relax breath support during the silence. If this is done, then the breathing muscles come into operation simultaneously with tongue action, resulting in an accent, and making it virtually impossible to develop a fast staccato. The following is a typical beginning staccato exercise.

etc. in scale patterns

Multiple Tonguing

Because on the flute the tongue acts as a true valve in the control of breath double tonguing and triple tonguing are possible and fairly commonly used just as they are on the brass instruments. These multiple tonguings are virtually impossible on the other woodwinds and their use is exceptional. Almost all advanced flute mehods include material for developing facility in these articulations.

A third type of multiple tonguing which the flute has in common with the other woodwinds is flutter tonguing. Introduction of any type of multiple tonguing on the flute must be delayed until the fundamental, legato and staccato acticulation styles are virtually mastered, and considerable technical facility has been achieved on the instrument. Double and triple tonguing are used only on the most rapidly moving passages where normal single tonguing is impossible.

Double Tonguing

Double tonguing is achieved by "tu-ku" (or "ti-ki," or "doo-goo"). The first syllable is pronounced with the tongue in the same position as for single tonguing, and the second syllable with the tongue striking the palate to stop the flow of air. The two syllables flow together in rapid succession in what is essentially a single movement of the tongue—hence the designation double tonguing. Needless to say this type of tonguing is restricted to use where the notes are grouped in two's. The alternation of the syllables allows the tongue to move much more rapidly and to articulate the notes much faster than is possible in using single tonguing. Double tonguing is used in rapid repetitions of the same note, or for rapidly moving passages in which there are pitch changes. These two types of usages are illustrated in the following.

Because the second of the two syllables tends to be a little weaker in sound than the first (although the differences can be almost completely eliminated with practice) it is common practice to have the "tu" fall on the metrically strong notes and the "ku" on the metrically weak ones. The following illustrates this procedure:

Double tonguing may be used with notes of uneven value if they move so rapidly that single tonguing does not give the right effect. The same syllables are used with this unequal rhythm. The following illustrates a typical use of this technique.

Triple Tonguing

Triple tonguing is used for rapidly moving passages where the notes are grouped in three's. The same two syllables used for double tonguing are utilized in order to alternate impulses between the tip and middle of the tongue, except that in the most common procedure one syllable is repeated. The syllables most commonly recommended and certainly those with which triple tonguing should begin are "tu-ku-tu," or its closest relation "doo-goo-doo." Using either of these it is possible to develop complete facility. An alternate method sometimes recommended for use on flute, as well as for use on brass instruments, is to simply use double tonguing but grouping the notes in three's as: "tu-ku-tu," "ku-tu-ku," "tu-ku-tu," "ku-tu-ku," etc. Triple tonguing is used for articulating rapidly repeated notes of the same pitch, or rapidly moving passages with pitch changes. The following shows a typical usage.

If the passage calling for triple tonguing begins on the second of the group of three notes, the first two notes are articulated with the syllables "tu-ku." If the passage begins with the third note of a group it is articulated with the syllable "tu."

Triple tonguing can be used in groups of three notes of unequal rhythmical value, just as double tonguing can be used with groups of two notes of unequal value, in passages where the music is moving so rapidly that single tonguing is difficult or doesn't give the proper effect. The same sequence of syllables is used for the unequal rhythm as for the patterns of equal rhythm. Following is a typical example for this technique.

Flutter Tonguing

Technically speaking flutter tonguing is not an articulation but a special tonal effect which has come into use in twentieth century music, and first used by Richard Strauss. Darius Milhaud uses it in the first movement of his Sonatine for Flute as well as in several orchestral compositions. Contemporary composers are making even more extensive use of the unusual effect flutter tonguing gives, not only on the flute but on all other wind instruments.

The flutter tongue is produced by rolling the tongue rapidly against the roof of the mouth as in rolling the letter "R" in "b-r-r-r,' producing a very rapid tremolo. There is no set speed for the roll, but the more rapid the tongue movement the more effective the sound. Some students have considerable difficulty in producing a satisfactory roll of the tongue, and some few will find it impossible as the rolled "R" is not natural to English speaking people. Some flutists resort to using the gutteral "R" in the manner of the German language where the "R" can be rolled by vibrations of the soft palate at the back of the throat. This does not produce a true flutter tongue sound, but is better than nothing.

There is no standard notation to indicate flutter tonguing, and notes or passages to be flutter tongued have directions in a language. Some of the words used in other languages to indicate this effect include: *flatterzung, coupe de langue roule, en roulant la langue, tremolo dental,* and *frullante.* Sometimes, on isolated long notes, a rapid tremolo is indicated by four or five strokes across the stem of the note. The following illustrates typical notations.

Flutter

Common Problems in Articulation

1. *Articulation too heavy.* In this type of sound each note starts with an accent, and is normally caused by too much pressure of the tongue against the teeth accompanied by too great a pressure of the breath against the tongue. The best solution is to have the student practice articulation at the pianissimo level, correcting first the legato articulation, then the fundamental articulation, and finally the staccato.

A second cause of this type of sound is found when the student is pushing his breath simultaneously with the beginning of the attack, and is normally accompanied by the inability to develop much speed in articulation. This condition is rather difficult to correct as it involves basic principles in breath support which require the student to begin at the beginning of this process and redevelop his responses. Practice in front of a mirror where the student can detect movements of the breathing mechanism is mandatory as students are not always aware of these movements. Slow practice and much patience is required to correct this condition.

2. *Sluggish tongue.* Inability to tongue rapidly should not be a major concern with beginners, since time and practice is necessary to develop speed in articulation, but in more advanced players where technique has developed past articulation ability, it is a matter of considerable concern. Sluggish tonguing in most instances, where tongue placement and breath support are correct, is a simple matter of insufficient practice devoted to developing speed and accuracy. Special articulation exercises should be assigned to these students, with specific instructions on how many times each day to practice them, to use a metronome, and with specific metronomic speeds to use. Any player can develop satisfactory speed and control if he is using his tongue and breath support properly and if he will spend enough time on the problem. enough time on the problem.

Some students lack speed in articulation because they are moving the back of their tongue as well as the front portion. Movements in articulation are confined to the forward portion of the tongue, with the center and back remaining static, and the primary concept of this motion is of the tip moving up and down rather than forward and backward. Movement of the back portion of the tongue almost invariably carries with it movements of the throat which can easily be seen. To correct, the entire process of tongue placement and development of articulation must be gone through from the very beginning to allow new muscular habits to be formed. Some students make the correction quickly while others are never able to completely overcome the problem.

3. *Lack of coordination between tongue and fingers.* This is frequent among more advanced students who have developed a fair amount of facility on the instrument without detailed attention to articulation. It is purely and simply the result of practicing too fast without first working out notes and tonguing slowly and carefully. These students must practice slowly, at whatever tempo perfect coordination between fingers and tongue is possible, and gradually increase the speed. The use of a metronome on such exercises is invaluable to maintain a steady tempo and to help in the gradual increase in speed. Major and minor scales and arpeggios, making use of various articulation patterns, are good media of practice for this purpose.

4. *Slow staccato.* Some players have difficulty in executing a true staccato rapidly. Other things being correct, this problem can be traced to the lack of breath support and maintaining continuous breath pressure against the tongue or through the aperture in the lips. Some players will be found to be relaxing abdominal support of the air at the end of each note, or cutting off the stream of air in the throat. The concept of the tongue stopping staccato notes as well as starting them with the breath pressure continuing against the tongue during the space of silence will help correct this situation. Once this is corrected, speed and control can be readily developed.

5. *Movement of the jaw in tonguing.* This is the result of too large or too violent movements of the tongue, which are frequently accompanied by changes in pitch of the tone as the embouchure is moved. Rather than confining the movement to the front part of the tongue, the student is moving the entire tongue. The solution is to ask the student, no matter what his technical advancement, to practice the basic exercises for developing articulation constantly checking in a mirror to eliminate all movements.

TECHNIQUE PROBLEMS

A good technical proficiency on the flute is one which is accurate, under complete control, and facile. In developing this proficiency the flutist must be aware of certain mechanical or technical problems peculiar to the instrument which must be approached logically. While some of the items which will be discussed are not introduced until the student is quite advanced, many of them will be quite valuable to students who are still in the early stages of their development. For this reason the school teacher as well as the private teacher must be fully aware of the various potentials and introduce them whenever the problem arises in the day to day work with the student, and even to provide an opportunity to include them in the instruction of the players.

The best organized and most logical presentation of all the problems connected with flute playing is found in the *Altes Method for Flute* (in two volumes) as revised by Caratge and published in 1956 by Alphonse Leduc, Paris. The text is printed in English as well as French, and every instructor who is seriously interested in the welfare of his flutists past the beginning stage should study the contents of this method thoroughly. Much of the material is quite difficult technically and the method itself is suitable for study only by advanced students.

Approached logically and with full information on available choices technical problems on the flute are neither difficult to solve, nor complex to use. Intelligent selection and use of alternate fingerings and other procedures will simplify technical problems to an extent undreamed of by the uninformed. Both the importance of the correct solution and the reasons for a particular solution must be impressed on the student. Each alternative must be practiced until it becomes an involuntary part of the player's technique and how each alternative is used must be made so much a part of his technique that the correct choice becomes involuntary and instantaneous. Both players and teachers should not hesitate to mark instructions on the printed pages as reminders.

Following are problems which occur frequently and their solutions.

1. *Use of D-sharp key.* The D-sharp key played by the right little finger has three important functions in flute technique: (1) it acts as a point of support and control in holding the instrument, (2) it acts as a vent key to improve tone quality and intonation in all three octaves, and (3) it plays the note D-sharp and E-flat. In performing these functions the key is depressed into its open position on all except a very few tones on the instrument. The notes on which the D-sharp key is *not* depressed are indicated in the following:

Failure to keep the D-sharp key depressed is one of the most common deficiencies of the beginning flutist. Unless the importance of this is continually stressed, difficulties first of all in holding the instrument securely and later in intonation present themselves.

There is a tendency on the part of the player to omit depressing the D-sharp key in passages involving the low C and C-sharp where these notes are combined with notes on which the D-sharp key should be depressed. The D-sharp key has a considerable effect on the right hand notes in the first octave, and must be used. This is one instance where it is necessary to slide a finger from one key to another, and the instruments are constructed in such a way to make this possible even if not convenient. If the finger will not slide, the old professional trick of rubbing the ball of the little finger at the side of the nose or in the hair to pick up lubrication can be resorted to.

The example below illustrates a sequence in which it is necessary to slide the little finger from one key to another. Gaining facility in the sliding is a matter of considerable practice and effort, but it must be done.

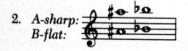

2. *A-sharp:*
B-flat:

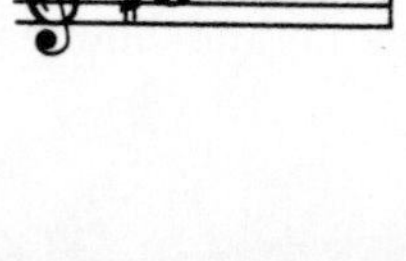

Three Fingerings: (1) T 100 400 D-sharp (diatonic & chromatic)

(2) TB-flat 100 000 D-sharp (for special situations)

(3) T 100 4x00 D-sharp (trills)

In establishing the correct hand position for the flute, it was emphasized that the left thumb should be placed on the B-natural lever, and that fingering 1 was the basic and only fingering which the student should use in the beginning stages of development. Early introduction of the use of the B-flat lever (fingering 2) leads to sliding the thumb back and forth between the B-natural and B-flat levers. This sliding is one of the worst habits a flutist can develop as the keys do not lend themselves to convenient sliding. Sliding makes technique rough, and the students play wrong notes because they don't remember which lever the thumb is on.

With fingering 1, to be used except in special situations, the question arises as to exactly when the thumb B-flat should be used. The thumb *must* be on the B-natural lever to play B-natural in the first and second octaves and F-sharp-G-flat in the third octave. Except for these notes the thumb may be placed on either lever without effecting any other note. When the B-flat is preceded or followed by one of these notes either directly or in a sequence of tones, the basic fingering 1 must be used. The rule to apply is simply that the thumb must not be used on the B-flat lever when the sequence of notes would require that the finger slide to the natural lever.

The thumb B-flat is, however, extremely useful in many situations, and the student must learn when to use it to facilitate technical smoothness. Theoretically, as well as in actual practice in most music, the thumb can be placed on the B-flat lever when playing in the keys of F major, d minor, B-flat major, g minor (the presence of an F-sharp in the third octave would present a problem), E-flat major, A-flat major and f minor. Its use in keys with more than four flats would be contingent on making adjustments in the thumb position for the G-flats in the third octave. The following illustrates a passage in which the thumb B-flat could be used.

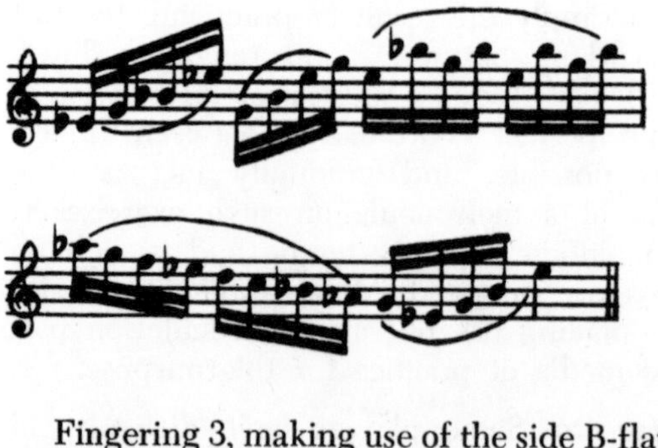

Fingering 3, making use of the side B-flat trill key with the fourth finger is a trill fingering, and its use is limited to this function.

3. *F-Sharp:*
G-flat:

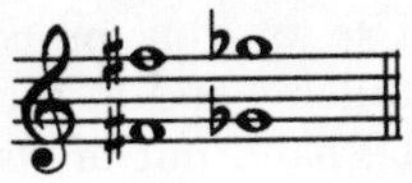

Two Fingerings: (1) T 123 006 D-sharp (basic)
(2) T 123 050 D-sharp (trill)

The first of these is the basic standard fingering while the second is a trill fingering. There is a widespread misunderstanding among non-flutists about the use of the fifth finger rather than the sixth for this note. This is probably because the fifth finger in the right hand is the basic standard fingering for F-sharp on the saxophone and in the clarion register of the clarinet and this fingering has been transferred to the flute by instructors who have not made a thorough study of the instrument.

Let it be understood once and for all that T 123 006 D-sharp is the fingering for F-sharp (G-flat) on the flute which *must* be used at all times except where circumstances demand the use of the trill fingering for technical reasons. These circumstances will occur when the notes are moving at a rapid rate of speed, where the use of the sixth finger for the note would make the passage rough or impossible to play. In the following passage played at a rapid tempo the trill fingering would be used.

4. *D and E-flat fingerings.*

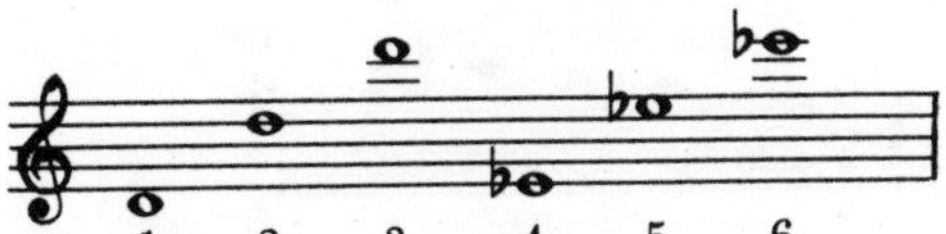

D: (1) T 123 456
(2) T 023 456
(3) T 023 000 D-sharp

E-flat: (4) T 123 456 D-sharp
(5) T 023 456 D-sharp
(6) T 123 G-sharp 456 D-sharp

Beginning flutists have a tendency to use inaccurate fingerings on these notes unless the instructor checks carefully. The fingerings for the D and E-flat in the second octaves (fingerings 2 & 5) are identical with those in the first octave (fingerings 1 & 4) except the first finger must be raised to vent the tone hole. Unless this finger is up on these notes, the student may have difficulty in getting the note to speak; and if it does, the sound is that of a pure harmonic and will be slightly different in quality from other notes in the second octave.

The fingering for the E-flat above the staff (fingering 6) is identical with that for the first octave "D" plus the two little finger keys. This is the only note on the instrument for which all fingers are used. The basic fingering for "D" in the third octave is quite different from those for the other two octaves and should pose no problem when it is introduced, although some beginners will tend to use a harmonic fingering.

5. *Special fingerings.* A few special fingerings are useful in certain circumstances. Because of the acoustical response of the instrument, these fingerings will respond better than the regular fingerings under special circumstances:

(a) In upward slurs from the second to third octaves the "E" will respond better without the low D-sharp key:

(b) For better control and intonation on these notes use the low C-sharp key instead of the D-sharp key:

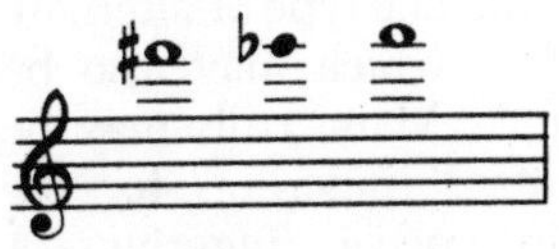

(c) Special fingerings for fortissimo attack. On some instruments these notes may be sharp when attacked at the fortissimo level. Use the fingerings indicated for correction.

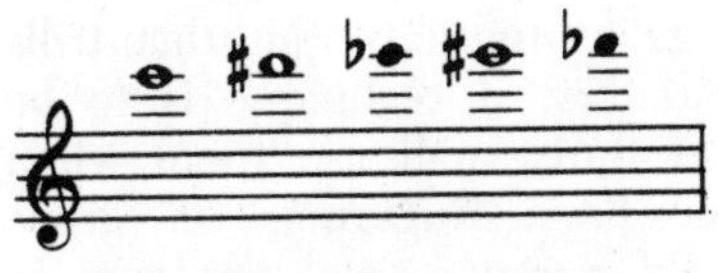

(1) E: T 120 450 no D-sharp
(2) F-sharp: T 103 050 D-sharp
(3) G-sharp: 0 023 G-sharp 056 D-sharp

6. *Selection and use of alternate fingerings.* Alternate fingerings are used to solve technical problems of facility, intonation, and response when the normal standard fingerings are unsatisfactory. When a student is playing a passage where the sequence of fingerings is awkward for him so that he cannot play it fast enough or smooth enough, or when he has difficulty in getting one of the notes to respond properly the solution can frequently be found by using an alternate fingering for one or more notes in the pattern. Selection of alternate fingerings for

intonation may occur in either extreme of the dynamic range and frequently on notes in the third octave.

The fingering chart at the back of this book includes all the normal alternate fingerings. Harmonic fingerings should also be considered alternate fingerings. Some of the notes in the first and second octaves and almost all notes above the second octave have alternate fingerings indicated. Not all the alternate fingerings will be useful for all students. Some of the fingerings will be out of tune to a greater or lesser degree for some players. Such fingerings can be used only when the sequence of notes in which they are used is moving so rapidly that the note is not sufficiently exposed for the ear to get an exact impression of the pitch. Some of the most commonly used alternate fingerings are discussed in this section; the potential is too great for all to be discussed.

Alternate fingerings should be added to the student's technique as the need for them arises. If a student on the intermediate or advanced level (beginning students should concentrate on standard fingerings) encounters a technical problem, standard procedure should be to check alternate fingerings for a solution. The more advanced the student, the more need for alternate fingerings. As alternate fingerings are introduced, the student should practice them until their selection for use in the appropriate situations becomes a matter of habit.

7. *Trill fingerings.* These are a special type of alternate fingerings intended for trilling but which may also be used in certain other circumstances. Many trills may be executed with standard or alternate fingerings for the notes involved, but others require special fingerings. A chart of these special trill fingerings is given following the standard flute fingering chart. These special fingerings may tend to sacrifice intonation and/or tone quality on the upper note for the sake of facility. Some are noticeably out of tune when played slowly, but this out of tuneness is tolerable at the rapid speed of the trill.

The use of trill fingerings in situations other than trills is most useful, even mandatory, if technique is to be smooth. The accomplished flutist will use them when needed as substitutes for basic fingerings on grace notes, mordents, turns and for upper neighbor tones in diatonic pasages. But as with any alternate fingering, trill fingerings must not be used when the ear can hear faulty intonation.

8. *Use of right hand trill keys.* Some auxiliary fingerings in the third octave and in the extended range of the flute call for the fifth or sixth finger to both close the tone hole and open the trill key simultaneously. This is done easily by moving the finger only slightly to the left so that it touches and operates both the trill key and closes the hole.

Some teachers for their advanced students, and under special circumstances of technical difficulties, recommend that the hand be moved to the *right* so that the fourth finger operates trill key 5x, leaving the fifth finger in its normal position. Similarly the fifth finger is moved to the right to operate trill key 6x, with the sixth finger in its normal position. Use of this procedure should be limited to advanced students and to those special conditions where moving the hand out of its normal position will not have an adverse effect on the fingerings of the notes which precede or follow.

9. *Leaving down one or more fingers throughout a passage.* Rapidly moving passages involving some tones can frequently be made smoother if certain fingers in the right hand which are not a part of the basic fingerings for all notes are kept down throughout. This device is used on the clarinet first as an aid to crossing the break and then for the sake of smoothness in facility, and the basic principle can be applied to the flute.

Advanced players frequently make use of this technique without being conscious of it, but it is frequently a great aid to less experienced flutists if they can be directed to make use of it. In some combinations of player and instruments leaving fingers down will affect the pitch of the other notes in the passage, while in other instances having the fingers down will have little or no effect.

Use of this technique is limited to those places where there is no appreciable change in intonation of any of the notes, but is always usable where the notes are moving so rapidly that the ear does not perceive an incorrect intonation. In order to use this device learn the following.

The right hand portion of any of these notes may be kept down.

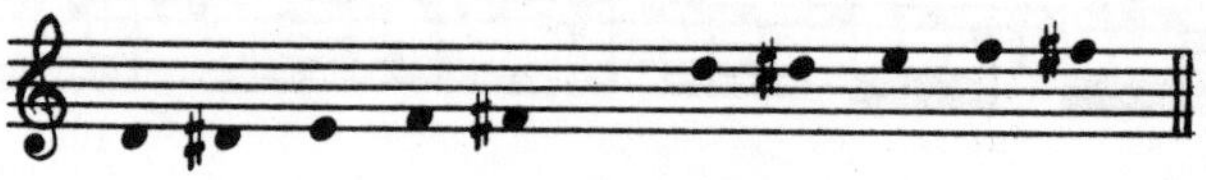

While playing any of these notes.

The following examples will illustrate the use of this technique.

Keep first finger of right hand down throughout.

Keep first and second fingers of right hand down throughout.

Keep all three fingers of right hand down throughout.

10. *Tremolo.* A tremolo involving the interval of a minor third or larger occurs occasionally and with increasing frequency in contemporary music. The problems involved in accomplishing the rapid alternation of notes are similar to those found in half and whole-step trills. Good tremolos are possible on most note combinations through the careful choice of fingerings.

Many tremolos may be executed with the normal fingerings for both notes and pose no problem other than finger coordination. Others may be executed easily by making use of the principle of leaving down one or more fingers throughout a passage.

The procedure for selecting the fingering for a tremolo is to select a basic standard fingering for the lower note in the interval, then a fingering for the upper note which involves the least movement of fingers. Avoid if at all possible opening and closing holes simultaneously for the upper. Some promises in intonation and/or tone quality on the upper note may be necessary to accomplish this. Tables of tremolo fingerings for intervals of a minor third through a perfect fifth can be found in Edwin Putnik's *The Art of Flute Playing,* pp. 54-60.

11. *Glissando.* The glissando is being used more and more frequently in contemporary flute music. When it is called for, the procedure is to play a rapid chromatic scale from the beginning to the final note. If the two notes which are connected by the glissando are a wide interval and in a rhythm which moves so rapidly that it is not possible to play the entire chromatic scale between the two, the glissando may consist of the major scale in the key, or the glissando may start and end with a short group of chromatic notes—the center being filled in by the major scale.

The portamento as defined and described in the clarinet chapter is not possible on the closed hole flute. An advanced player with a strong flexible embouchure and well-controlled finger action can develop the portamento to a limited degree on the French model instrument.

12. *Special problems of the extended range.* To the normal three octave range of the flute contemporary performance has extended the range an additional fifth.

Extended Range: 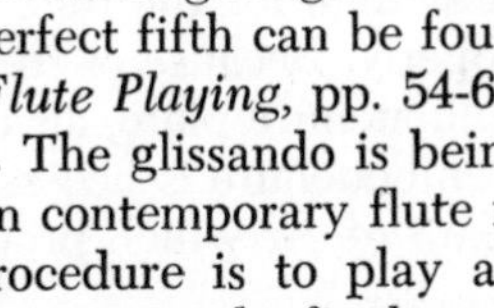

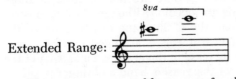

This range poses problems even for the advanced flutist, and only the most advanced students should undertake a systematic study of it. Notes in this range are called for only occasionally, but players performing music in contemporary idioms should be prepared. Tone production in this range requires a small intense stream of air (jaw forward to cover more of the embouchure hole and to direct more air across the embouchure plate) under extremely firm support. The feeling is quite similar to playing at the very top of the piccolo range.

Selection of fingerings from the special chart of the extended range is critical. There are great individual differences from player to player and from instrument to instrument. The chart at the end of the book supplies several possible fingerings for each note (except "D"). Not all fingerings will respond for all players. Once the player is producing satisfactory tones in this range, he should work with the various fingerings for each note until he finds one or more which will respond with good quality and intonation. Some players will develop fingerings which are not included on the chart. This is all to the good. If the fingering works, use it!

Some players will develop this range quite easily, some with considerable effort, while others may find it almost impossible. Some teachers recommend adding the notes in this range only as they occur in music which the student is playing, as this supplies the motivation. But all serious advanced students should consider this range essential to their performance and develop their control and facility little by little.

HARMONICS

Acoustically it is possible to produce harmonics on any woodwind instrument. Indeed the second octave of the flute is the normal first harmonic of the notes in the first octave, and a portion of the normal fingering for all the other woodwinds makes use of either the first harmonic (oboe, bassoon, saxophone) or the second harmonic (clarinet), and these instruments are spoken of as overblowing an octave or in the case of the clarinet of overblowing a twelfth.

As indicated in the discussion of acoustics, the harmonic series falls in a regular pattern above the fundamental, and is produced by forcing the column of air to vibrate in two, three, four or more equal segments, rather than as a single segment which produces the fundamental. Harmonics are relatively simple for a competent flutist to produce, and many teachers recommend the regular practice of harmonics as a means of developing flexibility and control of the embouchure.

Harmonics on the flute can be produced on all notes in the first octave, although the lower the pitch of the fundamental the easier it is to produce a greater number of notes in the series. They are produced by decreasing the size of the aperture in the lips, increasing the intensity of the air stream, and altering the direction of the air flow as the increasingly higher overtones are produced. Considerable practice is necessary to accomplish this with facility, and the student should practice on the lowest three or four notes first until they come easily before practicing on the remaining fundamentals.

Harmonics are notated with a small circle above the note to indicate that it is played as a harmonic. Sometimes, as in notation for string instruments, the fundamental is written beneath the harmonic in a smaller note size. The following musical example gives the harmonic series on the lowest three notes of the instrument. Although the series of harmonics can be extended for ten or twelve notes above the fundamental, four notes above the fundamental as in the illustration are those most practical and most commonly used on the flute. With experience the number may be increased, especially on these lower notes.

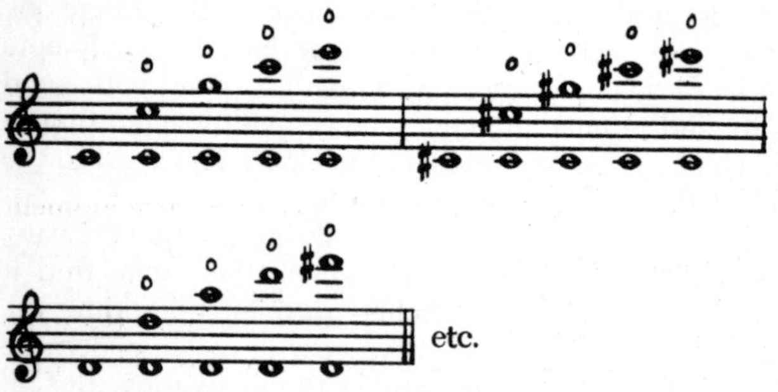

Special fingerings for harmonics for G (first space above staff) and above have been derived and accepted as standard. These appear in a special section at the end of the fingering chart, and should be learned and used by advanced students. Harmonics are used at the pianissimo level only. They are especially useful for this purpose as many of the tones in the third octave are difficult to sustain on pitch at the pianissimo level when the regular fingerings are used. Harmonics, on the other hand, will not drop in pitch when played softly. Their primary use is for sustained notes, but they may also be used for moving passages in the third octave which must be played pianissimo.

Contemporary composers are making more and more frequent use of harmonics on the flute for special effects, and the skilled flutist will make use of them on older music to facilitate its performance. The following are typical examples of the use of harmonics.

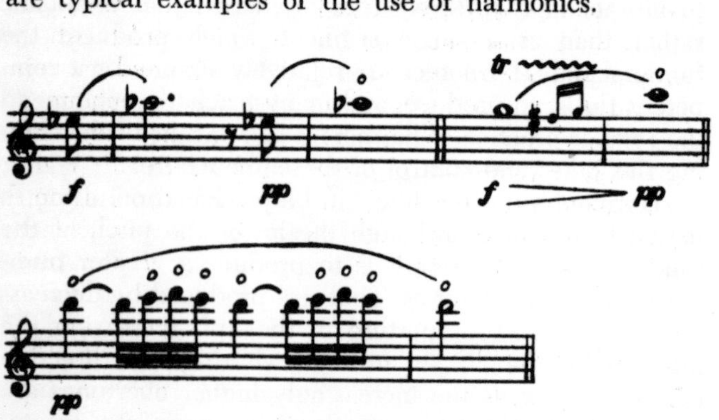

DOUBLING PICCOLO, ALTO AND BASS FLUTE

The basic approach to playing the piccolo, alto, and bass flutes should be the same as that for the "C" instrument, making appropriate adjustments in the placement of the embouchure plate on the lower lip, and the amount and velocity of air used to produce the tone. These are not beginning instruments. A student should at least be well into the intermediate level of flute performance before beginning the study of one of these instruments. There are no methods books for these instruments. The student uses those written for C flute, selecting first from studies which avoid the extreme low and high portions of the playing range. The Cavally *Melodious and Progressive Studies for Flute,* Vol. I. published by the Southern Music Company provides excellent material for starting the study of these instruments.

Piccolo

Because of the miniature size of the keywork, the piccolo (which lacks the low C and C-sharp of the flute) requires an adjustment of hand and finger positions, but the basic placement and shape of the hands must be the same as for flute. The placement of the embouchure plate on the lower lip is crucial to both pitch and tone quality. Most flutists will find that placing the embouchure plate somewhat higher on their lower lip than their flute placement will produce the best results.

The piccolo requires more breath pressure and air speed than does the flute, although the total amount of air used will be less than for the flute if the embouchure is functioning properly. Because of the very small size of the hole in the embouchure plate, air direction is critical, and a more firm embouchure is necessary to produce the small intense stream of air which produces the best piccolo tone.

As an aid to consistent embouchure placement, it is a good idea to scribe an alignment on the head and middle joint so that they can be kept in the same alignment each time the instrument is used.

A player beginning the study of the piccolo will find that intonation is a somewhat greater problem than on the flute. Intonation is especially sensitive in the upper portion of its pitch range. This can be controlled by the embouchure with practice and careful attention. The normal tendency of the flute to play sharp at loud dynamic levels and flat at soft ones is exaggerated on the piccolo.

Alto Flute

The alto flute in "G" is being used more and more in groups playing all styles of music. The problems in changing from C-flute to alto flute are not as great as those found in changing to piccolo. Although the alto instrument is longer than the C-flute, the construction of the keywork on most instruments is arranged in such a way that there is little increase in finger spread over that of the "C" instrument. For this reason, hand and finger positions can and should be virtually identical with those the player uses on the C-flute.

While the same embouchure formation as that on the C-flute should be used on the alto instrument, some experimentation with the exact placement on the lower lip to get the best tone quality and control may be necessary.

The exact placement should not vary greatly from that used on the "C" instrument. In general, the embouchure used with the alto flute is less tense than that used for playing the C-flute.

The first problem to be solved when a student begins the study of the alto flute is that of breath control. The instrument, especially in the first octave, requires a greater volume of air with less velocity than that used in the first octave of the C-flute. The direction of the air from the lips toward the embouchure hole is quite critical, and the student must be constantly aware of the need for matching tone quality and body over the range of the instrument. Too much air velocity or air improperly directed will cause the tone to break.

Bass Flute

The bass flute, a "C" instrument sounding an octave lower than the C-flute, remains a fairly uncommon instrument, although they are now being made in the United States. Its primary use is in flute ensembles, and as a solo instrument in special orchestrations where its tone can be electronically amplified. Because of its comparatively large size, the bass flute is heavy and somewhat awkward to hold. But the basic playing position must be the same as that for the C-flute.

The primary problem with playing the bass flute is in the great amount of air needed to produce a full tone. Indeed, the quantity of air needed for this instrument will be the primary factor for selecting a student to play it. Embouchure placement is critical to make the most efficient use of available breath. Intonation is dependent both upon breath support and embouchure flexibility. Tone studies from standard flute literature are most useful in developing tone and control.

TRANSPOSITION FOR THE FLUTIST

As the flute is a non-transposing instrument, the flutist is not required in the normal course of events to do any transposition. Advanced flutists, however, like advanced players on any instrument are expected to be able to transpose parts, etudes, and various exercises to different keys and should take advantage of any opportunity to develop this facility. Teachers must see to it that the more advanced flutists are assigned problems in transposition as a part of their regular course of study.

The most frequent occasion for transposition, and this is rare, is found in older band arrangements where the flutist who does not have a D-flat piccolo available is expected to transpose the part and play it on a C piccolo. This is a relatively simple transposition. Every note is played a half-step higher than written. The following example illustrates this process.

Written for D-flat piccolo

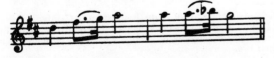

Played on C piccolo

SELECTION OF INSTRUMENTS

The modern flute was developed by Theobald Boehm (1794-1881), and the basic principles of key mechanism have been adapted and applied to the modern clarinet described as the Boehm System, and formed the basis for the development of the conservatory system for the oboe and the mechanism of the saxophone. Attempts to apply his principles to the bassoon produced an instrument called the Sarrusophone which has never been widely adopted. All modern woodwind instruments are indebted to Boehm for their high degree of development.

Theobald Boehm was a professional flutist who became dissatisfied with the tone quality and imperfect mechanism of the old style conical bore flute. He made his first instrument in 1832 based on the old system, and did no further study of the problems until 1846 when he resumed his work on perfecting the instrument. In his own words: "I finally called science to my aid and gave two years (1846-1847) to the study of the principles of acoustics. After making many experiments, as precise as possible, I finished a flute in the later part of 1847, founded upon scientific principles, for which I received the highest prize at the World's Expositions, in London in 1851 and in Paris in 1855."[1] He continued to refine his instrument and the present cylindrical bore instrument was perfected between the years 1870-1880. Only the most minor improvements have been made since that time.

Because of the almost universal acceptance of the Boehm System modern flutes have been standardized into a single mechanical model. There is not the wide variety of models such as are available for clarinet or oboe, although certain options described below are available. Primary differences in flutes within a wide price range are in the metal used in the body and finish, and in the amount of precision hand-work used to refine the mechanism and temperament of the instrument. The basic mechanism is identical in all models. By virtual common consent of professional flutists in this country the finest instruments are those made in Boston by Powell whose instruments have become the standard of comparison by which all other instruments are measured.

Various options available for flute are as follows:

1. *Closed tone holes.* This is the standard model instrument on which all tone holes are covered by pads

1. Theobald Boehm, *The Flute and Flute Playing* (originally published in German, 1871; English translation by Dayton C. Miller, 1922), p. 12.

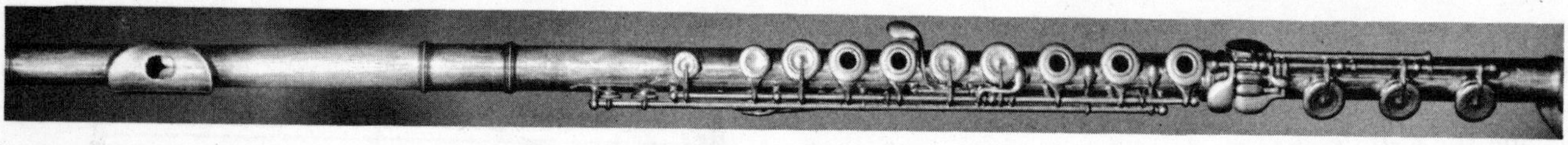

Figure F-34

in the same fashion that the plateau system for oboe is constructed. This model is recommended for all except the most advanced students and is available in a wide price range.

2. *Open tone holes (French model).* Most, if not all, professional flutists use the open hole model flute. In this model the keys operated by the second, third, fourth, fifth and sixth fingers are partially covered by a ring with a circular pad. The fingers themselves act as pads just as they do on the clarinet. Professionals and advanced students prefer this model because it gives a somewhat greater control over the tone quality, and permits certain alternate fingerings which are not available with the closed tone holes.[2] The difficulty in covering the open holes accurately makes it inadvisable for use except by the most advanced players. Figure F-34 is a Powell flute with open tone holes, and a low B-natural key.

3. *Low B-natural key.* The principal standard choice one has on the number of keys on the Boehm flute is the option of the low B-natural key. This key is added to the instrument by lengthening the foot joint so that the length of the tube produces B-natural rather than C-natural, and adding a key for the new note operated by the right little finger. This additional key is rarely called for in solos or orchestral literature of contemporary composers, and for this reason is not recommended for student use. Professional flutists, and the most advanced students who might be purchasing a new instrument should seriously consider a model instrument with this key. In addition to adding a half-step to the low range of the instrument, the additional length of the tubing adds resonance to the tone quality of the lower notes of the first and second octaves which makes it most desirable for professional calibre performance.

4. *Open G-sharp key.* On the standard instrument the pad of the G-sharp key operated by the little finger of the left hand is held in a closed position by a spring. On the model instrument with the open G-sharp the pad of the key is held in an open position by a spring, which means that the key must be depressed by the little finger on all notes except where the open position of the pad is needed. Over a period of years it was discovered that the use of the open G-sharp key had many disadvantages and this model has completely disappeared from the market except for instruments made on special order. In a school situation the open G-sharp key may appear on older instruments, and the teacher should be aware of their existence.

5. *Additional mechanical options.* Several other optional keys are available on some professional quality instruments. In general, these are of little value and complicate the mechanism. For this reason their inclusion on an instrument is not recommended unless there are special considerations. These options include a right hand G-sharp trill key and extra C-sharp trill key, replacing the B-flat lever (key 4x) with a key producing B-natural, an extra long lever to produce low C with the left little finger, etc.

6. *Piccolo.* The piccolo is made with either a cylindrical or conical bore of wood, metal, or plastic. The cylindrical metal instrument is almost the universal choice for school musicians because students find tone production easier and intonation more sure on this instrument than one with a conical bore.

Many professionals as well as advanced students prefer the wooden instrument with a cylindrical bore, feeling that the tone quality is smoother and richer than on the metal instrument, although there is no scientific evidence that this is true.

The conical bore piccolo is used less frequently, although some professionals feel that it produces a more brilliant tone as well as a larger tonal body in its lower range. Some notes in the third octave speak with greater difficulty on the conical instrument than on the cylindrical. Unless there is a strong personal preference otherwise, the metal cylindrical model is recommended.

STUDENT QUALIFICATIONS AND APTITUDES

The flute is an excellent beginning instrument. The closed tone holes make it possible for a student to begin study as soon as he is physically large enough to achieve a reasonably accurate holding and hand position. This can be tested by observing the left hand position. If, after some instruction, he can hold the instrument with his left hand in the proper position with the little finger touching the G-sharp key he can begin study of the instrument. The right hand poses no particular problem if the left hand is satisfactory.

Other than size of the hands, standards of physical aptitudes for the flute are not always reliable. Generally speaking a student who has even teeth and lips that are firm and not too large may have an advantage over those who do not possess these attributes. The rare individual who has a pronounced underbite will probably have difficulty in achieving much success on the flute.

2. Altes, *Complete Method for Flute.* Revised by F. Caratge. (Paris: Alphonse Leduc, 1956). The book has a table of the most useful of these fingerings on page 92 of volume I followed by material to develop their use.

Advisability of flute study may be determined by success in producing tones on the head joint alone after some instruction in embouchure formation. These tones should be strong and clear and produced with the end of the head joint closed and open in the manner described in the section on embouchure. When he can sustain them for ten to fifteen seconds, he is ready to proceed with the complete instrument.

The student who can immediately produce a satisfactory tone on the head joint may be said to have a natural aptitude for the flute. Others may fail for some time, but with instructive guidance may develop an equal aptitude. In the final analysis, it is not natural aptitude but desire and persistence which determines future success on the instrument.

The piccolo is not a beginning instrument, as tone production and control are much more difficult than on the flute. The piccolo should only be played by those who have been successful in their accomplishments on the flute.

CARE OF THE FLUTE

Assemble and disassemble with the greatest of care. Review the instructions on assembly of the instrument until they are thoroughly understood and the students are performing the operation easily. Keep the instrument in its case when not in use.

It is mandatory that the inside of the flute is thoroughly dried after each playing, and the habit of doing this thoroughly should be developed from the very first. Some flute players have the unfortunate habit of neglecting this process. Swabbing the instrument does not take much time, and will prevent the accumulation of dirt and grime inside the instrument, as well as helping to maintain sanitary conditions for playing. Disassamble the instrument in reverse order of assembly and put in the case carefully before starting the cleaning process.

1. *Use of cleaning rod.* Every flute case is, or should be, equipped with a metal cleaning rod. It is to be used with a soft lint-free cloth such as an old linen handkerchief. A corner of the cloth is put through the opening near one end of the rod, drawn over the tip of the rod and wound down the length of the rod so that all except an inch or so of the length is covered. The end of the cloth is held firmly in place by a finger or fingers.

2. *Head joint.* Shake the water out of the head joint. Insert the cleaning rod carefully so as not to move the end plug. Draw it back and forth several times so that all the inside area is wiped dry (Figure F-35). Put on the protective cap and replace the head joint in the proper place in the case.

3. *Middle joint.* Shake the water out of the upper end of the middle joint. Holding the joint as in the process of assembling the head joint, insert the swab and draw back and forth several times to clean the inside thoroughly (Figure F-36).

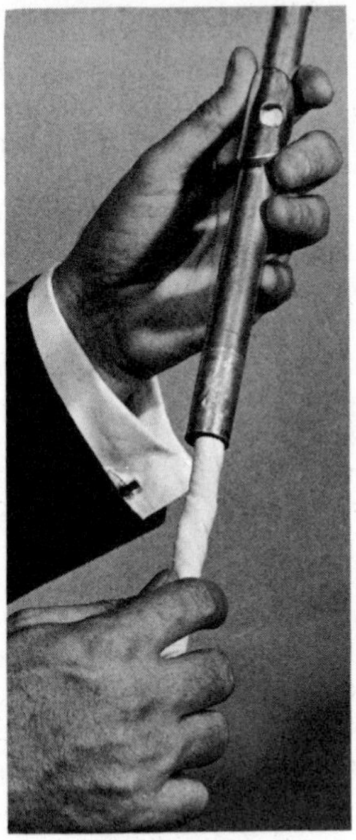

Figure F-35

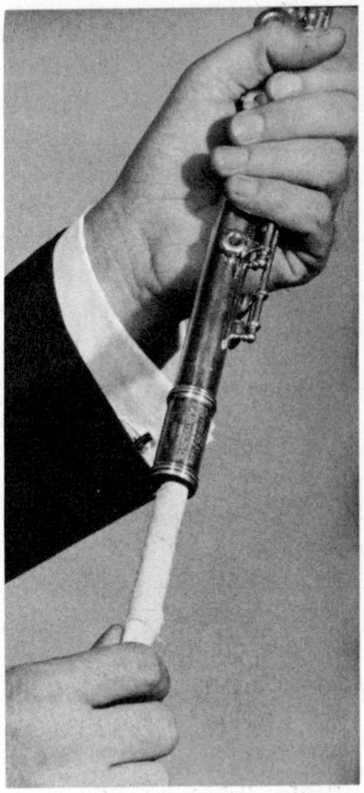

Figure F-36

To clean the other end of the middle joint hold it near the other end as in assembling the foot joint and repeat the swabbing process (Figure F-37). Put the protective cap on the end and return joint to case.

4. *Foot joint.* While very little moisture reaches the foot joint, it is well to clean it regularly. Hold it carefully so as not to put undue pressure on the key mechanism (Figure F-38).

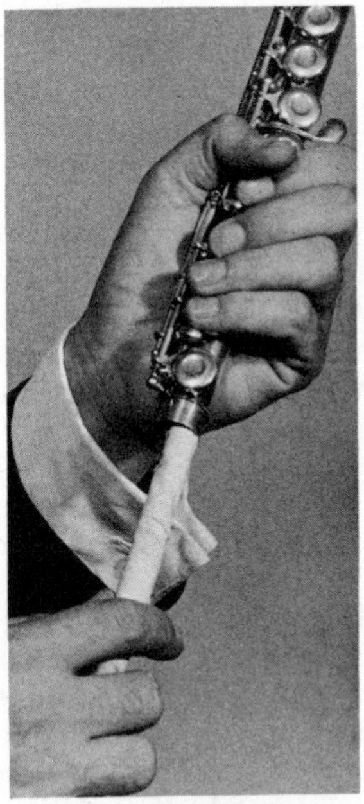

Figure F-37

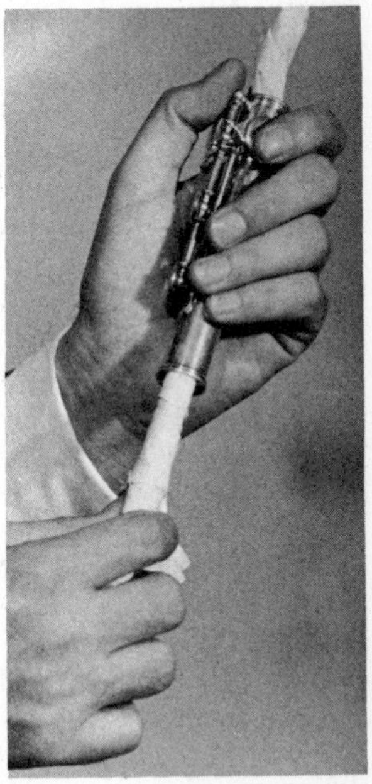

Figure F-38

5. With a soft cloth wipe clean the inside and outside of all the connecting joints so that they will remain in good condition for assembly. Under normal circumstances, the joints will not need lubrication. If, however, the instrument goes together with difficulty because the joints are too tight, they may be lubricated with cork grease until the situation can be corrected by a repairman. If cork grease is used over a period of time, the joints should be wiped clean and fresh grease applied.

6. Using a chamois or different cloth, preferably of flannel, wipe the entire outside of each joint carefully to remove finger prints and dust. If this is done regularly and thoroughly the instrument will never need polishing.

Regular Maintenance of the Instrument

If the flute receives good care and a regular schedule of maintenance is followed, it will remain in the best playing condition over a long period of time. Instruments which are in poor condition are difficult to play and result in poor players. Observing the following suggestions will help keep the flute in the perfect mechanical condition so necessary for success on the instrument.

1. *Oiling the mechanism.* The mechanism must be oiled regularly three or four times each year. A special oil, called key oil, is available under various brand names for this purpose. A drop of oil on the end of a needle or toothpick should be put at each pivot screw of each key. Do this carefully so that no oil can get onto the pads. This regular oiling keps pivot screws from excessive wear and from rusting into place, making any repairs and adjustments on the instrument easier to accomplish.

2. *Adjusting screws.* Most student model flutes have four adjusting screws on the keys closed by the second, fourth, fifth, and sixth fingers. The function of these screws is to coordinate the closing of another tone hole when these fingers are used. Observation of the instrument will show this correlation. These screws must be in perfect adjustment if the instrument is to respond as it should.

If the coordinated hole is not closing properly, the tone will be sharp, fuzzy in quality, and respond with difficulty or not at all. When an "A," "F," or F-sharp, in the first octave for example, does not respond properly, check immediately to see if any adjusting screws need attention. The screws can be adjusted visually and tested by playing. In addition to the adjusting screws, the pivot screws for each key should be checked regularly and tightened if necessary. New instruments are especially susceptible to developing loose pivot screws.

3. *Dusting the instrument.* If the instrument is wiped carefully after each use as suggested above, very little dust will accumulate. However, over a period of time some dust will be found beneath the key mechanism where the regular wiping does not reach. This dust can be removed with a soft watercolor brush. If a cloth is used, it must be handled very carefully so as not to snag on the needle springs which break under pressure.

4. *Shining the instrument.* The body and key mechanism of the flute will remain in good condition if wiped regularly. This will not only keep the keys and tube from tarnishing, but will prevent corrosion of the plates and keys in the event the player perspires excessively.

Silver polish must never be used on the instrument, nor should the instrument ever be polished while the keys are in place. Using silver polish while the keys are on the instrument will foul pivot screws in the mechanism, and damage pads so they will leak. Leave polishing up to a competent repairman. Caution students against polishing the instrument, but give them careful and repeated instruction to keep the instrument clean by wiping it regularly.

5. *Bent rods or keys.* In spite of the best of care, keys or rods sometimes become bent out of line. Bent keys or rods occur with alarming regularity on the instruments of young players, and cause unevenness in technique, or even prevent some tones from responding at all. No attempt should be made to straighten keys or rods while they are in place on the instrument. This puts excessive pressure on both the keys and their posts and the instrument may be damaged even more. Keys must be removed from the instrument by a repairman who has the proper knowledge and tools to straighten and align them. Caution students against trying to do it themselves.

6. *Sticking pads.* The flute is especially susceptible to sticking pads. If the instrument is not thoroughly dried before it is put into the case, or if the humidity is excessive even temporarily, some pads on the instrument may stick tightly, or will stick momentarily before they open, making technique uneven. If this happens, the first measure to take is to make sure that the student is doing a thorough job of cleaning the instrument each time it is put into the case.

Moisture can be removed from sticking pads by placing a cigarette paper between the pad and the tone hole, and pressing down on the key firmly. Release the key, move the paper and repeat the process until the key no longer sticks. If this does not relieve the sticking, put the cigarette paper in place, press the key, and pull the paper slowly from under the pad. Repeat the process several times.

If the cigarette paper does not relieve the sticking, dip the end of a pipe cleaner into a cleaning fluid such as carbon tetrachloride, benzine, or denatured alcohol. Wipe the pad with this fluid, and dry thoroughly with another pipe cleaner. Since this removes the natural oil from the pad, replace the oil by putting a very light coat of key oil over the pad with a pipe cleaner. Dry off excess key oil with another pipe cleaner.

If none of these procedures relieves the sticking, the pad should be replaced. Never use powder on pads in an attempt to stop sticking. It is rarely successful and damages the pad so that it begins to deteriorate.

7. *Leaky pads.* Pads on an instrument wear out with use. Some wear out more rapidly than others and begin

to leak, causing the instrument to respond with difficulty on certain notes. The pads on the foot joint of the flute are especially susceptible to leaking, with the result that the student has difficulty in producing these notes, if he is able to produce them at all. If a student cannot produce low C or C-sharp, suspect a leaky pad.

Some pads which are in good condition may leak because they are improperly seated over the tone hole. Pads deteriorate so slowly that the player is frequently not aware that the condition exists. For this reason a close inspection of the condition of the pads on every instrument should be made very three or four months.

If some notes respond with difficulty, with a change in tone quality and intonation in comparison with surrounding notes, there is a strong possibility of a leak in the instrument. Finding the exact source of a leak on a flute is a somewhat more awkward process than on some other woodwinds.

To test for leaks take the instrument apart. Close the bottom end of the middle joint with a cork, close all tone holes with the six fingers using no more than the normal amount of pressure against them, and blow through the open end of the tube. Leaky pads can be identified by the air leaking through, although the assistance of a second person is sometimes necessary to find the exact location of a leak.

If a tone hole which is normally covered by a key and a pad held closed by a spring leaks (the G-sharp key or a trill key for example) when maximum wind pressure is applied during the test, the spring on that key must be strengthened or replaced by a repairman. The joint should not leak no matter how much breath pressure is applied if it is in the best playing condition. The foot joint can be tested for leaks in the same manner.

If the leak is located, an examination of the pad will determine whether it should be replaced or simply reseated. Accuracy in seating pads is determined best by the use of commercial feeler papers or strips of cigarette paper about a quarter inch wide. Slide one end of the paper under the pad, put the normal amount of pressure against the pad if the key is not held closed by a spring, and slowly draw the paper out. As long as the pressure against the paper remains constant there is no leak. If the pressure suddenly lessens, the pad is not properly seated. Repeat the process completely around the pad so that all edges are tested.

The process of blowing cigarette smoke through the instrument to identify a leak by seeing the smoke come out of the leak is not recommended. The nicotine in the smoke coats the pads and if this is done frequently, will damage them so they harden and leak. Repairmen use a small light in the bore of the instrument to find leaks, as the light will shine through the open space of the leak.

8. *Regular overhaul.* The condition of every instrument must be checked at least once each year by the instructor or by a repairman. Regular maintenance keeps an instrument in playing condition over a period of years, rather than allowing it to gradually deteriorate becoming increasingly difficult to play. Every instrument must have a complete overhaul every three to five years depending on the amount of usage. If instruments receive a yearly checkup, a regular overhaul, and proper daily maintenance they will last in virtually perfect condition for many years. The service of a competent repairman are invaluable and a great asset to any program of instrumental instruction.

BIBLIOGRAPHY OF STUDY MATERIALS

The amount of teaching material available for the flute is quite extensive once the student is past the beginning stage of his development. The farther along in his studies the greater the variety of music available. In the sections which follow a cross section of the most widely used material (exclusive of solo and ensemble music) available for flute is listed. It is by no means all inclusive as such a list would fill an entire volume. Additional information on all classifications of flute music may be found in the volumes by Chapman, Coleman, Heller, Pellerite, Putnik, Rasmussen, Vester, and Wilkins listed in the bibliography at the end of this book and in the Selective Music Lists published by MENC.

Beginning Methods

Anzalone, Valentine. *Breeze-Easy Method for Flute.* Two Volumes. M. Witmark.

Bodegraven, Paul Van. *Adventures in Flute Playing.* Two Volumes. Staff Music Publishing Co.

Buck, Lawrence. *Flute Elementary Method.* Kjos Music Co.

Dalby, Cleon E. *All Melody Method for Flute.* Two Volumes. Pro Art Publications.

Eck, Emil. *Eck Method for Flute.* Two Volumes. Belwin, Inc.

Fair, Rex Elton. *Flute Method.* Two Volumes. M. M. Cole Publishing Co.

Gekeler, Kenneth. *Belwin Flute Method.* Three Volumes. Belwin, Inc.

Herfurth-Stuart. *A Tune A Day for Flute.* Two Volumes. Boston Music Co.

Hetzel, Jack. *Hetzel's Visual Method for Flute.* Oliver Ditson.

Moore, E. C. and A. O. Sieg. *Preparatory Instructor for Flute.* Carl Fischer.

Petersen, A. C. *Rubank Elementary Method for Flute.* Rubank, Inc.

Skornicka-Petersen. *Rubank Intermediate Method for Flute.* Rubank, Inc.

Voxman, H. *Rubank Advanced Method for Flute.* Two Volumes. Rubank, Inc.

Van Vactor, David and Kitti, Arthur. *Carl Fischer Basic Method for Flute.* Carl Fischer.

Weber, Fred and Douglas Steensland. *The Flute Student* (Student Instrumental Course). 3 vols. Belwin, Inc. Correlated with five other volumes of solos, studies and duets.

Standard Methods

Altes, Henry. *Method for the Boehm Flute.* Two editions. Carl Fischer, Inc. Two Volumes; edition wtih English text published by Alphonse Leduc. The Leduc edition revised and augmented by Caratge (1956) is the finest and most complete flute method available, and is recommended for study and reference. The Carl Fischer edition, published in 1918 has the original contents of the method, but is poorly edited and has very little explanatory material. Many duets in both editions.

Berbiguier. *Flute Method.* Two Volumes. Salabert. French Text.

Brooke, Arthur. *Modern Method for Boehm Flute.* Cundy-Bettoney. Available in two volumes, or complete edition. Published in 1912, this method is no longer "modern" but does have considerable useful material on both the intermediate and advanced technical levels.

DeLorenzo, Leonardo. *L'Indispensabile. A Complete Modern School for the Flute.* Two volumes. Carl Fischer, Inc. Text in English and Italian.

Langey. *Tutor for Flute.* Carl Fischer.

Soussmann, H. Revised by W. Popp. *Complete Method for Flute.* Carl Fischer, Inc. Three volumes. Volume two contains 12 duets, and volume three has 24 studies in major and minor keys which are quite advanced in technical difficulty.

Taffanel & Gaubert. *Methode Complete de Flute.* Alphonse Leduc. French text only. Contains much excellent material on an upper intermediate and advanced level. A few duets. There is very little text and the absence of an English translation will not be a handicap to its use.

Wagner. *Foundation to Flute Playing.* Carl Fischer. Suitable for the first intermediate book.

Additional Study Materials

Altes. *26 Selected Studies.* G. Schirmer.

Andersen. *25 Études, Op. 15.* Carl Fischer, International, Southern Music Co.

24 Studies in All Major and Minor Keys, Op. 21. International.

24 Instructive Studies, Op. 30. Southern Music Co., International.

24 Studies, Op. 33. International, Southern Music Co., Carl Fischer.

26 Little Caprices, Op. 37. International, Southern Music Co.

18 Studies, Op. 41. International, Schirmer, Southern Music Co.

24 Virtuosity Studies, Op. 60. Southern Music Co.

24 Technical Studies, Op. 63. Southern Music Co.

Andraud. *Modern Flutist.* South Music Co. Has études by Donjon, caprices by Karg-Elert and a number of orchestral studies, including some for piccolo and also flute.

Bach, J. S. *Twenty Concert Studies.* Southern Music Co.

Twenty-Four Flute Concert Studies. Southern Music Co.

Barrere, G. *The Flutist's Formulae.* G. Schirmer. A compendium of daily studies on six basic exercises.

Berbiguier. *18 Studies.* Schirmer, International, Carl Fischer.

Boehm, T. *Twelve Studies, Op. 15.* Carl Fischer.

Twenty-four Caprices, Op. 26. Carl Fischer.

Twenty-four Melodious Studies, Op. 37. Carl Fischer.

Camus. *42 Études.* Editions Salabert. Piano accompaniment available.

Cavally. *Melodious and Progressive Studies for Flute,* 3 vols. Southern Music Co. Selected from the works of Andersen, Garibaldi, Koehler, Terschak, Boehm, Kronke, Kohler and Mollerup. Volume one is suitable for lower intermediate level. Studies only generally progressive. An excellent collection. When in doubt use this series.

Original Melodious and Progressive Studies for the Beginning Flutist. Southern Music Co. A piano accompaniment for some of the studies is available.

Famous Flute Studies and Duets. Southern Music Co. Includes the Andersen Studies Op. 30 and 63 in addition to duets and solos.

Demersseman-Moyse. *Fifty Melodious Studies,* 2 vols. Leduc.

DeMichelis. *24 Exercises, Op. 25.* Ricordi.

Eck, E. *Flute Trills.* Belwin-Mills.

Practical Flute Studies. Belwin-Mills.

Tone Development for Flute. Belwin-Mills.

Endresen, R. *Supplementary Studies for the Flute.* Rubank.

Fanelli. *Authentic Latin Flute Technique.* Belwin-Mills.

Furstenau. *26 Studies for Flute, Op. 107.* 2 vols. Fillmore, Leduc.

Studies, Op. 125, edited by Eck. Belwin.

12 Grand Studies for Flute. Cundy-Bettoney.

Galli. *30 Exercises, Op. 100.* Ricordi.

Garibaldi. *Little Studies, Op. 131.* Leduc.

20 Little Études, Op. 132. International, Leduc.

20 Études Chantantes, Op. 88. Leduc.

Hovey, N. *Daily Exercises for Flute.* Belwin-Mills. Selected from works of Albert and Pares.

Hovey-Morsch. *Section Studies for Flute.* Belwin-Mills.

Hughes, L. *40 Studies, Op. 101.* International.

Jean-Jean, P. *16 Modern Études.* Leduc. Difficult, built on twentieth century harmonies. Standard literature for the advanced flutist.

Karg-Elert, S. *30 Studies, Op. 107.* International.

Kincaid, William. *The Art and Practice of Modern Flute Technique,* 2 vols. MCA Music. An important new method by the master performer-teacher, giving his personal method and technique of teaching in collaboration with Claire Polin. A total of five volumes is projected.

Koehler. *Progress in Flute Playing, Op. 107,* 3 vols. Carl Fischer, International, G. Schirmer, Southern Music Co.
Romantic Études. Southern Music Co.
Six Preludes for Flute Alone, 2 vols. McGinnis & Marx.

Kujala, Walfrid. *The Flutist's Progress.* Progress Press. A self-teaching method for the advanced beginner, including a recording. Somewhat limited in scope. Additional volumes are projected.

Kuhlau. *Six Divertissements, Op. 68.* Cundy-Bettoney.

Kummer. *24 Melodic Études, Op. 110.* Associated Music Publishers, Schott (Belwin-Mills).

LaPorta, John. *Developing the School Jazz Ensemble.* Berklee Press. Has a director's manual and a book for flute.
A Guide to Improvisation. Berklee Press. Has a director's manual, three l.p.'s and a book for C treble instruments.

Marquee, Andre. *Daily Exercises for Flute.* G. Schirmer.

Moore, E. C. *Daily Routine for Flute.* Carl Fischer.

Moyse, Marcel. *Tone Development Through Interpretation,* vol. 1, flute and piano. McGinnis & Marx. A second volume to consist of commentary and instructions was announced, but the publisher has no present plans for publication.
De La Sonorite: Art et Technique. Leduc. Marcel Moyse, former professor of flute at the Paris Conservatory, has made great contributions to the study literature for flute. This is one of the more than thirty volumes of original works and arrangements which have been published by Alphonse Leduc in Paris under the general title *Enseignement Complet de la Flute.* With the exception of his edition of the Demersseman studies, op. 4, his material is on the upper intermediate and advanced levels.

Nicolet, Aurele. *Learning with the Masters.* Edition Peters. Text, musical scores and two 10″ l.p. records illustrating the text.

Paganini. *12 Études and Caprices.* Fillmore.

Pares, G. *Technical Exercises for Flute.* Carl Fischer.
Modern Pares for Flute. Rubank. Two editions of the same music.

Peichler, A. *40 Grand Studies,* 4 vols. International.

Platonov, V. *30 Studies.* International.
24 Studies. International.

Prill. *24 Studies, Op. 12.* Carl Fischer.

Reichert, A. *Six Études, Op. 6.* Cundy-Bettoney.
Daily Exercises, Op. 5. Associated Music Pubishers.

Rynearson, Paul. *Eleven Contemporary Flute Études.* Avant Music. Excellent but difficult studies dealing with avant garde techniques applied to the flute.

Schade, W. *24 Caprices.* Southern Music Co., Cundy-Bettoney.
12 Impromptu Études. Southern Music Co.

Sieg. *Piccolo Preparatory Studies.* Carl Fischer.

Spiegl, F. *Bach for Unaccompanied Flute.* Oxford University Press.

Stokes, Sheridan and Richard Condon. *Illustrated Method for Flute.* Trio Associates. "Fundamentals of flute technique through discussion, illustration and photography."

Taffanel-Gaubert. *17 Daily Drills.* Leduc.

Terschak. *Daily Exercises, Op. 71.* Associated Music Publishers, Schott (Belwin-Mills).

Viola, J. *Developing Sight Reading Skills in the Jazz Idiom.* Berklee Press.

Vivian, A. *Scale Exercises.* Carl Fischer, Boosey & Hawkes.

Voxman, H. *Selected Studies for Flute.* Rubank.

Wilkins, Frederick. *The Flutist Guide:* D. & T. Artley, Inc. Has a phonograph recording of each of the musical excerpts in the book. Highly recommended.

Wood. *Studies for the Execution of Upper Notes.* Boosey & Hawkes.

Wummer, J. *12 Daily Exercises in all the Major and Minor Keys.* Carl Fischer.

Study and Achievement Questions

1. Identify the beginning, intermediate and advanced playing ranges of the flute and piccolo.
2. Assemble the flute, identifying each part and describing and demonstrating each step.
3. Observe one or more beginning, intermediate and advanced flute students in the process of assembly and fill out the check list for assembly. Describe corrections for any faults found.
4. Describe and demonstrate the holding and hand positions for the flute. Instruct a student unfamiliar with the instrument in how to achieve the correct positions.
5. Observe one or more, beginning, intermediate and advanced flute students and fill out the check list for holding and hand positions. Suggest corrections for any faults.
6. Discuss and demonstrate embouchure formation, setting the embouchure, and the effect of the four items which influence tone production on the flute.
7. Observe one or more beginning, intermediate and advanced flute students and fill out the check list for embouchure formation. Suggest corrections for any faults.
8. Discuss how the flute is tuned and the influence of the cork in the head joint on pitch and intonation.
9. What factors will make the over-all pitch of the instrument flat? sharp? What factors influence the pitch of individual notes?
10. Identify the three registers of the flute. Indicate

those notes produced by the fundamental vibration of the air column, and by the first overtone.

11. List the most frequently found deficiencies in tone quality together with their causes and corrections.
12. Describe placement and movement of the tongue in fundamental, legato and staccato articulation. Describe how multiple tonguing is achieved and used.
13. List the notes on the flute for which there are standard alternate fingerings. Give the fingering for each alternate and an example of how and when it is used.
14. What are the uses of harmonics on the flute?
15. Discuss the advantages and disadvantages of closed and open tone holes on the flute.
16. Discuss student qualifications and aptitudes for flute study. Demonstrate the use of the head joint in this respect.
17. Perform the process of disassembly and cleaning. Discuss the regular maintenance of the instrument.
18. How may sticking pads be corrected? How may leaky pads be discovered?
19. Make a comparative analysis of as many beginning flute methods as you have available. Select and rank them in order of preference.
20. Examine available standard methods and additional study materials for flute and list them with comments.
21. Prepare a suggested list of material to include all five types of material suggested for simultaneous study for an upper beginning level student. An intermediate level student. An advanced student.
22. Discuss the use of vibrato on the flute. When and how is a vibrato developed?
23. Listen to several phonograph records of flute literature. Comment and and compare tone quality, phrasing, articulation and general facility.
24. Attend a festival event which includes flute solos. Observe the players and make a detailed critique of as many as possible on details of holding positions, hand positions, embouchure formation, tuning, intonation, tone quality, articulation and technique. Describe any faults found in any of these, the possible causes, symptoms, and corrections for each.

Oboe and English Horn

The oboe and English horn have virtually the same written range and the fingering on the two instruments is identical. The discussions in this chapter will be concerned with both instruments, although the oboe specifically will be mentioned, and unless otherwise noted all comments apply equally to both instruments.

The oboe is a non-transposing instrument, sounding the note as written. The English horn is in F, sounding a perfect fifth lower than written. The transposition for the English horn, and the range of actual sounds produced by both instruments is as follows.

1. *Oboe*

Written Sounds Range of Actual Sounds

2. *English Horn*

Written Sounds Range of Actual Sounds

PLAYING RANGES

The playing ranges for the oboe are fairly generally accepted, and are classified as *Beginning*, the range a typical young beginner can be expected to play by the end of his first year of experience; *Intermediate,* the range commonly required for the average good high school player; and *Advanced,* the complete range of the professional caliber player. These ranges are determined not so much by the fingering problems involved, but in the development of a good strong standard embouchure plus the ability to make and/or adjust reeds which will respond both on the lowest and highest notes. The highest tones in the advanced range are rarely called for but are necessary in order to cover the range written in contemporary music of a difficult nature. The upper limits of an oboist's playing range should not be forced, but allowed to develop naturally as embouchure control grows. Forcing the upper notes before a player is ready causes serious embouchure problems since the student will make unnatural adjustments in order to reach the notes. The natural development of these tones comes when the student can play them without shifting or changing his embouchure except for the increased support necessary to control intonation.

Since the English horn is played by a competent oboist, the three stages of range development are given only for the oboe. Only the complete advanced range is given for the English horn. All ranges are as written for the instrument.

1. *Oboe*

Beginning Intermediate Advanced

2. *English Horn*

Playing Range

ASSEMBLING THE INSTRUMENT

Of all the woodwind instruments the oboe is the most susceptible to damage to the mechanism through careless handling in assembly or disassembly. The mechanism is extremely complicated and close fitting tolerances are necessary for certain keys to work properly. The slightest bent key or lever will cause difficulties in performance. For this reason care in handling must continually be emphasized. Beginners on the instrument have a tendency to assemble and disassemble the instrument without sufficient care or to handle the instrument as if it were ruggedly built. The proper method of putting the instrument together and taking it apart must be taught from the very beginning.

The following procedure is a standard one. Practice it until it is comfortable and natural. Before proceeding make sure that both corks are well lubricated with prepared cork grease, and that the metal lined joints into which the corks fit are wiped clean and smooth.

Parts of the Instrument

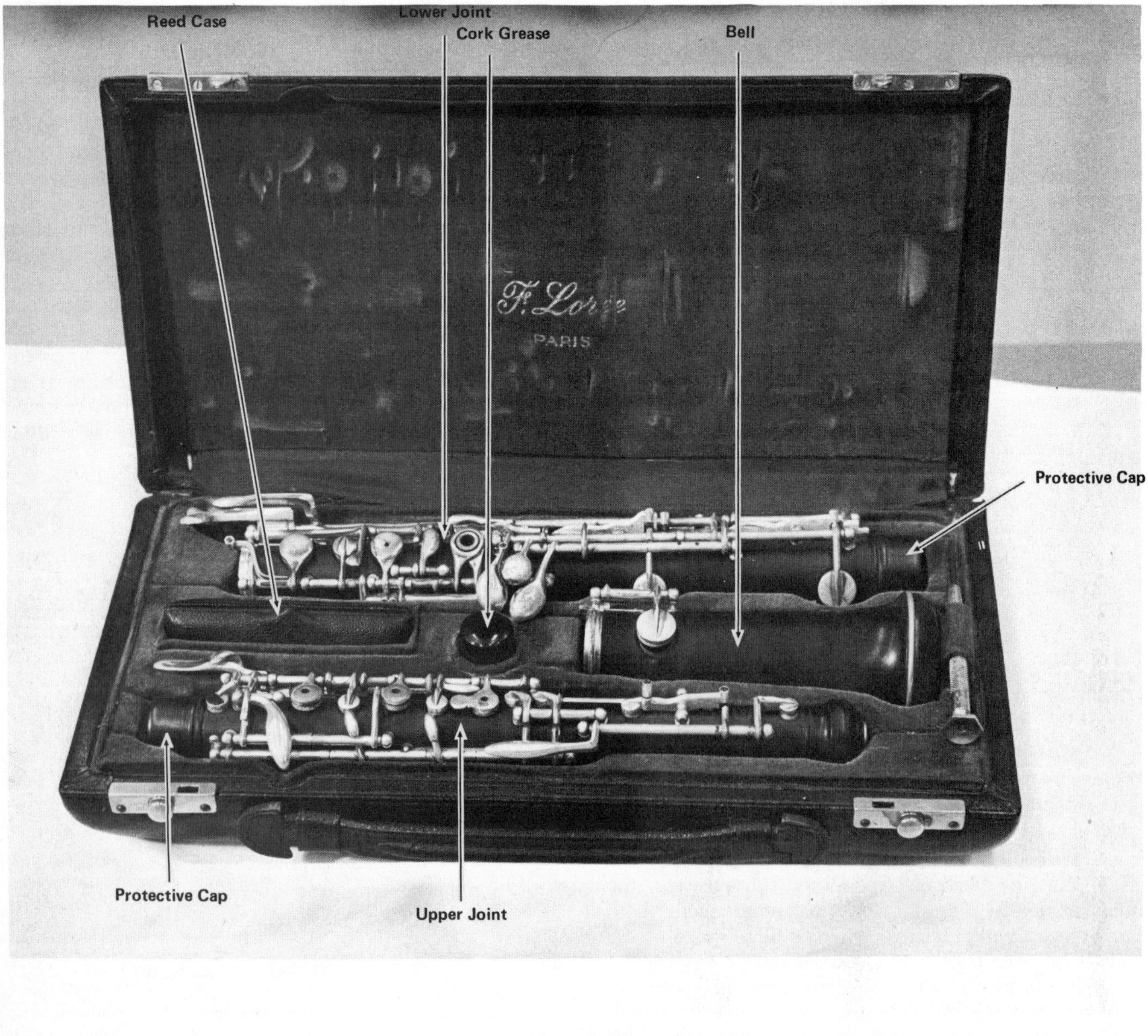

Figure O-1

A. Lower Joint and Bell Assembly

1. Figure O-2. Grasp the lower joint with the right hand, palm of the hand on the wood beneath the instrument, with the thumb around the thumb rest.

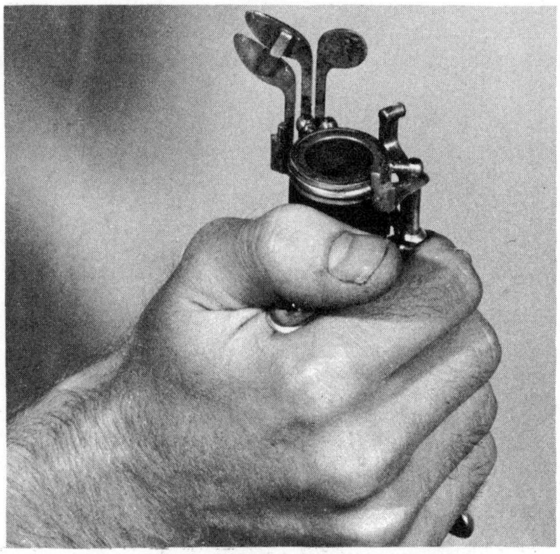

Figure O-2

2. Figure O-3. With the palm in position, the tips of the fingers press the plates over the tone holes in holding the joint firmly. Fingers are cupped so that there is no pressure against the rods on the side of the joint.

Figure O-3

3. Figure O-4. The left hand grasps the bell firmly in the palm, with the forefinger pressing on the key to raise the connecting lever so that it will slide over the portion of the lever on the lower joint.

Figure O-4

4. Figure O-5. The bell is then pushed on the lower joint and the two portions of the connecting lever aligned. The bell should be pushed with only the slightest back and forth motion keeping the connecting lever in view constantly. If the bell is twisted on, it will hit against the posts on the lower joint and be bent out of alignment.

B. Upper Joint and Lower Joint Assembly

1. Figure O-6. Grasp the upper joint with the left hand, palm of the hand on the wood beneath the instrument, with the thumb on the wood beside Octave Key A.

Figure O-5

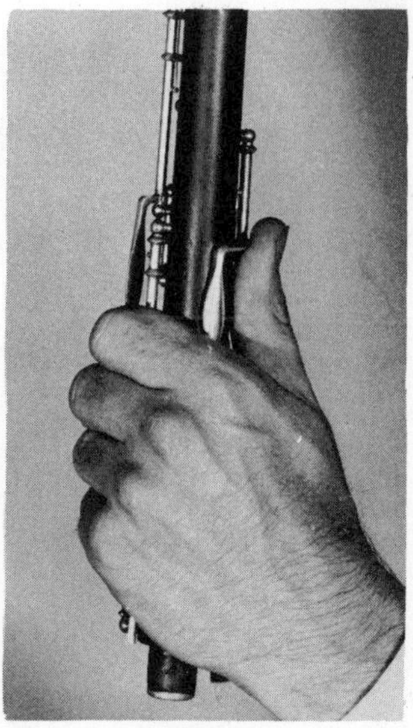

Figure O-6

2. Figure O-7. The index finger depresses the top trill key (if this key is on the instrument) to raise the connecting lever. Observe the connecting lever on the left side of the instrument to see that it is lifted as the key is pressed. The remaining three fingers cover the tone holes with the second finger over the second tone hole and press to hold the joint firmly. The heel of the thumb presses the B-flat-C rocker mechanism to raise the connecting lever. Observe the connecting lever on the right side of the instrument to see that it is raised.

Figure O-7

3. Figure O-8. Lower joint first alternate holding position. The grasp of the right hand on the lower joint is identical with that used for assembling the bell, except that the thumb is moved from around the thumb rest to hold down the connecting lever on the left side of the instrument.

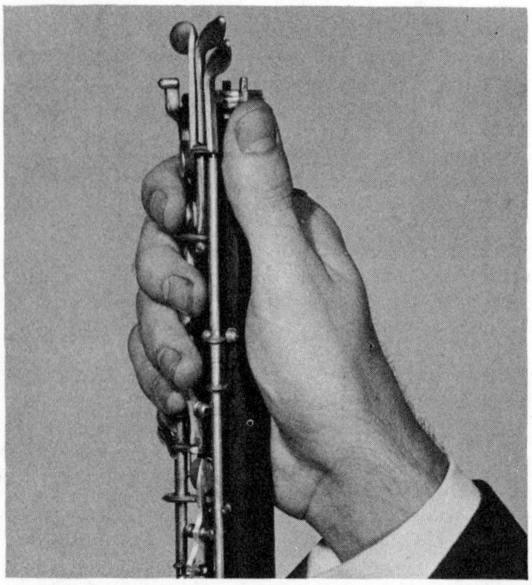

Figure O-8

4. Figure O-9. Lower joint second alternate holding position. The right hand grasps the assembled lower joint and bell with the bell held in the fingers. The forefinger is on the metal band of the bell, and the thumb presses firmly on the lower key of the upper joint. This section is held securely in this position so that the two joints can be pushed together.

Figure O-9

5. Refer back to Figure O-2. There are three connecting levers between the lower and upper joints. The placement of the hand on the upper joint raises two of these—the third on the top of the instrument is normally in a raised position. Keep your eyes on these while putting the two parts together so that there is no possibility of bending them.

6. Figure O-10. With the right hand in the first alternate position the two sections are pushed together. There must be no winding or twisting motion or one of the levers will be bent. Rest the bell against the body if necessary to hold the instrument firmly. If the cork is the right size and well greased, the sections can be pushed together without applying too much force. Check the alignment of the connecting levers.

Figure O-10

7. Figure O-11. With the right hand in the second alternate position the two sections are pushed together. There must be no winding or twisting motion or one of the levers will be bent. If the joints slide together with some difficulty, use only the very slightest back and forth motion with the lower joint, keeping the eyes on the connecting levers. Check the alignment of the connecting levers.

Figure O-11

8. Figure O-12. Push the reed into the socket as far as it will go and adjust to playing position. Grease the cork on the reed if necessary to make it fit easily.

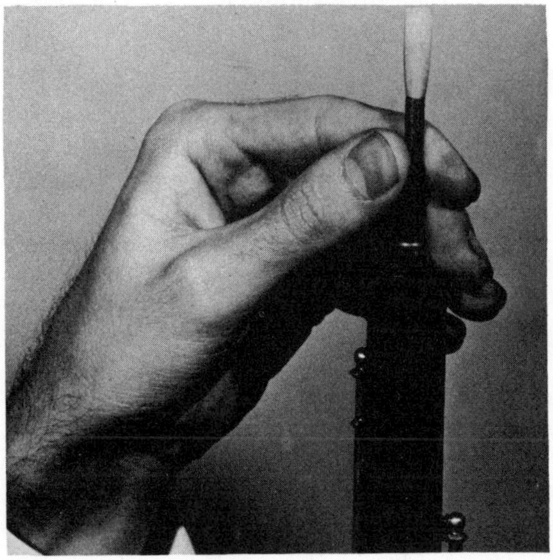

Figure O-12

English Horn. The assembly of the English horn is identical with that of the oboe, except that the bocal on which the reed fits is added to the end. A neck strap is helpful in holding the instrument and students should be encouraged to use it, although some professionals do not feel that it is necessary.

Common Faults in Assembly

There are, of course, several possible ways in which the oboe may be assembled, the only criteria for a good procedure being that no pressure is put on rods, plates, or keys during the process. The procedure outlined above is a common standard one and may be safely used for beginners who should practice putting the instrument together and taking it apart until the correct routine becomes comfortable and accurate. The following items are the most commonly found faults or inaccuracies in assembly of the oboe.

1. *Failure to grease corks.* A container of cork grease is a must for every oboe case, and the cork joints of the instrument and the reed staple must be kept well greased so that the connections may be made with ease. If the corks are not greased the instrument is assembled with difficulty and a great deal of pressure is necessary. This excessive pressure can easily cause the hand to grip the instrument too tightly and bend keys, rods, etc.

If, after the corks are well greased, a joint is still assembled with difficulty, then cork is too large. It may be fitted to the right size by sanding with fine grain sand paper either by the student or by taking the instrument to a repairman. If sanding is done, care must be taken not to sand any of the wood of the instrument, only the cork. Since the joints of many brands of oboes are metal lined, the instrument can be assembled with ease if the corks are properly fitted and well greased.

2. *Improper sequence of assembly.* Some students will assemble the upper and lower joints before putting the bell on the lower joint. While this procedure is quite satisfactory for experienced players, the inexperienced player will find it awkward to hold the assembled upper and lower joints without putting pressure on the mechanism when adding the bell. A further advantage of putting the bell on the lower joint first is that it provides an alternate holding position which gives the student a firm and safe place to hold the lower joint while the extremely critical connections are made between the lower and upper joints.

3. *Bending connecting levers.* A bent connecting lever is perhaps the most common result of improper assembly which makes some fingerings difficult or impossible to use. Unfortunately the younger players who should have the instrument in perfect playing condition are most frequently at fault. The connecting lever between the bell and the lower joint controls the closure of the pad which plays the low B-flat—the bottom of the oboe range. Young players have difficulty in producing this tone even under the best conditions and if the lever is bent or not centered properly in assembly the pad will not close completely and the student cannot produce the tone at all. If the student can play the low C and B-natural, but not the low B-flat it is almost inevitable that this pad is leaking.

Between the upper and lower joints there are three connecting levers on most instruments, two on others, which must be in perfect adjustment and perfectly aligned if the instrument is to respond properly on certain fingerings. These levers are bent during the process of assembly by twisting the joints so that the levers hit a post or key or the other portion of the lever. Insist that the students keep their eyes on these levers while these two joints are being assembled.

The lever on the right side of the instrument connects the plate or ring operated by the first finger of the right hand with two small pads between the first and second tone holes of the upper joint. Both of these pads must be opened for the basic fingering for third space C and the second for the third line B-flat. If this lever is bent so that these pads do not open sufficiently, these notes will be flat, if it is bent so they open too far, the notes will be sharp, if it is bent too much or not aligned, these notes will not respond at all.

The connecting lever on the top of the instrument is part of the articulated G-sharp mechanism, and its function is to close the pad of the tone hole which produces G-sharp when the fourth finger is down even though the G-sharp key is being held down by the left little finger. The articulated G-sharp is a very useful device in smoothing technique and is discussed later in this chapter. If this lever is bent so that it will not close the pad, then the articulation of this key is ineffective and can readily be detected. If, however, this lever is bent down so that it is too close to the pad, then the tone hole operated by the fourth finger will not completely close, and notes involving fingers down in the right hand will not respond or will respond with difficulty. If the student can play down to second line G, but has difficulty with the F-sharp or E-natural below the chances are that this pad is leaking and the cause of the leak may be this connecting lever.

The connecting lever on the left side of the instrument controls an alternate fingering for a trill key on the upper register, and is not on all models of the instrument. If this lever is bent down so that there is space between the two portions, no problem is involved, except that the rarely used trill fingering will not respond properly, and the student will resort to the identical key operated by the left hand. If however, this lever is bent up, the trill key will be held open and the instrument will not respond or will respond with difficulty.

Correcting the adjustment on any of these bent connecting levers, or indeed on any key on the instrument, must be done by a repairman who has the proper tools and uses the proper procedure to avoid putting excess pressure on the posts which hold the keys to the instru-

Checklist for Assembly

Observe the student in the operation of assembling the instrument and check the following items. Incorrect items for older students should not be called to their attention until the entire process is completed; younger students should be corrected immediately. If any mistake is made, the entire process should be repeated until perfect.

	Yes	No	Comments
1. Were corks examined to see if they were well greased?			
2. Bell held properly?			
3. Lower joint held properly?			
4. Connecting lever between bell and lower joint carefully aligned?			
5. Upper joint held properly?			
6. Lower joint and bell assembly held properly for joining upper joint?			
7. Eyes on connecting levers during this process?			
8. Upper and lower joints pushed together without twisting motion?			
9. Connecting levers between these two joints carefully aligned and tested?			
10. Reed pushed firmly into socket?			

ment. Putting pressure on the keys to straighten them may well cause more serious damage to the instrument.

4. *Holding the joints improperly.* Holding the parts of the instrument as described and illustrated in the assembly process avoids any pressure of any kind on the mechanism which would bend any portion of it. Any other manner of holding the parts which accomplishes the same thing would be equally satisfactory. Holding the parts improperly puts pressure on the delicate mechanism of the instrument and soon bends keys or rods out of line.

An instrument which is not in perfect alignment plays with difficulty, has certain notes out of tune, or simply doesn't respond at all. Beginners on the instrument must be taught to hold the parts correctly during the assembly and disassembly and checked frequently to see that they are doing so.

5. *Bent keys or rods.* The result of improper assembly, rough handling, or putting the instrument in its case carelessly is bent keys or rods. The keys and rods most frequently bent are those operated by the left little finger which makes certain notes difficult or impossible to produce. The cluster of three keys all operating on the same rod must operate smoothly and accurately. If the rod is bent, realignment is difficult and complicated and must be done by a repair man. The second octave key operated by the first finger is frequently bent down so that the pad is not opened sufficiently. This causes difficulty in producing the notes in the upper part of the second octave, and frequently makes them flat in pitch.

HOLDING POSITION FOR THE OBOE

The way in which the oboe is held has a direct effect on the type of tone quality produced, the embouchure, intonation, and the development of technical facility. The proper position is one in which the body is in a comfortable relaxed position, in which the hands and arms fall naturally into position; and which permits the formation and development of the best embouchure. There is virtually unanimous agreement among authorities on what the best playing position is, and the description and illustrations given here follow this standard. Seated, standing and rest positions are given here, with details of hand and finger positions following in the next section.

Seated Position

The oboe is held directly in the center of the front of the body. The instrument is at a forty degree angle with the body, with the weight of the instrument on the right thumb and balanced between the right and left thumbs and the mouth. Head erect, chin up, eyes straight ahead, with shoulders up but relaxed. Elbows, hands free from the body. Both feet flat on the floor. Shoulders and back must not touch the back of the chair when playing.

Figure O-13. Seated Position (Front View).

Figure O-14. Seated Position (Side View).

Adjust the height of the music stand so that the music can be easily read in this position. When two students are playing from the same music, angle the chairs slightly toward the center of the stand so that the position of the body and instrument can remain correct.

Figure O-15. Standing Position (Front View).

Figure O-16. Standing Position (Side View).

Standing Position

The position of the instrument when the player is standing should be identical with the seated position, only the position of the body itself is changed. Stand erect with feet slightly apart, one foot ahead of the other to help maintain balance. Head remains erect, with chin up and eyes straight ahead. Shoulders up but relaxed, and elbows free from the body. Raise the music stand, if one is being used, so that the head does not tilt downward. Every player should regularly spend a portion of his practice time standing to become at ease playing in a standing position.

Figure O-17. Standard Rest Position.

Figure O-18. Semi-rest Position.

Rest Position

In the standard rest position, the oboe is placed diagonally across the legs with the tone holes up to keep moisture from running into the tone holes. From this position it can be quickly picked up and returned to playing position. Protect the reed from damage while the instrument is moving to and from this rest position, and while it is in the rest position.

The semi-rest position is used during short rests in a composition when the player must be ready to resume playing immediately. This position permits some physical relaxation and helps prevent fatigue when performing over a period of time.

HOLDING POSITION FOR THE ENGLISH HORN

Figure O-19. Seated Position (Front View).

Seated Position

The English horn is held between the legs of the player directly in front of the body. The position of the instrument is adjusted with the bell back or forward from the absolute vertical according to the physical size of the student so that the right hand is in position comfortably, and the reed enters the embouchure at the best angle for the correct embouchure formation.

Most students prefer to have the weight of the instrument held by a neckstrap. The right thumb supports none of the weight, but simply controls the position of the instrument, and balances it in the mouth with the aid of

Figure O-20. Seated Position (Side View).

the left thumb. Advanced students may dispense with the neckstrap if they desire.

Head erect, chin up, eyes straight ahead, with shoulders up but relaxed. Elbows, hands free from the body. Both feet flat on the floor. Sit forward so the instrument does not touch the chair, and shoulders and back do not contact the back of the chair. Adjust the height of the music stand for easy reading.

Standing Position

When the player is standing, the position of the instrument itself and its relationship to the body should be identical with the seated position, only the position of the body itself is changed. Stand erect with feet slightly apart, one foot ahead of the other to maintain balance. Head remains erect, with chin up and eyes straight ahead. Shoulders up but relaxed, and elbows free from the body. A certain amount of regular practice time should be spent standing in order to develop ease playing in the standing position.

Rest Position

In the rest position, the neckstrap is unhooked and the instrument laid diagonally across the legs with the tone holes up. From this position the instrument can be quickly picked up and returned to playing position, although players must allow sufficient time for hooking the neckstrap. If the instrument is to be left in this position for any length of time, perhaps the bocal and the reed should be removed from the instrument for protection.

Common Faults in Holding Positions

The way in which the oboe and English horn are held has a great influence on the way in which the student progresses on the instrument. Progress can be facilitated or it can be hindered. For some reason the oboe holding position is subject to greater and more serious deviation from the normal by a greater percentage of students than those on any other instrument. The teacher must check continually, especially during the first few months of study on the instrument, to correct any deviations before they become habits. The players must learn to feel the right position, and a continual check will help them achieve this. Every player should be encouraged to observe his position daily in front of a mirror.

The following are the most commonly found faults in holding positions for the oboe, and to a great extent on the English horn. Since the English horn is normally played by an oboist, any deviations from the standard will be transferred to that instrument.

1. *Head inclined downward.* This is the most serious deviation from the normal because of the extreme effect it has on tone quality, and is, unfortunately, found in students at all stages of development. When the head is inclined downward, the reed enters the embouchure at a right angle rather than the forty degree angle unless the oboe is brought correspondingly closer to the body. This virtually eliminates effective control of the reed with the lips, puts the angle at which the breath enters the reed directly into the reed, and makes delicate tonguing impossible. The tone quality produced with this position is reedy, nasal, and lacking in body. It is, as well, extremely difficult to play in tune with the head in this position.

This habit must never be allowed to start. Correct it immediately and firmly to the forty degree angle. Raise the music stand so that the student will have to hold the heard erect, and insist on regular practice in front of a mirror until the position is corrected. Students should see themselves, since they frequently cannot feel this incorrect position.

2. *Instrument not centered on body.* Students will point the bell of the instrument toward one knee or the other rather than straight ahead. This is sometimes caused by not pointing the chair and the body toward the center of the music stand when two students are reading off of the same music. It may be caused by muscular tenseness in the arms, or by an incorrect hand position on the instrument. Whatever the cause it should be located and corrected immediately.

An instrument which is not centered puts the reed into the embouchure at a slight angle, making the lip support on the reed on a diagonal rather than a right angle on the blades. While the consequences of this may not be especially noticeable in the middle range of the instrument it produces a coarse tone quality on the lowest notes, and in the high register the tones will be thin. Any problem in intonation will be magnified.

3. *Bell resting on leg.* This, unfortunately, is not too common, and is caused by the student's desire to take the weight of the instrument off the right thumb, or because he must turn his head to read the music on the music stand. Most students, if the bell rests on a leg, will have to adjust their head up or down from the normal position in order to have the reed in the mouth. This causes changes in the way in which the embouchure controls the reed, with the resultant problems this situation leads to. If allowed to continue, this position becomes habitual and extremely difficult to correct. Locating the music stand and chair properly helps, and the use of a mirror helps the student establish the right feeling for position.

4. *Fingers assisting thumbs in holding the instrument.* During the earliest experience with the oboe, the student may feel insecure in holding the instrument and in gaining confidence in the balance between the thumbs and embouchure. This is especially true of students transferred from the clarinet to the oboe since the oboe is smaller and lighter in weight, and the finger spread is wider. Fingers will be found under the instrument, against the instrument, or moving back and forth from their proper guide position to the incorrect positions on the body of the oboe.

Correct through insistence on maintaining the guide positions for the fingers both through feeling the keys and through use of the mirror. Fingers which remain habitually out of position cause roughness in technique, and even make certain passages impossible to play.

5. *Slouched body.* Many different degrees of poor posture are found—spine curved against the back of the chair, shoulders curved forward, feet crossed or hung over a rung on the chair, etc. Poor posture affects breathing and breath control to the point that students may find it impossible to support the tone properly, and will become physically tired rather quickly while playing. It pulls the arms out of position making technique rough. Poor posture in any degree must be corrected immediately and firmly. Use of a mirror is helpful.

6. *Moving the body while playing.* Beating time with the bell of the instrument, swaying back and forth in time with the music, grandiose flourishes with the instrument at the end of difficult passages, etc., are extremely distracting to the conductor of a group and to the other players, and frequently humorous to an audience. All movements change the position of the reed in the mouth to a degree, interferes with the coordination of the muscles controlling breath support and in general makes for a less effective performance.

The habit of bodily movement during the performance is very difficult to correct once it becomes ingrained, since the player frequently doesn't realize he is doing it. Any such movements must be called to the attention of the player for immediate correction.

7. *English horn neck strap.* While some advanced players prefer not to use a neckstrap on the English horn, it is well to insist that younger students use one. It must be adjusted so that the reed falls naturally into the embouchure. A rule of the thumb is to adjust the strap so that the reed is in the center of the lower lip when the head is erect and the lips together. From this point the player will make slight adjustments up or down in order to accommodate his particular embouchure formation.

The strap must be adjusted so that the right thumb is not holding the weight of the instrument, but controlling the angle at which the instrument is held. An adjustment which is too high or too low forces the player to raise or lower his head into an unnatural position with consequent alterations of embouchure formations. The strap adjustment should enable the player to form and use exactly the same embouchure formation on the English horn that he uses on the oboe.

HAND POSITIONS

Since the oboe is usually played by a student with previous training on another woodwind instrument—usually clarinet—hand position may not be as much of a problem if the hand position on the previous instrument was good. Hand positions on all woodwind instruments are quite similar, i.e., the position in which the fingers fall naturally into place on the instrument, and in which there is no muscular tension in fingers, wrists, arms or shoulders. This naturally relaxed position allows facility to develop rapidly.

The following step-by-step procedure for establishing the hand position on the oboe should be studied thoroughly, preferably with an instrument so that a feel for the position can be developed. Study both the text and the photographs carefully until they are perfectly clear.

The "Guide Position" which is given is the fundamental position for hands and fingers and should be maintained at all times except when the fingering for a note involves moving a finger to another location. The guide position puts all fingers into the best position for developing speed and accuracy. If the proportions of finger lengths to hand size is on the large side, the student may have to raise his hand position to enable his fingers to cover holes and contact keys at the proper spots.

A. Right Hand Position

1. Figure O-21. The right thumb contacts the thumb rest on the flesh to the side of and at the base of the nail. The ball of the thumb is against the body of the instrument.

2. Figure O-22. The right little finger touches lightly the C key, and the remaining fingers fall naturally into position no more than an inch directly above the three tone holes. The tips of the fingers overlap the plates slightly so that the ball of the finger directly beneath the finger nail is in the center of the plate. This is especially important if the tone hole for the sixth finger is open, or if an open key model instrument is being used.

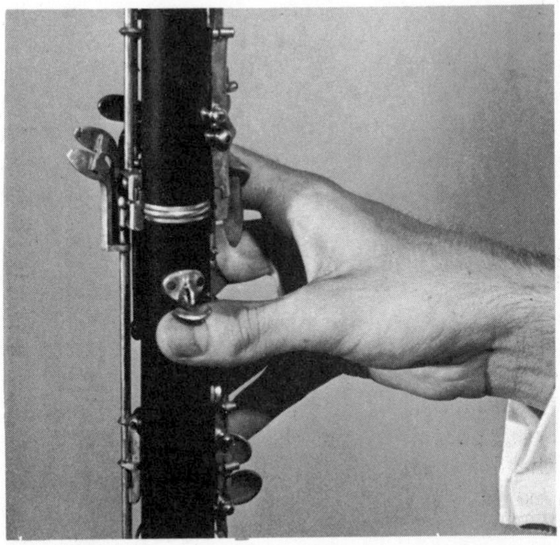

Figure O-21

Figure O-22

3. Figure O-23. The fingers fall into a natural curve without tension to permit maximum control and accuracy of movement.

B. Left Hand Position

1. Figure O-24. The left thumb assists in balancing the instrument and controlling the first octave key. It is placed at almost an angle across the instrument so that the fleshy part of the ball is against the wood of the instrument, and the side just touching, but not pressing

the octave key. The octave key is controlled by vertical movements of the first joint of the thumb. The ball of the thumb never loses contact with the wood of the instrument.

Figure O-23

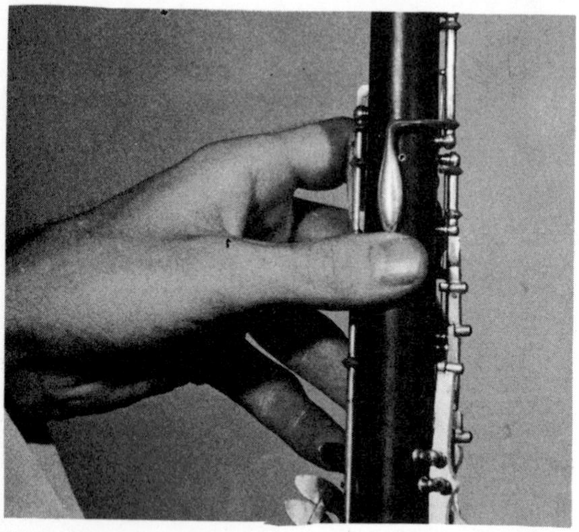

Figure O-24

2. Figure O-25. The left little finger touches lightly the B key, and the remaining fingers fall naturally into position not more than an inch directly above the three tone holes. The tips of the fingers overlap the plates slightly so that the ball of the finger beneath the finger nail is in the center of the tone hole to close the vent holes in the plates. The fingers are in a natural curve as shown for the right hand in Figure O-23.

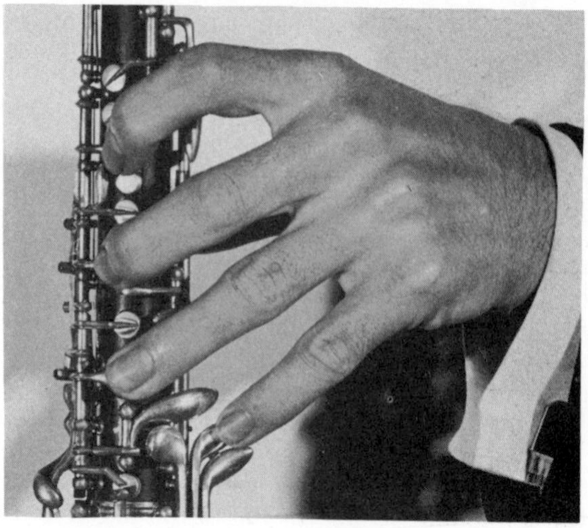

Figure O-25

C. Guide Position

Figure O-26. With the thumbs and little fingers in place as described above and the remaining fingers over the tone holes, a guide position is established which should be maintained constantly. Note that the fingers are approaching the instrument from a slight upper angle, and that the wrists are flat. The entire finger moves from the knuckle and closes the tone holes with a snap or click, pressing just hard enough to close the holes. Avoid too much pressure against the plates with the fingers.

Figure O-26

The oboe has certain fingerings which tend to pull the hands out of position unless the fingers are moved efficiently and with minimum motion. If the correct guide position is established and maintained, these finger movements will come naturally and can be readily developed. A constant check on the use and position of the fingers in these situations is necessary until the movements become habitual.

1. *Half-hole position for the first finger.* The half-hole position for the first finger functions as an octave key for the first three notes in the second octave;

The normal position for the finger is over the plate with the vent hole covered by the ball of the finger. For the half-hole position the finger is rolled downward—not slid—with a movement of the second joint of the finger so that the vent hole is open and the finger is on the extension plate of this key. Figure O-27 shows the first finger in the half-hole position. Notice that the remainder of the fingers are kept in the guide position.

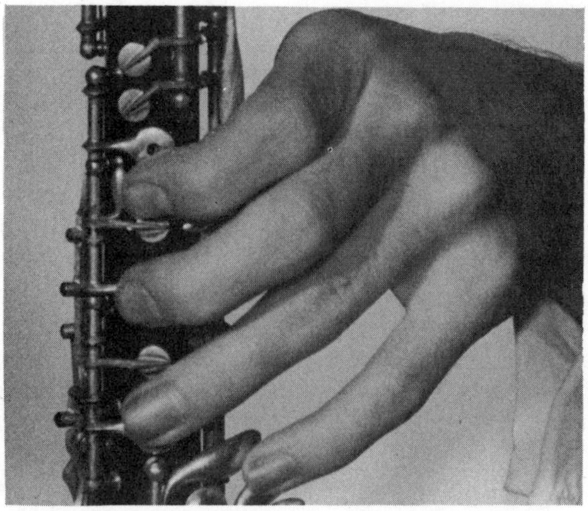

Figure O-27. First finger in half-hole position.

The following example illustrates a typical use of the half-hole:

2. *The first octave key.* This key (Octave key A on the fingering chart) is operated by the left thumb and is used for E-natural to A-flat inclusive in the second octave:

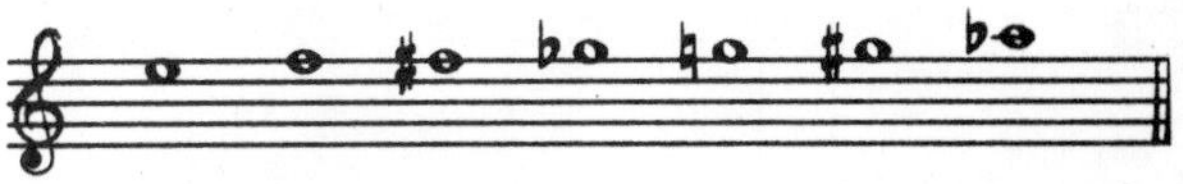

This key is opened by a vertical movement of the first joint of the thumb, with the corner of the thumb pressing the key. The thumb must not slide or roll. While this thumb is normally at a slight oblique angle with the body of the instrument, a player with short fingers will require a position more nearly straight across the body of the instrument. The position of the remainder of the fingers must be established first, and the thumb placed as close to the recommended angle as possible. No matter what angle is determined, it must be such that the octave key can be operated by the vertical movements of the first joint. The following musical example illustrates a typical use of this octave key.

3. *The second octave key.* The second octave key (octave key B on the fingering chart) is operated by the first finger of the left hand and is used for the notes A through C in the second octave:[1]

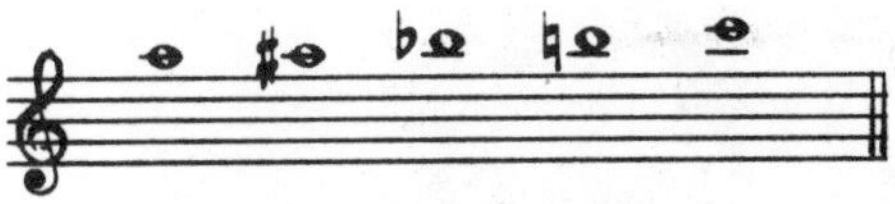

For the notes on which it is brought into use the first finger also covers the tone hole. The second octave key is operated by rolling the second joint of the finger upward, contacting the key between the first and second joints.

Figure O-28 shows the first finger in the normal position and Figure O-29 the first finger pressing the second octave key. Note carefully the point at which the finger contacts the key and that the remainder of the fingers maintain the guide position. The exact point of contact between the first finger and the second octave key varies slightly according to the length of the player's fingers.

1. On some English horns the A-flat must also be played with the second octave key.

Figure O-28. First finger in normal position.

Figure O-29. First finger operating second octave key.

The second octave key is operated differently on the various model oboes:

1. Instruments with an automatic octave key will not have this side octave key. Fingerings calling for either octave key to use the thumb key, and the mechanism of the instrument automatically shifts to the proper one.

2. On instruments with the semiautomatic octave key, it is not necessary to remove the thumb from the first octave key is open, hence the designation "semiauto-first octave key is automatically closed when the second octave key is open, hence the designation "semi-automatic."

3. Instruments without one of the automatic mechanisms require that the thumb release the first octave key when the second octave key is used to avoid having both keys open simultaneously.

The following example makes use of both the first and second octave keys:

Common Faults in Hand and Finger Position

A good hand position is a great asset to the study of the oboe. It will develop facility and control, while a poor hand position handicaps this development. The first experiences with the instrument must emphasize hand position, and it must be continually checked until the best position for that particular player is established. A beginning player who persists in quickly establishing the proper positions makes rapid progress. The use of a mirror of sufficient size so that the student can see the entire length of the instrument is actually mandatory in establishing position.

The common faults which are listed here are those which occur most frequently and are those which the instructor should look for. All of these faults have an adverse effect on facility and technique and a combination of several will be a severe handicap to progress.

1. *Right thumb.* The position of the right thumb against the thumb rest determines to a great extent the placement of the fingers over the tone holes. If the thumb is pushed too far under the instrument so that the thumb contacts the thumb rest away from the nail, the fingers are forced into an unnatural curve and cover the tone holes with the tips of the fingers rather than with the natural pad of the finger. This puts muscular tension on the fingers making them less flexible, and if an open hole instrument is being used the fingers will not properly close the tone holes. When this condition is corrected with advanced students an immediate improvement in right hand facility can be observed.

A second common fault in right thumb position is that of contacting the thumb rest with the nail itself so that the side of the finger rather than the ball is against the body of the instrument. This puts the weight of the

Checklist for Holding and Hand Positions

The following list of items provides a means of quickly checking holding positions and hand positions in the seated position for the oboe. The check should be performed while the student is playing and preferably when he is not aware that the check is being made. Any items which are checked "no" should be corrected with the deviation explained to the student, what effect it has on his playing, and why the correct position is important. Students make a more serious effort to correct mistakes if they thoroughly understand the reason for them.

A. Holding Position

	Yes	No	Comments
1. Oboe in center of body?			
2. At forty degree angle with body?			
3. Head erect with chin up?			
4. Shoulders up but relaxed?			
5. Elbows free from body?			
6. Body posture good?			
7. Feet well placed?			
8. Height of music stand correct?			
9. Uses proper rest position?			
10. Excessive body movements?			

B. Hand Positions

	Yes	No	Comments
1. Right thumb correctly placed?			
2. Left thumb correctly placed?			
3. Fingers in proper curve?			
4. Right little finger on guide key?			
5. Left little finger on guide key?			
6. Fingers covering holes with their natural pad?			
7. "U" shape between thumbs and forefingers?			
8. First octave key operated correctly?			
9. Second octave key operated correctly?			
10. First finger moving properly to half-hole position?			
11. Basic guide position maintained?			
12. Wrists flat?			
13. Muscular tension?			
14. Fingers no more than one inch above tone holes?			

instrument on the thumb in such a way that it is difficult to support, and the student tires quickly. Correct by insisting that the ball of the thumb be against the wood of the instrument, and a "U" shape formed by the thumb and first finger.

2. *Left thumb.* Two common faults in the use of the left thumb are removing it from contact with the instrument when it is not in use, or when the second octave key is being used, and in sliding the thumb to open the octave key rather than using the vertical movement of the first joint. A less common problem with the left thumb is found when the student places it parallel with the body of the instrument rather than at the right angle.

Removing the thumb from the instrument removes the support which holds the instrument into place in the mouth, and frequently puts additional pressure against the lower lip with the reed which has the same unfortunate result as biting the reed with the lower teeth. It also destroys the balance of the fingers of the left hand, leaving them free in the air rather than pivoting against the support of the thumb. In inexperienced students this causes the fingers to fall out of position on the tone holes and the notes do not respond. Correct this condition as soon as it is discovered, since most players will not be aware that they are doing it.

Sliding the thumb to open the first octave key produces sluggish, erratic, and undependable operation. With inexperienced players sliding the thumb will pull the fingers out of position over the tone holes, or even pull the third finger off of its plate. Practicing the study suggested for the use of this key, and similar studies while being aware of the movement of the thumb will help correct this condition. Students transferred from clarinet to oboe do not have this trouble as a rule if their use of the left thumb was correct on the clarinet.

Placing the thumb parallel with the wood of the instrument pulls the hand so far out of position that the development of any appreciable amount of facility is extremely difficult. This position is sometimes encouraged by the improper use of the first finger of the left hand in the operation of the second octave key. Correcting the way in which this octave key is opened, developing the relationship between the thumb and first finger to approximately a "U" shape, and insisting on the correct guide position for the hand will correct the condition, although slowly and with effort if it has been long established.

3. *Little fingers.* In the suggested guide position the little fingers are touching a key from which it is easy to move rapidly to another key when needed. If the little fingers are not in the guide position, then assurance in this movement is lost. Deviation of the little fingers from the guide position frequently puts the remainder of the fingers out of position as well. Beginners on the instrument will frequently take the instrument from the mouth and look at the keys to see which one they should use if the guide position is not maintained.

Some students take the little fingers off of the instrument and put them under the keys on the side, or even under the body of the instrument itself. All of these deviations cause problems in technical development, and the best remedial measure is to insist that the guide position be maintained. The use of a mirror, with slow practice will help establish the correct position.

EMBOUCHURE FORMATION

An embouchure may be defined as the formation of the performer's lips with supporting muscles, teeth and jaws in relation to the reed which have to do with tone production.

The criteria for a good oboe embouchure may be summarized as follows: A good embouchure is one which over the entire range of the instrument produces a rich, full-bodied, clear tone; plays perfectly in tune; allows the full scope of articulations; allows the full range of dynamics; plays and is controlled with a minimum amount of physical exertion when used in connection with a good reed.

A poor embouchure is one which violates one of these criteria: produces a thin, reedy nasal tone quality; plays certain notes out of tune; does not allow the full scope of articulation in all ranges; has a restricted dynamic range; or requires an undue amount of physical exertion.

Embouchure is inseparable from the reed and is entirely dependent on having a good, responsive reed. The best embouchure formation cannot play a poor reed, nor will an excellent reed respond properly with a poorly formed embouchure.

There are among authorities on the instrument, two basic types of embouchure formation recommended, although the differences between the two are not as great as those found between the two types of clarinet embouchure. Each of the formations is subject to infinite variation in small ways according to the teacher, and depend primarily upon the type of reed being used and the exact concept of tone quality desired.

The basic difference between the two points of view is found in whether the cheek muscles and the corners of the mouth are pushed in toward the reed, or whether the cheek muscles are pulled back into a slight "smile" position while at the same time the corners of the mouth are pushed in around the reed. For convenience and clarity the first is called a "Soft Cushion" and the second a "Hard Cushion," although these terms are relative and not to be taken literally.

The Soft Cushion Embouchure

The soft cushion embouchure seems to be the most widely used formation in many sections of the country, being taught by the teachers in many of the leading universities and schools of music and by many of the fine professionals. The basic formation of the soft cushion embouchure may be achieved through the following step-by-step procedure. Check each step with a small mirror on the music stand.

1. Keeping the lips relaxed, drop the lower jaw so that the teeth are about a half inch apart. Place the tip of the reed in the center of the lower lip as in Figure O-30.

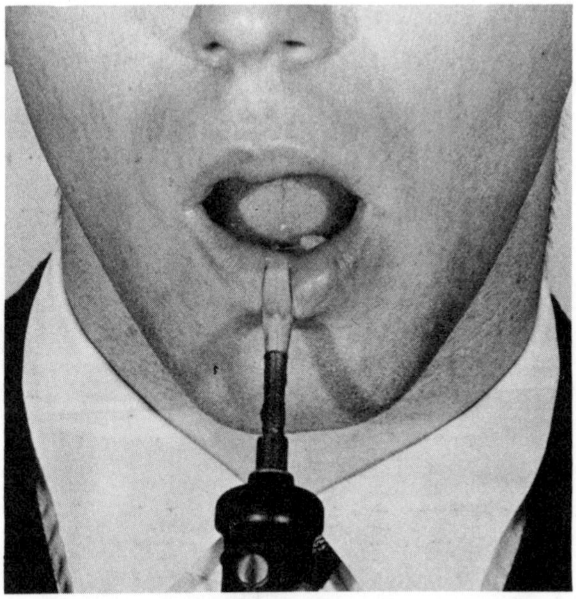

Figure O-30

2. Roll the lower lip over the teeth until the tip of the reed is sticking just past the lip as in Figure O-31. Keeping the lower jaw down, bring the upper lip barely over the teeth. Only a very little of the lip is over the teeth—just the skin in front of the rope muscle in the lip. No muscle is over the teeth.

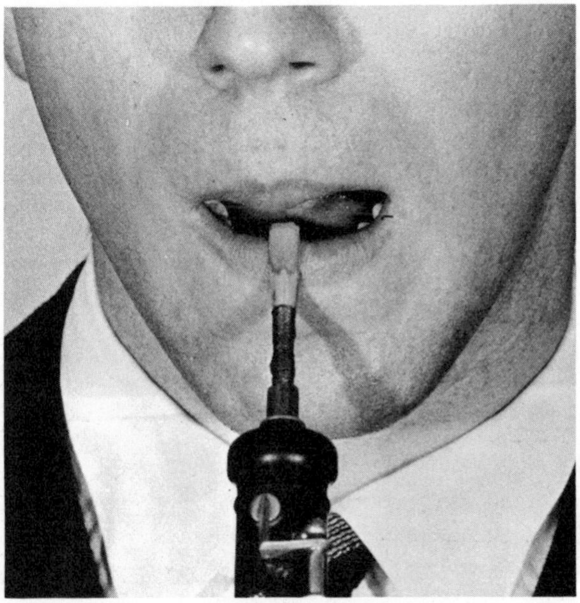

Figure O-31

3. Bring the lips together, pushing the corners of the mouth slightly toward the reed so that the reed is supported with slight pressure from all directions. The lower jaw must be kept open so that there is no pressure against the reed with the lower teeth. Just enough reed, about an eighth of an inch, protrudes past the lips in the mouth so that it can be touched with the tongue. Figure O-32 is in front view of this embouchure formation and Figure O-33 a side view. Both photographs were taken while the instrument was being played.

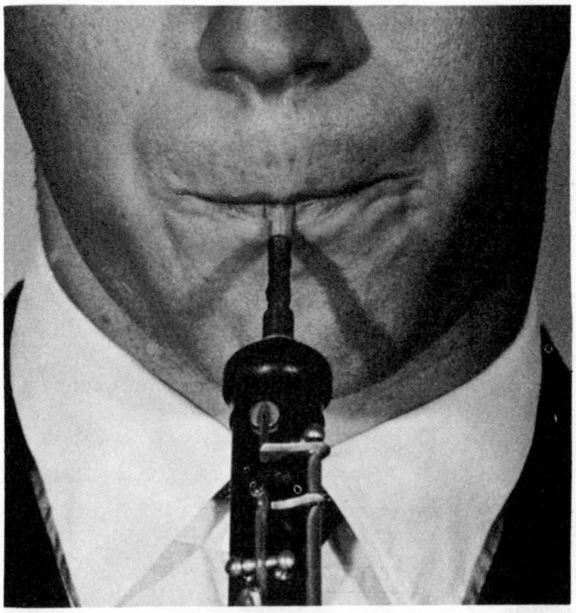

Figure O-32. Front View.

Figure O-33. Side View.

The embouchure used on the English horn is identical with that used on the oboe. Students playing both oboe and English horn must not change their basic embouchure when playing the English horn. Figures O-34 and O-35 are the front and side views of the same player taken while the English horn was being played.

Alternate Soft Cushion Embouchure

The most common alternative formation for the soft cushion, and one which is perhaps used just as often as that just described is the formation which puts the entire red of both lips over the teeth but which is otherwise identical. Using the entire lip over the teeth provides a larger cushion on which the reed can vibrate, and a greater amount of lip to control the reed. This formation when used with the proper reed produces a tone quality somewhat fuller and darker in color than that when a small amount of lip is used. For this reason it is preferred by many teachers.

The following step-by-step procedure illustrates this formation.

1. Figure O-36. Relax the lower lip and place the tip of the reed slightly past the center of the lip.

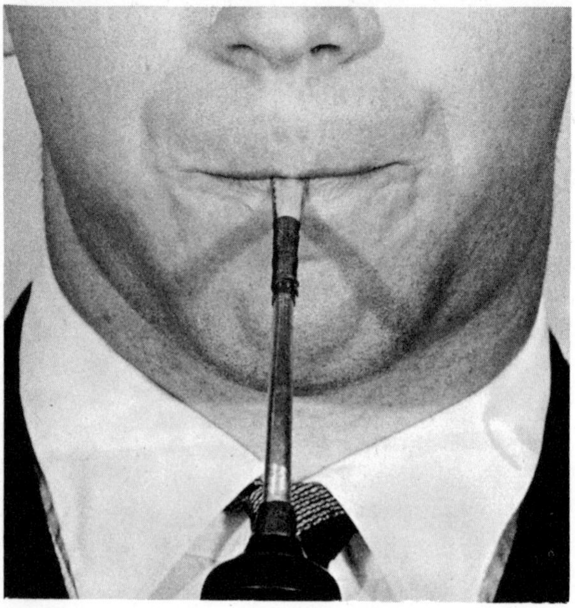

Figure O-34. Front View.

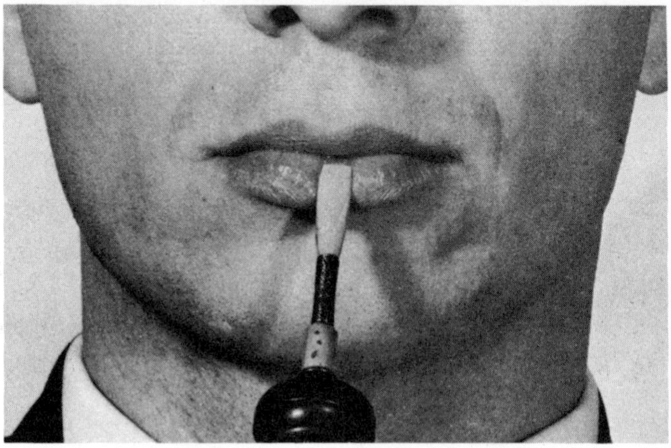

Figure O-36

2. Figure O-37. Drop the lower jaw and roll the lower lip over the teeth until the edge of the lip is over the front edge of the teeth. Note the amount of reed extending past the lip.

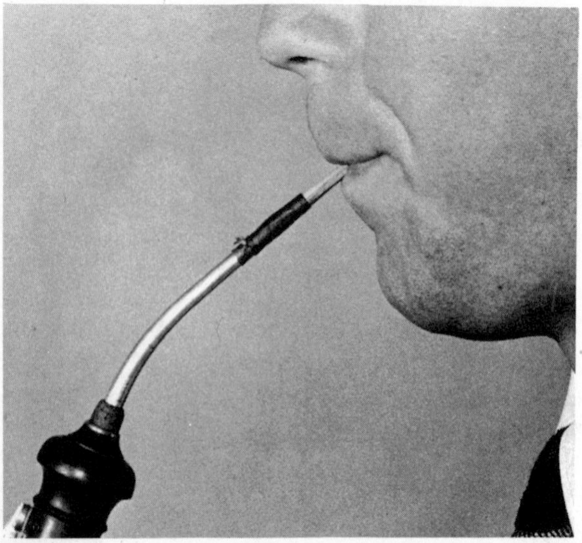

Figure O-35. Side View.

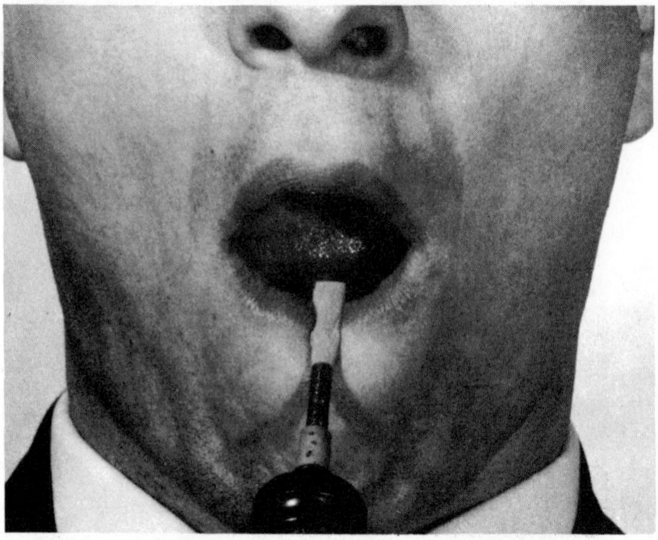

Figure O-37

3. Figure O-38. Draw the upper lip over the teeth so that no red is showing. Bring the lips together so that no air can escape. The corners of the mouth are pushed slightly toward the reed so that it is supported with slight pressure from all directions. The lower jaw must be kept open so there is no pressure against the reed with the lower teeth.

Figure O-38

The amount of reed varies with the octave which is being played, less reed for the lower octave, more for the third octave. Figure O-39 shows this embouchure position playing the low B-flat, and Figure O-40 third octave G (4 lines above staff). Note the difference in the amount of reed in the mouth.

Figure O-39

Figure O-40

The Hard Cushion Embouchure

The hard cushion embouchure for the oboe is less widely recommended than the hard cushion formation for the clarinet, although some fine performers make use of it. The basic formation of the hard cushion embouchure for the oboe may be achieved through the following step-by-step procedure. Check each step with a small mirror on the music stand. Continue to use the mirror constantly until the embouchure is established.

1. Drop the lower jaw until the teeth are about a half-inch apart. Pull back the corners of the mouth so that the lower lip is stretched. Place the reed on the lower lip, pushing it into the mouth so that none of the red of the lower lip is showing.

2. Pull the upper lip over the teeth so that about half the lip is covering the teeth.

3. Close the lips around the reed, maintaining the stretch positions of the lips. The cheek muscles are pulled back slightly into the "smile" position, and dimples are formed in the cheeks of most students. About a quarter-inch of the reed extends past the lips so that the tongue can touch it. The lower jaw must be held open away from the lip. There must be no upward pressure or biting with the teeth against the lower lip. Chin is held flat so that the lower lip will not bunch against the reed, and the lips closed or pushed around the reed so that no air escapes.

Setting the Embouchure

Before producing a tone on the instrument, practice with the reed alone. With a properly moistened reed (this is described under the section on reeds), form the embouchure as described, checking continually in a mirror to see that it is correct. Using a little more reed in the mouth than will be used in playing on the instrument, produce a tone using standard abdominal breath support. Continue blowing until the characteristic "double crow" can be produced and sustained for five to ten seconds, before putting the reed on the instrument and adjusting the amount of reed in the mouth to the proper playing position.

Since many oboists have had previous experience on clarinet, the same type of embouchure formation—soft cushion or hard cushion, will come quite naturally. A further advantage of a student with previous experience on the clarinet is that there is considerably less problem with holding the instrument and with fingering thus giving an opportunity to concentrate on embouchure formation and tone production.

A beginning student on the oboe should be given a softer reed at the start than will be used after he has developed. Such a reed will produce a rather reedy tone, but has the advantage of being easier to blow thus permitting the formation of the proper embouchure. As the embouchure develops the strength of the reed can be increased gradually. A mirror should be used constantly to check this formation until the embouchure is formed and developed.

Common Faults in Embouchure Formation

The teacher will have to check frequently to catch any deviations from the standard. Students are not always capable of discovering their own mistakes, or of actually knowing when they are right and when they are wrong, since it is just as easy for them to develop the wrong muscular formation as it is the correct one. The embouchure must be established by how it feels in the mouth and how the tone sounds, as well as how it looks in the mirror. The teacher must tell the student when he is right so he can discover the right feel, hear the right sound, and see the right shape.

Minute variations in embouchure formation are sometimes required to accommodate the physical characteristics of the student. The lower jaw should be adjusted so that the front of the lips are in a vertical line while playing. The lower lip must be neither forward or back of the upper lip.

Players with thick lips will cover more of the reed than players with thin lips. The amount of reed in the mouth—just enough for the tongue to touch it—is the criteria for the proper embouchure, not the amount of reed covered by the lips.

Players with uneven teeth—especially the lower ones—may need to turn the reed slightly to avoid more pressure against one side than the other, as it is necessary that the pressure against the flat of the reed be the same across its width and equal on both the upper and lower blades. If this is necessary, the amount the reed is turned is extremely slight, and care must be taken that the instrument itself is not turned but kept in position so that the hand position will be absolutely correct.

Problems encountered in embouchure formation may be summarized as follows:

1. *Dimples in cheeks.* While the presence of dimples in the cheeks when using the soft cushion formation on the clarinet is considered an indication of a poorly formed embouchure, this is not true of the soft cushion embouchure on the oboe. Because the reed is so small, and the teeth considerably closer together on the oboe embouchure, dimples need not be avoided as they will form naturally with some students when the corners of the lips are pressed together and inward to prevent air from escaping. For almost every student using the hard cushion formation dimples are virtually inevitable and should be considered a normal result of the formation. They have no effect directly one way or the other on the type of tone quality being produced.

2. *Amount of lip over teeth.* The amount of lip over the upper and lower teeth should be checked carefully until established. If the first soft cushion embouchure is being used, only enough of the upper lip is over the teeth to cover them. In the usual formation of this type none of the rope muscle in the upper lip is over the teeth, although a common variation is to put enough of the upper lip over the teeth so that the rope muscle itself is against the inner edge of the upper teeth. Students with thin lips often need this amount of lip in order to provide sufficient cushion for the reed, and the tone quality produced is the only criteria to determine the exact amount of the lip to be used.

The lower lip normally has more of the red over the teeth in order to get enough surface to control the vibration of the reed in optimum fashion. The step-by-step suggestion of putting the tip of the reed in the center of the lower lip and rolling the lip is the best starting point for determining the exact amount. The player himself will make minor deviations as the embouchure develops in order to produce the best tone quality on the type of reed being used. When using the alternate soft cushion formation check to see none of the red of the lip can be seen.

3. *Pressure against reed.* The amount of pressure against the reed with the lower teeth is frequently difficult to adjust. The reed is only supported by the lower lip, and biting with the lower teeth must be avoided. The lower teeth control to a degree the amount of support of the lip against the reed increasing the support for the upper and high registers and decreasing for the lower octave, making small adjustments to control intonation, and assisting in the control of dynamics.

If the lower teeth are biting, excessive breath pressure is necessary to produce a tone, the tone quality is rough, and the lower notes of the instrument difficult to produce. Evidence of biting can be seen by examining the inner part of the lips for imprints of the teeth. Temporarily using a very soft reed at the expense of tone quality will discourage biting since the reed will close up completely under excess pressure. Asking the player to play flatter will cause him to drop the lower jaw and gives him the feeling of playing flatter although little or no change in pitch will be apparent to the listener.

4. *Puffing cheeks.* Puffing cheeks is sometimes a

problem with oboe players as well as with other woodwind players. This is inevitably an indication of an embouchure problem since it indicates that the muscles involved in the proper embouchure formation are not supporting properly. Players with puffing cheeks virtually always have a very open tone quality which is more often than not reedy, because the breath is not properly focused and directed into the reed.

Frequently the players do not realize that the cheeks are puffed, especially if the amount of air between the teeth and cheek is small, and the use of a mirror is necessary. When the student can actually see that the cheeks are in the right position, and the embouchure formation itself is correct, he can then feel the muscular support that is necessary to keep the cheeks in position. Playing a note on the instrument with one hand while feeling the cheeks with the other is useful in helping the player feel the right position.

5. *Angle of instrument.* The angle at which the instrument is held has a great effect on the embouchure formation. Any deviation from the recommended forty degree angle of the instrument with the body will be magnified in the embouchure.

If the angle of the instrument is too wide, either because the head is dropped down or the instrument held too far out, much of the support of the lower lip is removed from the reed and the tone quality is open, rough, and difficult to control. Students with this problem automatically compensate by biting with the lower lip which brings on additional problems. Checking the angle with the use of a full length mirror until the student feels the right position is an excellent method of correction. If the angle is too great because the head is dropped, the same method may be used, or the music stand raised higher so that he will have to raise his head in order to see the music.

If the angle of the instrument with the body is smaller than forty degrees additional pressure is put against the reed with the lower lip, making the tone difficult to control, the lower notes difficult to produce, and results in a general sharpness in pitch in the higher notes. Players who habitually use the smaller angle usually make their reeds in such a way as to compensate for it in order to produce a pleasing tone quality. Unless adjustment is made in the reed the tone is small in body and frequently nasal.

This problem of the angle at which the instrument is held with the body is extremely difficult to correct once it has become habitual, and for this reason it is essential that the proper holding position be established at the beginning of oboe study.

6. *Escaping air.* Air escaping from one corner of the mouth while playing is clear indication that something is wrong with the embouchure formation. With the soft cushion embouchure this means that the lips are not being pushed around the reed, but that the corner where the air is escaping is released. With the hard cushion embouchure escaping air is the result of too much pulling back of the corner of the mouth, and is corrected by tightening the corner of the mouth and pushing slightly toward the reed.

Comparison of Soft and Hard Cushion Embouchure

It must be repeated that the words soft and hard are merely relative and not to be taken literally. The soft cushion uses a thick firm support and the hard cushion a thin and slightly harder base upon which the reed rests. Each of these formations is subject to infinite variation, all of which are slight, depending upon the training and experience of the teacher using them, and upon the physical characteristics of the student.

No two teachers will agree exactly on how to describe the correct formation, nor will two students respond exactly to the same type of instruction in their formation. A variety of explanations making use of various kinds of imagery is necessary to put across the idea of exactly what is desired. The production of pleasing musical sounds is the goal of every teacher and student, and the final judgment of whether an embouchure is good or poor cannot be made on how it is described or explained but on the results obtained.

The decision on whether to use the soft cushion or the hard cushion formation is in the end, dependent upon the ultimate type of tone quality desired. Some teachers prefer a tone which is dark in color and full-bodied without a reedy edge, others prefer a clear smooth tone with a slight edge on it. Both are equally pleasing when fully developed and used musically.

Generally speaking the soft cushion formation produces the dark full-bodied tone with little or no edge; while the hard cushion produces a clear smooth tone of less body with a slight edge. The soft cushion formation is the more flexible since the firmness of the cushion can be altered with very slight movements of the muscles which control the lower lip, while the stretched muscles used with the hard cushion are more difficult to alter without losing control of the tone. The more flexibility in an embouchure the more shadings of tone are possible, the better the control of intonation and dynamics. Many embouchures take a middle ground between the two formations described.

Any opportunity which arises to make direct comparisons of the two formations should be taken advantage of in order to hear the differences. Comparisons between the tone qualities of professional level performers are difficult, since it is virtually impossible to isolate the one element of performance—tone quality—from all the other elements such as phrasing, articulation, and general technique.

Teachers who do not have a strong personal preference for the hard cushion formation are urged to make use of the soft cushion embouchure since experience of many teachers has indicated that this embouchure is capable of more rapid development and achieves a more musical

Checklist for Oboe Embouchure Formation

The following check on oboe embouchure formation must be made while the student is playing and preferably when he is not aware that a check is being made. Any errors should be carefully explained to the student, and the correction worked out with him while he is observing the embouchure in a mirror. Remedial measures can be assigned on the basis of this list.

A. Soft Cushion Embouchure

	Yes	No	Comments
1. Reed proper distance in mouth?			
2. Corners of lips pushed inward?			
3. Proper amount of upper lip over teeth?			
4. Proper amount of lower lip over teeth?			
5. Are lower teeth biting?			
6. Cheeks puffed?			
7. Air escaping?			
8. Instrument held at correct angle?			

B. Hard Cushion Embouchure

1. Reed proper distance in mouth?			
2. Cheek muscles pulled back?			
3. Corners of mouth closed around reed in correct position?			
4. Proper amount of upper lip over teeth?			
5. Proper amount of lower lip over teeth?			
6. Are lower teeth biting?			
7. Cheeks puffed?			
8. Air escaping?			
9. Instrument held at correct angle?			

sound more quickly when used by school players of all ages than does the hard cushion.

TUNING

The problems of correct tuning for the oboe and English horn are discussed extensively in the chapter on reeds since it is the reed rather than the instrument which is tuned. Unlike the clarinets which are tuned by adjusting the various joints, the pitch of the oboe is subject to only the slightest alteration by using this prodedure. Refer to the chapter on reeds for information on tuning the reed.

In the orchestra the oboe has traditionally been the instrument to which all other instruments are tuned, and this practice has been carried over to some extent into the band field. The reason for this is the fact that professional oboists have always made their own reeds, and as a part of this process tune the reed and the instrument to a standard A-440 tuning fork. Thus the orchestra was reasonably sure of a standard pitch for tuning.

In the hands of a professional oboist the pitch can be expected to be accurate. Most advanced student oboists who make their own reeds, or who have developed the process of adjusting a reed to a fine point will also supply a reliable reference pitch provided the instrument and reed have been properly warmed up and prepared for playing. However, less experienced oboists cannot be relied upon to provide an accurate A-440 pitch for tuning, and most conductors prefer to use an electronic tuner which sounds a constant pitch or which operated on the stroboscopic principle providing a visual check of intonation.

As the oboe is a nontransposing instrument, music written for it sounds as written. The usual tuning notes of A for orchestra and either B-flat or A for band are used.

Oboe Plays Concert Pitch

Oboe Plays Concert Pitch

The English horn is a transposing instrument sounding a perfect fifth lower than the written note, tuning to a written E which sounds A-440, or for bands which use B-flat as the pitch reference, plays F sounding B-flat. Most players prefer to check tuning by comparing both the upper and lower octaves of the tuning note.

English Horn Plays Concert Pitch

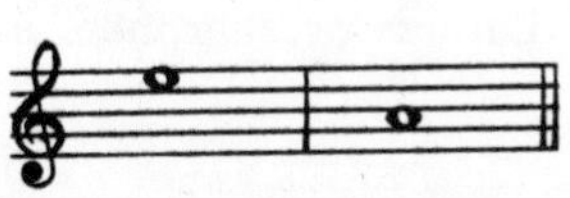

English Horn Plays Concert Pitch

The pitch of the English horn, as that of the oboe, is primarily dependent on the reed itself which must be adjusted and tuned to a particular instrument and embouchure formation. The pitch of the instrument may be slightly flattened by pulling the bocal a very little from its socket in the instrument, but this must be done with caution as both tone quality and intonation are susceptible to change by this procedure.

Many English horns are supplied with two bocals as are the bassoons, and larger pitch adjustments can be made by choosing the proper bocal. These bocals are of slightly different lengths, the shorter one raising the overall pitch of the instrument somewhat over the pitch produced by the longer one. Some experimentation with the two will soon indicate which of these a particular student should normally use.

INTONATION

The nature of the typical oboe tone quality seems to make the listener more acutely aware of slight deviations in intonation on this instrument than any of the other woodwinds. This is especially true of student oboists when tone quality has not progressed to the smooth quality of the professional, but tends toward a slight reediness. For this reason intonation on this instrument frequently becomes a major problem, although the oboe is no more difficult to play in tune than any other woodwind.

Natural Tendencies of the Instrument

Acoustically the first two octaves of the instrument, in which most of the playing is done, are produced by the fundamental frequency of the vibrating pipe and the first overtone. The example below gives those tones produced by the fundamental vibration and those which are the product of the first overtone (or partial vibration) when basic fingerings are used.

Fundamental

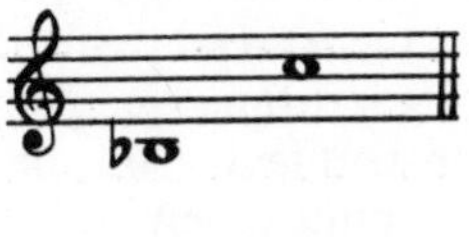

First Overtone

Theoretically the first overtone has exactly twice the number of vibrations as the fundamental, or exactly a perfect octave. Therefore, from the standpoint of pure theory, if the lower octave is in tune the upper octave will also be in tune. Thus the oboist has fewer acoustical problems to overcome in achieving perfect intonation than does the clarinetist.

Unfortunately the achievement of perfect intonation is not this simple. In the manufacturing of instruments certain mechanical problems will cause the instrument to respond slightly off the natural acoustical response. Each manufacturer has his own solutions to the problems of construction, and there is considerable variation from brand to brand in the temperament of the scale. A player who plays well in tune on one instrument will have intonation problems on one of a different brand. The reeds have considerable influence on intonation and one which is well in tune on one brand will not play in tune on another. The oboist must learn to control and adjust to the particular instrument he is playing, and to adjust reeds to fit it.

Each brand, or even each model, of instrument will have certain notes which have a tendency to be flat or sharp to a greater or lesser degree. These notes will be quickly discovered by the experienced player and the necessary adjustments made. Many of these tendencies for being slightly out of tune will be the product of embouchure, reed, or breath support rather than the acoustical properties of the instrument as an isolated factor. Stauffer[2] gives the following tendencies as a result of his experimentation, and they are generally, but not universally, accepted as the norm.

Tendency to be flat:

Tendency to be sharp:

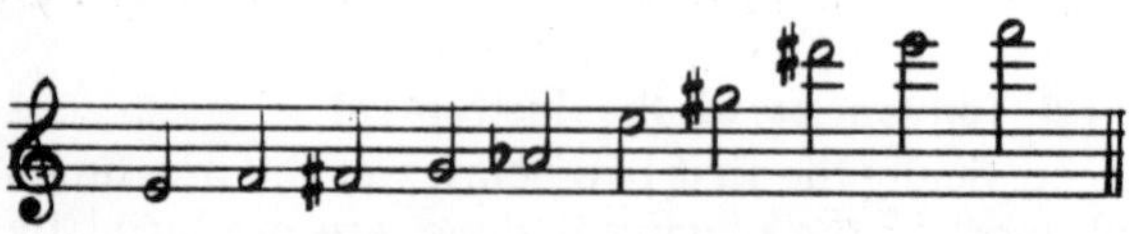

Reed and Intonation

The nature of the reed being used is of primary importance in intonation. The way in which it is cut, the type of cane used, and how well it fits the player's embouchure all have major effects on pitch. Thus the way in which the final adjustments are made on a reed will determine not only whether the instrument is properly tuned to A-440, but how well the instrument will play in tune with itself. Generally speaking a reed which responds well in all registers with a good tone quality will also play well in tune over the instrument. Consult the chapter on reeds for details of reed adjustment.

A reed which is too soft will play flat over the range of the instrument and minor adjustments in intonation will be difficult to make. Notes in the highest register will be quite flat in pitch, and the lowest four or five notes even flatter. Such a reed cannot be controlled by even the best players.

A reed which is too hard will play generally sharp over the range of the instrument. The natural tendencies for sharpness and flatness will be emphasized because the amount of control by the embouchure is limited. This condition can easily be corrected by properly adjusting the reed.

Many beginning students are deliberately started on the instrument with reeds which are too soft and pitch and intonation are intentionally made secondary to tone production and basic technique. These students should not be kept on a soft reed too long, but the strength of the reed they are using gradually increased with each new reed until the proper strength is reached. Most students will make this adjustment easily if it is brought about gradually. As an incentive to make this change there will be a parallel development toward a better tone quality to which the young player is frequently more sensitive than he is to intonation.

Intonation gradually becomes more and more difficult to control on reeds which have been played on too long, and which are worn out. Student oboists will need to be checked frequently for this condition, as the change in the reed is so gradual that they are frequently not aware that a change has taken place. Insist that a spare reed or two be prepared, broken in, and ready to play at all times.

Embouchure and Intonation

The embouchure coupled with the reed is a primary factor in intonation. Even the best of reeds will play out of tune if the embouchure is poorly formed or underdeveloped. An embouchure deficiency can be heard in the tone quality as well as being observed by visual examination. It is for the purpose of good intonation and tone quality that so much emphasis is given to embouchure formation and development. A well-formed and developed embouchure is a necessary foundation for good intonation.

The embouchure can correct slight intonation problems through adjusting the pressure with which the reed is held. To make a note higher in pitch contract the embouchure around the reed to increase pressure. To make a note lower in pitch relax the embouchure to reduce pressure. These slight changes in pressure are constant and involuntary in experienced players. Younger players need guidance to develop this facility.

The amount of reed taken into the mouth has considerable effect on pitch and intonation. If too much of the reed is in the mouth in relation to its cut the overall pitch tends to be sharp, especially notes in the second octave. If the half-step between third line B and third space C is too wide it is frequently an indication that there is too much reed in the mouth. Conversely, if too little of the reed is in the mouth in relation to its cut the overall pitch tends to be flat. In both instances the natural tendencies toward sharpness or flatness of certain notes on the instrument will be emphasized.

Dynamics and Intonation

On the oboe, as on most other wind instruments, there is a natural tendency for the pitch to get lower as the tone gets louder, and for the pitch to get sharper as the tone gets softer, with the degree of flatness or sharpness in-

2. Stauffer, op. cit., p. 111.

creasing as the level of dynamics approaches the extremes. This must be compensated for by adjusting the embouchure. In order to play louder the student tends to relax the embouchure so that the reed may open up to allow more wind to pass through or to tighten the embouchure as he gets softer to lessen the amount of wind passing through the reed. Since pitch is controlled to a considerable degree by the pressure of the embouchure around the reed there is a corresponding flatting or sharping.

Dynamics are properly controlled by breath support and pressure which controls the velocity of the wind passing through the reed. Students relax their embouchure to play louder rather than increasing breath velocity, and tighten the embouchure rather than decreasing breath velocity to play softer.

Pitch is maintained through balancing the velocity of the wind through the reed with the pressures of the embouchure around it. When playing fortissimo the slight relaxation of the embouchure is compensated for by an increased velocity of the wind. In a crescendo the wind velocity and embouchure pressure are kept in balance to maintain pitch stability. In playing pianissimo the embouchure pressure may be relaxed slightly if at all, with the pitch maintained through maintaining breath support while decreasing the velocity of the wind through the reed to achieve the proper dynamic level.

Developing the facility for maintaining a constant pitch through long crescendo and diminuendo is one of the ways breath control is developed in students. The tone exercises below are excellent practice in control of pitch through wide dynamic levels. They should be practiced slowly enough that an entire breath is used in each four measures. Maintain constant firm breath support while controlling the dynamics by changing the velocity of the breath through the instrument.

Practice exercise "a" in major or minor scale patterns to include the entire range of the instrument in which the student is proficient. Exercise "b" is best practiced chromatically first in the most comfortable range for the student, then extending upward and downward to the extremes of his range. This is also a good exercise for developing the use of the half-hole, and the two octave keys.

Playing Position and Intonation

The angle at which the oboe is held with the body can have considerable influence both on overall pitch and the intonation of individual notes. If the oboe is held at a too great an angle with the body, i.e., greater than forty degrees, the overall pitch is flat with the upper octave even flatter. The same effect results when the head is inclined downward so that the reed enters the mouth on a straight line rather than at the proper angle. The downward position of the head is quite common with beginning players, and must be corrected as soon as it occurs.

When the angle is too great or the head inclined downward good general overall pitch is virtually impossible to obtain, and good intonation completely impossible. Some students attempt to achieve a measure of correction by adjusting a reed to compensate but success with this is rare because complete control of the reed cannot be achieved.

If the instrument is held too close to the body, i.e., at an angle of less than forty degrees, the overall pitch is sharp with the upper octave still sharper in relation to the lower octave. This position also produces a pinched hard sound. The angle of the instrument with the body, whether too great or too small, must be corrected if good intonation is to be achieved. This basic holding position is arrived at very early in the beginning stage of playing the instrument, so it is important that the proper angle be established from the very beginning. Correction of an incorrect angle with an experienced player is a slow and demanding process.

Mechanical Factors and Intonation

The adjustment of the mechanism of the oboe is the most critical of all the woodwind instruments, and keys or plates which do not open wide enough or which open too much will affect the intonation on individual notes. If an individual tone is flat, check to see if the key is opening sufficiently, or if the plate of the first tone hole which is open on that note is raised high enough. If an individual tone is sharp, a key or plate may be opening too much.

Most brands of oboes have adjusting screws which control the amount of opening on various keys and plates.

a.
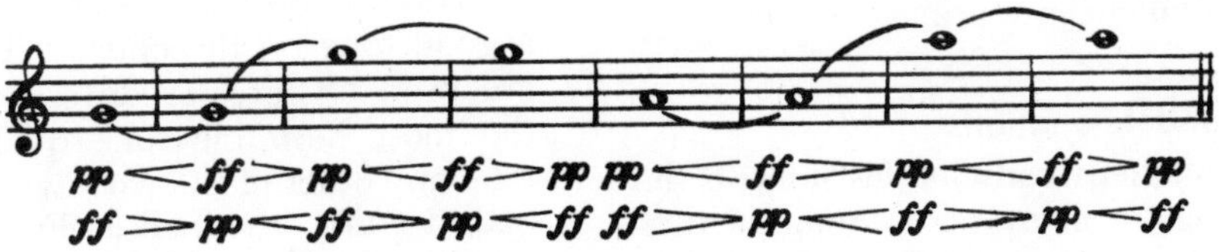

b.

These adjusting screws should be used to keep the mechanism in the best playing condition. It is well to check all adjusting screws frequently as they move with use and may put the mechanism out of adjustment frequently. If a tone hole or key does not have an adjusting screw, but is open too little or too much, the adjustment must be made by a competent repairman.

Notes in the upper octave which involve the use of the half-hole with the first finger of the left hand may be slightly flat or respond with difficulty if the small vent hole in the plate covered by the first finger is not clear. Check to see that it is open and clear the hole regularly with a broom straw or a small needle. Avoid increasing the size of this hole through using a needle which is too large since the size of this opening is critical for the best intonation.

The holes covered by the two octave keys are quite small and frequently clogged with foreign matter after a period of use. The keys may be removed from the instrument and the holes cleared with broomstraw or a small feather.

Summary

An overall sharpness in pitch of the oboe may be caused by one or more of these factors: (1) instrument held too close to the body, (2) too much reed in the mouth, (3) embouchure too tight, (4) a reed which is too sharp for the instrument on which it is being used, and (5) a reed which is too stiff.

An overall flatness in pitch may be caused by one or more of these factors: (1) instrument held at too great an angle with the body, (2) too little reed in the mouth, (3) embouchure too relaxed, (4) a reed which is too flat for the instrument on which it is being used, and (5) a reed which is too soft.

Intonation difficulties on individual notes may be caused by: (1) a poorly adjusted reed, (2) poorly formed embouchure, (3) improper balance between tightness of the embouchure and breath support, (4) keys or plates too open or too close, and (5) a clogged vent hole.

Good intonation is the result of the player's ability to hear intonation accurately and to control it through small variations in breath support and velocity coordinated with increases and decreases in the firmness of the pressure of the embouchure around the reed.

Alternate Fingerings and Intonation

The oboe, as well as other woodwind instruments, has more than one fingering for many notes. Some of these fingerings produce slightly different pitches (as well as tone quality) for the same note, although some produce an identical pitch. The player should be aware that there are alternate fingerings and be able to use them, and should check the pitch relationship between the fingerings for the same note. It is frequently necessary to choose an alternate fingering for the sake of perfect intonation, rather than the fingering which offers the best facility. The player must never hesitate to put intonation before facility.

Attention should be paid to the special trill fingerings which are for trilling only, and which must not be used where the note is sufficiently exposed to give an impression of definite pitch. Many trill fingerings are more than a little out of tune but must be used for the sake of facility.

Consult the fingering chart for alternate fingerings and compare their pitches. As the differences between fingerings will vary from instrument to instrument and from player to player, no positive statement as to which alternates are sharp or flat is possible.

TONE

The most valuable asset of any performer is a beautiful tone, and it is to this end that the student must direct his constant attention. The quality of the tone must be the same over the entire range of the instrument and at all dynamic levels. The better the balance of quality over the instrument the better the musical results and the more pleasing the performance to the listener.

The range of the oboe is divided into three registers, designated as the first, second and third octaves (or low, middle, and high register).

First octave Second octave Third octave

Notes in the lower octave are produced by the fundamental vibration of the air column, those in the upper octave by the column of air vibrating in two segments (the first partial). Notes in the high register are produced by the column of air vibrating in three, four, or five segments—the third, fourth, and fifth partials of the overtone series.

Beginners on the instrument tend to have a discernible different tone quality in each of the three registers. It is true that the quality of tone will be slightly different even in the hands of a professional, but the closer they match the more pleasing the results.

There is no single standard for determining what is a good tone on the oboe or English horn, in fact there are probably greater differences in what is considered the most desirable tone quality on these instruments than any other of the woodwind instruments. The various qualities are described as French, German, or American and all three have a place in the United States because so many fine musicians came from France and Germany in the early years of this century to take principal positions in our major symphony orchestras. These men taught the instrument in the way they had learned and the information and style has been passed on from generation to generation of players.

To describe a tone quality accurately in words is

impossible and the differences between the French and German sounds on the instrument can be easily heard on the high fidelity recordings made by musicians in these countries. In general the French sound is considered to be a light pure tone with a slight tendency toward reediness to our ears and capable of great variation, while the German sound is dark and heavy, with less potential variation. The American tone quality is a combination of the two combining the dark, full sound of the German tone with the flexibility of the French. These various qualities are a product of the type of reed and the embouchure formation being used. There are innumerable variations of both reed and embouchure, most of which are capable of producing what is considered a good oboe tone. No matter what the differences may be if the oboe still sounds like an oboe and if the tone is pleasing, it is a good one.

Every teacher and oboist should take advantage of every opportunity to hear live performances of fine instrumentalists. Or if this is not possible, to study the recorded performances of the oboe repertoire on a high quality phonograph. Compare the tone qualities of the various artists. A comparison of the performances of French, German, English, and American artists will be quite revealing. All will be quite different, all will be pleasing.

Common Problems in Tone

A good tone is the product of all the elements involved in performance: instrument, reed, embouchure and breath support. If any of these is defective, then the tone quality suffers accordingly. Problems of tone production and quality are many and varied, but may usually be traced to their source, and must be corrected immediately. Refer also to the sections on reed, embouchure, and breathing.

Following are some of the most prevalent problems or faults in tone:

1. *Small or pinched tone.* This is a common fault with beginning oboists, and may be traced to several possible causes. A frequent reason is that the opening in the tip of the reed is too small, a result of the original shaping of the cane or by weakening the sides of the reed during the adjustment process. Consult the section on oboe reeds for possible corrections.

If the opening in the tip of the reed is correct, then it is possible that the student is biting the reed through upward pressure with the lower teeth. This can be remedied by asking the student to play flatter by dropping his lower teeth but continuing the lip support around the reed. Unless he also relaxes the breath support, dropping the teeth will not flatten the pitch, but simply free the tone.

This fault may also be caused by not having sufficient reed in the mouth, by not having enough lip over the teeth for the reed cut and embouchure formation being used, or by putting too much pressure on the reed by holding the instrument too close to the body. All of these are physically visible and can be corrected. Instructing the student to check himself in a mirror so that he can actually see what he is doing is advisable.

2. *Squawky tone.* The squawky tone which can be described as lacking in body and focus, and generally uncontrolled is typical of the beginner although it is sometimes found as well among more advanced students. In the beginner it is caused by a weak, uncontrolled embouchure, but if the basic formation of the embouchure is correct, the undesirable tone will gradually disappear.

In the more advanced student this tone quality may be caused by a reed which is too stiff for his embouchure causing him to use a large amount of breath to produce a tone. This cause is confirmed if the student is unable to produce a diminuendo into the pianissimo level. Making the proper adjustments on the reed will correct the situation. A squawky tone may also be caused by having too much reed in the mouth, or by having too much lip over the teeth for the type of cut made on the reed.

3. *Hard, cold tone.* A tone which is inflexible and which lacks the intangible quality of vitality is described as hard and cold. If embouchure formation is correct this is almost invariably caused by the type of reed being used, usually too stiff for the student. If the usual adjustments on the reed to make it free blowing and responsive in all registers do not remedy the situation, try reeds which are made with a different cut. If the student is making his own reeds, have him test with different cuts, or if the reeds he is using are commercial or custom-made reeds, try reeds from one or more different makers until a satisfactory tone is achieved. This is a difficult solution for many players since different cuts may require major adjustments in embouchure formation and playing habits.

If the student is quite advanced and is playing well in tune with good tone quality except for the coldness of tone, introducing the use of a tasteful vibrato would be a solution worth trying. However, the use of the vibrato should be restricted to advanced players.

4. *Weak, colorless tone.* A tone which is otherwise smooth in quality, but is lacking in body and carrying power is most often due to lack of proper breathing and breath support. Check the fundamentals of good breath usage with the student, and assign long tone practice with diminuendo and crescendo. The student will need to be told when he is producing the proper sound so that he can associate his physical feeling with the desired sound. It is difficult for many even advanced players to know by listening to themselves when they are producing the proper tone quality and projection.

5. *Control of soft tone.* Difficulty in producing and controlling a soft tone is principally due to the inability of the player to project a steady concentrated small stream of air into the instrument. Check breathing and breath support, and have the student practice focusing a steady stream of air into the palm of his hand. Other

possible causes may be a reed which is too stiff, or a poorly shaped embouchure.

6. *Dynamics and tone quality.* Some students with otherwise good tone quality will lose it when playing at extremes of loudness or softness. This is caused by an undeveloped or poorly formed embouchure, or by lack of proper breath control or a combination of both. In making a crescendo the embouchure must gradually relax to allow the tip of the reed to open while at the same time increasing the velocity of the air. Good control is the product of the proper balance of these two factors, and if they are in the proper balance both tone quality and intonation will remain good.

To play a diminuendo the embouchure may tighten slightly around the reed, while decreasing the velocity of air through the instrument, but being very careful to maintain a strong abdominal support of the air stream. With the proper abdominal support, air velocity, and embouchure control tone quality will remain the same at any dynamic level.

TONGUING

Tonguing refers to the manner in which the tongue operates in relation to the reed and breath support in order to articulate the tones. The placement and action of the tongue must be rapid and under complete control at all speeds, and at all dynamic levels. It must, in coordination with breath support, be able to produce on the oboe all varieties of articulation from the hardest staccato to the softest legato.

The manner in which the tongue touches the reed, the place it touches, and how it moves is dependent somewhat upon embouchure formation. There are several points of view on how and where the tongue touches the reed, and each is effective if properly done. In essence the tongue acts as a valve to control the flow of air through the reed, stopping the flow and vibration when it touches the reed, and allowing the vibration to begin again when it is removed.

The effectiveness of the tongue is entirely dependent upon proper breath control and support. The interrelation between breath pressure and tongue action allows the production of every conceivable kind of attack from the hardest marcato-staccato to the very smoothest legato within the widest dynamic range. The amount of pressure of the tongue against the reed determines the hardness of the attack, the amount of wind pressure against the tongue determines the loudness of the attack.

Placement of Tongue

There are three standard methods of tongue placement used on the oboe, each subject to variations according to the personal desires of the teachers using them. They have several things in common however: (1) the tongue is relaxed. A tongue under tension cannot move rapidly enough, nor can it be controlled; (2) tongue movement is confined to the forward part of the tongue; and (3) the tongue acts as a valve for the air and is dependent on good breath support. The three methods may be outlined as follows:

First Method. With the reed in place and the embouchure properly formed, touch the lower blade of the reed at the tip with the top of the tongue just back of the tip. A slight pressure against the reed closes the tip. To start the tone put the tongue in place against the reed and build up air pressure against it. Release the air into the instrument with a tongue action similar to that in pronouncing the syllable "Too." The center of the tongue is depressed slightly so that the throat is well open. For a harder attack pronounce the syllable "Tee," and for a softer attack the syllable "Du."

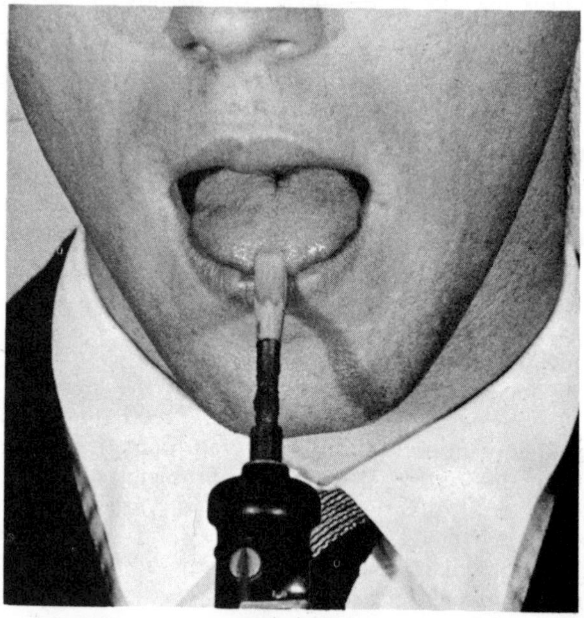

Figure O-41A. Placement of Tongue (Front View).

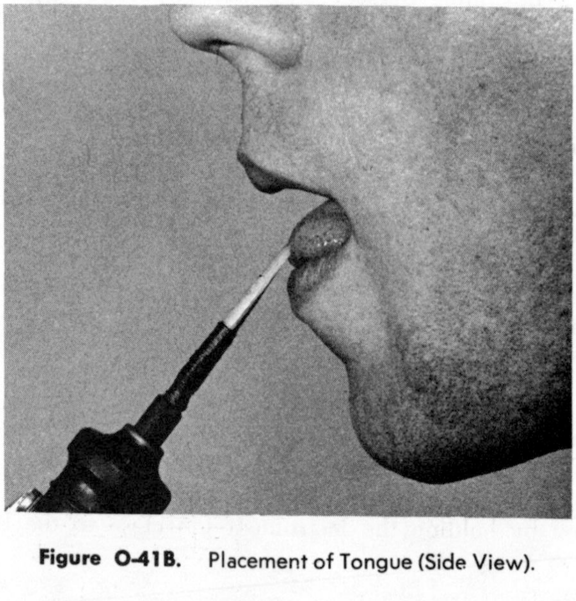

Figure O-41B. Placement of Tongue (Side View).

Figures O-41A and O-41B show the front and side view of the tongue in this position.

Second Method. With the reed in place and the embouchure properly formed feel the oval shape of the tip of the reed with the front of the tip of the tongue. This is the placement of the tongue for this style of articulation. The tongue acts physically as a valve to open and close the opening in the tip of the reed. The exact point of contact of the tip of the tongue with the reed varies from authority to authority and ranges from having the tongue close the tip of the reed by approaching it directly as described, to touching the lower blade as in the previous method but with the very tip of the tongue. To start the tone, put the tongue in place against the tip of the reed, build up air pressure against the tongue and release the air with a tongue action similar to that in pronouncing the syllable "Tu." For a softer attack use the syllable "Du" and for a harder attack the syllable "Tee."

Figure O-42 shows the front view of the tongue in this position.

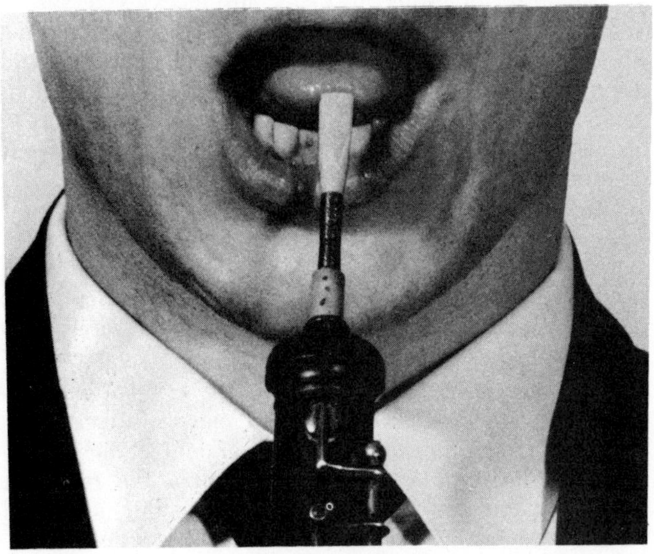

Figure O-42

Third Method. With the reed in place and the embouchure properly formed, touch the lower lip with the tip of the tongue. Keeping the tip of the tongue in place against the lip the forward part of the tongue moves up to touch the lower blade of the reed. To start the tone, build up air pressure against the tongue and release the air into the instrument with a tongue action similar to that in pronouncing the syllable "Dah." For repeated articulations the tip of the tongue remains in contact with the lower lip with the tongue pivoting against it. Harder attacks are produced by the syllable "Tah" and softer ones by the syllable "Du."

Developing Tongue Action

For the purpose of developing articulation the position of the tongue against the reed is considered the normal position, for it is from this position that it starts the tone. There is no forward or upward movement of the tongue preceding the beginning of the tone since breath support is against the tongue which is in place against the reed. The commonly used word "attack" to describe the articulation of a tone is most unfortunate since it implies both violence and forward movement. The action of the tongue may be gentle or hard depending on the type of articulation desired.

Various types of articulations demand varying lengths of silence between successive notes. The length of this silence is determined by how long the tongue remains in contact with the reed. Hardness of attack is determined by the breath pressure behind the tongue and by how hard the tongue is pressing against the reed. By varying these two factors the entire gamut of bow strokes used by string players can be reproduced on the oboe.

The introduction of tonguing or articulation should be delayed until the student is producing a steady tone of reasonable quality, and has developed facility within the limited range of the beginner. Do not allow the tongue to touch the reed during this preliminary study, but simply start the tone with the breath. This requires that the beginning study be done with music of legato style, and eliminates the rhythmic approach to the beginning study in favor of the melodic approach. The articulation of quarter and eighth notes in the typical beginning method patterns must be done with the tongue and not the breath. Do not allow articulation with the breath alone for once this habit is established it is extremely difficult to break.

Once the tongue is in the correct position against the reed and articulation begun attention must be focused on breath support so that there is a steady stream through the reed upon which the tones rest. The tongue simply interrupts this movement of air through the instrument to detach the notes. A legato style of articulation most successful in the beginning. (See illustration a.)

a.

b.

After the student is producing the legato articulation reasonably well, he can move to the normal detached sound in which the notes are well separated. There must be a continuing emphasis on a steady stream of air through the reed. The notes are separated simply by leaving the tongue in contact with the reed longer while breath pressure remains constant. This is the most common articulation, used when there is no other articulation indicated, and varied according to the musical demands of the composition. Example b (p. 147) illustrates a typical exercise for developing this type of articulation.

Staccato articulation should not be introduced until both the legato and normal detached articulations are well under control. The same tongue movement and placement and the same steady stream of air is used in staccato articulation. The only difference is that in staccato articulation the tongue returns to the reed to stop the vibration, but the air pressure against the tongue must remain the same during the period of silence as during the production of the tone.

Because of the longer period of silence between notes in this type of articulation students are frequently tempted to relax breath support during the silence. If this is done, then the breathing muscles come into operation simultaneously with tongue action, resulting in an accent, and making it virtually impossible to develop a fast staccato. If fairly rapid repetitions of notes are used to introduce the staccato, the concept of an uninterrupted flow of breath is developed and many of the problems involving movement of breathing muscles can be avoided. The following is a typical beginning staccato exercise.

etc. in scale pattern

Common Problems in Tonguing:

1. *Articulation too heavy.* In this type of sound each note starts with an accent or pop, and is normally caused by too great pressure of the tongue against the reed. The best solution is to have the student practice articulation in the pianissimo level, correcting first the legato type, then the normal detached, and finally the staccato.

A reed which is too soft will frequently produce this sound, since the blades do not respond instantly when released by the tongue. If pianissimo practice does not correct this difficulty, it is possible that the placement of the tongue against the reed is incorrect for the embouchure and type of reed being used. Vary the tongue placement or experiment with one of the other tongue placements previously described.

2. *Sluggish tongue.* Inability to tongue rapidly should not be a major concern with beginners, since time and practice is necessary to develop speedy articulation, but in more advanced players where technique has developed past articulation ability, it is a matter of considerable concern. In this condition the reed should be checked first, since a reed which is too stiff for the player makes rapid articulation difficult. If the reed is too stiff, there will probably be other symptoms in addition to sluggish articulation.

Some students lack speed in articulation because they are moving the back of their tongue as well as the front. Articulation is confined to the forward portion of the tongue, and the primary motion of the tongue is up and down rather than forward and backward in the mouth. Movement of the back portion of the tongue almost invariably carries with it movements of the throat which can easily be seen. To correct, the entire process of tongue placement and development of articulation must be gone through from the very beginning to form new muscular habits. Some students correct the problem quickly, others are never able to completely overcome the problem.

Sluggish tonguing in many instances is a simple matter of insufficient practice devoted to developing speed and accuracy. Special articulation exercises should be assigned to these students, with specific instructions on how many times each day to practice them, and to use a metronome, and with specific metronomic speeds to use. Any player can develop satisfactory speed and control if he is using his tongue and breath support properly, and if he will spend enough time on the problem. Scales, thirds, and arpeggios as found in most method books practiced with a variety of articulation patterns are the quickest and most efficient way of developing rapid articulation.

3. *Lack of coordination between tongue and fingers.* This is frequent among the more advanced students who have developed a fair amount of facility on the instrument. It is purely and simply the result of practicing too fast without first working out notes and tonguing carefully. These students must practice slowly, at whatever tempo perfect coordination between fingers and tongue is possible, and gradually increase the speed. Use of a metronome on such exercises is invaluable to maintain a steady tempo and to help in the gradual increase in speed. Major and minor scales and arpeggios making use of various articulation patterns are good media of practice for this purpose.

4. *Slow staccato.* Some players have difficulty in executing a true staccato rapidly. Other things being correct, this problem can be traced to the lack of breath support and a continuing stream of air through the reed. Such players will be found to be relaxing abdominal support at the end of each note, or cutting off the stream of air in the throat. The concept of the tongue stopping staccato notes as well as starting them with the breath pressure continuing against the tongue during the space of silence will help correct this situation.

5. *Movement of the jaw in tonguing.* This is the result of too large or too violent movements of the tongue, frequently accompanied by changes in pitch of the tone. Rather than confining the movement to the front part of the tongue, the student is moving the entire tongue. The solution is to ask the student, no matter what his technical advancement, to practice the basic exercises for developing articulation constantly checking in a mirror on the music stand to eliminate all movement. Jaw movements can occur with all methods of correct tongue placement, as well as with incorrect tongue placement, and prevent the development of speed in articulation.

Double and Triple Tonguing

Theoretically, double and triple tonguing in the sense of its use on flute and brass instruments is possible on the oboe, but in practice it is very unsatisfactory because it is virtually impossible to match the sounds of the beginnings of the two notes in the double pattern or the three notes in the triple pattern.

The double tonguing is done by using the letters "T" and "K" in rapid alternation, the "T" with the tongue in its normal position on the reed and the "K" pronounced with the middle of the tongue against the roof of the mouth which interrupts the flow of air. Triple tonguing uses the letters "T-K-T" or "T-T-K" in rapid succession.

Both double and triple tonguing are called for only in the most rapid passages. Most oboists prefer to develop the speed and control of the single tonguing to a degree that it can be used exclusively for both normal and the most rapid articulations. Most authorities agree that students need not be taught double or triple tonguing.

Flutter Tonguing

Flutter tonguing, produced by rolling an "R" so that the tongue flutters against the reed is called for in a few contemporary compositions. Some relaxation of the embouchure with perhaps a little less reed in the mouth will help achieve the best effect.

Accents, Sforzando, Forte-piano

Accents, sforzando, and forte-piano notes must be played in relation to the dynamic level of the musical phrase. A sforzando is not a note played as loudly as it is possible to play, but simply an isolated note one or two degrees louder than the note which precedes or follows it in the phrase. It demands assistance from the breath so that the breathing mechanism must supply additional support and velocity simultaneously with the release of the reed by the tongue.

The forte-piano requires immediate relaxation of velocity and pressure by the breathing mechanism, coupled with whatever degree of simultaneous support demanded by the musical content of the phrase at the instant the tone starts. Accents indicated above or below the notes must be only one dynamic level above the notes which precede or follow them. Many accents may be accomplished by only increased tongue pressure against the reed, others demand slight movements of the breathing muscles. It must be clearly understood that there are no rapid movements of any breathing muscles in support of tongue action except for accents, sforzando, and forte-piano notes.

TECHNIQUE PROBLEMS

A good technical proficiency on the instrument is one which is accurate, under complete control, and facile. In developing this proficiency the oboist must be aware of certain mechanical or technical problems peculiar to the instrument which must be approached logically. Both the importance of the correct solution and the reasons for a particular solution must be impressed on the student. Unfortunately the literature for the study of the oboe with the possible exception of the Alphonse Leduc edition of the Barret Method does not provide a particularly well-organized presentation of these problems, so it is incumbent upon the teacher to make an opportunity to include them in the instruction of the players.

Approached logically, these problems are neither complex to solve, nor difficult to use. Many of these technical problems on the instrument demand that the player make a choice between two or more alternatives. Each alternate must be practiced until it becomes an involuntary part of his technique and the use of each alternative made so much a part of his technique that the correct choice becomes involuntary and instantaneous. Players and teachers should not hesitate to mark instructions on the printed music as reminders.

1. *Use of left and right little fingers.* One or both of the little fingers are involved in the fingering for these notes in the first two octaves:

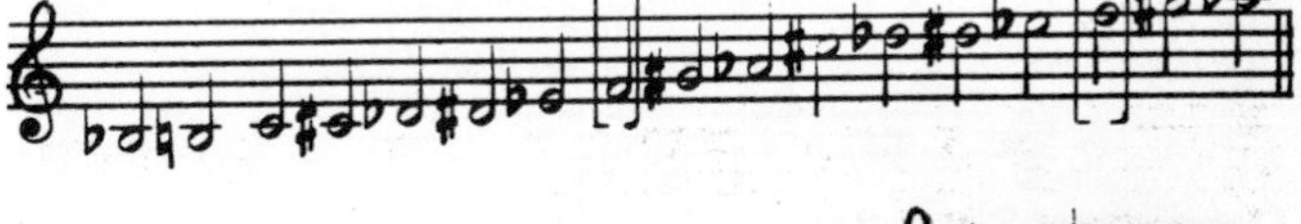

Of these notes only D-sharp–E-flat  can be played by either the left or right little fingers. (The G-sharp–A-flat has an alternate key operated by the first finger of the right hand which is discussed later.) The problem in playing a passage which has two consecutive little finger notes is to avoid sliding one of the fingers from one key to another if at all possible. Making use of both the left and right D-sharp–E-flat keys and planning ahead to alternate the little fingers will help to avoid excessive sliding. Students should begin using both the left and right D-sharp–E-flat keys very early in their beginning study so that correct use of the little fingers is firmly established as one of the basis for technical advancement.

However, some combinations of notes make it mandatory to slide a finger from one key to another. The proper sliding is done by increasing the curvature of the finger and pressing down so that it slides off the top of one key onto the next one. If the finger does not slide easily an old professional trick is to rub the finger beside the nose where the skin is oily and the finger picks up enough of this oil to slide easily. Rubbing the finger in the hair works equally well. The following example is typical of passages in which sliding the little fingers is mandatory.

2. *Use of half-hole and two octave keys.* Notes in the second octave and the high register are produced by using the half-hole with the first finger, or by one of the two octave keys. Using these correctly on each note as required by the fingering system is most important for the sake of both intonation and tone quality. Insist that students use the correct one from the very beginning of study. These keys are necessary to relieve the pressure in the column of air at a particular place in that column to force it to break into vibrating sections of the right length thus producing the 1st or a higher partial. The notes played with each are indicated below. Notes in the third octave may use any of the three depending on the fingering chosen. Consult the fingering chart for these.

1st finger half-hole:

Octave key A:

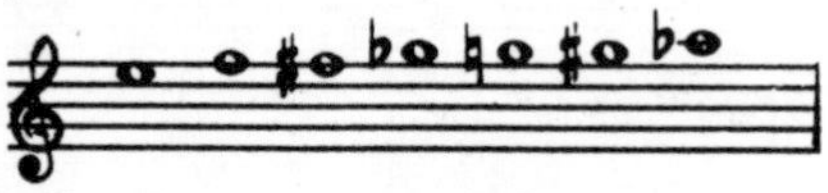

Octave key B:

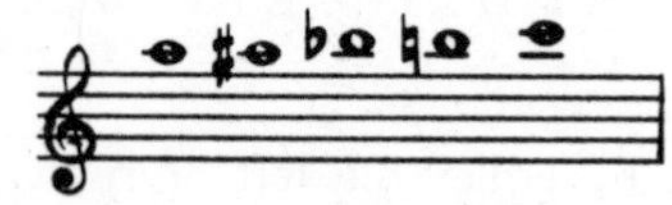

Considerable attention during the process of developing technique on the instrument must be given to developing the proper finger and hand movements used in changing back and forth from one to the other of these. Instruments with a single automatic octave key do not have Octave Key B, the instrument automatically changing vent holes as the notes are fingered. On instruments with semiautomatic octave key the thumb may be kept in contact with Octave Key A while the first finger opens octave Key B, since the mechanism automatically closes Key A when Key B is open. Instruments with no automation require that the thumb be removed from Key A simultaneously with the opening of Key B, and vice versa. The semiautomatic mechanism in the most satisfactory for student use.

3. *F fingerings:* 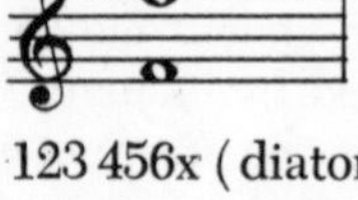

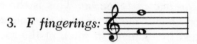

Two fingerings: (1) 123 456x (diatonic)

(2) 123 406 (D-sharp) (fork)

Every oboist from the early beginning stage of development should be familiar with and make constant use of both of the fingerings for F. Fingering 1 is the normal diatonic or chromatic fingering. Fingering 2 is called the "fork F." The D-sharp key with either the right or left little finger is necessary if the instrument does not have an F resonance key, but must not be used if the instrument has this key. (See the section on Selection of Instruments on how to determine whether or not a particular instrument has the F resonance key.) Fingering 2 or the "Fork F" is used when the sixth finger is used to cover the sixth hole on the note which precedes or follows the F to avoid sliding this finger from the 6x key to the hole.

On most oboes both fingerings produce identical tone qualities and are equally well in tune. It is necessary that both fingerings and directions for their use be introduced very early into the study of the instrument. The following illustrates typical uses of these fingerings:

Use diatonic fingering:

Use fork fingering:

4. *Alternate low C fingering:* 

Fingering: 123 4566p

Key 6p on the fingering chart is depressed by extending the sixth finger to depress it at the same time the finger is closing the tone hole. This plate closes the low C key and is a substitute for the C key played by the right little finger. When feasible and necessary, the plate is used instead of the C key to avoid sliding the right little finger.

The most common use of key 6p is in the trill:

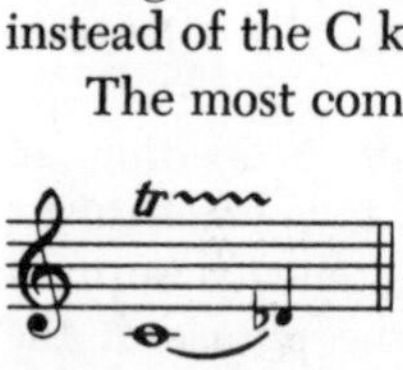

which is otherwise impossible to execute. In this trill the fingering for C is with key 6p and the D-flat is obtained by adding the D-flat key with the right little finger to the C fingering. The trill is made by the right little finger.

Figure O-43 shows the right hand in position for making this trill. Note the extension of the sixth finger to close the plate and the little finger on the D-flat key. Note also that the hand position is only slightly changed from the basic guide position.

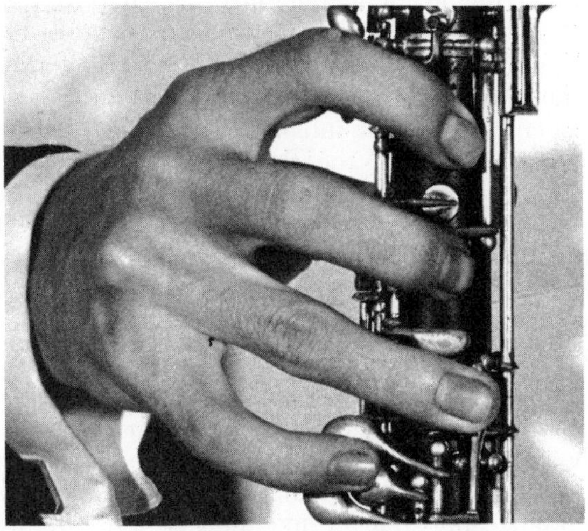

Figure O-43

5. *G-sharp:*
A-flat:

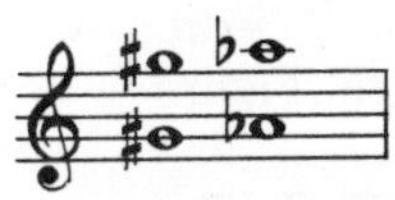

Two fingerings: (1) 123 G-sharp 000 (standard)
(2) 123 4x00 (trill)

Fingering 1 is the standard fingering used in both diatonic and chromatic passages. Fingering 2, using the key operated by the first finger of the right hand, is primarily a trill key.

6. *Articulated G-sharp key.* All standard system oboes have an articulated G-sharp incorporated into the mechanism. This mechanism automatically closes the G-sharp key when the fourth finger is down even though the little finger remains on the key. Use of this key smooths certain technical passages by allowing the little finger to remain stationary on the G-sharp key eliminating the possibility of poor coordination between this finger and others. The example below indicates a typical use of this key. The little finger remains down on the G-sharp key throughout.

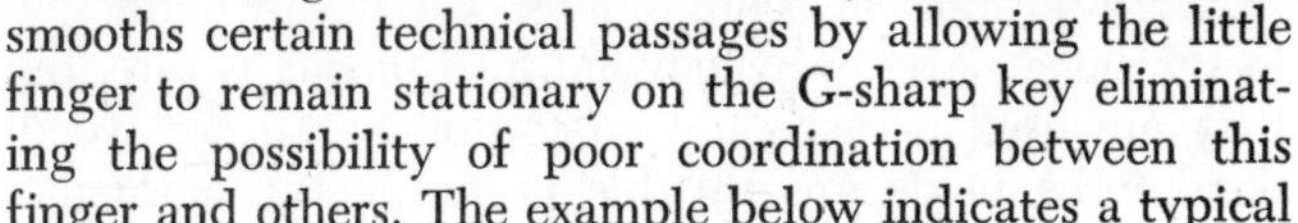

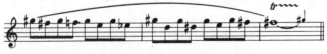

7. *Trill fingering for:*
Fingerings: (1) A-sharp—B-flat: 11p20 100
(2) B-natural—C-flat: 11p00 100

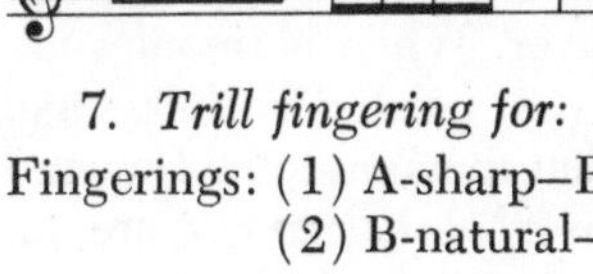

A special plate—1p on the fingering chart—used by extending the first finger so that it closes both the hole and this plate is incorporated into the mechanism of the instrument. The fingerings given above the trill are executed by the second finger.

8. *Use of left little finger on two keys simultaneously.* For slurring in the lower octave between B-natural and A-flat, or E-flat to A-flat in either the first or second octaves it is frequently advantageous to depress both the keys involved with the left little finger. Distribute the width of the finger between the two keys so that both are fully depressed. The articulated G-sharp key which is built into the instrument makes this technique possible. Certain fingerings for notes in the high register require two of these keys and depressing them both with the left little finger is advantageous as it frees the little finger of the right hand for other use. Figure O-44 shows the placement of the left hand with the little finger in both the G-sharp and D-sharp keys, in the fingering for E-natural in the third octave.

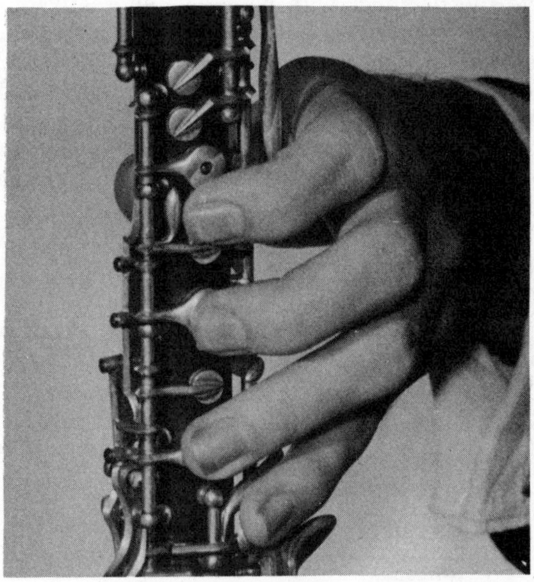

Figure O-44

The following excerpt from the slow movement of Dvorak's "New World Symphony" is a notable instance where leaving a finger in place on two keys simplifies the performance immeasurably. The left little finger holds down both the D-sharp and G-sharp keys throughout the entire example, taking advantage of the articulated G-sharp.

9. *Selection and use of alternate fingerings.* Alternate fingerings are used in specific instances to solve technical problems of facility, intonation, and response when the

normal standard fingerings are found unsatisfactory. When a student finds he cannot play a passage fast or smoothly enough with standard fingerings or when there is difficulty in getting one of the notes to respond properly, the solution can frequently be found by using an alternate fingering for one or more of the notes in the pattern. Selection of an alternate fingering for intonation occurs frequently at either extreme of the dynamic range and quite frequently on notes in the third octave.

The fingering chart at the back of this book includes all the normal alternate fingerings. Harmonic fingerings should also be considered alternate fingerings, especially at extremely soft dynamic levels. Not all the alternate fingerings will be useful for all students. Some of the fingerings will be out of tune to a greater or lesser degree for a particular player. Such fingerings can be used only when the sequence of notes in which they are used is moving so rapidly that the note is not sufficiently exposed for the ear to get an exact impression of the pitch.

Except for the special fingerings for certain notes previously mentioned in this section, there is little need to involve the beginner with numerous alternatives. Alternate fingerings are best added to the student's technique as the need for them arises. If a student on the intermediate or advanced level encounters a technical problem, standard procedure would be to check alternate fingerings for a solution. The more advanced the student, the more need for alternate fingerings. As alternate fingerings are introduced, the student should practice them until their selection for use in an appropriate situation becomes a matter of habit.

10. *Special uses of trill fingerings.* Trill fingerings may be used in certain passages, primarily upper neighbor notes, for smoothness in technical facility. The following illustrate their use in various situations.

(a) Trill fingerings may be used for the upper note in turns. In the following turn use the trill fingering for D:

(b) Use of a trill fingering for grace notes is a common practice. In the following example the trill fingering is used for C-sharp:

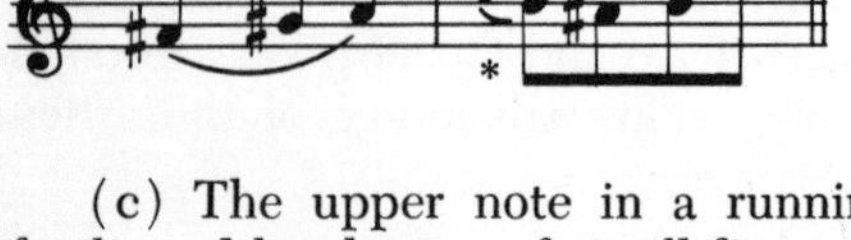

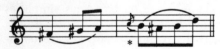

(c) The upper note in a running passage may be facilitated by the use of a trill fingering, as in the following where the B-flat trill fingering is used:

8. *High register.* Beginners on the oboe should not attempt to play above the top C in the second octave until the embouchure is firmly established and notes in both the first and second octave are played well in tune with good control. Notes in the third octave all have several alternate fingerings. In each instance the first fingering given in the fingering chart is the preferred one. Response of instruments in this register varies and it is well to try the alternate fingerings for each note to see if one of them responds on a particular instrument with better intonation and tone quality than the others. Notes in the third octave require greater embouchure support around the reed than those in the second octave. Avoid biting the reed. Use a firmer breath support. Notes in this register are produced with difficulty if the reed is too soft. If a student has difficulty producing these sounds, try a slightly stiffer reed.

In order for the embouchure to support the reed properly for notes in the third octave more reed is taken into the mouth. The simple process of using more reed in the mouth, even to the point where the upper lip touches the wrapping on the reed, will often make an astounding improvement in students who are having difficulty producing full tones of good quality in the third octave. A comparison of the photographs, Figure O-39 and 0-40 will show the extremes in the amount of reed taken into the mouth. Figure O-39 shows the position while playing  and Figure O-40, the position while playing 

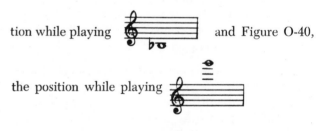

HARMONICS

The use of harmonics for special effects is standard procedure on all string instruments and they are found regularly in musical compositions. The use of harmonics in the same sense on woodwind instruments is rare, but they are used occasionally on the oboe. All the woodwind instruments are capable of producing harmonics on certain notes, but they are never called for on the clarinet and bassoon but appear occasionally in flute and oboe literature.

Harmonics are used on the oboe in piano or pianissimo passages where a light flute-like quality is called for at the discretion of the player. When harmonics are desired by the composer, they are printed with a small circle above them to indicate that they are to be fingered as harmonics in the same way that harmonics are indicated in music for string instruments. Harmonics are produced and controlled with some dififculty, and should be reserved for introduction only to advanced players.

These harmonics are frequently somewhat flatter in pitch than the same notes played normally. If this is the case they may be brought up in pitch by increasing embouchure support around the reed and by increasing breath pressure. Professional players will use harmonics for pianissimo notes which are hard to control with the regular fingering, or which are sharp at this dynamic level.

The example below gives the harmonics used on the oboe and the fingerings used to produce them. Finger the lower notes and overblow a twelfth to produce the harmonics. Oboes with a single automatic octave key cannot play the notes A through C.

The following is a melody which can be played entirely in harmonics. If an advanced oboist is available

have the example played first with normal full tone and then as harmonics.

TRANSPOSITION FOR THE OBOIST

The oboist is occasionally expected to transpose and play parts written for the English horn on the oboe, and rarely to play oboe parts on the English horn. Advanced players should develop some facility in both transpositions. The ability to transpose and play at sight is acquired only by doing it, slowly at first, and then with increasing speed.

1. *Playing English horn parts on the oboe.* As the English horn is in "F" and the oboe a nontransposing instrument in C, the English horn part is transposed down a perfect fifth when played on the oboe. Since the range of the English horn is lower than that of the oboe, some of the notes in the English horn part cannot be played down a perfect fifth as they actually sound, but must be played a fourth higher so that they sound an octave above the written notes. To make this transposition add one flat or subtract one sharp from the key signature of the English horn part and transpose down a perfect fifth or up a perfect fourth. The illustration below shows this type of transposition.

2. *Playing oboe parts on English horn.* This transposition involves the reverse of the previous process. To make this transposition add one sharp or subtract one flat from the key signature of the oboe part and transpose up a perfect fifth or down a perfect fourth according to the range of the music being played. The illustration on page 154 taken from the Bach "B minor Mass" illustrates the transposition.

SELECTION OF INSTRUMENTS

The system of fingering used on the present day oboes used in the United States developed from principles first applied to the flute by Boehm. This system, called the Conservatory System, was developed by the French firm of Triebert during the mid-nineteenth century, and brought to a high state of development by Loree around 1880. Since that time various improvements have been made on the instrument and its mechanism without, however, changing the basic sytsem.[3] Other systems used in Europe such as the German system, the true Boehm system seem to be gradually losing favor to the Conservatory system, and are never used in this country.

There is perhaps less standardization in mechanism of the oboe than in any other musical instrument, each maker having several models from which to choose, or with extra features which can be added at the option of the buyer. The various options are detailed in the following.

1. *Plateau keys and open tone holes.* The most fundamental difference in oboe models is found in the option of plateau, or covered tone holes, in contrast to the models with open tone holes as on the clarinet. The plateau system is standard and is used by oboists from

3. See Bate, Philip *The Oboe.* London: Ernest Benn Ltd. 1956 for a fascinating account of the various developments in the construction of the oboe.

beginners to the most polished professional. In it the tone holes are covered by vented plates with pads under them as on the flute rather than directly by the fingers. The open tone hole models require that the tone holes be closed by using the fingers as pads as on the clarinet. Some professionals prefer the open tone holes saying that the tone quality is superior, but these are in the minority. The plateau system is preferable for all school use.

2. *Octave keys.* The oboe requires two octave keys, and these are available in three different arrangements:

(1) The automatic octave key model in which a single octave key operated by the thumb automatically changes from one vent hole to another according to the fingering being used. This is the arrangement which is standard on the saxophone and on modern alto and bass clarinets. It has the advantage of simplicity for younger students, but the disadvantage of eliminating some excellent fingerings for certain notes in the third octave as well as some of the harmonics. The automatic octave key model is not recommended.

(2) The semiautomatic octave key model incorporates some of the advantages of both the automatic octave key and the double octave key. Two octave keys are provided on the instrument, one operated by the thumb, the other by the first finger of the left hand. The semiautomatic mechanism on this model allows the thumb to be kept on its octave key while the side octave key is being used, the mechanism automatically closing the vent hole of the first when the second is opened. This is the preferred arrangement for players on all levels and is the type recommended.

(3) Double octave key instruments have two independent octave keys which must be opened and closed independently by the thumb and first finger of the left hand. This involves complex movements of these fingers and a high degree of coordination which is difficult to develop. This system has no advantages over the semiautomatic arrangement, and is not recommended.

3. *Resonance keys.* The earlier models of the Conservatory system oboe required the addition of the E-flat key to the fork fingering for F in both the first and second octaves in order to match the resonance of this fingering with the other tones. Many models of oboes now have a resonance key on the side of the instrument which opens automatically when the fork fingering for F is used thus eliminating the necessity of adding the E-flat key with a little finger, and freeing the little finger for use on successive notes. An F resonance key is invaluable and is recommended for use on any level of performance.

When examining an oboe the presence of this resonance key can be ascertained by closing the three holes of the right hand, then opening and closing the middle hole while keeping the first and third closed. If there is a key on the side of the body of the instrument which opens and closes simultaneously with the middle hole, the instrument has an F resonance key, otherwise there is no F resonance key on the instrument.

The finest oboes of recent manufacture have an additional resonance key on the bell. This key improves the resonance, tone quality, and intonation of the low B-flat. If all other considerations are equal when considering the purchase of an instrument the resonance key on the bell is recommended. It is by no means essential, and many manufacturers do not feel that it is essential and do not offer it as an option.

4. *Extra keys.* Various keys in excess of what has become the standard mechanism are offered on many models. These include a left hand F key operated by the little finger of the left hand; a second G-sharp key operated by the first finger of the right hand which has virtually become standard on the better instruments; a third octave key used only for three notes in the high register; various trill keys, etc. These keys are useful if they are on the instrument, but unless the player is of professional calibre, they are not recommended because of the additional complexity of the mechanism and its accompanying problems.

Recommended standard model. The model recommended for use by student musicians on all levels is the Plateau System with the semiautomatic octave key and F resonance key. To this basic complement the better grades of instruments will automatically supply the standard and desirable trill keys, plates, and the extra G-sharp key. Lower grades of instruments which do not have these extras are satisfactory only for beginning and intermediate students.

STUDENT QUALIFICATIONS AND APTITUDES

The oboe is not a beginning instrument. Before being considered for playing the oboe, a student should have developed something more than basic facility on another woodwind instrument plus the ability to produce a good tone on the instrument, preferably the clarinet. This is the best criteria for advisability of study on the oboe.

Most authorities are in agreement that students should not start playing the oboe earlier than the seventh grade because of the stretches required of the fingers and the problems of controlling a small double reed. The benefits of the years of instrumental study prior to the seventh grade, if on another woodwind instrument, can be transferred quickly and easily to the oboe.

A natural aptitude for the oboe may be determined by success in producing a good "crow" on a reed adjusted and prepared for playing by the instructor after some brief instruction on embouchure formation and how to produce the crow. Students who are not immediately successful with some instructive guidance, may soon indicate a good natural aptitude. In the final analysis it is not natural aptitude but desire and persistence which are the greatest of all aptitudes for any instrument.

The English horn should be played only by competent oboists.

CARE OF THE OBOE

Assemble and disassemble with the greatest of care. Review the instructions on assembly of the instrument until they are thoroughly understood and the students are performing the operation easily. Keep the instrument in its case when not in use. Keep the instrument out of direct sunlight and away from all sources of heat. It is mandatory that the instrument be thoroughly dried after each playing, and the habit of doing this thoroughly should be developed from the very first. The process of swabbing does not take much time and will prevent cracks in the wood and help maintain sanitary conditions for playing.

Swabs. Three different types of swabs are available for drying the oboe. Each type has its advantages and disadvantages and its proponents and opponents. The principal problem revolves around the best method of thoroughly drying the very small diameter of the upper joint, and each type of swab gives a solution to this problem as well as for drying the lower joint. The only criteria is that the entire inside of the instrument be thoroughly dried, and the instructor and player are free to choose the type which they feel gets the best results. The three kinds of swabs are:

(1) *Double end wool swab.* A stiff wire with a large round wool swab on one end for drying the lower joint and the bell and a small conical shaped wool end for drying the upper joint. The small end of most of these swabs will not go completely through the upper joint but must be inserted and withdrawn from the larger end. This type of swab leaves moisture in the small end of the upper joint which must be cleared by a pipe cleaner, feather, or a special swab for the top joint such as the one made by Artley. The combination of the special top joint swab and the double end wool swab is ideal for younger players.

(2) *Cloth swabs.* These are small cloths on a drop cord with a weight similar in design to the typical clarinet swab. They usually come in pairs, one for the upper joint and one for the lower joint. Unless the smaller one will pull through the upper joint they are not satisfactory without an additional means of drying the upper part of the top joint as discussed previously. Combined with a top joint swab, however, they are quite satisfactory.

(3) *Feathers.* Using a turkey or pheasant feather is the traditional way of drying the oboe. These feathers must be long enough to reach through the lower joint. Only feathers with barbs of equal size on either side of the quill should be used. Pheasant tail feathers are equally as useful as the wing tip feathers of the turkey. These feathers may be purchased commercially or prepared by the student. Feathers prepared at home should be washed with lukewarm water and soap to remove the natural oils which prevent the feather from absorbing water. Since the turkey feather is the traditional swab it is used in the illustrations which follow, but wool or cloth swabs may be used with equal success.

The suggested step-by-step process which follows is efficient and should be checked regularly by the instructor until it is easily accomplished by the student.

1. Take the instrument apart in the reverse order of assembly, holding each part exactly as they were held during the process of assembling the instrument. Shake the moisture out of each end of each joint and place the parts carefully in the case before proceeding with drying the inside.

2. Upper joint. Holding the joint in the left hand as shown in Figure O-45, push the feather through from the larger end until the tip extends through the small end. Pull the feather back and forth rotating it at the same time to absorb the moisture. Put the protective cap over the cork and replace joint carefully in case.

3. Lower joint. Hold the lower joint as shown in Figure O-46 (or reverse the left and right hands). Insert the feather from the bottom, rotate, and pull back and forth simultaneously. Put the protective cap over the cork and replace joint carefully in the case.

4. Hold the bell as shown in Figure O-47. Insert the feather from the bell end, pulling back and forth and rotating simultaneously. Replace bell in case.

5. With a soft cloth or chamois dry the inside of each of the connecting joints.

6. The reed. Blow the moisture out of the reed and

place it carefully in a reed case so that it can dry properly. The inside of the reed should be cleaned once a week or so by drawing a wet pipe cleaner through it carefully (Figure O-48). Insert the pipe cleaner from the cork end pushing then pulling through the tip. Be very careful not to reverse the direction of the cleaner as it will damage the tip of the reed.

Figure O-45

Figure O-46

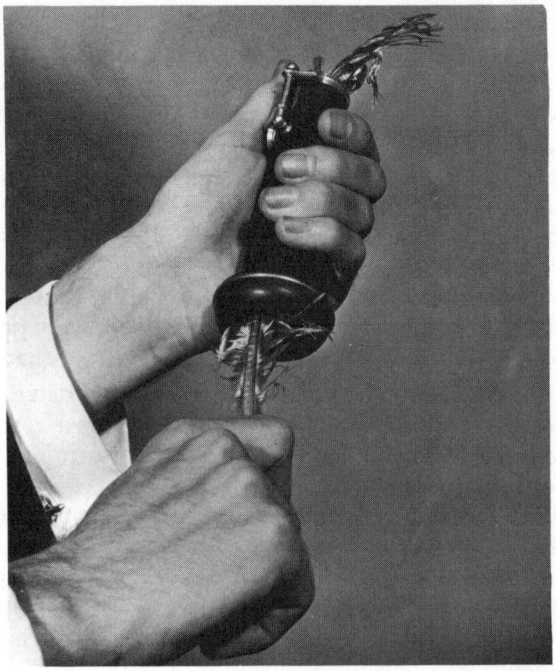

Figure O-47

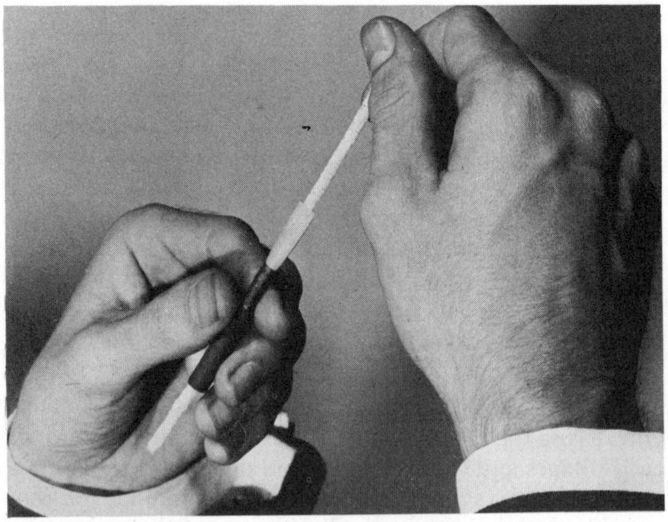

Figure O-48

Regular Maintenance of the Instrument

1. *Oiling the bore.* Even though they are made of the hardest wood available—grenadilla wood—wood instruments are subject to cracking. Careful drying after each playing will help avoid this but authorities recommend that the bore of a wood instrument be oiled with specially prepared bore oil. New instruments should be oiled every two weeks for the first three or four months of

use, once a month for the next six months, then four or five times a year. Only the very thinnest coating of oil is desired. The best means of oiling the bore is with a turkey feather kept for this purpose. Let three or four drops of oil run down the bottom of the bore of each joint, then distribute this over the entire inside of the joint by pushing the feather back and forth through the joint rotating it at the same time. Two drops of oil will be sufficient for the bell. Be sure that the upper portion of the top joint is covered well, since this is a critical area for moisture. Be careful that no oil gets into the tone holes or on pads or corks. The outside of the instrument may be oiled very lightly with a few drops of oil distributed by a small, soft cloth, again being very careful that no oil gets onto any pad or cork.

2. *Oiling the mechanism.* The mechanism, if it is to remain in the best playing condition, must be oiled regularly three or four times a year. Special oil called key oil for this purpose is commercially available. A drop of oil on the end of a needle or toothpick should be put at each pivot screw of each key. Do this carefully so that no oil can get onto the pads. This regular oiling keeps pivot screws from excessive wear and from rusting into place, making repairs and adjustments on the instrument easier.

3. *Adjusting screws.* These are screws which control the action and clearance of various keys and levers which act together. If a leaky pad is discovered, check first to see if it can be corrected with an adjusting screw. All these screws must be perfectly adjusted if the instrument is to respond as it should.

There are a number of such adjusting screws on the oboe. The standard model instrument recommended will have as many as fifteen of these screws including two on the semiautomatic octave keys, one on the articulated G-sharp, two on the F resonance key, etc. A visual check of the instrument will show how each is involved in the mechanism.

Every student past the beginning stage should have a small screwdriver in his case at all times. These screws can be adjusted visually and tested by playing, but the adjustment is critical for the height of open pads above the tone hole which will effect intonation as well as response. In addition to these adjusting screws, the pivot screws for each key should be tightened regularly to assure the best reliable action of the mechanism.

4. *Dusting the instrument.* After an instrument has been in use over a period of time, dust collects under the key mechanism. This can and should be removed with a soft watercolor brush. A cloth should never be used for this purpose as it will snag on the needle springs which will break under pressure.

5. *Shining the keys.* Keys may be kept in good condition if they are wiped regularly and gently with a soft cloth or chamois to remove perspiration and dirt. This will not only keep the keys from tarnishing, but will prevent corrosion of the plates and keys in the event the player perspires excessively. Silver polish must never be used on the keys, nor should the keys ever be polished while on the instrument. Using silver polish while the keys are on the instrument will foul pivot screws in the mechanism, and damage pads so that they will leak. Leave polishing up to a competent repairman. Caution students against polishing the keys, but give them careful instructions to keep the instrument clean by wiping the keys.

6. *Bent keys.* In spite of the best of care, keys sometimes become bent out of line. Bent keys or rods occur with alarming regularity on the instruments of young players, and cause unevenness in technique, or even prevent certain tones from responding at all. No attempt should be made to straighten keys or rods while they are on the instrument. This puts excessive pressure on both the keys and their posts and the instrument may be damaged even more. Keys must be removed from the instrument by a repairman who has the proper tools to straighten and align them.

7. *Sticking pads.* If the instrument is not thoroughly dried before it is put into its case, or if the humidity is excessive even temporarily, some pads on the instrument will stick tightly, or will stick momentarily before opening, making technique uneven. Moisture can be removed from sticking pads by placing a cigarette paper between the pad and the tone hole, pressing down on the key firmly. Release the key, move the paper and repeat the process until the key no longer sticks. If this does not relieve the sticking, put the cigarette paper in place, press the key, and pull the paper slowly from under the pad. Repeat the process several times. If the condition reoccurs regularly have the pad replaced. Never use powder on pads to stop sticking.

8. *Water in tone holes.* Some instruments tend to collect water in certain tone holes under pads that are normally closed, producing a bubbling sound when these keys are opened. This may be removed by opening the key and blowing into the hole. If time permits take the instrument apart and swab the joint on which this occurs. If a particular hole collects water regularly it may sometimes be corrected by removing the key and coating the inside of the tone hole lightly with vaseline. Avoid a heavy coat of vaseline as it will soak into the pad. Instruments which have the bore oiled regularly tend to collect less water in tone holes than those instruments with a dry bore.

9. *Leaky pads.* The keywork of an oboe is an extremely complex one in which almost every key and tone hole is part of a system made up of set screws, levers, or counter-balanced springs. If a note doesn't respond correctly or if the tone quality of a note or notes doesn't match, the problem may well be a leaky pad. Pads may leak because the adjusting screws (see number 3) are not properly set, or they may be worn because of use. Some pads wear out more rapidly than others and begin to leak,

causing the instrument to respond with difficulty on certain notes.

To test for leaks take the instrument apart. Plug the lower end of the joint with a cork or with the palm of the hand. Cover the tone holes and close all keys as if playing, avoiding using more pressure against the holes or keys than is used when playing. Blow through the other end with as much pressure as possible. Leaky pads can be identified by leaking air. If a tone hole normally covered by a key and pad held closed by a spring leaks when maximum wind pressure is applied during the test, the spring on that key must be strengthened or replaced by a repairman. A joint in perfect condition will not leak air no matter how much breath pressure is applied.

If the leak cannot be located by the above method, an alternative method which assures positive seating of all pads is to use commercial feeler papers, or strips of cigarette paper about a quarter inch wide. Slide one end of the paper under the pad, put the normal amount of pressure against the pad if the key is not held closed by a spring, and slowly draw the paper out. As long as the pressure against the paper remains constant there is no leak. If the pressure suddenly lessens the pad is not properly seated. Repeat the process completely around the pad so that all edges are tested.

The process of blowing cigarette smoke through the instrument to identify a leak through seeing the cigarette smoke coming out of the leak is not recommended. The nicotine in the smoke coats the pads and if this is done frequently will damage them so that they harden and leak. Repairmen use a small light in the bore of the instrument to find leaks, as the light will shine through the open space of the leak. Teachers responsible for numbers of woodwind instruments might find it advantageous to purchase such a light, as instruments may be tested quickly, accurately, and efficiently with this device.

Pads may leak because they are not seated properly, or because they are worn. A loose membrane on the bottom of the pad indicates that it should be replaced immediately, even though it is not leaking at that time. It soon will be, and if the condition persists it will produce a buzz when that particular key is used to play a note.

10. *Regular overhaul.* The condition of every instrument must be checked at least once a year by the instructor or by a repairman. Regular maintenance keeps an instrument in good playing condition over a period of years, rather than allowing it to gradually deteriorate becoming increasingly difficult to play. Every instrument must have a complete overhaul every three to five years depending on amount of usage. If fine instruments receive a yearly checkup and regular overhauls they will last in virtually perfect condition for many years. The services of a competent repairman are invaluable and an asset to any program of instrumental instruction.

BIBLIOGRAPHY OF STUDY MATERIALS

The amount of teaching material available for the oboe is not very extensive, although it is adequate if full advantage is taken of what is available. Material on the beginning and lower intermediate levels is particularly limited, with a greater variety of material becoming available as the student's technical facility progresses.

A complete list of study materials, solos, and ensemble material for oboe is too extensive to include here. Detailed information is available from various sources including the volumes by Cobbett, Coleman, Heller, Houser, Rasmussen-Mattran, Rothwell, and Stanton listed in the bibliography at the end of this book, and in the Selective Music Lists published by the MENC.

Beginning Methods

Anzalone, V. *Breeze-Easy Method for Oboe,* two volumes. Witmark.

Buck, L. *Elementary Method for Oboe.* Kjos.

Carey, Milburn. *Basic Method for the Oboe.* Carl Fischer.

Gekeler, Kenneth. *Oboe Method,* three volumes, Belwin.

Herfurth-Stuart. *A Tune A Day for Oboe.* Boston Music Co.

Hovey, N. W. *Elementary Method for Oboe.* Rubank, Inc.

Skornicka, J. E. and R. Koebner. *Intermediate Method for Oboe.* Rubank, Inc.

Voxman, H. and Wm. Gower. *Advanced Method for Oboe.* Rubank, Inc.

Weber, Fred and Blaine Edlefsen. *Oboe Student* (Student Instrumental Course), 3 vols. Elementary, Intermediate, Advanced Intermediate. Belwin, Inc. Correlated with four other volumes of solos, studies, and études.

Transfer Methods

Many fine school oboists are developed by transferring to the oboe a student who has had considerable experience and who has developed good technical facility and musicianship on clarinet or another woodwind. The beginning methods listed above are not the best choices for such a student as they progress much too slowly, nor are the Standard Methods suitable for the first few months of experience.

The Study of the Oboe by William D. Fitch, published by George Wahr Publishing Co. was designed for the beginner with previous experience and presents technical problems clearly and efficiently and develops facility rapidly. *A Method for Oboe* by Florian Mueller, published by the University Music Press would be an alternate choice when transferring experienced players to the oboe. The best choice to follow would be the Andraud *Practical and Progressive Oboe Method* because of the wealth of material it makes available.

Standard Methods

Andraud, Albert. *Practical and Progressive Oboe Method.* Southern Music Co. An extensive collection of exercises, technical studies, and études selected from the standard works for oboe. Includes many solos as well. An excellent choice for students who have completed the beginning stage of their development.

Barret, A. M. R. *Complete Method for Oboe.* Boosey & Hawkes, Alphonse Leduc. The material in this method is not arranged progressively, and very little of it is useful for other than advanced students. The Boosey & Hawkes edition is a reprint of the original nineteenth century edition. The first volume of the Leduc edition, in two volumes, is available only with text material in French, but the music calligraphy is considerably easier to read. Volume one of this edition (131 pages) is a considerable expansion of the first 56 pages of the original. Volume two has the Forty Progressive Melodies, Four Sonatas, and Fifteen Grand Studies reedited according to contemporary performance practices. However, in the Leduc edition the bass part for the Forty Melodies is transposed for English horn and the second part for the Sonatas and Grand Studies doesn't appear at all.

Langley. *Tutor for Oboe,* two editions. Carl Fischer or Boosey & Hawkes. An old standard method in the series written by Langey for many instruments. It is primarily in the intermediate level of difficulty.

Niemann. *Method for the Oboe.* Carl Fischer. Another old standard method. The material is mostly on the intermediate level of technical difficulty. Can be used in combination with the Langey to provide more intermediate level material.

Additional Study Materials

Andraud, Albert. *First Book of Studies for Oboe.* Leduc.
Vade-Mecum of the Oboist. Southern Music Co. A most important and extensive collection of selected studies from the standard writers for the instrument, and a number of orchestral studies for oboe and English horn. Basic for the oboist.

Bach, J. S. *Difficult Passages.* Ed Rothwell. Boosey & Hawkes.

Bassi, L. *27 Virtuoso Studies.* Carl Fischer. Transcribed from the original clarinet studies by Iasilli. Fairly difficult.

Blatt. *Fifteen Entertaining Études for Oboe.* Edition Musicus. These are also in the Andraud Practical and Progressive Method.

Bleuzet, L. *La Technique du Hautbois,* 3 vols. Leduc. English text. Scales in various forms, chromatic studies, arpeggios, staccato exercises, etc., for advanced student.

Bozza, E. *18 Études.* Leduc. Fine studies for advanced students.

Braun, C. A. P. *18 Caprices.* Breitkopf & Hartel.

Brod, H. *Études et Sonates,* 2 vols. Leduc.
20 Studies. International, Leduc.

Brown. *370 Exercises.* Leduc

Caillieret. *15 Études from Solo Violin Sonatas of J. S. Bach.* Leduc.

Capelle. *Twenty Grand Exercises,* 2 vols. Leduc. From the works of Rode, Fiorillo, Sivori, and Charpentier. For the advanced student.

Cavallini, E. *Thirty Caprices,* 2 vols. Carl Fischer.

Chopin, F. *Chopin Studies Transcribed for Oboe.* Gornston.

Debobdue. *Twenty-Four Melodic Studies.* Leduc. Most are of medium difficulty.
100 Exercises for Oboe. Leduc. Advanced studies.

Dubois. *Twelve Études.* Leduc.

Dufresne. *Develop Sight Reading.* Charles Colin. Like the volumes by Gates and Teal, the primary interest here is rhythmic. Intermediate.

Ferling. *144 Preludes and Studies,* 2 vols. Friedrich Hofmeister.

18 Studies, Op. 12. Southern Music Co.

48 Famous Studies. 2 books. Southern Music Co. Book I contains the 48 studies and first oboe parts for the Ferling 3 duos concertants. Book II has the 2nd oboe parts for the Ferling Duos plus the Trio, op. 87 of Beethoven and 10 Duets by Bernards. The 48 studies are a must for any student who reaches the upper intermediate level. The 18 studies are also in the Vade-Mecum.

Flemming. *60 Progressive Études,* 3 vols. Peters (Zimmerman).

Gallois-Montbrun. *Six Musical Études.* For oboe and Piano. Leduc.

Gates, Everett. *Odd Meter Études.* Gornston.
Odd Meter Duets. Gornston. Excellent studies in twentieth century meters.

Gekeler, K. *Practical Studies for Oboe,* 2 vols. Belwin-Mills.

Giampier. *Sixteen Studies for Oboe.* Ricordi.

Giampieri. *Progressive Method.* Ricordi.
6 Daily Studies for Perfection. Ricordi.

Gillet. *Twenty Minutes of Study.* Leduc. A daily routine to keep the oboist in shape.

Heinze. *Bach Studien für Oboe.* Breitkopf edition.

Karg-Elert. *25 Capricen und Sonate, Op. 153.* Zimmerman.
Études-Schule, Op. 41. Zimmerman.

Labate. *Études and Scales for Advanced Oboists.* Carl Fischer.

Lamorlette. *Twelve Études.* Leduc.
18 Études. Leduc.

Lamotte. *First Book of Scale and Arpeggio Studies for Oboe.* Josef Marx edition. McGinnis & Marx.

Loyan. *Thirty-Two Études.* Costallat.

Luft, J. H. *24 Études.* Peters, Costallat editions.

Mayeur. *21 Studies for Saxophone or Oboe.* David Gornston.

Pares, G. *Daily Technical Exercises for Oboe.* Carl Fischer.

Modern Pares Foundation Studies for Oboe. Rubank. Major and minor scales in various patterns an keys. Two editions of the same music.

Prestini. *Collection of Studies for Oboe.* Ricordi.

12 Studies on Modern Style with Chromatics. Ricordi.

12 Studies in Modern Style with Rhythmic Difficulties. Ricordi.

30 Studies for the Execution of Embellishments. Edizione Bongiovanni.

Rose. *22 Selected Studies.* Pro-Art Publications.

Rothwell, Evelyn. *A Book of Scales for the Oboe.* Oxford University Press.

The Oboist's Companion, 3 vols. Oxford University Press.

Salviani. *Studies from the Method,* 4 vols. Ricordi.

Schiemann. *Seven Characteristic Studies for Oboe.* Edition Musicus.

Singer. *Metodo Teorico-Practico per Oboe,* 3 vols. Ricordi.

Small, L. J. *27 Melodius and Rhythmical Exercises.* Carl Fischer.

Teal, L. *Studies in Time Division.* University Music Publishers.

Tustin, Whitney. *Technical Studies.* Peer-International. The most complete book of mechanical technical studies available.

Daily Scales. Southern Publishing Co.

Verroust, S. *24 Melodic Studies, Op. 65,* 2 vols. Costellat or Ricordi editions. Vol. I only McGinnis & Marx. Excellent standard intermediate level material. A two volume piano accompaniment to these is also available in the Costellat edition.

Voxman, H. *Selected Studies for Oboe.* Rubank, Inc.

Wiedemann, L. *45 Études for Oboe.* Breitkopf and Hartel.

Study and Achievement Questions

1. Identify the beginning, intermediate, and advanced playing ranges for the oboe.
2. Assemble the instrument, identifying each part, and demonstrating the correct holding position for each operation.
3. Observe beginning, intermediate, and advanced students in the process of assemblying their instruments and fill out the checklist for assembly. Describe corrections for any faults.
4. Describe and demonstrate the correct holding position for the oboe including the two rest positions. Demonstrate various common faults in holding positions and describe the effect of each on performance.
5. Demonstrate the correct hand positions for oboe.
6. List the three ways of venting the instrument to produce notes in the second and third octaves, and write on a staff the notes for which each is used.
7. Observe beginning, intermediate, and advanced students and fill out the check list for holding and hand positions. Describe the effect on performance which any faults will have. Prescribe corrections for any faults.
8. Discuss the three basic types of embouchure formation for oboe. Choose one of these and describe and demonstrate the step-by-step procedure to form it.
9. Observe beginning, intermediate, and advanced students and fill out the checklist for embouchure formation. Suggest corrections for any faults.
10. Discuss tuning and intonation for oboe and English horn. What factors will make the instrument flat? What factors will make it sharp? What influence does the mechanism of the instrument have on intonation?
11. Identify the three registers of the instrument with range of each.
12. List the symptoms and corrections for the most commonly found faults in tone quality.
13. Discuss the three methods of tongue placement for articulation and how tongue action is developed.
14. Write on a staff the notes in the first two octaves for which the fingering involves the use of one or both little fingers. Select a passage in which several of these occur and mark the use of the left and right fingers.
15. Identify and describe the use of the two fingerings for F.
16. Write on a staff the harmonics used on the oboe and the fingering for each. Under what circumstances are harmonics used?
17. As considerations for the selection of an instrument for a good high school player discuss the pros and cons of plateau keys vs. open tone holes; whether a single automatic octave key, a semiautomatic octave key, or double octave keys is preferable; and what extra keys should be recommended and why.
18. Discuss the merits of the various kinds of swabs which may be used for drying the oboe.
19. Perform the step-by-step process of disassembly and cleaning the oboe, having a colleague observe and rate the procedure.

20. Locate the various adjusting screws on an instrument, discover the function of each, and check to see that they are properly set.
21. Discuss the various things involved in the regular maintenance of the oboe.
22. Examine and compare various beginning oboe methods. Select one or two best suited for junior high beginner, one or more suitable for a high school student transferring from clarinet to oboe.
23. Examine available standard methods and additional study materials for oboe and list them with comments. Prepare a suggested list of material to include all five types of material suggested for simultaneous study for an advanced beginner. For an intermediate level student. For an advanced student.
24. Listen to several phonograph records of outstanding oboe soloists. Comment on and compare tone quality, phrasing, articulation, and general facility. If the players are other than American describe any nationalistic differences which are discernible.
25. Discuss the use of vibrato on the oboe, and when and how it should be developed.

Chapter 5

Bassoon

The Bassoon as the bass voice of the double-reed choir has a remarkably large usable range which has been exploited in contemporary music. The contra-bassoon (or double bassoon as it is sometimes called) sounds an octave lower than the bassoon and extends the woodwind range into that of the string bass, but has not been extensively used. The fingering for the contra-bassoon is identical with that of the bassoon, and it is played, when called for, by a bassoonist just as the English horn is played by an oboist.

The bassoon has defied mechanical development, and the mechanism and technique remain awkward in comparison to the other woodwind instruments. Numerous attempts to adapt the Boehm principles to the bassoon have failed. Today there are two rival fingering systems in use in Europe—the French and German—widely different both mechanically and in tone quality produced. In the United States only the German system, called the Heckel System, is used. The bassoon as we have it today was perfected in the Heckel factory in Germany through several generations since the beginning of the company in 1831. The Heckel mechanical system is made by many manufacturers under their own names. Bassoons made by the Heckel factory are prized possessions of many bassoonists.

The bassoon, written in the bass, tenor, or alto clef is a non-transposing instrument. The beginning, intermediate, and advanced playing ranges are indicated below.

Beginning Intermediate Advanced

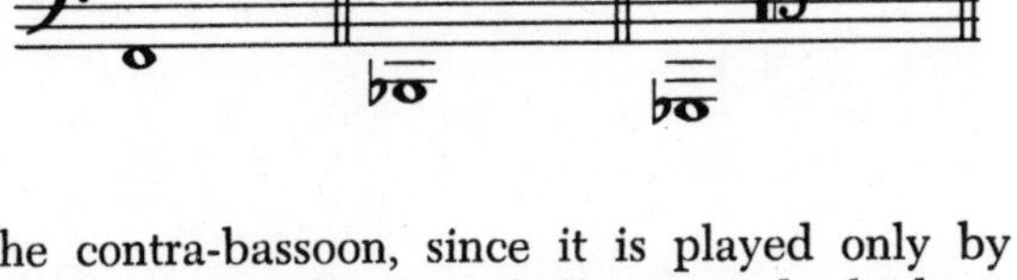

The contra-bassoon, since it is played only by advanced players, makes use of all except the highest portion of the advanced playing range indicated for the bassoon. Some instruments extend the range of the contra-bassoon to the written A one half-step lower than the lowest note on the bassoon. Sounding an octave lower than written, the actual pitch of this note is the same as the lowest note on the piano, making the contra-bassoon capable of producing tones lower than any other instrument of the orchestra or band. The contra-bassoon is written in the bass clef, and sounds an octave lower than written. The example below indicates this transposition.

Written Sounds

PARTS OF THE BASSOON

Parts of the bassoon are illustrated in Figure B-1. Since much of the literature about the bassoon uses the names, it is well to be able to identify them readily. The parts may be listed as follows:

1. Butt (or boot)—the end of the bassoon into which are fitted the long joint and the tenor joint.
2. Tenor joint (or Wing joint)—onto which the crook is fitted.
3. Long joint (or bass joint)—onto which the bell is fitted.
4. Bell joint.
5. Bocal (or crook) onto which the reed is fitted.

Most bassoons are equipped with two crooks of different lengths.

ASSEMBLING THE INSTRUMENT

Proper assembly and disassembly of the bassoon is of the utmost importance, and must be taught to students from the very first lesson. Probably more damage—bent keys, rods, bent connecting levers, etc.—is done by beginning students to the instrument in putting it together and taking it apart than by all other means combined. Instruments with damaged and out-of-line mechanism do not respond properly, and some of the difficulty that students, especially beginners, have in playing their instruments can be traced to damaged mechanism. The bassoon is, fortunately, somewhat less susceptible to this kind of damage than the oboe or clarinet, so that it is easier to avoid.

The assembly of an instrument must be accomplished without putting pressure on any key or rod which will bend it in any way. An instrument with as many keys as the bassoon is obviously impossible to put together without touching the keys. Before starting the process of assembly, be sure that all cork joints are well greased with prepared cork grease so that undue pressure will not have to be applied to put the parts together. The following step-by-step procedure is given in detail, and every student should practice it carefully until each procedure is correct and automatic. Study the photograph and directions for each step carefully and repeat the operation several times before proceeding to the next.

A. Butt Joint and Long Joint Assembly

1. Figure B-2. With the left hand grasp the long joint with the cluster of keys toward you. The palm of the hand is around the wood, thumb parallel with the long rod. The base of the thumb is near but not touching the rod.

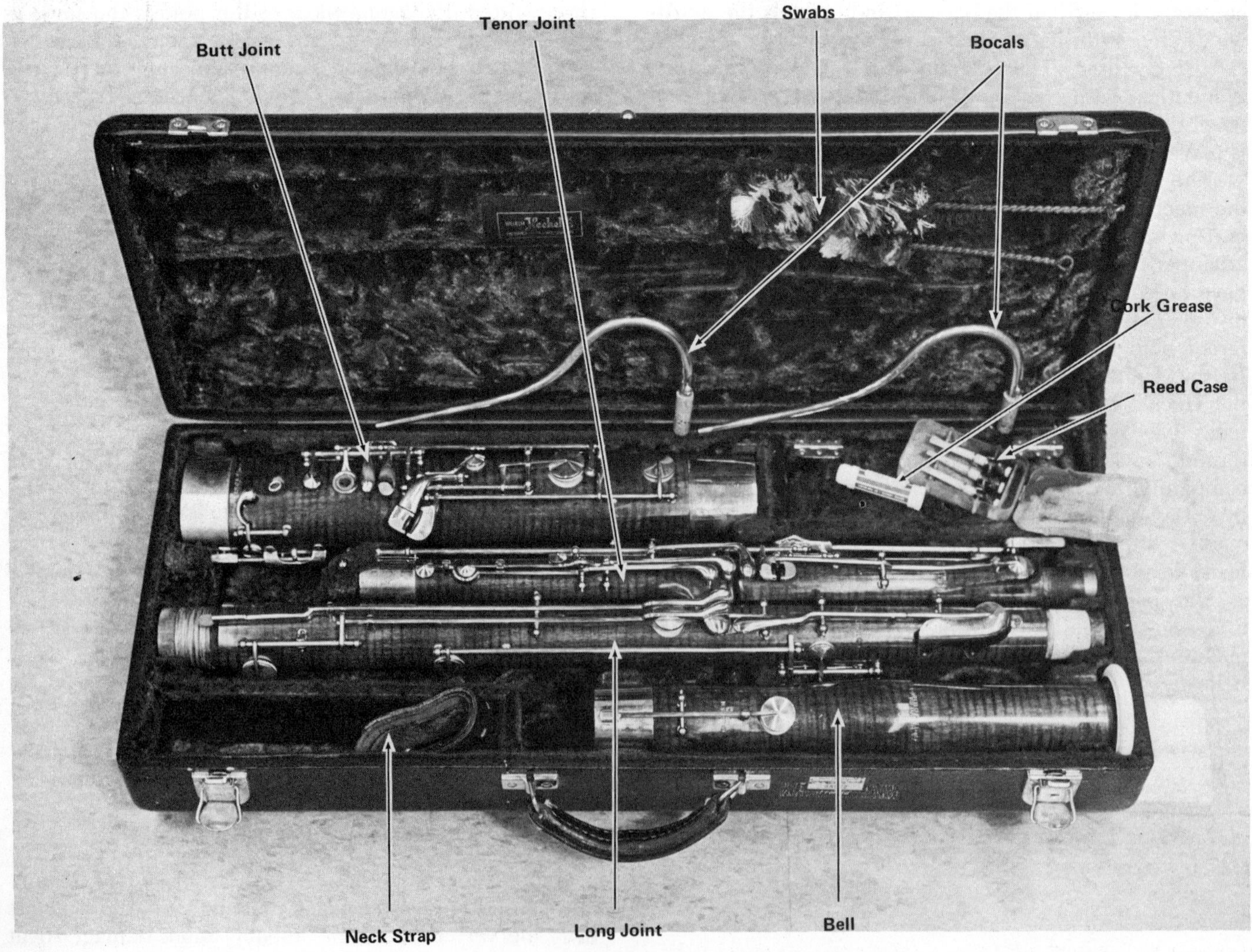

Figure B-1

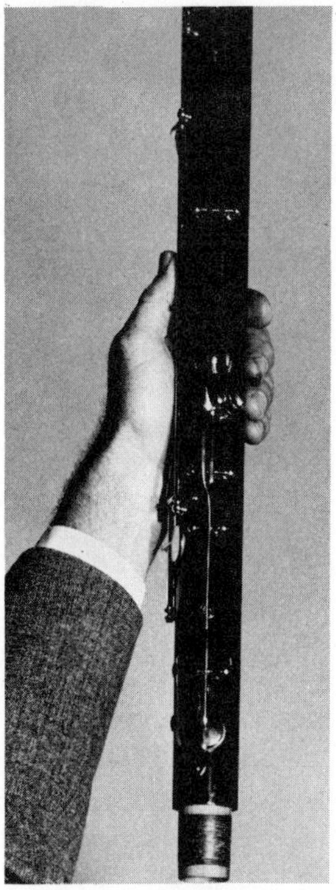

Figure B-2

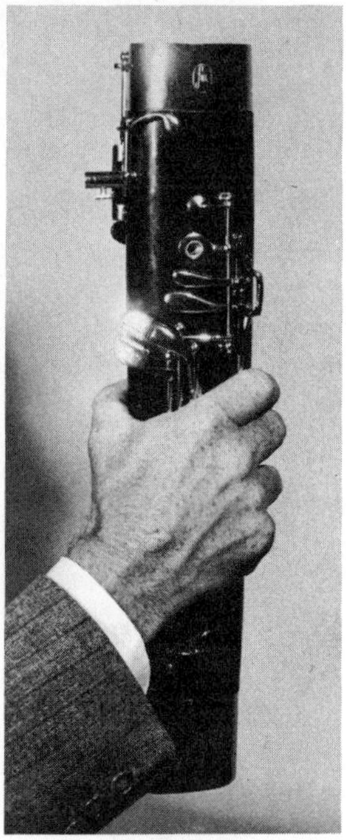

Figure B-3

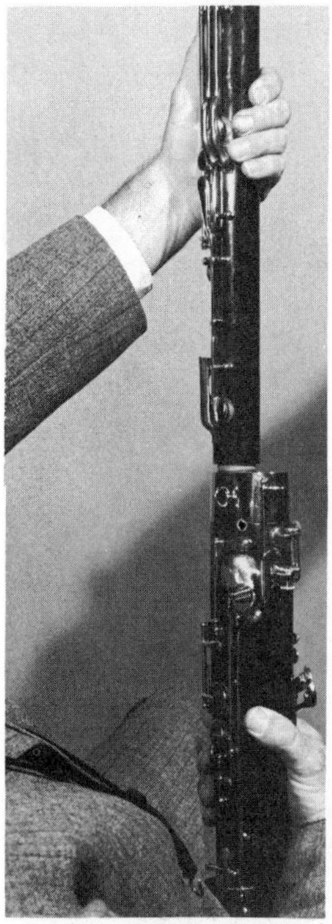

Figure B-4

Figure B-5

2. Figure B-3. With the right hand, take the butt joint with the palm over the keys on the tone hole side. The thumb and fingers grasp the wood to hold the joint firmly without pressure of the palm against the keys.

3. Figure B-4. With the end of the butt joint against the leg, and holding the two joints as described, push the two sections together with a slight back and forth twist until the long joint is firmly in place.

B. Butt Joint and Tenor Joint Assembly

1. Figure B-5. Take the tenor joint in the right hand as shown, with the thumb on the pivot screw and pressing the key against the guard. The tips of the fingers are against the wood, and the hand cupped to avoid pressure on the keys.

2. Figure B-6. The left hand holds the assembled butt and long joints against the left leg. Thumb and first finger are on the metal band at the top of the joint, tips of other fingers are on the wood, with second joint of fingers over the holes.

3. Figure B-7. Holding the tenor joint and butt joint as described push the two joints together with a slight back and forth motion. Keep the eyes on the connecting lever for the whisper key (indicated by an arrow in the photograph) so that it is not bent. When the tenor and long joints are in place in the butt, check to see that they are properly aligned with each other, and secure the lock which holds them together if the instrument has one.

Figure B-6

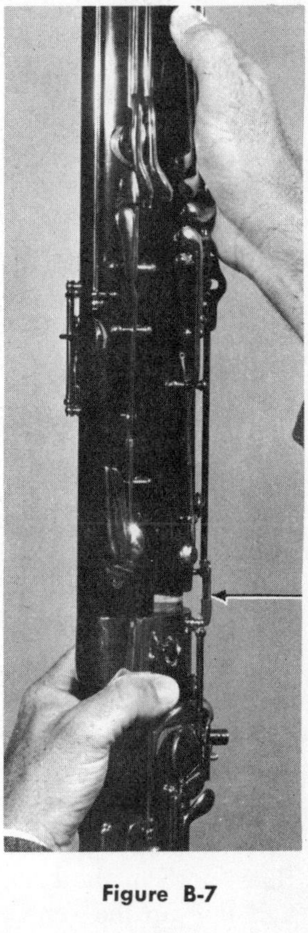

Figure B-7

C. Adding the Bell

1. Figure B-8. The bell is held in the left hand with the fingers on the wood and with the heel of the thumb depressing the single key on the bell to lift the connecting lever.

2. Figure B-9. Rest the heel of the bassoon on the floor and steady the instrument with the right hand. With the left hand holding the bell as indicated push it on and line up the two portions of the connecting lever.

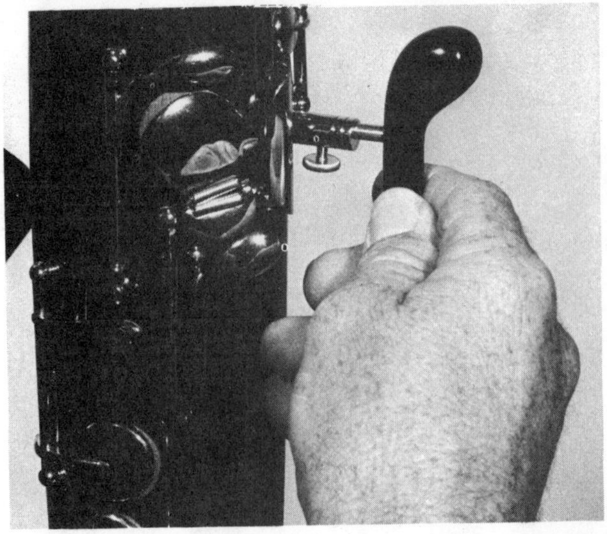

Figure B-10

Figure B-8

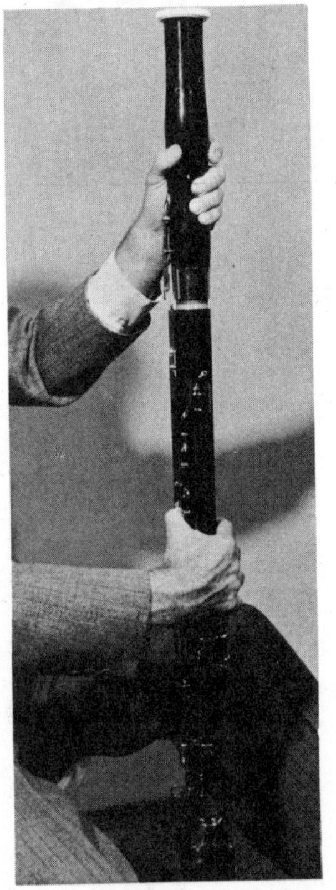

Figure B-9

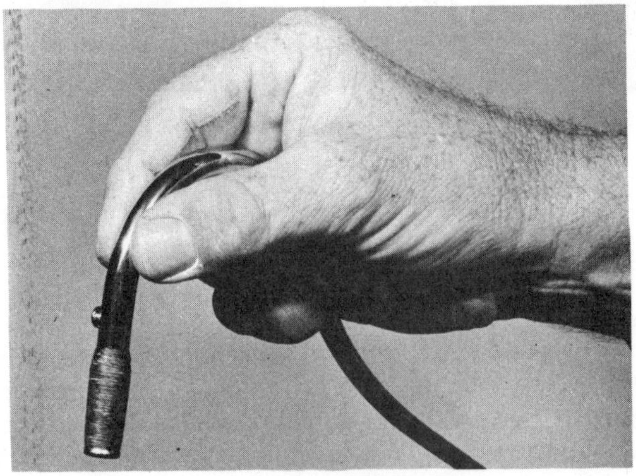

Figure B-11

D. Completing the Assembly

1. Figure B-10. Insert the thumb rest and line it up vertically with the bassoon, the larger part toward the bell. Adjust the height so the right thumb and fingers will fall into the correct holding position, and tighten the screw.

2. Figure B-11. Hold the bocal with the thumb and forefinger near the vent hold. The remainder of the fingers cup around the part, but control and pressure for adding this piece are in the thumb and forefinger.

3. Figure B-12. With the heel of the bassoon on the floor, push in the bocal with the thumb and forefinger, and line up the vent hole with the pad of the whisper key.

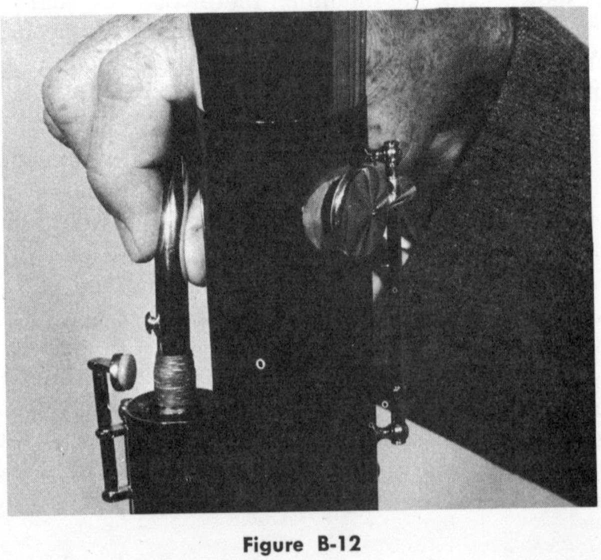

Figure B-12

4. Figure B-13. Hook the neck strap in the ring and adjust it to the proper length for playing. With the weight on the neck strap and the instrument in playing position balance the instrument with the right hand and add the reed with the left.

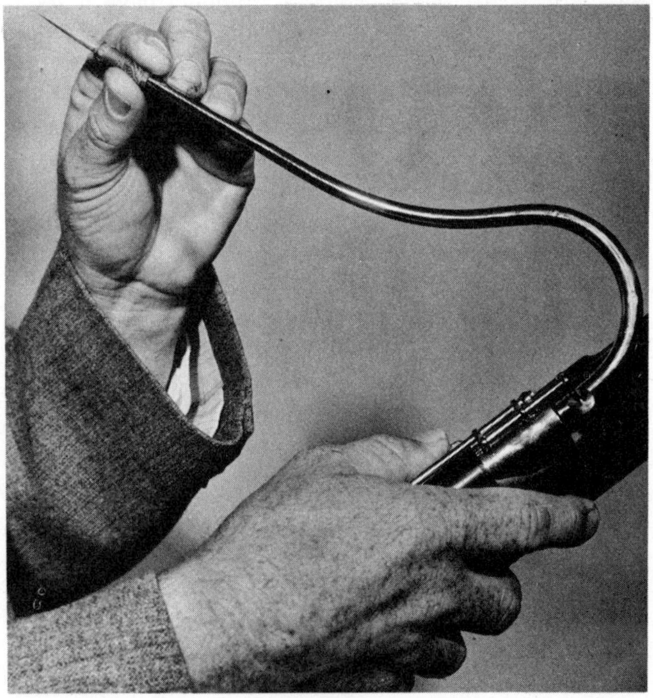

Figure B-13

Common Faults in Assembly

There are, of course, several possible ways in which the bassoon may be assembled, and various teachers have different methods and procedures. The only criteria for a good procedure is that no pressure is put on rods, plates or keys during the process. The procedure outlined above is a common standard one and may be safely used for beginners. As familiarity with the instrument increases, students may change the procedure to suit themselves. More advanced students will soon take the long joint and the tenor joint from the case together and assemble them with the butt joint at the same time. The following items are the most commonly found faults or inaccuracies in the assembly of the bassoon.

1. *Failure to grease cork or thread joints.* A container of cork grease is a must for every bassoon. The cork or thread joints of the instrument must be kept well greased so that the connections may be made with ease. If the corks are not greased, the instrument is assembled with difficulty and a great deal of pressure is necessary. This excessive pressure can easily cause the hand to grip the instrument too tightly and bend keys or rods. If, after the corks are well greased, a joint is still assembled with difficulty, then the cork is too large. A cork may be fitted to the correct size by sanding it with fine grain sandpaper, being careful not to sand any of the wood of the instrument. If a thread wound joint is too tight, a little of the thread may be unwound to make it the correct size.

If a thread wound joint is so loose that the joint is unsteady in its socket, additional linen thread of the same diameter or dental floss in an emergency may be wound on to make it the correct size. If the cork joint is too loose, wipe off all cork grease and moisten. Some corks will absorb enough water to swell to the correct size. Regrease and replace on the instrument. If the cork joint does not expand sufficiently from the additional moisture, apply a little heat entirely around it. This is preferably done with an alcohol lamp, but in an emergency can be applied with a match or cigarette lighter. Hold the match or lighter far enough away that the cork is not burned. If this procedure expands the cork sufficiently, apply cork grease and replace on the instrument. If neither of these procedures expands the cork sufficiently, it must be replaced.

2. *Holding joints improperly.* Holding the joints improperly puts pressure on keys and rods and soon bends them out of line. It is difficult to hold the various parts of the bassoon so that pressure in the wrong places is avoided, but the method described either avoids pressure on keys, or puts pressure on keys which are ordinarily in a closed position. An instrument which is not in perfect alignment plays with difficulty, has certain notes out of tune, or simply doesn't respond at all. Beginners on the instrument must be taught to hold the parts of the instrument properly during assembly and disassembly and checked frequently to see that they are doing so.

3. *Connecting levers out of line.* With only two connecting levers between the various joints to contend with, the bassoonist is not troubled with this problem as much as the oboist. The connecting lever between the tenor joint and the butt joint closes the whisper key when the right thumb is on the low E key. If this lever is not properly aligned, and the pad on the whisper key is not completely closed, notes in the lowest part of the instrument will be difficult to play and control. The remaining connecting lever, between the long joint and the bell closes the key on the bell to produce the low B-flat. This lever is sometimes bent out of alignment making it impossible to produce this note.

4. *Alignment of tenor and long joints.* The alignment of the tenor and long joints with each other is critical only to the extent that it effects the placement of the left hand and the ability of the fingers and thumb to reach out and operate the various holes and keys involved. In order to assure perfect alignment as well as to stabilize these two joints, many makes of bassoons are provided with a lock to lock the two sections together. Various kinds of locks are found, some in two separate pieces, others in a single piece with the lock

operated with a spring. The instructor must examine the lock in order to instruct the student exactly how to use it. Some students will ignore the lock or be unaware of its use. If there is a lock, it must be used. In the absence of a lock correct alignment is made by fitting together the wood projection on the tenor joint and the metal plate under the thumb keys on the long joint. Contact between these two points will help steady these two joints.

5. *The bocal.* The bocal is susceptible to bending if undue pressure is put on it near the reed end. It is common to see in school groups a bassoon bocal with a flat spot where it has been bent. A flat area in the bocal, or any alteration in its shape, changes the tone quality, intonation, and ease of playing. To avoid this kind of damage insist that the crook be held near the cork end as described. Younger students have a tendency to ignore the importance of aligning the vent hole in the crook with the pad which closes it. This should be carefully checked as ease of tone production in the lower register is dependent on its proper operation.

Checklist for Assembly

Observe the student in the operation of assembling the instrument and check the following items. Incorrect items for older students should not be called to their attention until the entire process is completed; younger students should be corrected immediately. If any mistake is made the entire process should be repeated until perfect.

	Yes	No	Comments
1. Were corks examined to see if they were properly greased?			
2. Long joint held properly during assembly with butt?			
3. Butt joint held properly during assembly with long joint?			
4. Tenor joint held properly during assembly with butt?			
5. Butt joint held properly on leg during assembly with tenor joint?			
6. Connecting lever on tenor joint properly aligned?			
7. Long and tenor joints properly aligned and locked?			
8. Bell held properly?			
9. Connecting lever on bell properly aligned?			
10. Crook held properly?			
11. Vent hole aligned with pad?			
12. Reed lined up and secured firmly?			

HOLDING POSITIONS FOR BASSOON

The way in which the bassoon is held has a direct relationship with the progress of the student, the embouchure formation, tone quality produced, control of intonation, and the development of technical facility. The proper position is one in which the body is in an erect position, with the body balanced comfortably, and in which the arms and hands fall naturally into a position in which there is no muscular tension. This position is one which can be maintained over a period of time without physical exhaustion and which permits freedom and control of the breathing mechanism.

Seated Position

The weight of the bassoon is supported by the neck strap or a seat strap[1] with the instrument balanced by the left and right hands as described in the section on hand position which follows. Adjust the height of the instrument with the strap so that when the head is erect the reed will touch the jaw at the bottom of the lower lip. The reed can be easily taken into the mouth from this position.

The butt joint rests against the right hip with the instrument held diagonally across the body so that music can be read with head and eyes straight forward. The bell of the instrument is held forward so that the angle of the crook permits the reed to enter the mouth at a very slight angle.

Head erect, chin up, eyes straight ahead, with shoulders up but relaxed. Elbows free from the body. Both feet flat on the floor. Shoulders and back must not touch the back of the chair when playing.

Figure B-14. Seated Position (Front View).

Adjust the music stand so that the music can be easily read from this position. When two students are playing from the same music, angle the chairs slightly toward the center of the stand so that the position of the body and instrument can remain correct.

Figure B-15. Seated Position (Side View).

Standing Position

The position of the instrument itself when the player is standing should be identical with that used in the seated position. Only the position of the body itself is changed. Stand erect with feet slightly apart, one foot ahead of the other to help maintain balance. Head remains erect, with chin up and eyes straight ahead. Shoulders up but relaxed, and elbows free from body. Raise the music stand, if one is being used, so that the head does not tilt downward. Every player should regularly spend a portion of his practice time standing to become at ease playing in a standing position.

1. Use of a seat strap is considered later in this chapter.

Figure B-16. Standing Position (Front View).

Figure B-17. Standing Position (Side View).

Rest Position

In the standard rest position, the neck strap is unhooked and the bassoon is placed diagonally across the legs with the crook up. The reed should be removed from the crook to prevent possible damage. From this position the reed can be returned to the crook and the instrument can be quickly picked up and returned to playing position, and the player is free to arrange music and to relax physically.

In the semi-rest position the strap is left hooked and the instrument tilted slightly forward in a relaxed position. This position is used during rests in the music, and when the player must be ready to resume playing immediately. This position, too, permits physical relaxation to avoid fatigue in performing for a period of time.

Figure B-18. Standard Rest Position.

Figure B-19. Semi-Rest Position.

Common Faults in Holding Positions

The holding position for an instrument can further rapid musical development, or it can make progress slow and difficult. The exact holding position depends upon and must be adapted to the physical characteristics of the player. Teachers must continually check student positions, especially in the early stages of learning, so that any deviations from the proper position can be immediately corrected before they develop into fixed habits. Once an incorrect position is established, it is extremely difficult to correct. Students themselves must and do learn to feel the right position, and should be encouraged to check their positions daily in front of a mirror both at school and at home. A full-length mirror is an integral part of the well-equipped instrumental room of any school.

The following are the most commonly found faults in holding positions for the bassoon. Check these points specifically and regularly with each student.

1. *Instrument at wrong angle with body.* Because of the two oblique angles, with the front of the body and with the side of the body, which are involved in the playing position there is considerable chance of error. The angle across the front of the body can be checked by looking directly at the student from the front to see that no part of the face is covered by the body of the instrument. If the instrument has a whisper key and most do, the fact that the vent hole in the crook and the pad on the key which closes it must be lined up makes this particular angle easier to arrive at correctly. A final check on this angle is to make sure that the reed is entering the center of the mouth at a right angle rather than entering from one side.

The angle with the side of the body involves more problems, and there is less unanimity of opinion among authorities on exactly what this angle should be. This angle is primarily determined by the angle with which the reed enters the mouth. Most authorities agree that the crook should tilt up slightly so that the reed enters the mouth at a slight angle. Others, and these are by far in the minority, ask that the reed enter the mouth directly, or ask for a greater upward angle. This angle affects tone quality and control and must be subject to constant scrutiny.

If the head is erect with the chin up as it should be, the reed angle determines how far forward or backward the butt end of the instrument is in relation to the body. If the butt is too far back, the left elbow is forced backward too far, putting tension on muscles and ligaments in the right hand. If the butt is too far forward, the right hand is pulled out of position, making it difficult for the fingers to operate the holes and keys. The angle of the arm at the elbow should be no less than 90 degrees and preferably greater than this. The physical characteristics of the individual student will help determine the exact angles best for him.

2. *Head inclined downward.* This is a most serious deviation from the normal because of the extreme effect it has on tone quality, and is, unfortunately found in students at all stages of development. When the head is inclined downward, unless the butt is drawn correspondingly farther back, the reed enters the embouchure at a downward rather than an upward angle. This puts the primary support for the reed on the upper lip rather than on the lower lip where the best and most accurate control is possible. This downward incline of the head makes the breath enter the reed at an angle and restricts the volume and support by bringing the tip of the reed closer to the tongue.

A related undesirable result is the effect this position has on articulation. Because the tip of the reed is close to the tongue, movements of the tongue are restricted, and the reed is contacted by the center of the tongue rather than the forward position. The result is a sluggish tongue and a lack of control and variety on articulation.

3. *Slouched body.* Varying degrees and kinds of poor posture are almost universal among student players. Common among these are the curved spine with the back against the chair, shoulders curved forward, feet crossed or hung over a rung on the chair. Poor posture affects breathing and breath control to the point that the student finds it impossible to support and control the tone properly. Students with poor posture will become physically tired rather quickly while playing. Poor posture pulls the arms, and consequently the fingers out of position making technique rough. Poor posture in any degree must be corrected immediately. The use of a mirror in correcting is helpful.

4. *Moving the body while playing.* Some students have the unfortunate habit of swaying or bouncing their body while playing. Any movement of the body changes the position of the reed in the mouth to a greater or lesser degree, interferes with the coordination of the muscles controlling breath support and in general has undesirable results in performance. Most players who move the body are not aware of the fact that they are doing so. Any movements noted should be called to the attention of the player and corrected immediately and firmly. A correct holding position without any bodily movement is necessary for complete success in performance.

5. *Adjustment of strap.* The neck or seat strap must be adjusted to support the entire weight of the instrument and so the reed enters the mouth at the correct angle. If the strap is adjusted so that it is too long, the student must duck his head or slouch to get the reed into his mouth. Any attempt to support the weight of the instrument with the hand rest or with the palm of the left hand pulls the hand out of position and tenses the muscles so that the fingers do not move freely. The condition of the strap should be checked when students are found to be having a problem with it to see that it

is not worn to the extent that the lock slides when weight is put on it. The strap must hold the desired length without slipping. Replace worn straps promptly.

HAND POSITIONS

Since the bassoon most desirably is played by a student with previous training on another woodwind instrument—usually clarinet—hand position may not be as much of a problem if the hand position on the previous instrument was good. The size of the student's hand and the length of fingers are more critical on the bassoon than on any other of the woodwind instruments because of the wide stretches necessary to reach and cover the holes and to operate the keys. Students with small hands and/or stubby fingers will have more difficulty achieving the best hand position than students with larger hands and longer fingers. The exact hand position, particularly of the left hand, will of necessity be determined by the size of the player's hands.

The following step-by-step procedure for establishing the hand position on the bassoon should be studied thoroughly with an instrument so that a feel for the position can be developed. Study both the text and the photographs carefully until they are perfectly clear. The "Guide Position" which is given is the fundamental position for hands and fingers and should be maintained at all times except when the fingering for a particular note involves moving a finger temporarily to another location. The guide position puts all fingers into the best position for developing speed and accuracy.

A. Left Hand Position

1. Figure B-20. The bassoon is balanced with the flesh at the base of the forefinger against the wood of the instrument. Position the hand so that the thumb comfortably reaches the whisper key as shown in the photograph. Be sure the hand is not touching the rod which extends up the side of the instrument.

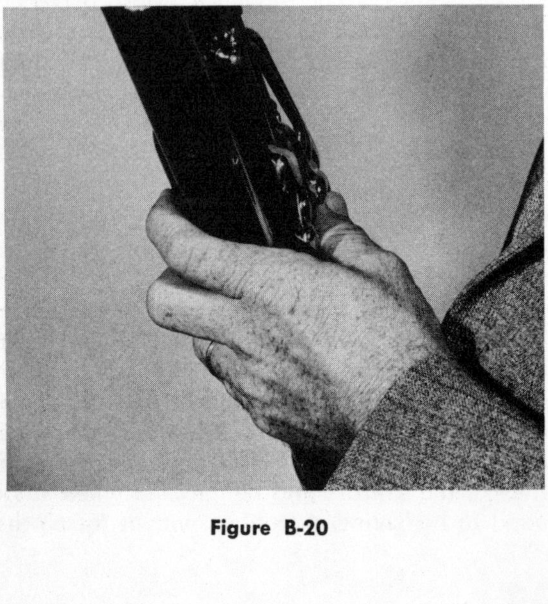

Figure B-20

2. Figure B-21. The left little finger touches lightly but does not press the D-sharp key. The remaining fingers fall into place covering the three tone holes with the ball of the fingers directly beneath the fingernails.

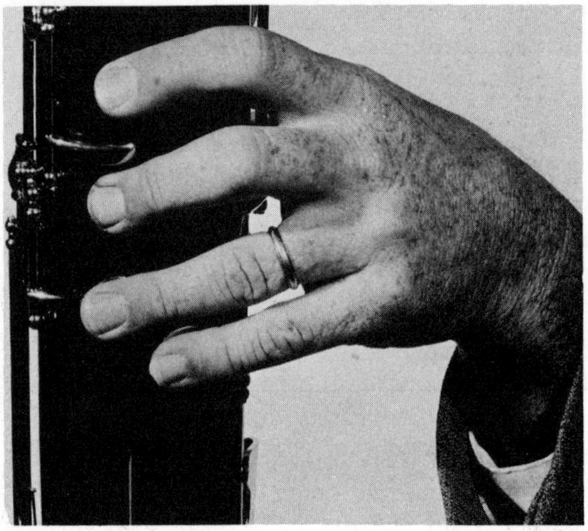

Figure B-21

B. Right Hand Position

1. Figure B-22. Adjust the height of the hand rest so that the fingers can reach the tone holes and the thumb can close the E key. The crotch of the thumb and forefinger should rest comfortably in the hand rest to help balance the instrument. Wrist should be flat. The thumb may rest on the metal guard plate near the E key when not in use.

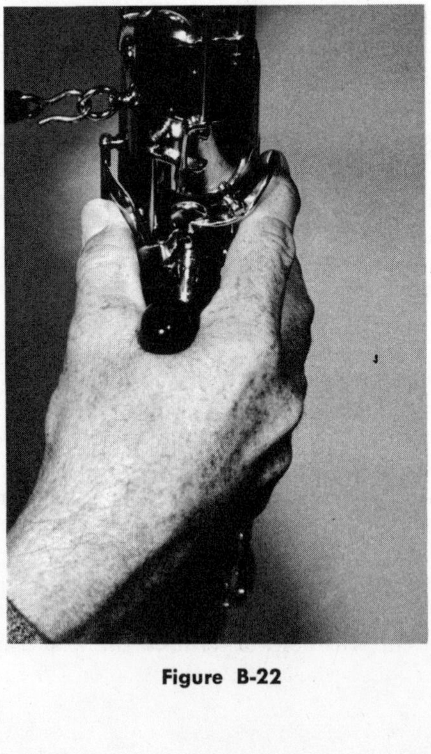

Figure B-22

2. Figure B-23. The little finger of the right hand touches lightly but does not press the F key. With the little finger in place the remaining fingers fall into place over the two tone holes and G key covering the tone holes with the ball of the finger directly beneath the fingernail.

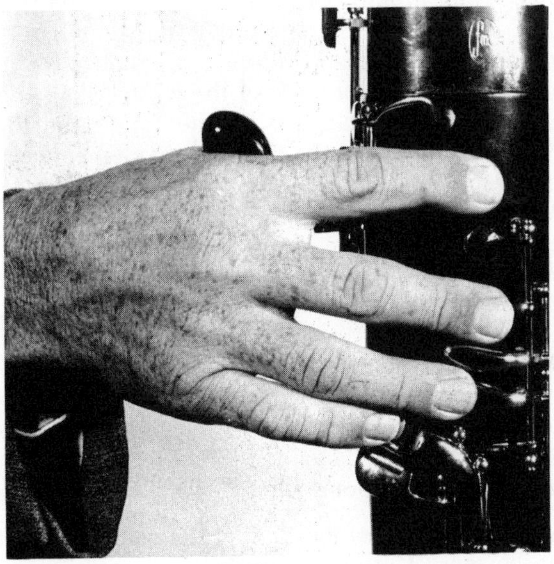

Figure B-23

C. Guide Position

With the hands in position as described and the balls of the fingers no more than one inch directly above the tone holes a guide position is established which should be maintained constantly. Wrists of both hands should be flat to avoid muscular cramping. In playing, the entire finger moves from the knuckle and closes the tone holes with a snap or click, pressing just hard enough to close the holes. Avoid too much pressure against the plates with the fingers.

D. Special Finger Positions

The bassoon has certain fingerings and keys to operate which tend to pull the hands out of position unless fingers are moved efficiently and with minimum motion. If the correct guide position is established and maintained, these finger movements will come naturally and can be readily developed. A constant check on the use and position of the fingers in these situations is necessary until the movements become habitual.

1. *Half-hole position for the first finger.*

The half-hole position of the first finger functions as a small vent to help secure positively fourth line F-sharp and fourth space G and G-sharp. To reach the half-hole position the finger is rolled downward by a movement of the second joint of the finger so that half of the tone hole is open and half closed by the finger. The guide

Figure B-24. Guide Position.

position for the remainder of the fingers of the hand must be maintained. Avoid sliding the finger instead of rolling. The motion is that of rolling down to open and rolling up to close. Sliding will slow the movement of the finger so that the notes will not respond.

2. *Right hand C-sharp.*

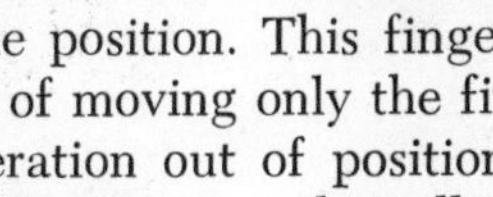

Key 4x operated by the first finger of the right hand is an alternate fingering for C-sharp used primarily as a trill fingering. Figure B-25 shows the position of the fingers when this key is being used. The first finger stretches slightly to reach the key, but the remainder of the fingers keep the basic guide position. This fingering illustrates the basic principle of moving only the finger or fingers involved in the operation out of position while maintaining the basic guide position so that all the fingers will be in the best position to play notes which follow.

3. *Left thumb.* With eight (or nine) keys to operate the left thumb requires considerable dexterity in manipulation. The four keys nearest the base of the thumb (D,C,B,B-flat on the fingering chart) are involved in the four lowest notes on the instrument. To play these

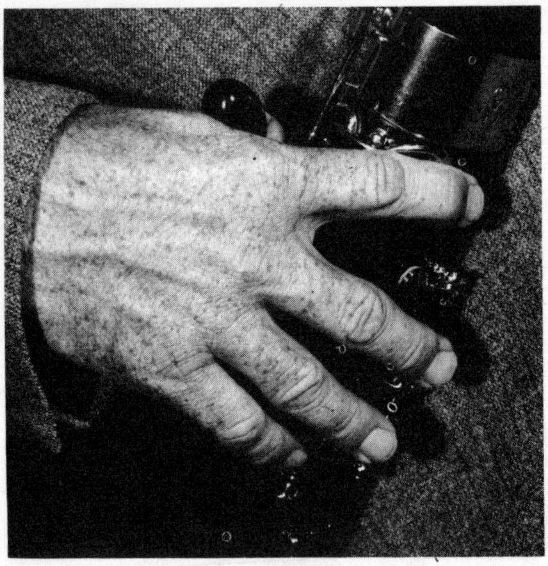

Figure B-25

notes downward the keys are added one at a time with the D key being depressed by the bottom of the thumb under the first joint, the thumb is slid up to depress the C key, and rolled for the B and B-flat successively. Figure B-26 shows the position of the thumb playing the low B-flat with all four keys depressed. Most modern bassoons have the D, C, and B keys interlocked so that when the C key is depressed the D key is automatically closed, and when the B key is depressed both the D and C keys are automatically depressed. It is not necessary to hold all three keys down with the thumb, although most available fingering charts will so indicate. Taking advantage of this interlocking of the keys simplifies and facilitates technique with these keys.

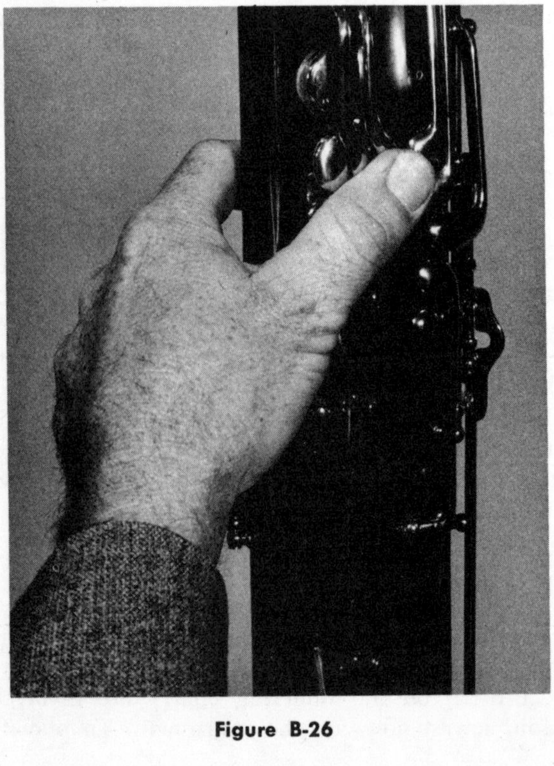

Figure B-26

The three or four keys toward the tip of the thumb are arranged so that the thumb can reach them by moving in a slight arc. These keys are depressed with the portion of the thumb between the ball and the tip, and using a slight arch in the joint of the thumb to clear the other keys. One of the alternate fingerings for fourth space E-flat calls for the use of the whisper key and the C-sharp key, both operated by the tip of the thumb. To do this the width of the thumb is divided between the two keys and both depressed simultaneously.

An alternate fingering for second space C-sharp calls for the use of the low D key with the middle of the thumb and the C-sharp key with the tip. For this the thumb should be flattened so that both keys can be depressed simultaneously. Other notes involve different combinations of right thumb keys. Some experimentation and practice is necessary to perfectly coordinate the operation of these two keys.

Common Faults in Hand and Finger Position

A good hand position is a great asset in the study of the bassoon. Unfortunately the wide stretches necessary to reach keys and holes force students whose hands are not large enough to assume unnatural or strained hand and finger positions. A student whose hand is quite small for the instrument will have difficulty in developing facility since the stretches which he will have to make will tense the muscles and make them slow to respond. However, a physically immature student who is still growing will succeed on the instrument despite small hands, if with the encouragement of his teacher he gradually changes his hand position toward the ideal.

The better the hand position the easier it is to develop facility and control. The first experiences with the instrument must emphasize hand position, and it must be checked continually until the best position for that particular student is established. A beginning player who persists in establishing the proper positions makes rapid progress. The use of a mirror of sufficient size so that the student can see the entire length of the instrument is an asset in establishing position.

The following are the most common faults and are those which the instructor should look for. All of these are involved in and help determine the progress of facility and technique.

1. *Hand rest.* Two common faults are considered in this connection: (1) improper height adjustment and (2) not using the hand rest if the instrument is supported by a neck strap. The height of the hand rest is most important. It must be adjusted so both the thumb and the fingers can reach the various keys and holes easily with the proper amount of curvature and still balance

Checklist for Holding and Hand Positions

The following list of items provides a means of thoroughly checking holding and hand positions while the player is seated. The check must be performed while the student is playing and preferably when he is not aware that the check is being made. Any items which are checked "no" should be corrected with the deviation explained to the student, together with what effect it has on the playing, and why the correct position is important. Students make a more serious effort to correct mistakes if they understand the reason for them.

A. Holding Position	Yes	No	Comments
1. Angle with front of body correct?			
2. Angle with side of body correct?			
3. Position of head correct?			
4. Neck strap properly adjusted?			
5. Hand rest properly adjusted?			
6. Shoulders up but relaxed?			
7. Elbows free from body?			
8. Body posture good?			
9. Feet in place?			
10. Height of music stand correct?			

B. Hand Positions			
1. Left hand contacting wood at proper place for supporting the instrument?			
2. Fingers of right hand neither stretched nor cramped because of hand rest adjustment?			
3. Proper part of left thumb contacting keys?			
4. Balls of fingers covering holes?			
5. Left little finger on guide key?			
6. Right little finger on guide key?			
7. Right thumb over E key?			
8. Fingers no more than one inch above open holes?			
9. First finger rolls properly to half-hole position?			
10. Basic guide position maintained?			
11. Wrists flat?			
12. Any signs of muscular tension?			

the instrument securely. The height can be adjusted by the lock screw provided on the instrument. If the student has a small hand, and the hand rest cannot be lowered sufficiently, measure and shorten it by cutting a little off the end. Hand rests are readily available as accessories for the instrument, and the school who has several beginning bassoonists could well have on hand several extra hand rests of varying lengths.

It is mandatory that the hand rest be used if the instrument is being supported by a neck strap. A hand rest is ordinarily not used if the instrument is being supported by a seat strap. Without the hand rest with the neckstrap the student is forced to balance the instrument with the thumb, or by putting a finger against the instrument, limiting technique of the right hand fingers and thumb. Teachers are advised to insist on the use of the hand rest with a neckstrap.

2. *Left thumb.* The most common problem in the use of the left thumb is that of depressing the D key or the C key with the tip of the thumb rather than beneath the joint. Using the tip of the thumb on these keys makes it impossible to roll the thumb onto the B and B-flat keys or to depress one of the others keys quickly and smoothly. The left thumb is difficult to observe while the student is playing, and it is necessary for the teacher to make a special effort to observe the action.

3. *Muscular tension.* Symptoms of muscular tension are easily seen, and must not necessarily be attributed to the effort of playing the instrument. Some symptoms are rigid little fingers, uncoordinated finger movements, etc. This tension can be caused by improper positioning of the instrument which puts too much weight on the left hand; not using a hand rest which puts pressure on the right thumb to support the instrument; wrists which are stretched into a curve rather than being virtually flat; a hand rest which is too high or too low; a neck strap adjusted too long or too short; elbows held up rather than relaxed, etc. Any muscular tension should be tracked down to its source and corrected immediately, since the most rapid progress on the instrument is possible only when the body is relaxed.

4. *Little fingers.* In the suggested guide position the little fingers are touching a key from which it is easy to move rapidly to another key as needed. If the little fingers are not in the guide position, then assurance in this movement is lost. Deviation of the little fingers from the guide position frequently pulls the remainder of the fingers out of position as well. Players with small hands will have difficulty in keeping the little finger of the left hand in position. If keeping the little finger on its guide key causes tension in the hand, then the student must be allowed to relax the little finger into a comfortable position for him. Insist, however, in maintaining the guide position as closely as possible for all students.

EMBOUCHURE FORMATION

An embouchure may be defined as the formation of the performer's lips with supporting muscles, teeth and jaws in relation to the reed which have to do with tone production. The criteria for a good bassoon embouchure may be summarized as follows: a good embouchure is one which over the entire range of the instrument produces (or is capable of producing) a rich, full bodied, clear tone; plays perfectly in tune; allows the full scope of articulations with minimum effort; allows the full range of dynamics to be played with complete control; plays and is controlled with a minimum amount of physical exertion when used with a well-adjusted reed.

A poor embouchure is one which violated one or more of these criteria and produces a thin, reedy, nasal tone quality; plays certain notes out of tune; does not allow the full scope of articulations; has a restricted dynamic range; or requires an undue amount of physical exertion. Embouchure is inseparable from the reed and is entirely dependent on having a good, responsive reed. The best embouchure formation cannot play a poor reed, nor will an excellent reed respond properly with a poorly formed embouchure.

The recommendation of various bassoon authorities can be summarized in two basic types of embouchure formation, although the differences between the two are not as great as those found between the two types of clarinet embouchure, and the preponderance of authority lies with one particular formation. As could be expected there are many small variations which are necessary and desirable depending upon the type of reed being used as well as the concept of the desired tone quality.

The basic difference between the two approaches to bassoon embouchure is found in whether the cheek muscles and the corners of the mouth are pushed in toward the reed, or whether the cheek muscles are pulled back into a slight "smile" position while the corners of the mouth are pushed in around the reed. For convenience and clarity the first is called a "soft cushion" and the second a "hard cushion," although these terms are relative and not to be taken literally.

The Soft Cushion Embouchure

The soft cushion embouchure has the preponderance of authoritative weight behind it, and is the one most widely recommended. The basic formation of the soft cushion embouchure may be achieved through the following procedure. Check each step with a mirror.

1. Keeping the lips relaxed, drop the lower jaw so that the teeth are about a half inch apart.

2. Pull the lower jaw back to increase the natural overbite. The jaw is kept back while playing.

3. Push the corners of the mouth toward the center as in whistling, forming wrinkles in the lips.

4. Maintaining the contracted position of the lips, roll them over the teeth so that virtually all of the lip is over the teeth. The exact amount of lip over the teeth

varies from student to student depending on whether the lips are average, thin, or thick. Thin lips will need all the lip over the teeth, while those students with thick lips may leave a line of the red of the lip in front of the teeth. Pull the chin muscles down—avoid bunching under the reed.

5. Put the reed between the lips. The reed should be in the mouth far enough that the upper lip is almost touching the first wire. Contract the lips around the reed like a drawstring.

The Hard Cushion Embouchure

The hard cushion embouchure for the bassoon is much less widely recommended than the similar formation on the other woodwind instruments, although some fine performers make use of it. The general experience with this formation has been that school age bassonists develop a good tone quality and control less rapidly than with the soft cushion formation. The hard cushion embouchure may be achieved through the following procedure. Check each step with a mirror.

1. Keeping the lips relaxed, drop the lower jaw so that the teeth are about a half inch apart.
2. Pull the lower jaw back to increase the natural overbite. The jaw is kept back while playing.
3. Pull the corners of the mouth back so that they and the attached cheek muscles are in a slight smiling position.
4. Roll both of the lips over the teeth, keeping the teeth open and the slight smiling position of the corners. The amount of lip over the teeth varies as indicated before according to the thickness of the student's lips. Pull the chin muscles down—avoid bunching under the reed.
5. Insert the reed into the mouth until the upper lip is almost touching the first wire. Tighten the lips around the reed, while maintaining the smile position of the corners.

Setting the Embouchure

Since most begining bassoonists will have had previous experience on another woodwind instrument the same type of embouchure formation used on the previous instrument, either the soft cushion or the hard cushion, will come quite naturally on the bassoon. Before attempting to produce a tone on the instrument, the embouchure must be set with the reed alone. Much time will be saved if this is done.

To find the proper amount of reed in the mouth is a fairly simple process which should be the first order of business. This is done with the reed alone. The well-adjusted bassoon reed when blown alone produces a buzz commonly called a "crow," of two distinct pitches —one high and one low pitched. Some good reeds produce more than two pitches but the high and low ones will predominate in the sound. The setting of the embouchure is aimed at finding the exact formation and amount of reed in the mouth which produces this double crow.

Use a reed which has been prepared for playing for either the soft or hard cushion embouchure described, checking in a mirror to see that it is properly formed. Starting with just the tip of the reed between the lips produce a sound using standard abdominal breath support. The sound produced will be a thin reedy buzz. Keeping the sound continuous gradually increase the amount of reed in the mouth until the upper lip touches the wire on the reed. Considerable differences in sound will be readily apparent as the amount of reed in the mouth increases. Try moving it back and forth to note the immediate differences. These differences in sound of the reed alone are magnified many times when the reed is producing a tone on the instrument. This points out the importance of setting the embouchure not only with the proper muscular formation, but with exactly the right amount of reed in the mouth.

Assuming that the reed is properly adjusted, at some point as the amount of reed in the mouth is increased the characteristic "double-crow" of the bassoon reed will be heard with maximum resonance. This is the critical point on the cut of the reed, normally more than halfway between the tip and first wire, and determines the amount of reed to be put into the mouth. This point should be approximately centered between the support provided by the upper and lower lips over the teeth.

Remember that no matter which embouchure formation is used the lower jaw is pulled back to increase the natural overbite. This means that the position of the upper lip on the reed is slightly forward toward the first wire of the point of maximum vibration while the lower lip and teeth are slightly back toward the tip of the reed in relation to this point. Under normal circumstances this adjustment will have the upper lip almost touching the first wire on the reed.

When this experiment has been completed, the student should continue producing a double-crow on the reed until it sounds freely and can be sustained for ten to twenty seconds. Once this is accomplished the reed can be put on the bocal and tones produced on the instrument itself. Continue to emphasize the importance of checking the embouchure formation with the use of a mirror until it is well established—a period of several months.

Checking the Embouchure

The teacher will have to check frequently to make sure the embouchure continues to be correctly formed and is developing properly. Students are not always capable of discovering their own mistakes, or of even knowing when they are right and when they are wrong, since it is just as easy for them to develop the wrong muscular formation as it is the correct one. The embouchure must be established by how it feels in the mouth and how the tone sounds, as well as how it looks in the mirror. The teacher must tell the student when he is right so he can discover the right feel, hear the right sound, and see the right shape.

1. *Physical characteristics.* Very small variations in embouchure formation are sometimes required to accommodate the physical characteristics of the student. Students with thicker than average lips will not need to put the entire lip over the teeth. Students with a small natural overbite will need to pull the lower jaw back further than students with a large overbite in order to put the points of support in their proper relationship on the reed.

2. *Uneven teeth.* Players with uneven teeth—especially the lower ones—may need to turn the reed slightly to avoid more pressure against one side than the other, since it is necessary that the pressure against the flat of the reed be the same across its width and equal on both the upper and lower blades. If this is necessary, the amount that the reed is turned is extremely slight, and care must be taken that the instrument itself is kept in the best playing position.

3. *Biting.* The amount of pressure or bite against the reed with the lower teeth is frequently difficult to adjust. The basic concept that the teeth must be kept apart and the reed supported only by the lips must be emphasized. Biting the reed restricts its vibration and prevents good tone production. The lower teeth do control to a degree the amount of support which the lip gives the reed, increasing support for the upper and high registers and decreasing for the lower octave, making small adjustments to control intonation, and assisting in the control of dynamics.

If the lower teeth are biting, excessive breath pressure is necessary to produce a tone, the tone quality is rough, and the lower notes of the instrument difficult or impossible to produce. Evidence of biting can be seen by examining the inner part of the lip for imprints of the teeth. Asking the player to play flatter will cause him to drop the lower jaw and gives him the feeling of playing flatter although little or no change in pitch will be apparent to the listener. A poorly made or adjusted reed will sometimes force the player to bite in order to control the tone, and for this reason, beginners must be provided with reeds that have been well adjusted and prepared for playing.

4. *Puffed cheeks.* Puffing cheeks is sometimes a problem with bassoon players as well as other instrumentalists. This is an inevitable indication of an embouchure problem since it indicates that the cheek muscles involved in the embouchure formation are not supporting properly. Players with puffing cheeks virtually always have an open unfocused tone quality combined with poor intonation. Frequently the player does not realize that his cheeks are puffed, especially if the amount of air between the teeth and cheek is small. The use of a mirror to check is necessary. When the student can actually see that the cheeks are in the right position, and the embouchure correctly formed, he can then feel the muscular support that is necessary to keep the cheeks in position. Playing a note on the instrument with one hand while feeling the cheeks with the other is useful in helping the player feel the right position.

5. *Holding position.* The holding position of the instrument is an important facet of embouchure formation. The bocal must be at a downward angle from the lips to the instrument. It should never be straight nor go upwards from the lips. The height of the instrument must be adjusted by the strap so that when the player's head is erect and straight the reed will touch his lower lip at about the line which divides the lip from the chin. From this position the player tilts his head downward just enough to take the reed into the mouth comfortably. This is the correct playing angle. The instrument must be held so that the reed enters the mouth at a right angle rather than approaching from either side. If the reed enters the mouth at an angle, even a very slight one, the support on the reed becomes slightly diagonal with resulting tone problems.

6. *Escaping air.* Air escaping from one corner of the mouth while playing is a clear indication that something, large or small, is wrong with the embouchure formation. With the soft cushion embouchure this means that the lips are not being properly tightened around the reed. The corner of the mouth is either relaxed or is being pulled back enough to release the air. With the hard cushion embouchure, escaping air is the result of too much pulling back of the corner of the mouth. This is corrected by tightening the corner of the mouth and pushing slightly toward the reed. The cause of the escaping air can be seen clearly by examining the embouchure while the student is playing, and corrective measures suggested.

TUNING

The problem of tuning the bassoon is discussed at length in the section on reeds since the basic pitch of the instrument is determined almost entirely by the reed and its relationship with an individual embouchure. Mechanical adjustment of the instrument itself can accomplish only the slightest changes in basic pitch. Refer to the chapter on reeds for information on tuning the reed, and to the section on embouchure for its influence on pitch.

All modern bassoons are made to play to the standard international pitch of A-440, but the construction of the reed and the player's embouchure can make the pitch of the instrument deviate several vibrations in either direction. Tuning is best done with the aid of an electronic tuner where a visual check on the pitch is possible. This is especially important for younger players who have not yet developed an accurate and dependable sense of pitch. Tuning bars, tuning forks or electronic devices which sound a single note are useful comparisons, but

Checklist for Embouchure Formation

The following check on embouchure formation must be made while the student is playing and preferably when he is not aware that a check is being made. Any errors should be carefully explained to the student, with the correction worked out wtih him while he is observing the embouchure in a mirror. Remedial exercises can be assigned on the basis of this list.

	Yes	No	Comments
1. Sufficient lip over lower teeth?			
2. Sufficient lip over upper teeth?			
3. Lips supporting around entire reed?			
4. Corners of mouth pushed toward center with soft cushion formation?			
5. Corner of mouth pulled back with hard cushion formation?			
6. Reed proper distance in mouth?			
7. Head inclined slightly downward?			
8. Crook at an upward angle toward the mouth?			
9. Cheeks puffed?			
10. Air escaping?			
11. Teeth sufficiently apart?			

are not as useful as a device which provides a visual check of the pitch of all the notes on the instrument.

The piano is probably the poorest source of tuning notes, unless it has been tuned by an expert tuner within the previous few days. Piano pitch is affected by temperature changes which cause the string to stretch or contract, raising and lowering the pitches, and over a period of time the overall pitch of the instrument gradually sinks lower than the standard A-440. Temperature changes alter the piano and wind instruments in reverse directions. A low temperature raises the pitch of the piano and lowers the pitch of the wind instrument, while a high temperature lowers the pitch of the piano and raises the pitch of the wind instrument. A player who is playing a solo with piano accompaniment must obviously tune and play in tune with it, but other than this the piano is best avoided for tuning purposes.

The bassoon tunes to the standard A for orchestra and either the B-flat or A for band, playing an octave lower than the pitch usually sounded for tuning purposes. The following illustrates this relationship.

Tuning Note Bassoon Plays Tuning Note Bassoon Plays

Bocals or Crooks

Once the reed itself is properly tuned, small adjustments on overall pitch of the instrument can be made by changing the bocal being used. All instruments are provided with two bocals, and an examination will reveal that they are a few millimeters different in length. Following the basic laws of acoustics the longer the bocal the flatter the overall pitch of the instrument. If a student consistently plays sharp over the instrument, he should use a longer bocal; if he consistently plays flat over the instrument, he should use a shorter bocal.

Bocals are numbered according to length, normally 1, 2, 3, in order of increasing length. Some manufacturers use the numbers 0, 1, 2, or 0, 1, 2, 3, but always the higher the number the longer the bocal, and the flatter the pitch. If it is necessary to replace a bocal or to purchase one of a different size, one made by the manufacturer of the instrument on which it is to be used should be purchased. There are slight differences in length, diameter, and shape from brand to brand, although basically all those used on Heckel System bassoons are copies of those made by the Heckel Company. If the length bocal needed is not available in the brand desired, substitute one made by Heckel.

The number is normally stamped on the face of the bocal for easy identification, since differences in length are so small that it is sometimes difficult to make a positive visual comparison of two different bocals. Instruments normally come supplied with number 1 and 2 bocals. If a shorter or longer bocal is needed, they must be purchased separately.

Tuning with Bocal Cork

Very slight adjustments in overall pitch of the bassoon may be made by adjusting the distance the bocal cork fits into the instrument. The further into the instrument the bocal is the sharper, and conversely farther out the cork is the flatter the instrument. The amount of tuning adjustment that it is possible to make in this manner is limited since the vent hole must be positioned so that it can be covered by its pad.

INTONATION

Even though an instrument is being played with a well-tuned reed and the proper bocal has been selected, intonation problems on individual notes still exist. Experienced players adjust to these individual notes automatically, and students must develop a keen sense of discrimination in intonation in order to develop this automatic compensation. The various factors which influence intonation are considered in the following.

Natural Tendencies of the Instrument

The bassoon, because of the combination of acoustical and mechanical factors, probably has more naturally out of tune notes than any other woodwind instrument. These notes may be very slightly or considerably out of tune, and vary somewhat from brand to brand and instrument to instrument. The teacher should be aware of these notes in order to understand the problems of the student and to help him solve them. The following indicates these notes as they are most commonly found.

(a) Notes with a natural tendency to be sharp

(b) Notes with a natural tendency to be flat

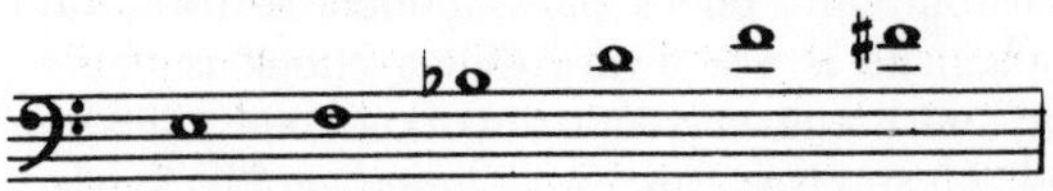

The notes from the lowest B-flat up a perfect fifth to F tend to be sharp on all instruments, and very sharp on some instruments and with some players. These notes pose the most difficult problem in control of intonation on the entire instrument since being sharp in this register is contrary to what the ear expects to hear and no alternate fingerings are available to help in adjusting the pitch. The natural tendencies toward sharping and flatting on the other notes can be compensated for by embouchure, breath support, or through choosing an alternate fingering which is better in tune.

Effect of Reed on Intonation

The nature of the reed being used is of primary importance in intonation. The way it is adjusted, the type of cane used, how it fits the player's embouchure all have an effect on pitch and intonation. The way in which the final adjustments on the reed are made will determine not only whether the instrument is properly tuned to A-440 but how well the instrument will play in tune with itself. Generally a reed which responds well in all registers of the instrument with a good tone quality will also be capable of good intonation over the instrument.

A reed which is too soft will play flat over the range of the instrument and minor adjustments in intonation will be difficult to make. Certain notes, third space E and fourth line F for example, are affected more than others. Notes in the highest register will be quite flat and cannot be brought up to pitch by embouchure adjustments, if indeed they can be played at all.

A reed which is too hard will play generally sharp over the range of the instrument. Here, as well as with the soft reed, certain notes—third space E-flat for example—are affected more than other notes. The lowest notes on the instrument will be difficult to play softly, and will be even sharper than their natural tendencies.

Reeds which have been played too long, and which are worn out gradually become more and more difficult to control in intonation. Student bassoonists will need to be checked frequently for this condition, as the change in the reed is normally so gradual that the student is not aware that a change has taken place. Insist that a spare reed or two be prepared and ready to play at all times.

Effect of Embouchure on Intonation

The embouchure coupled with the reed is a primary factor in intonation. Even the best of reed will play out of tune if the embouchure is poorly formed or undeveloped. An embouchure deficiency can be heard in the tone quality as well as being seen through examination. It is for the dual purposes of good intonation and tone quality that so much emphasis is given to embouchure formation and development. A well formed and developed embouchure is a necessary foundation for good intonation.

The embouchure can make slight corrections in intonation through adjusting the pressure with which the reed is held. This adjusting is made by the lips and their controlling muscles, and not by the lower jaw and teeth. To make a note higher in pitch contract the embouchure around the reed to increase support. To make a note lower in pitch, relax the embouchure to reduce the support. These slight changes in pressure are constant and involuntary in experienced players. Younger players need guidance to develop this facility.

The amount of reed taken into the mouth has considerable effect on intonation—even microscopic changes in the amount frequently can be heard. The skilled bassoonist makes use of the device of using slightly more or less reed in the mouth to help control intonation. For example, the very lowest notes on the instrument have been cited as having a natural tendency to be sharp, and one measure of correction is to take slightly less reed in the mouth when playing these notes. Care must be taken not to use too little reed as this will change tone quality as well as intonation.

The highest notes on the instrument are frequently flat in the hands of the student bassoonist. These can be brought up somewhat in pitch through using more reed in the mouth even to the point where the upper lip is actually touching the first wire on the reed.

The lower jaw can help control intonation by moving back and forth slightly under the lower lip. Pulling the lower jaw back slightly flattens the pitch and pushing it forward sharpens the pitch. Used in combination with the amount of reed in the mouth the jaw movement can increase the amount of pitch change possible. If for example, in addition to using less reed in the mouth for the lowest notes on the instrument the lower jaw is also pulled back, a considerably flatter pitch can be achieved than if only one of these changes were made.

Dynamics and Intonation

Like most other wind instruments, the bassoon has a natural tendency to get flat as the tone gets louder and sharper as the tone diminishes in volume, with the degree of flatness or sharpness increasing as dynamics approach the extremes. This must be compensated for by embouchure adjustments.

In order to play louder the student tends to relax the embouchure so that the reed tip may open up to allow a great volume of air to pass through, or to tighten the embouchure as he gets softer to lessen the amount of air passing through the reed. Since pitch is controlled to a considerable degree by the pressure for the embouchure around the reed, there is a corresponding flattening or sharping.

Dynamics are properly controlled by breath support and pressure which controls the volume or velocity of the air passing through the reed. Students relax their embouchure to play louder rather than increasing breath velocity, and tighten the embouchure to play softer rather than decreasing breath velocity. Pitch is maintained through balancing the velocity of the wind through the reed with the pressure of the embouchure around it.

When playing fortissimo the slight relaxation of the embouchure needed to open the tip of the reed more is compensated for by the greatly increased velocity of the air. In a crescendo the wind velocity and embouchure pressure are kept in balance to maintain pitch stability. In playing pianissimo the embouchure may be relaxed slightly, if anything, while the pitch is maintained through a continuing firm breath support while decreasing the velocity of the air through the reed to achieve the desired dynamic level.

Developing the facility for maintaining a constant pitch through long crescendo and diminuendo is one of the best ways to develop breath control. The tone exercises below are excellent practice in control of pitch through wide dynamic levels. They should be practiced slowly enough that an entire breath is used in four measures. Maintain constant firm breath support while controlling the dynamics by changing the velocity of the air through the instrument.

a.

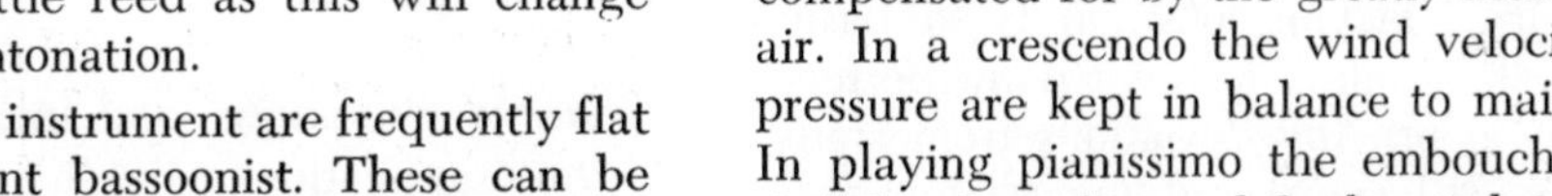

b.

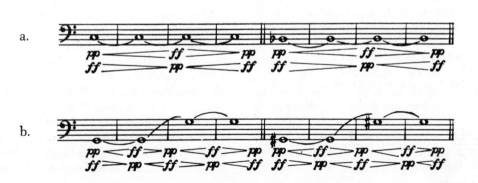

Practice exercise "a" (p. 181) in major or minor scale patterns to include the entire range of the instrument in which the student is proficient. Exercise "b" (p. 181) is best practiced chromatically first in the most comfortable range for the student, then extending upward and downward to the extremes of his range. Practicing with the use of a stroboscope which provides a visual check of pitch fluctuations is extremely valuable in connection with developing this facility.

Playing Position and Intonation

Body posture in its relationship with breathing and breath support is an important facet in the control of intonation. Poor posture makes good breath support impossible, and as a result limits its use in the control of intonation. Good posture is so basic that it must be given a high priority in teaching.

The position in which the instrument is held in relation to the body has been developed and standardized not only to provide the best playing position to eliminate muscular tension, but so that the embouchure could be formed in the best relationship to the reed and bocal. If the reed is not at a right angle with the lips then pressure is uneven across the reed and intonation problems develop. Similarly if the reed does not enter the mouth at a slightly upward angle control of intonation is difficult or impossible. Playing position is so basic to good performance that unless it is virtually perfect intonation is inevitably poor. Any deviations from standard playing position must be corrected immediately and firmly.

Mechanical Factors and Intonation

Adjustment of the mechanism on the bassoon can control intonation on various notes. Keys or pads which do not open wide enough cause the tone involved to be flat, and conversely if they open too widely these tones will be sharp. If an individual tone is sharp or flat, check first to see that the pads involved are being raised the proper distance from the tone hole. The distance a pad is raised from the tone hole is controlled by the thickness of a buffer cork on the bottom of its key which can be adjusted without too much difficulty.

The thickness of the pad itself is frequently involved. The pad may have been too thick when it was put on, or may have swelled through absorbing moisture. These should be replaced by a repairman. Pads which are too thin are rarely found because there is difficulty in seating them and they are replaced in the normal course of putting the instrument in playing condition.

There are several articulated keys on the bassoon where operating a single key opens and/or closes two pads which may be widely separated on the body of the instrument. If the articulation mechanism of these keys is not properly adjusted one of these pads may be too close or too far from a tone hole. The articulations are usually determined by the thickness of a cork beneath one or more of the keys which can be adjusted to give proper clearance.

Keys which are bent up or down or which are bent out of alignment will also cause one or more notes to be out of tune because of the distance of the pad from its tone hole. The instrument should be examined regularly to see that all keys are in the proper alignment. Students become accustomed to out of line keys and are not aware that they should be corrected.

Tone holes covered directly by the fingers frequently become clogged from various causes. A clogged tone hole will change both tone quality and intonation. As a matter of good maintenance all tone holes should be cleaned periodically with a soft cloth or a bent pipe cleaner. It is not always possible to see the foreign material in the holes, so do not depend on a visual examination to determine whether or not they are clean.

The vent hole on the bocal is particularly susceptible to clogging because it is so small. Even a slight bit of foreign material in it will change the intonation of some tones. This hole should be cleared regularly and carefully by running a small broom straw through it. Do this carefully to avoid enlarging the size of the hole, which is determined to a close tolerance by the acoustics of the instrument.

Alternate Fingerings and Intonation

An examination of the fingering chart for bassoon given in this book will show that there are alternate fingerings for many notes on the instrument. Some notes have three or four alternate fingerings. Many of these alternate fingerings will produce a tone slightly different in pitch from other fingerings for the same note. This is particularly true in the high register.

There is greater pitch variation in the alternate fingerings on the bassoon than on any of the other woodwind instruments. Players must be aware that there are alternate fingerings and be able to use them intelligently. They should, through comparing, be completely aware of the pitch differences between each fingering and choose the fingering which provides the best intonation in a specific musical situation.

Some of these special fingerings tend to be further out of tune than the regular fingerings, and should not be used where the duration of the tone is long enough to give a definite pitch impression. Do not use these special trill fingerings as a substitute for a regular fingering.

If a particular note is out of tune, consult the fingering chart for possible alternate fingerings which could correct the intonation. The intonation differences between fingerings will vary from instrument to instrument and from player to player. No positive statement as to which alternates are sharper and which are flatter is possible. The wise player will take advantage of alternate fingerings, and the more advanced the player the more of these fingerings he should know and use.

TONE

With a range of over three octaves, the bassoon rivals the clarinet in versatility. In spite of this wide usable range the basic quality of the tone produced must be essentially the same throughout. There is however considerable variation in extensity, a feeling of fullness or bigness of tone, between the lowest tones and the highest ones. The lowest tones tend to be large in feeling while the highest ones are smaller in feeling.

There is no particular standardization in the division of the entire bassoon range into registers as there is, for example, on the clarinet. Perhaps the most logical division is based on the acoustical response of the instrument, i.e., those notes produced by the fundamental vibration of the air column, those produced by the first overtone, and those produced by the second or third overtones.[2] Because of the extension of the instrument through the keys operated by the thumbs to extend the range downward an interval of a fifteenth is produced by fundamental vibrations. This is divided into the low register made up of the tones produced by adding thumb keys and the lower middle register made up of the remaining notes produced by six fingers over the holes plus the little fingers. The four registers thus obtained are called: (1) low register, (2) lower middle register, (3) upper middle register, and (4) high register. These are notated as follows:

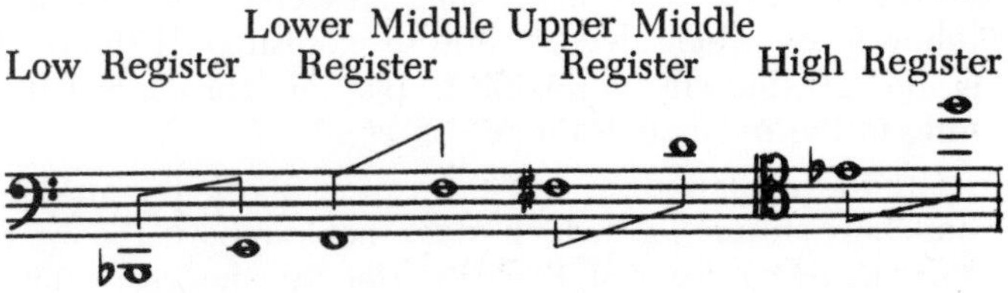

In the hands of the student bassoonist there is a tendency for each of these registers to have its own individual tone quality. The low register is thick and reedy, the lower middle register the fullest, the upper middle register a little thinner and reedier than the lower, and the high register thin and reedy. An interesting test of the capabilities of the bassoonist to match tone qualities is to make a comparison of the sounds produced on the fourth space F and F-sharp where the tones produced change from the fundamental vibration to the first overtone.

Notes in the high register, because they are products of partial vibrations, have a variety of fingerings available, each being the product of a different harmonic. It will be found that certain instruments produce certain notes with better quality and intonation than other instruments using the same fingering. There are large differences from instrument to instrument in the way in which notes in this register respond.

In the process of developing a good tone the bassoon student must direct his attention not only to producing pleasing sounds, but to matching the basic tone quality over the four registers of the instrument. Beginners have difficulty in producing good quality in both the low and high registers, and should not be forced to play in these sections until their embouchure has developed to the point that control in the middle register is sure and accurate and a good quality has been developed.

It is especially important not to force extension of the range upward. A student whose embouchure is not sufficiently developed will make drastic changes in his embouchure, including biting with the lower jaw, in order to play these notes. This changing of his basic embouchure formation slows down its development, and frequently produces a less desirable formation when it is fully developed.

The American concept of good bassoon tone quality as represented by the finest professional musicians in our major symphonies is derived almost entirely from the German school of performance. The French school of bassoon playing has been virtually rejected in this country, primarily because the system of fingering is so different from the Heckel System which we use. The differences in fingering systems are minor when compared to the differences in tone quality produced. The entire bore of the instrument is quite different in the French and Heckel Systems and the sounds produced are vastly different in quality.

In other chapters it has been suggested that the teacher and student study recorded performances to gain a concept of the best standard quality for the instrument under discussion. This can be done to a certain extent with the bassoon provided the inherent differences between the basic French and German schools of playing are clearly understood. It is virtually impossible to produce the typical good French sound on a Heckel System bassoon, and vice versa. Tone qualities to be desired are those produced by the players in various major orchestras of the United States. Even though the critical listener will hear differences from one player to another, the basic quality is the same—a big, dark tone quality which is capable of great variation and perfect control over the entire range of the instrument.

There are innumerable variations in embouchure formation, which, combined with the various reed cuts and adjustments produce slightly different tone qualities. No matter what combination of reed and embouchure is being used, if the tone produced has the characteristic bassoon sound and if the tone is a pleasing one, then

2. See Appendix on Acoustics for details of the overtone series.

it is a good tone. Teachers and bassoon students alike should take advantage of every opportunity to hear live performances of fine instrumentalists. Take advantage of workshops, demonstrations, and clinics sponsored by various educational groups. Every such contact with fine professionals can only be beneficial.

Common Problems in Tone

A good tone is the product of all the elements involved in performance: instrument, reed, embouchure and breath control. If any of these is defective, the tone quality suffers accordingly. Problems of tone production and quality are many and varied, but may usually be traced to their source, and must be corrected immediately. Refer also to the sections on reed, embouchure, and breathing.

Following are some of the most common problems in tone production:

1. *Small or pinched tone.* This is a very common problem of student bassoonists. It can be traced to several possible causes, with the reed itself the most likely cause. The tip of the reed may be the wrong shape as a result of poor scraping, or it may not be open sufficiently to vibrate enough to produce a full tone. If the tip is properly shaped but too close together, it may be opened by adjusting the wires on the reed. A reed with a tip which is poorly shaped is best discarded. A reed which is too soft either by scraping too much or which is worn out is difficult to adjust. If after performing the adjustment processes to correct this condition, it still doesn't respond, it must be discarded.

If the reed is in good condition and the tone is small or pinched, it is possible that the student is biting with the lower jaw, exerting too much pressure against the blades with the teeth. This can be identified by the presence of teeth marks on the inside of the lips which can be felt by the student and frequently seen by the instructor. Corrections for this condition include a review of embouchure information with the student to be sure that he understands that the support for the reed comes from the lips around the reed and not from the teeth pressing against it.

Asking the student to play flatter will frequently cause him to drop the lower jaw. If the lips are properly supporting the reed, the actual pitch of the tone will not drop, although the student will have the sensation of it doing so. Suggesting that he play a long crescendo will force the student to drop the lower jaw if he is to achieve a fortissimo level. The combination of playing louder and flatter brings the greatest degree of drop of the lower jaw so that the student can actually feel the difference. When the jaw is sufficiently down, the student should be asked to feel the difference and keep the jaw in that position in all his performance. Correction of this pressure with the lower jaw is a slow process which demands persistence by both student and teacher.

If the reed is good and the teeth sufficiently open, a small or pinched tone may be caused by having too little reed in the mouth. This is readily recognizable by close examination of the student. The correction is simply to insist that more reed be taken in the mouth. If the reed is a good one, the student will immediately hear the difference in the size of the tone he is producing. An additional measure to help find the proper amount of reed in the mouth is to work with the reed alone, moving it back and forth in the mouth to find the place where the best and most characteristic double-crow is heard, as previously explained in the section on embouchure.

2. *Open squawky tone.* This tone is described as lacking in body and focus, and generally uncontrolled. This sound is typical of the very beginner but is, unfortunately, found with more advanced students. In the beginner it is caused by a weak undeveloped embouchure, but if the basic formation of the embouchure is correct and remains correct, the undesirable tone will gradually disappear.

In the more advanced student this tone quality may be caused by a reed which is too stiff. Ask the student to remove the reed from the instrument for examination, and play to find the double-crow. If an excessive amount of breath is required to blow the reed or the double-crow is not controllable, make the necessary adjustments on the reed as explained in the section on reeds. A further confirmation of the fact that the reed is too stiff can be made by asking the student to play a long crescendo to fortissimo followed by a long decrescendo to pianisimo. If the reed is too stiff, he will be unable to play and/or control the tone in the pianissimo range.

If the reed itself is not the cause, check for an embouchure formation which does not support the reed sufficiently to control the vibration of the reed. This can be verified by asking the student to play notes in the upper register since these notes are difficult if not impossible to produce without the proper amount of embouchure support around the reed. Appropriate correctional measures include practice of long tones and other exercises for embouchure development.

3. *Hard, cold tone.* A tone which is inflexible and which lacks the intangible quality of vitality is described as hard and cold. If embouchure formation is correct, this tone quality is almost invariably caused by the type of reed being used, usually one which is too stiff for the student. If the usual adjustments on the reed to make it free blowing and responsive in all registers do not remedy the situation, try reeds which are made with a different cut. If the student is making his own reeds, have him test with different cuts, or if the reeds he is using are commercial or custom-made, try reeds

from one or more different makers until a cut is found with which the student can produce a satisfactory tone. This is a difficult solution for some players since different cuts may require adjustments in embouchure formation and playing habits.

If the student is quite advanced and is playing well in tune with good tone quality except for the coldness of tone, introducing the use of a tasteful vibration is a solution worth trying. Vibrato is discussed in another chapter. It is important that the use of the vibrato be restricted to advanced players.

4. *Weak, colorless tone.* A tone which is otherwise smooth in quality, but is lacking in body and carrying power is most often due to lack of proper breathing and breath support. Check the fundamentals of good breath usage with the student, and assign long tone practice with diminuendo and crescendo. The student will need to be told when he is producing the proper sound so that he can associate his physical feeling with the desired sound. It is difficult for many even advanced players to know by listening to themselves when they are producing the proper tone quality and projection.

5. *Control of soft tone.* Difficulty in producing and controlling a soft tone is principally due to the inability of the player to project a steady concentrated small stream of air into the instrument. Check breathing and breath support, and have the student practice focusing a steady stream of air into the palm of his hand. Other possible causes may be a reed which is too stiff, or a poorly shaped embouchure.

6. *Dynamics and tone quality.* Some students with otherwise good tone quality will loose it when playing at extremes of loudness or softness. This is caused by an undeveloped or poorly formed embouchure, or by lack of proper breath control or a combination of both. In making a crescendo the embouchure must gradually relax to allow the tip of the reed to open while at the same time increasing the velocity of air. Good control is the product of the proper balance of these two factors, and if they are in the proper balance both tone quality and intonation will remain good.

To play a diminuendo the embouchure may tighten slightly around the reed, while decreasing the velocity of air through the instrument, but being very careful to maintain a strong abdominal support of the air stream. To play a crescendo the embouchure may relax slightly around the reed while increasing the velocity of air through the instrument, maintaining proper abdominal support. With the best balance of abdominal support, air velocity, and embouchure control, tone quality will remain the same at any dynamic level.

TONGUING

Tonguing refers to the manner in which the tongue operates in relation to the reed and breath support in order to articulate the tones. The placement and action of the tongue must be rapid and under complete control at all speeds, and at all dynamic levels. It must, in coordination with breath support, be able to produce on the bassoon all varieties of articulation from the hardest staccato to the softest legato.

The manner in which the tongue touches the reed, the place it touches, and how it moves is dependent somewhat upon embouchure formation. There are several points of view on how and where the tongue touches the reed but the differences are not as great as those on clarinet or oboe, and each is effective if properly done. In essence the tongue acts as a valve to control the flow of air through the reed, stopping the air flow and vibration of the reed when it touches the reed, and allowing the vibration to begin again when it is removed and the air flow is resumed.

The effectiveness of the tongue is entirely dependent upon proper breath support and control. The interrelation between breath pressure and tongue action allows the production of every conceivable kind of attack from the hardest marcato-staccato to the very smoothest legato within the widest dynamic range. The amount of pressure of the tongue against the reed determines the hardness of the attack, the amount of wind pressure against the tongue determines the loudness of the attack.

There are two standard methods of tongue placement used on bassoon, each subject to small variations according to the personal desires of the teachers using them. Some authorities recommend that different parts of the tongue touch the reed for various types of articulation, a recommendation which makes a great deal of sense on a double-reed instrument. The tongue is simply a means to an end and the way it is used is not as important as the results obtained.

No matter what placement and usage of the tongue is recommended certain basic principles are common to all: (1) the tongue is relaxed. A tongue under tension cannot move rapidly enough, nor can it be controlled; (2) tongue movement is confined to the forward part of the tongue; (3) the tongue acts as a valve for the air and is dependent on good breath support. The two most common approaches to tongue placement on the bassoon may be outlined as follows:

First Method. With the reed in place and the embouchure properly formed, touch the tip of the lower blade of the reed with the top of the tongue just back from the tip. A slight pressure against the reed closes the tip. To start the tone put the tongue in place against the reed and build up air pressure against it. Release the air into the instrument with a tongue action similar to that in pronouncing the syllable "Too" or "Tu." The center of the tongue is depressed slightly so that the throat is open and there is no obstruction to the free flow of air. For a harder attack pronounce the syllable "Tee," and for a softer attack the syllable "Du."

Second Method. With the reed in place and the embouchure properly formed, touch the tip of the reed with the tip of the tongue. The exact point of contact of the tip of the tongue with the reed varies from authority to authority and ranges from having the tongue close the tip of the reed by approaching it directly, to touching the lower blade as in the previous method but with the tip of the tongue. To start the tone, build up air pressure against the tongue while it is in contact with the reed, and release the air into the instrument with a tongue action similar to that in pronouncing the syllable "Tu." For a softer attack use the syllable "Du," and for a harder attack the syllable "Te."

Developing Tongue Action

For the purpose of developing articulation the position of the tongue against the reed is considered the normal position, for it is from this position that it starts the tone. There is no forward or upward movement of the tongue preceding the beginning of a tone since breath pressure is against the tongue and not the reed. The commonly used word "attack" to describe the articulation of a tone is most unfortunate since it implies both violence and forward movement. The action of the tongue may be gentle or hard depending on the type of articulation desired.

Various types of articulations demand varying lengths of silence between successive notes. The length of this silence is determined by how long the tongue remains in contact with the reed. Hardness of attack is determined by the breath pressure behind the tongue and by how hard the tongue is pressing against the reed. By varying the relationship between breath pressure and tongue pressure articulations which simulate the entire gamut of bow strokes used by string players can be reproduced on the bassoon.

The introduction of tonguing or articulation should be delayed until the student is producing a steady tone of reasonable quality, and has developed facility within the limited range of the beginner. Do not allow the tongue to touch the reed during this preliminary study, but simply start the tone with the breath. This requires that the beginning study be done with music of legato style, and eliminates the rhythmic approach to beginning study in favor of the melodic approach. If the rhythmic approach is used the articulation of quarter and eighth notes in the typical beginning method patterns must be done with the tongue and not the breath. Do not allow articulation with the breath alone for once this habit is established it is extremely difficult to break.

Legato Articulation

When the tongue is in the correct position against the reed and the study of articulation has begun, attention must be focused on breath support so that there is a steady stream through the reed upon which the tones rest. The tongue simply interrupts this movement of air through the instrument to detach the notes. The following example illustrates the legato style of articulation most successful as the beginning experience with articulation:

Normal Detached Articulation

After the student is producing the legato articulation reasonably well, he can move to the normal detached sound in which the notes are well separated. There must be a continuing emphasis on a steady stream of air through the reed. The notes are separated simply by leaving the tongue in contact with the reed longer while breath support remains constant. This is the most common articulation and is used when no other articulation is indicated. It is, of course, varied according to the musical demands of the composition.

The example below illustrates a typical exercise for developing this type of articulation. This exercise may be practiced in scale patterns up and down or adapted to other note sequences in the playing range of the student.

etc.

Staccato

Staccato articulation should not be introduced until both the legato and normal detached articulations are well under control. The same tongue movement and placement and the same steady stream of air is used in staccato articulation. The only difference is that in staccato articulation the tongue returns to the reed to stop the vibration. It is essential that the air pressure against the tongue remain the same during the period of silence as during the production of the tone.

Because of the longer period of silence between notes in this type of articulation students are frequently tempted to relax breath support during the silence. If this is done, then the breathing muscles come into operation simultaneously with tongue action, resulting in an accent and making it virtually impossible to develop a fast staccato. For this reason the first introduction to staccato can well utilize as rapidly repeated notes as the student can produce, as well as slower repetition. A typical beginning staccato exercise can be constructed as follows:

Common Problems in Tonguing

1. *Articulation too heavy.* In this type of sound each note starts with an accent or pop, and is normally caused by too great pressure of the tongue against the reed. The best solution is to have the student practice articulation at the pianissimo level, correcting first the legato type, then the normal detached, and finally the staccato. A reed which is too soft will frequently produce this sound, since the blades do not respond instantly when released by the tongue. If pianissimo practice does not correct this difficulty it is possible that the placement of the tongue against the reed is incorrect for the embouchure and type of reed being used. Experiment by changing the part of the tongue which contacts the reed to see if a slightly different placement will remedy the situation.

2. *Sluggish tongue.* Inability to tongue rapidly should not be a major concern with beginners, since time and practice are necessary to develop speedy articulation. In more advanced players where technique has developed past articulation ability, sluggish articulation is a matter of considerable concern. In this condition the reed should be checked first, since a reed which is too stiff for the player makes rapid articulation difficult. If the reed is too stiff there will probably be other symptoms in addition to sluggish response in articulation.

Some students lack speed in articulation because they are moving the back or middle of their tongue as well as the front. Articulation is confined to the forward portion of the tongue, and the primary motion of the tongue is up and down rather than forward and backward in the mouth. Movement of the back portion of the tongue almost invariably carries with it movements of the throat which can be seen. To correct, the entire process of tongue placement and development of articulation must be repeated from the very beginning to form new muscular habits. Some students correct the problem quickly, others are never able to completely overcome the problem.

Sluggish tonguing in most instances is a simple matter of insufficient practice devoted to developing speed and accuracy. Special articulation exercises should be assigned to these students, with specific instructions on how many times each day to practice them, to use a metronome, and with specific metronomic speeds to follow. Any player can develop satisfactory speed and control if he is using his tongue and breath support properly and if he will spend enough time on the problem.

3. *Lack of coordination between tongue and fingers.* This is frequent among the more advanced players who have developed a fair amount of facility on the instrument. It is purely and simply a product of practicing too fast without first working out notes and tonguing carefully. These students must practice slowly, at whatever tempo perfect coordination between fingers and tongue is possible, and gradually increase the speed. Use of a metronome on such exercises is invaluable to maintain a steady tempo and to help in the gradual increase in speed. Major and minor scales and arpeggios making use of various articulation patterns are good media of practice for this purpose.

4. *Slow staccato.* Some players have difficulty in executing a true staccato rapidly even though other articulations are executed with sufficient speed. Other things being correct, this problem can be traced to the lack of breath support and a continuing stream of air through the reed. Such players will be found to be relaxing abdominal support at the end of each note, or cutting off the stream of air in the throat. The concept of the tongue stopping staccato notes as well as starting them with the breath pressure continuing against the tongue during the space of silence will help correct this situation. An improperly adjusted reed will also make rapid staccato impossible, particularly in the low and lower middle registers. Adjust according to directions in the section on reeds.

5. *Movement of the jaw in tonguing.* This is the result of too large or too violent movement of the tongue, frequently accompanied by changes in pitch of the tone. Rather than confine the movement to the front part of the tongue, the student is moving the entire tongue. The solution is to ask the student, no matter what his technical advancement may be, to practice the basic exercises for developing articulation constantly checking in a mirror on the music stand to eliminate all movements. Jaw movements can occur with all methods of correct tongue placement, as well as with incorrect tongue placement, and prevent the development of speed in articulation.

Additional Aspects of Articulation

Double and Triple Tonguing. Theoretically, double and triple tonguing in the sense of its use on brass instruments is possible on the bassoon, but in practice it is very unsatisfactory because it is virtually impossible to match the sounds of the beginnings of the two notes in the double pattern or the three notes in the triple pattern. The double tonguing is done by using the syllables "Tu-Ku" in rapid alternation, the "Tu" with the tongue in its normal position on the reed and the "Ku" pronounced with the middle of the tongue against the roof of the mouth. Some authorities recommend the syllables "Ti-Ki" because they put more of an arch in the position of the tongue putting it in a better position for the "K" attack.

Triple tonguing uses the syllables "Tu-Ku-Tu" or "Tu-Tu-Ku" (Ti-Ki-Ti or Ti-Ti-Ki) in rapid succession. Both double and triple tonguing are useful only in the most rapidly moving passages. Most bassoonists prefer to develop the speed and control of single tonguing to the point where it is used exclusively for both normal and the most rapid articulations. Authorities agree that bassoon students need not be taught double or triple tonguing.

Flutter Tonguing. Flutter tonguing, produced by rolling an "R" so that the tongue flutters against the reed is called for in a few contemporary compositions. It is an adaptation to woodwinds of the technique which is common and easy on the brass instruments. Among the woodwinds, the flute is the most successful in producing the flutter tongue sound. Some relaxation of the embouchure and complete relaxation of the tongue is necessary to achieve this effect.

Accents, Sforzando, Forte-piano. Accents, sforzando, and forte-piano notes must be played in relation to the dynamic level of the musical phrase. A sforzando is not a note played as loudly as it is possible to play, but simply an isolated note one or two degrees louder than the notes which precede or follow it in the phrase. It demands assistance from the breath so that the breathing mechanism supplies additional support and velocity simultaneously with the release of the reed by the tongue.

The forte-piano requires immediately relaxation of velocity and pressure by the breathing mechanism, coupled with whatever degree of simultaneous support at the instant the tone starts demanded by the musical content of the phrase. Accents indicated above or below the notes must be only one dynamic level above the notes which precede or follow them. Many accents may be accomplished by only increased tongue pressure against the reed, others demand slight movements of the breathing muscles. It must be clearly understood that there are no rapid movements of any breathing muscles in support of tongue action except for accents, sforzando, and forte-piano notes.

TECHNIQUE PROBLEMS

A good technical proficiency on the instrument is one which is accurate, under complete control, facile and which permits the performance of all types of musical demands with ease. In developing this proficiency the bassoonist must be aware of certain mechanical or technical problems peculiar to his instrument which must be solved. In teaching, both the importance of the correct solution and the reason for that particular solution must be impressed on the student. Unfortunately the literature for the study of the bassoon does not provide a particulary well-organized presentation of these problems, so it is incumbent upon the teacher to take every opportunity to include them in the instruction of his students.

Approached logically, these problems are not difficult to identify, nor complex to solve and put into use. Many of these technical problems demand that the player make a choice between two or more alternatives. Each alternate must be practiced until it becomes an involuntary part of his technical facility and the way and place in which each alternative is used must be made so much a part of his technique that the correct choice becomes automatic. Other technical problems are matters of procedure. Players and teachers should not hesitate to mark instructions on the printed music as reminders.

Following are problems which occur frequently:

1. *Left thumb.* A good portion of the smoothness of technique which the bassoonist develops is dependent in good measure upon how the left thumb is used. With so many keys to operate considerable dexterity in manipulation is required. The position of the left hand should be checked to see that the wrist is almost flat and that the fingers and thumbs can reach their proper positions without muscular tension.

In playing the notes in the low register of the instrument the forward half or two-thirds of the thumb is used so that each of the four keys involved can be depressed with an absolute minimum of sliding. The D and C keys are depressed by the thumb under the first joint, and the thumb is then rolled to the B and B-flat keys. Avoid sliding the thumb to these keys, although under normal usage the thumb must be slid from the D to the C key. The keys toward the tip of the thumb are depressed with the portion of the thumb near the tip. The thumb moves in a slight arc in order to contact all of these keys most efficiently.

2. *Whisper key.* The whisper key (sometimes called the pianissimo key) operated by the left thumb which opens and closes the small vent hole in the bocal of the bassoon is a fairly recent addition to the instrument. Some schools and players may have instruments without this valuable aid to playing tones in the upper middle register. It is not an octave key as on the saxophone and oboe, nor a register key as on the clarinet which force a node in the vibrating air column of the instrument. The hole in the bocal of the bassoon is much too small in diameter to do this, but when it is open it does relieve pressure on the air column at this point sufficiently to help the affected notes sound more clearly. Changes in octaves which use the same fingering are controlled primarily by the embouchure and not the whisper key (see use of half-hole below).

The whisper key is closed by the left thumb on all notes in this range:

Use of the whisper key is optional on certain notes in the high register which speak better on some instruments when it is closed. Experimentation with an individual player on his instrument is necessary to discover when the key should or should not be used in the high register.

The whisper key is automatically closed when the right thumb depresses the E key, and it is well to develop the habit of removing the left thumb from the whisper key when the right thumb is on this key. This frees the left thumb and makes it instantly available for use on another key.

Many beginners on the instrument neglect to use the whisper key properly since to them the instrument seems to respond just as well without it as with it. Teachers should be alert to this situation because as his facility and tone production develops use of this key becomes absolutely necessary if the best results are to be obtained.

3. *First finger half hole.* The standard fingering for these three notes calls for the first finger to cover only half of its hole:

A similar half-hole technique is found as standard procedure on the oboe, and under certain circumstances on the clarinet. Opening the hole half way helps force a node in the vibrating column of air making pitch and intonation more secure. The young bassoonist will soon find that the notes respond when the finger is completely off the hole (as on the flute) as well as when half of the hole is covered. A more advanced bassoonist will know and hear a difference in both tone quality and intonation between a half-hole and a completely open hole. For this reason the teacher must insist on the proper use of the half-hole from the very beginning, for it is difficult to start using it after technique has been developed.

In rapidly moving passages where the tone is not exposed sufficiently to make a firm impression of pitch and quality more advanced students make an exception to this rule. In this circumstance the finger may be taken completely off the hole rather than rolled to the half-hole position in order to facilitate technique. Like the whisper key, use of the half-hole is optional on certain notes in the high register, depending on the player and the instrument being used. Experimentation is necessary to discover when and where it is best used in this register.

With beginning students care should be taken that exactly half the hole is open. Too little or too much will effect response, quality, and/or intonation. If response is not correct, a more advanced player should check the exact amount of the hole he is opening, and experiment with opening more or less of a hole. With some players and instruments, there are occasional notes where opening more or less of the hole will better the response. Typical of these are:

(a) Open two-thirds of the hole: 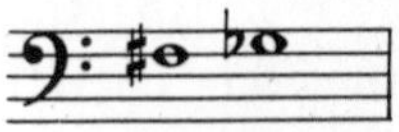

(b) Open one-quarter of the hole: 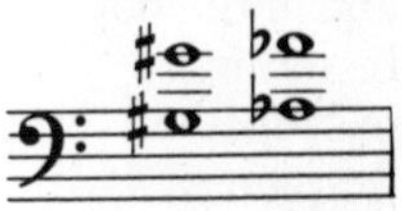

4. *Use of little fingers.* With only two keys to operate with the left little finger and three with the right, the little fingers have a much simpler operation on bassoon than on the clarinet and oboe. Fingers must be kept in a slight curve to depress the keys rapidly and without muscular tension. Occasionally the little finger will have to be used on different keys on successive notes in spite of the fact that there are alternate fingerings available for some of the notes involved.

If there is a satisfactory alternate fingering, it is always used in preference to sliding a finger. If it is necessary to slide the little finger from one key to another make use of the rollers placed on the keys for this purpose. In sliding from one key to the other, keep the finger slightly curved and continue the downward pressure while quickly sliding the finger over the rollers to the next key. The right little finger is never slid from the F to the F-sharp key or vice versa. Rather the regular F-sharp key played with the right thumb is used.

5. *High register.* Notes in the upper range of the high register are played with difficulty by many students. They should not be attempted nor should students be expected to play these notes until the other registers are well established and they are playing easily with a full tone. A reed which is too soft will make these high notes difficult or impossible to play. An embouchure which is incorrectly formed or immature in development will cause similar difficulties. If the embouchure is well formed and the reed stiff enough, playing these notes can be facilitated by taking more reed into the mouth, even to the extent that the upper lip is actually touching the first wire on the reed. This, combined with a more intense stream of air and firm support around the reed by the lips will help these notes respond with good quality and well in tune. There are many alternate fingerings in this register and the player should try all of them to see which responds with best tone quality and is best in tune for him.

6. *Flick keys* (also called flip or snip keys) are used as an aid for producing good slurs to the following notes.

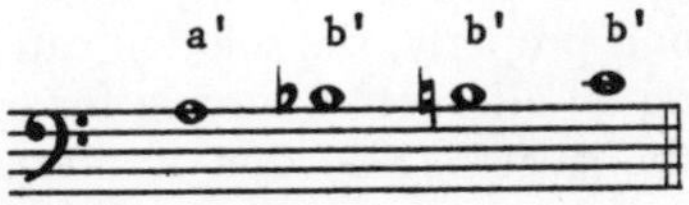

The need for using a flick key occurs when in slurring to one of these notes, that note drops to the lower octave, responds in the proper octave too slowly, or the fingering produces an indeterminate sound.

The left thumb flicks either key "a" or "b" (on the fingering chart in the back of the book) as indicated above the notes, so that it is open for just an instant at the beginning of the note. It functions as a momentary vent to help the vibrating column of air break into the desired frequency. If the thumb stays on the flick key too long, the note doesn't respond at all or responds out of tune.

The principal use for the flick keys is for slurs an interval of a fourth or more upward to the flick notes. Some teachers also recommend their use in downward slurs to these notes. Following are typical intervals which make use of the flick technique.

Flick key "a":

Flick key "b":

The flick keys are frequently useful in assuring a sfzorando attack on one of these four notes, but the player should experiment with this use of the flick keys only after the slurs have been perfected.

Intermediate students can learn the flick technique easily, and it is a must for advanced students. Some teachers have been successful in teaching it to students on the beginning level to help them develop a perfect slur. A word of caution—use flick keys only when necessary. They should never become an automatic part of the fingering, but a conscious choice in a particular situation.

Note that the flick key cannot be used for the C-sharp in this range. For slurs to this note, the alternate fingering C-sharp 123 056 F may be used if needed. If the "D" does not respond properly the alternate fingering 120 056 F may be used for slurs.

7. *Selection and use of alternate fingerings.* Because of its mechanism, the bassoon, more than any other of the woodwinds, has a great variety of alternate fingerings. Beginners should concentrate on basic fingerings, but as they advance technically, players will need to learn more and more alternate fingerings.

Alternate fingerings are used in specific instances to solve technical problems of facility, intonation, and response when the normal standard fingerings are found unsatisfactory. When a student finds that he cannot play a passage quickly or smoothly enough with the standard fingerings or when there is difficulty in getting one of the notes to respond properly, the solution can frequently be found by using an alternate fingering for one or more of the notes in the pattern. Selection of alternate fingerings occurs more and more frequently in the highest register of the instrument. The bassoonist will also choose alternate fingerings for control at both extremes of the dynamic range.

The fingering chart at the back of this book includes all the normal alternate fingerings. Examination of this chart will indicate that many are small variations of a basic fingering designed to accomodate variations in the response of a particular instrument and player. Not all the alternate fingerings will be useful for all players. Some of the fingerings will be out of tune to a greater degree for a particular player. Such fingerings can be used only when the sequence of notes in which they are used is moving so rapidly that the note is not sufficiently exposed for the ear to get an exact impression of the pitch.

8. *Basic alternate fingerings.* Among the alternate fingerings are some for four notes in the middle register of the instrument which should be introduced as part of the instruction on the beginning level. If their introduction and use is delayed, the student will develop poor habits of sliding fingers unnecessarily which is difficult to correct. The use of both fingerings for each of these notes is necessary for ease and smoothness of facility. The need for them, and the conditions under which each is selected for use should be made clear to the student at the earliest opportunity.

(a) F-Sharp:
G-Flat:

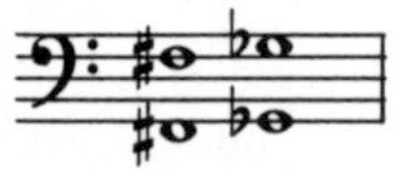

Two fingerings: (1) 123 F♯ 456 (Right thumb on F-sharp key)
(2) 123 456 F♯ (Right little finger on F-sharp key)

Fingering 1 is used except when the right thumb is needed as a part of the fingering of the note which precedes or follows the F-sharp. The most common situation for the use of fingering 2 occurs when the F-sharp or G-flat is preceded or followed by an A-sharp or B-flat. A typical use of the second fingering on all G-flats is the following arpeggio. Use of the half-hole for the upper octave and the whisper key for the lower is necessary.

(b) G-sharp:
A-flat:

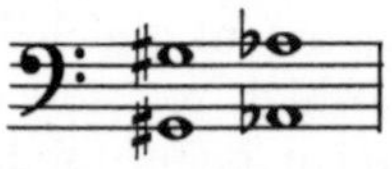

Two fingerings: (1) 123 456 G-sharp (Right little finger on G-sharp key)
(2) 123 G-sharp 456 (Right thumb on G-sharp key)

Use of the whisper key on the lower octave and the half-hole on the upper octave is necessary in addition to the fingering indicated.

The first fingering for G-sharp is always used except when the right little finger is needed on another key as part of the fingering for the note which precedes or follows the G-sharp. The most common usage of the second fingering is in the lower octave when the G-sharp or A-flat precedes or follows the low "F."

Use fingering 2:

(c) A-sharp:
B-flat:

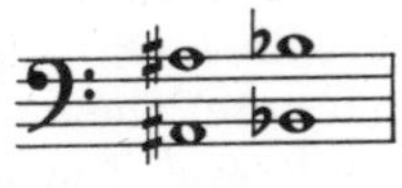

Two fingerings: (1) 123 A-sharp 450 (Right thumb on B-flat key)
(2) 123 456x (Sixth finger on B-flat key)

Use of the whisper key on the lower octave is necessary in addition to the fingering indicated.

The first fingering must always be used when the sixth finger must cover its tone hole as part of the fingering on the note following or preceding. Many students learn the second fingering as their standard fingering and treat the thumb B-flat as an alternate. This procedure causes many problems and teachers should be on the lookout for students who are doing this.

Situations arise in the music when no matter which fingering is selected either the thumb or sixth finger must slide to the next note. This forces the choice of whether it is better to slide the sixth finger from the B-flat key to the tone hole or to slide the thumb from the B-flat key to another key. Practices vary in this situation, but most students are able to develop facility in sliding the sixth finger easier than attempting to slide the thumb, although the thumb slides naturally from the B-flat key to the E-key.

The second fingering is used primarily as a chromatic fingering and for trills involving B-flat.

(d) D-sharp:
E-flat:

Two fingerings: (1) W 103 000 (standard)
(2) W 120 000 (alternate)
c♯

The problems in choosing between these two fingerings are as frequently found in tone quality and intonation as in technical facility. The first fingering tends to be out of tune and stuffy sounding with beginning bassoonists whose embouchure has not developed and who may be playing on a reed which is not properly adjusted (usually too stiff for them). For this reason, many beginners will use the second fingering to get the best quality and intonation rather than for facility. Students should be encouraged to use the first fingering in spite of how it sounds until they have developed the proper tone quality and intonation. The second fingering is used for smoothness in technique, in chromatic passages, and is mandatory for the trill from "D" to E-flat.

9. *Fingerings for control.* Certain notes on the bassoon are difficult for even more advanced players to control at extremely soft dynamic levels. To achieve control at this level, fingers and/or keys may be added to the standard fingering. The resultant fingering is referred to as a "long" or "resonance" fingering. The following examples for adding to a standard fingering will serve to illustrate this process. Others will be found in the fingering chart.

(a) D-sharp:
E-flat:

Standard fingering: W 103 000
For control: W 103 (D♯) B-flat 400

(b) E:

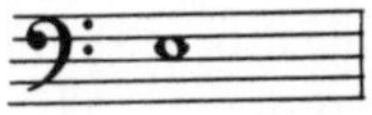

Standard fingering: W 100 000
For control: W 100 (E) 006 (F)

(c) F:

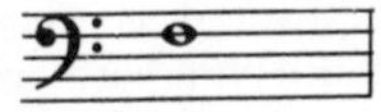

Standard fingering: W 000 000
For control: B-flat 000 E 406

(d) D:

Standard fingering: 120 000
For control: 120 056 F

10. *Trill fingerings* are special types of alternate fingerings intended for trilling, but which may also be used in certain other circumstances. Many trills may be executed with standard or alternate fingerings for the notes involved, but others require special fingerings. A chart of these special trill fingerings follows the standard bassoon fingering chart. These special fingerings tend to sacrifice intonation and/or tone quality on the upper note for the sake of facility. Some are noticeably out of tune when played slowly, but this out-of-tuneness is tolerable at the rapid speed of the trill.

The use of trill fingerings in situations other than trills is a common procedure for accomplished bassoonists, for their use is almost mandatory if rapid technique is to be smooth. The advanced bassoonist may use trill fingerings as alternate fingerings on grace notes, mordents, upper notes of turns and for upper neighbor tones in diatonic or chromatic passages when standard fingerings are not satisfactory. But as with any alternate fingering, trill fingerings must not be used when the ear can hear faulty intonation.

11. *Control in high register.* As the student's playing range is extended into the high register, he will frequently encounter problems in controlling the tone quality and intonation. When the music gets into the high playing range, breath support and velocity must increase and the reed must move slightly farther into the mouth. As the reed is moved inwards, the lip should roll inward with the movement rather than sliding along the reed. In the highest portion of the playing range, the upper lip will almost touch the first wire of the reed. It is frequently helpful to also move the lower jaw forward. Along with increased breath support and more reed, the embouchure support must be firmed. Avoid biting with the teeth for this causes thin tone quality and intonation problems.

12. *Tenor clef.* Because of the extremely wide range of the bassoon a large number of leger lines are necessary when musical passages in the highest portion of the range are rotated in the base clef. To avoid excessive leger lines the tenor clef is used in this range to make note reading easier. All bassoonists past the beginning stage should be able to read tenor clef, and in the course of their progress on the instrument should develop reading facility in this clef equal to that in the bass clef. The teacher should be sure that the tenor clef is introduced as soon as the student is playing in the upper register. The standard intermediate methods use some tenor clef, and all advanced studies for the instrument make use of it. If additional material is needed to develop facility in reading, useful studies can be found in both the cello and trombone literature. An example of this type of material using a step-by-step approach is *Introducing the Tenor Clef for Trombone (Bassoon)* by R. H. Fink, published by Accura Music Co.

13. *Alto clef.* The alto clef is rarely found in bassoon literature, and while the player should have knowledge of it, it is not considered necessary to develop equal facility with the other two clefs. Advanced players will find trombone literature useful in developing facility in both the alto and tenor clefs.

SELECTION OF INSTRUMENTS

Although the bassoon is historically one of the oldest of the woodwind instruments its fingering system is considerably less refined than any of them.[3] The system of fingering used in this country is the Heckel System, developed over a period of years by the Heckel Company in Germany. It is commonly conceded that those instruments made by the Heckel Company are the finest available. Other companies make Heckel System bassoons under their own trade names. While the finest clarinets and oboes available today are made in France, French bassoons are not used in this country. The reason for this is the fact that the French have a different fingering system called the French System which differs greatly both mechanically and tonally with the Heckel System.

The standard model bassoon is the Heckel System with twenty-two keys. Some older bassoons which are still in use have only twenty-one keys, lacking the whisper key which is now considered an integral part of the mechanism. Bassoons are made of maple rather than the grenadilla wood used in clarinets and oboes. The wood is sealed inside and out and the outside of the instrument is stained mahogany and finished as are fine pieces of furniture with several coats of lacquer to seal the wood against moisture. The interior of the instrument is specially treated to seal it against moisture.

Virtually all instruments now have the tenor joint lined with rubber or a plastic substance to further seal it against moisture, and the small side of the butt joint is lined with metal or rubber. These inner linings protect the instrument against moisture in the places where moisture tends to collect, and as a result cracks in the wood of a bassoon are considerably less frequent than in the wood of an oboe or clarinet. All instruments purchased for school use should have these inner linings.

The variety of models of bassoons available, unlike the oboe for example, is practically nil. If an instrument other than the standard twenty-two key Heckel System is desired, extra keys can be added on order from the factory, or added to the instrument after it is received by an expert repairman. The most useful of these additional keys is the high D key which is added to the tenor joint above the b′ key operated by the left thumb, and used for slurring to D second space above the bass clef. This key is a widely used addition to the instrument and is recommended for advanced players.

Other refinements of the mechanism which are found but rarely include a locking mechanism for the whisper key which locks the key in place leaving the left thumb free to operate other keys, an A-flat to B-flat trill key added to the cluster of keys played by the right thumb, etc. None of these and many others available are recommended for school use since the need for them is so limited, and they add complexity to the already complex key system of the instrument.

STUDENT QUALIFICATIONS AND APTITUDES

The bassoon is not a beginning instrument. The best criteria for advisability of study of the bassoon is the demonstration of fine tone production and basic technique on another woodwind instrument. The clarinet is an excellent pre-bassoon instrument. Physical size

3. For an interesting history of the development of the instrument see Lyndesay Langwill, *The Bassoon and Contrabassoon* (New York: W. W. Norton, 1965).

of the potential student is of primary importance because of the long reaches and stretches demanded of the fingers in playing the instrument. Most students younger than seventh grade are not physically large enough to play the instrument, and are best started on another woodwind and then transferred to the bassoon. In addition to size physical qualifications which will prove to be of advantage include fairly even teeth, an upper lip which is not too short to cover the teeth comfortably, a natural or greater than natural overbite (students with an underbite or protruding lower jaw have difficulty with the instrument), and fingers of normal or longer length.

A natural aptitude for the bassoon may be determined by his success in producing a good double crow on a reed adjusted and prepared for playing by the instructor after some brief instruction on embouchure formation and how to produce the crow. Students who are not immediately successful in producing the crow may, with instruction, soon exhibit a good natural aptitude. In the final analysis it is not natural aptitude but desire and persistence which are the greatest of all aptitudes for any instrument.

CARE OF THE BASSOON

The instrument must be assembled and disassembled with the greatest of care. Review the instructions on assembly of the instrument until they are thoroughly understood and the students are performing the operation easily. Keep the instrument in its case when not in use. The instrument is damaged by excess heat. Keep the instrument either in or out of the case out of the direct sun and away from all sources of heat. It is basic to good care of the instrument that it be thoroughly dried after each playing, and the habit of doing this thoroughly should be developed from the very first. The process of swabbing does not take much time, and will keep the instrument in good condition and maintain sanitary conditions for playing.

Swabs

The type of swab used and the way in which it is used determines the thoroughness with which the instrument is dried inside. Various kinds of swabs are used in cleaning the instrument, and the player chooses the type he likes best. These are described below.

Wool Swabs. Figure B-27 shows the pair of wool swabs which are the traditional type used for bassoon. The two sizes are to fit the large and small sections of the instrument. These have the advantage of maximum convenience in use, but must be used with care. The wire on which the wool is mounted can and does scratch the bore of the instrument unless handled carefully. For this reason many teachers advise against using them.

Figure B-27

Cleaning Rod. Use of an aluminum cleaning rod similar to the rod used in cleaning the flute is an excellent method of cleaning the bassoon. A piece of silk or soft lint-free cotton cloth of the dimensions shown in Figure B-28 is used. The small end of the cloth is pulled through the opening in the rod. To clean the tenor joint the rod is used as a weight to carry the cloth through the joint. To clean the butt joint the cloth is wrapped around the rod.

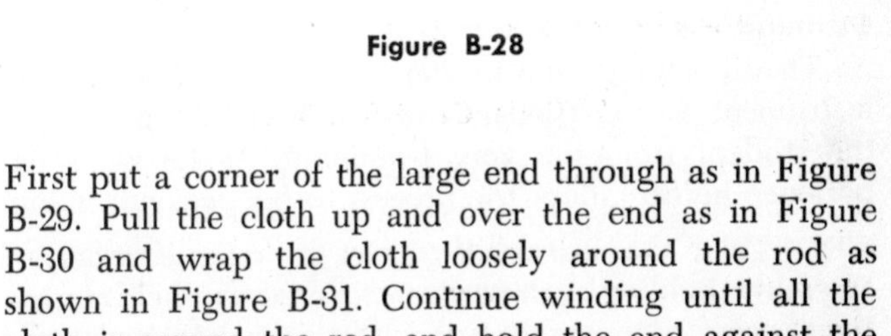

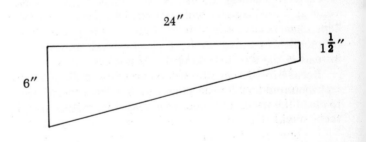

Figure B-28

First put a corner of the large end through as in Figure B-29. Pull the cloth up and over the end as in Figure B-30 and wrap the cloth loosely around the rod as shown in Figure B-31. Continue winding until all the cloth is around the rod, and hold the end against the rod with the forefinger while cleaning the butt joint.

Cloth and Drop Cord. A small piece of soft lint-free cloth, or a small triangle of chamois tied to a weighted drop cord similar to the typical clarinet swab is sometimes used for cleaning the tenor joint. The cord

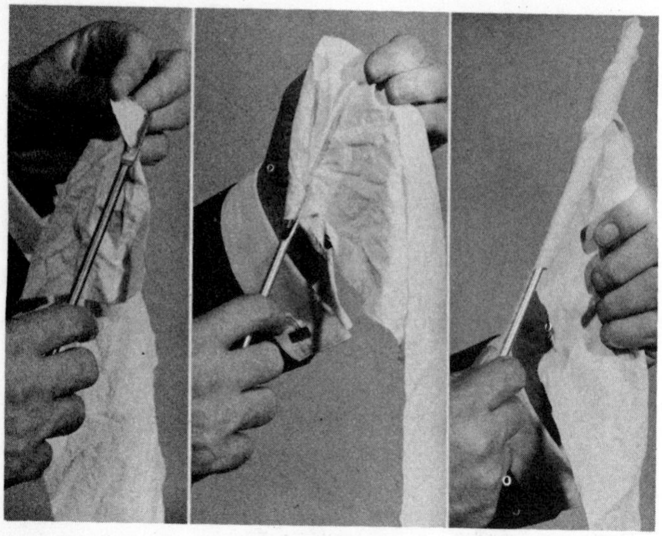

Figure B-29 Figure B-30 Figure B-31

must be long enough to drop completely through the tenor joint. The cord and cloth must *not* be pulled through the butt joint because of the small rods which go through the instrument to articulate keys on either side of the joint. The cloth can be pushed down into the butt joint with the end of a wool swab to the end and pulled out by the string simultaneously with the wool swab.

To summarize the pair of wool swabs traditionally used for cleaning the inside of the bassoon, while the most convenient, may damage the bore by scratching it and as they wear will drop lint into the bore and tone holes. The cleaning rod is recommended by a majority of bassoon teachers as it gives maximum flexibility to clean all parts equally well and the cloth used can be kept clean and lint-free. The cloth and drop cord are frequently combined with the cleaning rod and is used instead of the rod for drying the tenor joint.

Bocal Brush. A small brush about a half-inch in diameter mounted on a long flexible wire designed specifically to clean the inside of the bassoon bocal. Its regular use is recommended.

Cleaning the Bassoon

The following step-by-step process in cleaning the instrument is an efficient one which should be taught the student from the very beginning. As he gains experience he can adapt the process to his personal liking.

1. Take the instrument apart in reverse order of assembly, holding each part exactly as it was held during the process of assembling the instrument. As each joint is removed shake any moisture out of the ends. Place the parts carefully in the case before beginning the swabbing process.

2. Shake the moisture out of the bocal from both ends. Blow through it from the large end to force water out. Clean thoroughly with the bocal brush. The small end may be cleaned with a pipe cleaner (Figure B-32) on which the end has been bent to keep it from falling through.

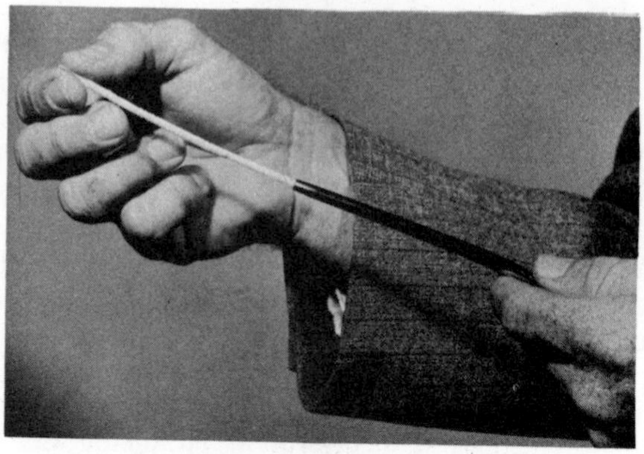

Figure B-32

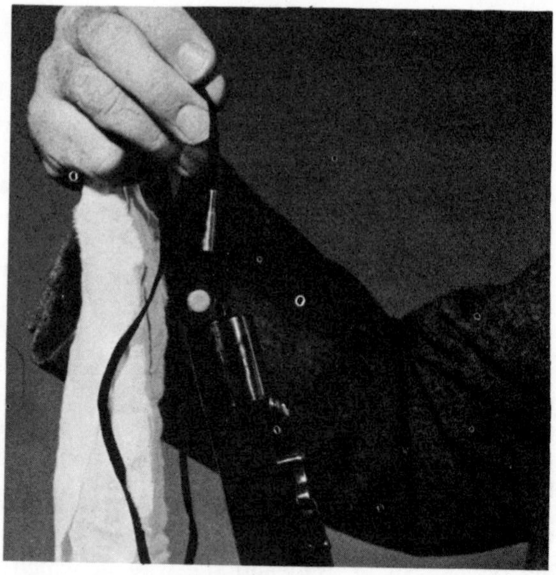

Figure B-33

3. Using the type of swab selected, dry the tenor joint. If a cloth and drop cord are being used drop the weight from the small end (Figure B-33). Pull the cloth through a couple of times being very careful that it does not snag the key which protrudes from the top (Figure B-34). If a cleaning rod and cloth are being used the rod is dropped into the joint from the top and the cloth pulled through a couple of times. If wool swabs are used the smaller wool swab is inserted from the large end of the joint (Figure B-35) and pushed back and forth to clean.

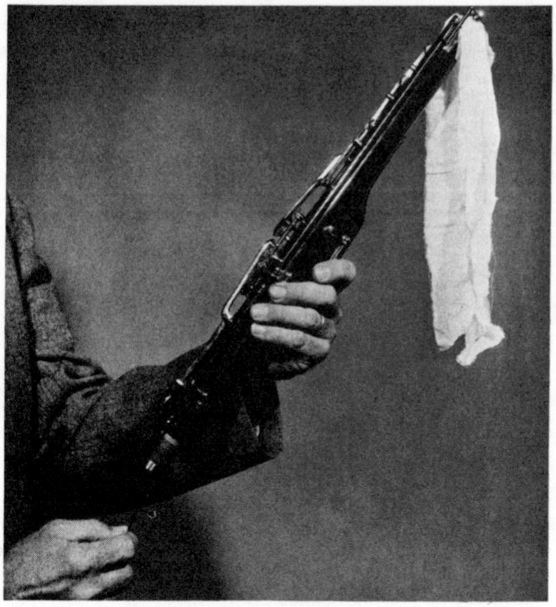

Figure B-34

Figure B-36

Figure B-35

Figure B-37

Figure B-38

4. Shake excess water from the small side of the butt joint. The small side of the joint is cleaned first with the smaller of the wool swabs, or with the cleaning rod on which the cloth has been wound as described (Figure B-36). Be sure to hold the end of the cloth with the fingers so that it will not unwind on the rod.

5. The larger side of the butt joint is cleaned with the larger of the two wool swabs (Figure B-37) or with the cleaning rod and cloth. Even though very little water collects in this side of the joint it should be cleaned as a matter of precaution.

6. The long joint and the bell rarely collect moisture but should be cleaned occasionally. They are cleaned with the larger of the two wool swabs (Figure B-38) or by the cloth and drop cord or the cleaning rod used as they were on the tenor joint.

7. Because of the way in which the tone holes for the fingers are bored into the body of the instrument water sometimes collects in them. The first tone hole

on the tenor joint is especially susceptible. During rehearsal or performance this water must be blown out. If there is sufficient time the hole affected can be dried with a pipe cleaner and the joint thoroughly swabbed as described.

8. With a soft cloth or chamois wipe the outside of the wood and keys to remove moisture and fingerprints. Place the instrument carefully in the case checking to see that each joint is properly positioned with the right side up.

9. Blow the moisture out of the reed and place it carefully in a reed case so that it can dry properly. The inside of the reed should be cleaned once a week by drawing a wet pipe cleaner through it carefully. Insert the cleaner from the bottom of the reed and pull it carefully out of the tip. Move cleaner from side to side as it is being pulled through to clean the entire surface of the blades. Repeat the process several times. Be very careful not to reverse the direction of the cleaner as it will damage the tip of the reed. A quick way to clean the reed is to run lukewarm or cold water through it from a tap. The pressure of the stream of water will force out accumulation although this is not a good substitute for the pipe cleaner.

Regular Maintenance of the Instrument

Oiling the Mechanism. The mechanism, if it is to remain in the best playing condition, must be oiled regularly three or four times a year. Special oil, called key oil, is available for this purpose. A drop of oil on the end of a needle or toothpick should be put at each pivot screw of each key. Do this carefully so that no oil gets on the pads. This regular oiling keeps pivot screws from excessive wear and from rusting into place, making repairs and adjustments on the instrument easier.

The Bore. The bore of the bassoon, unlike that of wooden oboes and clarinets, is not oiled. In the process of manufacture, both the inside and outside of the wood is treated to resist moisture. On most bassoons the tenor joint and the tenor side of the boot are lined with rubber to prevent moisture collecting. Because of this and the fact that the maple wood of which the instrument is made is more pliable than the grenadilla of oboes and clarinets, there is little danger of a bassoon cracking. The regular swabbing of the instrument is the best care for the bore.

Cleaning Bocal. Because of its shape, diameter, and location next to the reed, the bocal is much more susceptible to the accumulation of sediment than other parts of the instrument. If allowed to accumulate, this sediment soon changes the size and shape of the bore and makes playing more difficult and uncertain. Many performance problems which students have can be traced to this problem with the bocal.

In addition to the regular use of a bocal brush, the inside of the bocal should be washed out by running warm water through it once a month or oftener. Avoid damaging the cork in the process.

As part of this cleaning, check to see that the small vent hole on the side of the tube is clear. Do not use a needle or pin to clear the hole, for this may enlarge the opening which is of critical size. Use a broomstraw or a piece of a flat toothpick.

Dusting the Instrument. After the instrument has been in use over a period of time, dust collects under the key mechanism. This can and should be removed with a soft watercolor brush. A cloth should never be used for this purpose.

Shining the Keys. Keys will be kept in good condition if they are wiped regularly and gently with a soft cloth or chamois to remove perspiration and dirt as directed in the previous section. This will not only keep the keys from tarnishing, but will prevent corrosion of the plating in the event the player perspires excessively. Silver polish must never be used on the keys, nor should the keys ever be polished while on the instrument. Using silver polish while the keys are on the instrument will clog pivot screws in the mechanism and damage pads so that they will leak. Leave polishing up to a competent repairman. Caution student against polishing the keys, but give them careful instructions to keep the instrument clean by wiping the keys.

Bent Keys. In spite of the best care, keys sometimes become bent out of line causing unevenness in technique, or even preventing certain tones from responding at all. No attempt should be made to straighten keys or rods while they are on the instrument. This puts excessive pressure on both keys and their posts and the instrument may be damaged even more. Keys must be adjusted by a repairman who has the proper tools to straighten and align them.

Sticking Pads. If the instrument is not thoroughly dried before it is put into the case, or if the humidity is excessive even temporarily some pads on the instrument may stick tightly, or will stick momentarily before opening. This sticking can frequently be eliminated by placing a cigarette paper between the pad and the tone hole and pressing the key down firmly. Release the key, move the paper, and repeat the process until the key no longer sticks. If this does not relieve the sticking, put the cigarette paper in place, press the key, and pull the paper slowly from under the pad. Repeat the process several times.

If the cigarette paper does not relieve the sticking dip the end of a pipe cleaner into a cleaning fluid such as carbon tetrachloride, benzine or denatured alcohol. Wipe the pad with this fluid, and dry thoroughly with another pipe cleaner. Since this removes the natural oil from the pad, replace the oil by putting a very light coat of key oil over the pad with a pipe cleaner. Wipe off excess key oil with a dry pipe cleaner.

If none of these processes relieves the sticking, the pad should be replaced. Never use powder on pads in an attempt to stop sticking. It is rarely successful and damages the pad so that it begins to deteriorate rapidly.

Leaky Pads. Pads on instruments wear out with use. Some wear out more rapidly than others and begin to leak, causing the instrument to respond with difficulty on certain notes. Other pads which are in good condition may leak because they are improperly seated over the tone holes. If some notes respond with difficulty, with a change in tone quality and intonation in comparison with surrounding notes, there is a strong possibility of a leak in the instrument. Finding the exact source of the leak on a bassoon is somewhat more awkward than a similar operation on clarinet or flute.

To test for leaks take the instrument apart. Close one end of the joint to be tested with a cork or the palm of the hand, cover tone holes and close all keys as if playing and blow through the other end with as much pressure as possible. Leaky pads can be identified by the air leaking through. If a tone hole normally covered by a pad held closed by a spring leaks when maximum pressure is applied during the test, the spring on that key must be strengthened or replaced by a repairman. A joint in perfect condition will not leak no matter how much breath pressure is applied.

If the leak is located an examination of the pad will determine whether it should be replaced or simply reseated. Accuracy in seating pads is determined best by the use of commercial feeler papers or strips of cigarette papers about a quarter inch wide. Slide one end of the paper under the pad, put the normal amount of pressure against the pad if the key is not held closed by a spring, and slowly draw the paper out. As long as the pressure against the paper remains constant there is no leak. If the pressure suddenly lessens the pad is not properly seated. Repeat the process completely around the pad so that all edges are tested.

The process of blowing cigarette smoke through the instrument to identify a leak by seeing the smoke come out of the leak is not recommended. The nicotine in the smoke coats the pads and if this is done frequently will damage them so that they harden and leak. Repairmen use a small light in the bore of the instrument to find leaks as the light will shine through the open space of the leak.

Key Corks. Several keys of the bassoon have corks cemented on them so that the pads will close properly, controlling the amount of opening of a key or eliminating noise in the action. If a cork which closes a pad wears thin or breaks off, the pad no longer closes properly and there is a problem in tonal response on notes where that pad is involved. If a key is opening too far because of a missing cork, there is a change in intonation on that note. When these things occur or when the mechanism becomes noisy, corks should be replaced.

Loose Tenon Ring. The ring on the end of the bell joint may loosen if the wood of the instrument shrinks. The purpose of this ring is to reinforce the wood to keep it from cracking. If it is loose, it is no longer supporting the wood. To avoid the possibility of a crack in the bell, it should be tightened by a repairman.

Regular Overhaul. The condition of every instrument must be checked at least once each year by the instructor or by a repairman. Regular maintenance keeps an instrument in good playing condition over a period of years, rather than allowing it to gradually deteriorate and become increasingly difficult to play. Every instrument must have a complete overhaul every three to five years depending on amount of usage. If fine instruments receive a yearly checkup and regular overhaul they will last in virtually perfect condition for many years. The services of a competent repairman are invaluable and an asset to any program of instrumental instruction.

ACCESSORIES

There are certain accessories for the bassoon which are designed to make performance easier or more convenient for the player, or to protect the instrument against damage. The most common of these are further discussed.

Neck Strap. The traditional suspension of the instrument is by a neck strap which supports the instrument and which makes use of the right hand in the hand rest. Use of the hand rest is mandatory when a neck strap is used. Neck straps may be thick cords, or may have a wide leather neck piece which is more comfortable for the student as the cord around the neck frequently becomes uncomfortable when playing for long periods of time. The strap must be adjustable so that the instrument may be easily adjusted to the proper playing position, and the adjusting mechanism such that it will not gradually slip when the weight of the instrument is put on it. The instructor will need to check the condition of neck straps occasionally as they wear and do not stay in adjustment. This wear is so gradual that the students are frequently not aware of the problem and their playing suffers.

Seat Strap. A seat strap rather than a neck strap is becoming more and more widely used to support the weight of the instrument. This type of suspension of the instrument is advantageous in that it removes the weight of the instrument from the neck, and relieves the right hand of the necessity of assisting in the support of the instrument. A seat strap is simply a belt with a snap on the end which snaps into a ring holder on the cap at the bottom of the butt joint. The belt is placed over the chair, the amount of strap over the edge of the chair adjusted to hold the bassoon at the right height, and the player sits on the belt to keep it from slipping.

Bassoons do not come from the factory equipped for the use of a seat strap—they must be altered for this type of suspension. The most simple alteration is the addition of a metal band with a ring over the cap of the butt joint. This can be easily added by the student or the instructor, and the seat strap snaps into the ring to support the instrument. These add-on metal ring holders are commercially available and are not expensive.

Some bassoonists prefer to alter the cap on the butt end of the instrument by drilling a hole in the rib at the bottom and attaching a ring holder through the hole. This must be done by a professional repairman since special drilling tools are necessary.

The right hand rest is not used with the seat strap, freeing the right hand from its restrictive influence. It is desirable that a plate similar to the right-hand thumb plate be added to the instrument on which the first finger of the right hand can rest. On some bassoons the thumb rest can be shifted to serve this function, although it is advisable that it be left in place since the neck strap and the normal hand-rest for the right hand will be needed for playing the instrument in a standing position. A competent repairman can add the first finger rest plate. A protective plate over the A-sharp and F-sharp keys on the bottom of the butt joint is also a desirable addition when the instrument is adapted to the seat strap.

Floor Stand. Two types of floor stands may be used with the bassoon. The first type is used to hold the instrument safely when it is not being played. The bassoon is held in a fairly upright position so that water does not run into the holes, and the stand protects the instrument from possible damage through being knocked off of a chair, or stepped on if it is placed on the floor. This type of stand is highly recommended for safety of the instrument and is not expensive. Models are available which fold up compactly for convenience in carrying, although they will not fit inside the normal bassoon case.

The second type of floor stand holds the instrument in playing position so that neither a neck or seat strap is necessary. It functions similarly to the stand whcih holds the baritone saxophone in playing position. Regular use of this type of stand is not recommended for school use as it tends to put the student into an awkward and somewhat unnatural playing position. Use of this type of stand is normally used only by players in studio-type orchestras who are doubling on several instruments and must have them in position for rapid changes from one to another.

BIBLIOGRAPHY OF STUDY MATERIALS

In comparison to that available for the other woodwind instruments study material written especially for bassoon is meager. And unless it is carefully selected tends to lack stylistic variety and is frequently downright uninteresting. For this reason the wise instructor will make generous use of appropriate materials written for cello and trombone which frequently is ideal for bassoon when appropriate phrasing is added to put it into the woodwind idiom.

Following is a cross section of the most widely available material (exclusive of solo and ensemble music) for bassoon. Detailed information about music of all types for bassoon may be found in the books by Cobbett, Coleman, Camden, Heller, Rasmussen and Mattran, Risdon, and Spencer as listed in the bibliography at the end of this book and in the *Selective Music Lists* of the MENC.

Beginning Methods

Anzalone, V. *Breeze-Easy Method for Bassoon,* 2 vols. Witmark.

Buck, Lawrence. *Elementary Method for Bassoon.* Neil Kjos.

Gekeler-Hovey. *Bassoon Method,* 3 vols. Belwin, Inc.

Herfurth-Stuart. *A Tune A Day for Bassoon.* Boston Music Co.

Lentz, Don. *Method for Bassoon,* 2 vols. Belwin, Inc.

Skornicka, J. E. *Elementary Method for Bassoon.* Rubank, Inc.

Voxman, H. *Intermediate Method for Bassoon.* Rubank, Inc.

Voxman, H-W. Gower. *Advanced Method for Bassoon,* 2 vols. Rubank, Inc.

Weber, Fred-Henry T. Paine. *Bassoon Student* (Student Instrumental Course), 3 vols. Belwin, Inc. Correlated with four additional volumes of solos, études and technical studies.

Standard Methods

Bourdeau, E. *Grande Methode Complete de Bassoon.* Leduc. Text in English and French. For use by more advanced students. Scales, interval studies, scales in thirds in a wide range and making use of tenor clef. Concludes with a series of etudes on an advanced level and in all major and minor keys. Fingerings indicated in early portion of the method are for the French system bassoon. Fingerings for the Heckel system are not indicated.

Langey. *Tutor for Bassoon.* Carl Fischer. An old standard which contains much useful material in the traditional nineteenth century style. Useful on upper intermediate level. Some duets and a couple of trios.

Weissenborn, J. *Practical Method for the Bassoon.* Carl Fischer. The standard method for bassoon which all bassoonists use. Basic to the study of the instrument. Useful for early intermediate level.

Additional Study Materials

Bertoni, U. *12 Studies* (ed. Sharrow). International Music Co.

Bitsch. *20 Studies for Bassoon.* Leduc. Contemporary style, quite advanced.

Bozza. *15 Études Journalieres.* Leduc.

Dherin G & P. Pierne. *Nouvelle Technique du Basson,* 2 vols. Henry Lemone & Co. Volume one by Dherin is advanced technical exercises in all keys, volume two by Pierne is advanced études.

Ferling. *Forty-Eight Famous Studies.* Southern Music Company. The famous oboe studies transcribed for bassoon by Thornton.

Fink, R. H. *Introducing the Tenor Clef for Trombone (Bassoon).* Accura Music.

Flament. *Technical Exercises,* 7 volumes. Leduc. The volumes are classified as follows: (1) long tones, (2) staccato exercises, (3) exercises in accentuation, (4) miscellaneous studies, (5) cello studies of Duport, (6) daily studies, (7) study of reed adjustment.

Gambaro, J. B. *18 Studies.* International.

Haultier, J. *Le Débutant Bassoniste.* Leduc. For early intermediate level. Ranges to G in upper register. Basic technical exercises in all keys. Uses tenor and bass clef.

Jacobi, C. *Six Caprices.* International.

Jacobi, F. *Six Bassoon Exercises.* Boosey & Hawkes.

Jancourt, E. *26 Melodic Studies.* International.
Method for Bassoon, Op. 15, 2 vols. Costallat.
32 Progressive Exercises. Costallat.

Jancourt-Collins. *Bassoon Studies.* Belwin, Inc. Selected from the method, these are slightly more advanced studies than volume two of the Weissenborn studies.

Kopprasch. *60 Studies for Bassoon,* 2 vols. International, Cundy-Bettoney. The standard studies used for many instruments. The International edition adapted for bassoon by Kovar.

Kreutzer. *Studies, Op. 6.* Leduc. The famous violin studies transcribed for bassoon.

Louchez. *20 Études Faciles d'après Samie.* Leduc.

McDowell, P. *Daily Exercises for Bassoon.* Belwin, Inc.
Practical Studies for Bassoon, 2 vols. Belwin, Inc.

Milde, L. *25 Studies in Scales and Chords, Op. 24.* International, Cundy-Bettoney.
Concert Studies, Op. 26, 2 vols. International, Cundy-Bettoney.

Neukirchner, V. *23 Exercises for Bassoon.* Boosey & Hawkes.

Orefici, A. *Melodic Studies.* (ed. Sharrow) International.
Bravoura Studies. (ed. Weisberg) International.

Oromszegi, O. *10 Modern Études.* Boosey & Hawkes.

Oubradous. F. *Games et Exercises Journaliers,* 3 vols. Leduc. Tone studies, scales, thirds, fourths, arpeggios, articulation exercises in three octave ranges and in all major and minor keys. Excellent for lower advanced level.

Pares, C. *Scales and Daily Exercises for Bassoon.* Carl Fischer.
Modern Foundation Studies for Bassoon. Rubank, Inc. Two versions of the same material. The Fischer is the original. The Rubank edition revised by Harvey Whistler keeps the exercises in an easier range.

Petrov, I. A. *Scale Studies.* International.

Piard, Marius. *Enseignement Du Contre-basson.* Leduc. A volume designed to orient the bassoonist to the contrabassoon quickly and efficiently using exercises, études and presenting a large number of excerpts from orchestral works using the contrabassoon.

Pivonka. *Rhythmical Études.* Boosey & Hawkes.

Rode. *15 Caprices.* (ed. Sharrow) International. Famous violin studies for Bassoon.

Satzenhofer, J. *24 Studies for Bassoon.* International.

Slama, A. *66 Studies in All Keys.* International, Cranz editions.

Vaulet-Voxman. *Twenty Studies for Bassoon.* Rubank, Inc.

Vobaron. *34 Études for Bassoon.* Cundy-Bettoney.
Four Lessons and Seventeen Studies. Cundy-Bettoney.

Weissenborn, J. *Bassoon Studies, Op. 8,* 2 vols. Carl Fischer, International, Cundy-Bettoney. Volume one "for beginners" is useful on the intermediate level and has short technical studies in seven sections; essential kinds of expression, tenor clef, brief scale exercises, etc. These are basic studies every student should cover. Volume two is slightly more advanced. These studies are reprinted in the Carl Fischer edition of the method.

Study and Achievement Questions

1. Identify and write on a staff the beginning, intermediate, and advanced playing ranges for bassoon.
2. Assemble the bassoon identifying each part as it is taken from the case and demonstrating the correct holding position for each operation.
3. Observe beginning, intermediate, and advanced students (when available) in the process of assembling their instruments and fill out the check list for assembly. Describe corrections for any faults.
4. Demonstrate the correct holding positions for the bassoon. Demonstrate commonly found faults and describe their effect on performance.
5. Demonstrate the guide positions for the hands. Instruct a student who is unfamiliar with the instrument in how to arrive at this guide position.
6. Observe various students during performance and fill out checklists for holding and hand positions. Suggest appropriate corrections for any faults.
7. Discuss the two general types of embouchure formation for bassoon. Select one and demonstrate the step-by-step formation. Describe and demonstrate the process of how the proper amount of reed in the mouth is arrived at.
8. Observe various students during performance and

fill out checklists for embouchure formation. If any faults are observed describe their effect on performance, and suggest corrections.

9. How is the basic tuning of the bassoon done? How is the bocal involved in tuning?
10. What factors will make the overall pitch of the bassoon flat? Sharp? What factors influence the pitch of individual notes?
11. Identify the four registers of the bassoon range by writing the notes in each on a staff.
12. List the most common problems in tone production on the bassoon together with their causes and corrections.
13. Describe the two most common approaches to tongue placement on the bassoon. What basic principles do they have in common?
14. Describe and demonstrate the use and action of the left thumb. The right thumb.
15. What is the function of the whisper key? On what notes must it be closed by the thumb? On what notes does it close automatically.
16. On what notes is the first finger half-hole position used? What is the purpose of the half-hole?
17. What are flick keys? On what notes are they used? When and why are they used?
18. List the notes on the bassoon for which there are standard alternate fingerings. Give the fingering for each alternate and an example of how and when it is used.
19. Discuss student qualifications and aptitudes for study of the bassoon.
20. Discuss the advantages, disadvantages, and uses of the various kinds of swabs available for use with the bassoon.
21. Perform the step-by-step process of disassembly and cleaning the bassoon, having a colleague observe and rate the procedure.
22. List the items to be considered in the regular maintenance of the instrument.
23. Discuss the pros and cons of the neck strap, the seat strap, and the floor stand to hold the bassoon.
24. Examine and compare various beginning bassoon methods. Select one or two best suited for a junior high beginner, and one or two best suited for a high school student transferring from clarinet.
25. Examine available standard methods and additional study materials for bassoon and list them with comments. Prepare a suggested list of material to include all five types of material suggested for simultaneous study for an advanced beginner. For an intermediate level student. For an advanced student.
26. Listen to several phonograph records of outstanding bassoonists. Compare and comment on tone quality, phrasing, articulation. If the players are other than American describe any nationalistic differences which are discernible.
27. Discuss the use of vibrato on the bassoon, together with when and how it should be developed.

Chapter 6

Saxophone

Since its invention in 1846 by Adolph Sax of Paris the saxophone has received an acceptance in the musical world which is remarkable for the divergence of usages to which it has been put. Excepting only the flute among the woodwind instruments the saxophone is the most perfect instrument from the standpoint of both acoustics and mechanism. Only very minor alterations and additions have been made to its basic mechanism since its introduction. As a newcomer historically speaking, the saxophone lacks musical literature in various musical styles available for the other woodwinds.

Clearly defined schools or performance styles have not yet become as apparent as those for the other woodwinds. The development of performance styles and pedagogical approaches to the teaching of an instrument have always centered around fine performers in major symphony orchestras over the world or in various conservatories or schools of music. The saxophone has not had this treatment since it is not a regular part of the symphony orchestra, and it is only comparatively recently that students have been allowed to "major" on the saxophone at schools of music in the United States.

As a result of this situation, the saxophone in the United States generally speaking, has the lowest performance standards of any woodwind instrument. Educators who act as adjudicators for public school music festivals will affirm the fact that more often than not the saxophone section of a band is the weakest by far of all sections in the group.

An analysis of the problem reveals that while the technical facility of the players in the section is adequate, the concept of tone quality is woefully lacking. This is due primarily to two factors. First, there is a lack of professional saxophone players in the field of legitimate music to set the same high standard that is found on the other woodwinds. Second, the traditional association and use of the saxophone in the field of popular music where the concept of tone quality changes from year to year depending on the style of musical entertainment in vogue, and where many of the star performers who have not had a legitimate musical training and succeed on the basis of raw talent alone, develop highly individual tone qualities. This is not necessarily to be condemned as the entertainment business demands individuality of the kind no other personality can duplicate.

The fact remains, unhappy as it may be, that the saxophone as a medium of musical expression has not been developed in the United States to anywhere the extent found on other wind instruments. This situation can and must be remedied by intelligent and diligent teaching. It is no more difficult to produce beautiful sounds, fine phrasing, and all the other aspects of artistic performance on the saxophone than on any other woodwind instrument. Indeed, some teachers hold the view that progress toward this goal can be more rapid on the saxophone than on some of the other woodwind instruments.

The saxophone is an instrument deserving of serious study, of serious teaching, and sufficient literature exists to make this possible. A fine saxophone section is one of the most valuable assets a band can have. The sounds produced as a section and in the ensemble of the group will pay handsome rewards to the teacher who develops them. As a solo instrument or in ensembles the saxophone is a flexible and musically pleasing medium of expression.

THE SAXOPHONE FAMILY

While only the Alto, Tenor, and Baritone saxophones are widely used, the addition of the Soprano and Bass instruments to the choir produces a pitch range almost as great as that of the clarinet family. The Soprano saxophone is called for in many band scores, but the Bass instrument, unfortunately, has virtually disappeared from the symphonic band instrumentation.

Fingerings for all instruments in the saxophone family are identical, and a player may easily transfer from one to another. The basic embouchure is the same for all the instruments with adjustments made according to the size of the mouthpiece of the instrument.

Since the Alto saxophone is the most widely used, discussions in this chapter will center around it, with special problems and differences between it and the other instruments in the family noted in the course of the discussion.

Except for some models of the Soprano and Bass which do not have the two lowest notes, all the instruments in the family have the same theoretical *written* range:

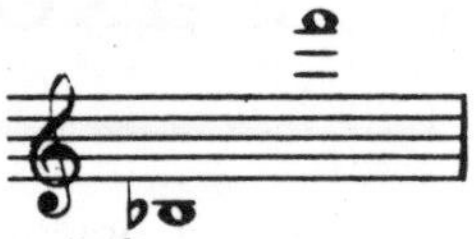

but all are transposing instruments and *sound* in different ranges.

The transpositions and ranges in which each instrument sounds is as follows:

1. *B-flat Soprano*: Sounds a whole step lower than written.

Written Sounds Range of Actual Sounds

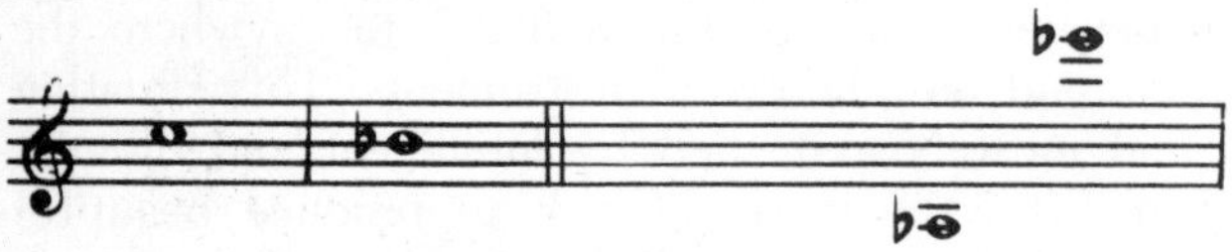

2. *E-flat Alto*: Sounds a major sixth lower than written.

Written Sounds Range of Actual Sounds

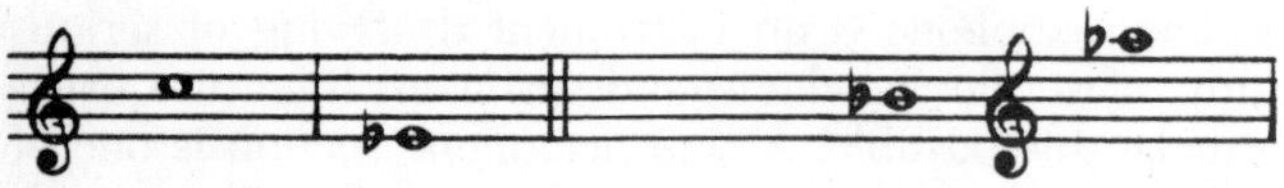

3. *B-flat Tenor*: Sounds a major ninth lower than written.

Written Sounds Range of Actual Sounds

4. *E-flat Baritone*: Sounds an octave plus a major sixth lower than written.

Written Sounds Range of Actual Sounds

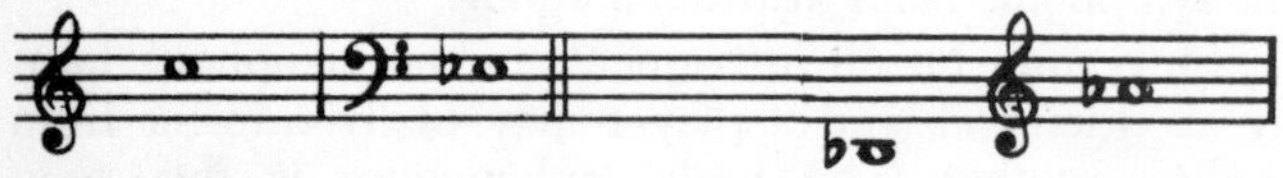

5. *B-flat Bass* (rarely found): Sounds two octaves plus a whole step lower than written.

Written Sounds Range of Actual Sounds

In addition to the preceding instruments a Soprano saxophone in C, sounding the pitch as written is occasionally found. The C-melody saxophone is a Tenor saxophone in C. Although it is obsolete an occasional beginning student will bring such an instrument from home since it is identical in appearance with the B-flat Tenor and considerable diplomacy is necessary on the part of the teacher to explain why it can't be used. The reason it can't be used is simply that there is no music written for it to play in a band or in a beginning class.

PLAYING RANGES

Because of the acoustics of the saxophone, the beginner on this instrument can extend his playing range more rapidly than on the other woodwinds. In actual practice, however, the highest notes are not utilized on the Tenor and Baritone instruments as much as they are on the Alto. A very advanced player on the Alto, and to some extent the Tenor through use of additional harmonics, can extend the playing range of his instrument above the normal high F. This is discussed later in this chapter, and fingerings for these notes given in an additional section of the fingering chart.

The three playing ranges on the instrument are described as the easy range, the normal range, and the extended range:

Easy Range Normal Range Extended Range

PARTS OF THE SAXOPHONE

Parts of all members of the saxophone family are the same: body, neck, mouthpiece, ligature, mouthpiece cap, reed, and neck strap, and differ only in size.[1] The instrument pictured is an Alto. The type of case illustrated provides a place for a fitted B-flat clarinet case on the shelf where the mouthpiece and neck are shown, and a flute case in the brackets on the lid as

1. The Soprano is normally straight and with body and neck as a single unit.

a convenience for those players who double these instruments.

ASSEMBLING THE INSTRUMENT

All members of the saxophone family are assembled in the same fashion, and the Alto saxophone is used in the photographs. Proper assembly and disassembly of the instrument is of the utmost importance, and must be taught to students from the very first lesson. Probably more damage—bent keys, rods, bent connecting levers, etc.—is done to instruments in putting them together and taking them apart than by all other means combined.

The mechanism of the saxophone is rugged, but the long rods, the large cups for the pads, the connecting levers as well as the side keys are easily bent out-of-line. Instruments with damaged mechanism do not respond properly. A great deal of the difficulty students, especially beginners, have in playing their instruments can be traced to damaged mechanism which causes leaky pads. For this reason, as well as for the simple necessity of keeping the instrument in perfect mechanical condition, proper habits of assembly must be firmly established.

The assembly of an instrument must be accomplished without putting pressure on any key or rod which will bend it in any way. It is obviously impossible to put together the saxophone without touching the mechanism, so in selecting the way in which the parts are held the hands and fingers must be in a position against parts of the mechanism which are not affected by the slight pressure put on them.

The following step-by-step procedure is given in detail, and every student should practice it carefully until each procedure is correct and automatic. After some experience with the instrument, the student will adjust this procedure to his personal tastes.

Before starting the process make sure that the cork end of the neck is well greased with prepared cork grease. Study the photograph and directions for each

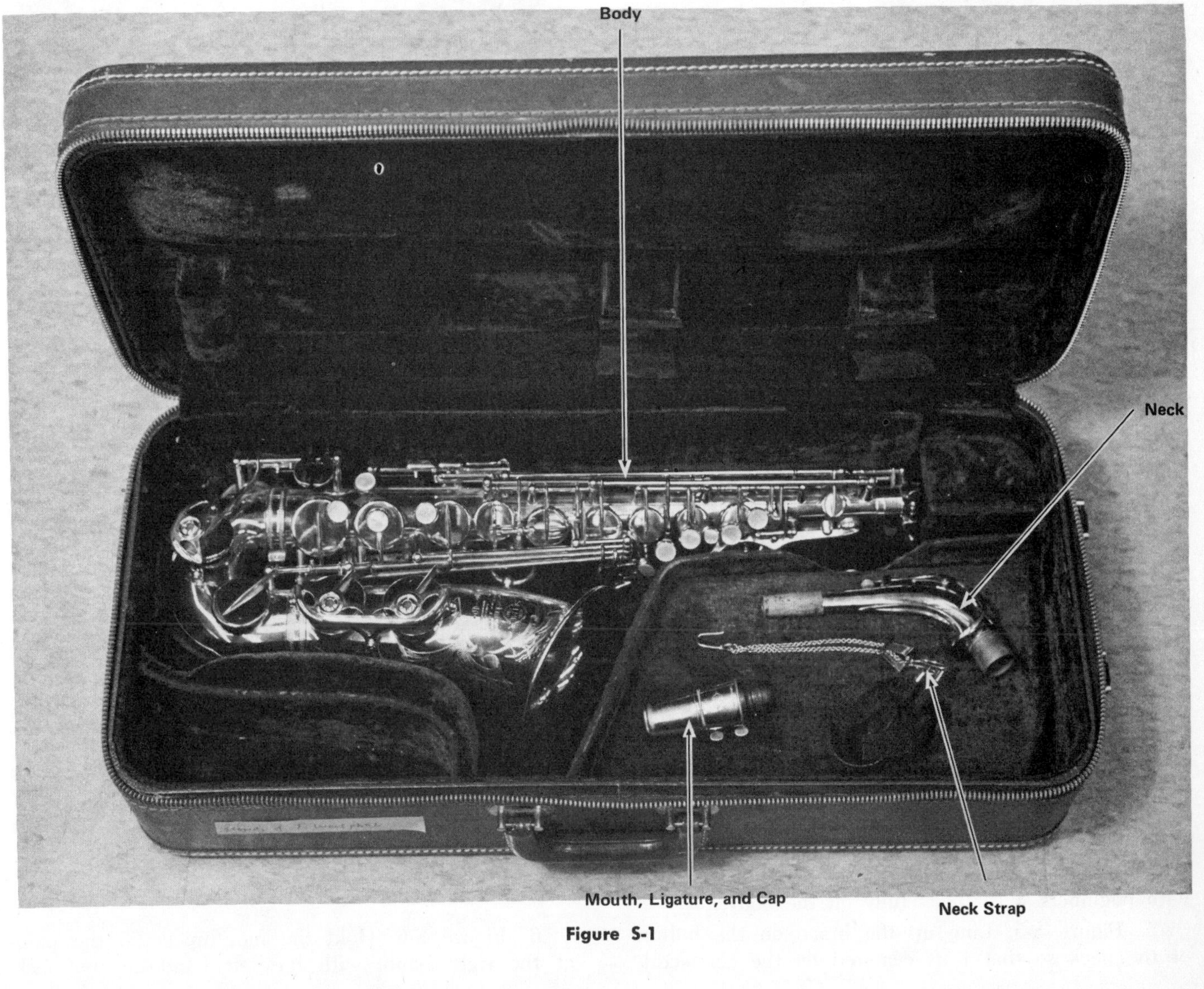

Figure S-1

step carefully and repeat the operation several times before proceeding to the next.

1. Take the neck strap out of the case and put it into position around the neck. Examine the device on it which adjusts its length, and operate it to become familiar with its adjustment. The exact length will be determined later.

2. Figure S-2. Grasp the instrument by the bell away from the keys and lift it from the case. Holding it by the bell, hook the neck strap on to the circle on the body of the instrument. Continuing to hold the bell, remove the end plug which protects the connective lever for the octave key.

Figure S-2

3. Figure S-3. Remove the neck from the case and hold it in the palm of the right hand so that the octave key is held down firmly. Check the tension screw which holds the neck in place on the instrument to see that it is loose. This screw appears either on the neck as in the photograph, or at the top sleeve of the body. Check to see that the sleeve which fits into the body is clean and polished. If it is clean but does not slide into place easily lubricate it with cork grease or vaseline.

4. Figure S-4. Holding the body of the instrument with the left hand, push the neck on, keeping the eyes on the connecting lever to avoid turning the neck in such a way that this lever will be bent. Bending this lever during this process is a very common problem with beginners. Push neck fully on the body.

5. Figure S-5. Line up the brace on the bottom of the neck so that it is centered on the connecting lever on the body of the instrument. The exact adjustment varies with the brand of instrument and with the playing position used by the student. Tighten the tension screw to hold the neck firmly in place.

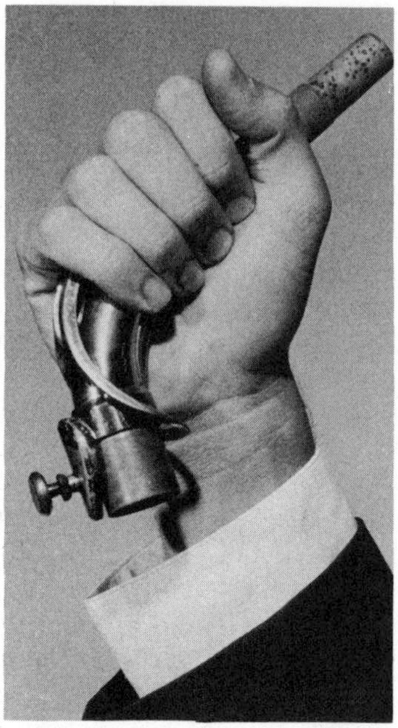

Figure S-3

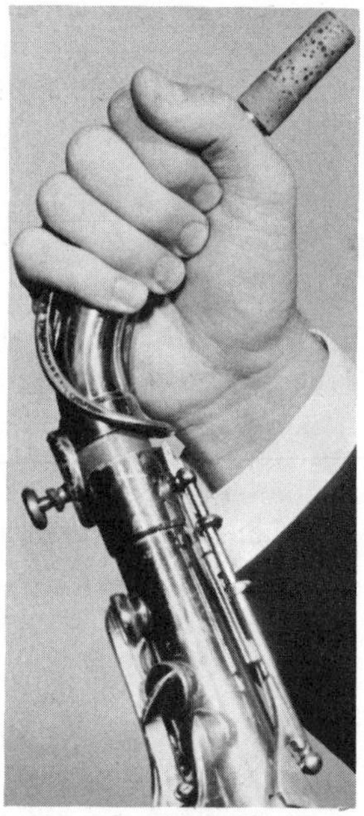

Figure S-4

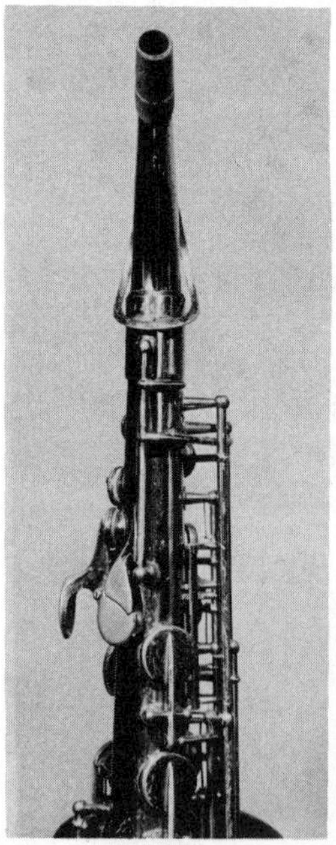

Figure S-5

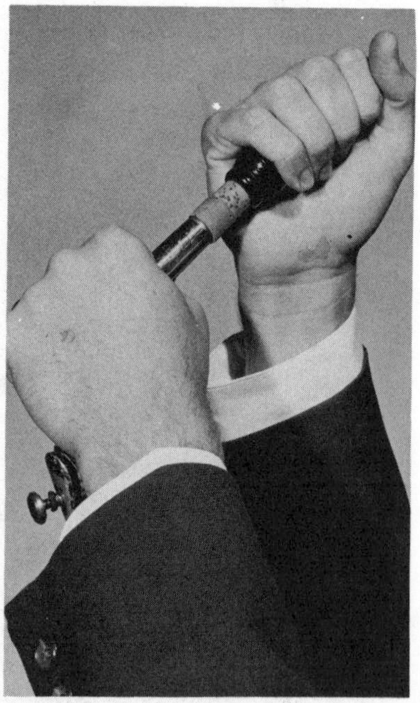

Figure S-6

6. Figure S-6. Hold the mouthpiece in the palm of the right hand, with the left hand on the neck,

palm holding down the octave key. The weight of the instrument is on the neck strap. Push on the mouthpiece so that at least half of the cork is covered. The exact distance of the mouthpiece is determined by the tuning process. If the instrument has a tuning screw on the neck in addition to a cork, the mouthpiece must be pushed on to cover the entire cork.

Placing the Reed on the Mouthpiece

Placement of the reed on the mouthpiece is highly critical since the way in which it is fitted to the mouthpiece affects its response and tone quality to a considerable degree. Placement and procedure is the same for all instruments in the saxophone family. If the reed is put on the mouthpiece and the ligature slipped over it, there is danger that the ligature will chip or split the reed if it touches it. Many reeds are damaged this way by students, and even advanced players have been known to ruin a good reed by inadvertently hitting it with the ligature. To avoid the slightest chance of damage, and as a matter of efficient procedure it is recommended that the ligature be put on first and the reed slipped under it.

The following step-by-step outline should be carefully followed by all saxophonists from the very beginning stage to the most advanced.

1. Figure S-7. Put ligature with loosened screws on the mouthpiece with screws on the flat side of the mouthpiece. With the weight of the instrument on the neck strap, hold the ligature forward on the mouthpiece with the left thumb and slide the reed underneath the ligature.

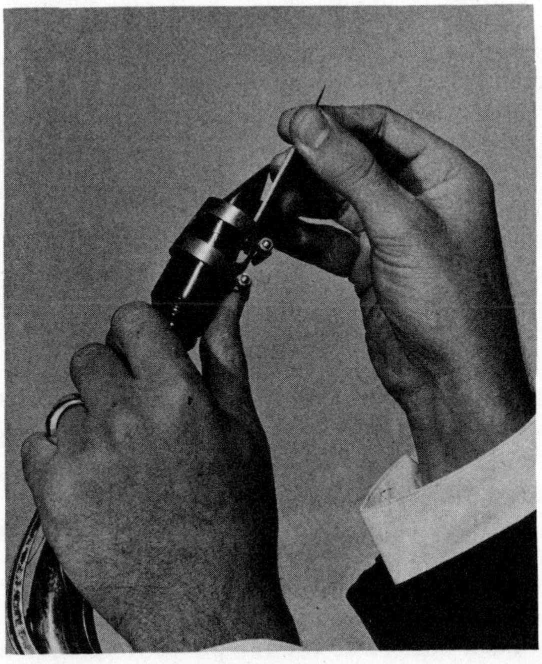

Figure S-7

2. Figure S-8. With the thumbs in the position shown in the photograph, line up the reed on the mouthpiece so that there is equal space from side to side and centered on the flat portion of the mouthpiece. About a sixty-fourth of an inch of the black of the tip should be seen when looking directly at the tip.

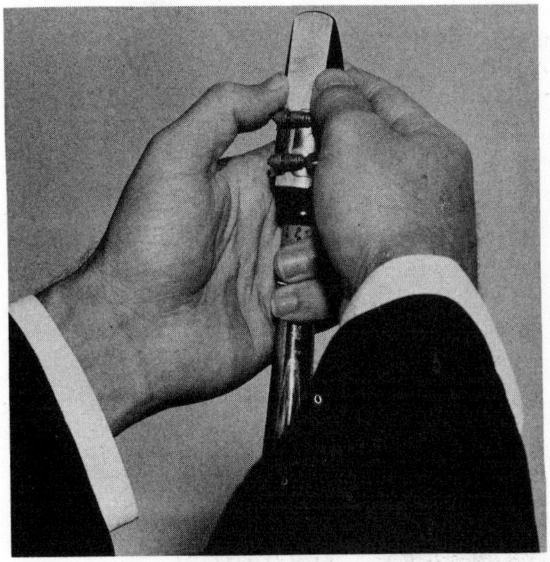

Figure S-8

3. Figure S-9. Hold the reed in place firmly with the left thumb and tighten first the upper screw and then the lower screw snugly. Avoid tightening them too much as this will pull the reed out of position and restrict its vibration.

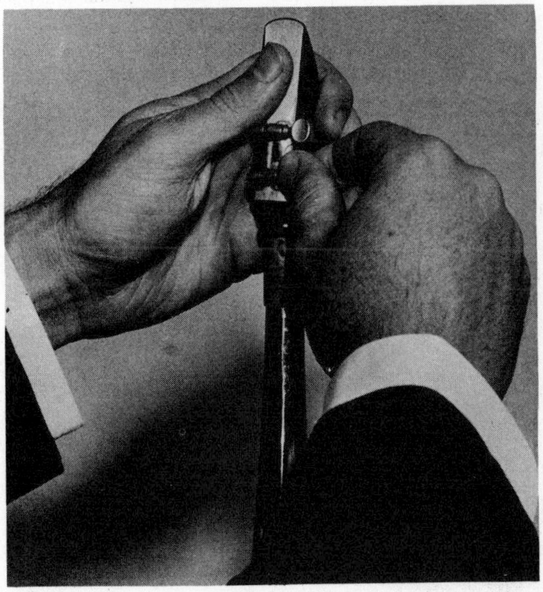

Figure S-9

4. Figure S-10. Turn the mouthpiece so that the reed is flat on the lower lip when the instrument is in playing position. The flat portion of the mouthpiece will be off center with the brace on the neck of the instrument.

Figure S-10

5. Figure S-11. When the instrument is not in use the mouthpiece cap should be in place. In order to avoid chipping the end of the reed with the cap, the upper portion of the cap should be placed lightly against the curved portion of the mouthpiece and slid into position keeping contact with the mouthpiece.

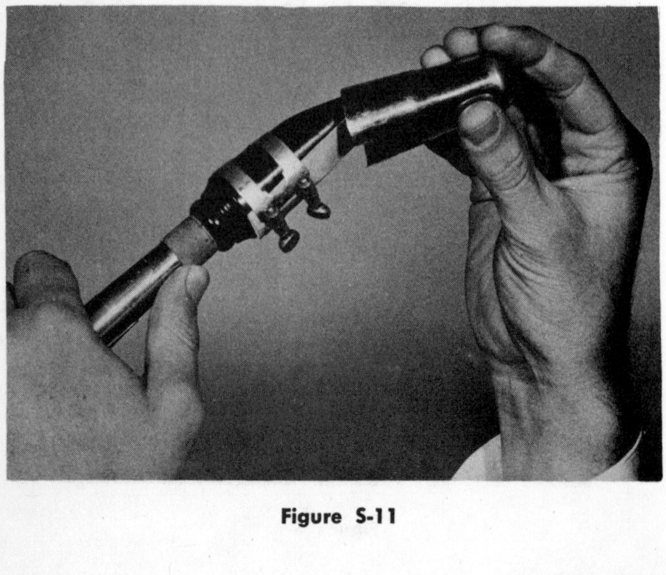

Figure S-11

Common Faults in Assembly

There are various incorrect procedures in assembling a saxophone which are commonly seen among students. The younger the student and the less experienced he is the more often he violates the best procedures. Advanced players have learned through experience the value of careful assembly, and rarely, if ever, deviate from an accepted method of preparing his instrument for playing, although he won't always follow exactly the procedures previously outlined. If the opportunity arises, observe carefully how a professional saxophone player takes his instrument from the case and puts it together, the care and detail with which the reed is put on the mouthpiece, and the way in which the instrument is tested to assure that everything is operating properly.

The following items are the most frequent faults:

1. *Holding the part incorrectly.* This puts undue pressure on keys and rods which eventually forces them out of adjustment. Bent keys rub against each other and move sluggishly or stick; bent rods cause the key to stick against its pivot screw; pad cups bent out of line even very slightly will cause the pad to leak.

2. *Failure to grease cork on neck.* Since there is only one cork which connects parts of the saxophone, unlike the clarinet, oboe, and bassoon, the young saxophone student frequently does not feel the necessity of having a container of cork grease in his case to the extent that players on the other instruments feel the need, and is apt to ignore this important procedure. Teachers should make sure that every student has cork grease in his case. Assuming that the cork is the proper diameter to fit the mouthpiece a small amount of grease applied once a week or oftener if necessary and spread evenly over the cork will make the mouthpiece slide into place easily. Excess grease must be wiped off with a soft cloth.

Corks which are too large for the mouthpiece, or which are not greased make it difficult to put the mouthpiece in place and cause excess pressure against the mechanism of the instrument with the result of possible damage. If a cork is excessively tight after being greased, it may be rubbed down with very fine sandpaper to the proper size. Corks which are not the proper size or which are not greased are easily damaged by forcing the mouthpiece on and will crack or tear making the mouthpiece even more difficult to put in place, and will eventually break off entirely.

3. *Bent or out-of-line connecting lever.* The connecting lever which projects from the top of the body of the saxophone, fitting under a metal circle on the neck to operate the upper octave key, is the most vulnerable key on the instrument because of its exposed position. It is frequently bent in the case because the student neglects to use the protective plug provided with the instrument. The instrument will fit solidly

Checklist for Assembly

Observe the student in the operation of assembling the saxophone and check the following items. Incorrect items for older students should not be called to their attention until the entire process is completed; younger students should be corrected immediately. If any mistake is made the entire process should be repeated until perfect.

	Yes	No	Comments
1. Protective plug in place in the end of the body?			
2. Cork on the neck examined to see that it was well greased?			
3. Neck strap put around neck before assembly started?			
4. Body of instrument picked up by bell away from any keys?			
5. Body of instrument immediately attached to neck strap?			
6. Connecting sleeve on neck examined and/or wiped clean?			
7. Neck held properly during placement on body?			
8. Neck properly aligned with body of instrument?			
9. Mouthpiece held properly during placement on cork?			
10. Ligature placed on mouthpiece before reed.			
11. Reed correctly placed on mouthpiece.			
12. Ligature tightened to proper degree.			

in the case only if this plug is in place. When the plug is missing the body of the instrument is free in the case and this connecting lever is bent.

A second cause of a bent connecting lever is the failure of the student to hold the neck properly during the process of assembly, allowing the ring under which the lever fits to hit the lever, or by twisting the neck too far from side to side which, on some instruments, will cause the ring to press against the lever. Remind the student to hold the neck properly, and to keep the eyes on this lever while the neck is being put in place. A bent lever will stick and cause difficulties in the operation of the octave key, or will cause the automatic second octave key to function improperly.

An out of line connecting lever, that is one which while it is not bent is not properly aligned with the neck through improper alignment of the neck and body of the instrument, will not allow proper operation of the octave key. Usually the result is that the pad on the octave key on the neck will not close firmly and it is impossible or difficult to play any notes on the instrument in the lower octave. Somewhat less frequently the result is that the connecting lever will not open the pad on the neck, and tones in the second octave are difficult or impossible to produce. The problem of an out-of-line connecting lever is usually a product of a poor holding and playing position for the instrument. Check the holding position, body position, and hand position and correct as needed.

4. *Bent keys or rods.* Bent keys or rods are most frequently the result of improper assembly of the instrument. The clusters of keys played by the left and right forefingers are the most vulnerable to damage because of their exposed location on the instrument. Other keys, especially the cups and pads covering the holes on the top of the instrument may also be bent

out-of-line during the process of assembly or disassembly.

Even if the keys or rods are not bent to the point of causing leaks they should be realigned by an expert repairman as soon as they are discovered. They must be removed from the instrument for straightening—never attempt to straighten a key while it is on the instrument. This puts tremendous pressure on the posts and pivot screws and can easily break them, making a major repair job out of a minor one. It is best to leave these adjustments to an expert who has the proper knowledge and tools.

5. *Reed improperly placed on the mouthpiece.* The way in which the reed is placed on the mouthpiece determines to a large degree how the instrument will respond. Inexperienced players do not understand the importance of perfect reed placement, and teachers must check constantly to see that it is done properly.

Check first to see that it is properly centered both at the tip and at the butt. A reed which is crooked is hard to blow, squeaks, and does not respond properly. If the reed is centered properly in relation to the sides of the mouthpiece, check the distance of its tip from the tip of the mouthpiece. When looking directly across the tip of the reed toward the mouthpiece just a hairline of black of the mouthpiece should be seen. Reeds which are too far down from the tip or which extend past the tip of the mouthpiece require greater wind pressure to produce a tone than when they are properly placed. There are minor deviations from this rule of placement which can be used in emergencies which are discussed elsewhere.

HOLDING POSITIONS FOR THE SAXOPHONE

The manner and position in which the saxophone is held affect both directly and indirectly such important musical items as tone quality, intonation, and technical facility. The proper position is one in which the body is in a comfortable erect position, in which the hands and arms fall naturally into position, and which permits the formation and development of the best embouchure, breath control, and technical facility.

Authorities are in virtually unanimous agreement on what the proper playing positions are for all the instruments in the saxophone family, and the ones given here follow this standard. Basic seated, standing, and rest positions are given here, with details of hand and finger positions in the next section.

Alto Saxophone

Seated Position. The saxophone is held to the right of the body with the instrument resting against the side of the leg. The body of the instrument is slightly out of the vertical position with the bottom slightly further back. The right arm is relaxed with the elbow pushed back very slightly to put the right hand into the best playing position. This angle is critical as it puts the mouth-

Figure S-12. Seated Position (Front View).

Figure S-13. Seated Position (Side View).

piece into the mouth at the slight upward angle to permit the best embouchure formation. The mouthpiece is adjusted on the neck cork so that the reed is absolutely flat with the lower lip and teeth.

The weight of the instrument is on the neck strap, and the instrument is balanced by the right and left thumbs and the mouth. Adjust the length of the neck strap so that the end of the mouthpiece touches the center of the lower lip. Head erect, chin up, eyes straight ahead, with shoulders up but relaxed. Elbows hang free from the body. Both feet flat on the floor. Shoulders and back must not touch the back of the chair when playing. Adjust the height of the music stand so that music can be easily read in this position. When two students are playing from the same music, angle the chairs slightly toward the center of the stand so that the position of the body and instrument can remain correct.

Standing Position. The position of the instrument when the player is standing should be identical with the seated position; only the position of the body itself is changed. Since the instrument doesn't rest against the body in the standing position, it is held in position by the right thumb. Stand erect with feet slightly apart, one foot ahead of the other to help maintain balance. Head remains erect, with chin up and eyes straight ahead. Shoulders up but relaxed, and elbows free from the body. Raise the music stand, if one is being used, so that the head does not tilt downward. Every player should regularly spend a portion of his practice time standing to become at ease playing in a standing position.

Figure S-15. Standing Position (Side View).

Rest Position. The Alto saxophone falls quite naturally into a rest position across the body with the curve of the bell resting on the right leg. The neck strap must be left in position on the instrument. In this position the player is relaxed, is free to arrange music, and the instrument can be returned to playing position quickly and efficiently.

Figure S-14. Standing Position (Front View).

Figure S-16. Rest Position.

Tenor Saxophone

Seated Position. The Tenor saxophone is held to the right side of the body with the instrument resting against the side of the leg, the weight of the instrument on the neck strap. Adjust the length of the neck strap so that the end of the mouthpiece touches the center of the lower lip. No weight should be supported by the right thumb. The Tenor saxophone is further out of a vertical line—the bottom being further back—than the Alto. The neck of the instrument is a different shape than that of the Alto so that the mouthpiece will enter the mouth at the same angle as that of the Alto instrument.

Adjust the neck of the instrument so that it is at right angles with the mouth when the head is turned very slightly to the right. Adjust the mouthpiece so that the reed is absolutely flat on the lower lip and teeth. The instrument is balanced on the neck strap by the left and right thumbs and by the mouth. Head erect, chin up, eyes straight ahead, with shoulders up but relaxed. Elbows hang free from the body. Both feet flat on the floor. Turn the chair slightly to the right so that the right arm is not against the back. Shoulders and back do not contact the back of the chair while playing. Adjust the height of the music stand for easy reading so that the head is tilted neither up nor down.

Figure S-18. Seated Position (Side View).

Figure S-17. Seated Position (Front View).

Standing Position. The position of the instrument when the player is standing is identical with that in the seated position; only the position of the body itself is changed. Since the instrument doesn't rest against the body in the

Figure S-19. Standing Position (Front View).

standing position, it is held in position by a forward pressure of the right thumb. Stand erect with feet slightly apart, one foot ahead of the other to help maintain balance. Head remains erect, with chin up and eyes straight ahead. Shoulders up but relaxed, and elbows free from the body. Adjust the music stand so that the head does not tilt downward. Practice in the standing position regularly.

Figure S-20. Standing Position (Side View).

Figure S-21. Rest Position.

Rest Position. The Tenor saxophone falls quite naturally into a rest position across the body with the curve of the bell resting on the right leg. The neck strap must be left in position on the instrument. From this position the instrument can be quickly returned to playing position.

Figure S-22. Seated Position (Front View).[2]

Baritone Saxophone

Seated Position. The Baritone saxophone may be supported by a neck strap or by a stand. These photographs show the instrument in position held by a neck strap, and the following series with a stand. The bulk of this instrument causes it to be considerably out of the vertical position in order to place the hands in a comfortable playing position. The exact angle is determined by the angle at which the mouthpiece enters the mouth. The instrument rests against the player's right leg or against the chair and is balanced by the right and left thumbs and the mouth. The right thumb must support no weight Adjust the length of the neck strap so that the tip of the mouthpiece touches the center of the lower lip.

2. The bell of the instrument photographed is longer than standard to provide for the optional low "A."

Adjust the neck of the instrument so that it is at right angles with the mouth when the head is turned very slightly to the right. Adjust the mouthpiece so that the reed is absolutely flat on the lower lip and teeth. Head erect, chin up, eyes straight ahead, with shoulders up but relaxed. Elbows hang free from the body. Both feet flat on the floor. Turn the chair slightly to the right so that the right arm is not against the back. Shoulders and back of the body do not contact the back of the chair while playing. Adjust the height of the music stand for easy reading so that the head is tilted neither up nor down.

Standing Position. The Baritone saxophone, because of its weight and bulk, is not comfortable to play in a standing position although some dance band players do so. If it is played in the standing position, the position of the instrument must be identical with that in the seated position so that the same embouchure, breath support, and hand position can be used.

Figure S-23. Seated Position (Side View).[3]

Rest Position. The Baritone saxophone must be lifted into its rest position across the legs, but once in this position it is comfortably balanced and held securely by the neck strap. The player must allow several seconds to put the instrument back into playing position.

Figure S-24. Rest Position.

Use of Stand. The use of a stand to support the Baritone saxophone and to hold it in the proper playing position is common with professional players and is highly recommended for school musicians. These stands are readily available, and are provided with rollers so that they can be easily moved into position. A metal band with a plate and a slot which fits onto the stand is put around the bell of the instrument. This remains on the instrument permanently and permits it to be taken from the stand and put into its case.

The height, the front to back angle with the player, and the side to side angle with the player must be adjustable so that the instrument can be adjusted to be in the same perfect playing position when on the stand as when it is held with the neck strap. These adjustments are critical and are different for each player, but once they are made they are locked into position. Young players are especially appreciative of the stand for the instrument as it removes the strain of the weight of the instrument and gives them complete freedom of movement. Since the stand holds the instrument securely, and moves easily on rollers no rest position is necessary.

3. Ibid.

Figure S-25. Front View of Instrument in Stand.

Figure S-26. Side View of Instrument in Stand.

Soprano Saxophone

The Soprano saxophone being small enough is constructed in a straight line like the oboe and clarinet. Some Soprano saxophones made in the same shape as the Alto with the up-turned bell are still in use, although this shape is no longer available in new instruments. If the curved bell instrument is used, the directions given for the Alto saxophone apply to it. If the straight Soprano is being used it is held directly in front of the center of the body, with the instrument at an angle of thirty-five to forty-five degrees with the body.

This makes a more acute angle at which the mouthpiece enters the embouchure, similar to that for the clarinet, but Soprano saxophone mouthpieces are constructed for this angle. Students transferring to the Soprano from another instrument in the saxophone family have a tendency to hold the instrument too far out from the body so that the mouthpiece feels the same in the mouth as it did on the previous instrument. This should be discouraged and corrected as an angle which is too great will produce an open uncontrolled sound. The Soprano saxophone properly played produces a clear, bell-like tone of great power and beauty.

Bass Saxophone

If the Bass saxophone is used, and it makes a valuable addition to any concert band, it must be held in a stand. The instrument is simply too heavy for anyone to play comfortably for long if the weight is supported by a neck strap. The stand for this instrument must be carefully adjusted in the same fashion described for the Baritone saxophone in order to get the proper angle of the reed with the embouchure. The size of the mouthpiece and reed permit little deviation from this angle if the proper tonal response is to be achieved.

Common Faults in Holding Positions

The holding position for an instrument can further rapid musical development, or it can make real progress difficult. Teachers must continually check student positions for it is important that any deviations from a normal position be corrected immediately before the incorrect position becomes habitual. Once an incorrect position is established, it is extremely difficult to correct. Students themselves must learn to feel the right position, and should be encouraged to check their positions daily in front of a mirror both at school and at home. A full-length mirror is an integral part of the well-equipped instrumental room of every school.

The following are the most commonly found faults in holding positions on the saxophones:

1. *Bottom of instrument too far back.* Perhaps the most common fault in the holding position, and one which causes problems both in embouchure and technique, is that of holding the bottom of the instrument too far back so that the side of the instrument is resting against the hip rather than the leg.

An instrument in this position pulls the right elbow so far back that it must be held up which develops muscular tension in the arm and shoulders which in turn causes problems in finger technique in the right hand as well as adversely affecting breathing. With the instrument too far back, unless the head is tilted downward which is highly undesirable, the angle at which the mouthpiece enters the embouchure is incorrect and results in a thin reedy tone quality in most instances. If the head is tilted downward to keep the angle of the mouthpiece in the proper relationship with the embouchure, breathing and breath control suffer because of the cramped position of the throat.

The correct angle of the saxophone in its front-to-back relationship with the body is determined by the angle at which the mouthpiece enters the embouchure with the chin up in the normal position. No other consideration is pertinent. The exact angle is somewhat dependent on the physical size of the player and adjustments may need to be made to achieve the proper angle of the mouthpiece. If the mouthpiece angle is correct then the instrument will fall into the correct position where both the right and left arms and hands will be in a comfortable relaxed position on the instrument, and the body held in an equally comfortable erect position.

This problem may be caused by having the neck strap adjusted so that it is too short which pulls the instrument back to release the pressure on the player's neck. Put the instrument in the correct playing position—then adjust the neck strap to the proper length. Check photographs to note the difference in the front to back relationship between the Alto, Tenor, and Baritone instruments.

The Soprano saxophone which is straight like an oboe or clarinet, must be held at an angle of approximately forty degrees with the body just as the clarinet is held. The mouthpiece of this instrument is designed for the clarinet angle in the embouchure rather than the angle called for on the other instruments of the family. The Baritone and Bass instruments on stands require that the stand be carefully adjusted for the angle under consideration, and the assistance of the teacher in making this adjustment, as well as the adjustment for height, is virtually mandatory for all but the most experienced players.

2. *Head inclined downward*. This problem is encountered in students on all stages of development, and may or may not be associated with the problem just discussed. When the head is inclined downward, the neck is constricted which restricts the flow of air through the instrument, and support of the embouchure around the mouthpiece is difficult to achieve. If the instrument itself is in the proper position and head is inclined downward the support of the lower teeth is moved to a point forward of that provided by the upper teeth on the top of the mouthpiece, producing an underbite with which it is virtually impossible to develop an acceptable tone quality. The correction for this condition is to insist that the instrument be in the proper playing position and that the head be erect with the chin up, and the eyes straight ahead. The use of a large mirror is a necessity so that the student can check his position frequently.

3. *Slouched body*. Varying degrees of poor posture occur almost universally—shoulders slumped or curved forward, leaning against the back of the chair with spine curved, bending forward so that the shoulders sag downward, feet crossed or hung over a rung on the chair or various combinations of these.

Poor posture affects breathing and breath control to the point that students may find it impossible to support the tone adequately. It pulls the arms, and consequently the fingers out of position making technique rough. The importance of good posture cannot be overemphasized. It is basic to musical development, and the wise instructor will maintain a continual vigilance to be sure that it is established and maintained by every student.

4. *Adjustment of neck strap*. The adjustment of the neck strap on the saxophone of any size allows little deviation from the correct length if it is to support the instrument with head and body in the best positions. The standard adjustment of the neck strap is one, with the instrument in playing position, which allows the mouthpiece to fall naturally into the embouchure without tilting the head up or down.

An adjustment which is too long or too short forces the student to raise or lower his head which is not only a muscular strain if continued over a period of time, but also forces the embouchure into an unnatural formation. It is important that the neck strap be one which will maintain the desired length without slipping when the weight of the instrument is put on it. The same comments made concerning the adjustment of the neck strap apply to the height of the stand used for the Baritone or Bass instrument.

HAND POSITIONS

The same basic hand position is used on all instruments in the saxophone family, the only difference being the slightly wider spread of the fingers as the size of the instrument gets larger. This position may be defined as one in which the fingers fall naturally into place and are completely relaxed without any muscular tension in the fingers, wrists, arms or shoulders. It is only in this perfectly relaxed condition that it is possible to develop rapid, accurate and dependable facility.

Proper position and shape of the hands on the instrument must be stressed from the very beginning of saxophone study, and checked in detail regularly until it is habitual. If the student is transferring to the saxophone from the clarinet or another woodwind instrument and has achieved correct hand positions on the previous instrument, achieving the proper positions on the saxophone will come quite naturally with some instruction.

Even the youngest students can achieve this correct position, and indeed, progress much faster with the correct placement than with one which deviates slightly. Many of the difficulties beginners have in playing from one octave range to the other, in crossing the break between C-sharp and D, in playing the lowest notes, etc., can be traced to faulty hand and finger positions. Poor hand position becomes even more of a handicap when the student attempts to extend the range into the third octave.

It is very easy for beginners who have not acquired a feel for the instrument to deviate to a position which temporarily feels better or gives them a greater sense of security. It is a truism that the proper placement of hands develops a faster sense of security and better technical facility sooner than an incorrect one. Perhaps the greatest service a teacher can give the student is to insist that he establish and maintain this correct position.

The following step-by-step procedure for establishing the hand position should be studied thoroughly, preferably with an instrument with which to experiment. Study both the text and the photographs carefully until they are perfectly clear. The "Guide Position" which is given is the fundamental position for hands and fingers and should be maintained at all times except when the fingering for a note involves moving a finger temporarily to another location. This position on the instrument may be compared to the position on the typewriter which makes it possible to develop speed and accuracy so quickly on that machine. It is used on the saxophone for exactly the same reason.

A. Right Hand Position

1. Figure S-27. The right thumb contacts the thumb rest on the flesh to the side of and at the base of the nail. The ball of the thumb is against the body or a plate on the instrument. Notice the "U" shape formation of the thumb and forefinger which put the fingers into position on the top of the instrument. Notice also that the thumb rest on this particular instrument can be adjusted up and down for the best and most comfortable position for the player's hand. Not all instruments have this feature.

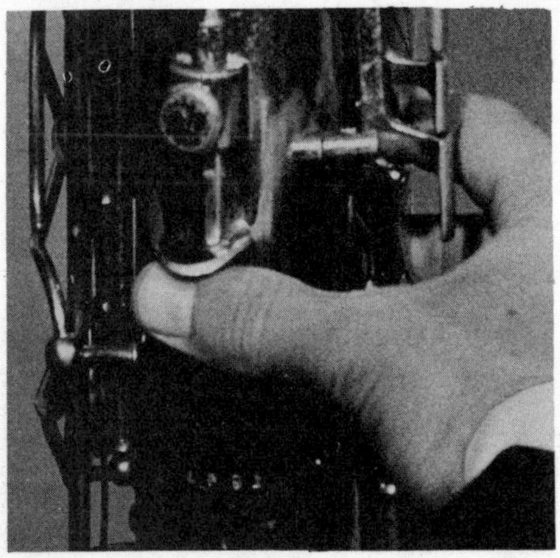

Figure S-27

2. Figure S-28. The right little finger touches lightly the C key, and the remaining fingers fall in a natural curve without tension and contact the pearl buttons of their tone holes with the bottom of the finger beneath the forward portion of the nail.

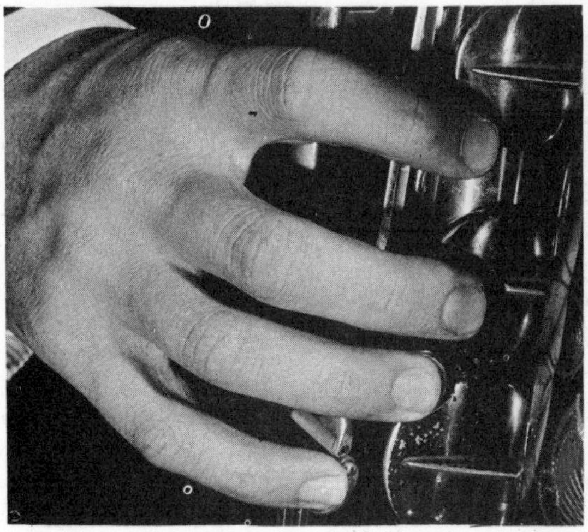

Figure S-28

B. Left Hand Position

1. Figure S-29 and Figure S-30. The left thumb has the function of operating the octave key. It is placed at

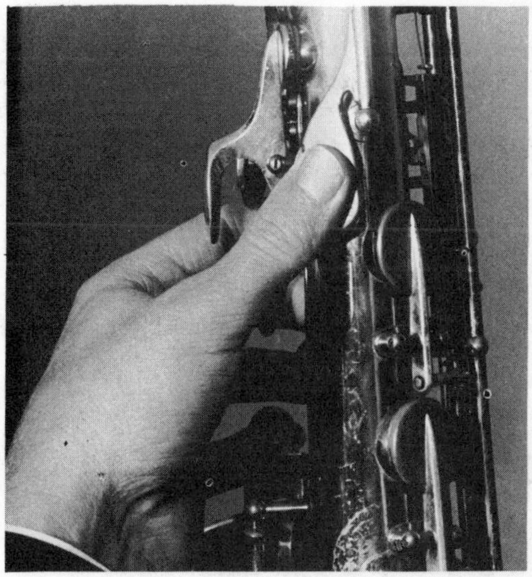

Figure S-29

a diagonal angle across the instrument so that the fleshy part of the ball is on the plate provided for it, and the tip of the finger is touching but not pressing the octave key.

Figure S-30

2. Figure S-31. The octave key is controlled by vertical movements of the first joint of the thumb. The placement of the octave key on some instruments requires that the thumb be lifted off the plate on which it rests as in the photograph, while others permit the octave to be depressed by a smaller vertical movement of the first joint so that the ball of the thumb remains in contact with the plate. The latter mechanical arrangement is somewhat more efficient from the standpoint of technique.

Figure S-31

3. Figure S-32. The left little finger touches lightly the G-sharp key, and the remaining fingers fall into a natural curve without tension to contact the pearl buttons of their tone holes with the bottom of the finger beneath the forward portion of the nail.

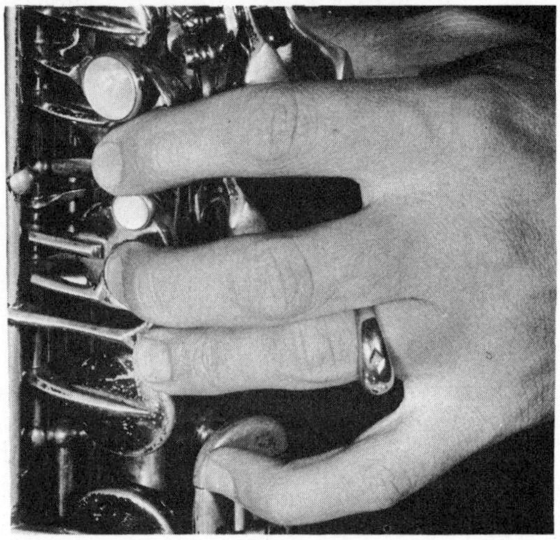

Figure S-32

C. Guide Position

1. Figure S-33. With the thumbs and fingers in the proper positions, the wrists are almost flat, and the thumbs and forefingers of both hands form a "U." If this shape is a "V" the wrists are out of place and the student will have difficulty reaching the little finger keys.

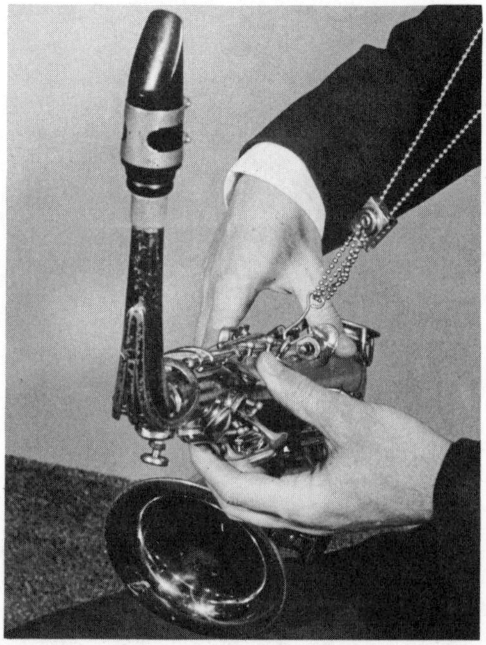

Figure S-33

2. Figure S-34. With the thumbs and little fingers in place as described above, and the remaining fingers touching their respective buttons, a guide position is established which should be maintained constantly. Note that the fingers are at approximately a ninety degree angle to the instrument. Avoid more than the slightest deviation from this right angle relationship. The entire finger moves from the knuckle and closes the tone holes with a snap or click, pressing just hard enough to close the tone holes. Avoid using too much pressure with the fingers. The fingers preferably should be in contact with their key or pearl button at all times. Avoid lifting the fingers high above the keys and closing them by pounding.

Figure S-34

Movement of Fingers from Guide Position

Fingerings for certain notes on the instrument tend to pull the hands out of position unless fingers are moved efficiently and with minimum motion of both the finger involved and the entire hand. Some keys on the saxophone require that the hand be pulled out of position in order to reach them, and when this occurs the hand should be returned immediately to the perfect guide position. These movements do not seem to come naturally to all students, but can be readily developed if they are understood and the teacher provides music to practice which isolates the problem. A constant check on finger positions for these keys is necessary until the movements become habitual. The following are the most commonly used movements in this respect. Study both the text and the photograph, and try the movement on an instrument if possible, until they are clearly understood.

1. Figures S-35 and S-36. First finger right hand playing B-flat: 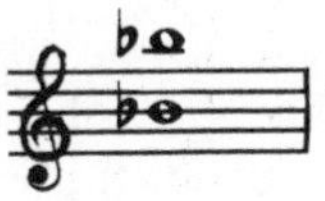 This key, called the side B-flat, is contacted and depressed by the first joint of the right forefinger. The finger is straightened and moved directly down from the knuckle to press the key. The second, third, and little fingers of the hand must remain in the basic guide position. Avoid pressing the key by rotating the wrist which pulls the remaining fingers out of position.

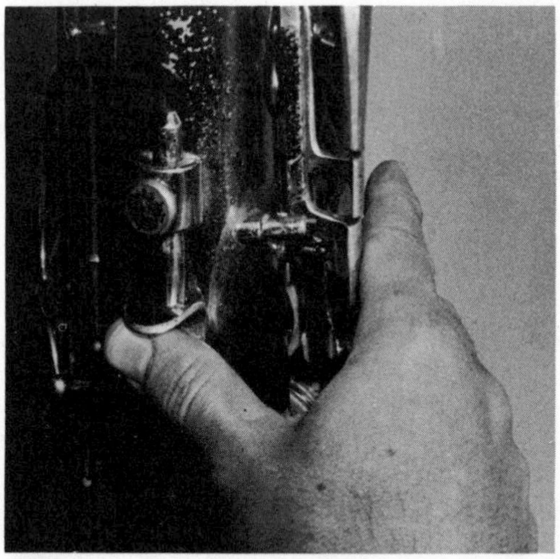

Figure S-35

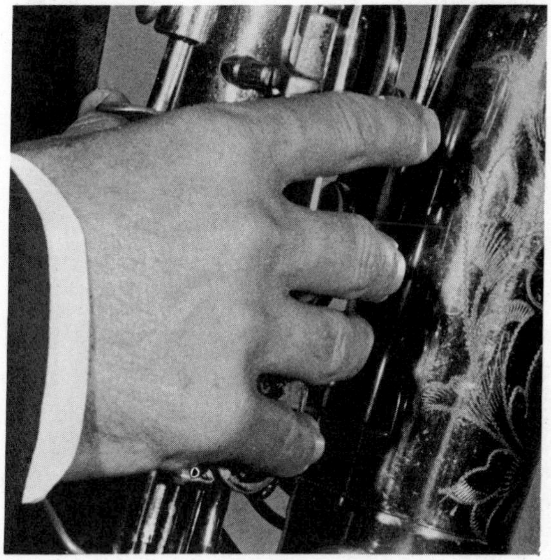

Figure S-36

2. The center key of this group of three operated by the side of the right forefinger is one of the two regular fingerings for C: 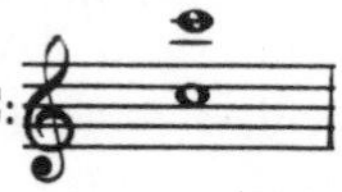. On most instruments it can be conveniently operated in the same way as the B-flat key, by extending only the forefinger slightly upwards. Keep the second, third, and little fingers in the guide position. Players with small hands and/or short fingers may have to use a movement similar to that described below for F. In any event, use a minimum of hand motion.

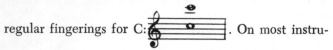

3. Figure S-37. First finger right hand playing E:  This is the top key played by the right forefinger and its distance from the finger requires that the wrist be rotated very slightly to the left in order that it can be reached. It is contacted by the left side of the finger between the knuckle and first joint. The little finger will be pulled off its guide key, but the movement of the wrist and hand must be as small as possible. Avoid large movements of the forearm, and elevating the elbow to reach this key.

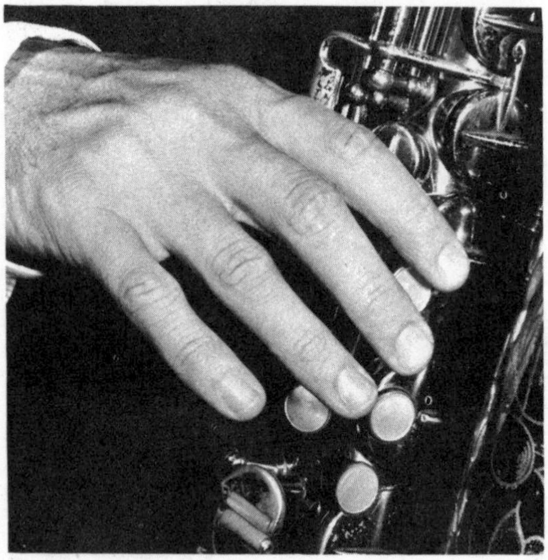

Figure S-37

4. Figure S-38. First finger left hand playing D:  This key lies directly beneath the knuckle of the first finger and is depressed by the bottom of the knuckle with a slight downward movement of the knuckles of the hand. The second, third, and little fingers of the hand must be kept in the guide position. Avoid straightening and lifting all the fingers of the hand while depressing this key. Avoid also depressing the key by rotating the wrist. Both of these are common faults with students.

Figure S-38

5. Figure S-39. First finger left hand playing E-flat:  Two keys operated by the first finger are involved in this fingering, and both lie conveniently beneath the finger when the hand is in the guide position. The D key, as explained above, is depressed by the bottom of the knuckle. The E-flat key is depressed by the finger beneath the first joint. Keep the second, third and little fingers in the guide position. Avoid both straightening all the fingers of the hand and a rotating of the wrist when playing this note.

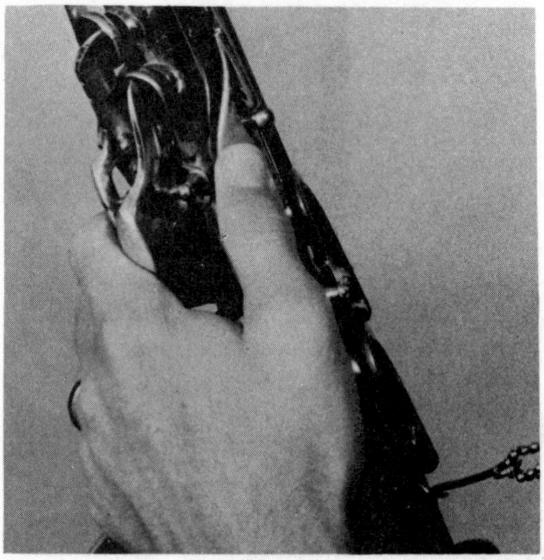

Figure S-39

6. The third side key of the cluster of three on the upper left side of the instrument lies directly beneath and is operated by the bottom of the *second* finger at the first joint. It is added to the D and E-flat keys played by the first finger of the left hand, and the E key operated by the first finger of the right hand to produce the high F: 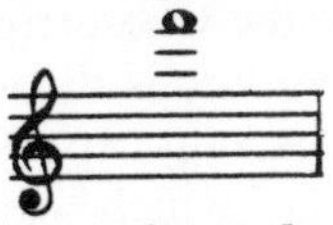 To open this key the second finger is straightened slightly and moved downward. The third and little fingers will have to be moved slightly from the guide position in order for this finger to operate the key, but this movement should be kept at a minimum. Avoid straightening all the fingers, rolling the wrist, and pulling the hand too far away from the guide position.

7. Figure S-40. First finger left hand on key 1x—the pearl button above the normal position for the first finger. This key is involved in a standard alternate fingering for the high F, and opens the same tone hole as the side F key. It is operated by moving the first finger from its normal position to this key, making a wider spacing between the first and second fingers. Use of this key is a valuable asset to good technique.

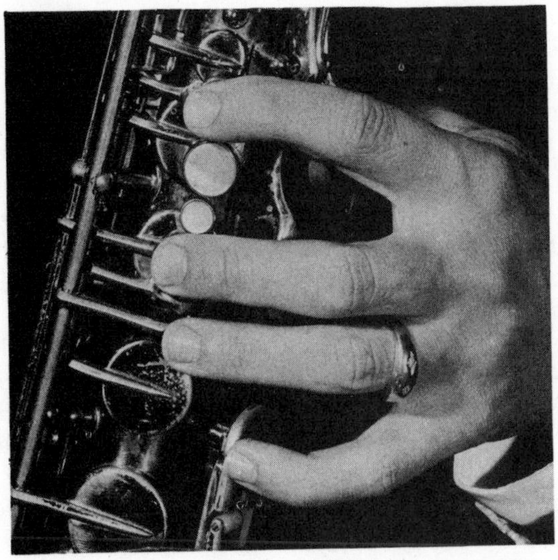

Figure S-40

8. Figure S-41. Little finger left hand on low B-flat key:  The cluster of keys played by the left little finger play, in addition to the G-sharp, low B-flat, B-natural and C-sharp. The shape of these keys varies considerably in different brands as a result of the effort to make them more accessible and easy to use. They are depressed by the bottom of the tip of the little finger which must be kept in a curved position. Students with small hands will have difficulty in reaching the low B-flat key which requires considerable extension of the finger. Avoid, if at all possible, rolling the wrist and hand down to put the little finger closer to these keys. Keep the hand as close to the guide position as possible. These keys are provided with rollers so that the finger may slide more easily from one to another in playing legato passages. Considerable practice is necessary to gain facility with these keys.

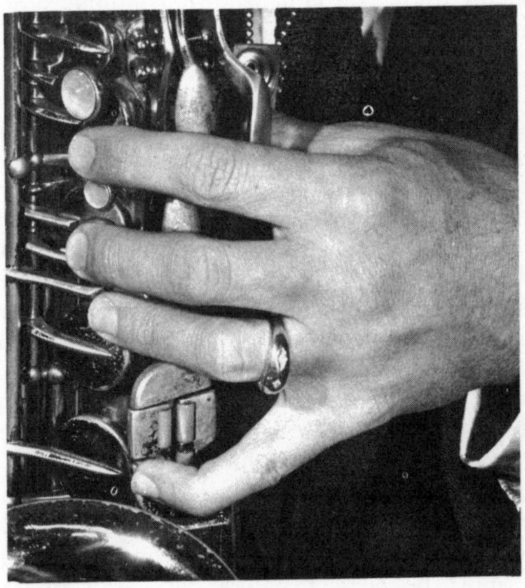

Figure S-41

Common Faults in Hand and Finger Position

Because of the nature of the mechanics of the instrument and the fact that the saxophone was invented rather than being the result of decades of devolpment by trial and error the hand and finger positions are worked out to best fit the human hand and the saxophone student has a considerable advantage over students of the other woodwinds in this respect. This relative perfection in the mechanical arrangement is disadvantageous in a way in that sounds can be produced and a small amount of technique developed with hand and finger positions deviating greatly from the proper positions to the degree which if applied to the clarinet or bassoon no sequence of sounds could be produced.

Unfortunately, the saxophone does not demand correct holding, hand or finger positions as a prerequisite to a minimum of success, and for this reason the teacher's attention is not called aurally to a poor position on the instrument. A conscious effort should be made to check position on the saxophone as regularly and with the same degree of exactitude as for other woodwind instruments.

A player whose hand and finger positions are poor develops facility slowly and seldom if ever progresses to the point where he would be considered a good performer. A beginning student who persists in quickly establishing the proper positions makes rapid progress in acquiring technical facility. There is a direct relationship between how the instrument is held, hand and finger positions and success on the instrument. Many potentially fine players are discouraged in the beginning stages because their teacher does not insist on the best position.

It is, therefore, of the utmost importance that proper positions be established from the very beginning of saxophone study, through careful continuous checking by the teacher and by the student himself who must check his positions in a mirror daily until they are established. Some teachers take the attitude that positions are not important for elementary school beginners, and that poor positions can be corrected when the student becomes more advanced. Nothing could be more unfortunate than this attitude, since many students are discouraged from continuing, and even those who do continue with the instrument have great difficulty in correcting nonstandard positions once the muscular pattern has been established incorrectly. It is so easy and simple to do it correctly in the beginning and so difficult to correct that every teacher who is truly interested in his pupil's progress will do everything possible to establish the proper habits from the very beginning.

The common faults which are listed here occur over and over again in students. Some of them are directly related to the holding position of the instrument itself which must be correct before hand and finger positions can be established. All of these faults have an adverse affect on facility and technique—making some progressions rough, some difficult and others impossible.

1. *Left thumb.* The left thumb must be held in the diagonal angle described in the holding position, with the pad of thumb on the button, and with the corner of the finger operating the octave key. The thumb must never lose contact with the instrument while playing. There are several common deviations from this standard position:

(a) The thumb is held almost parallel with the body of the instrument rather than diagonal. While it is possible to operate the octave key from this position, the fingers are pulled out of position on top of the instrument frequently to the point that the student cannot reach the keys operated by the little finger. Remedial measures include changing the direction of the thumb to the diagonal so that the thumb and forefinger form the "U" as pictured above, and insisting that the left little finger remain in contact with its guide key.

(b) The thumb slides back and forth over the button to open and close the octave key rather than operating it with a vertical movement of the joint. This results in sluggish and inaccurate operation of the octave key with resultant technical difficulties. The best remedial measure is to position the thumb properly and then have the student play octave intervals up from the first to the second octaves in which the only difference in fingering is the opening of the octave key. Scales in octaves provide readily accessible material. It should be noted that slurring the octave interval down from the second to the first octave on notes where the fingering is the same except for the octave key is difficult on the saxophone so the slurs should be only up. The following is typical of other material which can be used for this purpose:

(c) The thumb is removed entirely from the button and held free from the instrument when playing in the first octave. Beginners especially are susceptible to this difficulty, and frequently have trouble replacing the thumb in the proper position when it is needed for the octave key. Insist that the left thumb be in contact with its button at all times, for if it isn't the basic holding position of the instrument is difficult to maintain.

2. *Right thumb.* The position of the right thumb is critical for both balancing the instrument in the proper playing position, and for putting the fingers of the right hand into the best guide position for developing facility. The position of the right thumb on the saxophone is easier to achieve and maintain than on the oboe and clarinet where the thumb actually supports the weight of the instrument. There are two common faults with the position of the right thumb on the saxophone:

(a) Pushing the thumb too far under the instrument so that it contacts the rest too far from the end of the finger. Some students contact the support at the first joint of the thumb and some even higher. The thumb support should contact the side of the finger at the base of the nail as shown in the photograph illustrating the right hand position. This condition of contacting the support too far up on the thumb can frequently be detected by merely looking at the student's thumb since an incorrect position will cause a callous on any player who spends enough time playing the instrument to be considered an average performer. No callous will develop if the thumb is in the proper position. When the thumb is too far under the instrument the fingers on top are forced into an unnaturally acute angle so that the fingers contact the key buttons with the tip rather than the natural pad on the finger beneath the nail. Younger players especially have difficulty in contacting the buttons with the natural pad since their fingers are short, so it is even more important for them to have the thumb properly positioned. Further, when the fingers are at an acute angle which approaches the instrument directly, there is considerable muscular tension which makes rapid and accurate coordination of the fingers difficult.

When this condition is corrected with intermediate or advanced students there is a noticeable improvement in facility and smoothness of technique in the space of a few days.

(b) A second, and less frequent fault, is that of contacting the thumb rest with the nail itself so that the side of the finger rather than the ball is against the body of the instrument. This puts the pressure of the forward support of the instrument in such a way that a great deal of muscular tension is needed to steady the instrument and the student tires quickly. It also turns the hand slightly downward making it dififcult for the fingers to contact their keys in the correct way. Fortunately this faulty position is easy to correct if discovered before it becomes habitual. Students are grateful for the correction since they are immediately more comfortable playing the instrument.

3. *Little fingers.* The guide position calls for each little finger to be in contact with a key so that they will be in a position to move rapidly and easily to other keys which they operate. If they are not on the guide keys, then there is a slight delay in putting the finger in place, making for rough technique. Beginners whose little finger positions have not been established frequently go so far as to take their instrument out of the mouth to look at the keys to see exactly where the little finger should go. If the fingers are on the proper guide key they soon move naturally to the desired location.

The most frequently found fault in the placement of the little fingers is to find them sticking straight up in the air—a tense position which also tenses up the other fingers. The left little finger is frequently placed underneath the keys, apparently to help keep the instrument in playing position. The best, and perhaps the only, remedial measure is to insist that the fingers remain in the guide position actually touching their respective keys.

4. *Finger positions.* If the thumbs and little fingers are properly located, the remaining six fingers should fall naturally into place on their respective buttons. The best procedure for keeping these fingers in position is to insist that they remain in contact at all times with the buttons during the beginning stage of development. It is permissible for more advanced students to lift the fingers no more than one-half inch directly above the buttons. There are three commonly found faults in the positions of these fingers, each having an adverse effect on technical development.

(a) The fingers are not curved into the most natural relaxed position, where there is a complete absence of tension so they move quickly and accurately from the knuckle. The correct curve is established by the "U" shape formed by the thumb and forefinger, with the other fingers following the curve of the forefinger. An incorrect position of these fingers is caused by an incorrect position of the thumb or by the wrist being either too low (usually) or too high. Check and correct as necessary although some persistence will be needed to correct a long established habit.

(b) Lifting the fingers too high—more than one-half inch above the buttons—is rather common, even among advanced players, and causes unevenness in rapidly moving passages. Since the fingers usually are unequal distances above the buttons, it takes a slightly longer space of time for the finger highest above to close the key than it does for the finger which is closest. This space of time is microscopic, but it is enough that unevenness can be heard, and in less advanced players actually produces the unwanted grace note. It is signicant to note that this fault is never found among the finest players.

(c) Contacting the buttons with the tips of the fingers is most frequently encountered with inexperienced players, but is occasionally found with more advanced students. It happens when the fingers do not fall in the natural curve described above, and may occur even though the remainder of the hand position is correct. It is frequently the result of a faulty position of the right thumb (see above), and if this is the case is easily corrected. Using the tips of the fingers to contact the buttons causes the fingers to be in an unnatural position creating muscular tension and stiff movements. The remedial action for this problem is to insist that the front portion of the pad of the finger directly beneath the nail be centered on the button.

On most instruments these pearl buttons are slightly concave which assists in finding the best position. It should be noted at this point that procedure of centering the ball of the finger tip over the pearl button in the same manner in which the finger is centered over a tone hole of the clarinet and bassoon is not necessary on the saxophone, although players with small hands will find it convenient to do so. Mature players should contact the buttons somewhat forward on the finger in relationship to the center of the natural pad of the finger.

5. *Angle of hands.* The standard placement of the hands on the saxophone places the fingers of both hands at an almost perfect right angle to the instrument. The mechanism of the instrument is constructed in such a way that this approach is easily achieved. With the hands in this position the keys, with the exceptions previously discussed, lie well under the fingers and hand so that all can be reached with a minimum of displacement of the hand. Insist on the correct angle from the very beginning of study, having the student check this in a mirror if he is having a problem.

6. *Side keys.* The side keys played by the first finger of the right hand and the first and second fingers of the left hand are normally not introduced until the student has established his basic hand positions and has acquired some technical facility on the intsrument.

Checklist for Holding and Hand Positions

The following list of items provides a thorough check of holding positions and hand positions, and is limited to the seated positions for the instruments. The check should be performed while the student is playing and preferably when he is not aware that the check is being made. Any items which are checked "No" should be corrected with the deviation explained to the student, what effect it has on his playing, and why the correct position is important. Students make a more serious effort to correct mistakes if they thoroughly understand the reasons for them.

A. Holding Position

	Yes	No	Comments
1. Angle with front of body correct?			
2. Angle with side of body correct?			
3. Position of head correct?			
4. Neck strap properly adjusted?			
5. Shoulders up but relaxed?			
6. Elbows free from body?			
7. Body posture good?			
8. Feet in place?			
9. Height of music stand correct?			

B. Hand Positions

1. Right thumb contacting thumb rest properly?			
2. Left thumb at diagonal across instrument?			
3. Tip of left thumb above or touching octave key?			
4. Fingers curved?			
5. Right little finger touching guide key?			
6. Left little finger touching guide key?			
7. Thumbs and forefingers form a "U"?			
8. Fingers across instrument at right angle?			
9. Wrists virtually flat?			
10. Octave key operated by vertical movements of the first joint?			
11. Fingers contacting buttons at right place?			
12. Left side keys properly operated?			
13. Right side keys properly operated?			
14. Guide position consistently maintained?			

If the player has established his position properly, introduction and operation of these keys will pose no problem provided he is given careful instruction on how they are used along with study material with which to develop facility. Unless this is done, there is a tendency for students to pull the entire hand out of position to operate one of these keys which has an adverse effect on the entire basic hand position.

The key to success with the left-hand keys is to depress the key with the right part of the finger—the D key with the bottom of the knuckle of the first finger, the E-flat key the first finger at the first joint, the F key by the second finger at the first joint, while keeping the other fingers in or as close to the guide position as possible. When this is done properly students can acquire just as much facility with these keys as with any other keys on the instrument, and failure to do so is a product of improper operation.

The three side keys operated by the first finger of the right hand—B-flat, C, and high E require a minimum of movement with the hand, keeping as close to guide position as possible. The most common fault in their operation is found where the player removes his entire hand from the instrument and depresses these keys with the side of the finger with the rest of the hand helping to push. This makes slow, rough, and uncertain technique because of the time it takes to replace the hand in the guide position. To correct, first establish correct use of the B-flat key with the second, third, and little fingers in the guide position, and finally the F key pulling the hand as little from the guide position as necessary to reach the key.

EMBOUCHURE FORMATION

An embouchure may be defined as the formation of the performer's lips with supporting muscles, teeth and jaws in relation to the mouthpiece and reed which have to do with tone production. The criteria for a good embouchure may be summarized as follows. A good embouchure is one which over the entire range of the instrument: (1) produces (or has the potential of producing) a rich, full bodied, clear tone; (2) plays perfectly in tune; (3) allows the player to use the full scope of articulations from the hard short staccato to the smoothest legato at all dynamic levels and without adverse effect on the tone quality; (4) allows the player to use the full range of dynamics from the very softest to the very loudest under complete control and without affecting either pitch or tone quality; (5) and is controlled with a minimum amount of physical exertion; (6) once developed can be maintained with a reasonable amount of practice.

Conversely a poorly formed embouchure is one with which: (1) the tone quality is reedy, thin, nasal, or which changes quality from register to register on the instrument; (2) plays the upper register or lower register out of tune consistently, or with which it is difficult or impossible to adjust the pitch of individual tones; (3) produces staccato notes which are hard, with mechanical noises, or which have poor tone quality; (4) has a restricted dynamic range in which tonal body is lost at soft levels, and very loud levels impossible to produce or control; (5) requires an undue amount of physical exertion; (6) deteriorates rapidly without persistent practice.

There are considerable differences in the kinds of embouchure formations used on the saxophone, primarily because of the lack of any great number of artist-teachers to develop and set a standard. Investigation reveals, however, that there are only two basic saxophone embouchures in use by the better players, each subject to minor variations depending primarily on the concept of the desired tone quality. The major difference between the two is found in the shape of the lower lip, one embouchure bunches the lower lip to a greater or lesser degree, the other stretches it to a lesser or greater degree. For convenience and clarity the bunched lower lip formation is called a "Soft Cushion" and the stretched lower lip a "Hard Cushion," although the words soft and hard must not be taken literally.

The Soft Cushion Embouchure

The basic formation of the soft cushion embouchure can be achieved through the following step-by-step procedure: Check each step with a small mirror on the music stand.

1. Keeping the lips lightly together drop the lower jaw so that the teeth are about three-eighths of an inch apart.

2. Shape the lips as if saying the letter "O." The corners of the mouth are slightly compressed and there are wrinkles in the lips, especially the lower one.

3. With the teeth open and the lips in the "O" position the rim of the lower lip which divides it from the chin should be directly in front of the top edge of the front teeth. Feel this with a finger and raise or lower the jaw until this relationship is correct.

4. Maintaining this position insert the mouthpiece of the saxophone into the mouth allowing the reed to push the lower lip over the teeth. If the winkles on the lower lip are maintained, the line dividing the lip from the chin is directly over the front edge of the lower teeth. Students with thicker than average lips will probably adjust so that less lip is over the teeth. Contract the lips and especially the corners of the mouth inward and around the mouthpiece so that no air can escape.

5. In order to vibrate freely the end of the reed must be clear of any contact with the lip for three-eighths to a half-inch on the Alto saxophone, more on the Tenor, and still more on the Baritone instrument. The amount of mouthpiece in the mouth is determined by

the mouthpiece itself. As a rule of the thumb, the support of the lower teeth against the lip should be at the point on the reed where the lay of the mouthpiece starts breaking away from the reed. Some deviations from this are possible, but examine the mouthpiece to find this point, and apply the principle to all instruments in the saxophone family. This distance varies from one-half to three-fourths of an inch on the Alto saxophone.

6. The upper teeth rest, but do not press, on the top of the mouthpiece somewhat forward of the position of the lower teeth.

7. The lower teeth remain in the open position established in step three above, and must not bite or exert pressure against the lower lip. The reed and mouthpiece are supported and controlled by inward pressure toward the center of the mouthpiece by the upper and lower lips and by the corners of the mouth.

8. The first efforts at tone production should be with the mouthpiece alone. Check the embouchure formation in the mirror, and using standard breath support produce a tone by blowing without using the tongue. Continue practicing with the mouthpiece alone until a steady natural tone of the highest pitch can be sustained for at least ten seconds. Check constantly in the mirror to be certain that the effort of blowing and producing a tone does not change the shape of the embouchure. When this is accomplished the student is ready to proceed with tone production on the entire instrument.

Any experienced teacher will verify the fact that while it is fairly simple to explain and form the embouchure in the manner given above, maintaining it in perfect condition over a period of weeks and months while the student is struggling with tone production and fingering problems is an entirely different matter. For this reason it is suggested that every student who is working on embouchure formation, whether he is at the beginning, intermediate, or advanced level, have a small mirror on the music stand for constant reference. The embouchure must be established by how it feels in the mouth and how the tone sounds, as well as how it looks in the mirror, and this is done only with the careful assistance of the teacher.

Common Faults in Soft Cushion Embouchure Formation. Analyzing the problem a student is having with his embouchure must be done both visually and aurally since some faults are not apparent to the eye but must be heard. It is frequently difficult to analyze and isolate an embouchure problem since the tonal symptoms indicating a difficulty in embouchure formation may indicate as well a problem with breath support or with the reed or mouthpiece being used which must also be discovered and corrected. These factors are virtually inseparable in performance. Following are some of the most frequent mistakes in embouchure.

1. *Dimples in cheeks.* Perhaps the most frequent mistake in the formation of the soft cushion embouchure is indicated by the presence of a dimple in one or both cheeks. These are caused when one muscle is pulling back the corner of the mouth to stretch the lip, while at the same time another muscle is attempting the proper contraction of the lips. This is a serious problem since the pulling back of the corner or corners of the mouth lessens the support of the lip against the reed with a consequent loss of tone quality.

Students with this condition tire easily because of the muscular tension resulting from muscles pulling against each other rather than working together. Unfortunately this condition is difficult to correct, and the only solution is to practice long sustained tones while the student watches himself in a mirror to see that the dimple doesn't return. Because it is so difficult to correct, it is of the utmost importance to avoid the problem from the beginning rather than letting it develop.

2. *Amount of lip.* The amount of lower lip over the teeth depends on the size of the lips of the student, although all should start as directed in the embouchure formation with the line separating lip from chin directly over the front edge of the teeth, as this will be correct for the normal lip. The student will make an adjustment himself, or can be directed to do so if his progress on the instrument indicates that such an adjustment should be made.

If there is too much lip over the teeth the tone is open and squawky, but too much mouthpiece in the mouth produces the same symptoms so a visual check is necessary. Too little lip over the teeth produces a cushion which is too small to control the vibrations of the reed and a very nasal reedy tone quality is produced which is quite flat in pitch, especially in the upper register. Too little mouthpiece in the mouth produces much the same sound so a visual check is necessary.

3. *Biting.* Biting the reed with the lower teeth is another fault which is frequently found in students on all stages of advancement. This excess pressure against the reed restricts the amount of vibration possible, and produces a thin stuffy tone with little body, and requires considerable more breath pressure to produce a tone than the correct procedure. Reducing this pressure by dropping the lower jaw back into the open position immediately frees the tone and improves both body and quality. The strength of reed being used may need to be changed at the same time.

4. *Amount of mouthpiece.* The amount of mouthpiece to put in the mouth is dependent on several variables—facial characteristics, mouthpiece, and reed—and the final determination is made by ear, moving the mouthpiece back and forth slightly to secure the best tone quality. The length and amount of the curvature of the lay, the size of the opening at the tip, and the strength of the reed being used help determine the exact location of the mouthpiece.

Regardless of the size of the mouthpiece, whether for

the Soprano saxophone or for the Baritone saxophone, the lower teeth must be slightly in back of the point at which the lay starts breaking from the reed in order that the cushion of the lip may control its vibration. A mouthpiece with a slight curvature and small opening at the tip requires that the lower teeth be fairly close to the breakaway point, while a mouthpiece with a larger curvature and wide opening at the tip requires that the lower teeth support the cushion closer to the tip of the mouthpiece and farther away from the breakaway point.

5. *Puffing cheeks.* Puffing cheeks is a problem with many beginners as well as with some more advanced students. They indicate a lack of support by the cheek muscles which may or may not affect the amount of support the corners of the mouth are giving the mouthpiece and reed. Puffed cheeks are always an indication that breath support necessary to produce a good tone is not properly focused and directed into the mouthpiece. Frequently the student does not realize that the cheeks are puffed, and the use of a mirror to check is invaluable. When the student can see that the cheeks are not puffed he can then feel the muscular support which is necessary to keep them in place and make the correction.

6. Escaping air from one corner of the mouth while playing is another clear indication that something is wrong with the embouchure formation. Normally it means that the lips are not being kept in a circle with pressure against the mouthpiece from all directions, but are being relaxed at that corner. The imagery of suggesting that the lips act as a draw-string closing around the mouthpiece is frequently helpful.

The Hard Cushion Embouchure

The hard cushion embouchure is formed in virtually diametric opposition to the soft cushion, and like the soft cushion is subject to many variations. The basic formation of this embouchure can be achieved through the following step-by-step procedure. Use a mirror on the music stand to check each step.

1. Drop the lower jaw so that the teeth are about three-eighths of an inch apart, allowing the lips to open also.

2. Draw the lower lip over the teeth so that approximately one-half of the red of the lips is covering the teeth. Test by putting a finger against the lip to see that the front edge of the upper teeth is in the center of the lip.

3. Using the "smile" muscles pull the corners of the mouth back in a smiling position.

4. The chin is held firm in a flat and pointed position pulling the lower lip against the teeth, forming a hard cushion upon which the reed rests.

5. Put the mouthpiece in the mouth so that the upper teeth are resting approximately three-fourths of an inch from the tip for the Alto saxophone, more for lower pitched instruments. This distance is determined and adjusted by following the previous discussion on how much mouthpiece to use in the mouth.

6. The corners of the mouth are pushed together to prevent air from escaping while maintaining the smiling position.

7. A slight downward pressure of the upper lip and a slight upward pressure of the lower lip provide the support for the mouthpiece and reed.

8. First efforts at tone production should be made with the mouthpiece alone as previously described.

Common Faults in Hard Cushion Embouchure Formation. Problems encountered in forming the proper hard cushion embouchure may be summarized as follows:

1. *Amount of lip.* The amount of lip over the lower teeth is dependent on the size and thickness of the lips of the individual student. Students with very thin lips may need to put the entire lip over the lower teeth, while students with thick lips may need to use as little as one-third of the lower lip. The correct distance can be determined by a visual check and by the tone quality produced.

2. *Amount of mouthpiece.* The amount of mouthpiece in the mouth is determined by the nature of the teeth of the student as well as factors previously discussed in connection with the soft cushion formation, and is equally important to the success of the hard cushion formation.

3. *Chin.* The chin must be kept pointed at all times as it is this muscular tension in a downward direction which maintains the hard cushion over the lower teeth. If the chin is relaxed or pushed up, the cushion is lost and there is too much pressure against the reed which restricts its vibration and results in poor tone quality. A stretched soft cushion produces the poorest imaginable tone quality on the instrument.

4. *Corners of mouth.* The corners of the mouth should maintain the smile position and the most frequently encountered problem in this connection is that they are pulled back too far into a position similar to the makeup on a happy clown. This exaggerated position makes control difficult and often causes air leakage around the mouthpiece. This condition can be corrected by pushing the corners of the mouth slightly toward the mouthpiece, while relaxing the tension on the smile muscles.

5. *Biting.* Biting or excess pressure of the lower teeth against the reed is quite frequent. Excess pressure restricts the reed vibration, demands excess breath pressure to produce a tone, makes high tones difficult to play in tune, and inhibits the development of a good tone quality. Insist that the teeth remain apart as described. If there is too much pressure the student can feel well-defined indentations on the inside of his lower lip with his tongue and will complain of a "sore lip."

The problems involving the mouthpiece, the reed, and puffing cheeks are similar with those encountered with soft cushion formation and need not be repeated here.

CHECKLIST FOR EMBOUCHURE FORMATION

The following check on embouchure formation must be made while the student is playing and preferably when he is not aware that a check is being made. Any errors should be carefully explained to the student, the correction worked out with him while he is observing the embouchure in a mirror. Remedial exercises can be assigned on the basis of this list.

A. Soft Cushion Embouchure	Yes	No	Comments
1. Lips rounded with wrinkles?			
2. Mouthpiece proper distance in mouth?			
3. Corners of lips pushed inward?			
4. Sufficient lip over lower teeth?			
5. Are lower teeth biting?			
6. Cheeks puffed?			
7. Dimples in cheek?			
8. Air escaping?			

B. Hard Cushion Embouchure

1. Mouthpiece proper distance in mouth?			
2. Proper amount of lip over lower teeth?			
3. Chin firm and pointed?			
4. Cheeks in proper smiling position?			
5. Lower lip smooth and firm?			
6. Corners pushed in slightly?			
7. Are lower teeth biting?			
8. Cheeks puffed?			
9. Air escaping?			

TUNING

All saxophones must be carefully and regularly tuned to the standard international pitch of A-440. The instruments are made to be in tune with themselves at this pitch, and playing sharper or flatter than this standard will cause intonation problems on the instrument. Tuning for saxophones as for all wind instruments is best when done with an electronic aid which provides a visual check on the pitch. Tuning bars and tuning forks are useful for checking single notes through the use of "beats" or direct comparisons but are not as useful as an instrument which can check the pitch of all the notes on the instrument, nor are they as useful for beginning players who have not developed a sense of pitch discrimination on their instrument.

The saxophone is tuned with the mouthpiece. If the instrument is flat when tuning, push the mouthpiece further on the cork, if the instrument is sharp when tuning pull the mouthpiece out so less cork is covered. The amount of cork covered by the mouthpiece is to some extent determined by the nature of its construction, but in general saxophones are made to sound A-440 when approximately half the cork is covered by the mouthpiece. Some brands of saxophones are provided with an adjustable tuning screw on the neck of the instrument in place of a long cork. On these instruments the mouthpiece must be placed completely over the cork and against the tuning screw. Such instruments may be sharpened by turning the screw to the left, and flattened by turning the screw to the right. This type of construction has the advantage of being able to return the mouthpiece to the neck and play at the same pitch previously determined.

Following are the standard band B-flat tuning notes and the note which each instrument plays for tuning purposes.

1. *Soprano Saxophone*

Concert Pitch Soprano Plays

2. *Alto Saxophone*

Concert Pitch Alto Plays

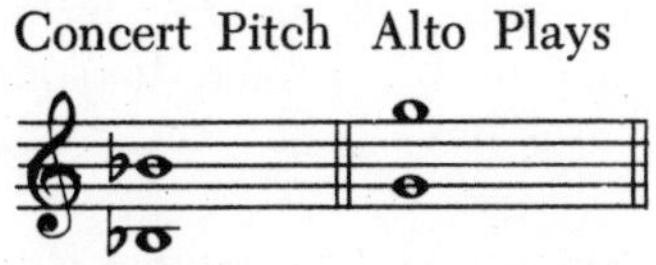

3. *Tenor Saxophone*

Concert Pitch Tenor Plays

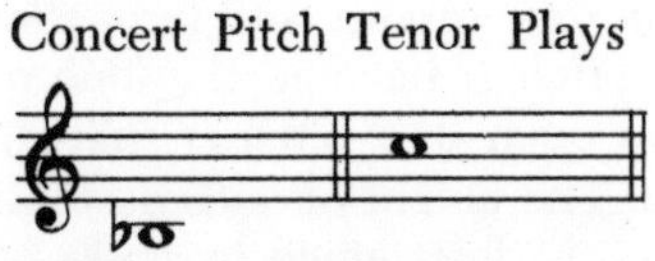

4. *Baritone Saxophone*

Concert Pitch Baritone Plays

5. *Bass Saxophone*

Concert Pitch Bass Plays

INTONATION

Accoustically the saxophone, in its normal range, uses only pitches which are products of the fundamental vibration of the air column or of the first harmonic (an octave higher). Since the octave harmonic is double the frequency rate of the fundamental in both the tempered scale and the natural scale, from a theoretical point of view every note on the instrument should be perfectly in tune. Instrument manufacturers have gone to great lengths to produce such an instrument, and it is probable that almost all intonation problems experienced on the saxophone are due to factors other than the physical acoustics of the instrument. Among the woodwind instruments only the flute approaches these ideal conditions. Following are some factors which bear on the problems of intonation:

Natural Tendencies of the Instrument

Generally speaking, because of the effect of the embouchure, reed, and mouthpiece on the pitch, the saxophones have a tendency to be sharp on both the lowest and highest notes in their range and flat in the upper portion of the second octave. Not all players will play all notes in these ranges sharp or flat, but these are areas to watch. These tendencies are the same on all instruments in the saxophone family.

Tendency to be sharp

Tendency to be flat

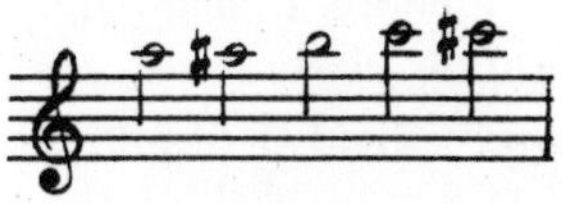

Effect of Reed on Intonation

A reed which is too hard tends to make the instrument sharp while a reed which is too soft tends to make the instrument flat. A soft reed emphasizes the natural tendencies of the notes and does not respond well to embouchure adjustments, so in addition to a general pitch flatness the instrument is out of tune with itself. A student who consistently plays flat, but whose embouchure formation is correct, is playing on a reed which is too soft. If he is given a harder reed the overall flatness disappears rather quickly, although he will probably protest that it is too hard to blow, but most students will make the adjustment to a slightly stiffer reed quite readily.

The student who has been using a reed which is too hard compensates for the overall sharpness by pulling out the mouthpiece. This in turn makes the instrument out of tune with itself making multiple intonation problems which are impossible to solve. Providing the embouchure formation is correct, a student who has to pull the mouthpiece out an excessive amount to play at the standard pitch is playing on a reed which is too stiff. This tuning habit is frequently the best clue to an overly stiff reed. If he is given a softer reed the pitch will be lowered although he will complain about the tone quality he is producing, even though no change will be apparent to the listener.

Effect of Embouchure on Intonation

The embouchure is the primary controlling factor in intonation on any woodwind instrument. The pitch of most tones on the saxophones can be considerably altered either up or down by the embouchure. A properly formed and developed embouchure playing on a reed of the correct strength for the mouthpiece can control the pitch of individual notes on the instrument within the normal deviations easily and with facility to achieve perfect intonation.

The amount of mouthpiece in the mouth is critical to good intonation. If there is too little mouthpiece in the mouth restricting the amount of reed which is vibrating the upper octave in the range will be flat in spite of the natural tendencies of the highest tones to be sharp. It is virtually impossible to play in tune in this range without sufficient mouthpiece in the mouth no matter how hard the student bites with his lower jaw. This biting in an attempt to play in tune, needless to say, causes other serious complications.

Too much mouthpiece in the mouth tends to make the general pitch of the instrument flat, but even more important makes pitch control of individual notes difficult because the support of the reed by the lower lip is placed so far forward on the reed that embouchure adjustments have little or no effect on the vibration of the reed.

The angle at which the saxophone is held determines the way in which the embouchure can control it. If the instrument is held too far forward so that the mouthpiece enters the mouth almost straight rather than at the recommended upward direction, the embouchure does not support the reed sufficiently and there is an overall flatness in pitch. If the bell of the instrument is held too far back the mouthpiece enters the mouth at too much of an upward angle and the resulting unequal support of the mouthpiece by the embouchure causes the overall pitch to be sharp.

Both of these positions affect certain notes on the instrument to a greater extent than others and the embouchure can not make the necessary adjustments for correct intonation. The importance of the angle at which the instrument is held can be verified by experimenting with the student sustaining an open C-sharp while moving the instrument back and forth. There will be a marked change in both pitch and tone quality, and the best position can be discovered.

Effect of Mouthpiece on Intonation

Mouthpieces with a close lay tend to be sharper than mouthpieces with an open lay, although the player through proper reed selection and embouchure formation can compensate for these natural tendencies of the mouthpiece. A close lay restricts the amount of compensation the embouchure can make in pitch, while an open lay although allowing sufficient compensation to be made is difficult to control because of the kind of reed it is necessary to use. This is only one of the reasons why it is necessary to select a mouthpiece with a medium length lay with medium tip opening.

All mouthpieces do not have the same internal dimension—i.e., throat and bore size and shape—and all brands of mouthpieces do not fit all brands of instruments. They will, of course, physically fit over the cork on the neck, but may be acoustically unsuited for the instrument. This problem is especially acute on the saxophone where there are so many different brands of mouthpieces available, some designed to produce the type of tone quality currently in vogue in the popular field professional circles.

If a student is having serious intonation problems and other possible causes have been checked, have him try other mouthpieces of different brands. If the mouthpiece construction is the problem, some quite serious intonation difficulties can be solved by changing mouthpieces, although the student will not suddenly cease playing out of tune and start playing in tune because of the automatic adjustments his embouchure has been making to accommodate the out-of-tune mouthpiece. These automatic embouchure adjustments can be changed in a short space of time if the student concentrates on intonation. However, the mouthpiece has its greatest influence on tone quality, and is not to be blamed for poor intonation until all other causes have been checked and corrected.

Mechanism Adjustment and Intonation

The distance an open pad is above the tone hole has an effect both on tone quality and intonation. If the pad is too close, the pitch is flat and the tone quality stuffy; if the pad is too open, the pitch is sharp and the tone quality too open. The height of pads on tone holes which are normally open is determined by corks on the mechanism; the distance which a normally closed tone hole may be opened is determined by bumper corks. The normal height of keys on the bell is determined by felt bumpers. If individual notes are consistently out of tune, check the adjustment of the mechanism involved in these notes to see if adjustment in thickness of cork or felt is necessary.

Dynamics and Intonation

There is a universal tendency for the saxophonist to play flatter as he gets louder and sharper as he gets softer, the degree of flatness or sharpness increasing as the degree of dynamics approaches the extremes. This must be compensated for by embouchure adjustments. The student has the tendency to increase the pressure of the lower lip against the reed when playing softly and to decrease the support of the lip as he gets louder. This tendency is especially apparent in students who do not use the proper abdominal breath support.

To overcome sharpness when playing softly relax the embouchure slightly, decrease the velocity of the air through the instrument but maintain the same firm support of the breath with the diaphragm and abdominal muscles that is used when playing with full tone. To prevent becoming progressively flatter and flatter as the loudness of a tone increases, drop the lower teeth slightly to allow a greater width of vibration of the reed, but slightly increase the pressure of the lips around the mouthpiece to retain control of this greater amplitude of reed movement.

Relaxing the embouchure when playing softly allows a greater length of the reed to vibrate which lowers the natural pitch of the reed itself and hence the pitch of the tone being played and overcomes the sharpness. Dropping the lower jaw and increasing the pressure around the mouthpiece when playing loudly allows the maximum length of the reed to vibrate in order to produce a loud tone while the increased pressure of the lower lip against it raises its natural rate of vibration to maintain the proper pitch. The dynamic levels between a normal mezzo-piano and a mezzo-forte usually require little or no adjustment for intonation.

The tone exercises below are excellent practice in control of pitch through wide dynamic levels. Practice them slowly enough to use an entire breath on each slur. Maintain constant firm breath support while controlling dynamics by changing velocity of the breath through the instrument at the same time embouchure compensations are made.

Practice exercise "a" in major and minor scale patterns to include the entire range of the instrument in which the student is proficient. Exercise "b" is best practiced chromatically using a restricted range which the student is capable of controlling well, and gradually extending the range upward and downward to cover his entire proficient range. This is also a good exercise for developing change of octaves. Check to see that the student is operating the octave key by vertical movements of the joint of the thumb.

Adjusting Intonation of Individual Notes

Occasionally when playing in an ensemble, the saxophonist will find it necessary to make slight alterations in the pitch of individual notes in order to correct intonation. While the fingerings for notes in the extended range will produce pitch differences, the alternate fingerings in the standard playing range do not normally produce significant pitch differences on the saxophone.

Slight pitch adjustments on the normal playing range may be made by opening or closing one or more tone holes in addition to those involved in the standard fingering. Each player will need to experiment, but the following basic principles apply.

1. In general, opening tone holes will raise the pitch and closing tone holes will lower the pitch.
2. At least one tone hole, preferably two, below the last closed hole involved in the fingering must remain open.
3. The closer to this tone hole that additional holes are opened or closed, the greater the effect on the pitch; the farther from this tone hole, the less effect on the pitch.
4. One or more fingers may be added to the basic fingering to correct the pitch.
5. The degree of correction which may be needed varies from player to player and with the musical situation at a given time.
6. The amount of correction needed, if any, varies with the dynamic level being used.
7. Such corrections are considered temporary expe-

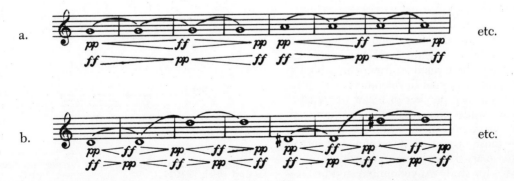

a.

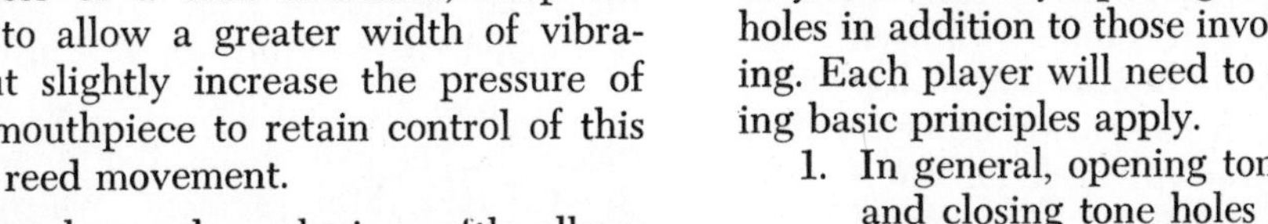

etc.

b.

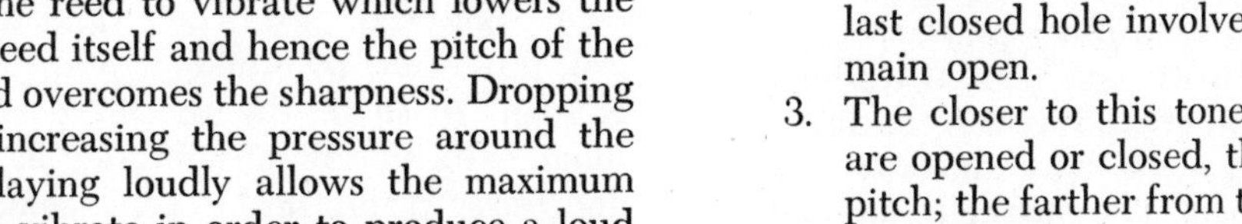

etc.

dients and must not become a part of the standard fingering for the note. If a particular note is always out of tune other remedial measures are called for.

The following examples will illustrate the process.

(a) F-sharp:
G:

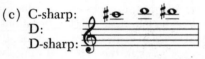

To sharpen: Open E-flat key with right little finger.
To flatten: Close "C" key with right little finger.

(b) C:
C-sharp:

To flatten: Add any combination of fourth, fifth or sixth fingers.

(c) C-sharp:
D:
D-sharp:

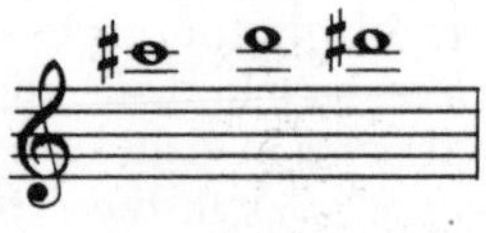

To sharpen: Add key 4C.

Intonation in Ensemble

The ability to tune the saxophone to the standard pitch and to play the instrument in tune with itself is essential. However, very few saxophonists do much playing alone, but rather with other instruments in ensemble. For this reason, playing the instrument itself in tune is only the starting point for good intonation. The player must listen to other instruments and make slight adjustments so that he is exactly in tune with other players.

Other woodwind instruments have natural tendencies toward out of tuneness which are different from those on the saxophone; brass instruments have different problems, and the piano still others. The musically intelligent player will recognize these different problems, and will compromise his intonation for the sake of perfect ensemble intonation.

Training in listening and hearing intonation is the most valuable contribution an instrumental teacher can make to his students. But it must be emphasized that the basis for good ensemble intonation must be the ability to play the instrument in tune with itself at the standard pitch.

TONE

The slow acceptance of the saxophone as a legitimate subject of study on the collegiate level has made the emergence of what may be termed an American school of saxophone playing a fairly recent development. The presence of artists-teachers at a number of major universities is beginning to show results in increasingly high standards of saxophone performance which, with advanced students, is equal to those on any of the woodwind instruments. Many of these artists have made recordings which are readily available for study. Anyone interested in saxophone performance should make strenuous efforts to attend clinics or workshops conducted by one of these artist-teachers to get a clear concept of the American saxophone sound.

The prevalence of the saxophone in the jazz field tends to obscure its use in other fields of music, and to in effect, set in the minds of the student performers a bewildering multitude of constantly changing concepts of tone quality. Where as serious music tone quality is constant and unvarying in its development with use, concepts, and standards widely known and accepted, the tone quality of the saxophone in the dance band fluctuates from year to year, from style to style, and from individual to individual.

The saxophonist must apply the same standards of tone quality expected on the other wind instruments: body, brilliance, control, smoothness, consistency, etc., to his instrument, and reject highly individualized and transient concepts of quality used by entertainers.

The eminent saxophone virtuoso, Sigurd Rascher, points out in one of his books for the instrument[4] that Adolphe Sax, the inventor of the saxophone, had in mind an instrument that should be as flexible as a string instrument, as powerful as one of the brasses, and possess an expressive power equal to that of the cello. This ideal can be attained provided serious study and effort is applied to the study of the instrument.

In order to identify the exact notes intended when discussing the saxophone, the range of the instrument is divided into three segments which are understood and remembered if called simply the first octave, the second octave, and the third octave. The notes in the first octave are produced by fundamental vibrations of the air column, those in the second octave by the first harmonic (the air column vibrating in two equal segments), and those in the third octave—actually only a part of an octave—by side keys operated by the first and second fingers of the left hand and by the first finger of the right hand. These three segments of the saxophone's playing ranges are sometimes called low register, middle register, and high register and should be understood to have the same meaning as first, second, and third octaves.

These three octaves are identified as follows:

First Octave   Second Octave

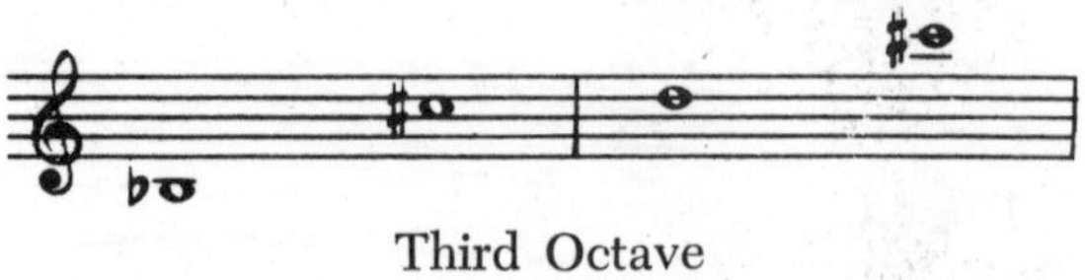

Third Octave

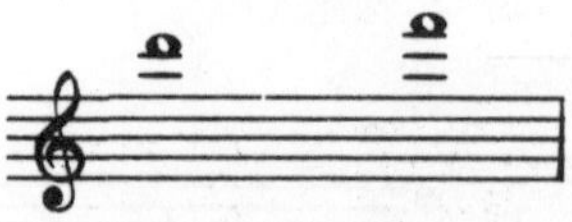

4. Sigurd M. Rascher, *Top Tones for the Saxophone* (New York: Carl Fischer, 1941).

Extended Range

The playing range of the Alto and Tenor saxophones can be extended a full octave above the high F. Only the most experienced and advanced students should attempt to develop this extended range for it demands a concentrated effort over a period of time. A discussion of developing this range is included in the section on Technique Problems, and a special fingering chart for notes in this range is included with the fingering charts at the end of the book.

Common Problems in Tone

A good tone is the product of all the elements involved in performance: the instrument, mouthpiece, reed, embouchure, and breath support. If any of these is defective than the tone quality suffers accordingly. Problems of tone production and quality are many and varied, but may usually be traced to their source and steps taken to correct the problem immediately. Following are some of the most prevalent problems or faults in tone:

1. *Small, pinched, or muffled tone.* Assuming a good mouthpiece and reed, a small, pinched, or muffled tone may be caused by too much pressure on the reed with the lower jaw, or by having too little mouthpiece in the mouth. Adjust the distance in the mouth by experimentation to the point of optimum quality and fullness, yet avoiding the tendency of the tone to break into a higher partial which is caused by too much mouthpiece in the mouth. Too much pressure against the reed can be remedied by asking the student to play flatter. This will cause him to relax the pressure of the lower jaw and free the vibration of the reed. Unless he also relaxes the support of the lip against the reed, he will not actually play flatter in pitch, the effect will simply be a freer tone quality.

2. *Squawky tone.* The squawky tone which can be described as lacking in body and focus, generally uncontrolled, and commonly flat in pitch is caused by or a combination of three things. Not enough pressure on the reed with the lower lip; poor embouchure formation evidenced by not enough support around the mouthpiece with the upper lip, and the corners of the mouth, as well as the lower lip, or by a poor reed. Corrections for these have been discussed previously.

3. *Hard, cold tone.* A tone which is inflexible and which lacks the intangible quality of vitality is described as hard and cold. This is caused by a mouthpiece which has a lay which is too open and too long, or by a reed which is too hard.

4. *Squeaking.* Squeaking on the saxophone is not a common problem with most students as it is on the clarinet, but when it occurs it is caused by a leaky pad which must be identified and replaced; by a reed which has a built-in squeak; or by an incorrect embouchure which is putting unequal pressure across the reed because of irregular length lower teeth or because the mouthpiece is not adjusted to be parallel with the teeth.

5. *Weak, colorless tone.* A tone which is otherwise smooth in quality but is lacking in body, quality and carrying power is most often due to lack of proper breathing and breath support. If all other conditions are good, the breath support can be corrected with diligent effort.

6. *Loud, raucous tone.* This quality is always the result of too much breath support, combined frequently with a very open mouthpiece and stiff reed, which overblows the instrument and presses it beyond the controllable dynamic range of the player. Insisting on a full dynamic range extending well into the pianissimo level, and limiting the volume the student is allowed to produce will correct this problem. In making this correction it is important to see to it that the student continues to use the proper breath support, and achieves the lower dynamic levels by reducing the velocity of air through the instrument rather than the support for the air.

7. *Control of soft tone.* Difficulty in producing and controlling a soft tone is principally due to the inability of the player to project a steady concentrated small stream of air into the instrument. Check breathing and breath support, and have the student practice focusing a steady stream of air into the palm of his hand. Other possible causes may be a reed which is too stiff, a mouthpiece which is too open, or a poorly shaped embouchure. Check all three if breath support is not the solution.

8. *Dynamics and tone quality.* Some students will lose their tone quality when playing at extremes of loudness and softness. This is normally due to an undeveloped embouchure. Keep the volume of tone within the ability of the embouchure to retain control, and concentrate on embouchure development through the use of the proper exercises.

TONGUING

Tonguing refers to the manner in which the tongue operates in relation to the reed and breath support in order to articulate the tones. This placement and action must be rapid and under complete control at all speeds. It must, in coordination with breath support, be able to produce on the saxophone all varieties of articulation from the hardest staccato to the softest legato. In short, at least the Alto saxophone must be able to match sound for sound the effects of the entire gamut of bow strokes used on the violin. As the instruments in the saxophone family get physically large the complete variety of articulations available for the Alto become more and more difficult to produce. The large mouthpiece and reed of the Baritone instrument responds somewhat more slowly and with a less variety of attacks than are available on the Alto instrument, although few school musicians take full advantage of its potential in this respect.

The manner in which the tongue touches the reed, the place it touches, and how it moves is dependent somewhat upon the embouchure formation, on the lay of the mouthpiece, and the stiffness of the reed being used. There are several ways in which the tongue touches the reed and in the way in which it moves, each with backing from fine woodwind instructors, and each effective within the style of performance being taught.

The function of the tongue is simply to act as a valve to control the flow of breath through the mouthpiece, stopping the breath and vibration when it touches the reed, and allowing the vibration to begin again when it is removed and the air flow begins again. Effective tonguing and articulation is entirely dependent upon the flow of air, and hence upon proper breath support and control. The interrelationship between breath pressure and tongue pressure against the reed allows the production of a broad range of attacks from the hardest marcato-staccato to the very smoothest legato within the widest dynamic range. The amount of pressure of the tongue against the reed determines the hardness of the attack, the amount of wind pressure against the tongue determines the loudness of the attack.

There are three basic methods of tongue placement used on the saxophone, each subject to many variations according to the personal desires of the teachers using them. All are effective if properly executed. All standard methods have at least three things in common: (1) the tongue is relaxed. A tongue under tension cannot move rapidly enough, nor can it be controlled; (2) tongue movement is confined to the forward part of the tongue. The base or root of the tongue is down to permit an open throat and does not move; (3) the tongue acts as a valve for the air and is dependent on good breath support.

The three basic methods may be outlined as follows:

First Method. This method is used with the soft cushion embouchure previously described and is the method taught by many fine saxophone teachers. When properly developed and used it produces maximum flexibility and facility, and is adaptable to solo, ensembles, band, and orchestra performance. This method in combinaiton with the soft cushion embouchure is recommended by the author. This method of tonguing is discussed in some detail in Lucien Calliet's *Method for Saxophone, Book One* published by Belwin, Inc. where material for its development is presented.

With the mouthpiece in playing position, and the embouchure correctly formed, feel with the tip of the tongue the junction of the reed and lower lip. The reed and lip form a small "V" shaped pocket. The tongue should be in this pocket with the top of the tip of the tongue curved up and touching the reed lightly about a half-inch from the tip on the Alto.

To start the tone, build up wind pressure against

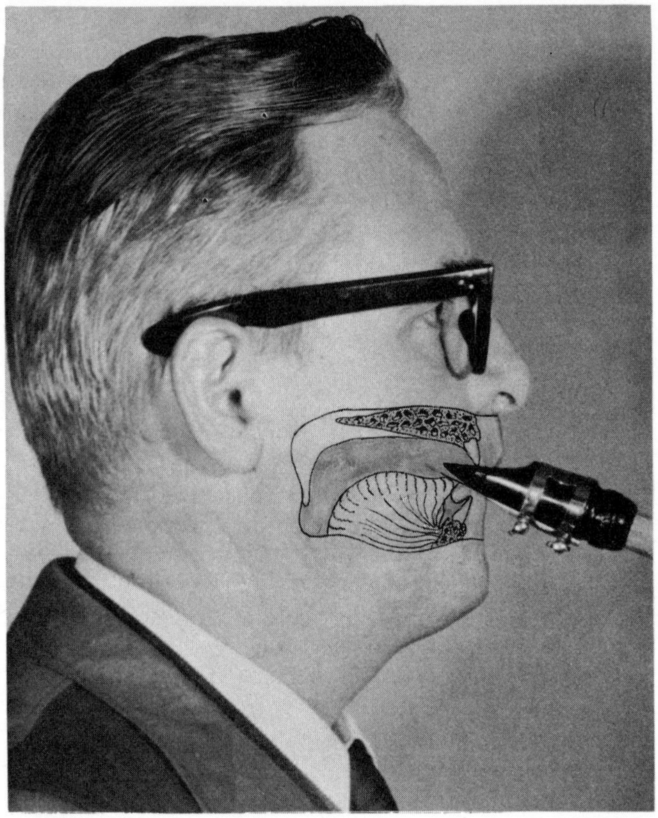

Figure S-42

the tongue. Release the air into the instrument with tongue action similar to that in pronouncing the syllable "Too." The center of the tongue is depressed slightly so that the tongue will not lie flat on the reed. Figure S-42 above shows this tongue position.

Second Method. This method is used with the hard cushion embouchure previously described, and is recommended by the many fine teachers who use the hard cushion. It is less successful when used with the soft cushion embouchure. It produces considerable flexibility and is adapted to all types of performance.

With the mouthpiece in place and the embouchure properly formed, the tongue is drawn up and back with the tip pointed. The center of the tongue is arched and the throat kept open. Action of the tongue is forward contacting the reed about a quarter of an inch from its tip with the top of the tongue about an eighth of an inch from its tip. Pressure of the tongue against the reed may be light or heavy depending on the type of articulation desired. To start the tone place the tongue against the reed, build up air pressure against it, and release the air with a tongue action similar to that in pronouncing "Du."

Third Method. This method is used with either the soft cushion or the hard cushion embouchure. With the mouthpiece in place and the embouchure properly formed, the tip of the tongue is anchored against the base of the lower teeth. Keeping the tip anchored against the teeth the tongue moves up and forward to contact the reed between a quarter and a half-inch from its tip.

The point on the tongue which contacts the reed is found naturally and is determined by its natural placement. Experience with advanced students who use this method has indicated that this technique of using the tongue does not have the potential of as great a variety of articulations as either of the previous methods, nor is speed and control developed as rapidly or to as great an extent. Unless there is a strong personal preference for this method, it should be used with caution.

Soprano, Tenor, Baritone, and Bass Saxophone

Any of the three methods of tongue placement and action described above for the Alto saxophone can be successfully used on the Soprano, Tenor, Baritone and Bass instruments. Normally the Soprano, Baritone or Bass saxophone are played after some experience on either the Alto or Tenor instrument, and the same method of tongue placement and action should be used on them that the student has already developed.

The difference in tongue placement between the various sizes of saxophone will be found in the point at which the tongue contacts the reed. As the reeds and mouthpieces get larger there is more reed in the mouthpiece and the point of contact of tongue and reed is further away from the top of the reed. The placement of the tongue in relation to the lower lip and teeth remain essentially the same regardless of size of the mouthpiece. Because of the larger reed and the fact that its response is slower it becomes increasingly difficult to produce a short staccato or to articulate as rapidly as we go from the Soprano to the Bass instrument.

Variety in Articulation

Once correct tongue action is established according to the method selected, variety in articulation can be developed. The exact sounds desired are determined by musical taste and style. A great variety of articulations is possible on the saxophone through the use of varying degrees of pressure of the tongue against the reed combined with varying amounts of breath support and velocity of wind through the instrument. This can be illustrated by a student playing in the following ways:

1. Sustain a second line G at a good solid *forte* level. While maintaining this dynamic level and keeping the length of the notes the same start with maximum tongue pressure against the reed and play a series of notes with gradually diminishing pressure of the tongue.

2. Do the same maintaining a *piano* level for the second line G, but starting with minimum pressure against the reed and play a series of notes with gradually increasing pressure of the tongue. It will be found that tongue pressure beyond a certain point will introduce an objectionable amount of mechanical noise.

3. Using the second line G softly play a series of staccato notes simultaneously increasing both loudness of the tone and pressure of the tongue against the reed. Be sure to eliminate any movement of the breathing muscles. Experimentation will show that the louder the staccato note the greater the tongue pressure needed to control it, and if the result is to be musically pleasing, the louder the staccato the longer duration it must have.

The success of these experiments depends on the degree of advancement of the player performing them. An advanced player will be able to carry the illustrations much farther and show a greater variety of articulated sounds.

Common Articulation Problems

There are several common problems in connection with articulation on the saxophone, some of them occurring in combination. Articulation is so basic to satisfactory performance that it must be accomplished well if the player is to have any measure of success with the instrument. The following are the most commonly found problems.

1. *Hard attack.* This is the result of either too much tongue pressure against the reed in relation to the amount of breath support, or too much tongue in contact with the reed. The interrelationship between tongue pressure and breath support is rather easy to correct.

The problem of too much tongue contact with the reed—sometimes to the point of laying flat against considerable portion of the reed—is much more of a problem to correct. A special effect on the instrument, the slap tongue, is produced with the tongue in the flat position on the reed, but in normal articulation only a very small area of the tongue must contact the reed. The correction involves a return to the basic procedures and concepts of tongue placement, and a gradual retraining of the muscles of the tongue to the correct position.

The hard, percussive attack is frequently associated with movements of the lower jaw which must also be eliminated.

2. *Sluggish tongue.* A sluggish tongue which does not permit rapid articulations may be the result of incorrect placement and movement of the tongue, moving the breathing muscles simultaneously with the tongue, or simply a matter of insufficient practice to gain speed.

If a variety of articulations can be controlled and successfully produced at slow speeds, it is probable that the placement and movement of the tongue is correct. If this is the case, speed may be gained by diligent practice making use of various articulation patterns with major and minor scales, thirds, and arpeggios. Use of a metronome for maintaining a constant tempo and to increase speed gradually is essential.

An incorrect placement and movement of the tongue usually produces a sluggish response because the tongue is tense or is making too large motions with the entire tongue rather than only the front portion moving. If this is the case, then a return to the basic position of the tongue and a gradual development of articulation from the beginning is required.

Moving the breathing muscles simultaneously with the movement of the tongue from the reed is relatively easy to detect since there will be visible body movements. This may occur with either correct or incorrect breathing. The habit of moving breathing muscles with the tongue can be corrected by reviewing correct breathing to get support and by emphasizing the concept that the pressure of the air against the tongue must be constant throughout a series of articulated notes with the function of the tongue that of a valve.

3. *Poor staccato.* A poor staccato or no staccato at all, if tongue placement is otherwise correct, is caused by lack of sustained, continuous breath support to the tip of the mouthpiece. The support is being relaxed between staccato notes and then tightened simultaneously with the beginning of the note by the tongue. Check breathing carefully, since if this is the cause the air is most frequently being inhaled with a chest movement rather than by the diaphragm and abdominal muscles. A good dependable staccato is rarely possible with incorrect breath placement.

If a check reveals that placement of breath is correct and the support continuous, then a poor staccato is the result of incorrect tongue placement or movement. Frequently the cause is simply that the student is not returning the tongue quickly enough to its place on the reed to stop the vibration. This can be developed by practicing slow repeated notes at a very soft dynamic level, increasing the dynamic level as proficiency is attained. Many students are simply afraid to stop a note with their tongue and need encouragement to do so in the case of the staccato.

4. *Lack of coordination between tongue and fingers.* This is the result of practicing and playing too fast without the essential slow working out process. Slow down the tempo until the tongue and fingers are perfectly coordinated, and increase speed gradually. Do not allow the student to exceed the maximum tempo at which there is perfect coordination between tongue and fingers. Use of a metronome to maintain a constant tempo is mandatory.

5. *Movement of the jaw in tonguing.* This is the result of too large or too violent movements of the tongue. Rather than confining the movement to the front portion of the tongue the student is moving the entire tongue. The solution is to require the student, no matter what his technical advancement, to practice basic exercises for developing articulation constantly checking in a mirror on the music stand to eliminate all movement. Jaw movements can occur with all methods of correct tongue placement, as well as with incorrect tongue placement.

Double and Triple Tonguing

The standard technique of double or triple tonguing used for very rapid articulations on the flute and on all brass instruments is becoming a desirable tool for advanced saxophonists. The development of good double and triple tonguing on the instrument requires considerable persistence and should be studied only by advanced players who have virtually mastered the standard staccato articulation.

Double tonguing is executed by rapid movements of the tongue as in pronouncing the syllables "tu-ku." The "tu" is articulated in the usual fashion on the reed, while the "ku" is pronounced by the tongue against the palate to stop the flow of air. The problem in developing a useful double tonguing technique is in matching the attack and tone qualities of the two syllables.

Practice slowly at first on

repeated notes in the range: 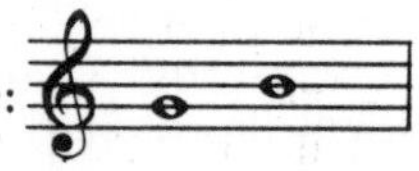

Breath support must be firm. Avoid any movement of the jaw and any changes in the embouchure. Increase the speed of the repeated notes gradually, making sure that the attacks of all notes match. In addition to the syllables "tu-ku," some teachers recommend "ti-ki" or "du-gu." Any of these will give satisfactory results.

Triple tonguing is done with the same syllables as those used in double tonguing. The syllables may be used in any of three patterns. The player should experiment to see which works best for him.

Patterns for triple tonguing:

1. 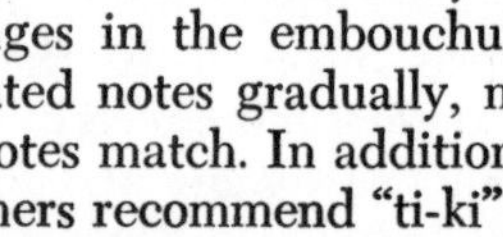

2. 

3. 

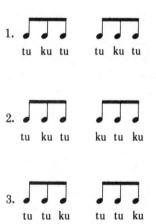

Unfortunately, the standard literature for saxophone does not include specific material for the development of double or triple tonguing. Saxophonists who are developing this technique can make use of material written for trumpet to good advantage.

Flutter Tonguing

Technically speaking flutter tonguing is not an articulation but a special tonal effect which is being used more and more by twentieth century composers, although considerably less frequently for saxophone than for flute or clarinet. Flutter tonguing seems to come naturally to some players while many have difficulty in developing the technique. Only advanced players should attempt to develop it.

In developing flutter tonguing which is dependable and under control certain things must be observed: (1) the tongue should always be as relaxed as possible; (2) the embouchure must not move out of its normal position although it may be relaxed to open the reed; and (3) the stream of air must be very firmly supported and move rapidly through the mouthpiece.

There are three methods of flutter tonguing on the saxophone. The player should experiment with each to see which method works best for him. Some players may want to use more than one method to meet the various musical requirements they will find.

1. *Tongue on reed.* In this method the flutter is produced by rolling the tongue rapidly against the reed as in rolling the letter "r" in "b-r-r-r." This method changes the basic tone quality less than the other methods.

2. *Dental flutter.* Place the tip of the tongue above the mouthpiece against the upper edge of the upper teeth. A fast stream of air will flutter the tongue against the teeth, producing what amounts to an intensity flutter.

3. *Hard palate flutter.* Flatten the tongue and place the front portion against the front of the hard palate. A fast, well-supported stream of air will vibrate the tongue rapidly against the palate. This method produces a greater change in normal tone quality than the other two methods.

TECHNIQUE PROBLEMS

A good technical proficiency on the saxophone is one which is accurate, under complete control, and facile. In developing this proficiency the saxophonist must be aware of certain mechanical or technical problems peculiar to the instrument which must be understood and approached in a logical fashion.

While in the training of the saxophone student, some of the problems or technical procedures which will be discussed are not introduced until the student is quite advanced, many of them will be quite valuable to students who are still in the intermediate stage of their development, while still others are suitable for introduction even earlier. For this reason every instructor must be fully aware of the various possibilities of solving certain technical problems, and introduce them whenever the problem arises in the day-to-day work of the student.

Among the most important things in developing a fine technical proficiency is to have a command of all the fingerings possible for every note together with the knowledge of how and when to use each. The book by Jay Arnold *Modern Fingering System for the Saxophone* published by Shapiro, Bernstein & Co. has the most complete listing of fingerings available together with musical examples illustrating the use of each, although the book does not provide enough musical material to fully develop their use. Any teacher responsible for saxophone students past the beginning stage should be familiar with the book and have it available for ready reference.

Approached logically and with full information on available choices technical problems on the saxophone are neither complex to solve, nor complex to use. Intelligent selection and use of alternate fingerings and other devices will simplify technical problems to an extent undreamed of by the uninformed. Both the importance of the correct solution and the reasons for a particular solution must be impressed on the student. Each alternative must be practiced until it becomes an involuntary part of the player's technique and how each alternative is used must be made so much a part of his technique that the correct choice becomes involuntary and instantaneous. Both players and teachers should not hesitate to mark instructions on the printed pages as reminders.

1. *Use of little fingers.* Two problems arise in connection with the use of the little fingers in achieving technical facility. The first of these is that of having them in the proper position to reach and depress any key involved with a minimum of motion. The guide position is established for this purpose, but care should be taken to see that the fingers remain in the natural curved position in so far as possible. This curved position gives them maximum strength since on some instruments the number and strength of the springs involved in playing low B-flat for example, requires considerable pressure to close the key.

Avoid too much curve which makes the finger contact the key with its tip. There is little strength in this motion. The right little finger with only two keys to operate poses little problem, but the four keys operated by the left little finger require accuracy, dexterity, and strength to operate properly. Many players never gain much facility in using the lowest notes on the instrument because of faulty use of the little fingers.

The second problem in the use of the little fingers is that of sliding from one key to another when successive notes require the same finger to be in two different locations, especially when the notes are slurred. Almost all brands of instruments provide rollers on these keys to facilitate this process.

To slide from one key to another, keep the little finger curved and without relaxing the downward pressure on the key, slide the finger with a sideways motion to the new location. Do not roll the hand to move the finger, do not flatten the hand or the little finger to contact the second key with the middle or side of the little finger. Considerable practice is necessary to perfect the technique of sliding, and most teachers find it necessary to assign particular exercises for this purpose.

2. *Left thumb.* The position and movements of the

left thumb previously described are those which, if carefully observed, will eliminate any problems with this finger. However, many beginners find it difficult to establish this and fall into a variety of bad habits which are a detriment to their technical advancement. A constant check of this finger is advisable throughout the beginning stages of study.

Emphasize to the student that the thumb must remain in contact with its button at all times, and that the octave key is operated by vertical movements of the first joint. Assigning exercises which cross back and forth between the first and second octaves so that the student's attention is focused on the operation of the octave key will help correct a poor habit, although if the habit is firmly established its correction will take a period of time.

3. *Leaving down one or more fingers throughout a passage.* Rapidly moving passages involving certain combinations of notes can frequently be made smoother if some of the fingers and/or keys can be kept down throughout even though they are not involved in the basic fingerings for all the notes. This basic principle can be applied to all woodwind instruments. Advanced players make use of this technique without being conscious of it, but it is frequently a great aid to less experienced players if they can be directed to make use of it.

Some combinations will affect the pitch of other notes in the passage, while others will have no effect. Use of this technique is limited to those instances where there is no appreciable change in intonation of any of the notes, but is always usable where the notes are moving so rapidly that none of the notes are sufficiently exposed for the ear to detect incorrect intonation. Following are some examples illustrating this technique.

(a) leave first two fingers of right hand down throughout.

(b) leave three fingers of right hand down throughout.

(c) leave three fingers and little finger of right hand down throughout.

(d) leave right little finger on C key and left little finger on D-flat key down throughout.

4. *Articulated G-sharp Key.* The G-sharp key played by the left little finger is articulated in two ways on the saxophone: (1) If the G-sharp key is depressed by the little finger, the pad which opens a tone hole to produce the note will automatically close when any of the tone holes operated by the three fingers of the right hand are closed. Thus in a sequence of notes containing several G-sharp's (or A-flat's) and notes fingered by the right hand the left little finger depresses the G-sharp key throughout, making the progression smoother and easier technically than if the little finger released and depressed the key each time a G-sharp appeared. Keeping the little finger down has no effect on the pitch of the other notes in the right hand and this technique may be used at any speed. The following example illustrates a typical use of this procedure:

(2) When the B-flat, B-natural or C-sharp keys are depressed by the left little finger the G-sharp key is automatically depressed.[5] With this type of articulated mechanism the G-sharp can be played with the three fingers of the left hand down plus any of the four keys operated by the left little finger. This eliminates the necessity of sliding the little finger back and forth in sequences of notes which involve the left little finger and permits a smooth legato technique in situations where a legato would otherwise be impossible. Fingering the G-sharp with any one of the other keys of the left little finger has no appreciable effect on intonation and this device may be used regardless of the speed of the notes.

Following is a typical example. Finger the G-sharp with the left little finger key used on the note which precedes it if that finger is involved in the fingering of that note, or if the left little finger is not involved in the note preceding the G-sharp, prepare for the note which follows it by using that key for the G-sharp. Left little finger keys to be used for each G-sharp (or A-flat) are indicated above the note in the example.

Without the use of this articulation of the G-sharp this example would be impossible to play legato, but using the fingerings indicated a perfect legato is possible and the rapid movement of notes no problem at all. This procedure should be introduced to students when the need arises in music which they are playing and referred to until it becomes an automatic part of their technique.

5. Not all instruments have this interlocking mechanism.

5. *Selection and use of alternate fingerings.* There are alternate fingerings for some notes in each of the three octave ranges of the saxophone which match the standard basic fingerings perfectly in tone quality and intonation. If the smoothest and most useful technique is to be developed it is necessary that these alternates be learned, when and how they are to be used, and the best choice made each time there is a choice. This choice should be the one which gives the smoothest progression and the best facility.

These are all fingerings which should be learned and facility developed by the student before or during the intermediate stage of development. Unless full advantage is taken of the potentials of the instrument, technical development is slowed, or smooth facility never achieved. Following is a consideration of each fingering and its uses:

(a) F-sharp:
G-flat:

Two fingerings: (1) 123 050 (diatonic)
(2) 123 406x (chromatic)

Use of the chromatic fingering is mandatory where F and F-sharp (or G-flat) follow each other if perfect smoothness is to be achieved. The only exception to this rule is found when the fingering of the note preceding or following the F-sharp involves the sixth finger on the button of the tone hole. Following are typical passages using these fingerings:

Use fingering 1:

Use fingering 2:

(b) A-sharp:
B-flat:

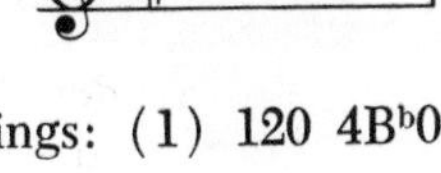

Four fingerings: (1) 120 4B♭00 (Regular diatonic and chromatic fingering.)

(2) 100 400 (When interval F to B-flat is involved.)

(3) 100 050 (When interval F-sharp to A-sharp is involved [slightly sharp on some instruments].)

(4) 11y00 000 (For facility and smoothness in any passages where there is no B-natural.)

The first fingering, the regular diatonic and chromatic fingering, is the most frequently used of all the fingerings. It is the preferred fingering in chromatic passages, in sharp keys, and in any passage where B-natural occurs. The second fingering produces a perfectly in tune B-flat and is useful when the interval of F to B-flat or B-flat to F occurs, as well as certain passages in which notes fingered with the right hand skip to the B-flat. The third fingering, a cross fingering, is slightly sharp on some instruments but may be used on these when the B-flat is not an exposed note. It is useful in passages involving the interval of F-sharp to A-sharp or A-sharp to F-sharp. Both the second and third fingerings should be introduced rather early in saxophone study as they permit students with limited facility to play these intervals more smoothly and accurately than when the regular diatonic fingering is used.

The fourth fingering in which the first finger of the left hand closes both the first tone hole and key ly is one of the most useful, but at the same time one of the most neglected fingerings on the instruments. It provides a fingering for B-flat which utilizes only one finger on the instrument and makes this note as convenient to play as B-natural with the resultant smoothness and rapid facility not possible with the use of the regular diatonic fingering. The only limitation on its use is that the passage not contain B-natural since to produce B-natural the finger would have to slide off of key ly. In this respect its use is analagous to the use of the thumb B-flat lever on the flute. This fourth fingering is considered as a useful alternate, perhaps even the standard fingering for flat keys. Use of this fingering should be delayed until the regular diatonic fingering is established, but then introduced and established in the student's technique. Following are typical passages in which each of the four fingerings are used:

Use fingering 1:

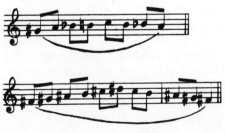

Use fingering 2:

Use fingering 3:

Use fingering 4:

(c) *C-natural* 

Two fingerings: (1) 020 000 (diatonic)
(2) 100 4C00 (chromatic)

The first fingering is the standard fingering for C, while the second is for chromatic passages and where the C follows or precedes B-natural if the right hand is not involved in the fingering of the note immediately preceding or following the C. It is difficult to release key 4C and depress a tone hole simultaneously with the right hand. Use the second fingering, when possible to overcome the inherent roughness which results in the rapid changes from B-natural to the diatonic fingering for C. Following are typical usages of these two fingerings:

Use fingering 1:

Use fingering 2:

(d) *E-natural:* 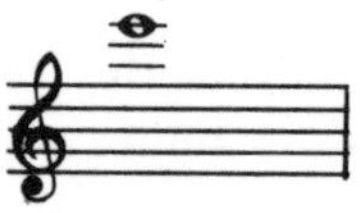

Two fingerings: (1) T D E-flat 000 4E 00 (diatonic and chromatic)
(2) T 1x23 000 (special alternate)

The first fingering is the standard one used except in rare circumstances where a special technical passage calls for the use of the alternate. This alternate "E" is derived from the standard alternate fingering for the high "F," discussed below, but is less stable tonally than the "F" and is not recommended for sustained notes. Breath support and embouchure are critical in this fingering.

The second fingering is primarily useful in rapidly moving passages involving skips from "C" or C-sharp to the "E." It cannot be used where the fingering for the preceding or following note requires that the first finger be in its normal position on the tone hole.

Following are typical uses of this alternate fingering:

Use fingering 2:

(e) *F-natural:* 

Two fingerings: (1) D E-flat F 000 4E00 (diatonic and chromatic)
(2) 1x20 000 (alternate)

Even though it is the highest note in the normal range of the saxophone this F occurs with considerable frequency in the music written for the Alto instrument, with some frequency for the Tenor but rarely for the Baritone. The regular fingering, involving three side keys with the left hand and one in the right is awkward and considerable practice and experience is necessary to gain facility. The regular fingering is used almost exclusively by most saxophonists.

The alternate fingering which provides a tone of equal quality and intonation is valuable in situations where it can be used. This fingering calls for the first finger to be moved from its normal location and stretched upward to key 1x. Virtually every brand of saxophone has this key located in such a way that it is impossible to slide the finger to it—the finger must be picked up from the first tone hole and replaced in its new location. If this key could be moved so that the finger could conveniently roll or slide, it would be of far greater use. It was added to the instrument as an auxiliary key many years after the invention of the instrument by Sax primarily for the interval of C to F in the major arpeggio and for instances where the high F is isolated. This fingering cannot be used conveniently when the first finger is in place on its tone hole on the preceding note, or must be on the tone hole on the note following. This example illustrates typical uses of both fingerings:

Use fingering 1:

Use fingering 2:

6. *Trill fingerings.* Although most trills on the saxophone may be done with the basic and alternate fingerings previously discussed, some notes require special fingerings in order to provide smoothness and speed. Many of these special trill fingerings sacrifice either tone quality or intonation for the sake of facility and must not be used on notes which are sufficiently exposed to give a true impression of pitch and quality.

In addition to the use of trilling these special fingerings are valuable in playing grace notes, mordents, or turns which would otherwise be difficult or impossible to execute. In a trill the lower note is played with a regular fingering and the upper note with the trill fingering. A special chart of trill fingerings is provided following the fingering chart.

7. *Developing the extended range.* The playing range of the Alto and Tenor saxophones can be extended a full octave or more above the high "F" usually indicated as the top limit of the range. For many years such notes were considered a curiosity to be indulged in by a few professionals. But in the past few years their use in contemporary music both "serious" and "popular" has greatly increased, and today most advanced students as well as professional players are expected to have facility in this range.

Only advanced students who have developed a strong flexible embouchure, have mastered breath control and support, and have excellent technical facility and tone control below the high "F" should undertake a study of the extended (or altissimo) range. The student must also be playing on a mouthpiece-reed combination which will respond in this range. If the mouthpiece lay is too short or too close, or the reed too soft the instrument will not respond. But the mouthpiece with the medium lay, medium open tip combined with medium strength reeds—the combination which most advanced players use—will function properly if technique for playing in this register is developed properly.

Notes in this range are in the upper harmonics and the approach to them is through the harmonic series. As an introduction, the student might play the following series of notes using the fingering for the low B-flat. The notes are produced by varying degrees of firmer than normal embouchure pressure and breath support.

Similar patterns can be played using the fingering for the low B-natural, low C, etc. The player should soon be able to play typical bugle calls such as "Reville" or "Taps."

The best presentation of materials, and the most widely used book, for the development of control and facility in the extended range is Sigurd Rascher's *Top-Tones for the Saxophone* published by Carl Fischer. The fingering chart included in the book has only a single fingering for each note. Students may find other fingerings among those included in this text which will respond better for them, or will want to develop their own personal fingerings for these notes.

In developing this register of the saxophone the player will find that: (1) intonation is extremely sensitive and greatly dependent upon fine embouchure control; (2) the fingerings are more complex than fingerings in the lower ranges; (3) these complex finger patterns of many of the fingerings cause technical problems both in facility and accuracy; and (4) considerable persistence over a long period of time is necessary to achieve a useful degree of facility.

A special fingering chart for notes in the extended range is included in this book. There are several fingerings for each note. Response, intonation, and tone quality of the fingerings varies greatly from player to player. Only with experimentation and practice can a player discover the best fingering for him in a given situation. Alto and Tenor saxophones may respond somewhat differently with the same fingering, even with the same player.

TRANSPOSITIONS FOR THE SAXOPHONE

While the saxophonist in the normal band or orchestra routine is rarely called upon to transpose and play a part written for another instrument, the situation does occasionally arise. In those schools which include a dance band in the curriculum the need for facility in transposition frequently becomes a matter of importance, and in the professional dance band field various transpositions are so common as to be considered an essential part of the performer's skill. Certainly the advanced school player should develop facility in the more common transpositions for his instrument. This facility is acquired only by doing it, slowly at first, and then with increasing speed. Regular assignments in transposition of study material should be a part of every advanced student's lessons. The transpositions which are most commonly encountered include:

1. *Playing B-flat clarinet parts on the Alto saxophone.* The need for this transposition is so frequent that the Alto saxophonist who plays or expects to play in a dance band should develop accurate facility in sight-reading this transposition. The process of making the transposition from the B-flat clarinet part to the Alto saxophone is to play the clarinet notes a perfect fifth higher. The Alto saxophone key signature is one sharp more or one flat less than that of the clarinet. This interval gives exactly the same concert pitch sounded by the clarinet. Since the range of the Alto saxophone does not extend as high as that of the clarinet, notes for the clarinet above B-flat above the staff cannot be produced on the Alto saxophone and must be transposed down a perfect fourth and will sound an octave lower than the pitches written for the clarinet. The example below illustrates the interval and key signature transpositions.

2. *Playing Bass clarinet parts on the Baritone saxophone.* In large studio bands the Baritone saxophone player frequently doubles on Bass clarinet. If in the school band this player does not have a Bass clarinet, the parts written for it may be transposed and played on the Baritone saxophone with exactly the same transposition as that used for the B-flat clarinet to Alto saxophone. As both the Bass clarinet and Baritone saxophone sound an octave lower than written this transposition will have the Baritone playing exactly the same pitches as those written for the Bass clarinet. The same limitation in the upper range applies as for the Alto saxophone transposition.

3. *Playing Alto saxophone from piano music.* Playing from a piano part or scales, tuning chords, etc., from a given concert key or from parts written for a non-transposing instrument such as flute is a useful facility to acquire. Flute and oboe are frequent doubles for the Alto saxophone in the studio band, and playing from piano music is frequently recreational in nature which helps encourage development. To sound the same note as the concert key the Alto saxophone plays a major sixth higher than written. The key signature is obtained by adding three sharps or subtracting three flats from the signature of the piano. Example No. 1 (p. 241) illustrates the interval and key signature transpositions. The same transposition is used for playing Baritone saxophone from piano music, but the saxophone sounds an octave lower than the piano note.

4. *Playing Tenor saxophone from piano music.* The need for transposing from a concert key for the Tenor saxophone is as great as that for the Alto saxophone both in the normal school band routine and for recreation, and for those players in the school dance band. The problem with this transposition is that the range in which the Tenor saxophone sounds is an octave lower than those of the oboe, flute, or voice lines on piano sheet

Clarinet Key: C | Saxophone Key: G | Clarinet Key: G | Saxophone Key: D | Clarinet Key: E-flat | Saxophone Key: B-flat

Piano Key: C | Saxophone Key: A | Piano Key: B-flat | Saxophone Key: G | Piano Key: A-flat | Saxophone Key: F

(1)

Piano Key: C | Saxophone Key: D | Piano Key: A-flat | Saxophone Key: B-flat | Piano Key: D | Saxophone Key: E

(2)

Alto Key: C | Tenor Key: F | Alto Key: D | Tenor Key: G | Alto Key: E-flat | Tenor Key: A-flat

(3)

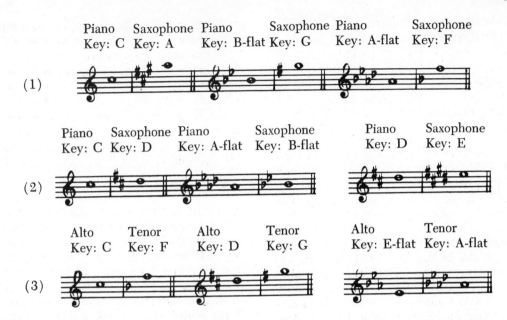

music. With this transposition the Tenor saxophone will sound an octave lower than the written pitches for the original part. This transposition is a major second higher than the written note, sounding an octave lower. The key signature for the Tenor saxophone is obtained by adding two sharps or subtracting two flats from the original signature. Example No. 2 illustrates the interval and key signature transpositions.

5. *Playing Oboe parts on B-flat Soprano saxophone.* Since the oboe cannot be played satisfactorily in a marching band, many directors ask the oboe players to play a Soprano saxophone when marching. As the playing range of the Soprano saxophone is almost identical with that of the oboe, it is a most satisfactory substitute for this purpose and the student transposes the oboe part. The same transposition can be used when playing from a piano, violin, or flute part. This transposition is accomplished in the same way as that described above for playing Tenor saxophone from piano music. The Soprano saxophone will sound the same pitch as the original part.

6. *Playing B-flat clarinet parts on Tenor saxophone.* As both instruments are B-flat instruments the clarinet part may be read as written but will sound an octave lower when played on the Tenor saxophone. Not all parts are satisfactory in the musical texture when sounding an octave lower than written, and the Tenor saxophone should play the notes an octave higher where possible if he is to blend with other B-flat clarinets. In dance band the Tenor saxophone player is expected to double on B-flat clarinet, and playing clarinet parts on the saxophone is not a desirable substitute.

7. *Playing Alto saxophone parts on the Tenor saxophone.* This procedure will be necessary very infrequently in the school dance band, although advanced players who play professionally should have this facility. The need for this transposition arises most frequently in the "Tenor band" style which uses no Alto saxophones but which may play some arrangements in which parts are written for the Alto. In this case the original Alto saxophone part is transposed and played on the Tenor. The problem of the differences in range of actual sounds of the two instruments can be solved only by having the Tenor saxophone play those notes which are out of range an octave lower. To sound the same pitch as the Alto, the Tenor saxophone transposes the note written for the Alto a perfect fourth higher, or a perfect fifth lower to sound an octave below the Alto pitch. The transposed key signature is obtained by adding one flat or subtracting one sharp from the Alto saxophone signature. Example No. 3 illustrates the interval and key signature transposition.

8. *Playing Tenor saxophone parts on the Alto saxophone.* There is very little need for this transposition as the difference in the pitch range of the two instruments does not lend itself to good musical results in most circumstances. The transposition for playing Tenor saxophone parts on the Alto saxophone is the same as that described for transposing from B-flat clarinet parts. With the transposition up a perfect fifth, the Alto saxophone will sound an octave higher than the Tenor saxophone pitch, and the Alto saxophone should play his transposed note an octave lower whenever the range of the instrument permits.

9. *Playing Bassoon parts on Baritone saxophone.* With the chronic shortage of bassoon players in many school systems, some directors who have good Baritone saxophone players available ask them to transpose and

Bassoon Key: C — Baritone Key: A — Bassoon Key: A-flat — Baritone Key: F — Bassoon Key: G — Baritone Key: E

(4)

play the bassoon parts in band or orchestra. This must be considered a temporary expediency as the tone quality of the Baritone saxophone is quite different from that of the bassoon, but it does cover the part and get the job done.

Transposing from the bassoon part, or any other part written in bass clef, is the simplest of all transpositions. To accomplish this, change the bass clef to a treble clef and add three sharps or subtract three flats from the bass clef signature. Other than this purely mechanical process the player must adjust for accidentals in the original part by raising or lowering the pitch of his note in the same way and to the same degree that the written accidental altered the original. With some instruction and experience the average school musician is able to do this accurately. Example No. 4 (above) illustrates the interval and key signature transposition.

Summary of Transpositions

1. *B-flat clarinet parts on Alto saxophone:* Up a perfect fifth (down a perfect fourth), add one sharp.
2. *Bass clarinet parts on Baritone saxophone:* Up a perfect fifth (down a perfect fourth), add one sharp.
3. *Piano music on Alto saxophone:* Up a major sixth (down a minor third), add three sharps.
4. *Piano music on Tenor saxophone:* Up a major second, add two sharps.
5. *Oboe parts on Soprano saxophone:* Up a major second, add two sharps.
6. *Clarinet parts on Tenor saxophone:* Octave higher (where range permits) or unison to sound octave lower.
7. *Alto saxophone parts on Tenor saxophone:* Up a perfect fourth (down a perfect fifth), add one flat.
8. *Tenor saxophone parts on Alto saxophone:* Down a perfect fourth (up a perfect fifth), add one sharp.
9. *Bassoon parts on Baritone saxophone:* Change bass clef to treble clef. Add three sharps. Accidentals inflected same degree as original part.

SELECTION OF INSTRUMENTS

The saxophone was invented by the great artisan of wind instruments, Adolphe Sax, who patented the instrument in 1846. It was the result of his experiments with applying a single reed mouthpiece to the ophicleide, a now obsolete brass instrument played with a cup mouthpiece but having tone holes and pads rather than valves. He was fascinated with the mixture of woodwind and brass tone qualities which resulted and gradually evolved the shape and mechanism of the saxophone which he patented. In general appearance the modern saxophone is little different from the original, but many refinements in the mechanism have been made to expand its technical potentials. The original Sax instruments' range was from low B-natural to the high D. A low B-flat has been added as well as the high notes from D to F. Other changes include the articulations for the G-sharp key, the alternate F-sharp key, and a single automatic octave key replacing the two separate octave keys of the original.

Today the mechanism of the saxophone is so standardized that there is a single model available from all manufacturers, differing mechanically only in shape and placement of keys and finger buttons. The teacher and student are not forced to make a decision between various models having different numbers of keys as they are when selecting a clarinet or oboe.

The same three different grades of instruments, determined by musical standards, are found in the saxophone just as in the other woodwinds. These grades are determined by tone quality produced by the instrument, by the accuracy of its intonation, by the mechanism which must be rugged and capable of easy and long lasting adjustment, by beauty and permanence of its finish, and by the general standards and control of production reflected in the amount and skill of the hand work involved. The grade of instrument must be selected to fit the use to which the student will put it. An instrument suitable for the elementary school beginner is not necessarily suited to the advanced high school or college player. There are considerable differences in the quality of instruments produced by various manufacturers as well as in the various lines of instruments produced by the same manufacturer. Price is not always, even though it is frequently an indication of quality. The higher the standard of tone quality and other musical values expected of the student, the more carefully the instrument must be selected. Select a saxophone with the same high standards and care used in selecting the best oboe or clarinet.

The standard finish for all the saxophones is a brass lacquer, which although giving virtually the same appearance on every brand, is subject to great fluctuation in lasting quality. Until recent years a gold lacquer, giving the instrument a gold rather than a brass color, was an optional choice in finish. This gold lacquer is still available from some manufacturers. Until the development of the gold and brass lacquer, the instruments were silver plated. The silver plate gave a permanent finish to the instrument, while lacquer deteriorates and wears and must be replaced periodically, but was dropped apparently because of the higher cost. The type of exterior finish on the body and keys of the instruments has no effect at all on the tone quality, and is selected for other reasons. The heavy brass lacquer is recommended for all student instruments.

An optional extra key to extend the range down a half-step to A is available in some brands of Baritone saxophones. The Baritone instrument used for illustrations in this chapter has this extension to low A. This extra key requires lengthening the bell of the instrument, and some redistribution of tone holes on the lower part of the instrument. It has no effect on the tone quality of the instrument, nor upon its intonation. This extra key is useful in symphonic bands and in dance bands playing special arrangements where it is called for. It is recommended only for advanced students. This extra key is available only on the Baritone instrument.

STUDENT QUALIFICATIONS AND APTITUDES

The Alto and Tenor saxophones are good beginning instruments, and the comments in this section refer only to them. The Soprano, Baritone, and Bass saxophones should be played only by competent performers on either the Alto or Tenor saxophone. It should be noted that because of the great differences in the cost of a saxophone and a clarinet suitable for young beginners, many teachers prefer to place elementary school age beginners on the clarinet rather than the saxophone. Students who have demonstrated good tone production and basic technique on the clarinet will make rapid progress on the saxophone.

Standards of physical aptitudes for the saxophone are not always reliable. Any student with normal teeth, lip, and chin formation can play the saxophone successfully. Thick lips and thin lips, crooked teeth and straight teeth, and to some extent overbite and underbite can all be accommodated within the normal embouchure formation without any adverse results on future development.

It is obvious that the student must be physically large enough so that he may hold the instrument with the proper hand position before he begins to study the saxophone. Students who are too small to play the instrument develop poor hand positions which are extremely difficult to correct, make slow progress and tend to become discouraged because of the physical handicap.

Whether or not the student is large enough to play the instrument can be easily determined by asking him to hold the assembled instrument with the assistance of a properly adjusted neck strap. Place his right hand in position. If the thumb is in the right place, can he reach the three tone hole buttons with the fingers curved and contact the buttons properly. If he can do this, see if he can reach the C key with the little finger without pulling the hand out of position.

If he is successful in all of this, test the left hand with the thumb in position; will his fingers reach over the side keys to reach the tone buttons and retain their curved shape? Students who can do this can easily reach the G-sharp and C-sharp keys with the little finger. Small hands will have trouble extending the little finger to the B-natural and B-flat keys, but this should be of little concern as these notes do not normally appear very early in the study of the instrument.

Having been checked for physical size, a natural aptitude for the instrument may be determined by the success of the prospective student in producing a steady natural tone of the highest pitch with the mouthpiece and reed alone after some instruction on embouchure. Students who are immediately successful and who are able to produce and sustain a strong clear tone for five to ten seconds may be said to have a natural aptitude for the instrument, and are ready to begin study. Other students may fail this test for some time, but with instruction and guidance may develop an aptitude. Such students should not be denied the opportunity to study saxophone on this basis alone, since the difference between those who quickly accomplish this tone production and those who must work to develop it disappears soon after formal study of the instrument begins. Success or failure on the instrument is determined by many other factors. In the final analysis desire and persistence are the greatest of all aptitudes for any instrument.

CARE OF THE SAXOPHONE

Simple but regular and careful maintenance of the saxophone will keep it in the best playing condition over a long period of time. Careless handling, sporadic cleaning, and lack of attention soon begins to have an effect on how the instrument plays and responds. It is important that the basic procedures for care of the instrument be emphasized from the very beginning of saxophone study so that they are correctly done and become habitual.

Care of the instrument starts with the assembly and disassembly of the instrument. Review the instructions on assembly of the instrument until they are thoroughly understood and the students are performing the operation easily. Disassembly is done in the same manner, but in the exact reverse order of assembly. Keep the instrument in its case when not in use for maximum protection. Heat is the greatest enemy of the instrument. Keep it, in or out of its case, out of direct sunlight and away from radiators and other sources of heat.

Cleaning the Instrument

It is mandatory that the inside of the saxophone—body, neck, and mouthpiece be thoroughly dried after each playing. Establish this routine from the very beginning of study. Many saxophone players have the unfortunate habit of entirely neglecting this process. Swabbing the instrument does not take much time, and will prevent the accumulation of dirt and grime inside the instrument, as well as helping to maintain sanitary conditions for playing.

To dry the instrument properly each case should be equipped with the following:

1. *A swab.* To clean the inside of the body of the instrument. The best and most efficient is a chamois with a center brush attached to a cord with a weight to pull the cord through the instrument. The cord must be long enough to drop entirely through the body of the instrument. This type of swab comes in two sizes, one for Alto and one for Tenor. The Tenor swab can be adapted for use on the Baritone by replacing the cord with one of sufficient length. The Soprano saxophone can be cleaned with the Alto swab, or with a clarinet chamois swab provided the cord is long enough.

2. *A neck cleaner.* A flexible metal wire with a soft wool swab on one end and a stiff brush on the other. The wool swab end is pushed through the neck to dry moisture, while the brush end is used to clean out any accumulated deposits. The neck is the most critical portion of the swabbing process; using a neck cleaner is the only way it can be kept clean. These come in only one size, and can be used on all saxophones.

3. A *chamois of soft cloth.* To clean the inside and outside of the mouthpiece. Because of the danger of chipping the mouthpiece neither the swab or the neck cleaner can be used on the mouthpiece. This chamois or cloth, but preferably another, is used to wipe the upper part of the bell and the outside of the instrument.

The following routine for cleaning the saxophone is a standard one which should be followed carefully until the player is sufficiently advanced to make satisfactory changes to suit himself. The instrument pictured is the Alto saxophone, but the same process is followed on all instruments in the family.

1. *Mouthpiece.* Remove the mouthpiece from the instrument. Loosen the ligature and slide the reed from under it; then remove the ligature. Wipe off the reed with the chamois and put it in a reed case or aside to be returned to the mouthpiece. Roll the chamois to fit the inside of the mouthpiece. Push the smaller end through the mouthpiece, and pull through carefully as in Figure S-43, or push back and forth until the mouthpiece is completely dry.

Return the ligature to the mouthpiece and slide under the reed if it is not kept in a reed case. If the reed is returned to the mouthpiece, put it in playing position, and tighten the ligature screws just enough to hold the reed. If the ligature screws are too tight, there is a danger of damaging the facing of the mouthpiece if the instrument is exposed to heat. Put the mouthpiece cap in place as shown in the directions for assembly, and return the mouthpiece to its place in the case.

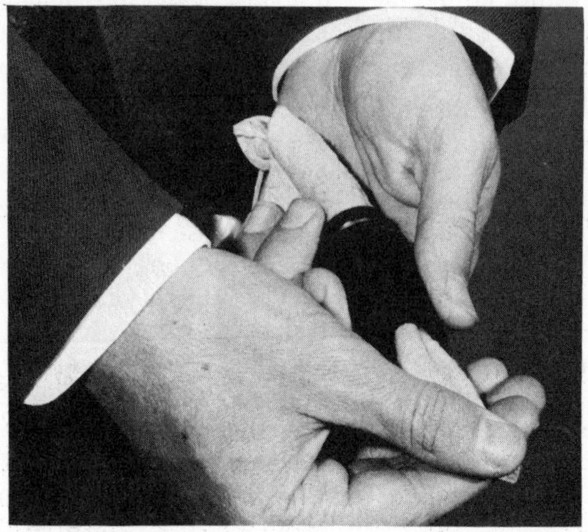

Figure S-43

2. *Neck.* Loosen the tension screw and remove the neck from the body of the instrument. Carefully shake the moisture out of each end. Then holding the neck as shown in Figure S-44 push the wool swab of the neck cleaner into the neck from the large end and back and

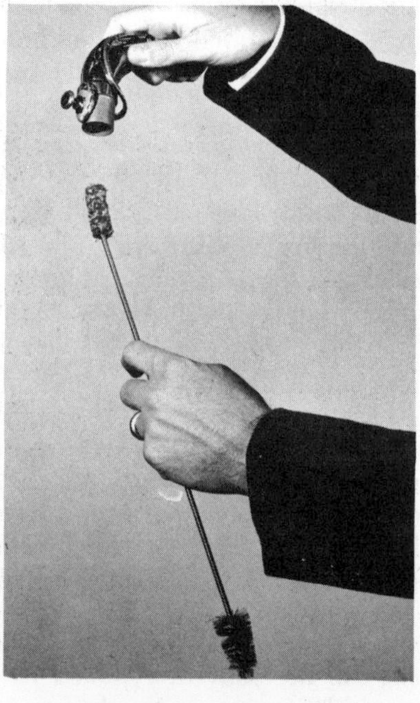

Figure S-44

forth through the neck to thoroughly dry it. Once each week this should be followed by a thorough brushing with the brush end of the neck cleaner. Return neck to its place in the case.

3. *Body.* Holding the body of the saxophone by the bell away from the keys unhook the neck strap. Tilt and shake the body to remove excess moisture from small end. Drop the weight on the end of the swab cord into the bell and rotate the instrument so that it falls out the other end. Pull the swab through the body as in Figure S-45. Repeat this process several times if necessary to remove all moisture.

4. *Connecting joint.* Using a portion of the chamois around the index finger clean the inside of the connecting joint on the top of the body as in Figure S-46. Insert the end plug for storage in case.

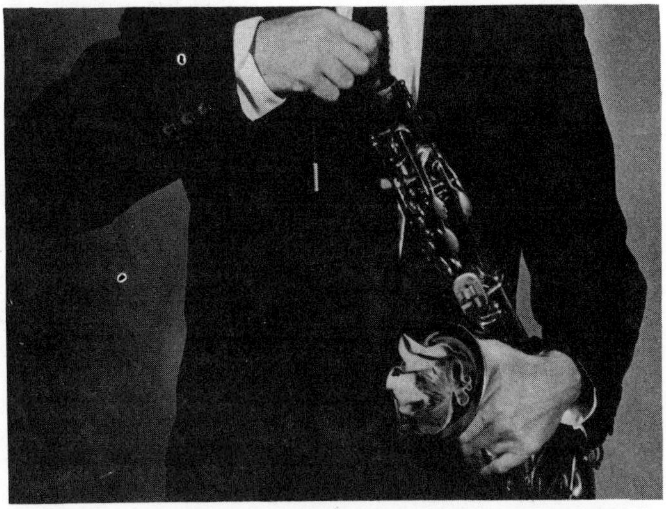

Figure S-45

Figure S-46

5. *Outside of instrument.* Using the chamois or soft cloth wipe the inside portion of the bell that can be reached with the hand, then the outside of the bell to remove finger prints. Continue to wipe the body of the instrument on which no keys are attached. Once a week the entire key mechanism should be wiped free of fingerprints and dust. If this is done regularly and thoroughly the instrument's finish will remain in good condition.

Regular Maintenance of the Instrument

If the saxophone received good care and a regular schedule of maintenance is followed it will remain in the best playing condition over a long period of time. Instruments which are in poor condition are difficult to play and result in poor players. Observing the following suggestions will help keep the saxophone in the perfect mechanical condition so necessary for success on the instrument.

1. *Oiling the mechanism.* The mechanism must be oiled regularly three or four times each year. A special oil, called key oil, is available under various brand names for this purpose. A drop of oil on the end of a needle or toothpick should be at each pivot screw of each key. Do this carefully so that no oil can get onto the pads. This regular oiling keeps pivot screws from excessive wear and from rusting in place, making any repairs and adjustments on the instrument easier to accomplish.

2. *Corks and felts.* A casual examination of the saxophone will reveal a number of bumper corks or felts against which keys rest either in an open or a closed position. These not only keep the mechanism silent in operation but determine the height to which the pads rise above the holes. This height is critical as it has a considerable adverse effect on intonation if it is incorrect.

Two very critical adjusting corks appear on the cup of the tone hole just above the first finger of the right hand. One of these closes a tone hole on the articulated G-sharp, the other a tone hole higher on the instrument when the first or second finger of the right hand is used for a fork B-flat fingering. If either of these are worn or damaged the tone holes do not close and that fingering will not respond. If either of the fingerings does not operate properly suspect these corks first. Some of the better instruments have adjusting screws in connection with these two corks so that they may be kept in perfect adjustment by the player. If any of the corks or felt bumpers are lost or badly worn they should be replaced by a repairman.

3. *Dusting the instrument.* If the instrument is wiped carefully after each use as suggested above, very little dust will accumulate. However, over a period of time some dust will be found beneath the key mechanism where the regular wiping does not reach. This dust can be removed with a soft watercolor brush. If a cloth is used, it must be handled very carefully so it will not snag on the needle springs which break under pressure.

4. *Polishing the instrument.* The body and key mechanism of the saxophone will remain in good condition if wiped regularly as directed. After a long period of use the lacquer is worn away in places where the hands contact the keys and body, and the lacquer begins to loose its sheen. When this occurs the old lacquer must be removed and the entire instrument relacquered—a job for an expert. Students must be cautioned against attempting to polish a lacquered instrument with silver polish or a polishing cloth as such a procedure damages or removes the lacquer entirely, calling for an expensive relacquer job.

5. *Bent rods or keys.* In spite of the best of care, keys or rods sometimes become bent out-of-line. This occurs with alarming regularity on the instruments of young players, and cause unevenness in technique, or even prevent some tones from responding at all. The long rods on the right side of the instrument are especially susceptible to damage. No attempt should be made to straighten keys or rods while they are on the instrument. This puts excessive pressure on both the keys and their posts and the instrument may be damaged even more. This adjustment must be made by a repairman who has the proper knowledge and tools to straighten and align them. Caution students against trying to do it themselves.

6. *Sticking pads.* The saxophone is not especially susceptible to sticking pads because of the large size of most of the pads and the fact that they have rather strong springs. If a student is having a problem with sticking pads, it is probably because he has failed to dry the instrument thoroughly before returning it to the case. Excessively high humidity might also be the cause. The pad most likely to stick is that of the G-sharp key as it is both opened and closed with a spring because of its articulation with other keys. This is discovered when the student fingers G-sharp, but the instrument plays G-natural. It can be unstuck by depressing the G-sharp key and lifting the pad from the hole with the forefinger of the right hand.

The moisture which causes pads to stick can be removed by placing a cigarette paper between the pad and the tone hole, and pressing down firmly on the key. Release the key, move the paper, and repeat the process until the key no longer sticks. If this does not relieve the sticking, put the cigarette paper in place, press the key, and pull the paper slowly from under the pad. Repeat the process several times. If the pad persists in sticking, it should be replaced. Never use powder on pads in attempt to stop sticking as it damages the pad so it deteriorates.

7. *Leaky pads.* Pads on an instrument wear out with use. Some wear out more rapidly than others and begin to leak, causing the instrument to respond with difficulty on certain notes. Pads deteriorate so slowly that the player is frequently not aware that the condition exists. For this reason a close inspection of the condition of the pads on every instrument should be made every three or four months.

There are two methods of determining whether a pad is seated properly or whether it is leaking. The first is by the use of commercial feeler or papers or strips of cigarette paper about a quarter-inch wide. Slide one end of the paper under the pad, put the normal amount of pressure against the pad if the key is not held closed by a spring, and slowly draw the paper out. As long as the pressure against the paper remains constant there is no leak. If the pressure suddenly lessens the pad is not properly seated. Repeat the process completely around the pad so that all edges are tested. The second method is that used most frequently by professional repairmen. This is through the use of a small electric light on the end of a rod which is dropped into the bore of the instrument. When the light is held close to a leaky pad, it will shine through the pad and the exact source of the leak can be determined. Teachers responsible for the condition of numbers of woodwind instruments will find it advantageous to purchase such a light.

Regular Overhaul

The condition of every instrument must be checked at least once each year by the instructor or by a repairman. Regular maintenance keeps an instrument in playing condition over a period of years, rather than allowing it to gradually deteriorate becoming increasingly difficult to play and more expensive to repair. Every instrument must have a complete overhaul every three to five years depending on the amount of usage. If instruments receive a yearly checkup, a regular overhaul, and proper daily maintenance, they will last in virtually perfect condition for many years.

BIBLIOGRAPHY OF STUDY MATERIALS

The amount of study material available for saxophone is considerably more extensive than the casual observer would believe, although it doesn't yet approach the amount and variety available for flute and clarinet. The saxophone student may also take advantage of the instructional material published for oboe. It is in the same playing range demanded of the saxophone and will greatly expand the possibilities for variety in musical styles and content.

In the sections which follow, a cross section of the most widely available material (exclusive of solo and ensemble music) for saxophone is listed. Additional information can be found in a variety of sources including the books by Coleman, Gold, Heller, Hemke, Rasmussen and Mattra, and Teal listed in the bibliography at the end of the book and in the Selective Music Lists of the MENC.

Beginning Methods

Anzalone, V. *Breeze-Easy Method for Saxophone,* 2 vols. Witmark.

Bodegraven, Paul van. *Adventures in Saxophone Playing,* 2 vols. Staff Music Publishing Co.

Calliet, Lucien. *Method for Saxophone,* 2 vols. Belwin, Inc.

Colin-Lindeman. *Saxophone Made Easy,* 2 vols. Charles Colin.

Dalby, M. *All Melody Method,* 2 vols. Pro-Art Publications.

Gekeler-Hovey. *Saxophone Method,* 3 vols. Belwin, Inc.

Gornston, David. *Very First Saxophone Method.* Edward Schuberth & Co.

Henton, H. B. *Beginners Method for Saxophone.* Theodore Presser.

Herfurth, C. P. *A Tune a Day for Saxophone.* Boston Music Co.

Hovey, N. W. *Elementary Method for Saxophone.* Rubank, Inc.

Pease, D. J. *Saxophone Method,* 2 vols. Pro-Art Music Publications.

Rousseau, E. *Saxophone Method for Beginning Students.* Leblanc Music Publications, Inc.

Skornicka. *Intermediate Method for Saxophone,* Rubank, Inc.

Voxman-Gower. *Advanced Method for Saxophone,* 2 vols. Rubank, Inc.

Vereecken, Ben. *Junior Saxophone Method.* Rubank, Inc.

Weber, Fred and Willis Coggins. *Saxophone Student* (Student instrumental Series), 3 vols. Belwin Inc. Separate volumes for alto, tenor, and baritone saxophones. The alto volumes are correlated with five other volumes of solos, studies, études, and duets. The tenor and baritone series of correlated books is the same except no volume of duets.

Standard Methods

Klose-Gay. *Méthode Complète pour Saxophone.* Leduc. English and French text. Modeled after and making use of much of the material in the Klose clarinet method with considerable additional material this is by far the best method for the serious student who has recahed the upper intermediate stage of development. Material is too difficult to follow directly after an "advanced" beginning method.

Iasilli, G. *Modern Conservatory Method for Saxophone.* Two Volumes. Carl Fischer.

Mayeur, A. *Method for Saxophone.* Carl Fischer or Leduc.

Vereecken, B. *Foundation to Saxophone Playing.* Carl Fischer.
The Saxophone Virtuoso. Carl Fischer.
The first of these, while described as an elementary method on the title page, is not a beginning method in the present-day understanding of the word. It is suitable to follow a beginning method. The second has more advanced material in the form of twenty-four advanced studies. The first portion of this book is concerned with transpositions (including for C-melody saxophone!), and the second section with transposing for any saxophone through the use of the seven c clefs.

Ville, Paul de. *Universal Method for the Saxophone.* Carl Fischer. The best and most complete of the American publications, but is not arranged in progressive order of difficulty.

Wiedoeft, R. *Modern Method for Saxophone.* Two Volumes. Robins. With a copyright date of 1950 the Klose is the only one of these methods which presents a modern viewpoint and material. The deVille was copyrighted in 1908, the Vereecken in 1917 and 1919, the Mayeur in 1911, the Iasilli in 1927, the Wiedoeft in 1927, and the Henton in 1928. These dates reflect the tremendous popularity of the saxophone in the United States during the first part of this century, but unfortunately are woefully out of date for contemporary teaching techniques and interests.

Addition Study Material

Ajosa. *8 Grand Études.* Edizioni Zanibon (Franco Colombo).

Allard. *60 Varied Études Based on Gabucci Clarinet Divertimenti.* Belwin-Mills.

Ameller, A.. *Études Expressives.* Peters.

Arnold, Jay. *Fingered Scales for Saxophones.* Shapiro, Bernstein & Co.
Modern Fingering System for Saxophone. Shapiro, Bernstein & Co.
25 Klose Daily Exercises for Saxophone. Shapiro, Bernstein & Co.

Bach-Corroyez. *24 Studies.* Leduc.

Bach, Teal. *15 Two Part Inventions.* Theodore Presser.

Barnards. *24 Virtuoso Studies.* Zimmerman.

Bassi, L.-Iasilli. *27 Virtuoso Studies.* Carl Fischer.

Bates. *Advanced Staccato Studies.* Robbins.

Blatt. *15 Entertaining Études.* Edition Musicus.

Blemant. *20 Melodic Studies,* 2 vols. Leduc.

Bosch, A. *Concert Studies.* Molenaar (Henri Elkan).

Bona. *Rhythmical Articulation Studies.* Schirmer.

Bozza, E. *Twelve Études-caprices.* Leduc.
Eighteen Études. Leduc.

Busser-Paquot. *12 Études Melodiques.* Leduc (with piano).

Capelle. *20 Grand Studies for Saxophone.* Leduc.

Caillieret. *15 Études from Bach Sonatas for Violin Alone.* Leduc.

Cavallini-Iasilli. *30 Caprices,* 2 vols. Carl Fischer.

Chopin. *Chopin Studies Transcribed for Saxophone.* Gornston.

Cragun. *Thirty Melodic Caprices.* Rubank, Inc.
Twenty Études. Rubank, Inc.

Decruck-Breilh. *École Moderne Du Saxophone.* Leduc.

Douse. *How to Double and Triple Staccato.* Baron.

Endresen. *Supplementary Studies for Saxophone.* Rubank, Inc.

Ferling. *48 Studies.* Southern Music Co.

Ferling-Mule. *Studies.* Leduc.

Faulx, J. *20 Virtuoso Studies after Bach.* Henri Elkan.

Gabucci-Allard. *60 Varied Études.* Ricordi.

Gates, E. *Odd Meter Études.* Gornston.
Odd Meter Duets. Gornston.

Gatti. *35 Melodious Technical Exercises.* Carl Fischer.
Studies on Major and Minor Scales. Carl Fischer.

Giampieri. *16 Daily Studies for Perfection.* Ricordi.

Gornston-Paisner. *Fun With Scales.* Leeds.

Hovey, N. *Practical Studies for Saxophone,* 2 vols. Belwin.
Daily Exercises for Saxophone. Belwin.

Karg-Elert. *25 Capricen & Sonate.* Zimmerman (Peters).

Klose. *25 Daily Exercises for Saxophone.* Carl Fischer.

Klose-Mule. *25 Daily Exercises.* Leduc.
25 Technical Studies. Leduc.
15 Melodious Studies. Leduc.
12 Études Chantantes. Leduc.

Kupferman. *Seven Inversions for Saxophone.* Boston Music Co.

Labanchi. *33 Concert Études,* 3 vols. Carl Fischer.

Lacour. *8 Études Brillantes.* Leduc.

Lang. *Beginning Studies in the Altissimo Register.* Lang Music Publishers.

Lamotte, A. *First Book of Scale and Arpeggio Studies.* McGinnis & Marx.

Lazarus. *Grand Virtuoso Saxophone Studies.* Belwin, Inc.

Lefevere. *20 Melodious Studies.* Ricordi.

Luft, J. H. *24 Études.* Editions Costallat.

Massis, A. *Six Études-Caprices.* Leduc.

Mausy, F. *10 Studies of Medium Difficulty.* Henri Elkan.
10 Difficulty Studies. Henri Elkan.

Mayeur, A. *50 Exercises.* Carl Fischer.
Grand Collection of Scales, Arpeggio Exercises and Studies in Interpretation. Carl Fischer.

Mayeur-Chauvet. *Grande Méthode for Saxophone,* 2 vols. Editions Philippi-Combre. (M. Baron).

McCathren. *Daily Routine for Saxophone.* Leblanc.

McKusick. *Supplementary Studies for the Modern Saxophonist.* Belwin, Inc.

Mule, M. *24 Easy Studies after Samie.* Leduc.
Scales and Arpeggios, 3 vols. Leduc.
18 Studies after Berbiguier. Leduc.
Daily Exercises after Terschak. Leduc.
30 Grand Studies after Soussmann, 2 vols. Leduc.
52 Studies After Boehm, Terschak and Furstenau, 3 vols. Leduc.
Miscellaneous Studies in All Keys: After the works of Campagnoli, Dont, Gavinies, Kayser, Kreutzer, Mazas, Paganini, and Rode. Leduc.
The works of Mule are basic for serious saxophone study. These are listed roughly in progressive order of difficulty.

Nash. *Studies in High Harmonics.* Leeds

Pares, C. *Scales and Daily Exercises for Saxophone.* Carl Fischer.
Modern Foundation Studies for Saxophone. Rubank.
Two versions of the same material.

Pantaleo. *Six Virtuoso Caprices.* Carl Fischer.

Paquot. *School for Style: 10 Melodic Pieces for Tenor Saxophone.* Piano accompaniment for each available separately. Leduc.

Parisi-Iasilli. *40 Technical and Melodious Studies,* 2 vols. Southern Music Co.

Perrin. *22 Transcendental Studies.* Leduc.
Daily Practice for Scales and Arpeggios. Leduc.

Rascher, S. *Top-Tones for the Saxophone.* Carl Fischer.
158 Saxophone Exercises. Wilhelm Hansen.
24 Intermezzi. Alto and piano. Bourne.
Scales for the Saxophone. McGinnis & Marx.

Rose-Gornston. *22 Selected Rose Studies.* Pro-Art Publications.

Rossari-Iasilli. *53 Études,* 2 vols. Southern Music Co.

Ruggiero. *15 Studies for Perfection.* Leduc.
20 Technical and Melodious Studies. Edizioni Zanibon. (Franco Colombo)

Runyon. *Dynamic Études.* Gornston.

Salviani. *Exercises for Saxophone.* Carl Fischer.

Samie-Mule. *24 Easy Studies.* Leduc.

Schiemann. *7 Characteristic Studies.* Edition Musicus.

Schmidt, W. *10 Contemporary Études.* Avant.

Sellner. *Method for Saxophone,* 2 vols. Costallat.
Progressive Studies in Articulation. Costallat.

Small, L. J. *27 Melodious and Rhythmical Studies.* Carl Fischer.

Soussman-Mule. *30 Grand Studies,* 2 vols. Leduc.

Spear. *Basic Syncopation.* Pro-Art Publications.

Teal, L. *The Saxophonist's Workbook.* University Music Press.
Studies in Time Division. University Music Press.

Terschak-Mule. *Daily Exercises.* Leduc.

Traxler-Lazarus. *Virtuoso Studies.* Belwin, Inc.

Tustin, W. *Technical Studies.* Peer International Corp.

Verroust. *24 Melodic Studies,* 2 vols. Editions Billaudot. McGinnis & Marx.

Vivard. *Grand Method,* 2 vols. Salabert editions.

Voxman, H. *Selected Studies for Saxophone.* Rubank, Inc.

Lyon. *32 Études.* Costallat.

Zietk. *Studies.* Boosey & Hawkes.

Special Studies in the Jazz Idiom

Many teachers and students are interested in special studies for developing performance practices and style in the jazz idiom. A special body of material is available for this purpose and is being used quite successfully. The following are the most widely used.

Baker, J. *Jazz Improvisation.*

Coker, J. *Improvising Jazz.* Prentice-Hall.

LaPorta, J. *A Guide to Improvisation.* Berklee Press. Has a director's manual, three seven-inch LPs and books for B-flat and E-flat instruments.

Developing the School Jazz Ensemble. Berklee Press. Has a director's manual and books for various instruments including alto, tenor and baritone saxophones.

Nelson, O. *Jazz Patterns for Saxophone.*

Niehaus, L.. *Jazz Conception for Saxophone,* 3 vols. The most widely used of these books.

Viola, J. *Technique of the Saxophone,* 3 vols. Berklee Press. Vol. I. Scale Studies, Vol. II. Chord Studies, Vol. III. Rhythm Studies.

Developing Sight Reading Skills in the Jazz Idiom. Berklee Press. Has books for B-flat and E-flat instruments.

Study and Achievement Questions

1. Discuss the possible reasons for the lack of performance standards for the saxophone.
2. What is the theoretical written range for the saxophone?
3. Select a band arrangement scored for a full complement of saxophones. Transpose the saxophone parts to the pitches they actually sound and make a two-line piano score of these parts.
4. Identify the easy and complete range for the instrument.
5. Assemble a saxophone identifying each part as it is taken from the case and demonstrating the correct holding positions for each operation. Show how the neck strap is correctly adjusted.
6. Demonstrate the correct procedure for placing a reed on the saxophone mouthpiece. Add the protective cap.
7. Observe one or more beginning, intermediate and advanced saxophone students and fill out the check list for assembly. Suggest corrections for any faults.
8. Describe and demonstrate the correct holding and hand positions for the saxophone. Instruct a student unfamiliar with the instrument in how to achieve the correct positions.
9. Observe one or more beginning, intermediate, and advanced saxophone students and fill out the checklist for holding and hand positions. Describe the effect any faults will have on performance and suggest appropriate corrections.
10. Discuss and demonstrate correct and incorrect placement and use of the left thumb. The correct placement of the right thumb. Demonstrate hand positions for correct use of the side keys.
11. Describe and discuss the two basic embouchure formations for saxophone. Select one and demonstrate the step-by-step procedure in its formation. Do the same with a student who is unfamiliar with the instrument.
12. List the most commonly found faults in the type embouchure selected and describe the effect of each on performance.
13. Observe various students during performance and fill out check lists for embouchure formation. If any faults are observed identify their effect on performance, and suggest corrections.
14. What are the factors which will make the pitch of a saxophone flat? Sharp? Instruct an advanced player on how to demonstrate some of them.
15. Identify by writing on the staff the three registers in the saxophone's range.
16. What is meant by an "extended range" for the saxophone? How is this achieved?
17. List the most common problems in tone production on the saxophone together with their causes and corrections.
18. Describe the three basic methods for tongue placement for articulation. How does this placement differ on the Alto, Tenor, and Baritone instruments?
19. What is an articulated G-sharp key? How does it function?
20. List all the notes which have alternate fingerings, demonstrate each, and illustrate how each is used.
21. Identify the various transpositions which may be required of a saxophonist and describe how each is made.
22. What three items are needed for the regular cleaning of the instrument?
23. Perform the process of disassembly and cleaning. Discuss the regular maintenance of the instrument.
24. How may sticking pads be corrected? How may leaky pads be identified?
25. Make a comparative analysis of as many beginning saxophone methods as you have available. Select and rank them in order of preference.
26. Examine available standard methods and additional study materials for saxophone and list them with comments. Examine and list oboe study material which you consider suitable for saxophone.
27. Prepare a suggested list of study material to include all five types of material suggested for simultaneous study for an upper beginning level student. For an intermediate level student. For an advanced student.

28. Attend a music festival event which includes saxophone solos and ensembles. Observe the players and make a detailed critique of as many as possible on details of holding positions, hand positions, embouchure formation, tuning, intonation, tone quality, articulation, and technique. Describe any faults found in any of these, the symptoms, possible causes, and corrections for each.

Chapter 7

Mouthpieces and Reeds

The quality, intonation, and control of the tone of the clarinet and saxophone are influenced by and, to a great extent, determined by the mouthpiece together with the reed and the embouchure. Of these basic factors involved in the production of the tone, only the mouthpiece remains constant. Further, it can be measured and produced so that under careful quality control in production any number can be made which will respond exactly alike.

Embouchures vary considerably from player to player, and even from day-to-day with the same player. The quality of response in reeds cannot be predicted. They wear out and must be replaced. Because of the variation in embouchure and reed it is most important that the one stable item—the mouthpiece—be carefully selected and cared for.

A tone is produced on the clarinet and saxophone by the vibration of the reed which acts as a flap beating against the mouthpiece alternately opening and closing the tip opening. When the tip opening is closed, the stream of air is interrupted, and when the reed breaks free from its contact with the mouthpiece the air stream flows into the instrument. This rapid pulsation of air into the instrument sets the column of air into vibration and produces a tone. The length of the column of air is determined by the fingering being used for a particular note, and forces the reed to vibrate in the natural frequency of the note being fingered.

The mouthpiece must be constructed so that the vibration of the reed can be controlled by the embouchure in such a way as to produce the desired pitch and tone quality. The length of the table (or lay) and the amount of curvature determine how much of the reed moves and how far it must move. The opening at the tip determines how far the flexible tip of the reed must move to stop the flow of air. The size and shape of these parts of the mouthpiece in relation to the vibration of the reed becomes of the utmost importance when it is realized that the reed strikes the mouthpiece 146 times each second for the Chalameau F and 1,395 times each second for the G in the high register on the clarinet. For this to occur such a large number of times each second in such a way as to produce the best sounds, demands a fine mouthpiece.

Achieving the proper number of vibrations per second to produce the desired pitch is the most simple of the problems. A poor mouthpiece, even combined with a poor reed and embouchure formation will produce a pitch. A pitch is not enough. The tone must be of a pleasing characteristic quality for the instrument. The quality of a tone is determined by the form of the sound wave produced. The best wave form will produce a good quality, another shape wave will produce a poor quality. The basic forms of the sound waves which can be produced are determined by both the internal and external shape and dimensions of the mouthpiece. This basic form determines the limits within which the reed and embouchure can operate to produce and control the type of sound produced. If the physical characteristics of a mouthpiece do not produce a basic wave form which is capable of being controlled and shaped to produce the desired tone quality even with the best embouchure and the finest reed, it will not be possible to develop a good tone.

The loudness of the tone produced on a single reed mouthpiece is determined primarily by the amplitude of the vibration of the reed. The greatest amplitude, hence the loudest tone possible, is determined by the length and amount of curve on the facing and by the amount of tip opening. From this maximum amount of vibration, the embouchure working with the flow of breath tightens and controls the amplitude for less volume of tone. If the greatest amplitude is not large enough the student cannot play with a full tone no matter how much the embouchure is relaxed. If the facing is long and the tip quite open an embouchure which is quite strong is required to play a soft tone with good quality and control. Selecting a reed to fit the mouthpiece will sometimes aleviate this situation, although usually at the expense of tone quality.

PARTS OF THE MOUTHPIECE

The construction of mouthpieces for all clarinets and saxophones is basically the same. The size is changed to fit the instrument on which it is being used, but the identification of parts and the influence of these parts is the same on all. Figure R-1 which is a drawing of a B-flat clarinet mouthpiece identifies in standard nomenclature the parts of the mouthpiece.[1]

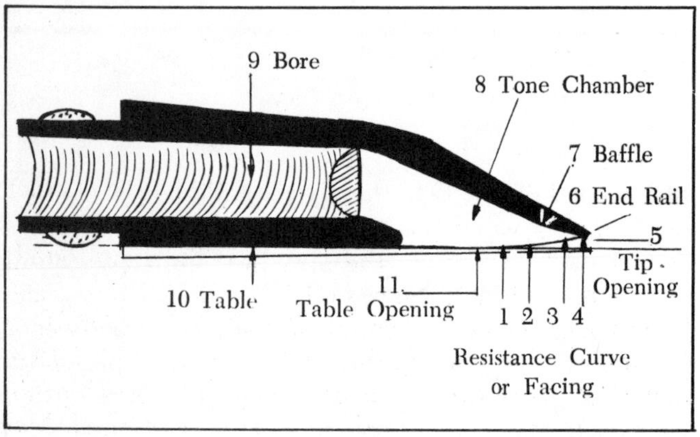

Figure R-1. Clarinet Mouthpiece—Cross Section.

The manner in which the mouthpiece is constructed, i.e., the shape of the tone chamber, the size of the bore, the length and shape of the table opening, and the size of the tip opening determine the kind and quality of tone the mouthpiece is capable of producing. Upon this potential the reed and embouchure are selected and developed to produce the desired tone quality. There is no scientific evidence that a mouthpiece needs to be fitted to a particular individual or to a particular embouchure formation in order to achieve a desired tone quality. A mouthpiece with a medium facing and a medium tip opening, provided it is constructed accurately with all specifications correct, will be the best choice for every student.

The parts of the mouthpiece identified in the drawing may be described as follows:

1, 2, 3, 4. *The facing*, resistance curve, or lay is the portion on the flat side which slants away from the reed. The facing varies greatly both in length and in the amount of curvature. A short lay requires less mouthpiece in the mouth, and frequently produces a stuffy tone quality with little volume or projection. An excessively long lay requires more than the normal amount of mouthpiece in the mouth. Because of the greater length of reed which is vibrating it is more difficult to control, demands more than normal breath pressure, frequently produces a rough tone and is tiring to play. A long facing usually requires a soft reed, while a short facing calls for a stiff reed.

5. *Tip opening*. This is the distance between the mouthpiece and the reed at the tip. The tip opening is described as close, medium, or wide, each with some variation depending on the length of the facing. The amount of tip opening is determined by the amount of curvature on the facing as well as its length. It is this opening which provides the resistance to the flow of breath into the instrument. A close opening offers great resistance, requires a stiff reed, and produces a small stuffy tone quality. A wide opening offers little resistance, requiring a soft reed, a strong embouchure, and is difficult to control. A medium opening is recommended for all students at all levels of advancement. It provides optimum resistance, uses a medium stiff reed, and normal embouchure support. The medium opening produces the tone quality commonly accepted as typical of the instrument regardless of the type of embouchure formation used.

6. *End rail*. The end rail is the edge of the mouthpiece tip against which the tip of the reed beats. This is a critical portion of the mouthpiece, which must be perfectly smooth, not too wide, and the same width from side to side. The width varies with the instrument for which the mouthpiece is made. On the B-flat clarinet it should be no wider than one thirty-second of an inch. If the end rail is too wide the reed responds slower because it has a tendency to stick on the surface, and it is difficult to articulate properly. The shape of the end rail must correspond exactly with the shape of the reed for that instrument. The mark of a well-made mouthpiece is in the finishing of this end rail which must be carefully done by hand.

7. *Baffle*. The baffle is produced when the end rail is completed and the inside of the mouthpiece is leveled off to fit the tone chamber. The height of this baffle is critical in tone production. If it is too high the mouthpiece squeaks. If it is too low it is difficult to produce and control notes in the upper register of the instrument. Some mouthpieces which are otherwise well made, will be unusable because of the height of the baffle.

8. *Tone chamber*. The tone chamber is the interior of the mouthpiece under the facing, extending from the tip to the beginning of the bore. The proportions of the tone chamber determine to a degree the type of response the mouthpiece will give and the quality of tone it will produce. Most brands of mouthpieces use the same shape tone chamber for all models for a particular instrument, varying only the facing and tip opening. A few will have a choice of tone chambers, and if they are available will make this fact known. The size and shape of the tone chamber varies considerably from brand to brand, and is one aspect of the mouthpiece which may be seen easily with a visual examination.

1. Reproduced by permission of Mr. Arlie Richardson.

It is wise to stay with a medium bore and to avoid radical variations from the standard.

9. *Bore.* The bore is the cylindrical, or mostly cylindrical, portion which fits on the barrel joint. The size and shape of the bore must be a continuation of the bore of the instrument upon which it is used. All instruments of the same type do not use exactly the same bore, nor is the size of the mouthpiece bore identical in all cases. If the tone of the instrument is uneven, or if there are serious intonation problems which cannot otherwise be identified the student should try another mouthpiece preferably of another brand which has a different bore.

10. *Table.* The table is the flat portion of the mouthpiece on which the reed is held by the ligature. If the reed is to respond properly it is important that the table be perfectly flat. A well finished mouthpiece will have a perfectly symetrical shaped table on which the reed can be centered.

11. *Table opening.* The table opening is the space over the tone chamber on which the reed vibrates. Its size is the result of the basic side of the tone chamber and the length of the table. On mouthpieces for a particular instrument the width is determined by the standard reed size for that instrument and by the width of the side rails. The width may vary slightly without influencing the tone. If the opening is too wide or too narrow reeds will not fit properly, and such a mouthpiece should be promptly discarded.

12. *Side rails.* The side rails are not shown in the illustration. They are the edges of the table opening which are shaped to make the facing of the mouthpiece. These rails must be perfectly smooth if the reed is to vibrate properly. A slight bump in a side rail will cause air to leak through the edge of the reed. The facing on the side rails must be absolutely identical on either side of the opening. If they are not, more of one side of the reed vibrates because it is damped by contact with the rail further back than the other side. This irregular vibration causes many problems in tone production and control which must be compensated for by the embouchure.

CRITERIA FOR A GOOD MOUTHPIECE

While the physical specifications of a mouthpiece determine how it will respond, the criteria by which a mouthpiece may be judged are musical ones. As such, they are subjective rather than objective in nature, and may be summarized as follows.

A good mouthpiece is one which:

1. Produces a tone which has good body, typical of the best produced on the instrument, and matching in quality in all registers.

2. Plays perfectly in tune in all registers with no more than normal embouchure adjustments.

3. Allows the easy production of all types of articulations from hard short staccato to broad legato at all dynamic ranges.

4. Has a wide dynamic range over which the tone quality remains constant.

5. Does not require too much or too little mouthpiece in the mouth so that a standard embouchure may be formed.

6. Is not highly critical of reeds, but is one for which it is fairly easy to find and adjust a satisfactory reed of medium strength.

RECOMMENDATION FOR A MOUTHPIECE

Authorities do not all agree unanimously on the brand or facing of the mouthpiece to be used. One standard brand offers thirteen different combinations of facings and tip openings for the clarinet and seven combinations for the saxophone. Another offers eleven for the clarinet and thirteen for the saxophone. It is interesting to note that while all brands offer a wide selection, most brands indicate which are their most popular facings. Regardless of the brand, three out of four of the facings indicated as being the most popular fall within the recommendation of a medium length with a medium tip opening.

This confirms the most general consensus of authorities that all students on any level of advancement should play on a mouthpeice with a medium facing and medium tip opening. Mr. Arlie Richardson who has done intensive research in the field of single reed mouthpieces makes the statement in connection with clarinet mouthpieces: "In recording and observing many national and regional bands composed of students selected from all over the United States, I have found that the chairs held after auditions to be in direct ratio to the type of mouthpiece played, and that as few as two of forty-eight players played anything but a medium facing."

Even more important than the maker's designation of medium facing and medium tip is how closely the individual mouthpiece meets the maker's specifications for that particular model of mouthpiece. The facing is put on by hand following preset dies, rather than being put on automatically by machine. The various measurements on a mouthpiece must be accurate within a thousandth of an inch, and the necessary handwork allows for considerable error. Quality control in the matter of facings seems to vary from day-to-day.

Measurements made of twenty-eight B-flat clarinet mouthpieces made by a famous company and having the same model number revealed that no two were exactly alike in all their dimension. Measurements made of a number of clarinet and saxophone mouthpieces made by another well-known company failed to turn up a single one which was not defective in some critical part or another. This explains the experience of most teachers that no two mouthpieces play exactly alike even though they have the same model number.

In selecting a mouthpiece the more advanced students should thoroughly test a number of mouthpieces by playing on them. In this test various reeds must be used for not all reeds fit all mouthpieces. This testing must be done over a period of several days since the embouchure compensates for variations in both reed and mouthpiece. When the choice is narrowed down to two or three, the player should try many reeds on each, for one of the best criteria for a good mouthpiece is its quality for responding to various kinds of reeds rather than being highly critical of the type of reed with which it will respond.

In addition to the playing test, it is well to actually measure the physical characteristics of the mouthpiece. Until recently this has been possible only with home made or laboratory instruments. The LeBlanc company has available a mouthpiece gauge kit for B-flat clarinet mouthpieces at the present time, and it is anticipated that similar kits for the other clarinets as well as for the saxophones will become available in the future. This kit consists of a tip gauge, and three metal shims of different thicknesses to measure the curvature of the facing.

The mouthpiece is measuerd by holding it table down on a piece of plate glass marked off with sixteenths of an inch. A B-flat clarinet medium tip will measure .0431 inches in height with the gauge in the center. A medium curve facing will measure .0015 inches at 10/16 inch, .010 inches at 7/16 inch, .024 inches at 4/16 inch, and .034 inches at 2/16 inch. These measurements are average and slight deviations in either direction would also indicate medium measurements. Use of the metal shims are especially useful to indicate whether or not the lay is warped. Teachers responsible for a number of clarinet students, or responsible for purchasing mouthpieces for schools will find the kit most useful in securing mouthpieces which are not defective. Checking student mouthpieces will often reveal that the mouthpiece is defective and changing mouthpieces will result in a rapid and startling improvement.

There are many brands of mouthpieces available today, and some of them are excellent musical tools. Generally speaking, the best mouthpieces are made of machined rod-rubber or of crystal glass. Inferior mouthpieces are made of poorer quality rod-rubber or molded plastic. However, with the proper manufacturing methods and quality control it is theoretically possible to make mouthpieces of molded rubber or plastic which are equal in quality to the best rod-rubber and crystal. The buyer has no way of knowing the playing qualities of any mouthpiece without a trial and measuring.

The rod-rubber and crystal mouthpieces are considered better because of the amount of handwork and the quality control which goes into the production of first-line mouth-indicate a mouthpiece of high quality.

There is no evidence that the material of which a mouthpiece is made has any effect at all on the type of tone quality it produces. Rod-rubber, crystal, or molded rubber or plastic will all produce equally good tone quality if the dimensions of the mouthpiece—the bore, tone chamber, resistance curve, and tip opening—are identical.

MOUTHPIECE DEFICIENCIES

Many difficulties students have in performance could be remedied if they would change to a good mouthpiece. Even the youngest beginner must have a good mouthpiece since he will progress much faster and be more satisfied with the results if he does have one. It is recommended that the mouthpieces which the makers supply with the inexpensive school instruments be replaced with a good quality mouthpiece, or that the instruments be purchased with the brand and model mouthpiece specified. It is obvious that the further advanced the student is in his performance the more important it is that he have the best possible mouthpiece with which to work.

It must be pointed out, however, that many problems which are attributed to mouthpieces are actually caused by embouchure formation, tongue placement, or reeds. If all these are correct, or if it is virtually impossible to find a reed which responds satisfactorily then it is the mouthpiece which should be suspected. Some common problems in connection with mouthpieces are the following:

1. *Warped lay.* A lay is warped when the rail on one side touches the bottom of the reed at a different distance from the tip than the rail on the other side. Some mouthpieces come from the maker with the facing warped. A mouthpiece may be tested for a warped lay by running a thin paper such as a cigarette paper between the mouthpiece and the reed. When the paper has reached as far as it will go it should be straight across the reed. If not the facing is warped at this point. The lay may be warped at any point on the facing as well as the end tested at the paper. Other locations may be tested for warping by using metal shims similar to those mentioned in the clarinet mouthpiece gauge kit with the mouthpiece held against the plate glass.

A warped lay may be caused during the process of making it, by a ligature which is consistently too tight, by subjecting the mouthpiece to excessive heat, or by washing the mouthpiece in hot water. A mouthpiece with a warped lay requires that the embouchure adjust to it, needs specially adjusted reeds, and may squeak. A warped mouthpiece can be avoided by keeping it away from heat, removing the reed and storing it in a reed case after playing, tightening the ligature just enough to hold the reed firmly in place rather than as tight as it will go, and making sure by testing and measuring that it is in perfect condition before it is purchased.

2. *Refacing the lay.* A warped mouthpiece may be corrected by having it refaced. There are many special-

ists over the country who have the knowledge and tools to not only correct warping but to put an entire facing on the mouthpiece. They can duplicate in a mouthpiece the exact dimensions of another. Many teachers have worked out formulae for the facing which works best for their students, and recommend that the students use this facing put on by a specialist. If a mouthpiece is otherwise a good one, then it is worth having refaced.

3. *Blows too hard.* This is caused by a mouthpiece with a lay that is too long or by a tip that is too close. The length and tip opening may be determined by measurements. The condition of blowing too hard may also be caused by a reed that is too stiff. The first remedy is to attempt to find a reed which fits the mouthpiece and responds according to the criteria for a good reed. If this does not correct the difficulty, other mouthpieces should be tried or the mouthpiece refaced.

4. *Too little resistance.* When a mouthpiece has too little resistance measuring the tip opening and the length of the facing will indicate a tip which is too open, or a reed which is too soft on a long lay, or both. Attempt first to correct the condition with a reed. If this fails try other mouthpieces, or have the mouthpiece refaced to a medium length lay and medium open tip.

5. *Stuffy tone.* This is the product of a short lay or a close tip, or a combination of both. A stiffer reed may remedy the situation, however the tone and intonation will be controlled with difficulty. A mouthpiece which produces a stuffy tone is best discarded.

6. *Intonation.* A properly proportioned mouthpiece will play with good intonation, assuming a good embouchure and reed. A mouthpiece with a tone chamber which is too large will cause the instrument to play sharp. This condition is most often found in "novelty" mouthpieces rather than in standard brands. If the size and taper of the bore of the mouthpiece does not properly match the bore of the instrument there will be intonation problems. This again is found frequently in novelty brands rather than in standard brands.

Most of the serious intonation problems attributed to a standard mouthpiece of the medium dimensions will, upon careful investigation, be found to be embouchure problems. Or if only the throat tones are sharp or flat in relation to the rest of the instrument the barrel joint is too short or too long. Defective barrel joints are the result of using a joint which the manufacturer did not provide for that instrument, or because it has been shortened by being cut off in the repair shop. The various registers of the instrument cannot be played in tune if the barrel joint is too short or too long.

REEDS

The reed has been described as the "soul" of the instrument by a player who had just found a good one, a "nightmare" by another, and various other terms both complimentary and uncomplimentary. But the fact remains that the reed poses a problem for every player from the rank beginner to the most seasoned professional.

Excellent mouthpieces and instruments can be purchased and kept in perfect condition, a good embouchure formed and developed, smooth and facile technique acquired—all of which remain more or less permanent

Single Reeds

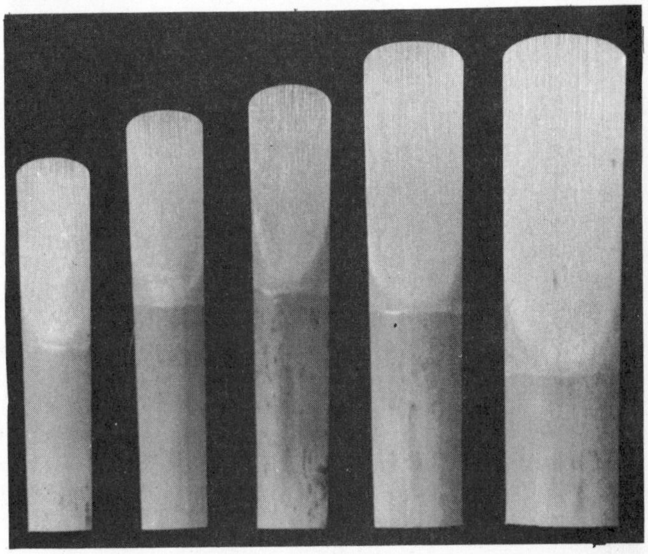

Figure R-2. Clarinet Reeds—Left to right: E-flat clarinet, B-flat (or A) clarinet, Alto clarinet, Bass clarinet, and Contra-bass clarinet.

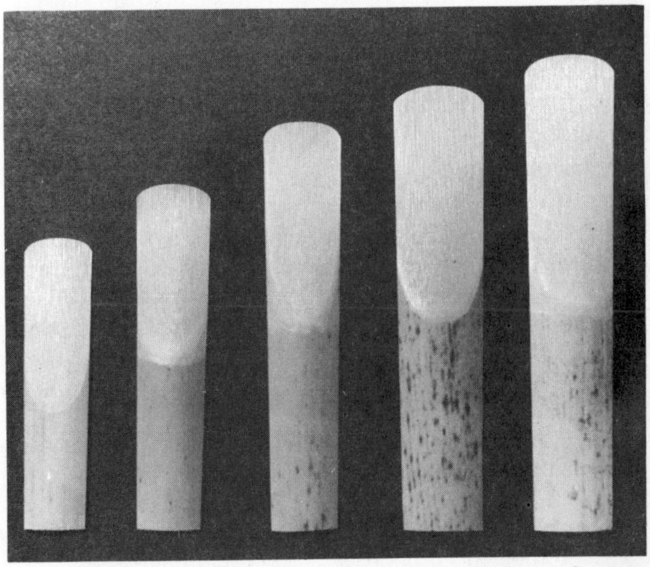

Figure R-3. Saxophone Reeds—Left to right: Soprano saxophone, Alto saxophone, Tenor saxophone, Baritone saxophone, and Bass saxophone.

acquisitions of the performer. But even the best of reeds may last only a few days or a few weeks at the most, and the player is faced with the necessity of finding another one on which to play, and then another, and another endlessly. No wonder some players have the chronic disease known as "reeditis," which can and should be avoided at all costs.

Oboe and bassoon students usually learn the art of reed making and adjustment as a regular part of the study of their instrument, and soon gain enough experience to make their own reeds from a blank piece of cane. Even if the oboe and bassoon students are not making their own reeds, they can be taught how to test and adjust the reeds which they acquire from commercial sources.

Clarinet and saxophone students rarely make their own reeds because of the ready availability of commercial reeds at relatively low costs. For this reason it is wise to give these students instructions on how to select, test, and adjust their reeds. This information is well known, fairly standardized, and easily accessible. There are no secrets of the trade, and the selection and adjustment of single reeds is not particularly time consuming.

It is not the purpose of this book to go into great detail or into an involved discussion of reeds. Rather it is the intent to present the basic facts of selecting, testing, and adjusting in organized fashion those facts which both teachers and players need to know and use in their everyday activities. A list of books which go into more details are listed in the bibliography.

CRITERIA FOR A GOOD REED

Whether a reed is or isn't a good one for an individual player is a subjective judgment. Players themselves can judge how a reed responds when they play it, but frequently can't judge exactly how it sounds to others because vibrations which are not heard by another person are transmitted through the upper teeth to the ear. The teacher can be of great assistance to the student through listening and commenting on how various reeds sound. The student will soon learn how the best reeds feel to him when he is playing and will be in a better position to judge the final tone quality for himself.

Whether the student makes his own reeds or buys them already made, the criteria for a good reed are the same. These critria are applied to the musical results obtained by a specific student. Therefore, for the individual using it, a good reed is one that:

1. Responds freely and easily over the entire range of the instrument.
2. Plays all octaves of the instrument well in tune without undue adjustments in embouchure or lip pressure.
3. May be controlled throughout the full dynamic range in all octaves of the instrument.
4. Produces the correct resistance to wind pressure.
5. Allows the complete scope of articulations from hard staccato to soft legato to be played in all octaves.

Every player should have three or more reeds adjusted, broken in, and ready to play at all times. Some authorities recommend that clarinet and saxophone players rotate reeds, rather than playing on a single reed until it is no longer satisfactory. It is not recommended that oboists or bassoonists rotate reeds from day-to-day, but it is dangerous to play on the same reed until it completely deteriorates. As the reed deteriorates, the embouchure makes adjustments to compensate for the reed deficiencies; and when a new reed is selected to play, the embouchure must be readjusted to it. For this reason, oboists and bassoonists, as well as clarinetists and saxophonists, should practice ocassionally on a reed which is not being used in performance in order to break it in as well to help maintain an embouchure which is not set inflexibly to a particular reed.

CLARINET AND SAXOPHONE REEDS

All clarinet and saxophone reeds are machine made, and as a result are not tested and adjusted as are oboe and bassoon reeds which are mostly hand made. As a result the cost of single reeds is considerably less than the double reeds, which makes it possible for the clarinet and saxophone player to exercise greater selectivity as to the reeds he actually uses. The best procedure for selecting single reeds is to buy them by the box of twenty-five in order to have enough from which to select. A good player will find four or five reeds in a box which he can use with very little adjustment. Another four or five can be used, but require more adjustment. The remaining reeds he will discard as being unusable. If it is impossible for students to buy reeds by the box, they should purchase them a half dozen at a time, and expect to discard three of them.

The selection of a reed is a highly personal matter, since only the person who is to play it can make the selection. The reasons for this are numerous, and perhaps help explain why reeds are such a problem for some players and no problem at all for others. How a reed responds is determined by the player's embouchure and mouthpiece as well as the inherent characteristics of the reed itself. A reed which does not respond at all for one individual on his instrument plays beautifully for another. A mouthpiece which is defective in any of several respects will make it difficult if not impossible to find a satisfactory reed. Thus the first prerequisite for a good reed is a good mouthpiece.

The individual embouchure formation has a tremendous effect on reed response, although the nearer to a standard formation the embouchure is the less difficulties there are in finding a satisfactory reed to produce the desired tone quality. A good embouchure, then, is the second prerequisite for finding a good reed. This, unfortunately, eliminates the beginner who has only a start toward developing an embouchure, but even he can make study on the instrument infinitely easier by having a reed which best fits his needs. The instructor must assume responsibility for seeing that he has a suitable reed, for a reed which is to hard or too soft or poorly proportioned can have disastrous results on a beginning embouchure.

Before discussing the points to be considered in selecting a reed a vocabulary for identification of the various parts of the reed should be established. The illustration shown below identifies parts of the reed which will be referred to throughout this discussion.

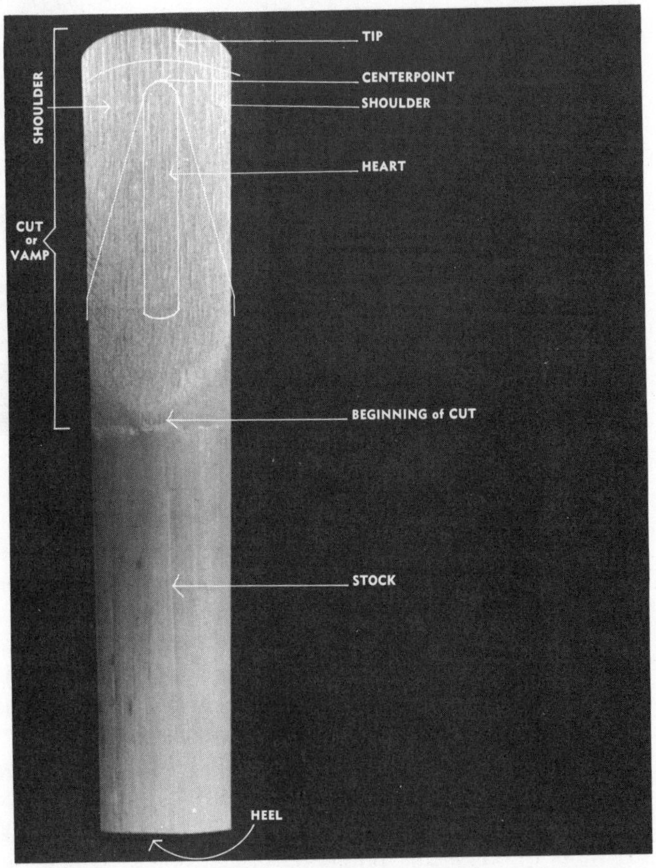

Figure R-4

Reed Strength

The first thing to consider in the selection of a reed is its strength. Most brands of reeds are classified by strength: 1, 1½, 2, 2½, 3, 3½, 4, 4½, 5 according to the resistance of the tip to bending as measured on a standard reed gauge, with number 1 being the softest and number 5 the hardest. In addition some brands use the designations "soft," "medium-soft," "medium," "medium-hard," and "hard," either with or without the number designation. These classifications are extremely unreliable since they represent only a general indication of the resistance of the tip and not the general shape of the vamp, do not consider the inherent characteristic of the cane itself, and are made when the reed is dry and unplayed although it is common knowledge that a reed, moist as it is in playing, responds quite differently than a dry one.

Testing reeds in a box marked no. 2 or medium strength will easily show that every range of strength from very soft to very hard is included among them. It must be clearly understood that selecting a reed simply by number or classification is no guarantee of getting the exact strength desired, however since they are merchandised in this fashion this must be the starting point.

For the average student, beginning, intermediate, or advanced, playing with a standard embouchure on a good mouthpiece of medium facing and medium opening the medium or medium-soft classification should be used. There is a widespread old wives tale that beginners must start with very soft reeds and gradually increase the strength of the reed used as they gain proficiency until they are playing on a very hard reed. This fallacy should be dispensed with once and for all. Beginners are frequently deliberately given a reed which is too soft until breath support and embouchure are set, and this is to be commended but they do not progress from strength no. 1 to 2, 3, 4, 5 in the way they must increase their shoe size as their bodies grow.

The hardness or softness of a reed in relation to a particular mouthpiece is determined by the nature of the lay on that particular mouthpiece, as well as the type and formation of embouchure being used by the player. In general, an open lay calls for a softer reed and a close lay for a harder reed. Only by a careful experimentation with many reeds can the clarinetist determine the type of reed best suited to his mouthpiece and embouchure.

A reed is too stiff for a player when it is hard to blow, offering too much resistance, and requiring more than normal breath pressure to produce a tone. A second symptom of a reed which is too hard is that it produces a heavy, hard, and coarse quality of tone in the low register.

A reed which is too soft produces a thin, reedy tone quality, and frequently won't play the higher notes at all. The clarion register is difficult to play in tune, generally being flat in pitch, and the lower notes in the chalameau register buzz. It requires less than normal breath pressure to produce a tone. Some soft reeds may be adjusted to play well, and this type of adjustment is discussed later.

Both hard and soft reeds frequently squeak. Squeaks are caused by faulty cutting of the vamp during the manufacturing process which makes it vibrate out of balance. The cane is thicker on one side of the center point than on the other, one side of the tip is thicker than the other, or the cane is inherently faulty in the heart section. A reed which is either too hard or too soft and squeaks as well poses a difficult problem in adjustment which cannot always be carried out. On the other hand a reed which is of the right strength and which possess the other attributes of a good reed but squeaks can frequently be adjusted so that it plays well.

The Cane

The color of the cane from which the reed is made can offer some criteria of quality. The bark on the stock of well-seasoned cane from which the best reeds come is a deep golden yellow color, and irregular brown or dark colored marks in the bark do not affect its quality. Indeed, some players feel that these indicate the best quality cane. Reeds on which the bark on the stock is light yellow or has a greenish look are usually improperly seasoned, or simply poor cane. Immature cane is also indicated by extreme roughness in the grain of the vamp which can be both seen and felt.

An even better indication of the quality of cane is the way in which the grains run. This can be seen by holding the reed up to the light or using a shadow box with a ground glass. The best cane has the grain running absolutely straight, with the hard grains (the darker streaks) evenly distributed across the vamp and with part of them running entirely to the tip of the reed. Reeds in which the grains run at an angle across the vamp play unevenly and frequently squeak. Reeds which have no hard grains extending to the tip tend to be too soft, or if playable, to wear out rapidly.

Shape of the Vamp

The way in which the vamp is cut or shaped determines how the reed will play, regardless of the quality of the cane from which it is made. The Vandoren reed has been the standard against which all single reeds have been measured for many years, and the style of vamp used on these reeds is generally accepted as being the best.

The way in which the reed is cut can be determined by holding it up to a light and observing the light and dark areas. The darker the area, the thicker the cane. If an imaginary line is drawn from the heel to the tip down the center of the reed the shadows should be exactly the same on either side. If they are not, one side is thicker than the other, and adjustments are made until both sides are identical. The more nearly symetrical the reed the better the cut. The difference between soft and hard reeds can clearly be seen by comparing the amount and shape of the light and dark areas.

The basic cut of the reed is as follows. The tip is a very thin area extending back about an eighth of an inch from the end which must be the same thickness for the entire width of the reed. When held to the light it is a very pale color.

The flexibility of the tip of the reed is all-important in the selection of a reed. It is determined not only by the thickness of the tip, but by the general proportion of the entire vamp—the shape and thickness of the heart, the location and thickness of the center point, the thickness of the shoulders, and how they are graduated.

If there is a single test of the hardness or softness of a reed it is in the response of the tip. The most accurate way of testing this flexibility, aside from playing the reed, is to gently move the tip across the thumbnail to ascertain how much pressure is necessary to flex it back. The more pressure needed, the harder the reed. It should flex evenly across the entire width, and if it does not, should be adjusted until it does.

The tip area is identified in Figure R-6.

Figure R-5

Figure R-7 shows the heart of the reed which extends from the stock to the center point and which gradually becomes thinner as it approaches the center point. It is graduated toward the edge with the edges considerable thinner than the center line. The shape is roughly that of an inverted "V" which shows clearly as a shadow when the reed is held toward the light.

The shoulders, Figure R-8, extend from the heart toward the edges and toward the tip, gradually growing thinner (lighter in color when held toward the light) as they approach the points on either side at which the edges and the back line of the tip meet. The shadows shown by the shoulders should be identical and symetrical. Much of the control of the vibration, and much of the adjusting of the reed is done in the shoulder area.

In summary the selection of a reed is made by (1) the color; (2) the way the grains run; (3) an examination of the cut by holding it toward the light; (4) testing the resistance of the tip by running it across the thumbnail; and (5) testing it on the instrument.

Considerable experience is needed both in judging a reed from its physical characteristics and hearing various kinds of reeds played on the instrument. How it plays on the instrument is the final determining factor. Regardless of how it looks, if it plays well it is a good reed, and players must, as part of the selection of a reed, give it a playing test on the instrument to make a final judgment, and to ascertain what adjustments, if any, need to be made, or if adjustments are possible at all if it is a poor reed.

Tip of Single Reed.
Heart Area of Single Reed.
Shoulder Area of a Single Reed.

Figure R-6 **Figure R-7** **Figure R-8**

ADJUSTING THE SINGLE REED

Proficiency in making adjustments on the reed is virtually mandatory for every teacher involved in teaching single reed instruments, because the students must be taught how to do it for themselves, and they must learn by example. This technique can only be learned by experience, and every teacher should experiment and work with reeds at great length. A great many reeds will be ruined but the knowledge and technique acquired are well worth the cost in time and money.

Tools and materials used in adjusting single reeds are simple to acquire and the following must be available:

1. *Scraping knife.* A reed knife such as those sold for making oboe and bassoon reeds; or a pocket knife; or a single-edged razor blade. The knives must be kept honed to a sharp edge, and the razor blades discarded when they become dull. Many players carry a razor blade in their cases so that it will always be available.

2. Plate glass. A piece of plate glass at least two-by-four inches, or some other hard material which can be kept absolutely flat.

3. *Sandpaper.* Fine grained sandpaper No. 8/0.

4. *Dutch rush.* Also known as Swamp Grass which grows wild around rivers, lakes, and swampy areas in many sections of the United States. It is commercially processed and is available in music stores. It is normally used wet, and must be soaked in water for several minutes so that one end can be pressed flat in order to obtain sufficient working surface. It may be used dry although the small working surface on the rounded material makes slow progress. Dutch rush is used for smoothing and polishing the vamp, and for making smaller adjustments to the shoulder or tip area of the reed than are possible with a knife.

5. *A reed clipper.* This is used for trimming the tip of soft reeds. The type and model should be selected carefully so that the shape of the cut it makes matches exactly the shape of the tip of the mouthpiece and/or the original shape of the reed. In addition it must have a screw adjustment for small adjustments in the amount of reed to be clipped off. Take along several useless reeds for testing shape, adjustment, and sharpness of the cutting blade when the clipper is being selected.

Reed trimmers are made for B-flat clarinet, Alto clarinet, Bass clarinet, Alto saxophone, Tenor saxophone, and Baritone saxophone reeds. Players on these instruments should have their own reed trimmer, and the well-equipped teacher will have a full set available for his students.

The purpose of adjusting a reed is to make corrections in the proportions of the vamp which are imperfect. The adjustments are made by scraping or sanding parts of the shoulders, adjusting and relocating the center point of the cut, reproportioning the heart, and, rarely, evening the thickness across the tip. All scraping or sanding movements are made in one direction with the grain of the wood and only toward the tip of the reed. All adjustments are made with the reed moist in playing condition.

The reed selected for adjustment should be the most nearly perfect reed selected from a group of six or more. Many players prefer to select the best three or four reeds from a box for final adjusting. Not all reeds can be adjusted for satisfactory playing and the better the response at the time the adjusting process is started, the better the final success will be in adjusting the reed. Only a very few reeds will be found that respond perfectly without some adjusting being necessary. The chances are practically a hundred percent that if a student is handed or purchases two or three reeds at a time all of them will require adjustment to a greater or lesser degree.

It should be emphasized again that proficiency in reed adjustment can only be learned by experience. Each single operation must be small and the reed tested on the instrument before making another adjustment. The process is one of continual testing by playing. It is easy to ruin a reed with even the slightest too much scraping, or rubbing or clipping. Proceed cautiously!

Soft Reeds

Soft reeds are identified by a thin reedy sound which requires little breath pressure for tone production, and which usually play out of tune. They are reeds on which the tip is too flexible. This can be seen when tested against the thumb nail, and when the reed is held to the light the tip section is almost transparent and extends farther than normal from the end putting the center point of the cut too far from the tip. This condition is corrected by clipping the tip with the reed clipper.

Put the reed in the clipper carefully being sure that both the heel and tip are exactly centered. Adjust the reed so that only a hair line of cane is cut off. The biggest danger in using the reed clipper is in cutting off too much of the reed. Very small amounts of cane removed make enormous differences in how the reed responds. It is better to clip twice to get the desired response than it is to risk taking off too much at once. When this is done test the reed again. If it is still too soft repeat the process. Once the reed is clipped to the desired strength it may play properly, or it may show need for further adjustment of any of the kinds discussed in the following paragraphs. Clipping a soft reed doesn't automatically make it a good reed.

Slightly Hard Reeds

These are the reeds which meet the general criteria for good reeds except that they blow a little hard, or on which the chalameau register tone quality is rough while the clarion register is good. Fortunately a good many reeds fall into this category. Many players deliberately choose this type of reed since it may soften to the desired strength after a few hours of playing, and if not, have sufficient reserve strength to allow the necessary minor adjustments. Reeds of this kind will generally have a perfectly formed tip section, but may be slightly too thick in one or both shoulder areas. If the reed doesn't play in, then the shoulder areas should be scraped gently with the knife to lighten the shadow when held to the light. The two shoulders should match perfectly. Polish the entire vamp with the Dutch Rush.

Medium Hard Reeds

These reeds required a greater breath pressure to produce a tone than do the slightly hard class and are somewhat rough not only in the chalameau register but also in the clarion register. The degree of hardness is such that they are uncomfortable to play on, and as a consequence cannot be brought into playing condition through use. This type of reed will have shoulders and tips which are thicker than the slightly hard group, and the center point of the cut may be closer to the end of the reed than is necessary for the best response.

Corrections on this kind of reed should be made in the following order:

1. Using the knife, scrape the shoulder areas so that both have identical shadows but not as light in color as the finished reed will be. The reed should respond a little freer when tried on the instrument.
2. With the Dutch Rush, thin the tip area uniformly across the width of the reed until its color is almost that desired for the finished reed. It should be tested several times during this process to avoid taking off too much.
3. With the knife, scrape the front portion of the heart section if the center point is closer than one-eighth inch to the tip, or if the general area of the center point is dark. Make this adjustment very gradually and test frequently.
4. Hold the reed to the light and check the color and shape of the shoulders and tip. Remove uneven dark spots with the knife, making sure that both sides of the center line are identical. Test.
5. When these operations are completed, the reed should respond as a slightly hard reed and treatment continued as suggested for that classification of reed. Conclude the adjustment by polishing the entire vamp with Dutch Rush.

Very Hard Reeds

These are reeds which require an extraordinary amount of wind pressure to produce a tone, and with a hard, rough, and squawky tone quality. These reeds have an overall thickness which is much greater than normal, some to the extent that this additional thickness is readily noticeable at the heel. Some have the overall vamp too thick—the tip area is dark, the shoulders dark, and the heart section much wider and longer than normal. Some few simply have a tip section which is little or no thinner than the shoulders.

The adjustments on this type of reed should be done in this sequence, testing frequently.

1. Using very light strokes of the knife and following the line of the grain remove the excess cane from the tip section. Test on the instrument frequently and continue until the thickness of the tip is almost that of the normal reed.
2. With Dutch Rush, work the tip section down to normal thickness. Test.
3. If this process doesn't complete the adjustment of the reed, thin the shoulder sections with the knife, keeping the graduation from the center line to the edge correct and balancing each side. Test frequently. If when the graduation and thickness is near normal and reed doesn't respond, proceed to the next step.
4. With light strokes of the knife thin the heart section, paying particular attention to the area near the center point so that it blends into the shoulders and tip. Test frequently.
5. Perform steps three and four alternately, testing frequently, until the reed responds as a slightly hard reed.
6. Make final adjustments on shoulders and tip area with the knife and then Dutch Rush.
7. Polish the entire vamp with Dutch Rush.

Squeaky Reeds

Reeds which are otherwise perfect may squeak. Soft reeds squeak and reeds of varying degrees of hardness may squeak. The process of bringing soft or hard reeds to the proper playing condition frequently removes the squeak. If when the proper degree of stiffness is reached and they still squeak, the same remedial measures as for a good reed can be applied to them.

Squeaks may also be caused by leaky pads, faulty position of fingers over the tone holes, or by fingers touching keys so not all squeaks can be attributed to a faulty reed. If a student doesn't squeak on several reeds, but does with one, then it is safe to assume that the squeak is built into the reed. Reeds normally squeak when slurring across the break, especially open G to third line B-natural, and rapid slurring back and forth between these two notes will identify most, but not all, squeaky reeds.

Squeaks are the result of uneven vibrations by the reed. These may be caused by a heavy or thick spot on one of the shoulders, by a thick spot in the tip area, or by a thick spot in the heart near the center point. These thick places in the tip and in the shoulders show up as dark spots when the reed is held to the light. When they are located rub them down to the proper thickness with the Dutch Rush, or if they are especially thick begin the process with the knife and finish with the Dutch Rush. Only the Dutch Rush should be used on the tip area. Test frequently during the process.

If when any heavy areas in tip or shoulders are removed and blended into the surrounding areas the squeak still remains the squeak is in the heart of the reed. Rub the heart with Dutch Rush over its entire length. Test frequently, since small changes in the heart area make large differences in reed response. If after all these operation are performed the squeak persists throw the reed away! Reeds are inexpensive and the apprehension of playing on a reed that may squeak at any time puts a severe strain on the performer.

CARE OF THE REED

A good reed is worth preserving, and a few simple measures will lengthen its useful life. Some students persist in using a reed long past its useful life, and a regular weekly reed inspection should be part of the regular routine of the instrumental class, band, and orchestra.

A simple inspection will reveal reeds with chips out of the tips, splits, dirty reeds, reeds on instruments played by girls coated with lipstick, reeds with jagged tips, etc. etc., ad infinitum. Any one of these conditions has an affect not only on how the instrument sounds, but on the ease with which it plays. Many students do not realize the importance of having a good reed to play on and it is the responsibility of the teacher to see that they do have good reeds until this importance becomes apparent to the player. Any reeds with any of the conditions mentioned above should be replaced immediately.

Much damage to reed of younger players occurs while on the instrument. The tip is brushed against the clothing, hit against a chair, or music stand or any one of a number of other contacts any one of which will damage it beyond reasonable use. Reeds are frequently split or chipped by the ligature if it is put on the mouthpiece after the reed is in place. It is for this reason that the ligature should be put over the mouthpiece and the reed slipped under it as standard practice. Putting the cap over the mouthpiece, if carelessly done often chips or splits the reed. The importance of avoiding this type of accident through reasonable care must be emphasized continuously, but especially with beginning students.

When the instrument is taken apart reeds should always be removed from the mouthpiece and stored in a reed case or reed holder. Cane is susceptible to warpage when drying out after use, and the reed is preserved best if it is held firmly in place on a flat surface after being wiped dry of excess moisture. Several commercial reed containers which do this efficiently are available and hold two to four reeds thus providing ready accessible storage for reeds which are ready to use.

Keeping the reed in a reed case rather than on the mouthpiece will also protect the mouthpiece from possible damage if it is exposed to heat while the ligature is tightly in place. Some teachers recommend a piece of plate glass of the size to fit into the instrument case on which the reeds are held by wide rubber bands. This is

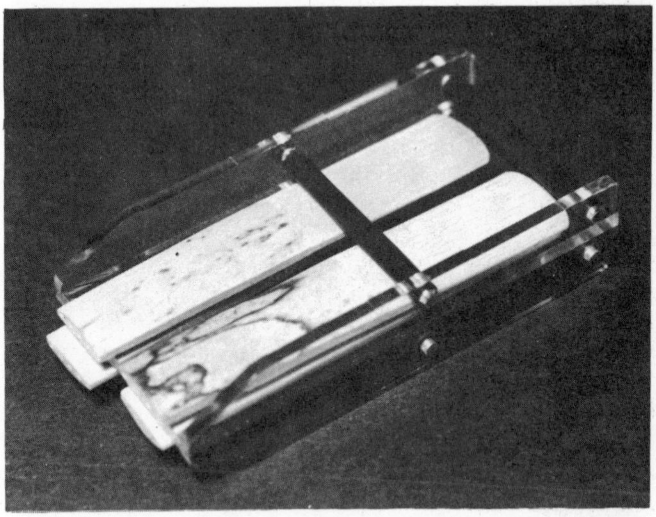

Figure R-9

more usable with the Chesterfield model case than with the fitted cases which do not have much excess storage in them. Plate glass or commercial reed cases are inexpensive and well worth the slight investment to preserve the reeds. Figure R-9 shows an excellent commercial reed case.

After a reed has been used several times the underside, or flat side, may warp. Or you may be able to see the shape of the tone chamber of the mouthpiece on the underside of the reed, since it tends to sink into the hollow space in the mouthpiece. This latter condition may be caused by having the ligature too tight which puts too much pressure against the reed. But whatever the cause the warp or unevenness should be removed if the reed is to continue to play well. This may be done by scraping the bottom of the reed with a knife or razor blade, or rubbing it gently over the sandpaper. If the sandpaper is used, protect the tip of the reed by sliding a piece of paper between it and the sandpaper.

The reed must be kept clean of accumulated dirt and saliva deposits or the pores of the cane become clogged and the reed loses response. These deposits may be washed off with warm water, or scraped off with a knife or Dutch Rush. If the scraping method is used care must be taken not to take off any of the wood which would weaken the reed.

In recent years many experiments have been made with plastic reeds, and there are several brands on the market. Plastic reeds are still in the developmental stage and do not give as good results as cane reeds. The plastic reeds have the higher overtones present in great intensity which gives them a rather thin and brittle tone. They lack the flexibility and depth of tone of a good reed of French cane. Because of their many shortcomings, plastic reeds as yet cannot be recommended for use on any of the woodwind instruments.

OBOE AND ENGLISH HORN REEDS

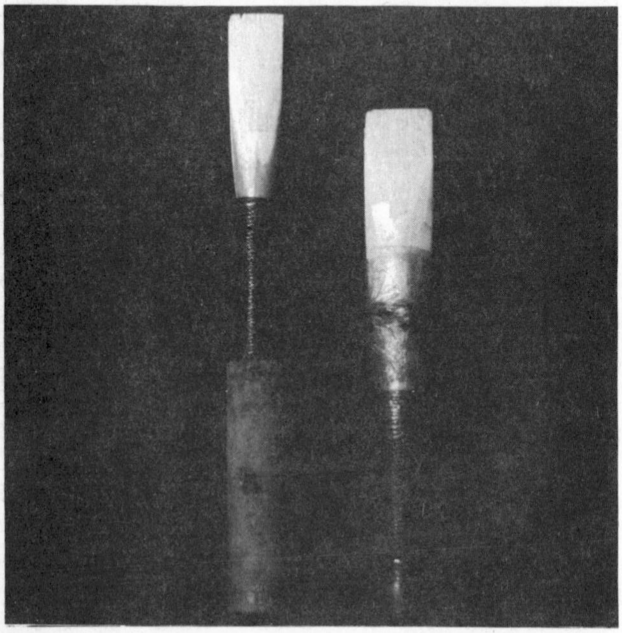

Figure R-10. Oboe Reed (Left) Compared with an English Reed.

The selection, adjustment, and care of the reed for the oboe or English horn is a subject which should be thoroughly understood by every player on these instruments, and by every teacher who is responsible for students on these instruments. The double reed functions both as a mouthpiece and as the tone generator for the instrument, and as such its response is highly critical. The type of reed being used determines tone quality, influences embouchure formation, and all aspects of performance. For these reasons the reed should be carefully selected and adjusted to fit both the student and the instrument he is using.

Every oboist past the beginning stage should be able to adjust commercial reeds, and if he is a serious student of the instrument, should learn how to make his own reeds from the blank cane. Most oboists learn the art of reed making and adjustment as a regular normal part of the study of their instrument. Many teachers consider this as important a part of their learning as developing technique, tone quality, or phrasing. No oboist's training is considered complete until he is proficient in making and adjusting reeds. Beginners on the instrument will first develop the facility for adjustment and then progress into the complete production of reeds.

The present discussion is limited to selection, adjustment, and care of the oboe reed. The problems involved in making reeds are beyond the scope of this book, and are best learned through personal instruction from one who is skilled in the art. The considerations here will be limited to those aspects of the problem which the teacher needs to know and use in his everyday activities.

Before discussing the oboe reed it is necessary to establish a vocabulary for identification of the various parts of the reed. The designations are the standard ones widely found in published literature. Figure R-11 identi-

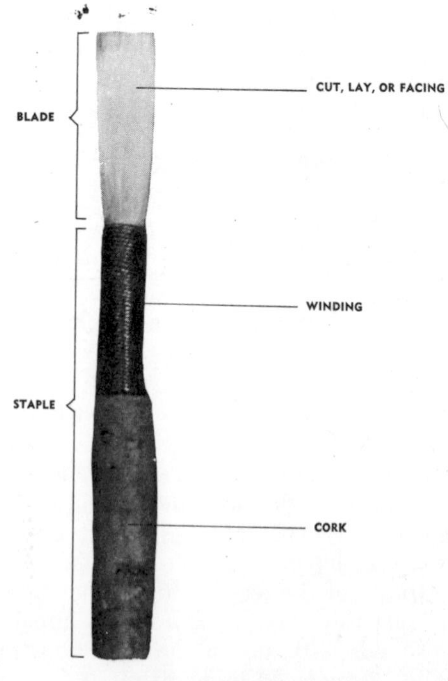

Figure R-11

fies the parts. The *staple* is the metal tube on which the cane is fitted, and has a cork on the end to fit into the socket on the oboe. The *blades* are the two pieces of cane which make the reed. The *winding* is the thread which holds the blades onto the staple. The portion of the blades from which the bark has been cut is known as the cut (scrape, lay, or facing).

HOW AN OBOE REED IS MADE

In order to adjust and care for oboe reeds it is desirable to understand the complete process of how they are made, even though skill in performing these operations is expected only of advanced oboists. Understanding the procedures will provide a basis upon which adjustments can be made. The following sequence of photographs illustrates a standard procedure in making an oboe reed as performed by a professional oboist and highly skilled reed maker.

1. Figure R-12. Cured, uncut cane from which oboe reeds are made is available in various diameters. The diameter of the cane determines to some extent the shape of the oval tip of the finished reed. The diameters of the pieces of cane illustrated are 14 mm, 12 mm, and 10 mm. The 12 mm is considered the standard size.

2. Figure R-13. The cane is split into three equal sections with a three blade knife called a splitting arrow.

3. Figure R-14. Three pieces of cane produced when the cane is split.

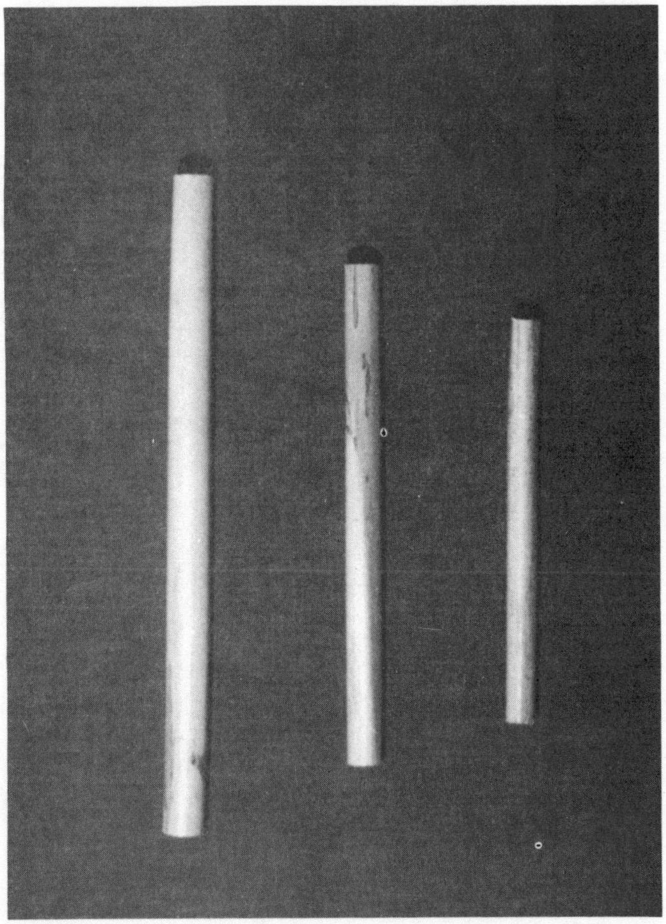

Figure R-12

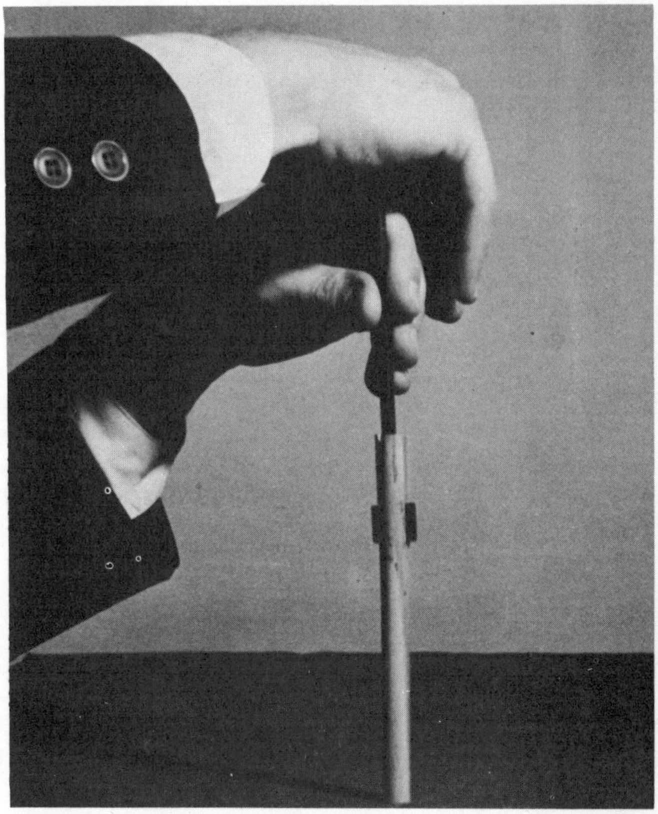

Figure R-13

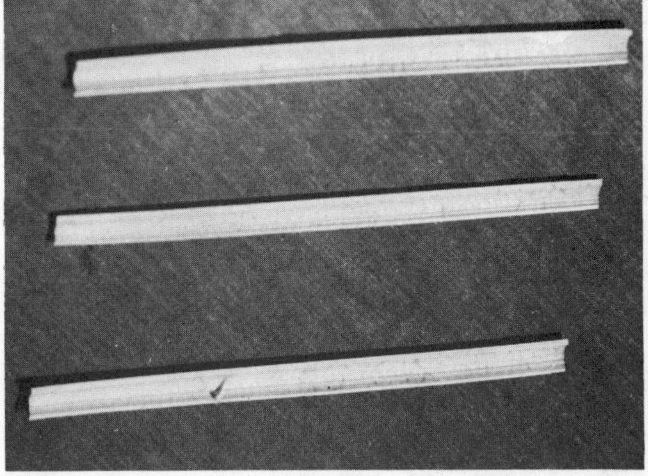

Figure R-14

4. Figure R-15. Each piece of cane is cut to size by pushing it through a plane-like instrument called the filiere. Beginning with this procedure, all subsequent operations are done with the cane thoroughly soaked so that it is pliable.

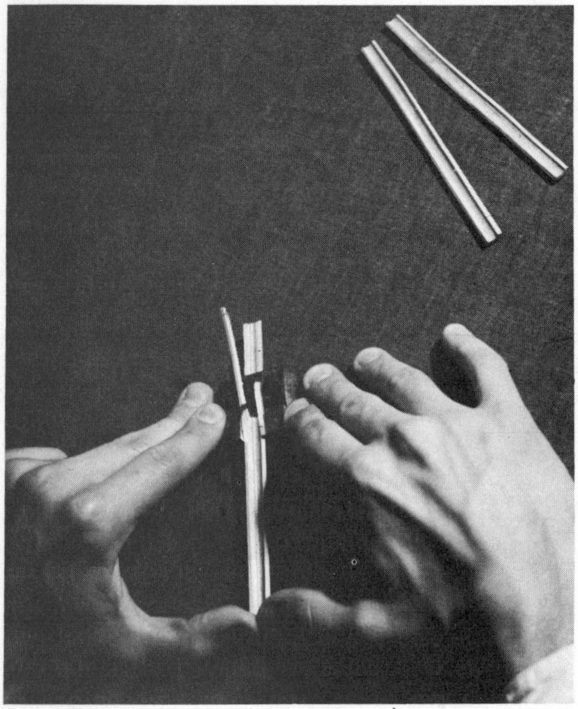

Figure R-15

5. Figure R-16. The cane is then cut to the correct length on a machine known as a guillotine.

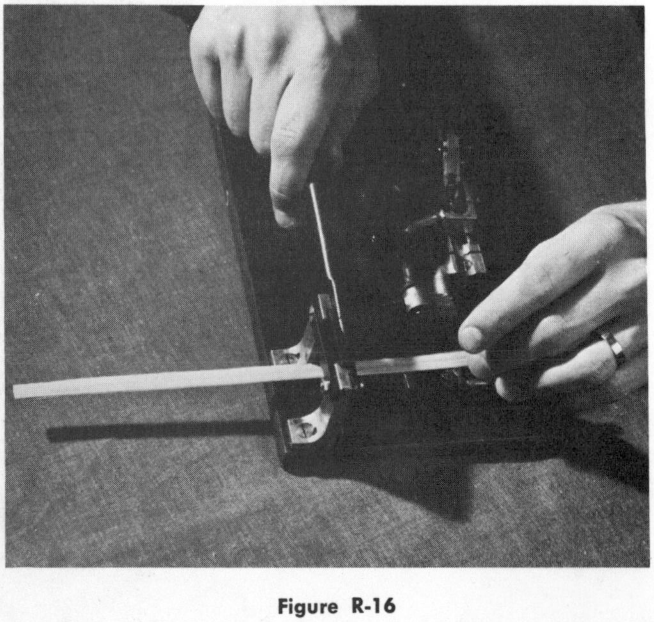

Figure R-16

6. Figure R-17. When the cane is the correct length it is placed in the gouger and the inside is planed to the correct shape and thickness.

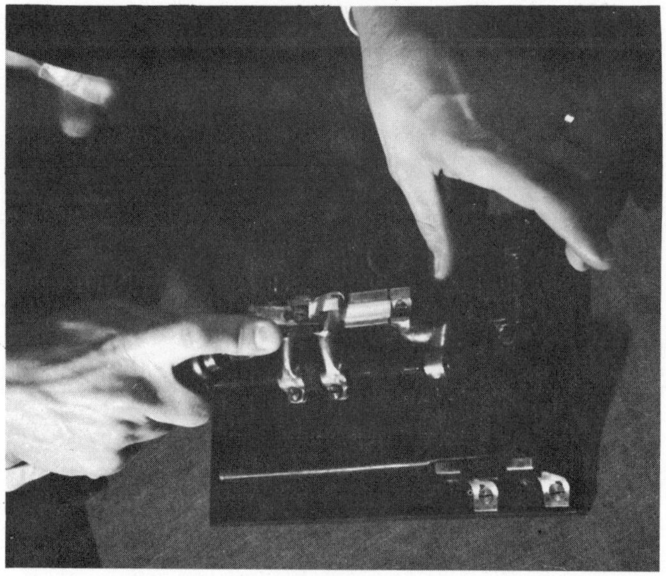

Figure R-17

7. Figure R-18. The gouged cane is placed on the cane easel which has an etched line marking the exact center of the length. With the cutting knife a notch is made through the bark at this point which will become the tip of the finished reed. Some players buy cane which has been finished to this point from which to make their own reeds. It is described as "gouged cane."

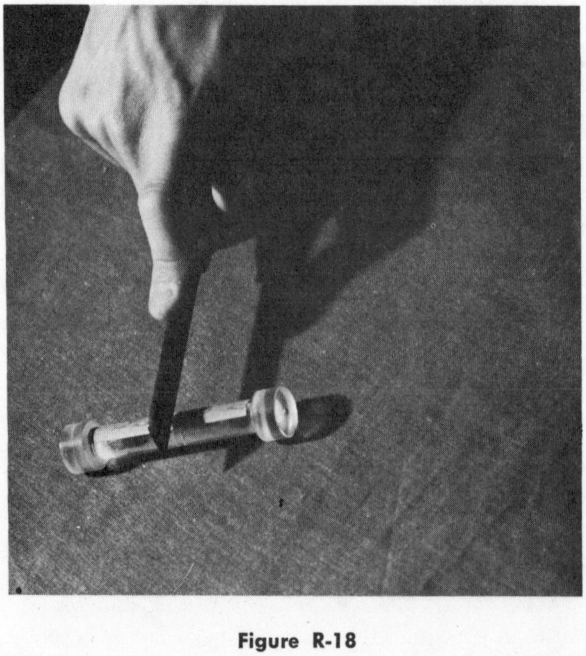

Figure R-18

8. Figure R-19. The cane is folded over the knife blade at the point where the notch was made.

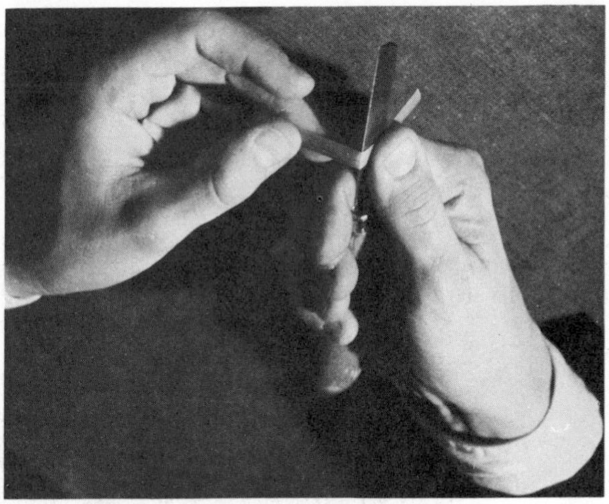

Figure R-19

9. Figure R-20. The folded cane is placed on an instrument called a shaper and the edges are cut with a knife or single edge razor blade to the exact shape of the finished reed. When this process has been completed the cane is described as "gouged, shaped and folded" and it is this type of prepared cane that most oboists purchase to make their own reeds.

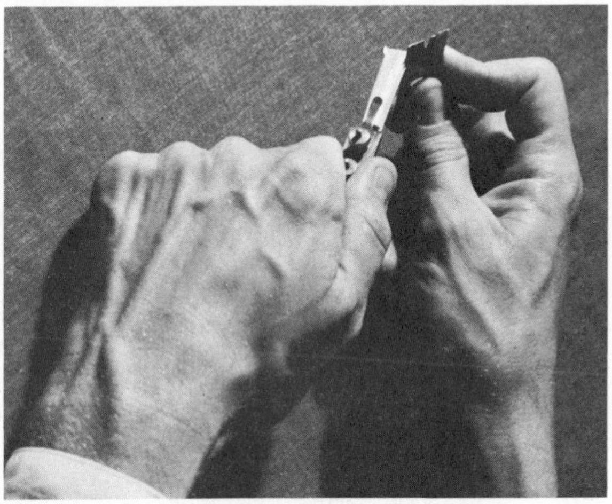

Figure R-20

10. Figure R-21. This photograph compares the cane in three stages. From bottom to top: filiered and cut to size, gouged, and shaped.

11. Figure R-22. The shaped cane is returned to the easel and the narrow ends of the cane which will be bound on the tube are thinned with a knife so that they will be flexible enough to fit tightly on the tube.

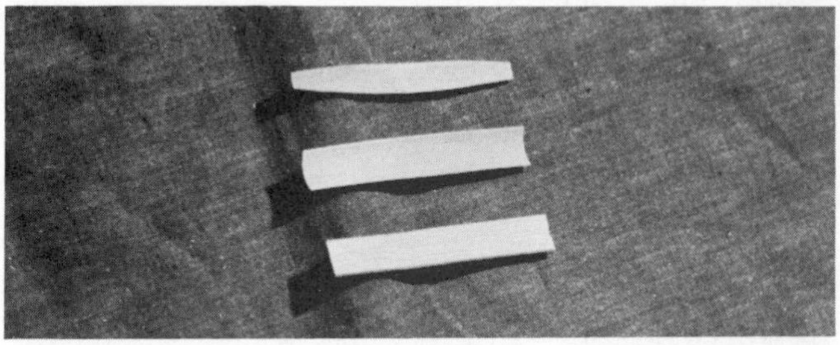

Figure R-21

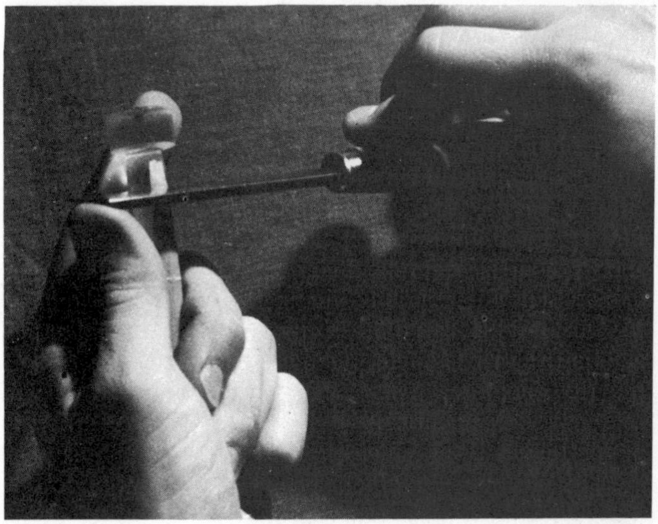

Figure R-22

12. Figure R-23. The cane is folded over the tube which is oval rather than perfectly round in shape. The cane is fitted to the flat sides.

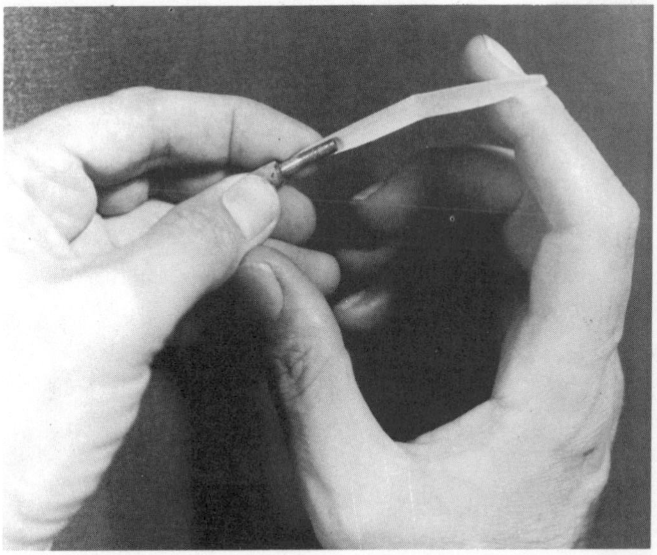

Figure R-23

13. Figure R-24. With the end of the binding thread attached to something which will hold it securely the thread is wrapped once around the reed at the edge of the tube. With the thread in place the cane is straightened and positioned on the tube and the thread secured.

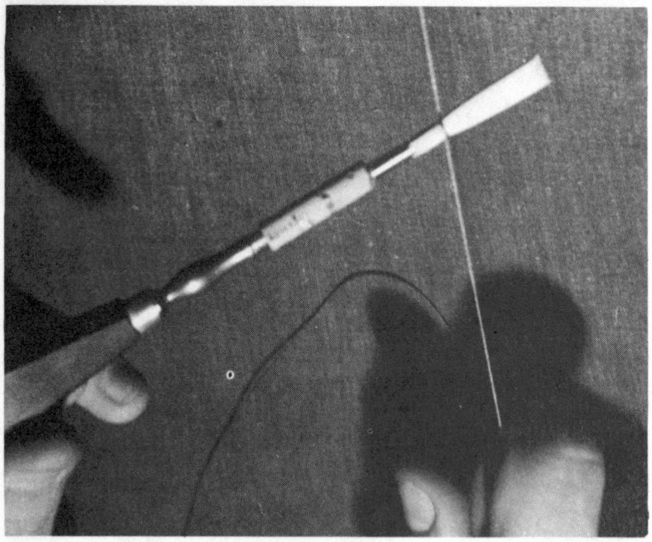

Figure R-24

14. Figure R-25. The thread is wound tightly around the reed and stapled down to the cork where it is tied securely. At this point the blank cane is ready for scraping.

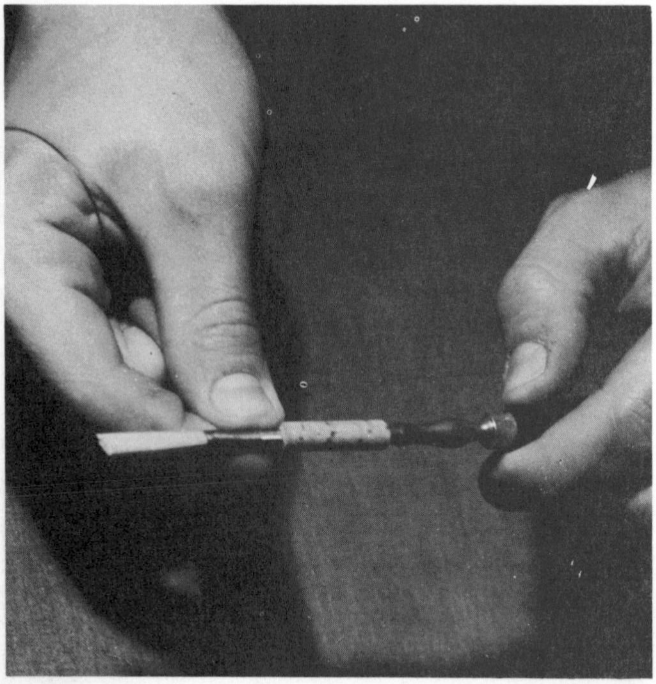

Figure R-25

15. Figure R-26. The back of the cut is scraped on either side of the spine of the red to form the general outline of the final cut. Both blades are scraped in identical fashion. This reed will be made in what will be described later as a long "W" cut. In the photographs the reed is being held with the fingers during the scraping process. Some professionals and most students feel more secure when the reed is held on a mandrel during all scraping, and this is the general recommendation.

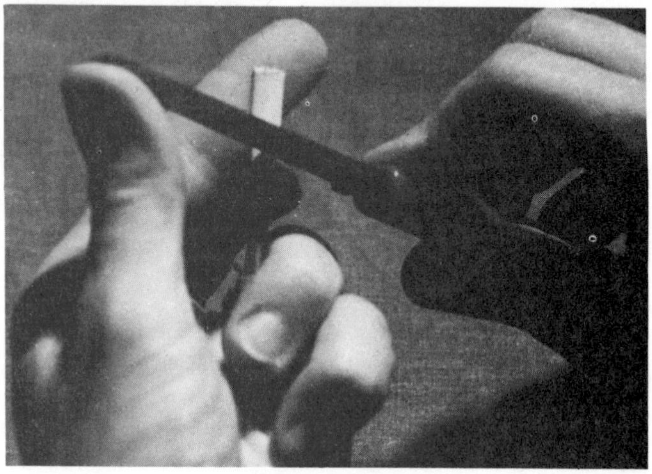

Figure R-26

16. Figure R-27. The tip of each blade is thinned and shaped.

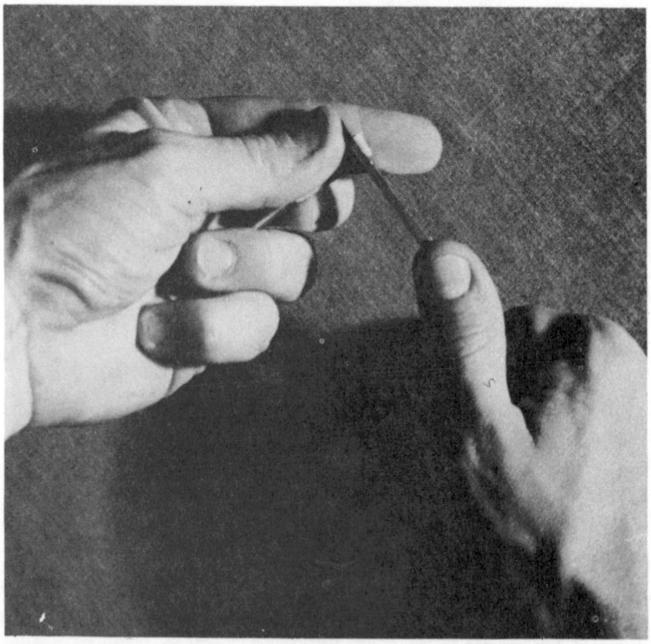

Figure R-27

17. Figure R-28. The end of the reed is split with the plaque, and we now have the basic double reed. At this point the reed is classified as "semifinished" and will produce a tone.

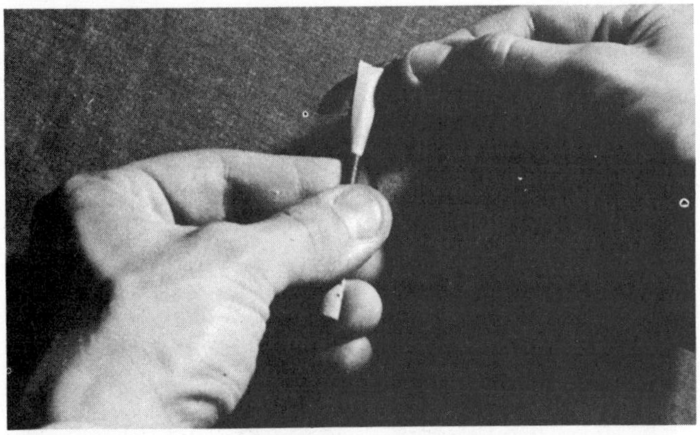

Figure R-28

The steps which are necessary to finish the reed and put it into perfect playing condition are similar to those described later in the adjusting process and are not shown here. The process of making an oboe reed is demonstrated by Blaine Edlefsen in an excellent 16 mm color film.[3] Those interested in the detailed process of making oboe reeds should consult books on the subject listed in the bibliography at the end of this book.

TYPES OF OBOE REEDS AVAILABLE

Although the advanced oboist is expected to make his own reeds, the great majority of student oboists will purchase reeds which are ready-made. Many schools purchase oboe reeds by the dozens for their oboists. Since the success of these students is dependent upon how the reed responds it is most important that they be purchased wisely and with full knowledge of the choices available. There are three general types of ready-made reeds available which can be described as follows:

1. *Semifinished commercial reeds.* These are mass produced for general retail distribution in much the same way that single reeds are produced and distributed. On some brands the lay is cut by machine rather than by hand. The designation "semifinished" indicates that the purchaser must put the finishing touches on the reed himself, as the reed is in the same state of adjustment as the reed in step fifteen in the preceding outline of how an oboe reed is made. These finishing touches include tuning the reed to fit his embouchure and instrument, finishing the cut on both blades, and smoothing the surfaces.

Reeds of this type vary greatly in the amount of finishing necessary. Unless the teacher or the student has developed some skill in adjusting reeds, this type of reed is seldom satisfactory. Unfortunately some semifinished reeds which have very little work remaining to be done are not designated as such when they are sold and many players attempt to play them without making the finishing touches. Many of the difficulties student oboists have can be traced to this situation. If the brand of reeds being used responds poorly, and requires considerable adjustment to achieve a good response, they are most certainly of the semifinished class.

2. *Finished commercial reeds.* Other types of commercial reeds generally available in music stores are classified as "finished" reeds. That is, the scrape has been finished and the reed tuned either by measurement or by actually playing it on an instrument. Some brands of these finished commercial reeds are graded according to strength in the same way single reeds are graded in strengths 1, 2, 3, 4, 5, with the number 1 the softest and the number 5 the hardest. The grading of oboe reeds in this fashion is a more reliable indication of their actual strength than is the grading of single reeds. The oboe reed probably will have been tested by a player and sterilized before shipment. This is not always the case however, since other and less accurate means of determining strengths are available.

It is not always possible to judge by merely looking at the reed whether it is finished or semifinished. It must be tried on the instrument. Even the finished reeds frequently need adjustment to suit the individual player. If a teacher or player finds a brand of commercial reeds which are consistently satisfactory without adjustment he is indeed fortunate. The way in which commercial reeds are adjusted is the same as that for all oboe reeds and these processes are discussed later in this chapter.

3. *Custom-made reeds.* These are reeds made by professional players to individual order. Professional players in all sections of the country cater to school musicians and will make reeds for beginning, intermediate, or advanced students which are fitted and tuned to a particular brand and model of oboe (or English horn). These reeds are usually made in the same way and with the same care the professional makes reeds for himself and are finished and ready to play when received.

It is highly recommended that this type of reed be secured for all school oboists until they learn to make their own, or at least have arrived at the place where they are competent to make adjustments on their reeds. If there is not a nearby professional oboist to supply reeds, the names and addresses of professional players who specialize in making reeds for school use can be found in the classified advertisements in such magazines as the *Instrumentalist* and *School Musician.* Try reeds

3. *Making the American Scrape Oboe Reed.* 27 minutes. Champaign, Illinois: University of Illinois Visual Aids Service.

from several makers until those best suited for the student and instrument are found.

Figure R-29 shows three typical oboe reeds. Number 1 is a custom-made reed with a long "W" cut which is ready to play without further adjustment. Number 2 is an imported finished commercial reed with a medium long "U" cut. The lay of this reed was cut by machine and completed with a minimum of handwork. Note that the blades are not aligned. This reed would need considerable adjusting before responding properly. Number 3 is a domestic finished commercial reed using a long "U" cut. The lay is cut by hand even though the reeds are made on an assembly-line basis. This reed would require some adjusting in order to respond properly.

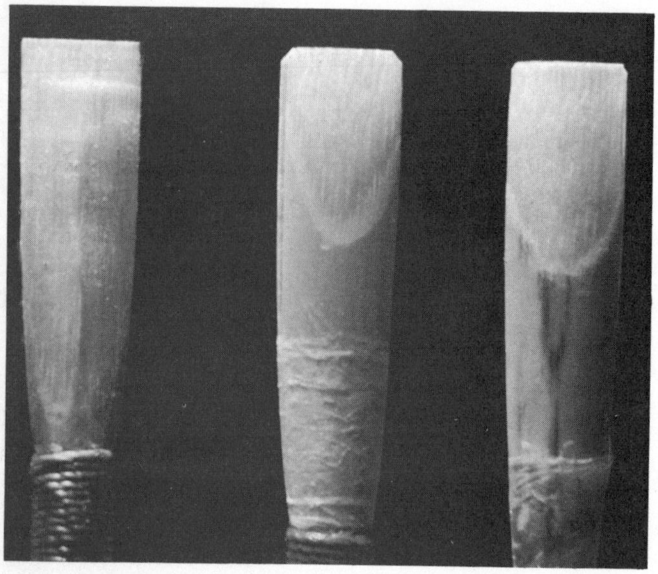

1 2 3

Figure R-29

TYPES OF CUT

The term *cut* (scrape or facing) refers to the portion of the blades from which the bark of the cane has been removed, and specifically to the shape and proportion of the tip, shoulders, back, and spine. There are various standard and basic cuts for the oboe reed, each subject to considerable variation in the hands of the individual maker. These variations are made to achieve the response, control, and tone quality desired by the individual player. Each professional oboist, and eventually each student oboist who makes his own reeds, will arrive after much experimentation at a cut which best suits his individual needs.

Variations in cuts are found in the length of the blade from which the bark has been removed, in the shape of the bark remaining where the cut begins, as well as the proportions of the thickness of the cane at various places on the cut. The cut gets its name from the shape of the bark at the beginning of the cut. This bark takes on the general shape of a "U," a "V," or a "W," and the reeds are described as having a "U," "V," or "W" cut.

The length of the cut as well as its shape varies considerably and is described as short, medium or long. The length is added to the designation of shape and we find the designations of short "U" cut, medium "U" cut, long "U" cut, and similar designations for the "W" and "V" shapes. This gives the designations for the nine basic types of cuts for oboe reeds. Figure R-30 illustrates some the various cuts.

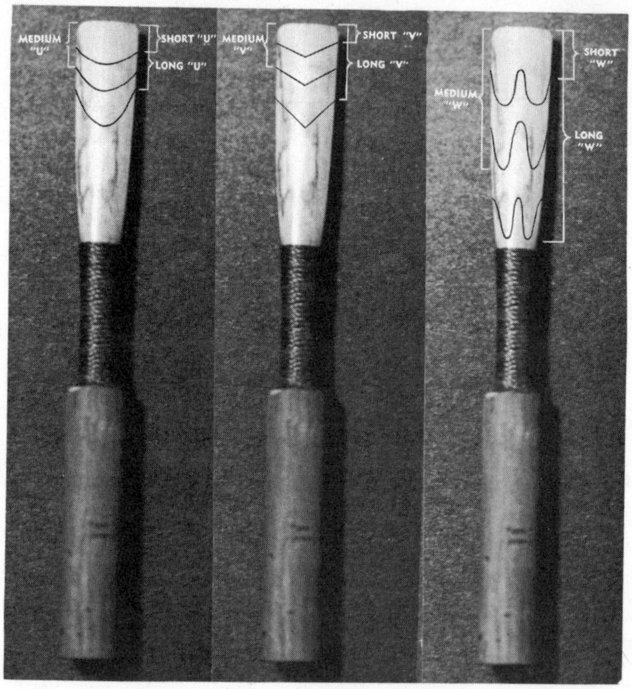

A. "U" cut B. "V" cut C. "W" cut

Figure R-30

When the innumerable variations in the proportions of the thickness of the cane at various points on the cut is added to the nine basic types a bewildering multitude of different cuts becomes available. Each type of cut responds somewhat differently for an individual player and will produce a slightly different tone quality. The type of cut which is best for a specific player is a highly personal decision and is primarily dependent upon the tone quality desired, and the shape and development of the embouchure. Any player can learn to play successfully on any type of cut so long as the reed is well made and adjusted for optimum response. It must be emphasized that the type of cut is a primary factor in determining the ultimate tone quality which the player will produce. Experience with listening to advanced players who use various types of cuts will soon clearly indicate the tone quality each cut produces, and the teacher can make a choice on this basis.

Both the semifinished and finished commercial reeds as well as custom-made reeds are available in a variety of cuts. In the commercial brands each brand will feature a particular cut, although the semifinished reeds tend to be mostly short or medium "U" cuts. The professional who makes custom-made reeds will make only that cut which he has found most successful for his purposes. One of the reasons why it is recommended that custom-made reeds from several makers be given a trial is to provide experience on several types of cuts. Teachers are urged to try a variety of makers in order to discover one or two types of reeds which are consistently good and which respond easily and produce the best quality of tone for their students.

SELECTING THE REED

Reeds must be suited to the individual who is going to use them—to his embouchure, his instrument and, for more advanced players, to fit the demands of the type of music he is playing. The reed must be made to play in tune at A-440 on the instrument on which it is being used. Different makes of oboes require reeds and/or staples of different lengths to play at the standard pitch. The oboe itself is not tuned, the reed is tuned so that the instrument is at the correct pitch.

Some embouchures require certain types of reeds so that the high notes or the low notes can be played in tune. Since it is not possible for an oboist to try many reeds to find one which is satisfactory, he must be able to adjust a particular reed in order to make it respond correctly. He must know how to care for it so that its useful life will be prolonged.

TOOLS AND MATERIALS FOR ADJUSTING OBOE REEDS

In order to perform the operations necessary to adjust the response of an oboe reed certain tools and materials are necessary. Additional tools and materials are necessary to produce a finished reed from blank cane. The complement of tools and materials for making adjustments should be a part of the equipment of every teacher responsible for oboe instruction. As soon as the student has progressed to the place where he is mature enough and his oboe playing has been stabilized he too should acquire these tools and begin to adjust reeds for himself. Figure R-31 shows the basic tools and materials for oboe reed adjusting. From left to right these are: file, cutting knife, scraping knife, mandrel, billot (above), plaque (below), and fishskin (or goldbeater's skin).

A description of these and additional items is summarized as follows. Details of their use in adjusting appears in the section on adjustment.

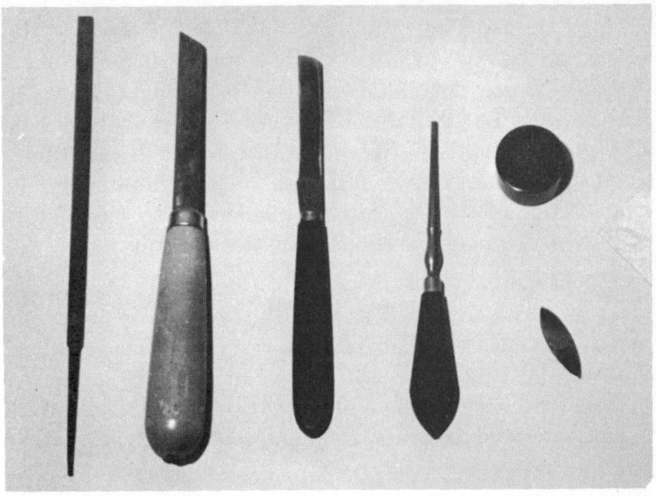

Figure R-31

1. *File.* A fine file or emery board is used for taking cane off the sides of the reed, or for making major adjustments to the cut.

2. *Cutting knife.* One of the two knives needed for reed adjustment, the cutting knife is used for cutting off the tip of the reed. The edge of the cutting knife is honed to a razor sharp straight edge. The scraping knife has a rolled edge and must not be used as a cutting knife.

3. *Scraping knife.* The scraping knife, or reed knife as it is also designated, is used only for scraping the cane. The scraping knife must have a rigid blade and be made of steel which will hold a sharp edge. Hollow ground blades are not satisfactory, and a special reed knife is an investment which will last indefinitely. A folding reed knife which folds like a pocket knife is available and is preferred by some players because the cutting edge is protected when it is closed. The edge of the scraping knife is rolled into a slight "J" shape as the final operation in the sharpening process in order that it will catch the wood evenly. Because of this rolled edge and the fact that it is designed to scrape only in one direction models for right-handed and left-handed use are available.

4. *Mandrel.* The mandrel fits into the tube of the reed and is used to hold the reed while working on it. The mandrel must fit the inside of the staple perfectly, and may be used to straighten bent staples as well as for holding the reed. The use of a mandrel when working on oboe reeds is optional, although many players prefer to use one. A different mandrel of the proper size to fit the tube is necessary for the English horn reed.

5. *Billot.* The billot, or cutting block, is a round block about an inch in diameter with a slightly convex upper surface. It may be made of grenadilla wood or plastic, and is used to provide a firm shaped surface for trimming the tip of the reed.

6. *Plaque.* The plaque is inserted between the blades of the reed whenever any scraping is being done in order to prevent damage to the tip section. The same plaque may be used for oboe and English horn reeds. It is pushed gently between the blades about a half-inch or until it extends an eighth to a quarter inch on either side of the reed. The correct placement of the plaque is shown in photographs later in this section.

7. *Fishskin.* Fishskin or goldbeater's skin is a tough clear material wrapped around the reed away from the cut to prevent air leaks. This wrapping is not a standard part of the finished reed, but is added only if testing of the reed indicates air leaks. Addition of fishskin to a finished reed is quite frequently a necessary part of its final adjustment.

8. *Clear fingernail polish.* Clear fingernail polish or lacquer or a special reed cement is applied over the goldbeater's skin and the thread wrapping to seal it and to keep the skin in place. A half and half mixture of clear fingernail polish and fingernail polish remover is as effective as fingernail polish alone and dries much more rapidly.

9. *Soft brass wire.* Soft brass wire is sometimes applied to the oboe reed to hold the tip of the blades open. The application of a wire to an oboe reed is a last resort measure and is not recommended as a common practice. The English horn reed is normally supported by the wire which is a permanent part of the standard reed construction.

10. *Small pliers with wire cutter.* For applying wire to oboe and English horn reeds. The special bassoon reed making pliers may be used for this purpose.

11. *Dutch rush.* Dutch rush is sometimes recommended for making fine adjustments to the cut of the reed and for the final polishing of the entire scrape. It is used wet and removes extremely small amounts of cane. For this reason it can be more safely used by inexperienced players than a reed knife.

12. *Knife sharpening materials.* The cutting knife and especially the scraping knife must be kept razor sharp at all times. A dull cutting knife will not cut the tip of the reed cleanly, and may even split one of the blades. A dull scraping knife cannot be controlled when scraping the reed, and may do more damage than good. A fine oil stone is necessary for keeping the knives sharp. Some reed makers use a leather strop in conjunction with the oil stone.

The sharpening of the scraping knife is an especially important process. The first step in this process is to polish the flat side by rubbing the entire side flat against the stone as shown in Figure R-32. This removes the rolled edge or "J" hook which is necessary for the scraping process. When this is accomplished the bevel edge is polished so that there is a fine, razor sharp straight edge on it. When the bevel edge is sharp, slowly straighten the knife to the vertical position as shown in Figure R-33 for about six light strokes to roll the edge slightly into the "J" hook.

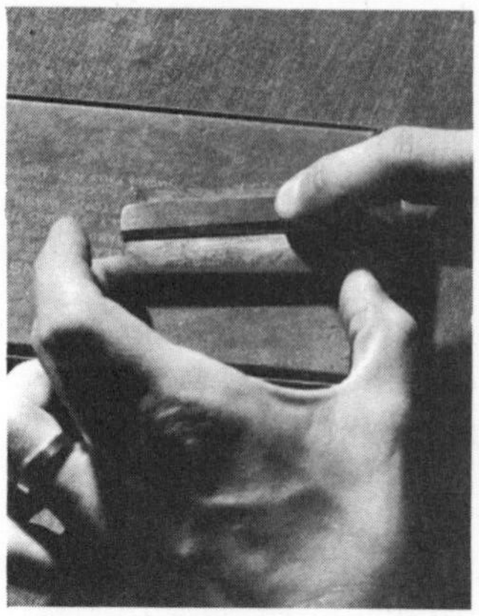

Figure R-32

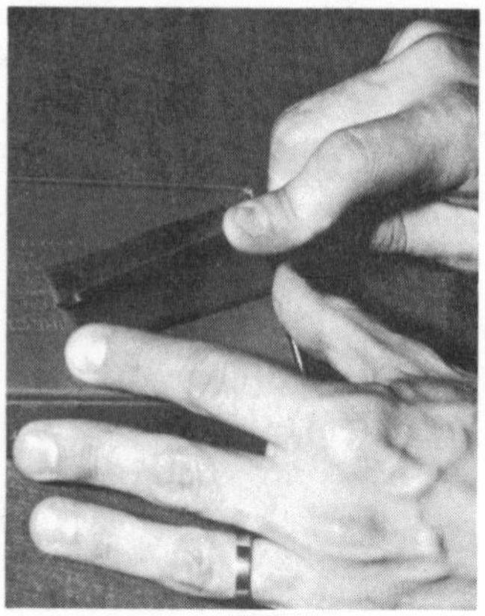

Figure R-33

AREAS OF REED TO BE SCRAPED FOR ADJUSTMENT

The areas of the reed which may need adjustment are well defined no matter which type of cut is being used. The exact size and shape of each area will vary with the type of cut and with the individual reed maker. Examine the reed carefully to locate the size, shape and proportions of each area before attempting to make an adjustment. Figures R-34 and R-35 show the various areas for adjustment. Each area influences a particular aspect of the reed's response. Figure R-34 identifies the areas as they appear on a "W" cut reed and Figure R-35 as they appear on a "U" cut reed. The areas of the "V" cut are similar to those on the "U" cut.

The areas and their function are as follows:

1. *Tip.* The tip must be uniformly thin across the entire width of the reed, except for the short "U" cut which

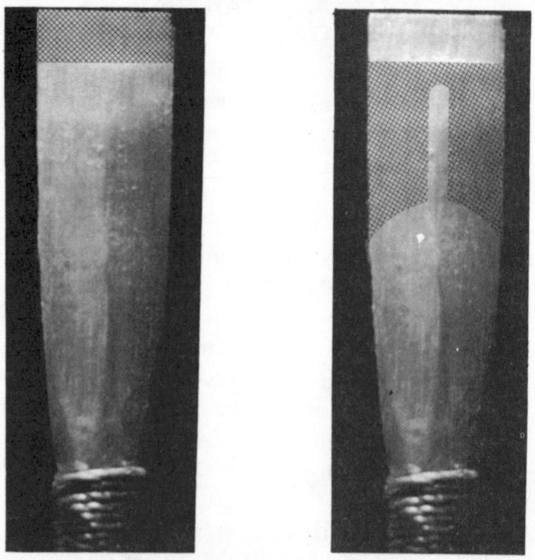

A. Tip B. Shoulders

Figure R-34. "W" Cut Reed.

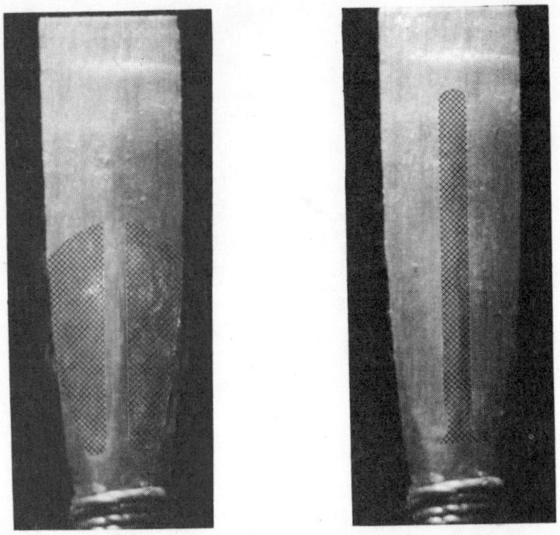

C. Back D. Spine

Figure R-34 (Con't). "W" Cut Reed.

uses a half moon shape tip. Scrape toward the tip with the knife parallel with the tip, very little at a time, and testing frequently. The thinner the tip the easier the reed will blow and the more reedy the sound will be. The adjustment of the thickness must be determined by balancing tone quality and easy for blowing with the other areas of adjustment as described in the testing routine.

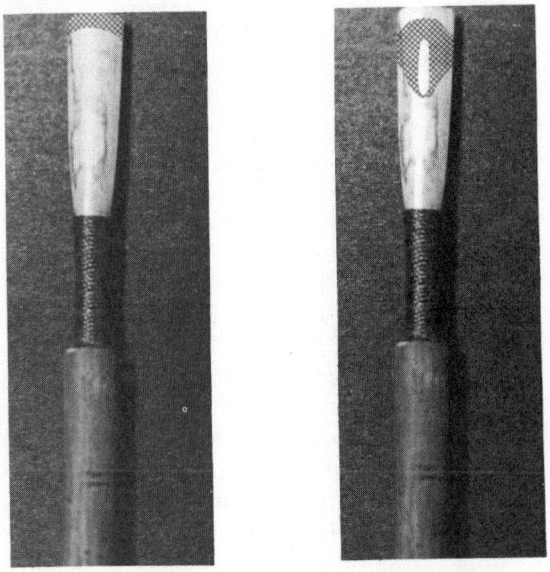

A. Tip B. Shoulders

Figure R-35. "U" Cut Reed.

In scraping the tip, the scraping knife is held in the tips of the fingers as shown in Figure R-36. Figure R-37 illustrates how the reed is held securely against the forefinger by the thumb. Note the placement of the plaque in the reed. The knife rests against the thumb and in this illustration is in position for scraping the center section of the tip. The scraping is done by rotat-

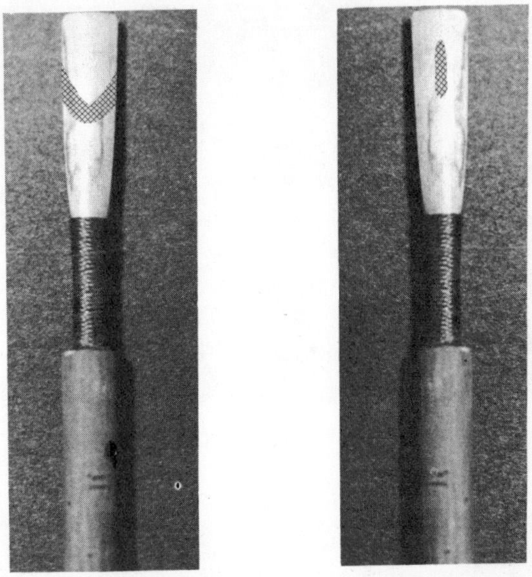

C. Back D. Spine

Figure R-35 (Con't). "U" Cut Reed.

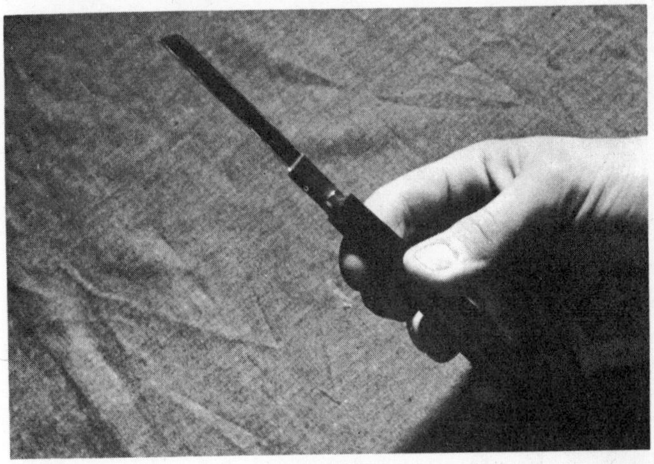

Figure R-36

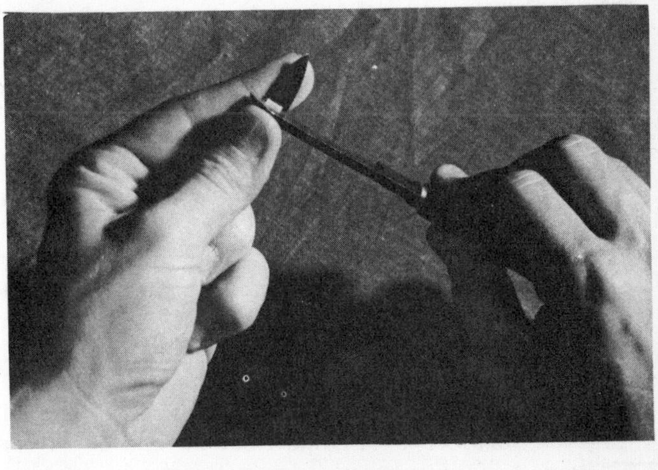

Figure R-37

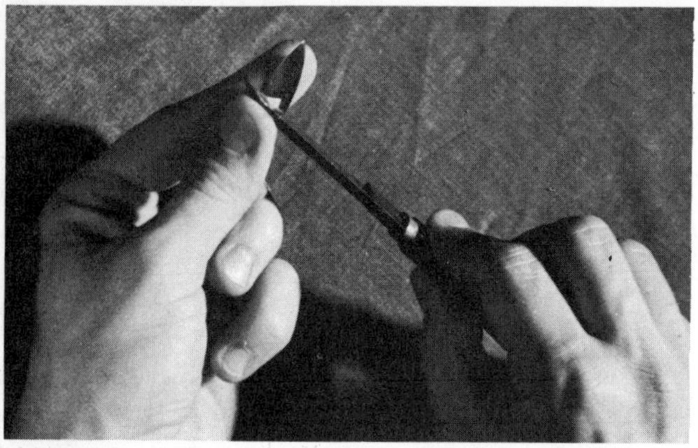

Figure R-38

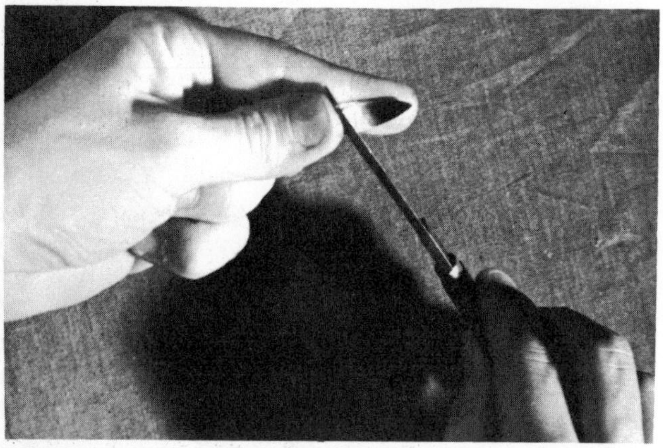

Figure R-39

Figure R-40

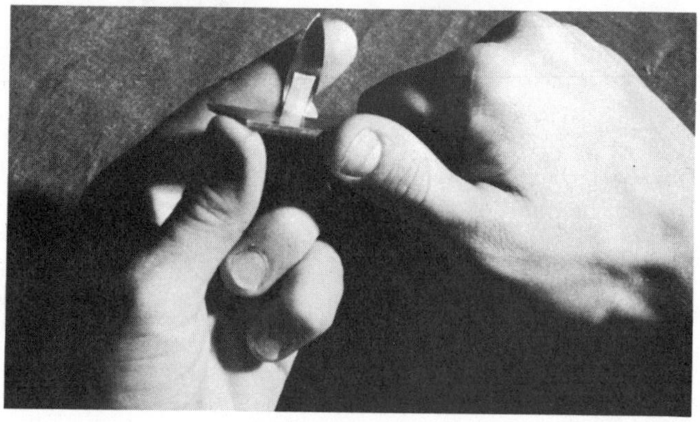

Figure R-41

ing the cutting edge toward the tip with the fingers and wrist, with the knife pivoting against the thumb.

The corners of the tip are scraped with the reed held in the same position as for the center scrape. The angle of the knife is changed to move diagonally toward the corner of the tip being scraped. The direction of the scrape is toward the corner with the cutting edge of the knife rotated by the tip of the fingers and the wrist and pivoting against the thumb. Figure R-38 shows the position of the knife for scraping the right corner of the tip, and Figure R-39 the position for scraping the left corner. The tips of both blades must be scraped to identical proportions.

2. *Shoulders.* The shoulders determine to a great extent the basic flexibility or strength of the reed. The two shoulders are thicker at the spine and at the base of the cut getting progressively thinner toward the sides and tip. Figure R-40 shows the way in which the scraping knife is held for scraping the shoulders. It is held firmly in the fingers with the thumb braced on the top. Figure R-41 shows the reed in place for scraping the left shoulder area. Notice that the end of the knife is against the thumb and is in position for beginning the scrape. This scrape is done toward the corner of the tip rather than straight forward with a forward motion of the forearm with the knife pivoting on the thumb.

3. *Back.* The back supports the vibration of the shoulders and is slightly thicker. The length of the scrape of the back helps control the basic pitch of the reed. The further back it is extended within the basic cut the flatter the reed. The thinner the back is, the thinner the shoulders will be and the softer the reed's strength which will make the tone quality more reedy. The back also affects the response of the low notes on the instrument. The back is scraped with the knife and reed held as for the shoulder scrape. The knife is held parallel with the tip and the scraping is done toward the tip while moving the knife from the center to the side of the reed with a movement of the thumb.

4. *Spine.* The spine is the center or heart of the reed which tapers in thickness toward the tip. Some types of cuts for oboe reeds do not have a clearly defined spine section, but if there is one it should be scraped only as a last resort. If in spite of other adjustments, the reed continues to be too stiff, the thickness and taper of the spine must be brought into the proper relationship with the remainder of the cut. It is scraped with the knife held as for the shoulder cut parallel to the tip, and very lightly. A very little cane removed from this section will have a great effect on the response of the reed.

TESTING AND CORRECTING REED RESPONSE

An oboe reed may be tested in several ways to see what adjustments, if any, need to be made to make it suitable for a particular player. All of the following tests can be performed in sequence, and if the reed does not respond properly on any one of them, adjustments should be made to correct the response before proceeding to the next test. The reed must be moistened to the proper playing condition before starting the testing. No adjustments are ever made on a dry reed.

The reed is soaked in a small amount of fresh water to put it in playing condition. A small glass vial deep enough to hold enough water to immerse the reed up to, but not touching the fishskin if the skin has been applied, or up to the end of the cut. The winding must never under any circumstances be soaked. The length of time needed to soak a reed into playing condition varies with the reed and type of cane. Soak until the sides close, but avoid soaking too long. The longer the reed has been played the longer it will take to soak it.

1. *Air leakage*

Test: Testing for leakage of air through the sides of the reed is done by stopping the end of the tube with a finger and blowing into the reed with some pressure. If air escapes from between the blades this should be corrected before proceeding to the next test.

Correction: Wrap goldbeater's skin around the reed in the area shown in Figure R-42. Cut a piece of the skin about an inch long and wide enough (a half inch is usually sufficient) to cover the affected area. Moisten with saliva the area of the reed where the skin is to be wound. Locate one end of the strip of skin carefully in place in the center of one of the blades and wrap tightly around the reed. A slight spiral downward so that the skin covers at least a quarter inch of the thread wrapping will help keep it in place. When the skin is wound in place moisten the entire surface of the skin with saliva. When this is dry apply a coat of clear fingernail polish over the skin and the wrapping to seal the skin permanently in place. Keep the polish off of the cane.

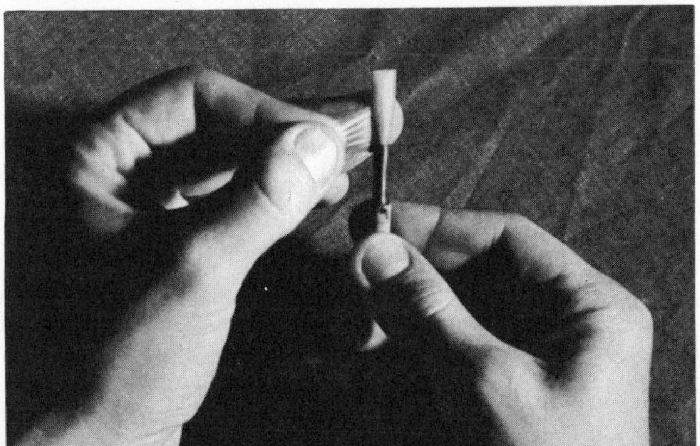

Figure R-42

2. *Basic strength of reed.*

Test: Stop the end of the tube with a finger and suck the air out of the reed. When taken from the mouth the blades of a properly adjusted reed will stay closed for a second and then open with a slight pop. If the end remains closed the reed is too soft, if the end does not close at all to form the vacuum the reed is too stiff, or a leak has not been sealed.

Corrections: (1) If the tip does not close test the thickness of the tip. First moisten the inside with saliva, then insert the plaque. The thickness of the tip can be seen when the plaque is pressed gently against each blade as shown in Figure R-43. The tip should be sufficiently transparent so that the plaque can be seen through it, and should be the same thickness entirely across the reed. Scrape the tip section of both blades until they are equally transparent. Retest the reed and if this procedure has not corrected the condition proceed with the next correction.

Figure R-43

(2) If, after the tip has been tested and adjusted as directed the reed will not form a vacuum, test, then the flexibility of the cut by pressing the blades together with the thumb and forefinger about a half-inch from the tip as shown in Figure R-44. If the blades require considerable pressure to close the tip they are too thick and must be scraped. Experience will quickly indicate the proper pressure needed to close the tip. While this test is performed the tip should close from the edges toward the center, with the exact center being the last place to close. If the tip does not close last in the exact center a diminuendo is difficult to play.

This condition is corrected by cutting the back of the lay to relieve the side which closes last. This procedure will sometimes be the only adjustment needed to correct the strength of the reed. If this does not make the correction scrape the shoulders of both blades to a uniform thickness and blend them into the tip area to maintain balance.

Be sure that the reed remains moist. Test the reed frequently during the scraping both with the vacuum test and the crow of the reed as outlined later.

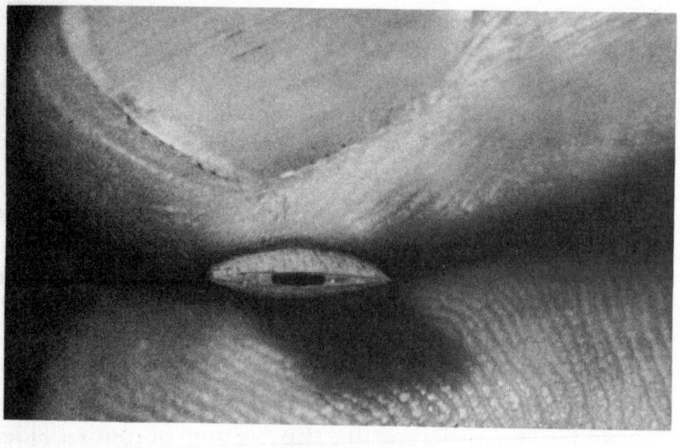

Figure R-44

(3) A tip which remains closed when the vacuum test is made may be much too soft, or the curvature of the blades may be so slight that there is not enough spring in them to open the tip. A tip which remains closed in the vacuum test will more often than not close easily when it is played so that no sound can be produced. A reed which is in this condition for either cause can seldom be adjusted for excellent response, although adjustments can be made so that it can be played.

If the curvature of the blades is satisfactory a tip which is too soft can be identified when the plaque is inserted as directed in number one above. A tip which is too soft will be almost completely transparent. The correction is to cut off a portion of the tip and if necessary rescrape the reed to the proper pitch and response.

If the reed which is otherwise satisfactory closes because of the slight curvature of the blades and generally weak shoulder areas, the tip may be held open by adding a wire as far back on the reed as possible. Figure R-45 shows a typical location. Use two turns of wire around the reed and twist the ends together. The twist controls the pressure against the reed and the amount the tip is held open. Adjust to achieve the desired opening. A wire is seldom necessary with a medium or long "W" cut, but is more frequently used with a medium or short "U" cut. Many oboists prefer to discard a reed rather than using a wire to hold the tip open, while others will use a wire as part of the normal process of making a reed.

English horn reeds may have a wire as part of its regular construction. The objection to wiring a reed is due to the fact that basic dynamic changes are made by opening and closing the tip. If the tip is naturally open it can be easily closed by the embouchure, but if it is held open by a wire it is difficult to control with the embouchure. Usually only quite soft reeds need a wire and the tone quality is not good, and is not improved by the wiring.

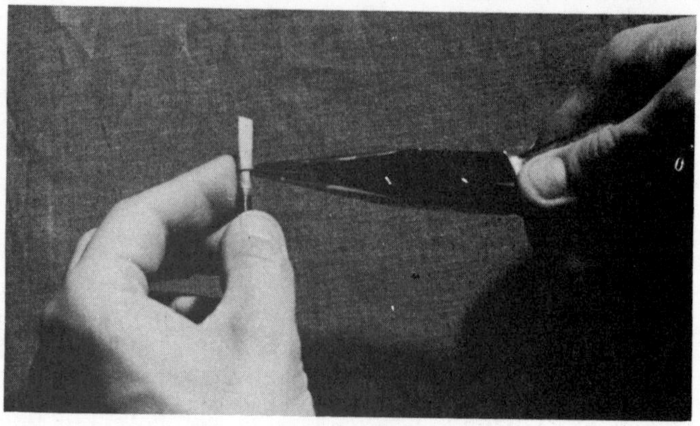

Figure R-45

3. *Crow or cackle of the reed*

Test: Testing the crow or cackle is done by placing the reed a little further into the mouth than it is placed for playing. Blow with a steady, but unfocused stream of air. When a sound is produced in this way a good reed will have a characteristic even and well-defined double crow. The correct crow must have both the high sound and the low sound present in about equal balance. Experience will enable a player to determine a great many things about a reed from the way in which it crows. Many reed makers will not even put the reed on the oboe until the crow is satisfactorily adjusted.

Corrections: (1) A high pitched squeak is produced by a reed that is too stiff. This may be accounted for by a tip which is too thick, a tip which is too short, or by shoulders or back being too thick. Test and adjust the tip area as previously described to the proper length and thickness, testing the sound of the crow frequently. If the high pitched sound persists after the tip is adjusted scrape the shoulders and back section a very little at a time, testing the crow frequently. Unless the reed is an exceptionally stiff one this should produce the proper crow.

If the reed is very stiff it may be necessary to take a little cane off the spine section. This must be done extremely carefully, very little cane at a time, and the reed tested frequently. Keep the length, shape, and proportions of both blades the same. Do not touch the tip section of the reed if it has been previously adjusted.

(2) If only a low pitch is present the tip is too long, too soft, or both. If the tip section is properly cut then the facing is too long. In both instances the pitch of the reed will probably be flat. The correction for a too long or too soft tip is to trim the tip back very very little at a time until the correction is made. Once the tip is responding correctly, the basic strength and pitch of the reed may be adjusted if necessary.

If the tip area is not the cause a facing which is too long is corrected by cutting off a little of the tip and reshaping the forward portion of the cut and tip. This process may make the reed play sharp and must be carefully done.

The tip may be trimmed with the cutting knife and billot. With the reed in place on the billot, prepare for the cut with the knife flat on the blade of the reed. With the knife in this position the cutting edge may be lined up exactly parallel with the tip and the amount to be removed determined accurately. When the edge is in position, roll the knife up to the vertical position for the cutting as shown in Figure R-46. The cutting is done with pressure of both hands on the blade.

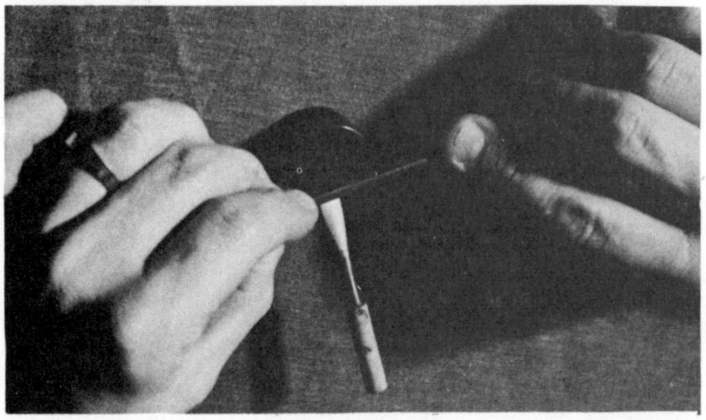

Figure R-46

Some oboists prefer to trim the tip with a pair of ordinary sewing scissors. When the scissors are used the two blades are pressed firmly together with the thumb and forefinger of the left hand. The reed is placed against the lower scissor blade, lined up parallel with it and the amount to be clipped determined as in Figure R-47. The trimming is done by holding the reed firmly against the lower scissor blade and cutting with a single movement of the scissors.

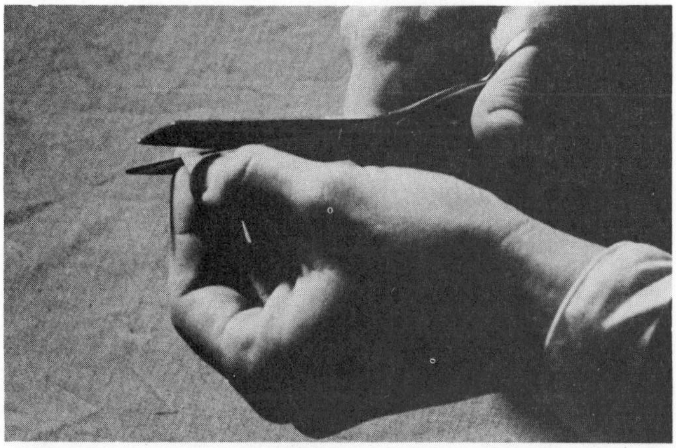

Figure R-47

4. *Matching the blades.*

Test: Test the reed in correct playing position in the normally formed embouchure without the instrument. (Note the difference between this position and the crow position). It should produce a clear tone. Turn the reed over so that the position of the blades is reversed in the mouth. The tone produced in this position should be identical with the previous sound.

Correction: If the tones produced with the reed in both positions are not identical then the blades are scraped unevenly and do not match. A careful visual examination will usually show the difference between the blades so that they can be scraped to match. Not all oboe reeds match exactly or respond identically when the blades are reversed. If, in spite of careful adjustments the response is still slightly different—one position responding better than the other—mark the upper blade of the better position so that the player can always play with this blade up.

5. *Checking pitch.*

Test: Put the reed on the instrument, warm up the instrument, and test the pitch to see that the reed plays exactly at A-440 when the tube is pushed into the instrument as far as it will go. All oboists should have a tuning fork for this purpose. A stroboscopic tuner where a visual check of the pitch can be made is more convenient and may be used when available.

Corrections: (1) If the reed is very slightly sharp, the tube can be pulled no more than a sixteenth of an inch from the instrument without adverse effect on the way in which the instrument will respond. If the tube is pulled more than a sixteenth of an inch, the instrument will be out of tune with itself, some notes will respond poorly, and tone quality on some notes will suffer.

(2) If the reed is too sharp to be corrected by pulling the tube, then the pitch can be flattened by slightly lengthening the cut. Scrape lightly the back area an equal amount on both blades. Test frequently and continue until the reed is brought to the correct pitch.

(3) If the reed is flat, the pitch may be raised by trimming a small amount off the tip, as previously described. Cut off only the smallest amount of the tip at one time. Test carefully, and repeat the process if necessary. Be very careful not to cut off too much so that the reed is sharp. If the trimming process to bring the reed up to pitch makes it stiff and difficult to blow, first scrape to reform the proper tip area. If reforming the tip does not correct the stiffness the entire cut may require scraping and adjusting.

6. *Intonation of upper octave.*

Test: If the A-440 is in tune, test to see if the octave above can be played perfectly in tune with normal adjustment in embouchure pressure. If the upper A is flat in relation to the lower one, then all the upper notes will be flat and the reed must be adjusted to compensate for this.

Correction: Assuming that the player's embouchure is properly formed and developed, there are several possible corrections for flatness in the upper notes. Perform the following operations in sequence until the situation is corrected:

(1) The tip of the reed may be too open, i.e., too round. If this is the case, correct as described under correction two of the basic strength tests previously described.

(2) Narrow the reed by filing both sides lightly with a file or emery board. Place the reed solidly on a table top. Holding it firmly, file parallel with the table, moving the file back and forth gently as shown in Figure R-48. Test the reed frequently to avoid taking too much off. Watch the tip opening during this process to see that it does not become too close.

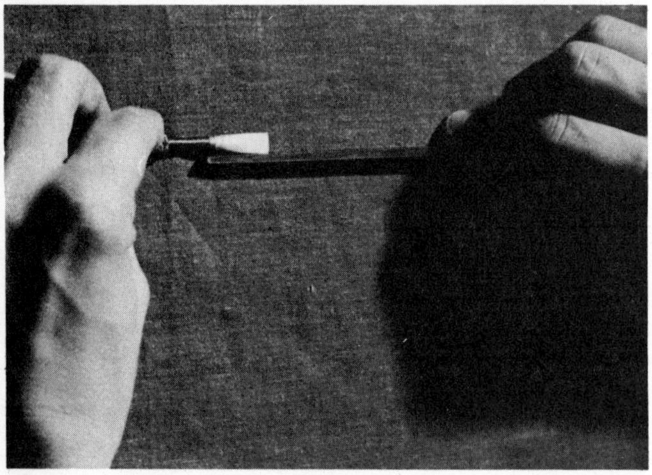

Figure R-48

(3) Slide one blade sideways so that they are very slightly out of parallel. If this does not help the intonation, shift them in the other direction and retest.

(4) Cut a sixty-fourth of an inch off the tip of the reed. This will solve the out-of-tune upper octave which is caused by a tip which is too thin and/or too long without changing the overall pitch of the reed.

If the reed otherwise responds well with satisfactory tone quality and none of these procedures solves the problem of flatness in the upper octave, then it is caused by the student's embouchure being undeveloped and/or poorly formed and the solution lies in the embouchure rather than the reed.

The upper A will almost never be sharp, this sharpness can be corrected by the appropiate adjustment in the embouchure. If this sharpness occurs regularly on several different well-adjusted reeds, check the embouchure formation of the student. It is likely that he is biting the reed with his lower teeth or wedging it between the upper and lower teeth.

7. *Response of lowest notes.*

Test: Test the response of the reed on the lowest four or five notes of the instrument. They should speak readily at a piano level and should not have a reedy quality.

Correction: If the low notes do not speak at a piano level or respond with difficulty thin the blade by scraping lightly the portions of the shoulder near the spine. Test frequently during this process since if too much is taken off response of other notes of the instrument will change. Be sure that both blades are scraped equally.

ENGLISH HORN REEDS

English horn reeds have the same basic cuts and adjustments as those described for oboe reeds. It normally has a shorter tip proportionately than an oboe reed to respond better on the higher notes and for better intonation. It will, as well, have a more pronounced spine. The English horn reed is made on a staple which fits directly on the crook of the instrument, and usually has a wire in place to adjust the tip opening.

All the tools except the mandrel used in adjusting oboe reeds can be used for adjusting English horn reeds. A special English horn mandrel to fit the staple is necessary to hold the reed while working on it. The tests and corrections used for the oboe reed apply also to the English horn reed with adjustments for its slightly different proportioned cut. Students who are skilled in adjusting oboe reeds can easily adapt this skill to the English horn reed with some experience.

CARE OF THE OBOE AND ENGLISH HORN REED

A good, well-responding oboe or English horn reed is a valuable possession and should have meticulous care if it is to have a long useful life. The rules for caring for reeds are simple and if followed will prolong their useful life.

1. Keep the fingers off the tip of the reed.

2. Keep reeds in a reed case so that they will dry out slowly and completely. Plastic tubes seal too tightly for this purpose. If such a tube is used punch a small hole in the cap. Figure R-49 shows a typical oboe reed case.

3. Always soak the reed as directed before playing. Never play on a dry or partially moist reed. Clear water is better than saliva for this purpose. Most oboists carry a small water-tight bottle in their case for this purpose.

4. Clean the inside of the reed every week or two with a wet pipe cleaner when the reed is well soaked. Insert the wet pipe cleaner through the tube from the cork and and force it gently through the tip of the reed. Then pull it through the reed slowly moving it from side to side so that all inside surfaces are cleaned. Re-

peat the process two or three times. Figures R-50 and R-51 illustrates this procedure.

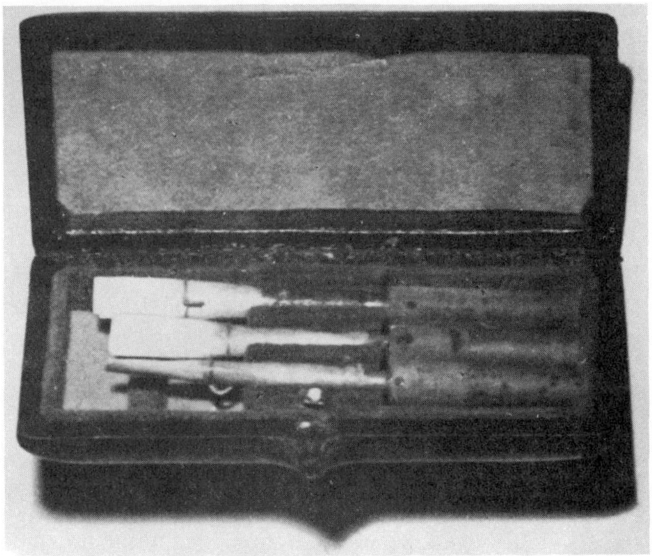

Figure R-49

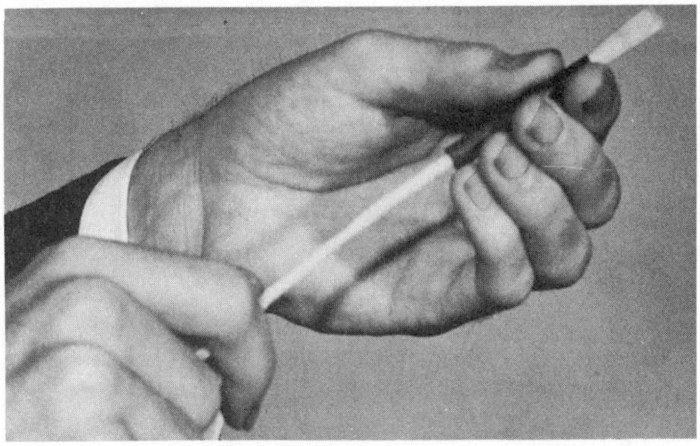

Figure R-50

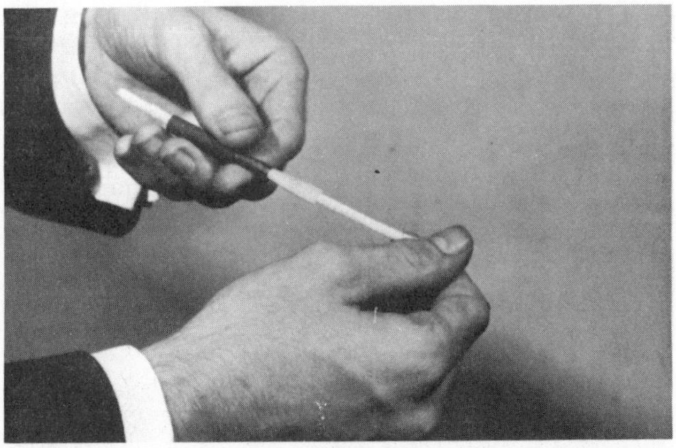

Figure R-51

BASSOON REEDS

The reed is perhaps the most important part of the bassoon, since in combination with the embouchure and the instrument itself, it is the determining factor in how the instrument will sound. Even the best embouchure cannot make a poor reed sound well, while a good reed is a valuable assistant for an undeveloped embouchure. The response of a good reed is limited by a poor instrument or an instrument in poor condition. The finest instrument cannot make a poor reed sound or respond correctly.

In order to isolate the influence, response, and control of the reed it is necessary to have the instrument in good playing condition, and a properly formed embouchure which has been developed past the beginning stages. If the embouchure is poorly formed or undeveloped it is impossible to isolate and identify many incorrect factors as being caused specifically by the reed. Many of the symptoms of a poorly responding reed may be caused by the embouchure.

The selection, adjustment, and care of the bassoon reed is a subject which should be thoroughly understood by every player and by every teacher who is responsible for these students. This is a widely neglected and misunderstood subject possibly because the information is not readily available. There is no mystery to the bassoon reed. Its selection and adjustment is no more complicated than for the oboe and single reeds, and is readily understood and performed after some experience by anyone familiar with the instrument. One writer on the subject is of the opinion that anyone, after making a dozen reeds from blank cane will be able to turn out a reed which will be very playable. Not everyone will agree with this statement, but certainly the subject of bassoon reeds is not one which should be considered difficult or impossible to understand.

Every bassoonist past the beginning stage should be able to adjust ready-made reeds. If he is a serious student of the instrument he should learn how to make his own reeds from the blank cane. Most bassoonists who are fortunate enough to study with a teacher skilled in reed making learn the art of reed making and adjustment as a regular normal part of the study of their instrument. Many teachers consider this as important as any other aspect of study. Certainly no bassoonist's training can be considered complete until he is proficient in making and adjusting reeds. Beginners on the instrument will first develop the facility for adjustment and then progress into the complete production of reeds.

The present discussion is limited to the selection, adjustment, and care of the bassoon reed. The problems involved in making reeds are beyond the scope of this book, and are best learned through personal instruction from one who is skilled in the art. The considerations here will be limited to those aspects of the problem which the teacher needs to know and use in his everyday activities.

PARTS OF THE BASSOON REED

Before discussing the bassoon reed it is necessary to establish a vocabulary for identification of the various parts of the reed. The designations here are the standard ones which are in almost universal use. Figure R-52 identifies these parts.

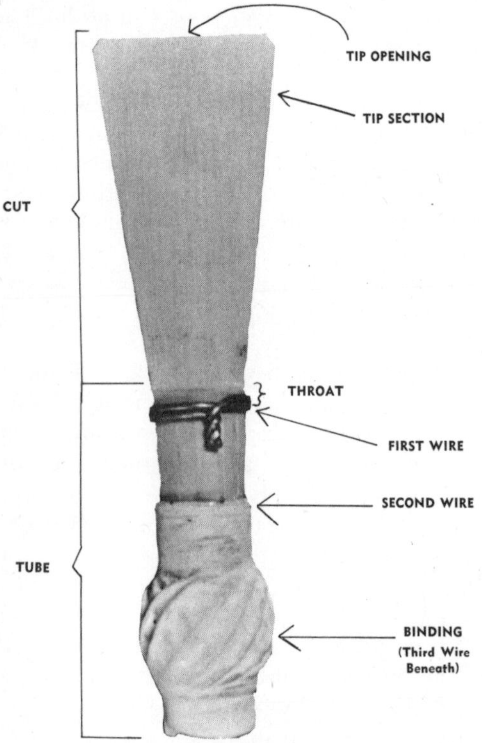

Figure R-52

The *tip* section is an inverted "U" similar to that found in single reeds and will be illustrated later. The *tip opening* refers to the space between blades. The *cut* (also called the facing, lay, or scrape) is that portion of the reed from which the bark has been cut. Its length, contours and thickness control the vibration of the blades and must be carefully controlled. The *shoulder* is the point at which the cut begins. The *throat* is the interior of the reed from the first wire to the shoulder. Its shape may be perfectly round or slightly elliptical when observed from the back of the reed. The function of the throat section is to blend the tube into the cut blades and it determines to some extent the amount of arch in the blades. Its shape may be adjusted by the first wire. The *tube* extends from the first wire to the bottom of the reed. Regardless of the shape of the throat the tube section, both inside and out, must be perfectly round.

The two halves of the reed are held together by three wires. The *first wire* is near the shoulder, the *second wire* about a half inch down the tube from it, and the *third wire*, beneath the binding, is about a quarter of an inch from the end. The first and second wires influence the response of the reed and are used in making certain adjustments. The function of the *binding* is to help hold the two pieces of cane together, to seal possible leaks in this area, and to provide a place for the fingers to grip the reed securely. The binding is nylon or cotton thread wound in a ball over the third wire, with a single layer extending to the second wire. It is covered with a coat of reed cement, or collodion to seal the reed and binding against air leaks. The wrapping is traditionally red in color, but some makers use other colors. The neatness and skill with which the binding is applied to the reed is one obvious way to judge the quality of workmanship in a reed.

HOW A BASSOON REED IS MADE

The process of making a bassoon reed from cane tubes is quite similar to that described in making an oboe reed. The diameter of the cane used is about nine-eighth inches—somewhat larger than that used for oboe reeds. A few more steps are necessary because the bassoon reed is not mounted on a staple.

The steps in producing the bassoon reed are performed in this order: splitting, gouging, sanding the inside, scoring on the easel, removing the bark from the center inch of cane on the easel, filing this portion which will become the tip of the reed, notching either side of the cane at the center, folding over shaper, shaping, beveling the edges, cutting the tube section to the correct length, applying the three wires, with the reed on the mandrel finishing the blades with knife and file, wrapping the thread, reaming the tube to fit the bocal and final tuning and adjustments. This process is demonstrated by Russell Pugh in an excellent 16 mm color film.[5] Those interested in the detailed process of making a bassoon reed may consult the books by Artley and Popkin-Glickman listed in the bibliography at the end of this book.

Cane for making bassoon reeds is available in five different forms in decreasing order of the amount of work remaining to complete the reed: (1) bulk, (2) straight gouged, (3) gouged and shaped, (4) gouged, shaped, and folded, (5) gouged, shaped, folded, and profiled. The profiled cane has the basic cut of both blades completed, usually by machine, and requires only wiring, wrapping, and completing the cut to produce a finished reed. The profiling is often referred to as "roughing out the tip" and should be understood as having the same meaning.

The more proficient and particular the bassoonist is in making reeds the more work he wants to do himself on the reeds. Professionals will start with bulk cane. An ex-

5. *Bassoon Reed Making.* 29 minutes. Champaign, Illinois: University of Illinois Visual Aids Service.

cellent way for a student bassoonist to learn the art of reed making is to start with the fifth class of cane listed above and work his way back through the list as his proficiency develops.

The fourth type—gouged, shaped, and folded—is that most frequently used by experienced student bassoonists as it saves a great deal of time while giving them complete control over the shape and contours of the lay. There are considerable differences in brands of cane available in all five forms. Several brands should be tried until the one best suited is found.

TYPES OF BASSOON REEDS AVAILABLE

Although the advanced bassoonist is expected and wants to make his own reeds, the great majority of students will purchase reeds which are ready-made. Many schools purchase them by the dozens for their bassoonists. Since the success of these students is dependent upon how the reed responds it is most important that they be purchased wisely and with full knowledge of the choices available. There are three general types of ready-made reeds available which can be described as follows:

1. *Semifinished commercial reeds.* These are mass produced for general retail distribution in the same way that single reeds are produced and distributed. Several machines have been perfected which produce a semi-finished bassoon reed virtually without handwork. The value of these machined reeds lies in the consistency of the cut and in producing reeds at a lower cost.

The description "semifinished" indicates that the purchaser must perform the final adjustments for the best response. This includes tuning the reed to fit his embouchure and instrument, finishing the cut on both blades, and smoothing the surfaces. Unless the teacher or student has developed some skill in adjusting reeds, this type of reed is seldom satisfactory. Many semifinished reeds are not designated as such when they are sold and many students attempt to play them without making the final adjustments, with the consequent multitude of problems a poorly adjusted reed brings.

2. *Finished commercial reeds.* Other types of commercial reeds generally available in music stores are classified as "finished" reeds. That is, the cut has been finished and the reed is in playing condition. Some brands of these finished commercial reeds are graded according to strength in the same way single reeds are graded. Strengths, 1, 2, 3, 4, 5, etc., are available. The lower the number the softer the strength. Even though the reed is classified as finished it must be tried on the instrument and adjustments made to suit the individual player. If this kind of reed is used several brands must be tried to find the one which is most consistently satisfactory and needs the least adjusting.

3. *Custom-made reeds.* This class of reeds is made by professional players to individual order. There are many professional players in all sections of the country who will make reeds for students, and who will adapt the reed to the level of advancement of the student. These reeds are normally made in the same way and with the same care the professional makes reeds for himself. Since they are not mass produced the quality is consistently high.

It is highly recommended that this type of reed be secured for all school bassoonists at least until their embouchure and facility has developed to the point that they have enough assurance to learn how to adjust their own reeds. If there is not a nearby professional bassoonist to supply reeds, the names and addresses of professional players who specialize in making reeds for school use can be found in the classified advertisements in such magazines as the *Instrumentalist* and *School Musician.* Try reeds from several makers until those best suited for the student and instrument are found.

TYPES OF CUT

There are two basic types of bassoon reeds, the French and the German. In the chapter on the bassoon vast differences are pointed out between the French system instruments and the Heckel system or German instruments both in mechanics of the key work and in the type of tone quality produced. Only the German or Heckel system bassoon is used in this country. Since the German type reed is designed for the Heckel bassoon it is the only type which should be used. The French cut reed will not respond or produce the desired tone quality when it is used on a Heckel bassoon. Unless the finished reeds are imported from a French maker it is highly improbable that the French cut will be found on the market. Avoid using any bassoon reed described as having a French cut.

Within the basic German cut which is universally used in this country, there are probably as many variations in length, width, shape, and overall size as there are people making bassoon reeds. Reeds for no other instrument vary so greatly. In spite of this the general shape of the cut remains the same, with only the proportions of the various areas changed. For this reason the areas described for adjustment, and the way the adjustments are made can be applied to any standard reed.

SELECTING THE REED

Reeds must be suited to the individual who is going to use them—to his embouchure and his instrument. The reed must be made to play in tune on his instrument since the pitch of the instrument itself can be changed very little with other adjustments. Unlike the clarinetist, the bassoonist cannot try a dozen or more reeds to find one that responds well, but must learn to adjust a particular reed to make it fit his needs. He must know how to care for it so that its useful life will be prolonged.

TOOLS AND MATERIALS FOR ADJUSTING THE BASSOON REEDS

In order to perform the operations necessary to adjust the response of a bassoon reed certain tools and materials are necessary. This complement should be a part of the equipment of every teacher responsible for bassoon students. When the student has progressed far enough he should acquire these tools and learn to adjust his reeds. Figure R-53 shows the basic equipment for adjusting bassoon reeds. From left to right the items are: file, cutting knife, scraping knife, reamer, mandrel, shaped plaque, billot (above), and pliers (top).

A description of these and additional items is summarized as follows. Details of their use in adjusting appears in the section on adjustment.

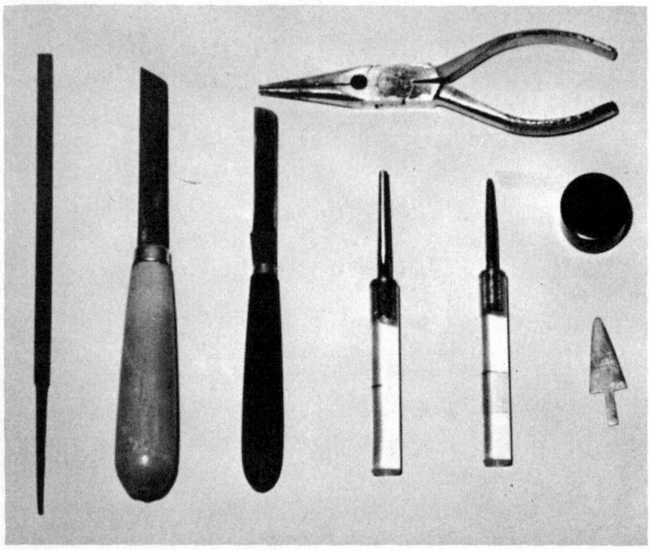

Figure R-53

1. *File.* For finishing the cut, rather than using the scraping knife. A "piller" file which has the serrations completely to the end is preferred.

2. *Cutting knife.* Used for cutting off tip of reed. Must not be used for scraping.

3. *Scraping knife.* The scraping or reed knife is used only for scraping the cane. It is identical with the oboe scraping knife. Refer to the section on oboe reeds for details of its shape and how it is kept sharp.

4. *Mandrel.* Fits into the tube of the reed, and is used to hold the reed while working on it. One with a short handle is preferable for the adjusting process. It must be the same size as the small end of the bocal being used.

5. *Reamer.* For enlarging the end of the tube so that the reed will fit the bocal properly. Like the mandrel, the reamer should match the size of the bocal.

6. *Plaque.* The plaque is inserted between the blades of the reed whenever any scraping is being done in order to prevent damage to the tip section. There are two shapes of plaques available, an oval shape similar to the standard oboe plaque and a shaped plaque as illustrated in the photograph. The shaped plaque is identical with the shape of the reed and is advantageaus in that it supports the blades more firmly than the flat oval shape, and its smaller size has a minimum protrusion around the blades so that the knife or file can be worked to the edge of the reed. Both are useful in the adjusting process.

7. *Billot.* The billot, or cutting block, is a round block about an inch and a half in diameter made of wood or plastic, and with a slightly convex upper surface. It is used to provide a firm shaped surface for trimming the tip of the reed.

8. *Pliers.* For adjusting the wires on the reed. A small, narrow end pair with a cutting edge is desirable. The special pliers made for use with bassoon reeds have a hole in them for shaping the cane over the mandrel, but are not necessary for simple adjustments.

9. *Dutch rush.* Used for making fine adjustment in the cut and for the final polishing of the entire lay. It may be used wet or dry and is recommended for beginners learning the art of adjustment because it removes cane very slowly. Fine grain sandpaper or a fine grain emery board may be used instead of the Dutch Rush.

10. *Soft brass wire.* For replacing the wire bindings on the reed in the event this becomes necessary.

AREAS OF REED TO BE SCRAPED FOR ADJUSTMENT

The areas of the reed which may need adjustment are well defined no matter what the size and shape of the reed. The exact size and shape of each area will vary slightly with each type of reed. Examine the reed carefully to locate the size, shape, and proportions of each area before attempting to make an adjustment. Figure R-54 shows the various areas for adjustment. Each area influences a particular aspect of the reed's response.

The areas and their function are as follows:

1. *Spine.* The spine is the center or heart of the reed which tapers in thickness toward the tip. It controls the vibrations of the sides and influences the strength of the reed. If the reed is too stiff this portion of the reed should be scraped only after the tip and sides have been properly proportioned. Scrape very little at a time and test frequently. This portion of the reed has its greatest influence on the low register of the instrument.

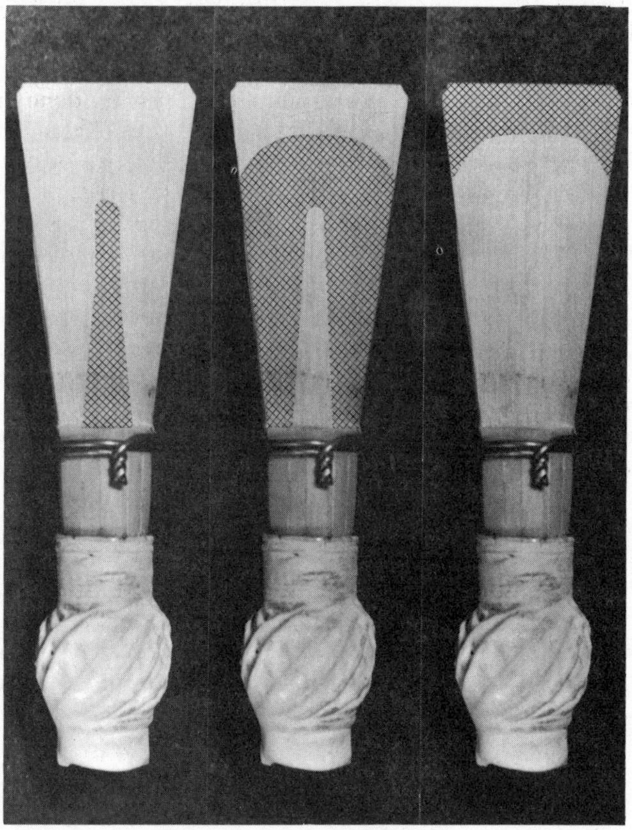

Figure R-54

In scraping the spine and the back portion of the sides, the knife is held between the fingers and thumb. It is held parallel with the tip of the reed. The scrape is made straight forward toward the tip and keeping the blade parallel with the tip. Figure R-55 shows the starting position for this scrape.

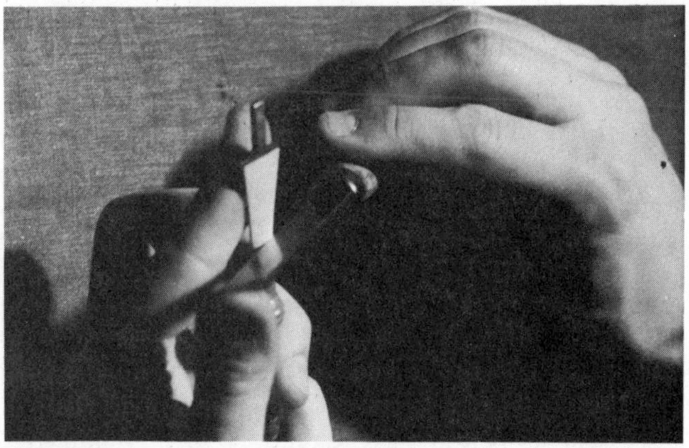

Figure R-55

2. *Sides.* These areas are tapered in thickness from the spine to the edge of the reed and toward the tip area. The sides along with the tip determine the stiffness of the reed. If the tip is properly proportioned and the reed is too stiff scrape the sides to make it softer. The sides must be blended smoothly into both the heart and tip sections.

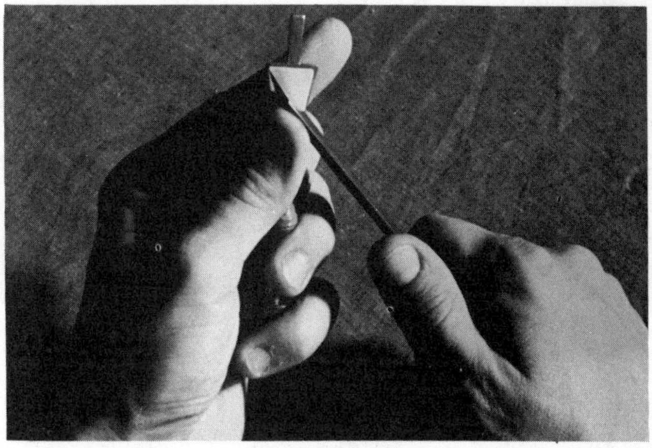

Figure R-56

In scraping the forward portion of the sides the knife is held as shown in Figure R-56 and braced against the thumb. The direction of the scrape is diagonally toward the edge of the reed.

3. *Tip.* The tip area is in the shape of an inverted "U" and tapers in thickness toward the corners. When looking at the tip opening the blades should curve evenly, and must match exactly. The blade is thickest in the center and gradually tapers to a very thin line at the corners. Both sides of the center of the blade should be identical, and both blades should match. Figure R-57 shows the shape of the tip opening. The

Figure R-57

two blades should be approximately one-sixteenth of an inch apart in the center of the tip opening.

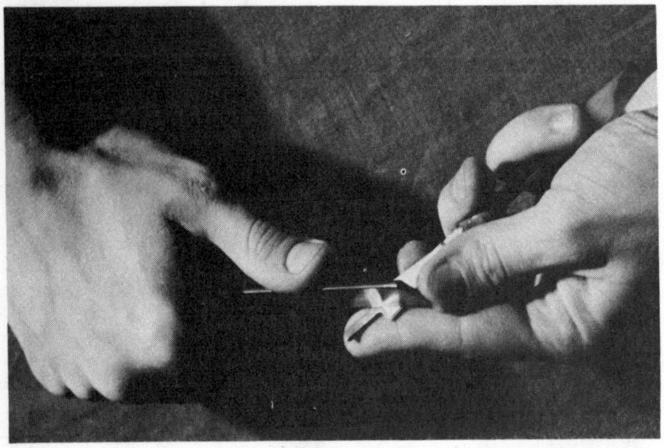

Figure R-58

In scraping the tip, the scraping knife is held as shown in Figure R-58 in the cupped fingers with the thumb on top. Notice how the knife rests against the thumb. The knife rotates against thumb and the direction of the knife is toward the corner of the reed.

ADJUSTING THE BASSOON REED WITH WIRES

The two visable wires on the bassoon reed bind the two sections of the reeds together as their primary function. In doing so they exert pressure against the top and bottom as well as the sides of the blades. These pressures control the amount of curvature in the blades and thereby the size and to some extent the shape of the tip opening. The two wires are adjusted to control both the tip opening and curvature of the blades.

The wires are squeezed from either the top and bottom or from the sides with the pliers. Do not tighten the wires by twisting the ends. If the wires are too tight either by twisting the ends or by squeezing, the reed may crack. The first wire is especially susceptible to cracking the reed, even to the point of extending the crack into the cut. When tightening the second wire the circular shape of the tube must not be disturbed. If this wire is tightened very much it may be necessary to ream the end of the reed so that it will fit on the bocal.

Changing the tip opening affects both tone quality and pitch, so adjusting with the wires must be done gradually and cautiously. A tip which is more open will produce a fuller and darker tone, be slightly higher in pitch, and have more resistance. A tip which is more closed will produce a thinner, reedier sound, be slightly flatter in pitch and have less resistance.

The first wire when squeezed on the sides will open the tip. When squeezed on the top and bottom the first wire will close the tip. The second wire when squeezed on the sides will close the tip. When squeezed on the top and bottom the second wire will open the tip. Notice that the two wires have an opposite effect on the tip when squeezed on the top and bottoms and on the sides. To open the tip squeeze the sides of the first wire or the top and bottom of the second wire. To close the tip squeeze the top and bottom of the first wire or the sides of the second wire.

The reed may be opened or closed an even greater amount by using both of the wires. The decision on whether to make the adjustment with the first or second wires or both of them depends on the nature of the reed itself. The first wire makes a greater change in the curvature of the blade and tip than does the second while opening and closing it. Therefore if the tip opening is too round or too flat in shape begin by adjusting the first wire. If the curvature of the blades is correct and the tip is too open or too close begin by adjusting the second wire. If the adjustment of one wire does not correct the problem, both should be used. Experience will quickly indicate whether or not adjustment of the wires is called for and how this adjustment should be done.

TESTING AND CORRECTING REED RESPONSE

A bassoon reed is tested in several ways to see what adjustments, if any, need to be made to make it suitable for a particular player. The testing and adjustments must be done slowly and carefully, testing the reed after each adjustment. Students have a tendency to over adjust in the learning stage. While some over adjusting can be corrected, cane which is scraped away cannot be put back. Emphasize the process of small adjustments between each testing of the reed.

All adjustments, including those made with the wires, must be made with the reed soaked to the proper playing condition. The reed is soaked in a small amount of fresh water. A small glass vial deep enough to hold sufficient water to immerse the reed up to the first wire is sufficient, and all bassoonists should have one in their case. The length of time needed to soak a reed varies with the reed type of cane, anywhere from three to twenty minutes. The reed is sufficiently moist when the sides close. This is the only dependable criteria for the length of time needed. Avoid soaking the reed too long. Do not wet the circular tube section, for if it becomes soaked and expands the binding tends to come loose after it dries.

After the reed has been soaked make the following tests. The tests for leaks should be first, followed by the "crow" test. The remainder may be performed in any sequence.

1. *Air leakage in reed.*

Test: Stop the end of the reed with a finger and blow air into the tip with considerable pressure. If air leaks out the seams make one or both corrections.

Correction: (1) Soak the reed longer—as much as twenty minutes—to see if the sides will close firmly. Many leaks will be stopped by this simple process.

(2) If soaking the reed does not stop the leak, the wires must be tightened. With the pliers twist the end of each wire, one-half turn and test the reed. If it still leaks twist each another half-turn and test. Continue until the leak stops, but avoid tightening the wires so much that the shape of the throat or tube is changed or the vibration of the blades is damped.

2. *Air leakage at bocal connection.*

Test: Using the bocal alone, put the reed in place with a slight twisting motion. Close the cork end of the bocal and the whisper key vent hole with the fingers and blow firmly through the reed. If the air leaks at the juncture of reed and bocal correct as follows.

Correction: Ream the end of the reed very carefully (Figure R-59) so that it is perfectly round and will fit further on the bocal. It should fit at least a quarter of an inch over the bocal.

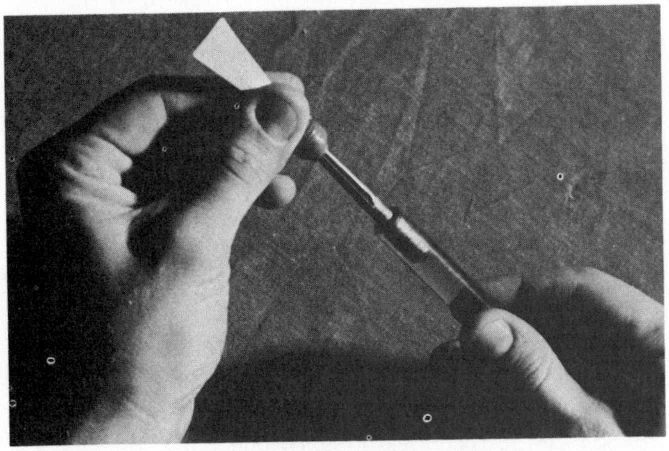

Figure R-59

3. *Crow of the reed.*

Test: Testing the crow of the reed is done by putting the reed between the lips with just enough pressure around it to keep the air from escaping, and with the lips almost touching the first wire. Blow with a steady, unfocused stream of air. When a sound is produced in this way on a good reed it will produce the characteristic double crow. This sound must have both high and low pitch sounds in it with the low pitch somewhat more prominent.

With some experience the bassoonist can judge the quality of the reed quite accurately from how it crows. No further tests should be made on the reed until attempts have been made to produce a satisfactory crow. If the high pitch predominates and the sound takes more than normal breath pressure to produce, the tip is too open and/or the reed is too stiff. If little or no high pitch is present and the sound takes less than normal breath pressure to produce, the tip is too close and/or the reed is too soft.

Correction: (1) If the reed is well soaked alter the tip opening by squeezing it with the thumb and forefinger. Squeeze the top and bottom of the tip for less opening. Squeeze the corners of the tip for a greater opening. This must be done with a gentle pressure in order not to crack the reed. If the reed is basically a good one the tip opening can be adjusted with this procedure. Make the adjustment and test the crow. Repeat two or three times if necessary. If the tip opening is still incorrect adjust with the wires.

(2) If adjusting the tip as directed in the first correction does not produce the correct crow, proceed with the test of the basic strength of the reed.

4. *Basic strength of reed.*

Test: The test will help verify the crow test. Stop the end of the tube with a finger and suck the air out of the reed. When taken from the mouth the blades of a properly adjusted reed will stay closed for a second or two and then open with a slight pop. If the end remains closed the reed is too soft or the tip opening too close. If the end does not close at all to form the vacuum the reed is too stiff, or a leak has not been sealed.

Correction: Repeat the test for air leakage to eliminate this as a cause. Check the tip opening to see that it is correct. If there is no air leakage and the tip opening is correct this test should confirm the conclusion made in the crow test, that the reed is too stiff or too soft. Proceed with the appropriate test and adjustment given for a stiff reed or soft reed.

5. *Stiff reed.*

Test: The crow test reveals a stiff reed when the high pitch predominates and it is hard to blow. The basic strength test indicates a stiff reed when the vacuum fails to form. For an additional test, put the reed in place on the instrument and play third space E-flat with the 103 000 fingering. Compare this pitch with the octave below. If the third space note is sharp the reed is too stiff. Play the notes in the low register—B-flat to F below the staff. If the reed is too stiff it responds slowly and these notes will have a rough quality and be impossible to play softly.

Correction: (1) Most commercial reeds are deliberately left stiff so that the purchaser can adjust them to his needs. If the tip opening is correct and the reed is stiff, the entire facing must be scraped or filed to make the blades thinner. This must be done evenly over both blades so they are in perfect balance. Remember, it is easy to take off too much cane. Make the crow and basic strength test frequently during this process until the reed successfully passes them. When it does, test the E-flat and the low register. If the E-flat responds properly but the low register does not, proceed with the next correction.

(2) The response of the lower octave on a reed which is otherwise correct is adjusted by additional scraping on the side areas of the reed. Scrape both sides of both blades evenly, a very little amount at a time. Test frequently so that too much cane is not removed. Continue until the proper response is achieved.

6. *Soft reed.*

Test: The crow test indicates a soft reed when there is little or no high pitch present and the sound takes less than normal breath pressure to produce. This basic strength test identifies a soft reed when the end remained closed. For an additional test, put the reed in place on the instrument and play third space E-natural starting softly and making a gradual crescendo. If the tone cracks before the fortissimo is reached the reed is too soft. Notes in the low register will have a very reedy quality on a soft reed, and notes in the high register will be difficult or impossible to play in tune. The basic pitch of the reed will be flat, and difficult to control.

A reed is too soft because the tip area alone is too thin, the sides and tip area both are too thin, or because the spine alone or in combination with the sides and tip is too thin. Adjustment is difficult or impossible and it is for this reason that testing the reed after each minute adjustment has been emphasized. In some areas, the spine, for example, a very little cane removed has a great effect on the strength of the reed. Since most commercial reeds are deliberately left too stiff and the usual problem is to bring them down to the desired strength, almost all reeds which are too soft are that way because of over adjustment on the part of the player.

Correction: (1) If the reed is only slightly soft work with the wire adjustments to see if it can be brought to the proper strength by increasing the curvature of the blades and the tip opening.

(2) Put the reed on the billot and with the cutting knife cut off a sixteenth of an inch from the tip. Starting with the crow test repeat the adjusting process. Pay careful attention to the basic pitch of the reed as cutting off the tip may make it too sharp.

(3) If the reed has been used for a period of time and has become too soft because the blades have lost some of their elasticity clean the inside of the reed with a pipe cleaner as directed in the section on care of the reed and put it aside to dry out for a week or more. If the reed is still too soft, try the first two corrections.

(4) If none of these corrections brings the reed to the proper strength discard it. Nothing is more useless and discouraging for a player than a soft reed which produces a poor tone quality, and cannot be controlled or played in tune.

7. *Pitch of reed.*

Test: Generally, but not always, the pitch of a stiff reed is sharp, the pitch of a soft reed is flat. During the process of adjusting the reed the pitch must be checked frequently. If the response of the reed is good and needs no further adjustment, but the pitch is sharp or flat make the appropriate correction. If a particular brand of reed is consistently sharp or flat for the instrument on which it is being used it is too long or too short for that instrument. Try other brands.

Correction: (1) If the reed is slightly flat ream the tube so that it fits further on the bocal. Increase the depth very little at a time and test frequently. This distance is critical for if it goes on too far the response of the instrument is altered. The reed under no circumstances must be reamed to the extent that the end of the bocal is any further into the reed than the first wire, and even this is risky.

(2) If reaming does not bring the reed up to pitch change to a shorter bocal. Bocals are discussed in the bassoon chapter. If this doesn't bring it up to pitch the reed should be discarded, for the student will begin biting in order to play in tune.

(3) If the reed responds well in all ways, but is sharp use a longer bocal if a longer one is available. If this does not bring it to the correct pitch continue with the following corrections which will change the response of the reed somewhat so that attention must be given to the response as well as the pitch.

(4) If the reed is slightly sharp check the thickness of the tip area and remove a very little cane. Check the response of the reed in articulation so that the tip is not made too thin. Readjust wires as needed.

(5) If the reed is still sharp check the thickness of the side areas and remove a little cane, but keep the sides and both blades in balance.

(6) If this does not correct the sharpness remove a very little cane from the forward portion of the spine section of each blade, and blend into the side sections. Do this very slowly and carefully and test frequently for the pitch and strength of the reed changes rapidly with this adjustment.

8. *Matching the blades.*

Test: During this discussion of adjusting the reed the point has been repeatedly made that both blades must be identical in shape and thickness at all points. The greater the deviation in the perfect symmetry of the two blades the poorer the reed. This matching of the blades should be a consideration in each step of the adjusting process.

Three tests can be applied. First, with the reed wet and saliva inside the reed insert a flat plaque. Press the plaque against the entire tip area to observe the thickness at the tip and to feel the resistance to the pressure at various points in the area. Test the corners of the tip area. Alternate the process between the two blades. The more transparent the cane the thinner it is. Adjust by scraping to balance as necessary.

Second, the side areas and the forward portion of the spine is tested by pressing these areas against the plaque with the thumb and forefinger. Alternate blades to compare. A little experience will soon enable the player to feel the relative resistance to the pressure at various points.

Third, polish the entire cut of the reed by rubbing it with dry Dutch Rush. An observation of the polished cane will reveal any irregularities, unevenness, or bumps in the cut. This polishing has an additional advantage of sealing the pores of the cane.

Correction: Adjust as necessary to balance the blades. Major adjustments can be made with the scraping knife. Minor adjustments and adjustments to small areas are best done with wet Dutch Rush with the end pinched to make a flat surface. Fine grain sandpaper or a fine grain emery board may be used instead of the Dutch Rush if handled carefully.

9. *Intonation of reed.*

Test: A reed on which the response has been adjusted according to the previous tests and which is responding well will normally play with good intonation. If the reed is a good one but plays out of tune, the fault almost always lies in the embouchure or in the instrument itself. The relationships of embouchure and the instrument to intonation are discussed in the chapter on bassoon.

Correction: Repeat various tests, especially the crow and basic strength tests, to see if further adjustments need to be made in the response of the reed. If response checks out and the student has intonation problems on several reeds the correction lies elsewhere than the reed. If a student who has been playing well in tune has intonation problems with a new reed which has been adjusted for response the construction of that particular reed is faulty and it should be discarded or have major alterations made.

10. *Articulation and the reed.*

Test: Play major scales and arpeggios through all registers of the instrument with legato and staccato articulations. If the reed does not respond as desired make corrections.

Correction: Articulation response is controlled almost entirely by the tip area of the reed. If the reed does not articulate properly, assuming of course that the student's tongue placement and action is correct, adjust the tip area for balance over the various registers of the instrument. Check tip opening in the center which should be one-sixteenth to three thirty-seconds. If the tip opening is too small articulation in the low register is difficult, if the tip opening is too wide articulation in the high register is difficult. Adjust the opening to balance these.

The thickness of the blades at the very tip is critical. They must be thicker in the center of the blade and thin toward the edges, with both blades identical. Using wet Dutch Rush thin the forward quarter inch of the blade as necessary, testing frequently. Good response in articulation is the result of the best balance and relationship between the size of the tip opening and the thickness of the forward portion of the blades. If articulation response is satisfactory except for excess reed noises, cut off a small portion of both corners of the reed.

11. *Response of lowest notes.*

Test: Test the low register—B-flat to F below the staff—in scale and arpeggio passages both slurred and legato. If the notes respond with difficulty the reed is too stiff or the tip opening too close.

Correction: (1) Check first the tip opening. Notes in this register articulate sluggishly when the tip is too close. Adjust the tip opening with the wires if necessary.

(2) If tip opening is correct and the reed responds well in other registers of the instrument but not in the low register the spine of the reed is too thick. Thin the entire spine section of both blades very gradually and testing frequently until correct response is achieved.

CARE OF THE BASSOON REED

Once the reed is adjusted and responding well it can be kept in good condition with care. The rules for caring for the reeds are simple and if followed will prolong their useful life.

1. Always soak the reed as directed before playing or adjusting. Clear water is better than saliva for this purpose. A small water tight glass should be kept in the case for this purpose.

2. Keep the reeds in a reed case so that they will dry out slowly and completely to retain their form. Some reed cases have a mandrel on which they are stored. The plastic tubes in which commercial reeds are merchandised are not a suitable substitute for reed storage unless a hole is punched in the cap. Otherwise they seal too tightly for the proper drying of the reed. Figure R-60 shows a typical bassoon reed case.

3. Clean the inside of the reed every week or ten days with a wet pipe cleaner when the reed is well soaked. Insert the pipe cleaner from the round end and force it gently through the tip of the reed. Then pull it through the reed slowly moving it from side to side so that all inside surfaces are cleaned. Repeat the process two or three times.

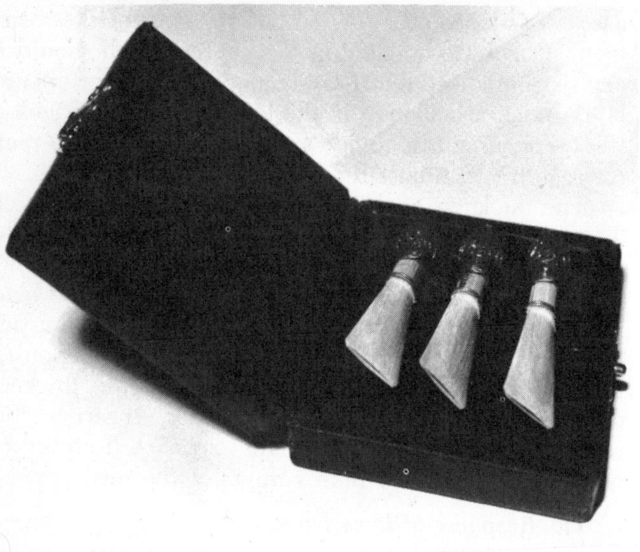

Figure R-60

4. Keep the outside of the blades clean so that the vibration of the blades is not restricted. A light polishing with Dutch Rush will clean the surface. Girls who play bassoon should remove their lipstick before playing, and remove any accumulation with the Dutch Rush or with the edge of an emery board. The discoloration of the blades which remains after the lipstick is removed will not harm the reed.

5. Protect the reed when it is in place on the bocal. When the instrument is to be in the rest position for a few minutes remove the reed from the bocal and put it in the mouth or behind an ear for protection.

STUDY AND ACHIEVEMENT QUESTIONS

Mouthpieces

1. Define and identify on a single reed mouthpiece: facing, tip opening, end rail, baffle, tone chamber, bore, table, table opening, and side rails. Describe effect of each on response.
2. Obtain several B-flat clarinet or Alto saxophone mouthpieces of different brands. Compare the shape and size of the various parts. Determine whether or not the end rail and side rails meet specifications. Have a member of the class who is proficient on the instrument play on each of the mouthpieces to compare tone quality and general response.
3. Using a gauge kit for B-flat clarinet mouthpieces measure the tip opening and facing of as many as you can. Number each mouthpiece and prepare a chart of these measurements. Indicate any which have a warped lay. Indicate on the chart whether the tip opening is close, medium, or open and whether the lay is short, medium, or long. Have a member of the class who is proficient on the instrument play each of these to compare measurements with tone quality and general response.

Single Reeds

4. Identify parts of a single reed: tip, shoulder, heart, center point, cut, stock, and heel.
5. Select at random six B-flat clarinet or Alto saxophone reeds from a box of medium strength, and number them on the back. Describe each in terms of color, grain, cut, and tip resistance. Estimate their probable quality and arrange them in progressive order from best to poorest.
6. Using the same reeds have a competent player on the instrument test them. On the basis of the playing test and the previous visual examination describe any adjustments which need to be made on each to bring them to the best playing condition, after indicating the degree of hardness of each.
7. Secure the minimum tools and equipment for adjusting single reeds. Practice the following operations: (1) scraping and balancing the shoulders; (2) scraping and balancing the tip; (3) adjusting the heart section to put the centerpoint in the proper place and of the right thickness; and (4) trimming the tip.
8. Select a reed which is too soft. Deliberately cut off too much of the tip. Reshape the entire lay to bring tip, shoulders, and heart section into the proper balance.
9. Adjust a reed for someone who is proficient on the instrument having him play on the reed after each adjustment. Experience will enable you to hear as well as see the adjustments which are necessary.
10. From a mixed collection of reeds for various sizes of clarinets identify the instrument for which each is intended. Do the same for a mixed collection of saxophone reeds. Mix the clarinet and saxophone reeds together and identify the instrument for which each is intended.
11. Describe in detail the care of a single reed.

Oboe Reeds

12. Define and identify on an oboe reed: staple, blades, winding, and cut.
13. Outline the shape of the blade of an oboe reed, draw and label the various types of cuts available.
14. Examine a collection of oboe reeds from various sources and describe the shape and length of cut on each.
15. Secure the minimum tools and equipment for adjusting an oboe reed. Identify each and practice holding it or putting it in place without adjusting a reed.
16. Practice the following scrapes: center and sides of the tip, shoulders, back (if clearly defined on the type of cut selected), and spine.

17. Perform the following, which can be done even though you are not an oboist, on one or more oboe reeds: (1) test for air leakage, (2) practice applying goldbeaters skin, (3) test for basic strength of reed and make necessary corrections, and (4) test the crow and make necessary corrections. Use commercial reeds for this as custom-made reeds will need little or no adjustment.
18. Adjust a reed for someone who is proficient on the instrument having him test after each adjustment. Perform the step-by-step test and correction procedure until the reed is responding properly.
19. Discuss how an oboe reed may be kept in good playing condition over a period of time.

Bassoon Reeds

20. Define and identify on a bassoon reed: tip, tip opening, cut, shoulder, throat, tube, first wire, second wire, and binding. On the cut identify: spine, side areas, and tip area.
21. Practice adjusting the bassoon reed with the first and second wires. Observe and describe how each adjustment effects the reed.
22. Secure the minimum tools and equipment for adjusting a bassoon reed. Identify each and practice holding it or putting it in place without adjusting a reed.
23. Practice the following scrapes on a reed: center and sides of the tip area, front and back portion of each of the sides, and front portion of the spine. Be sure reed and knife are properly held for each operation.
24. Perform the following, which can be done even though you are not a bassoonist on one or more reeds: (1) test reed for air leakage, (2) test for air leakage at bocal connection, (3) the crow test, and (4) the test of basic strength. Make the necessary corrections after each test.
25. Adjust a reed for someone who is proficient on the instrument having him test after each adjustment. Perform the step-by-step test and correction procedure until reed response is correct.
26. Discuss care of the bassoon reed.

Chapter 8

Vibrato

In the instruction of woodwind instruments, the subject of vibrato frequently arises with students as early as the intermediate level. This is natural, for if the students have listened critically to professional performers, in person or on record, they are aware of the use of vibrato. They realize that a good vibrato adds expressiveness to the tone of the instrument.

The vibrato is an integral part of all vocal tones; in fact, one authority states that there can be no true vocal tone without it. It is the lyric vocal vibrato that provides the inspiration and model for a good woodwind vibrato. The use of vibrato is universal on string instruments, and the development of a satisfactory vibrato is part of all string instruction. Virtually all brass instruments make use of a tasteful vibrato, but restrict its use primarily to solo passages. A well-developed and controlled vibrato is now part of the basic technical equipment for all advanced woodwind players.

DEFINITION

A good vibrato may be defined as a regular pulsation added to the basic tone of the instrument involving changes in pitch, in intensity (loudness), or in a combination of pitch and intensity. Traditional definitions of vocal vibrato also indicate that changes in timbre may also be involved, but discernable changes in tone quality in connection with woodwind vibrato are undesirable.

CONFUSION ABOUT VIBRATO

Among musicians there is more disagreement and confusion about vibrato and its uses than any other single factor in performance. Most of the confusion results because the ear, even of a trained musician, does not hear vibrato as it actually exists in the tone. Many people cannot hear vibrato as a separate entity, but hear it only as part of tone quality in general. Because of the intangibles of the musical tone, the ear does not hear the speed of the vibrato as it actually exists, nor the amount of pitch fluctuation as being as large as it actually is.

The vibrato is also frequently confused with tremolo, defined as a rapid and wide dynamic variation of the tone without any pitch deviation. Many of the objections to the use of vibrato should be aimed at the tremolo. Some students who attempt to develop a vibrato on their own develop instead a tremolo produced in the throat with its objectionable sounds. This is extremely difficult to correct. The tremolo should not be confused with the intensity vibrato which has a much slower rate of speed and a small and carefully controlled amount of dynamic variation.

WHAT IS GOOD VIBRATO

The primary factors in a good vibrato are the rate of speed of the pulsations and the degree of fluctuation in pitch and/or intensity. The rate of speed of the vibrato gives it life. If the rate is too slow, the tone gives an effect of laboriousness, heaviness, and sluggishness. Very slow pulsations are heard as a wobble in the tone. If the rate is too fast, its effect is lost and frequently approaches the tremolo in sound.

Both a scientific analysis of the vibrato of outstanding artists and the recommendations of woodwind authorities are in agreement on the most desirable rate of speed. This speed is between five and seven pulsations per second. Speeds either slower or faster occur in performances by artists only rarely. The same artist will vary the rate of speed within the suggested limits at times, depending on the nature of the music he is performing, but these variations are not too obvious to the ear.

The amount of pitch fluctuation in vocal vibrato has been established at about one half-step—one quarter below and one quarter above the actual pitch. In singing, small deviations on either side of the half-step interval are common, but too great a deviation is considered poor taste.

The amount of pitch deviation on string instruments is half that of vocalists—one quarter-step. The amount of actual pitch deviation on woodwinds where pitch rather than intensity is the primary basis of the vibrato has not been established. Considering the small pitch of adjustments which are possible with embouchure or breath on woodwinds, it is probably no more than a quarter-step. Critical listening must be the final judge as to whether the performer is using too much or too little pitch deviation.

METHODS OF PRODUCING A VIBRATO

There are three basic methods of producing a vibrato on woodwind instruments, along with many variations and combinations of them. In fact, the same player may use more than one method at various times depending on the effect he wishes to produce. However, most players will prefer to develop one type which will be flexible enough to cover any situation which might arise.

The standard ways of producing the vibrato may be described as follows:

1. *Diaphragmatic vibrato.* This type of vibrato is produced by increasing and decreasing the wind pressure against the embouchure by controlled motions of the diaphragm and abdominal muscles.

As we have seen in the study of acoustics an increase in wind pressure raises the pitch of a tone slightly and at the same time makes it louder. Decreasing the wind pressure lowers the pitch slightly while making it softer. This method produces parallel simultaneous fluctuations in both pitch and intensity.

No change in embouchure formation is necessary. This kind of vibrato can be freely used and controlled throughout the entire pitch and dynamic ranges of the instrument.

2. *Jaw vibrato.* This type of vibrato is produced by slight up and down motions of the lower jaw which produce changes in the pressure of the lips against the reed; or in the flute, slight changes in the direction of the wind across the embouchure hole.

When the pressure increases, the pitch is raised slightly; and when the pressure decreases, the pitch is slightly lower. As with the diaphragmatic vibrato, the jaw vibrato involves no changes in embouchure formation and may be easily used throughout the entire pitch and dynamic ranges of the instrument. There is a danger in getting too much movement of the jaw which would result in too wide fluctuations in pitch.

3. *Throat vibrato.* In this method the vibrato is produced by successive contraction and expansion of the throat muscles. When singers use this type of vibrato, the motion is quite visible.

A very dramatic vibrato is produced in this manner, but it is the least desirable of the methods for use on woodwind instruments. Its use impairs the breathing, the player using it tires quickly and the vibrato produced in this fashion is difficult to control and is capable of but little variation. Unless this type of vibrato is perfectly controlled, the result will be an objectionable tremolo rather than a vibrato.

This type of vibrato is not recommended for use on woodwind instruments. It is mentioned here because many students, especially flutists, will produce this type of vibrato when they attempt to learn without the guidance of a teacher.

Flute Vibrato

The need for a tasteful vibrato as part of the basic flute tone is universally accepted. Equally standard is the recommendation for the use of the diaphragmatic vibrato which can be quite easily and naturally produced on the flute.

In developing this type of vibrato, the attention of the student should be focused entirely upon varying the intensity or loudness of the note. The player should not make any attempt at all to vary the pitch. Overt attempts to change the pitch will cause intonation problems and embouchure changes. The desirable amount of pitch change for a typical good flute vibrato will come automatically with the increasing and decreasing breath support.

The problem area in developing vibrato on the flute is that many students will involve the throat muscles in addition to diaphragm movement. Or they will use throat motion alone. The throat vibrato should be avoided at all costs. Involvement of throat muscles in the diaphragm is also undesirable because of adverse effects on both tone and vibrato control.

Jaw vibrato must not be used on the flute because of the changes it makes in embouchure formation which will effect both tone quality and control.

Oboe Vibrato

Both the diaphragmatic and jaw vibratos are used successfully on the oboe. Some professional players use a combination of the two, or even one or the other of the methods depending on the musical content of what is being performed.

The use of the diaphragmatic vibrato on the oboe is recommended by a majority of teachers, and is recommended as the first approach to be tried with a student. As with the flute, in developing this type of vibrato, the attention of the student should be entirely upon varying the intensity or loudness of the note with no attempt at all to vary the pitch. Attempts to involve pitch changes will cause intonation problems and embouchure changes. This type of vibrato is somewhat easier to produce and control over the entire range of the instrument than the jaw vibrato.

If the student is having difficulty with developing the diaphragmatic vibrato, then jaw motion may be introduced either alone or in combination with the diaphragm.

Some teachers recommend the jaw vibrato alone for oboe because it is simple and easy to learn, and comes quite naturally to some players. If the jaw vibrato is being taught, the attention of the student must be upon the changes in pitch, with no attempt at changing loudness. The slight changes in intensity will come naturally with the small changes in tip opening resulting from increased and decreased embouchure pressure.

Clarinet Vibrato

Because the vibrato has so recently been accepted as a part of clarinet performance, there has been no standardization of approach. Standard references to the instrument avoid all mention of vibrato. The use of vibrato on clarinet has, in fact, been the subject of discussion and some controversy for many years. During the years in which vibrato was becoming a standard part of the performance practices of the other woodwinds, professional clarinetists for the most part refused to adopt the vibrato.

There is ample evidence that this attitude has changed and that the vibrato is beginning to be considered a part of the clarinetists technique to be used when it is needed. In a recent survey of college, university, and professional clarinetists, Cecil Gold reported that 71% said they used vibrato occasionally, 11% usually used vibrato and only 20% reported that they never used vibrato in performance.[1]

The survey indicated that in reporting the type of vibrato used 47% indicated they used the jaw-lip vibrato, 30% used the diaphragm vibrato, and 23% used the intensity vibrato. Since, as we have seen, the intensity vibrato must be produced by movements of the diaphragm and an intensity vibrato without some pitch change is almost impossible to produce on a woodwind instrument, it is probably safe to combine the responses on diaphragm and intensity and conclude that 53% of these professional performers and teachers used the diaphramatic vibrato.

On the basis of this evidence we can conclude that opinion on the best method for producing vibrato on the clarinet is almost equally divided between the jaw and diaphragmatic vibrato. Either method, or a combination of the two, produces equally satisfactory results.

The fact that the majority of these players made use of vibrato only occasionally indicates that the use of the vibrato on clarinet has not reached the degree of use as on other woodwinds. The results of the survey could be influenced by the fact that so many professional clarinetists double flute and saxophone. Those players who had developed a fine diaphragmatic vibrato for their flute playing adapted it to clarinet. Those who had developed a fine jaw vibrato for their saxophone playing adapted that method for their clarinet playing.

For students who are learning vibrato for the first time, the author recommends the jaw method. It develops more readily, can be controlled by students not on the professional level and if the student is going to do any doubling at all, it will probably be on the saxophone where the jaw method is also preferred. Alto and Bass clarinetists will find the jaw method easier to control.

The study of vibrato on clarinet need not be begun as early in the student's training as it is on other woodwinds where its use is more prevalent. It is advisable to wait until the player has reached the advanced level. Advanced clarinetists who are performing a wide repertoire will find that some contemporary scores call for vibrato. If they are playing show music, vibrato is desirable both stylistically and to blend with the other woodwinds.

In teaching the jaw vibrato, the attention of the clarinet student must be upon the changes in pitch, with no attempt at changing loudness. Attempts to change the loudness will involve the diaphragm and abdominal muscles and result in a combination of jaw and diaphragm vibrato. The slight changes in intensity needed for the vibrato will come naturally with the small changes in the amount of tip opening between reed and mouthpiece resulting from increased and decreased embouchure pressure.

Saxophone Vibrato

The development of a good vibrato which is always under control is mandatory for saxophones. Most authorities would agree that no player has fully developed his tone unless he has a vibrato available for use when needed. Statistics prove this point.

In a survey of prominent college, university, and professional saxophonists, Cecil Gold found that 49% of the respondents said they *always* used vibrato while the other 51% said they *usually* used vibrato.[2]

In the survey the types of vibrato being used was the subject of more variation than was found in the similar survey among clarinetists. Fifty-eight of the respondents reported using the jaw vibrato, fourteen the lip, thirteen the throat, nine the diaphragm, five the intensity, and three other types.

Interpretation of the results of the types of vibrato reported must be made on the basis of surmise, for the designated types may well have had different meanings to different respondents. In the minds of most players the lip and jaw vibrato are the same thing, for the lip is involved inevitably in any jaw movement. Combining the results of these two, we find that approximately 71% of these professional player-teachers use the jaw vibrato. Combining the response indicating diaphragm and intensity, which are also inseparable in the minds of many, we find approximately 14% making use of the diaphragm vibrato as described in this chapter.

On the basis of this evidence the first choice of method of producing vibrato on the saxophone would be the jaw vibrato, with the diaphragm vibrato as second choice. Some players reported using a combination of the two. A player who doubles flute, for example, will have developed a diaphragmatic vibrato for that instrument which would transfer naturally to the saxophone, perhaps in combination with some movement of the lower jaw.

---

1. Cecil V. Gold, *Clarinet Performing Practices and Teaching in the United States and Canada* (Moscow, Idaho: University of Idaho, School Music, 1972).
2. Cecil V. Gold, *Saxophone Practices and Teaching in the United States and Canada* (Moscow, Idaho: University of Idaho, School of Music, 1973).

In teaching jaw vibrato the attention of the student must be focused upon changing the pitch. Do not attempt to consciously change loudness. Any involvement of intensity fluctuations will require movement of the diaphragm and abdominal muscles. The result would be a combination of the two types of vibrato which some players use. The slight desirable changes in intensity needed for the vibrato will come automatically with the small changes in the amount of tip opening between reed and mouthpiece resulting from increased and decreased embouchure pressure.

Bassoon Vibrato

As was the case with the oboe, in common performance practices on the bassoon both the diaphragmatic and jaw vibratos are used, either singly or in combination. There is some evidence that a majority of professional players and teachers prefer the diaphragmatic method for producing bassoon vibrato, but this evidence is not conclusive. Some fine players use a combination of diaphragm and jaw movement while some will use jaw movement alone.

It is recommended that when starting with a student to add vibrato to the bassoon tone, the diaphragmatic approach be used first. Some students have problems with this approach and the development is a slow and difficult process, but with persistence it can be developed. If after a period of time the student has not achieved satisfactory results, jaw movement can be added to the diaphragmatic movements, or can be used alone.

In developing the diaphragmatic vibrato, focus the attention of the student entirely on making variations in the loudness of tone. The player should not make any attempt at all to vary pitch. Overt attempts to change pitch will cause intonation and embouchure problems.

Some teachers recommend the jaw vibrato alone for bassoon because it is simple and easy to learn, and comes quite naturally to many players. If the jaw vibrato is being taught, the attention of the student must be upon the changes in pitch, with no attempts at changing loudness. The slight changes in intensity needed for the vibrato will come naturally with the small changes in tip opening of the reed resulting from increased and decreased embouchure pressure.

DEVELOPING A VIBRATO

No attempt should be made to develop a vibrato until the player has not only developed a good technique, but has also developed a strong embouchure and is producing a tone of quality without a vibrato. And most important, not until the player has developed sufficient musicianship to know exactly when and how the vibrato should be used.

A good vibrato cannot be developed overnight. Rather it must be slowly and carefully developed over a period of weeks and months until it is under perfect control. Do not attempt to rush the process.

One successful approach to developing a vibrato may be outlined as follows:

1. Use a strong clear tone in the middle register of the instrument. If using the diaphragmatic method, slowly increase and decrease the pressure of the air against the embouchure with the abdominal muscles. The movements should be sufficient enough so that definite changes in loudness of the tone can be heard. If using the jaw method, move the jaw slowly up and down (avoid any back and forth motion) until definite pitch changes are heard. Be sure that with either method the embouchure formation itself does not move or change. Repeat this on other notes in the middle register until the changes in loudness or pitch can be initiated comfortably.
2. Set the metronome at sixty beats per measure. Practice a scale passage in the middle register using one fluctuation of the tone to each beat.
3. After the fluctuations come easily at this speed, increase the metronome speed little by little to 120 beats per minute, keeping one complete movement of the tone per beat.
4. After the tone fluctuations per beat come easily at these speeds, move the metronome back to sixty beats per minute. Practice successive vibratos of one, two, three, and four fluctuations per beat. Do the same thing gradually increasing the metronome tempo to 100 beats per minute. Do not go faster than the speed at which the vibrato is under perfect control.
5. The speed of the ideal vibrato ranges from four pulsations per beat at a speed of 72 to four pulsations per beat at a speed of 104. The speed must be under the control of the player, and not automatic. The speed of vibrato to be used in performance depends upon the musical content of the composition.
6. After the vibrato is under control practice slow melodies—folk tunes, chorale melodies, slow études, etc.—using vibrato only on the half and whole notes.

In conclusion, keep the following points in mind when working with vibrato:

1. The ear is the final judge of whether or not a vibrato is a good one and is being used correctly.
2. The vibrato embellishes a good basic tone quality; it will not make a poor sound better.
3. The vibrato must be the same and pulsate at the same rate of speed in all registers of the instrument.
4. The vibrato must be smooth and even and pulsate at the same rate of speed regardless of the dynamic level.
5. The amount and speed of the vibrato must be adapted to the content of the music being performed.
6. A vibrato must be consciously added to the tone. It must never be an automatic part of every tone.

Acoustics and Woodwind Instruments

A knowledge of *why* a woodwind instrument sounds and responds as it does is as important as knowing *how* it sounds and responds to adjustments. This *why* is the product of the study of acoustics of music and forms an essential basis for completely understanding how the instruments operate. The finest woodwind teaching is based on a thorough knowledge of what to do and how to do it as well as why it is being done. A complete course in the acoustics of music should be a part of every instrumental teacher's training. Such a complete consideration of acoustics is beyond the scope of this book, but the basic aspects of the subject as they concern the woodwind instruments are presented.

PERCEPTION OF SOUND

In order that a sound may be heard three things are necessary: (1) a vibrating object, (2) a medium of transmission, and (3) a receiver. The vibrating object in the woodwind instruments may be a single reed as on the clarinets and saxophones; a double reed as on the oboe, English horn and bassoon; or an edge tone which produces the tone on the flute. In each instance the vibrating object is reinforced by the enclosed column of air inside the instrument to amplify the tone so that it can be heard.

The medium of transmission is normally the air, but sound travels through any substance which has elasticity. Through the walls from one room to another, for example. Sound vibrations travel at the rate of 1,132 feet per second (almost 800 miles per hour) through the air when it is at 70 degrees Fahrenheit, faster when the air is warmer and slower when the air is cooler.

The receiver is normally the ear which can hear vibrations as slow as twenty per second and as fast as twenty thousand per second. The receiver may also be a microphone which changes the vibrations into electrical energy and makes it possible to record the sounds for future study.

PITCH

The fundamental pitch of a note is determined by the frequency of the vibration stated in terms of the number of vibrations per second. The faster the vibration the higher the pitch; the slower the vibration the flatter the pitch. The standard pitch to which all instruments is tuned is A-440, meaning that there are four hundred and forty vibrations per second for this note. The A an octave above has 880 vibrations per second, and the A an octave lower 220 vibrations per second.

In woodwind instruments the frequency of the vibration is determined primarily by the length of the enclosed air column. The longer the column the lower the pitch. Thus if we start with all the holes on the instrument closed and open them one by one the pitch is raised as each hole is opened. This is the physical basis for the fingering of a woodwind instrument. In addition to the fundamental pitches of the air column, woodwind instruments make use of harmonics of this fundamental which will be considered in the following section.

The fundamental pitch of a note on any woodwind instrument is the product of the *ratio* of the distance from the tip of the mouthpiece or flute embouchure hole to the first open hole on the instrument. For this reason the distance between the tone holes becomes less and less as they become closer to the mouth, and their diameter decreases. A brief examination of any of the woodwinds but especially the B-flat clarinet will indicate the extent of these differences.

The importance of understanding the effect of this ratio and how it affects both pitch and intonation can be illustrated on the B-flat clarinet. If the tuning barrel is pulled out one-eighth of an inch the third-line B-flat will be lowered one-fourth of a half-step while the third-line B-natural will be lowered only one-twelfth of a half-step. This adjustment has three times as much effect on the shortest length of pipe as it does on the longest. The more the barrel joint is pulled the greater the differences between the amount of change in these two notes. So that the ratios could be kept constant the three note three-place tuning procedure which is presented in the clarinet chapter is important, and must be used for the best intonation.

Double reed instruments are tuned to the basic pitch primarily through reed adjustments rather than adjusting the connections between the various joints and the ratios in the air column maintained. This is also the reason why the importance of the placement of the end plug on the flute was stressed in the flute chapter. If it is out of place the ratios are wrong and the instrument out of tune with itself.

A further relationship between the length of the enclosed air column is illustrated by the differences in sizes of the instruments in the clarinet family as we go down in pitch from E-flat, to B-flat, to A, to Alto, to Bass, to Contra-Bass. The importance of the ratio between the mouth and the first open hole on pitch can be seen by comparing the size of the Alto and Baritone saxophones. The Baritone saxophone sounds an octave lower than the Alto saxophone, but is more than twice the size.

Other factors which influence pitch to a slight degree are:

1. *Temperature.* It has been previously indicated that the speed at which a sound vibration travels is determined by the temperature of the air. The colder the air the slower the vibration travels. The warmer the air the faster the vibration travels. The slower it travels inside an instrument the fewer vibrations per second and the flatter the pitch and conversely for warmer temperatures. An instrument which is tuned to A-440 at a temperature of 70 degrees Fahrenheit with the same adjustment will sound approximately A-435 at 60 degrees Fahrenheit.

The implications of this effect of temperature on woodwind instruments are most significant, and point out the importance of having the instrument properly warmed up before tuning. Instruments which are tuned at the beginning of a rehearsal before they are warmed up, will play considerably sharp when they have been warmed up by playing. Playing in rooms which are overheated, or playing outside at cold or hot temperatures not only influences the basic pitch of the instruments, but makes playing them in tune virtually impossible.

2. *Humidity.* Humidity affects the fundamental frequency of a wood instrument in that a high humidity will cause the wood to swell and low humidity will cause it to shrink. Fortunately, the wood used in woodwind instruments is treated to minimize this condition. A further precaution is found in the suggestion that the bores of certain wood instruments be oiled regularly. The same condition of high humidity in the instrument prevails when it is not thoroughly swabbed before it is put in its case, and this is one of the reasons why this process is so important.

Rapid changes from low to high humidity will cause the wood to expand and shrink and eventually crack. All cracks are the result of this expansion and contraction. The result on pitch of the expansion of an instrument under conditions of high humidity when the wood expands is to make it flatter.

Conversely, when low humidity shrinks the instrument the pitch becomes sharper. The consequences of playing a wood instrument in the sun on a hot dry day in summer combines high temperature and low humidity to the point that no amount of adjusting could possibly bring the fundamental pitch down to A-440.

3. *Wind pressure.* An increase in the amount of wind pressure into the instrument will sharpen the fundamental pitch of a woodwind instrument slightly. This does not occur with most players as the natural sharpening is counteracted by embouchure adjustments. If, however, the wind pressure is increased too much the instrument will break into a harmonic which in the case of the single reed instruments is called a squeak. The flute makes use of this breaking into a harmonic by using increased wind pressure as one of the means of playing in the second and third octaves.

TONE QUALITY

The tone quality or timbre of an instrument is determined by what harmonics are present in the tone and their relative intensities. Harmonics are the result of partial vibrations of the air column. At the same time it is vibrating in two, three, four, five, six or more parts. The vibration as a whole produces the fundamental and is the pitch we hear. When it vibrates in two equal parts a tone one octave above the fundamental is produced, when vibrating in three equal parts a tone a twelfth above the fundamental is produced, when vibrating in four equal parts a tone two octaves above the fundamental is produced, etc. All these and more may be produced simultaneously in various strengths and, combined, determine the tone quality. When all the overtones are combined with the fundamental and graphed the curved line is called the wave form. The potential overtone series which is identical for every fundamental tone on every musical instrument is shown on page 276.[1]

The series is given on C. A similar series may be constructed for every fundamental on the instrument. The portion of the range of each instrument which is produced by the fundamental vibration is indicated in the section on Tone in the chapter for that instrument.

In addition to the fundamental vibration, each woodwind instrument makes use of partial vibrations of the air column to increase its playing range. When a partial is used in the playing range the air column is forced

1. The black notes indicate harmonic frequencies which only approximate these pitches.

to vibrate in its frequency and the vibration frequency of the fundamental itself is eliminated.

The partial is produced as the predominant sound through the use of vent holes which force the column of air to vibrate in segments rather than as a whole. These vent holes are called the register key on the clarinet, the octave key on the oboe and saxophone. In addition the first finger halfhole position on the oboe, and bassoon and the first finger entirely open on the flute function as vent holes, and are a part of the regular fingering for certain notes.

The complicated fingerings for notes in the highest registers of each instrument are the result of selecting the harmonic from one of the fundamentals to produce the pitch, opening a key to vent the air column so that it will vibrate at the correct speed, and finally opening or closing other tone holes which will make the note exactly in tune without altering the fundamental fingering. The multiplicity of fingerings for a particular high note is the product of using various fundamentals to produce it—plus the addition or subtraction of tone holes to correct intonation.

Special harmonic fingerings for a few notes are presented in the chapters on oboe and flute where they are used for limited functions. The extension of the range of the Alto saxophone above the normal high F is done through the utilization of additional harmonics which are not normally used on the instrument. Additional fingerings for many notes on any woodwind instrument can be discovered by applying the principle of harmonics.

The nature of the construction of the clarinets causes them to produce only every other harmonic. The first harmonic above the fundamental which can be produced on the clarinet is the twelfth. The octave is missing. For this reason the clarinet is described as overblowing a twelfth, while all the other woodwinds can produce all the notes in the harmonics, and overblow an octave. Thus on the clarinet the fundamental fingering is duplicated on notes a twelfth above, while on the flute, oboe, saxophone, and bassoon the fundamental fingering is duplicated an octave above.

Each instrument in the woodwind group characteristically produces tones with a particular complex of harmonics. Since this basic complex is a product of the instrument itself rather than the player, a saxophone tone is clearly recognizable as a saxophone tone even though it may be also described as an excellent, average, or poor tone quality. The same can be applied to the other woodwinds.

With the general nature of the harmonics a product of the instrument itself, the relative intensities and the interrelationships between them are controlled by the individual player. It is the interrelationship which determines whether a tone is a striking beautiful one or a sound which is downright bad. The nature of the number and format of harmonics present is a product of the size and shape of the mouthpiece or flute embouchure hole, the shape, proportions and response of the reed, the control of the wind pressure, and the formation and control of the embouchure. Each of these is considered elsewhere in its relationship to tone quality.

LOUDNESS

Loudness is the product of the amplitude of vibration, and/or the force of vibration in the air column. The wider the vibration the greater the force in the air column and the louder the tone is. In the case of the reed instruments the amplitude of vibration is determined by the distance the reed moves in vibrating.

A mouthpiece with a close lay does not permit the reed to vibrate as far as a mouthpiece with an open lay and thus in general does not permit the production of a full volume of tone. This is only one of the reasons why the lay of a mouthpiece is so important. The tip opening of the double reeds will determine how far the blades can vibrate. If the tip opening is too small there is sufficient amplitude to produce only a weak tone. This is one reason why tip opening is stressed.

The extent of the amplitude of vibration of a reed, and the force of the vibration of the air column on both the reeds and flute is primarily a product of wind pressure. Hence, the player blows harder to play louder, and less hard to play softer. The infinite variety in loudness of various tones which is so essential to good musical phrasing is dependent upon subtle changes in wind pressure. In order that these can be controlled it is necessary that breathing, breath support and breath control be developed if artistic performance is to be achieved.

DURATION

The duration of a tone, or how long it sounds, is determined by how long the vibratory source continues to vibrate. Or to put it more simply how long the wind pressure is continued. Since rhythm in music is determined by duration of tones, and by the infinite subtle variations which are inherent in good musical style duration becomes a matter of importance. Duration of tones in addition to the continuing wind pressure is determined by the articulation process on woodwinds. Various articulations are used for notes of different lengths, and the tongue functions as a valve to start and stop the flow of air into the instrument and thereby the duration of the notes.

Summary

The various aspects of musical sounds exist as physical phenomenon of the sound wave produced by the instrument and are heard by the ear which produces a psychological reaction. The corresponding physical and psychological attributes of a sound can be summarized as follows:

Physical	*Psychological*
Frequency	Pitch
Harmonic content (wave form)	Tone quality
Amplitude	Loudness
Duration	Duration

The following audiovisual material provides a useful explanation and demonstration of the various aspects of sound. The films in the *Science in the Orchestra* series and the two-record *The Science of Sound* provide the greatest detail and elaboration.

1. *Science in the Orchestra.* British Information Service, Distributed by McGraw-Hill Text Films. Black and White prints only.

   Part I. "Hearing the Orchestra." 13 minutes. Frequency, amplitude, timbre and transmission.
   Physiology of hearing.

   Part II. "Exploring the Instruments." 12 minutes.
   Vibrations, playing ranges of instruments, experiments in harmonics.

   Part III. "Looking at Sounds." 10 minutes.
   The harmonic structure of the tones of several instruments is shown and compared. An oboe tone is made to sound like a flute by electronically altering its harmonic structure.

2. *The Science of Musical Sounds.* 12 minutes. Academy Films. Makes use of three instruments—harp, flute, and saxophone—to explore basic principles of sound production.
3. *The Sounds of Music.* 11 minutes. Coronet Films. Uses string, wind, and percussion instruments to illustrate the characteristics of musical sound.
4. *The Science of Sound.* 2-12″ L.P. Records. Folkways 6007. (One record, shortened version, Folkways 6136.) These recordings, produced by the Bell Telephone Laboratories demonstrate frequency, pitch, intensity, loudness, fundamentals, overtones, and tone quality.

An excellent source of more detailed information written clearly and in nontechnical language is the paperback book *Horns, Strings, and Harmony* by Arthur H. Benade published by the Anchor Book division of Doubleday & Company.

Phonograph Recordings

The general availability of phonograph recordings of excellent quality and the high quality reproduction units which are widely available make possible an important adjunct to woodwind teaching. The opportunity to hear fine artists in performance is essential to the learning process of any instrument. This helps the student arrive at a concept of tone quality and phrasing which he could not acquire in any other way. Students should be encouraged to listen carefully and often to recorded performances. If a copy of the musical score is available at the same time, it should be used.

In selecting recordings, the differences in concept of the best tone quality and performance style between artists in various countries should be kept in mind. French, German, Italian, Dutch, Scandinavian, and to some extent, English artists, have quite different concepts from each other and from the American concept. For this reason, it is generally advisable to select recordings by American artists for study purposes, although the comparison in sounds from nation to nation is in itself an interesting study.

Records come and go on the market so rapidly it is impossible to provide a standard discography. The best source of information on available records is the monthly *Schwann Record Catalog*. The annual *Art Issue* of this catalog is especially valuable. It has a section on Instrumental Soloists where records currently available are listed by instrument, then by artist under the instrument heading. This is the fastest source for information on available recordings.

In order to assist the reader in locating recordings of particular instruments the following section contains the names of composers whose works have been available on recordings in the past. To ascertain current availability of a recording, consult the composer listing in the Schwann catalog. The instrument will be identified in the title.

FLUTE

Sonata and Sonatine: C.P.E. Bach, J. S. Bach, Blavet, Dutilleux, Handel, Hindemith, Marcello, Mozart, Muczynski, Piston, Poulenc, Prokofiev, Schubert, Telemann.

Sonatas with Other Solo Instruments: W. F. Bach, Elliott Carter, Chedeville, Debussy, Fasch, Handel, Telemann, Vivaldi.

Concerto and Concertino: C.P.E. Bach, J. S. Bach, Barger, Boccherini, Gluck, Gordeli, Hasse, Haydn, Ibert, Leclair, Mozart, Pergolesi, Quantz, K. Stamitz, Tartini, Telemann, Vivaldi.

Concertos with Other Instruments: J. S. Bach, Boismortier, Cimarosa, Honegger, Mozart, Telemann, Vivaldi.

Other Compositions Including Chamber Music: C.P.E. Bach, J. S. Bach, Balazas, Beethoven, Berio, Boulez, Caplet, Castiglioni, Cowell, Debussy, Dutilleux, Feldman, Foote, Grétchaninoff, Griffes, Hansen, Hindemith, Honneger, Hüe, Kennan, Kuhlau, McBride, McCauley, Mozart, Quantz, Ravel, Roussel, Saint-Saëns, Schubert, K. Stamitz, Stockhausen, Telemann, Templeton, Varese.

OBOE

Sonata and Sonatine: Albinoni, C.P.E. Bach, Handel, Hindemith, Hotteterre, Jacob, La Vigne, Loeillet, Poulenc, Saint-Saëns, Sammartini, Telemann, Vivaldi.

Concerto and Concertino: Albinoni, C.P.E. Bach, J. S. Bach, Bellini, Cimarosa, J. Fischer, Foss, Goossens, Handel, Haydn, Maderna, Marcello, Martinu, Mozart, R. Strauss, Telemann, Vaughan-Williams, R. Woodcock.

Other compositions including chamber music: Barlow, J. C. Bach, J. S. Bach, Ben Haim, Beethoven, Bitsch, Bliss, Boccherini, Britten, Dorati, Donovan, Duke, Fiocco, Francaix, Haieff, Henze, Ibert, Kolinski Loeffler, Mozart, Piston, Porter, Rimsky-Korsakov, W. Schuman, R. Schumann, Telemann, Vaughn-Williams, Wolf-Ferrari.

ENGLISH HORN

Sonata: Hindemith, Wilder.

Concerto: J. S. Bach (oboe d'amore), Donizetti.

CLARINET

Sonata and Sonatine: Bax, Bernstein, Brahms, Cage, Cushing, Devienne, Doran, Hindemith, Hoddinott, Honneger, Hughes, Karg-Elert, Koechlin, Kubik, Lefebvre, Martinu, Mason, Milhaud, Perle, Pillin, Pisk, Poulenc, Reger, Saint-Saëns, Stanford, Szalowski, Tate, Templeton, Wanhal, Weis.

Concerto and Concertino: Arnold, Beon, Blatt, Busoni, Copland, Etler, Finzi, Francaix, Hindemith, Hoddinott, Hovhaness, Krommer, Kurpinski, Larsson, Manevich, Milhaud, Molter, Mozart, Neilsen, Porkorny, Rivier, Schibler, Sieber, Spohr, J. Stamitz, K. Stamitz, Stevens, Stravinsky, von Weber, Winter.

Other Solos Unaccompanied or with Piano: Arnold, Ben-Haim, Benjamin, Berg, Boulez, Bozza, Busser, Campo, Cheslock, Danzi, Debussy, Doran, Finzi, Golestan, Kaplan, Kosteck, Krenek, Martino, Milhaud, Montbrun, Osborne, Oubradous, Perle, Pierne, Rabaud, Reger, Schmidt, Schumann, W. O. Smith, Starer, Stravinsky, Tomasi, Tuthill, Vaughan-Williams, Ward-Steinman, von Weber, Weis, F. Whittenberg, Weiner.

Chamber Music: C.P.E. Bach, Bartok, Bassett, Bavicchi, Beethoven, Bliss, Boydell, Brahms, Bruch, Copland, Glinka, Harris, Hindemith, Holbrooke, Hummel, Ireland, Ives, Kaplan, Kelterborn, Khachaturian, Martino, Messiaen, Migot, Milhaud, Mozart, Poulenc, Prokofiev, Ravel, Rawsthorne, Reger, Rosen, Rudolph Archuke of Austria, F. Schmidt, Schubert, Schumann, Simpson, W. O. Smith, Spohr, K. Stamitz, R. Strauss, Uhl, Villa-Lobos, von Weber, Weiss, Winter.

Other Compositions with Orchestra: Ben Haim, Binet, Boydell, Debussy, Delacroix, Finzi, Francaix, Keller, Krenek, Lutoslawski, Roren, Rossini, Saint-Saëns, Stravinsky.

BASSOON

Sonata and Sonatine: Cascarino, Etler, Galliard, Hindemith, Saint-Saëns.

Concerto and Concertino: J. C. Bach, Boismortier, Devienne, J. G. Graun, Hummel, Mozart, Rosetti, K. Stamitz, Vivaldi, Weber.

Concertos with other instruments: Couperin, Danzi (Sinfonia Concertant), Etler, W. Kraft, Haydn (Sinfonia Concertant), Mozart (Sinfonia Concertant), Scarlatti, Vivaldi.

Other Compositions including Chamber Music: Beethoven, Bozza, Brehm, Cervetto, Duke, Mozart, Phillips, Pierne, Poulenc, Swartz, Telemann, Villa-Lobos, von Weber.

SAXOPHONE

Sonata and Sonatine: Anderson, Cilea, Creston, Delden, Eccles, Galliard, Handel, Heiden, Hindemith, Kohler, Lazarus, Moritz, Pescal, Platti, Tcherepnin.

Concerto and Concertino: Dubois, Farberman, Glazunov, Hartley, Ibert.

Other Compositions including Chamber Music: Babdek, Bentzon, Bonneau, Bozza, Debussy, Decruck, Desenclos, Dubois, Fiocco, Francais, Granados, Handel, Jolivet, Lautier, Maurice, Orrego-Salas, Ruggiero, Tomasi, Villa-Lobos.

The catalogs of the following companies have recordings of particular interest to woodwind players and teachers.

Coronet Recording Company
4971 North High Street
Columbus, Ohio 43214

Of special interest is "The Art of the Oboe" a two-record set by Marcel Tabuteau. Check the "Artist in Residence Series" which has recordings by three flute artists, two oboists, two clarinetists, one bassoonist, and a saxophonist.

Crystal Record Company
P.O. Box 65661
Los Angeles, California 90065

Features artists from the Los Angeles area.

Golden Crest Records
220 Broadway
Huntington Station, New York 11746

This company has three series of records containing items of interest: the "Recital Series," the "Laboratory Series," and the "Clinician Series. . . ."

Selmer, Inc.
Advertising Department
P.O. Box 310
Elkhart, Indiana 46514

Special recordings of repertoire for clarinet, alto saxophone, flute, and clarinet choir.

Zalo Publications & Services
P.O. Box 913
Bloomington, Indiana 47401

Recordings of interest to flutists.

Accompaniments Unlimited, Inc.
20259 Mack Avenue
Grosse Pointe Woods, Michigan 48236

Provides tape recordings of piano accompaniments of solos on every level for every instrument. Many tapes have the accompaniment both at slower than normal tempo for practice as well as at the composer's intended speed.

Music Minus One
43 W. 61st Street
New York, N.Y. 10023

The *Laureate Series* is a group of recordings of compositions selected with the assistance of music educators in styles from Baroque to the present and from beginning to advanced levels. Scores are included with the recordings. Each composition is performed by a professional soloist. This is followed by a recording of the piano accompaniment so that the student can rehearse with it. Some compositions also have the piano accompaniment at a slower tempo for working out technical difficulties.

This is a continuing series. At present there are nine records for flute, eight for alto saxophone, and nine for clarinet. Flute performers are Julius Baker, Murray Panitz, and Donald Peck. Alto saxophone performers are Vincent Abato and Paul Brodie. Clarinet performers are Stanley Drucker, Harold Wright, and Jerome Bunke.

The *Standard Series* is a series of recordings of piano accompaniments, and some chamber music with one part missing, to compositions from the standard repertoire for flute, oboe, clarinet, bass clarinet, bassoon, alto saxophone, tenor saxophone, and baritone saxophone. Music for parts missing is included with the record. These are invaluable aids to learning the repertoire.

Sources of Music for Woodwinds

Your regular music dealer is the best source of supply. He can obtain music of any publisher through his usual channels. A request for music should identify composer, exact title, opus number if available, publisher, and the instrument or instrumental combination for which it is written.

Sources for lists of music for woodwinds alone or in chamber music are listed in the Bibliography, and pointed out in the Study Materials section for each instrument.

The catalogs of the following publishers (among many) contain music of interest in the woodwind field.

Associated Music Publishers, Inc.
609 5th Avenue
New York, N.Y. 10017

Belwin-Mills Publishing Corp.
250 Maple Avenue
Rockville Center, N.Y. 11571

Berklee Press Publications
1140 Boylston Street
Boston, Mass. 02215

Big 3 Music Corporation (Robbins-Feist-Miller)
1350 Avenue of The Americas
New York, N.Y. 10019

Boosey and Hawkes, Inc.
Oceanside, New York 11572

Carl Fischer, Inc.
56-62 Cooper Square
New York, N.Y. 10003

Henri Elkan Music Publisher
1316 Walnut Street
Philadelphia, Pennsylvania 19107

Elkan-Vogel Co., Inc.
1712-16 Sansom Street
Philadelphia, Penn. 19103

Franco Colombo Publications
16 West 61st Street
New York, N.Y. 10023

Highland Music Company
1311 N. Highland Avenue
Hollywood, Calif. 90028

The Instrumentalist
1418 Lake Street
Evanston, Ill. 60201

Interlochen Press
Interlochen, Michigan 49643

Neil A. Kjos Music Company
525 Busse
Park Ridge, Illinois 60068

G. Leblanc Corporation
7019 30th Avenue
Kenosha, Wisconsin 53141

MCA Music
445 Park Avenue
New York, N.Y. 10022

Edward B. Marks Music Corp.
136 West 52nd Street
New York, N.Y. 10019

Mills Music, Inc.
250 Maple Avenue
Rockville Center, N.Y. 11571

Oxford University Press
200 Madison Avenue
New York, N.Y. 10016

C. F. Peters Corporation
373 Park Avenue, South
New York, N.Y. 10016

Theodore Presser Company
Presser Place
Bryn Mawr, Pennsylvania 19010

Pro Art Publications, Inc.
469 Union Avenue
Westbury, L.I., N.Y. 11590

Rubank, Inc.
16215 N.W. 15th Avenue
Miami, Florida 33169

G. Schirmer, Inc.
609 Fifth Avenue
New York, N.Y. 10017

Southern Music Company
1100 Broadway
San Antonio, Texas 78215

Southern Music Co., Inc.
1619 Broadway
New York, N.Y. 10019

Bibliography

GENERAL

Baines, Anthony. *Musical Instruments through the Ages.* London: Penguin Books, 1961.

———. *Woodwind Instruments and Their History.* New York: W. W. Norton & Co., 1963.

Bartolozzi, Bruno. *New Sounds for Woodwind.* London: Oxford University Press, 1967.

A discussion of the sounds used in avant garde music, with fingerings and how to produce them.

Brand, Erick D. *Band Instrument Repair Manual.* 4th ed. Elkhart, Indiana: Erick D. Brand, 1946.

Cahn, M. M. *The Instrumentalist's Handbook and Dictionary.* San Francisco, Calif.: Forman Publishing Co., 1958.

Carse, Adam. *Musical Wind Instruments.* New York: Da Capo Press, 1965. (Reprint of the 1939 edition)

Cobbett, Walter W. *Cyclopedic Survey of Chamber Music.* 2 vols. London: Oxford University Press, 1929-30.

The standard reference work in this field. Out of print but available in most libraries.

Coleman, Leo R. *An Annotated Bibliography of Woodwind Study Materials Which Deal With Performance Problems Encountered in Contemporary Music.* Unpublished Doctorate dissertation, State University of Iowa, 1969. University Microfilms Reference No. 70-4342.

Dalby, Max F. *Psychology and Method in Teaching Woodwind Instruments.* Unpublished Doctorate dissertation. Utah State University, 1961. University Microfilms Reference No. 61-4925.

Galpin, Francis W. *A Textbook of European Musical Instruments: Their Origin, History, and Character.* New York: J. DeGraff, 1956.

Geiringer, Karl. *Musical Instruments, Their History in Western Culture.* New York: Oxford University Press, 1945.

Heller, George N. *Ensemble Music for Wind and Percussion Instruments: A Catalog.* Washington, D.C.: Music Educators National Conference, 1970.

Extensive graded lists for all combinations of instruments from duets to large ensembles.

Helm, Stanford M. *Catalog of Chamber Music for Wind Instruments.* New York: Da Capo Press, 1969. (Reprint of the 1952 edition)

Langwill, Lyndesay. *An Index of Musical Wind Instrument Makers.* 2nd ed. Edinburgh: The author, 1962.

Houser, Roy. *Catalogue of Chamber Music for Woodwind Instruments.* New York: Da Capo Press. (Reprint of the 1962 edition)

Keller, Hermann. *Phrasing and Articulation.* Translated by Leigh Gerdine. New York: W. W. Norton, 1965.

Palmer, Harold G. *Teaching Techniques of the Woodwinds.* Rockville Center, N.Y.: Belwin, Inc., 1952.

Peters, Harry B. *The Literature of the Woodwind Quintet.* Metuchen, N.J.: The Scarecrow Press, 1971.

Porter, Maurice M. *The Embouchure.* London: Boosey & Hawkes, 1967.

Rasmussen, Mary, and Mattran, Donald. *A Teacher's Guide to the Literature of Woodwind Instruments.* Durham, New Hampshire: Brass and Woodwind Quarterly, 1966.

Separate chapters on solos; ensembles; and methods and studies. Highly personalized commentary.

Sachs, Curt. *The History of Musical Instruments.* New York: W. W. Norton, 1940.

Sawhill, Clarence, and McGarrity, Bertram. *Playing and Teaching Woodwind Instruments.* Englewood Cliffs, N.J.: Prentice-Hall, 1962.

Squire, Alan P. *An Annotated Bibliography of Written Material Pertinent to the Performance of Woodwind Chamber Music.* Unpublished Doctorate dissertation. University of Illinois, 1960. University Microfilms Reference No. 60-3999.

Teide, Clayton. *The Practical Band Instrument Repair Manual.* 2nd ed. Dubuque, Iowa: William C. Brown Company Publishers, 1970.

Thornton, James. *Woodwind Handbook.* San Antonio, Texas: Southern Music Co., 1963.

Timm, Everett. *The Woodwinds: Performance and Instructional Techniques.* 2nd ed. Boston: Allyn & Bacon, 1971.

Weerts, Richard. *Handbook for Woodwinds.* 3rd ed. Kirksville, Missouri: Simpson Printing & Publishing Co., 1966.

———. *How to Develop and Maintain a Successful Woodwind Section.* West Nyack, N.Y.: Parker Publishing Co., 1972.

Woodwind Anthology. New York: Woodwind Magazine, 1952. Reprinted by McGinnis & Marx.

Woodwind Anthology: A Compendium of Articles from the Instrumentalist Magazine. Evanston, Illinois: The Instrumentalist Co., 1972.

Selected from past years of the magazine this anthology has 467 articles which discuss almost every topic related to woodwinds, each by an expert in the field.

FLUTE

Arnold, Jay. *Modern Fingering System for Flute.* New York: Shapiro, Bernstein & Co., 1963.

Bate, Philip. *The Flute.* New York: W. W. Norton, 1969.

Boehm, Theobald. *The Flute and Flute Playing.* New York: Dover Press, 1964.

A facsimile reprint of the revised edition of 1922 translated by Dayton C. Miller. Boehm's original version in German was published in 1871. An extremely important book on the development of the Boehm system as well as Boehm's views on flute playing.

Chapman, F. B. *Flute Technique.* 3rd ed. London: Oxford University Press, 1958.

Chapters on breath control, finger control, tongue control, practice care of the flute, and an extensive list of flute music.

DeLaney, Charles. *Teacher's Guide to the Flue.* Elkhart, Indiana: H. & A. Selmer, Inc., n.d.

DeLorenzo, Leonardo. *My Complete Story of the Flute.* New York: Citadel Press, 1951.

Fitzgibbon, H. Macaulay. *The Story of the Flute.* New York: Charles Scribner's Sons, 1914.

Hotteterre, Jacques. *Principles of Flute, Recorder and Oboe.* Translated by David Lasocki. New York: F. A. Praeger, 1968.

First published in Paris in 1707, this charming book by a famous flute and recorder player of the period provides precise instructions on how the flute, recorder, and oboe are to be played and how to interpret the intricate rhythms of the French style. This book is important for the performance practice of Baroque music.

LeJeune, Harriet. *A Flutist's Manual.* Evanston, Illinois: Summy-Birchard Co., 1964.

According to the acknowledgements it "embodies the teachings of Georges Laurent, presented as a guide to professional flute playing." Includes a discography, a fingering chart, and some recommended literature in its modest 38 pages.

Mellott, George K. *A Survey of Contemporary Flute Solo Literature With Analysis of Representative Compositions.* Unpublished Doctorate dissertation. State University of Iowa, 1964. University Microfilms Reference No. 64-7932.

Miller, Dayton C. *Catalog of Books and Literature Relating to the Flute.* Cleveland, Ohio: The Author, 1935.

Pellerite, James. *A Handbook of Literature for the Flute.* 2nd ed. Bloomington, Indiana: Zalo Publications, 1965.

An annotated and graded list of methods, study materials, solos, and ensemble literature.

———. *A Modern Guide to Fingerings for the Flute.* Bloomington, Indiana: Zalo Publications, 1964.

———. *Performance Methods for Flutists: A Notebook of Techniques for Recorded Flute Recitals.* 2 vols. Bloomington, Indiana: Zalo Publications, 1967, 1968.

Discussions correlated with performances on recordings available from the same company. Has detailed instructions on each composition.

Putnik, Edwin. *The Art of Flute Playing.* Evanston, Illinois: Summy-Birchard, Co., 1970.

———. *Flute Pedagogy and Performance.* Part I: Basic Essentials. Chicago: Estes Music Co., 1955.

Quantz, Johann J. *On Playing the Flute.* Translated by Edward R. Reilly. New York: Free Press, 1966.

A recent translation of one of the basic resource books on flute playing.

Reilly, Edward R. *Quantz and His Versuch: Three Studies.* American Musicological Society, 1971. New York: Galaxy Music Corporation.

Designed by Dr. Reilly to complement his translation of the Quantz treatise listed above.

Rockstro, Richard S. *The Flute.* London: Musica Rara. (Reprint of the 1890 edition)

Complete title page reads: "A treatise on the construction, the history and the practice of the flute, including a sketch of the elements of acoustics and critical notices of sixty celebrated flute players." One of the important standard books on flute.

Stevens, Roger. *Artistic Flute Technique and Study.* Hollywood, Calif.: Highland Music Company, 1967.

Vester, Frans. *Flute Repertoire Catalogue.* London: Musica Rara, 1967.

The most extensive listing of flute music available. The title page says it has 10,000 titles!

Vinquist, Mary, and Neal Zaslaw. *Flute Performance Practice: A Bibliography.* New York, W. W. Norton.

Welch, Christopher. *History of the Boehm Flute.* London: Rudall, Carte & Co., 1896. Reprint; McGinnis & Marx.

Wilkins, Frederick. *A Catalog of Music Literature for the Flute.* Nogales, Arizona: D. & T. Artley, Inc., n.d.

Study materials, solos, and ensembles graded.

———. *The Flutist's Guide.* Nogales, Arizona: Artley, Inc., 1963.

A book of 84 pages with accompanying illustrative long playing record.

OBOE

Bate, Philip. *The Oboe:* An Outline of its History, Development and Construction. London: Ernest Been, Ltd., 1956.

Ernest, David J. *An Analysis of the French Style of Oboe Performance.* Unpublished Doctorate dissertation. University of Colorado, 1961. University Microfilms Reference No. 62-1284.

Jackson, Marjorie. *The Oboe:* A Study of its Development and Use. Unpublished Doctorate dissertation. Columbia University, 1962. University Microfilm Reference No. 63-2259.

Lehman, Paul R. *Teacher's Guide to the Oboe.* Elkhart, Indiana: H. & A. Selmer, Inc., 1965.

Mayer, Robert M. *Essentials of Oboe Playing.* Des Plaines, Illinois: Karnes Music Company, 1970.

McAninch, Daniel A. *Technical Problems of the Oboe in the Woodwind Quintet.* Rochester, New York: University of Rochester Press, 1957. Microprint copy of original thesis.

Rothwell, Evelyn. *Oboe Technique.* London: Oxford University Press, 1943.

Chapters on producing a sound, breath control, embouchure control, tongue control, finger control, care of the instruments, reeds and their care, practice and an extensive list of music for oboe and English horn.

Russell, Myron E. *The Oboe: A Comparison Study of Specifications with Musical Effectiveness.* Unpublished Doctorate dissertation. The University of Michigan, 1953. University Microfilms Reference No. 5723.

Sprenkle, Robert, and Ledet, David. *The Art of Oboe Playing.* Evanston, Illinois: Summy-Birchard, 1961.

Includes a major section on reed making.

Stanton, Robert E. *The Oboe Player's Encyclopedia.* Oneonta, New York: Swift-Dorr Publications, Inc., 1972.

The title is deceptive. This is primarily an ungraded listing of solos and ensembles for oboe and English horn.

CLARINET

Caringi, Joseph J. *The Clarinet Contest Solos of the Paris Conservatory With a Performance Analysis of Selected Compositions.* Unpublished Doctorate dissertation. Columbia University, 1963. University Microfilms Reference No. 64-1466.

Eby, Walter M. *The Clarinet Embouchure.* New York: Walter Jacobs Co., 1955.

Gilbert, Richard. *The Clarinetists Solo Repertoire: A Discography.* New York: Richard Gilbert, 1972.

Gold, Cecil V. *Clarinet Performing Practices and Teaching in the United States and Canada.* Moscow, Idaho: University of Idaho, School of Music, 1972.

Hovey, Nilo. *Teacher's Guide to the Clarinet.* Elkhart, Indiana: H. & A. Selmer, Inc., 1967.

Kroll, Oskar. *The Clarinet.* Revised by Diethard Riehm, translated by Hilda Morris. New York: Taplinger Publishing Co., 1968.

McCathrey, Don. *Playing and Teaching the Clarinet Family.* San Antonio, Texas: Southern Music Co., 1959.

Mazzeo, Rosario. *The Clarinet Master Class: A Guide to Scale Studies.* Elkhart, Indiana: H. & A. Selmer, Inc., 1969.

Miller, Jean R. *A Spectrum Analysis of Clarinet Tones.* Unpublished Doctorate dissertation. The University of Wisconsin, 1956. University Microfilms Reference No. 19120.

Mills, Ralph L. *Technical and Fundamental Problems in the Performance of Clarinet Solo Literature.* Unpublished Doctorate dissertation. University of Southern California, 1965. University Microfilms Reference No. 65-10100.

Opperman, Kalmen. *Repertory of the Clarinet.* New York: G. Ricordi & Co., 1960.

Osborn, Thomas M. *Sixty Years of Clarinet Chamber Music (1900-1960).* Unpublished Doctorate dissertation. University of Southern California, 1964. University Microfilms Reference No. 64-13504.

Pace, Kenneth L. *An Analysis of Comprehensive Method Books for Clarinet.* Unpublished Doctorate dissertation. George Peabody College for Teachers, 1965. University Microfilms Reference No. 67-8002.

Pound, Gomer J. *A Study of Clarinet Solo Concerto Literature Composed Before 1850: With Selected Items Edited and Arranged for Contemporary Use.* 2 vols. Unpublished Doctorate dissertation. The Florida State University, 1965. University Microfilms Reference No. 65-9410.

Rendall, Francis G. *The Clarinet:* Some Notes on its History and Construction. 3rd ed. revised by Philip Bate. New York: W. W. Norton, 1971.

Richmond, Stanley. *Clarinet and Saxophone Experience.* New York: St. Martin's Press, 1972.

Rousseau, Eugene E. *Clarinet Instructional Materials from 1732 to CA 1825.* Unpublished Doctorate dissertation. State University of Iowa, 1962. University Microfilms Reference No. 63-961.

Seltzer, George A. *A Study of Some Technical Problems for the Clarinet Family in Orchestral Literature.* Rochester, N.Y.: University of Rochester Press, 1959. Microprint of original typescript.

Stein, Keith. *The Art of Clarinet Playing.* Evanston, Illinois: Summy-Birchard, 1958.

Stubbins, William H. *The Art of Clarinetistry.* Ann Arbor, Michigan: Ann Arbor Publishers, 1965.

Thurston, Frederick. *Clarinet Technique.* 2nd ed. London: Oxford University Press, 1964.

Tuthall, Burnet. *Concertos and Sonatas for Clarinet.* Washington, D.C.: Music Educators National Conference, 1972. (Reprinted from the *Journal of Research in Music Education*)

Titus, Robert A. *The Solo Music for the Clarinet in the Eighteenth Century.* Unpublished Doctorate dissertation. State University of Iowa, 1962. University Microfilms Reference No. 62-2412.

Walker, B. H. *Recordings for the Clarinet and the Recording Artists.* Augusta, Georgia: The Author, 1969.

Warren, Charles S. *A Study of Selected Eighteenth-Century Clarinet Concerti.* Unpublished Doctorate dissertation. Brigham Young University, 1963. University Microfilms Reference No. 64-3475.

Weston, Pamela. *Clarinet Virtuosi of the Past.* London: Hale, 1971.

Willaman, Robert. *The Clarinet and Clarinet Playing.* New York: Carl Fischer, Inc., 1949.

BASSOON

Bartlett, Loren W. *A Survey and Checklist of Representative Eighteenth-Century Concertos and Sonatas for Bassoon.* Unpublished Doctorate dissertation. State University of Iowa, 1961. University Microfilms Reference No. 61-5544.

Camden, Archie. *Bassoon Technique.* London: Oxford University Press, 1962.

Cooper, Lewis, and Toplansky, Howard. *Essentials of Bassoon Technique.* Union, N.J.: Howard Toplansky.

A 370 page compendium of bassoon fingerings. Clearly presented with directions for use.

Heckel, Wilhelm H. *The Bassoon.* Stamford, Conn.: Jack Spratt. Revised edition 1940. Translated from the German by Langwill and Waples.

Klitz, Brian K. *Solo Sonatas, Trio Sonatas, and Duos for Bassoon Before 1750.* Unpublished Doctorate dissertation. The University of North Carolina at Chapel Hill, 1961. University Microfilms Reference No. 61-6125.

Langwill, Lyndesay. *The Bassoon and Contrabasoon.* New York: W. W. Norton, 1965.

———. *The Bassoon and Double Bassoon.* London: Hinrichen Edition, Ltd., 1948.

Munsell, Donald T. *A Comprehensive Survey of Solo Bassoon Literature Published after CA 1929 with Analysis of Representative Compositions.* Unpublished Doctorate dissertation. State University of Iowa, 1969. University Microfilms Reference No. 69-13,170.

Pence, Homer. *Teacher's Guide to the Bassoon.* Elkhart, Indiana: H. & A. Selmer, Inc., 1963.

Risdon, Howard. *Musical Literature for the Bassoon.* Seattle, Washington: Berdon, Inc., 1963.

Spencer, William. *The Art of Bassoon Playing.* 2nd ed. rev. by Mueller. Evanston, Illinois: Summy-Birchard, 1969.

SAXOPHONE

Eby, Walter M. *The Saxophone Embouchure.* New York: Walter Jacobs, 1953.

Gold, Cecil V. *Saxophone Performance Practices and Teaching in the United States and Canada.* Moscow, Idaho: University of Idaho, School of Music, 1973.

Hemke, Fred. *A Comprehensive Listing of Saxophone Literature.* Elkhart, Indiana: H. & A. Selmer, Inc., 1961.

———. *Teacher's Guide to the Saxophone.* Elkhart, Indiana: H. & A. Selmer, Inc., 1966.

Londeix, Jean Marie. *125 Years of Music for the Saxophone.* Paris: Alphonse Leduc & Co., 1970.

McCathren, D. *The Saxophone Book.* Kenosha, Wisconsin: G. Leblanc & Co., n.d.

Richmond, Stanley. *Clarinet and Saxophone Experience.* New York: St. Martin's Press, 1972.

Snavely, Jack. *The Saxophone and Its Performance.* Heritage Publishing Co., 1969.

Teal, Larry. *The Art of Saxophone Playing.* Evanston, Illinois: Summy-Birchard, 1963.

REEDS

Bonade, Daniel. *The Art of Adjusting Reeds.* Kenosha, Wisconsin: G. Leblanc Co., n.d.

Eby, Wm. M. *Reed Knowledge.* New York: Walter Jacobs, Inc. 1925.

Hedrick, Peter and Elizabeth. *Oboe Reed Making: A Modern Method.* Oneonta, N.Y.: Swift-Dorr Publications, Inc., 1972.

Jaffrey, K. S. *Reed Mastery.* Summer Hill, Australia: The Author, 1956.

Considers clarinet and saxophone reeds.

Mayer, Robert, and Rohner, Traugott. *Oboe Reeds: How to Make and Adjust Them.* Evanston, Illinois: The Instrumentalist Co., 1953.

Opperman, Kalmen. *Handbook for Making and Adjusting Single Reeds.* New York: Chappell & Co., 1956.

The best and most complete book on the subject.

Popkin, Mark, and Glickman, Loren. *Bassoon Reeds.* Evanston, Illinois: The Instrumentalist Co., 1969.

A companion book to the Mayer-Rohner book on oboe reeds.

Russell, Myron E. *Oboe Reed Making and Problems of the Oboe Player.* Stamford, Conn.: Jack Spratt Co., 1963.

Sprenkle, Robert, and Ledet, David. "Problems and Techniques of Oboe Reed Making." In *The Art of Oboe Playing,* pp. 41-96. Evanston, Illinois: Sunny-Birchard, 1961.

Spratt, Jack. *How to Make Your Own Clarinet Reeds.* Stamford, Conn.: Jack Spratt, 1956.

Weait, Christopher. *Bassoon Reed-Making: A Basic Technique.* New York: McGinnis & Marx. (Pietro Deiro Music Headquarters).

ACOUSTICS

Benade, Arthur H. *Horns, Strings & Harmony—The Science of Enjoyable Sounds.* Garden City, N.Y.: Anchor Books, Doubleday & Co., Inc. (paperback)

Backus, John. *The Acoustical Foundation of Music.* New York: W. W. Norton, 1969.

Barber, J. Murray. *Tuning and Temperament: A Historical Survey.* New York: Da Capo Press. (Reprint of the 1951 edition)

Bartholomew, W. T. *Acoustics of Music.* New York: Prentice-Hall, 1942.

Culver, Charles A. *Musical Acoustics.* 4th ed. New York: McGraw-Hill, 1956.

Nederveen, Cornelius. *Acoustical Aspects of Woodwind Instruments.* Amsterdam: Frits Knuf, 1969.

Olson, Harry F. *Elements of Acoustical Engineering.* New York: Dover Publications, 1967. (Reprint of 1947 edition)

Richardson, G. W. *Acoustics of Orchestral Instruments and the Organ.* London: Edward Arnold & Co., 1929.

Stauffer, Donald W. *Intonation Deficiencies of Wind Instruments in Ensemble.* Washington, D.C.: Catholic University of America Press., 1954.

Journal of the Acoustical Society of America. Consult the indicies to the Journal for the many articles of interest.

Note: Unpublished Doctorate dissertations listed in the bibliography are available either on microfilm or Xerographic Copy (a 6″ by 8″ hardbound book copy of the original typescript). When ordering identify by the reference number given from: University Microfilms, Ann Arbor, Michigan 48106.

MAGAZINES AND JOURNALS

The following magazines and journals have articles of interest to woodwind teachers and players. Consult the *Music Guide, Readers Guide* and *Education Index* for specific articles in these and other periodicals.

The Instrumentalist
Journal of Research in Music Education
Journal of the Music Educators National Conference
Music Journal
NACWPI Bulletin (Quarterly Bulletin of the National Association of College Wind and Percussion Instructors)
School Musician
Woodwind World

The following magazines are no longer published but if back files are available in libraries they have considerable material of interest in the woodwind field.

Clarinetist Magazine
Etude Music Magazine
Symphony Magazine
Woodwind Magazine
Woodwind Quarterly

FINGERING CHARTS FOR

FLUTE

OBOE

CLARINET

BASSOON

SAXOPHONE

Flute Fingering Chart

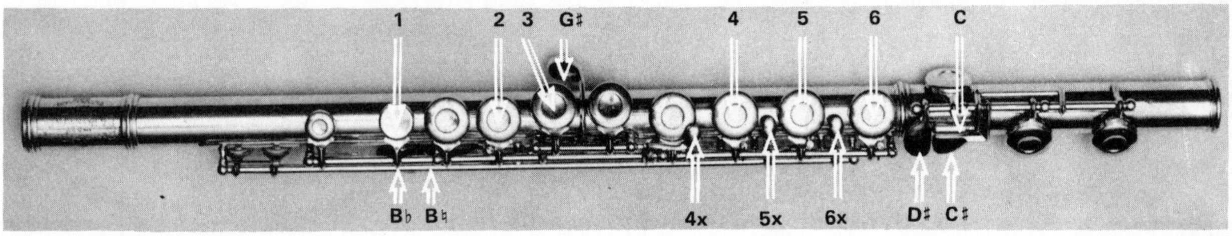

X—indicate keys operated by fingers normally covering holes. When these keys are used the hole operated by that finger remains open.

T—Left thumb on either lever except where indicated otherwise. Normal position is on the B-natural lever.

The D-sharp key is down on all notes except Low C, C-sharp, the two D-naturals, and the highest B-flat, B natural, and C.

( )—Parenthesis indicate that the use of that key or hole is optional in that fingering, depending on intonation and resonance on a particular instrument.

			Left Hand	Right Hand
C		1.	T 123	456 C
C♯		2.	T 123	456 C♯
D		3.	T 123	456
D♯		4.	T 123	456 D♯
E		5.	T 123	450
F		6.	T 123	400
F♯		7. 8.	T 123 T 123	006 050
G		9.	T 123	000
G♯		10.	T 123 G♯	000

			Left Hand	Right Hand
A		11.	T 120	000
A♯		12. 13. 14.	T 100 TB♭ 100 T 100	400 000 4x00
B		15.	TB 100	000
C		16. 17.	100 (T) 123	000 456 C
C♯		18. 19. 20.	000 123 T 023	000 456 C♯ 456 C♯
D		21. 22.	T 023 (TB) 100	456 05x0 D♯
D♯		23. 24.	T 023 (T) 100	456 D♯ 006x D♯
E		25.	T 123	450
F		26.	T 123	400

Left Hand	Right Hand					Left Hand	Right Hand
F♯		27.	T 123	006		E		46.	T 120	45 0
		28.	T 123	050				47.	T 120	45 6x
								48.	T 103	456
G		29.	T 123	000		F		49.	T 103	400 D♯ or C♯
								50.	T 103	406
								51.	TB 000	000
G♯		30.	T 123 G♯	000		F♯		52.	TB 103	006 (C♯)
								53.	TB 103	050
								54.	T 123	400
A		31.	T 12 0	000		G		55.	123	000
								56.	T 023	456
A♯		32.	T 100	400		G♯		57.	023 G♯	000
		33.	TB♭ 100	000				58.	023 G♯	056
		34.	TB 100	4x00				59.	T 023 G♯	450
B		35.	TB 100	000		A		60.	T 020 (G♯)	400 (D♯)
								61.	T 020	406 C♯
								62.	T 103	45x6x
C		36.	100	000		A♯		63.	T 000	45x0 (D♯)
		37.	T 023	450 D♯				64.	T 000	406x (D♯)
								65.	TB 103	05x6
C♯		38.	000	000		B		66.	TB 103	006x (D♯)
		39.	T 023	05(6)				67.	TB 103	05x6x D♯ or C
		40.	003	456						
D		41.	T 023	000 D♯		C		68.	123 G♯	400 (C)
		42.	T 123	000 D♯				69.	(T) 123 G♯	406 C
							8va—	70.	123	45x6 (C)
								71.	123 (G♯)	406x (C)
D♯		43.	T 123 G♯	456				72.	123 G♯	456
		44.	T (1)23	456				73.	123 G♯	456x C
		45.	T (1)23 G♯	05x0				74.	103	006x (D♯)
								75.	123 G♯	456x C

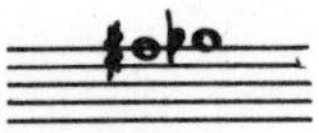

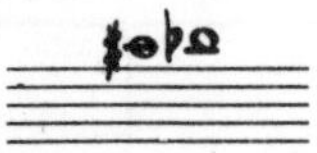

Flute Extended Range

			Left Hand	Right Hand
C♯		76.	020	406 (C)
		77.	020 (G♯)	400 (C)
		78.	(1)20	406 (C)
D		79.	T 003	45 0 C
D♯		80.	T 003 G♯	0 55x0 C
		81.	T 123 G♯	4(5x)6 (D♯)
		82.	T 003	4(5x) D♯ or C
E	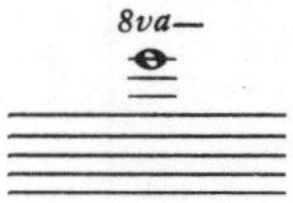	83.	(T) 120 G♯	0 06x6 D♯ or C
		84.	T 120 (G♯)	45 0 C
		85.	120	(4)56x
		86.	123	0 5x6x6 C
		87.	120	0 56x
		88.	120	0 56
		89.	120 (G♯)	0 56x6
		90.	120 (G♯)	0 5x56x6 C
		91.	120	0 5x56 C

			Left Hand	Right Hand
F	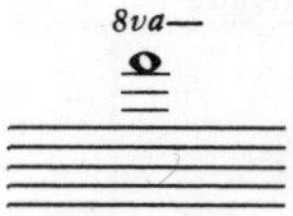	92.	020	056x
		93.	120 (G♯)	456x
		94.	120 (G♯)	45x6x C
		95.	123	45x6x
F♯		96.	T 023 G♯	450
		97.	T 023 G♯	056
		98.	T 103	406x6 C
G	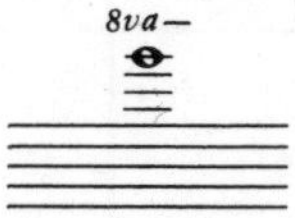	99.	T 023 G♯	0 5x5 0

Flute Harmonic Fingerings

			Left Hand	Right Hand
G		1.	T 123	456 C
G♯	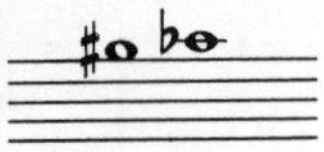	2.	T 123 G♯	456 C♯
A	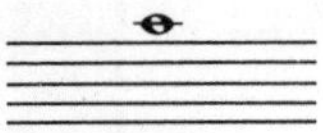	3.	T 120	456 (no D♯)
A♯		4.	T 103	456 D♯
B	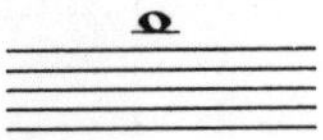	5.	T 103	450 D♯
C	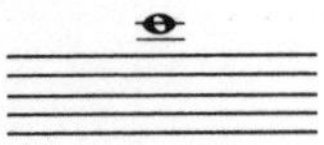	6. 7.	123 T 123	400 D♯ 456 C
C♯	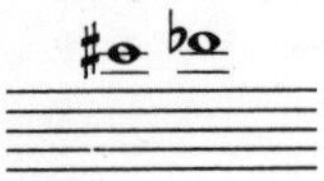	8.	T 023	456 C♯

			Left Hand	Right Hand
D		9. 10. 11.	T 023 T 123 T (1)23	05x0 D♯ 000 D♯ 456 no D♯
D♯	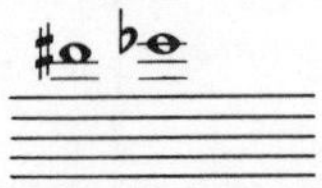	12. 13.	T 023 G♯ T (1) 23 G♯	006x D♯ 000 D♯
E	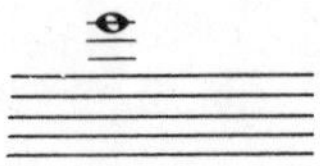	14. 15.	T 120 T 123	456x D♯ 450 D♯
F		16. 17.	T 103 T 123	400 C♯ 400 D♯
F♯	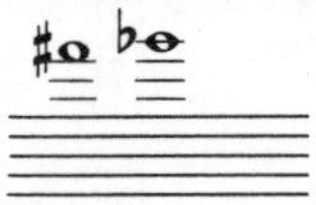	18. 19.	TB 103 T 1(2)3	050 C♯ 456 no D♯
G	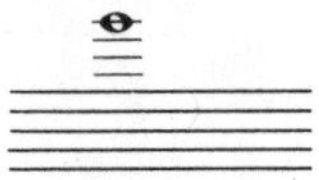	20. 21. 22.	100 (T) 123 123	000 no D♯ 456 C 456 D♯
G♯	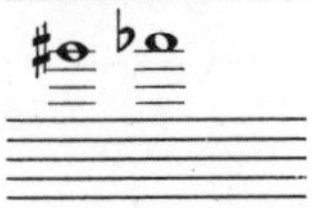	23.	(T) 123 G♯	456 C♯

Flute Trill Fingerings

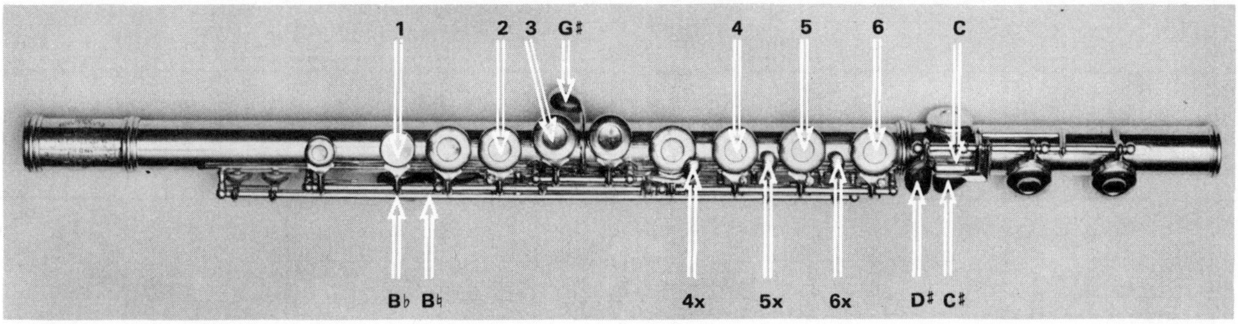

A composite fingering is given for the notes in a trill. The trill is made with the fingers and/or keys circled. Only special trill fingerings are included. Trills which are executed with regular fingerings are not included.

Notes	No.	Left Hand	Right Hand
E F♯	1.	T 123	(4) 50
F G♭	2.	T 123	(4) 06
F♯ G♯	3.	T 123 (G♯)	006
G♯ A♯	4. 5. 6.	TB♭ 1(2)3 G♯ T 1(2)3 G♯ T 1(2)3 G♯	000 4x00 1 00
A B♭	7. 8. 9.	T 1(2)0 T 1(2)0 TB♭ 1(2)0	100 4x00 000
A♯ B	10. 11.	TB♮ 100 TB♮ 100	(4)00 (4x) 00
B♭ C	12. 13. 14.	(T) 100 (TB♭) 100 (T) 100	400 000 4x00
B C♯	15.	(T) (1)00	000
C D	16.	100	0(5x)0
C D♭	17.	(1)00	000
C♯ D	18.	000	0(5x)0
C♯ D♯	19.	000	00(6x)
E F♯	20.	T 123	(4)50
F G♭	21.	T 123	(4) 06
F♯ G♯	22.	T 123 (G♯)	006
G♯ A♯	23. 24. 25.	TB♭ 1(2)3 G♯ T 1(2)3 G♯ T 1(2)3 G♯	000 4x00 1 00
A B♭	26. 27. 28.	T 1(2)0 T 1(2)0 TB♭ 1(2)0	400 4x00 000
A♯ B	29. 30.	TB♮ 100 TB♮ 100	(4)00 (4x) 00

Trill		No.	Left Hand	Right Hand
B♭ C		31. 32. 33.	Ⓣ 100 ⓉⒷ 100 Ⓣ 100	400 000 4x00
B C♯		34. 35. 36.	TB 100 ⓉⒷ ① 00 TB 100	0 ⑤x 0 000 00 ⑥x
C D♭		37. 38.	① 00 123	000 ④ 50
C D		39. 40.	100 100	00 ⑥x 0 ⑤x 0
C♯ D		41.	000	0 ⑤x 0
C♯ D♯		42.	000	0 ⑤x ⑥x
D E♭		43. 44. 45.	T 023 Ⓖ♯ T 023 T (1)23	000 00 ⑥x 0 ⑤x ⑥x
D E		46.	T 02③	000
D♯ E		47. 48. 49.	T 12③ G♯ T 12③ Ⓖ♯ T 123 G♯	456 456 45⑥
E♭ F		50. 51.	T 1②3 G♯ T 1② ③G♯	456 456
E F		52. 53.	T 1②0 TB♭ 1②0	450 000
E F♯		54. 55. 56.	Ⓣ120 T 1②0 T 1②0	450 056 056x

Trill		No.	Left Hand	Right Hand
F G♭		57.	T 103	④06
F G		58. 59. 60.	Ⓣ 103 T 123 T 123	400 ④00 C♯ ④00 D♯
F♯ G		61. 62.	Ⓣ 103 123	006 ④00 C♯
F♯ G♯		63.	Ⓣ ①03	006
G A♭		64. 65.	123 ①23	0 ⑤x 0 000
G A		66. 67. 68.	T 123 T 12③ T 02③	④ ⑤x 0 (C♯) 000 (C♯) 056
G♯ A		69. 70. 71. 72.	023 G♯ T 02③ G♯ 02③ Ⓖ♯ 023 G♯	05x0 000 000 00 ⑥x
A♭ B♭		73. 74.	023 G♯ T 0② ③	0 ⑤x ⑥x 45
A B♭		75. 76.	TB 0②0 T 02 0 (G♯)	400 40 ⑥x
A B		77. 78. 79.	T 123 T 1②3 T 1②0 G♯	④0⑥ ④06 000
B♭ C		80. 81.	T 1② ③G♯ Ⓣ 100	400 006 (C)
B C		82.	ⓉⒷ 103	00 ⑥x

Oboe Fingering Chart

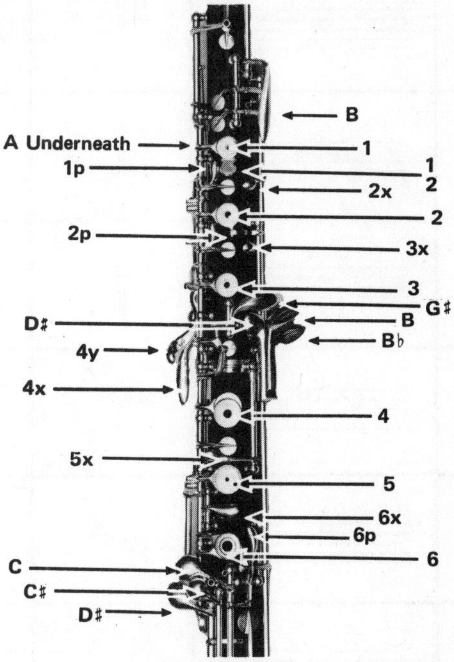

( )—Keys or fingers in parenthesis indicate its use in that fingering is optional, depending on intonation and resonance on a particular instrument.

x, y—indicate keys operated by fingers normally covering holes. When these keys are used the hole operated by that finger remains open unless specifically indicated that they are to be closed.

		Left Hand	Right Hand
B♭	1. 2.	123 B♭ 123 B♭	456 C 4566p
B	3. 4.	123 B 123 B	456 C 4566p
C	5. 6.	123 123	456 C 4566p
C♯	7. 8.	123 123	456 C♯ 4566p C♯
D	9.	123	456
D♯	10. 11.	123 D♯ 123	456 456 D♯
E	12.	123	450

		Left Hand	Right Hand
F	13. 14.	123 123	456x 406 (D♯)
F♯	15.	123	400
G	16.	123	000
G♯	17. 18. 19.	123 G♯ 123 *123	000 4x00 4y00
A	20.	120	000
A♯	21. 22. 23. 24.	120 *103 G♯ *103 **103	400 000 4x00 000
B	25. 26. 27. 28.	100 11p00 103 B♭ 120 B	000 400 456 C 456 C

*Plateau model only.

**Open hole model only.

			Left Hand	Right Hand
C		29. 30. 31. 32.	100 020 103 ½23	400 000 456 C 456 C
C♯	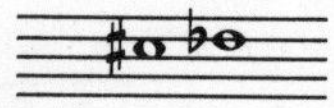	33. 34.	½23 000 103 103x	456 C♯ 400 456 C♯ 000
D		35.	½23 100 12x	456 45x0 400
D♯	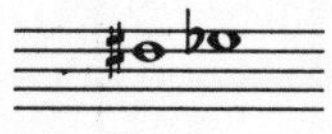	36. 37.	½23 D♯ ½23	456 456 D♯
E		38.	A 123	450
F		39. 40.	A 123 A 123	456x 406 (D♯)
F♯		41.	A 123	400
G		42.	A 123	000
G♯ **	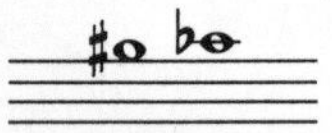	43. 44. 45.	A 123 G♯ A 123 *A 123	000 4x00 4y00
A		46.	B 120	000
A♯	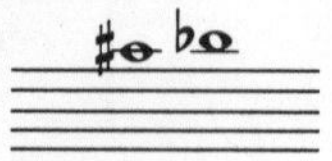	47. 48.	B 120 B 103	400 000
B		49. 50. 51.	B 100 B 11p20 B 103	000 400 456 (D♯)
C		52. 53. 54.	B 100 023 B 020 B 103	400 450 400 406

			Left Hand	Right Hand
C♯	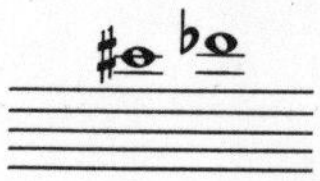	55. 56. 57. 58. 59.	023 B 000 ½23 B 003x ½23	400 C 400 400 000 406 C♯
D		60. 61. 62. 63.	½23 023 B 100 B 12x0	000 (C) 000 (C) 45x0 400
D♯		64. 65. 66. 67. 	½23 B ½23 G♯ ½23 ½23 A ½23	056 000 C 4x00 (C) 4y00 000
E	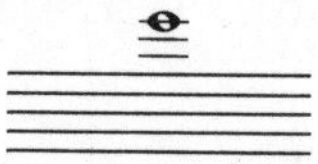	69. 70. 71. 72.	A ½23 G♯ D♯ A ½23 (B) ½20 A ½23 G♯	056 4x56 D♯ 000 056 D♯
F		73. 74. 75. 76.	A ½20 G♯ D♯ A ½20 (B) A ½20 G♯ A 11p23	056 4x56 D♯ 056 D♯ 400 C
F♯		77. 78. 79. 80.	A 120 A ½20 A 11p20 A 120	456x (C) 400 C 400 C 406
G		81. 82. 83. 84. 85.	A 103 A 11p00 (G♯) A ½00 G♯ D♯ A 100 A ½20	400 400 C 400 C 400 406x
G♯		86. 87. 88.	A 103 B A 100 A 103	056 400 (C) 006 C
A	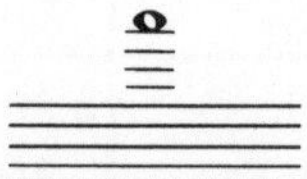	89. 90. 91. 92. 93. 94.	A 003 (B) A 000 A ½03 G♯ A ½03 B A 023 A ½03	056 (D♯) 400 006 D♯ 4x06 050 4y56 D♯
A♯	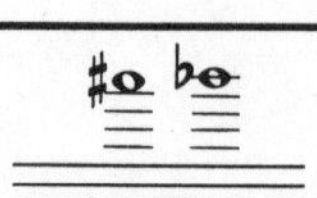	95. 96. 97.	A 02x3 G♯ A 020 G♯ A 020 G♯ D♯	006 D♯ 050 D♯ 050
B		98.	A 02x3 G♯	05x6 D♯
C	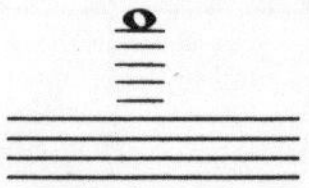	99. 100. 101.	A 02x3 G♯ A ½20 A ½20	45x6 D♯ 55x0 120

*Plateau model only.

**English Horn use octave key B.

Oboe Harmonic Fingerings

			Left Hand	Right Hand
F		1.	A 123 B♭	456 C
F♯		2.	A 123 B	456 C
G		3.	A 123	456 C
G♯		4.	B 123	456 C♯
A		5.	B 123	456
A♯		6.	B 123	456 D♯
B	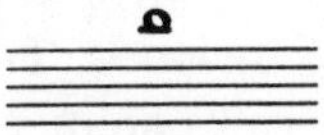	7. 8.	B 123 B 103 B♭	450 456 C
C		9.	B 123	456x

Oboe Trill Fingerings

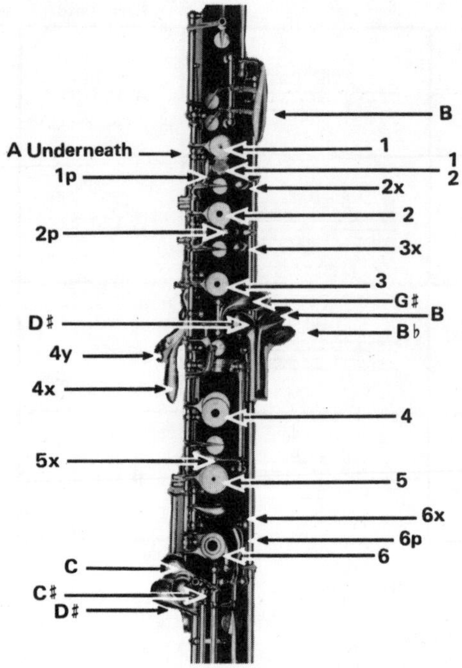

A composite fingering is given for the notes in a trill. The trill is made with the fingers and/or keys circled. Only special trill fingerings are included. Trills which are executed with regular fingerings are not included.

			Left Hand	Right Hand
B C♯		1. 2.	123 (B) *123 B	456 C♯ 4566p (G♯)
C D♭		3.	123	4566p (C♯)
C♯ D♯		4.	123 D♯	456 (C♯)
D♯ E		5.	123 D♯	45(6)
E♭ F		6. 7.	123 123 D♯	4(5)6 D♯ 4(5)6
F G		8. 9.	123 123	(4)56x (4)06
F♯ G♯		10.	123 G♯	(4)00

			Left Hand	Right Hand
G A♭		11.	123 123 (G♯)	(4x) 00 000
G♯ A		12.	*12(3) 12(3) G♯	4y00 000
A♭ B♭		13. 14. 15.	1(2)3 G♯ *1(2)3 **123 G♯	006 4x00 (4y) 00
A♯ B		16. 17.	1(2)0 G♯ 11p(2)0	400 400
B C♯		18.	10 (3x)	000
C D♭		19. 20.	(1)00 10 (3x)	400 400
C D		21. 22.	1 (2x) 0 100	400 4(5x)0

*Plateau model only.
**Open hole model only.

Trill	Notation	No.	Left Hand	Right Hand
C♯ D♯		23.	½23 D♯	456 (C♯ circled)
D♯ E		24.	½23 D♯	45⑥
E♭ F		25. 26.	½23 ½23 D♯	4⑤6 D♯ 4⑤6
F G		27. 28.	A 123 A 123	④56x ④06
F♯ G♯		29.	A 123 G♯	④00
G A♭	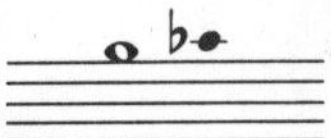	30. 31.	A 123 A 123 (G♯ circled)	(4x circled) 00 000
G♯ A		32. 33.	*A 12③ A 12③ G♯	4y00 000
A♭ B♭	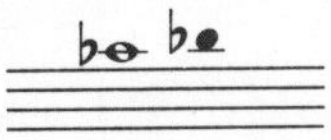	34. 35.	A 1②3 G♯ A 1②3	000 4x00
A♯ B	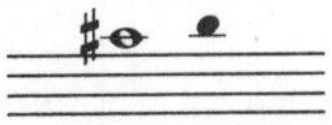	36. 37.	B 11p②0 B 1②3 (G♯)	400 400
B C♯		38.	B 10 (3x circled)	000
C D♭	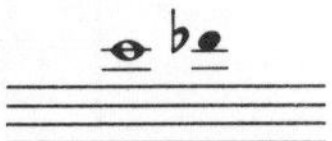	39. 40.	B 10 (3x circled) B ①00	400 400
C D	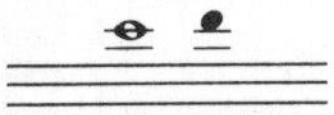	41. 42.	B 1 (2x circled) 0 B 100	400 4 (5x circled) 0
C♯ D	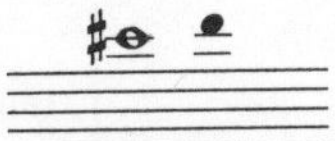	43.	023 ½23 G♯	④00 C ④06 C♯
C♯ D♯		44.	023 G♯	④00 C
D E♭	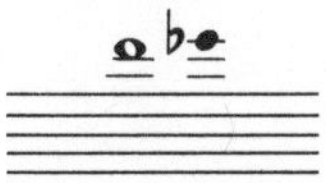	45. 46.	½23 ½23 (G♯ circled)	(4x circled) 00 C 000 (C)
D E		47. 48.	½2③ A 023 G♯	000 ④06x
D♯ E		49. 50. 51.	½2③ B ½2③ G♯ ½2③	056 0(5)(6) 4y00 C
E♭ F		52. 53.	½2③G♯ ½2③	000 C 4x00 C
E F		54. 55. 56.	A ½2③B A ½2③ G♯/D♯ A ½20 (G♯ circled)	4x56 D♯ 056 000
E F♯		57. 58.	A ½② ③ G♯/D♯ A ½② ③B	056 4x56 (D♯)
F G♭	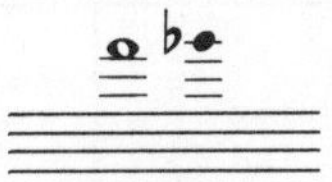	59. 60. 61.	A ½②0 B A ½②0 G♯/D♯ A ½②0 G♯	4x56 (D♯) 056 000 D♯
F G		62. 63. 64.	A (½ circled) ②0 G♯/D♯ A (½ circled) ②0 B A 11p② ③	056 4x56 D♯ 400 C
F♯ G		65. 66.	A 11p②0 **A 11p②0	400 C 406x
F♯ G♯		67. 68. 69.	A 1②0 A 1②0 A 11p②0	400 C 456x 450
G A♭	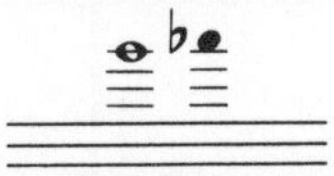	70.	A 10③	400
G A		71.	A ①0③	400

*Plateau model only.

**Open hole model only.

Clarinet Fingering Chart

x, y, z, zz–indicate keys operated by one of the fingers normally covering a hole. When they are used the hole is left open.

A, G-sharp operated by 1st finger; T-thumb hole and R–Register key by left thumb; E, F, F-sharp and G-sharp by little fingers.

( )–Parenthesis indicate that the use of that key or hole is optional in that fingering, depending on intonation and resonance on a particular instrument.

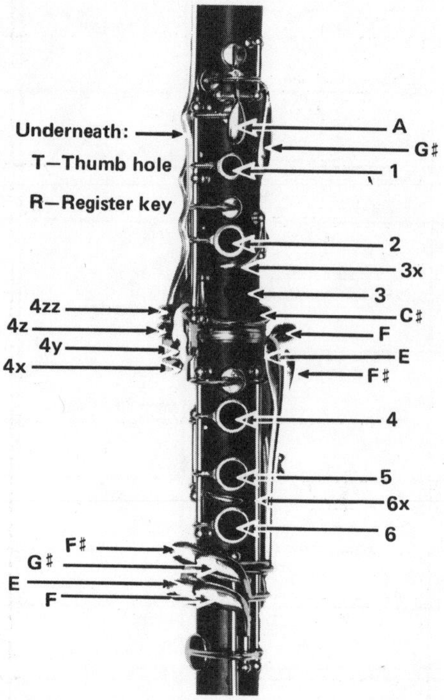

			Left Hand	Right Hand
E		1.	T 123 E	456
F		2. 3.	T 123 T 123 F	456 F 456
F♯	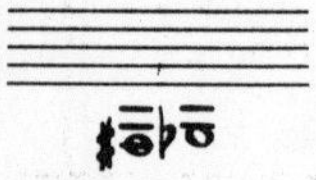	4. 5.	T 123 F♯ T 123	456 456 F♯
G	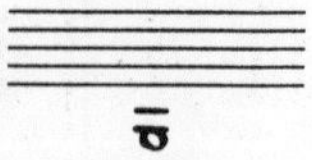	6.	T 123	456
G♯	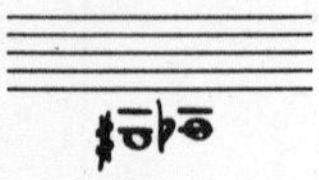	7.	T 123	456 G♯
A		8.	T 123	450
A♯		9.	T 123	400

			Left Hand	Right Hand
B		10. 11.	T 123 T 123	050 406x
C		12.	T 123	000
C♯	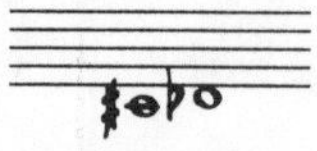	13.	T 123 C♯	000
D	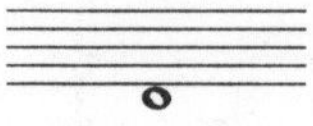	14.	T 120	000
D♯	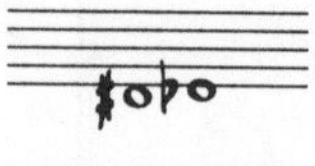	15. 16. 17. 18. 19.	T 120 T 123x T 100 T 100 *T 103	4x00 000 400 050 000
E	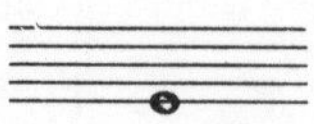	20.	T 100	000
F		21.	T 000	000

*7 ring model only.

	No.	Left Hand	Right Hand
F♯	22. 23.	100 T 000	000 4xy 00
G	24.	000	000
G♯	25.	G♯ 00	000
A	26.	A 00	000
A♯	27. 28.	R A00 A00	000 4z00
B	29. 30. 31. 32.	TR 123 E TR 123 A00 R A00	456 456 E 4zz00 4z00
C	33. 34. 35.	TR 123 TR 123 F R A00	456 F 456 4zz00
C♯	36. 37.	TR 123 F♯ TR 123	456 456 F♯
D	38.	TR 123	456
D♯	39.	TR 123	456 G♯
E	40.	TR 123	450
F	41.	TR 123	400
F♯	42. 43. 44.	TR 123 TR 123 TR 123	050 406x 006
G	45.	TR 123	000
G♯	46. 47.	TR 123 G♯ TR 120	000 450
A	48.	TR 120	000
A♯ B♭	49. 50. 51. 52. 53. 54. 55.	TR 120 TR 123x TR 100 TR 100 TR 103 TR 023 C♯ *TR 103	4x00 000 400 050 006 000 000
B	56.	TR 100	000
C	57.	TR 000	000
C♯	58. 59. 60. 61.	TR 023 TR 000 TR 100 100	450 4xy00 4z00 000
D	62. 63. 64.	TR 023 TR 000 TR G♯ 00	400 G♯ 4z00 (4x)00
D♯	65. 66. 67. 68.	TR 023 TR 023 TR 023 TR A00	406x G♯ 006 G♯ 050 G♯ 000 G♯
E	69. 70. 71.	TR 023 TR G♯ 23 TR A00	000 G♯ 000 4200
F	72. 73. 74.	TR 023 C♯ TR 123 C♯ TR G♯ 23 C♯	000 G♯ 456 000
F♯	75. 76. 77.	TR 020 TR 120 TR 120	000 G♯ 456 G♯ 42200 G♯
G	78. 79. 80. 81. 82. 83. 84.	TR 020 TR 100 TR 100 TR 023 TR 023x TR 020 TR 003 C♯	450 G♯ 450 G♯ 400 G♯ 450 G♯ 000 G♯ 4x00 G♯ 000 G♯
G♯	80. 81. 82. 83. 84. 85. 86.	TR 023 F♯ TR 023 TR 023 TR 023 TR 003 TR 023 TR 020	406 050 F 406x G♯ 400 F♯ 400 G♯ 006 F 050 G♯

*7 ring model only.

			Left Hand	Right Hand
A	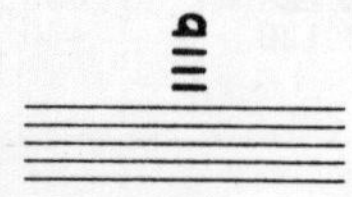	87. 88. 89.	TR 023 TR 023 TR 023	000 F 000 F♯ 4x00 F♯
A♯	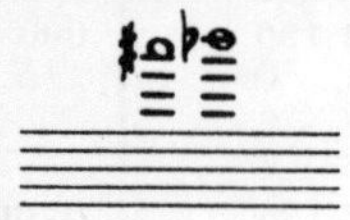	90. 91. 92.	TR G♯23 C♯ TR 123 C♯ TR 123	000 G♯ or F♯ 456 F or G♯ 456 F

			Left Hand	Right Hand
B		93. 94. 95.	TR G♯120 (F♯) TR G♯120 C♯ TR 020 F♯	450 (G♯) 450 G♯ 450 G♯
C	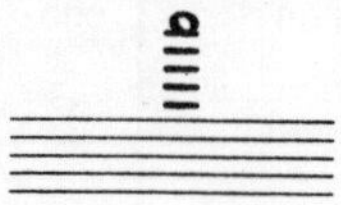	96. 97. 98. 99.	TR G♯ 100 TR G♯ 000 TR 103x TR A 100	400 F♯ 400 G♯ 406x G♯ 4(5)0 G♯

Clarinet Trill Fingerings

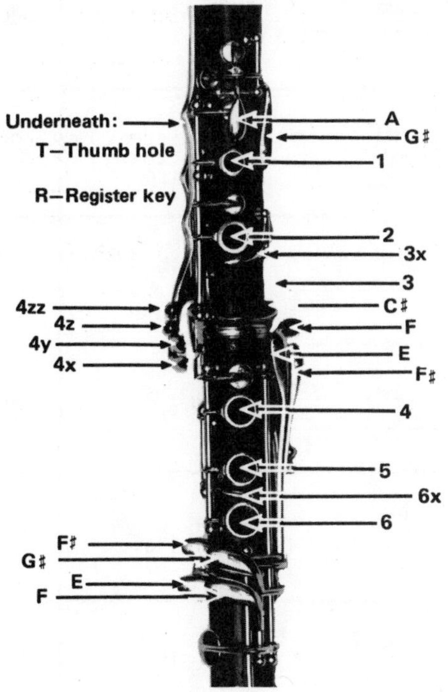

A composite fingering is given for the notes in a trill. The trill is made with the fingers and/or keys circled. Only special trill fingerings are included. Trills which are executed with regular fingerings are not included.

Trill	No.	Left Hand	Right Hand
E F	1. 2.	T 123 Ⓔ T 123 F	456 F 456 Ⓔ
E F♯	3. 4.	T 123 (F♯) T 123 E	456 E 456 (F♯)
F G♭	5. 6.	T 123 (F♯) T 123 F	456 F 456 (F♯)
F♯ G♯	7.	T 123 F♯	456 (G♯)

Trill	No.	Left Hand	Right Hand
A♭ B♭	8.	T 123	4⑤6 G♯
A♯ B	9.	T 123	40 (6x)
B C♯	10. 11. 12. 13.	T 123 (C♯) T 123 (G♯) T 123 Ⓒ **T 123 C♮	050 406x 006 0⑤0
C D	14. 15.	T 12③ T 123	000 (4x) 00
C♯ D	16. 17.	T 12③ C♮ T 12③ (C♯)	000 000
C♯ D♯	18. 19.	T 123 C♮ *T 1②3 C♮	4x00 000
D E	20. 21. 22.	T 1②0 T 100 *T 10③	4x00 400 000
E F	23. 24.	T ① ②0 T 123x	4x00 (4xy) 00
E F	25. 26.	Ⓣ 100 T 100	000 (4xy) 00
F G	27.	T 000	(4xy) 00
F G	28.	T (G♯) 00	000
F♮ G	29.	T (G♯) 00	4xy00

*7 ring model only.
**Model with articulated C#-G# key only

Trill	Notation	No.	Left Hand	Right Hand
G♯ A		30.	G♯ 00	(4z) 00
A♭ B♭	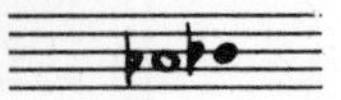	31. 32.	G♯ 00 G♯ 00	(4zz) 00 (4z) 00
A B♭		33.	A00	(4z) 00
A B		34.	A00	(4zz) 00
A♯ B		35.	R A00	(4z) 00
B♭ C		36.	R A00	(4zz) 00
B C	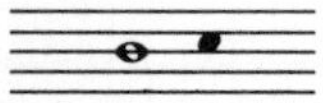	37. 38.	TR 123 Ⓔ TR 123 F	456 F 456 Ⓔ
B C♯	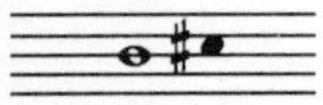	39. 40.	TR 123 (F♯) TR 123 E	456 E 456 (F♯)
C D♭		41. 42.	TR 123 (F♯) TR 123 F	456 F 456 (F♯)
C♯ D♯		43.	TR 123 (F♯)	456 (G♯)
E♭ F		44.	TR 123	4⑤6 G♯
F G♭		45.	TR 123	40 (6x)
F♯ G♯		46. 47. 48. 49.	TR 123 (C♯) TR 123 (C♯) TR 123 (C♯) **TR 123 C♯	050 006 406x 0⑤0
G A	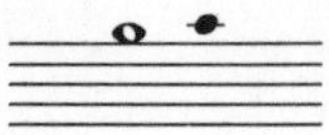	50. 51.	TR 12③ TR 123	000 (4x) 00
G♯ A		52. 53. 54.	TR 12③ (C♯) TR 123 C♯ TR 120	000 (4x) 00 ④ ⑤0
A♭ B♭	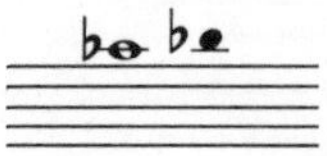	55. 56. 57. 58.	TR ①23 C♯ TR 123 C♯ TR 1②3 C♯ TR ①23	000 (4x) 00 000 450
A♯ B		59. 60.	TR 1②0 TR 100	4x00 ④00
B♭ C		61. 62.	TR ① ②0 TR 123x	4x00 (4xy) 00
B C♯		63. 64. 65. 66.	(TR) 100 TR 103 TR 100 TR 100	000 45⑥ (4xy) 00 (4x) 00
C D♭	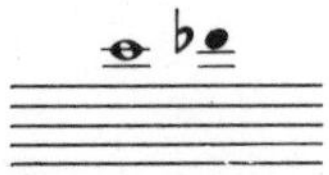	67.	TR 000	(4xy) 00
C D	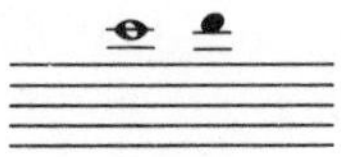	68. 69.	TR (G♯) 00 TR 000	000 (4z) 00
C♯ D♯		70. 71.	TR 023 TR Ⓐ23	④50 450
E♭ F		72. 73. 74. 75. 76.	TR 02③ TR 02③ TR 02③ **TR 023 G♯ **TR 023 C♯	406x G♯ 050 G♯ 006 G♯ 0⑤0 G♯ 00⑥ G♯
E F		77. 78.	TR 023 (C♯) TR 023	000 G♯ (4x) 00 G♯
F G♭		79. 80.	TR 02③ (C♯) TR 023 C♯	000 G♯ (4x) 00 G♯
F G		81.	TR 0②3 C♯	000 G♯

Left Hand	Right Hand
F♯ G	82.	TR 020	④x 00 G♯
	83.	TR 1②0	456 G♯
	84.	TR 123 C♯	4⑤ ⑥
	85.	TR 1②0	4zz00 G♯
F♯ G♯	86.	TR 023	4⑤ ⑥G♯
	87.	TR 020	④xy00 G♯
	88.	TR 020	⑤00 G♯
	89.	TR ① ②0	4zz00
G A♭	90.	TR 023	④50 G♯
	91.	TR 003 C♯	④x 00 G♯
	92.	TR 020	4⑤ ⑥F
G A	93.	TR 023	④ ⑤0 G♯
	94.	TR 020	④ ⑤0 G♯
	95.	TR ①00	450 G♯
G♯ A	96.	TR 023	0⑤0 G♯
	97.	TR 023 F♯	④06
	98.	TR 023	④00 F♯
	99.	TR 003	④00 F♯
	100.	TR 023 F	00⑥
	101.	TR 020	0⑤0 G♯

		Left Hand	Right Hand
A♭ B♭	102.	TR Ⓐ ② ③	4xy00 G♯
	103.	TR 023	050 G♯
A B♭	104.	TR Ⓐ23	000 G♯
	105.	TR Ⓖ♯ 23	000 (G♯)
A♯ B	106.	TR Ⓐ G♯ 23 C♯	000
	107.	TR 123 C♯	4⑤ ⑥F
B♭ C	108.	TR 1② ③ Ⓒ♯	4⑤ ⑥ Ⓕ
B C	109.	TR G♯ 1②0	4⑤0 G♯

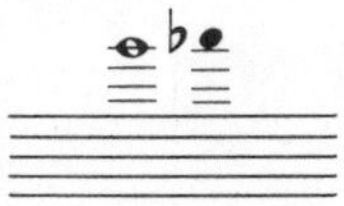

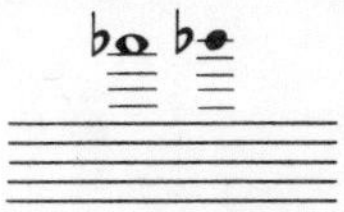

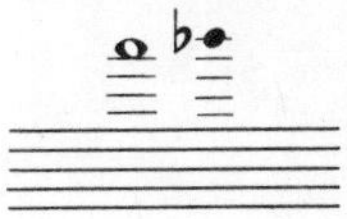

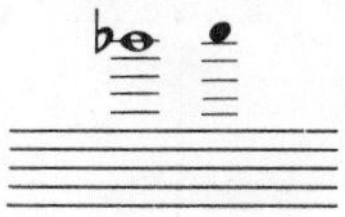

Bassoon Fingering Chart

Left Thumb

x–indicates key operated by one of the fingers normally covering a hole. When they are used the hole is left open.

( )–Parenthesis indicate that the use of that key or hole is optional in that fingering, depending on intonation and resonance on a particular instrument.

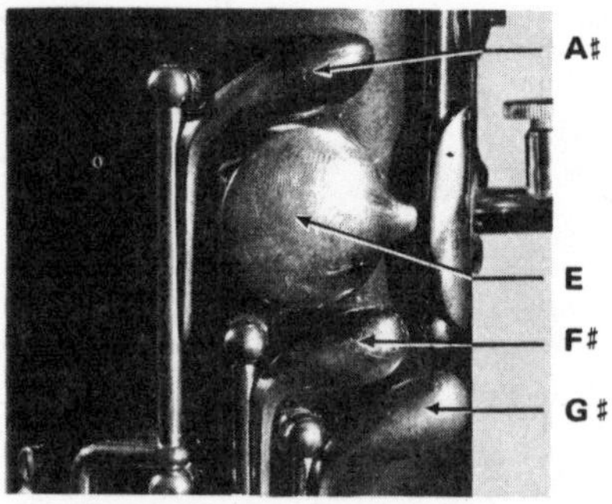

Right Thumb

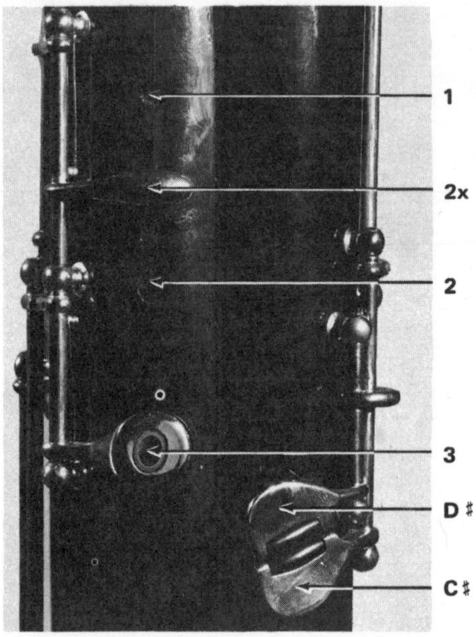

Left Hand

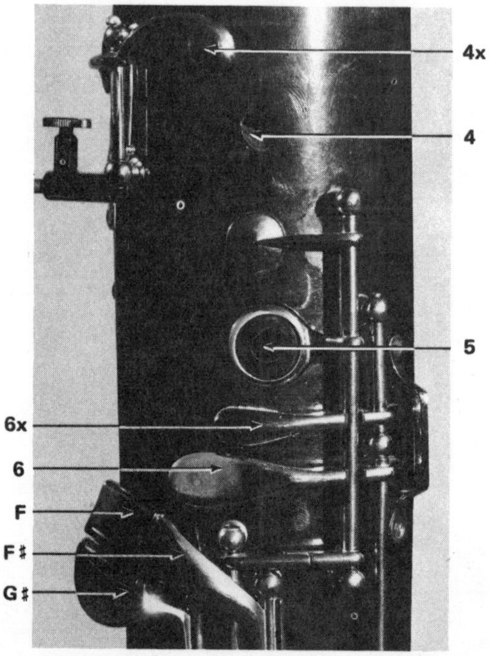

Right Hand

			Left Thumb	Left Hand	Right Thumb	Right Hand
B♭	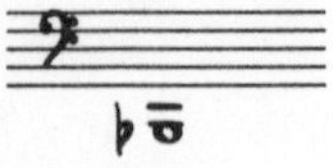	1.	B♭	123	E	456 F
B	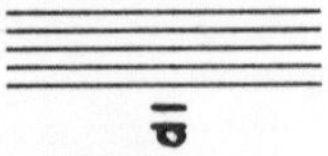	2.	B	123	E	456 F
C		3.	C	123	E	456 F
C		4.	C	123 C♯	E	456 F

Note	Notation	No.	Left Thumb	Left Hand	Right Thumb	Right Hand
D	(notation)	5.	D	123	E	456 F
D♯	(notation)	6.	D	123 D♯	E	456 F
E	(notation)	7.		123	E	456 F
F	(notation)	8.	W	123		456 F
F♯	(notation)	9.	W	123	F♯	456
		10.	W	123	E-F♯	456 F♯
		11.	(W)	123	E-F♯	456 F♯
G	(notation)	12.	W	123		456
G♯	(notation)	13.	W	123		456 G♯
		14.	W	123	G♯	456
A	(notation)	15.	W	123		450
A♯	(notation)	16.	W	123	A♯	450
		17.	W	123		456x
B	(notation)	18.	W	123		400
C	(notation)	19.	W	123		000
C♯	(notation)	20.	Dc♯ W	123		000
		21.	(W)	123	E	4x00 F
D	(notation)	22.	W	120		000

Note	Notation	No.	Left Thumb	Left Hand	Right Thumb	Right Hand
D♯	(notation)	23.	W	103		000
		24.	Wc♯	120		000
		25.	W	103 D♯	A♯	050
E	(notation)	26.	W	100		000
F	(notation)	27.	W	000		000
F♯	(notation)	28.	(W)	½23	F♯	456
		29.	(W)	½23		456 F♯
		30.	(W)	½23	E F♯	456 F♯
G	(notation)	31.	(W)	½23		456
G♯	(notation)	32.	(W)	½23		456 G♯
		33.	(W)	½23	G♯	456
A	(notation)	34.		123		450
A♯	(notation)	35.		123	A♯	450
		36.		123		456x
B	(notation)	37.		123		400
C	(notation)	38.		123		000
C♯	(notation)	39.	C♯	123		056 F
		40.	C♯	123		000
		41.		123	A♯	050 F♯
D	(notation)	42.		120		000
		43.		120		056 F
D♯	(notation)	44.		120		(4)56
		45.	C♯	120		000
		46.		120		0(5)6
		47.		103 D♯		000

Note		No.	Left Thumb	Left Hand	Right Thumb	Right Hand
E		48.		103 D#		(4)56
		49.		100 (D#)		000
F		50.		103 (D#)		450
		51.		023 (D#)		450
		52.		100		450
F#	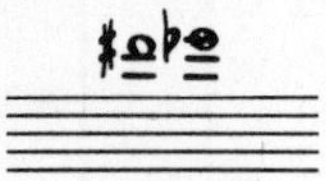	53.	W	½23 (D#)		400
		54.		02(3) D#	A#	450
		55.		103 (D#)	A#	450
		56.		020 D#		450 F
		57.		020		400
		58.		000 D#	G#	(4)50
G		59.	W	½23 (D#)		400 F
		60.	W	½23 (D#)		000 (G#)
G#	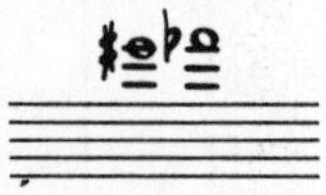	61.	W	½23 (D#)		006
		62.	W	½23 (D#)	A#	000 F
		63.	W	½23 (D#)	A#	056
A		64.	a c#	123 (D#)		006
		65.	a c#	123 (D#)		000 F
A#		66.	a c#	123 (D#)		450 F
		67.	Wc#	123 D#		050 F
		68.	Wc#	123 D#	E	(4)50 F

Note		No.	Left Thumb	Left Hand	Right Thumb	Right Hand
B	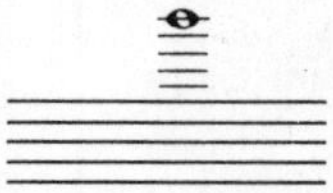	69.	C	120 D#	A#	450
C	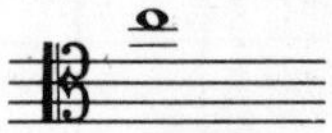	70.	C	100 D#	A#	450 F
C#		71.	C	103 D#		406 (G#)
		72.	C	103 D#	E	406 (G#)
D	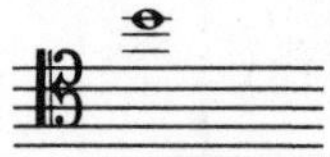	73.	C	003 D#		006 G#
		74.		003 D#		006 F
D#		75.	C	02x3 D#	(A#)	00(6) G#
		76.	C#	½23		(4x)00 G#
E		77.	C#	½23	G#	456 F

Bassoon Trill Fingerings

Left Thumb

A composite fingering is given for the notes in a trill. The trill is made with the fingers and/or keys circled. Only special trill fingerings are included. Trills which are executed with regular fingerings are not included.

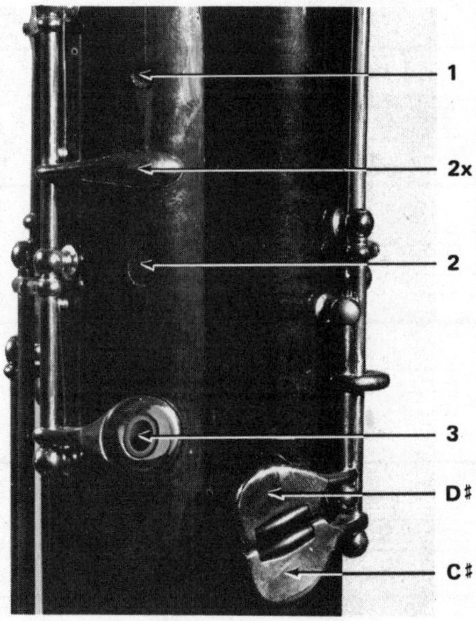

Left Hand

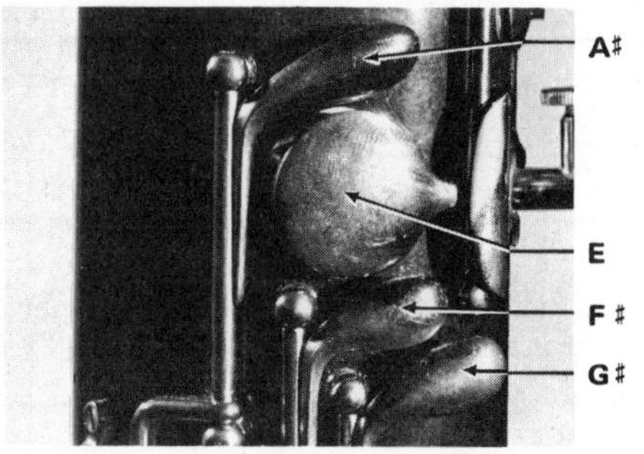

Right Thumb

			Left Thumb	Left Hand	Right Thumb	Right Hand
B C♯		1.	B	123 (C♯)	E	456 F
D♯ E		2.	(D)	123 D♯	E	456 F
E♭ F		3.	Dw	123 D♯	(E)	456 F
F♯ G♯		4. 5.	W W	123 123	F♯ (G♯)	456 (G♯) 456 F♯

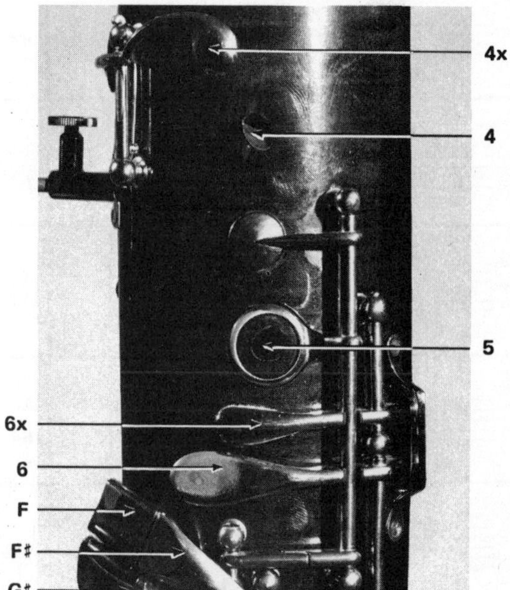

Right Hand

Notes	No.	Left Thumb	Left Hand	Right Thumb	Right Hand
G♯ A	6.	W	123		45⑥ G♯
	7.	W	123	G♯	45⑥
B C♯	8.	(D)W	12③		400
C D♭	9.	(D)W	123		④x 00
	10.	C♯	123		000
C♯ D	11.	W	12③	E	4x00 F
	12.	W	12③	F♯	006
	13.	W	12③		006 F♯
C♯ D♯	14.	Dc♯ W	①23		000
	15.	Dc♯ W	12③		000
D E♭	16.	Ⓒ♯	120		000
E♭ F	17.	W	103		④⑤⑥ Ⓕ
	18.	W	1②x 3 D♯		000
E F♯	19.	W	1②x 00		000
F G♭	20.	W	0②x 0		000
	21.	W	000		④⑤⑥ Ⓕ
	22.	W	000		④⑤ 6 F
F G	23.	ⓐ	000		000
	24.	W	0②③		456
F♯ G♯	25.	W	½23	Ⓖ♯	456 F♯
	26.	W	½23	F♯	456 Ⓖ♯
G A	27.	W	½23 D♯		45⑥
G♯ A	28.	W	½2③		456 G♯
	29.	W	½2③	G♯	456
	30.	W	½23	Ⓐ♯	456 G♯
	31.	W	½23	G♯	45⑥

Notes	No.	Left Thumb	Left Hand	Right Thumb	Right Hand
A♭ B♭	32.	(b)	123	A♯	45⑥
A♯ B	33.		123	A♯	4⑤0
B♭ C	34.		12③	A♯	450
	35.		123	A♯	④⑤0
B C♯	36.		12③		400
C D♭	37.		123		④x 00
	38.	Ⓒ♯	123		000
C♯ D	39.		12③		056 F♯
D E♭	40.		120		00⑥
	41.		120		0⑤⑥
D E	42.		1②0 D♯		000
D♯ E	43.		120	Ⓖ♯	056
	44.		120		056 Ⓖ♯
	45.		1②0 (D♯)		456
E♭ F	46.		①②0		456
	47.		103 (D♯)		0⑤0
E F♯	48.		103 D♯		4⑤⑥
	49.		103 D♯		40⑥
F G♭	50.		103 D♯		4⑤0
	51.		023 D♯		450 Ⓕ
F G	52.	W	½23 D♯		④⑤0
	53.	ⓐ	103 D♯		450

Trill	Notation	No.	Left Thumb	Left Hand	Right Thumb	Right Hand
F♯ G		54.	W	½23 D♯		400 Ⓕ
		55.		020 D♯	A♯	4⑤0
F♯ G♯		56.		023 D♯	A♯	④⑤0
		57.	W	½23 D♯		40⑥
		58.	ⓐ(c♯)	020 D♯	A♯	450
G A♭		59.	W	½23		00⑥
		60.	W	½23 D♯		④00 F
		61.	ⓐ	½23 D♯		400 F
G A		62.	W	½23 D♯		00⑥ G♯
		63.	W	½23 D♯		(4x)0⑥ G♯
G♯ A		64.	ⓐ(c♯)	½23 D♯		006
A♭ B♭		65.	ⓒⓐ	½23 D♯		006

Trill	Notation	No.	Left Thumb	Left Hand	Right Thumb	Right Hand
A B♭	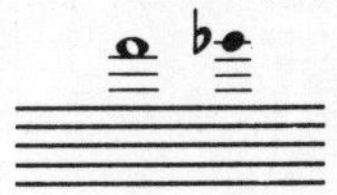	66.	aC♯	12③		006
		67.	aC♯	123 D♯		④⑤0 F
A B		68.	aC♯	123	A♯	④⑤0 F
A♯ B		69.	aC♯	12③ (D♯)		450 F
		70.	aC♯	123 (D♯)	(A♯)	450 F
B♭ C	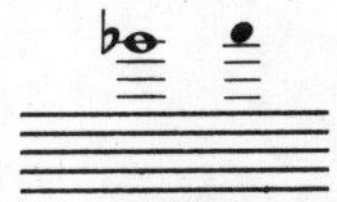	71.	b	1②③		450 F
B C♯		72.	c	①②0 D♯	A♯	450 F

Saxophone Fingering Chart

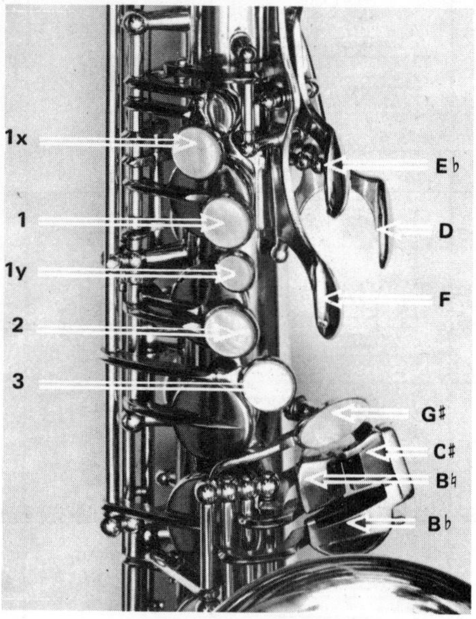

Left Hand

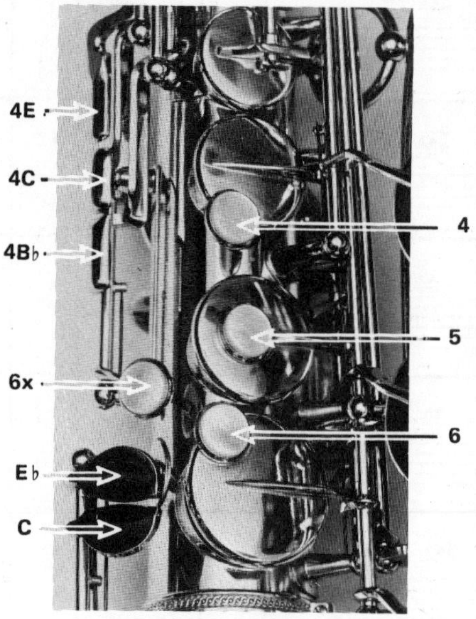

Right Hand

x, y—indicate keys operated by one of the fingers normally covering a hole. When they are used the hole is left open.

( )—Parenthesis indicate that use of that key is optional in that fingering, depending on intonation and resonance on a particular instrument.

			Left Hand	Right Hand
Bb		1.	123 Bb	456 C
B		2.	123 B	456 C
C		3.	123	456 C
C#		4.	123 C#	456 C
D		5.	123	456

			Left Hand	Right Hand
D#		6.	123	456 Eb
E		7.	123	450
F		8.	123	400
F#		9. 10.	123 123	050 406x
G		11.	123	000

			Left Hand	Right Hand
G♯		12.	123 G♯	000
A		13.	120	000
A♯		14. 15. 16. 17.	120 11y00 100 100	4B♭00 000 400 050
B		18.	100	000
C		19. 20.	020 100	000 4C00
C♯	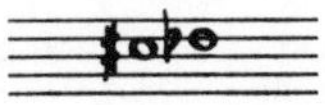	21. 22.	000 T 123 C♯	000 456 C
D		23.	T 123	456
D♯		24.	T 123	456 E♭
E		25.	T 123	450
F		26.	T 123	400
F♯		27. 28.	T 123 T 123	050 406x

			Left Hand	Right Hand
G		29.	T 123	000
G♯		30.	T 123 G♯	000
A	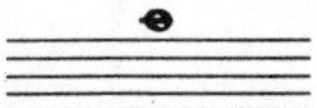	31.	T 120	000
A♯	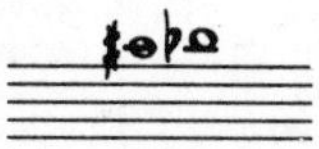	32. 33. 34. 35.	T 120 T 11y00 T 100 T 100	4B♭00 000 400 050
B		36.	T 100	000
C		37. 38.	T 020 T 100	000 4C00
C♯	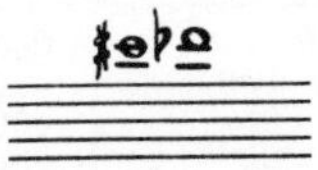	39.	T 000	000
D		40.	T D000	000
D♯		41.	T DE♭000	000
E		42. 43.	T DE♭000 T 1x23	4E 000 000
F		44. 45.	T DE♭F 000 T 1x20	4E 000 000

Saxophone Extended Range

			Left Hand	Right Hand
F♯		46.	T 1x20	4B♭ 00
		47.	T 1x20	400
		48.	T 1x20	4B♭ 456
		49.	T 1x03	4B♭ 450
		50.	(T) 1x20	4B♭ 400
		51.	(T) 103	400
		52.	T 100	450
G	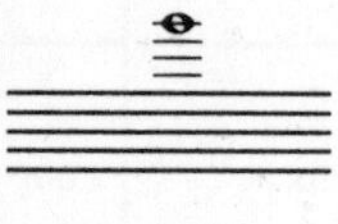	53.	T 103	006
		54.	T 020	450
		55.	T 1x00	4B♭ 400
		56.	T 1x00	4B♭ 450 E♭
		57.	T 103	406
		58.	T 103	406x
		59.	T 1x00	400
G♯		60.	T 103	000
		61.	T 020	050
		62.	T 1x00	4B♭ 00
		63.	T 103	4C400
		64.	T 103	4C450
		65.	T 1x00 G♯	4B♭ 00
		66.	T 103	4C06
		67.	T 020	400
A		68.	T 023	000
		69.	T 023	456
		70.	T 023 B♭	456 C
A♯		71.	T 003	4C00
		72.	TD 023	456
		73.	TD 023	4C50 E♭
		74.	T 003	450
		75.	TD 023	4B♭ 456
B	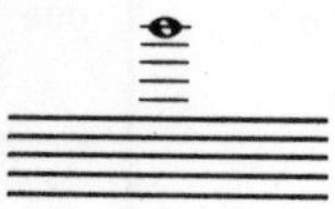	76.	TDE♭ 000	000
		77.	TE♭ 100	450
		78.	TD 003	450
		79.	TD 003	000
		80.	TDE♭ 120	456
		81.	TD 023	4C00
		82.	T 120 B♭	450
		83.	TD 023	400

			Left Hand	Right Hand
C		84.	TDE♭ 000	000
		85.	T 100	450
		86.	T 103	406
		87.	T 103	406 E♭
		88.	TDE♭ 023	4E00
		89.	T 103	400
		90.	T 103	056
		91.	T 1x03	400
		92.	TDE♭ 023	4C00
C♯	8va 	93.	T DE♭ 000	4E00
		94.	T E♭ 100	450
		95.	T 1x00	400
		96.	T 1x20	4B♭ 400
		97.	T 1x00	400 E♭
		98.	T 1x00	4E400
		99.	TDE♭ 023	4E00
D	8va 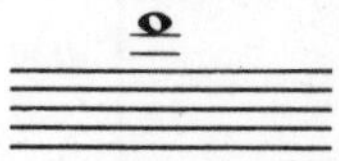	100.	T E♭ 100	000
		101.	T 1x00 B♭	050 C
		102.	T 1x00	4B♭ 00
		103.	T 1x00	000
		104.	T 1x00	4E00
D♯	8va 	105.	T 1x20	400
		106.	T E♭ 1x00	4C00
		107.	T 020	400
		108.	T 020	050
E	8va 	109.	T 020	450
		110.	T 000	406
		111.	T D120	4B♭ 56
		112.	T 020	050
		113.	T 1x00	400
F	8va 	114.	T 103	406
		115.	T D100	4B♭ 56
		116.	T 103	400
		117.	T DE♭ 020	450

Saxophone Trill Fingerings

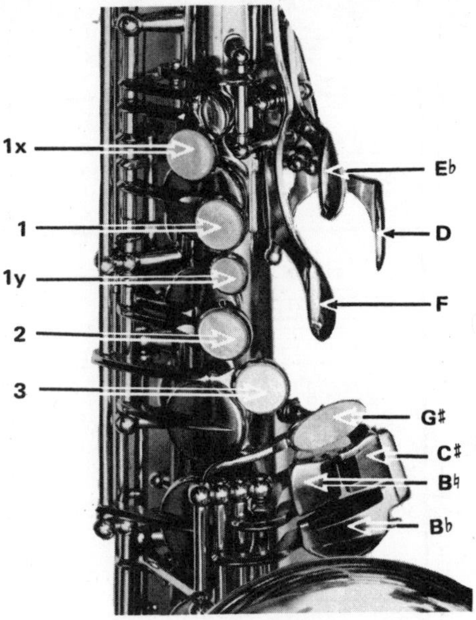

Left Hand

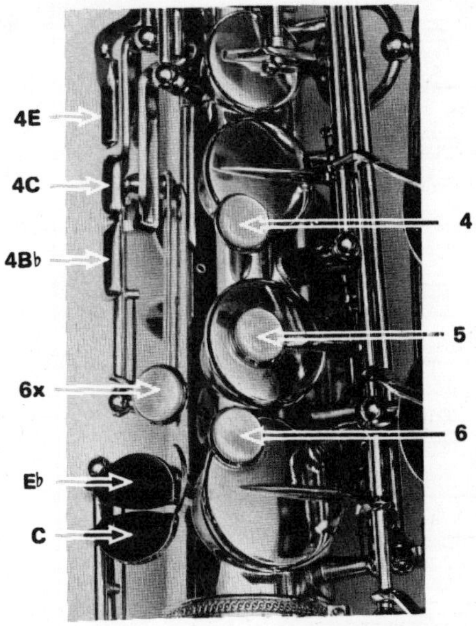

Right Hand

A composite fingering is given for the notes in a trill. The trill is made with the fingers and/or keys circled. Only special trill fingerings are included. Trills which are executed with regular fingerings are not included.

			Left Hand	Right Hand
C♯ D		1.	123 C♮	456 Ⓒ
D♯ E		2.	123	45⑥ E♭
E♭ F		3.	123	4⑤ ⑥ E♭
F G♭		4.	123	40 (6x)
F♯ G♯		5.	123 G♯	0⑤0

			Left Hand	Right Hand
G♯ A		6.	12③ G♯	000
A♭ B♭		7. 8.	12 3 G♯ 11y ② ③ G♯	(4B♭) 000 000
A B♭		9. 10.	120 11y②0	(4B♭) 000 000
A♯ B		11. 12. 13.	1②0 100 100	4B♭00 ④00 0⑤0
B♭ C		14. 15.	①20 11y00	4B♭ 00 (4C) 00

			Left Hand	Right Hand
B C		16.	100	(4C) 00
C D		17. 18.	(E♭) 020 T 123	000 456 Ⓒ
C♯ D		19.	Ⓓ 000	000
C♯ D♯		20.	000	(4E) 00
D♯ E		21.	T 123	45 ⑥ E♭
E♭ F		22.	T 123	4 ⑤ ⑥ E♭
F G♭		23.	T 123	40 (6x)
F♯ G♯		24.	T 123 G♯	0⑤0
A♭ B♭	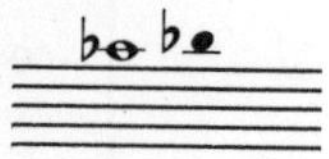	25. 26.	T 123 G♯ T 11y ② ③ G♯	(4B♭) 00 000
A B♭	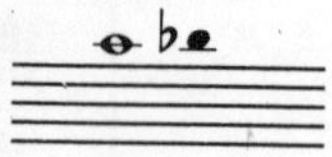	27. 28.	T 120 11y ②0	(4B♭) 00 000

			Left Hand	Right Hand
A♯ B		29.	T 1②0	4B♭00
B♭ C		30.	T ①20	4B♭00
B C		31.	T 100	(4C) 00
C D♭	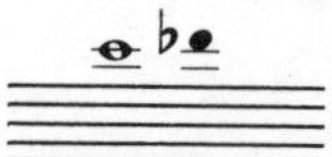	32. 33.	T 1②0 T ①04C	000 000
C D	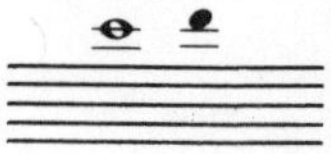	34.	T Ⓔ 020	000
C♯ D♯		35.	T 000	(4E) 00
D E		36. 37.	TD Ⓕ 000 TD 000	000 (4E) 00
E♭ F		38.	TDE♭ Ⓕ 000	000
E F		39. 40.	TDE♭ Ⓕ 000 T 1x2③	4E00 000